G000280007
Kwak
Anno 1791
BLONDE
Limburgse Witte
MARTENS PILS
Sloeber
GROTTENBIER
GRIMBERGEN
BOCKOR
poperings hommelbier
Abdij - Abbaye
ENAME
WITKAP-PATER
Tripel

All Belgian Beers

Les Bières Belges

Alle Belgische Bieren

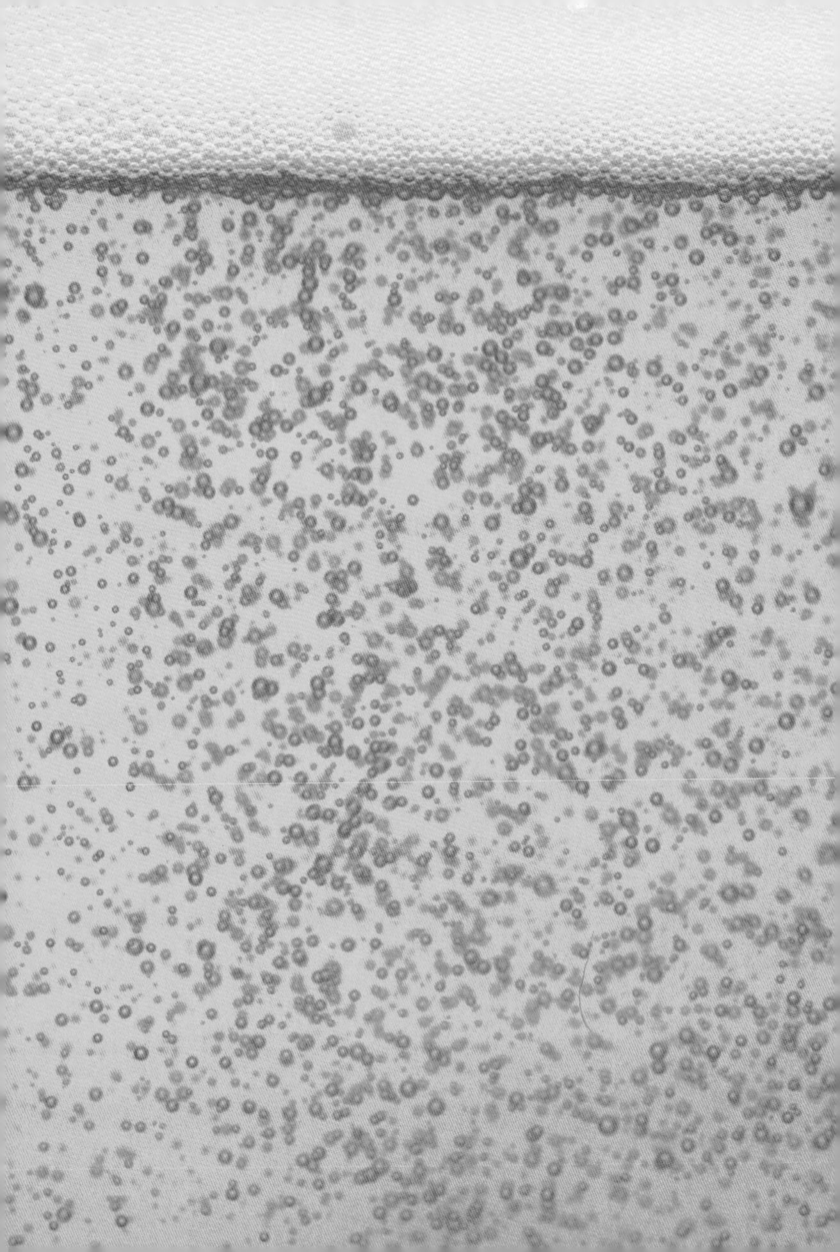

All Belgian Beers
Les Bières Belges
Alle Belgische Bieren

Belgian beer ...
La bière belge ...
Belgisch bier ...

The idea appeals to everyone's imagination all over the world. Countless tourists collect crown caps, beer mats, glasses and bottles, taking a little piece of Belgian pride back home. Worldwide, beer lovers come together to swap tips and tasting notes. In the United States and Japan specialised literature on the subject is quite common, although those publications seldom reach the Belgian public. Never before has such an extensive selection been written about as in this reference book. It will undoubtedly become your personal beer bible, an indispensable guide to the tremendously diverse Belgian beer world.

➤ pg 6

Parle à l'imaginaire de tout un chacun dans le monde entier. De nombreux touristes collectionnent des capsules, cartons, verres et bouteilles de bières et véhiculent ainsi notre fierté belge hors des frontières. Des amateurs de bière se réunissent partout. Ils la décrivent en détail et échangent des notes d'appréciation. Aux Etats-Unis et au Japon, une littérature spécialisée paraît même régulièrement, alors qu'on l'ignore souvent. Mais jamais auparavant, une telle somme de connaissances n'avait été rassemblée dans un ouvrage de référence comme celui-ci. Il deviendra sûrement votre 'bible du goût' et le guide indispensable dans le vaste paysage de la bière belge.

➤ pg 8

De idee spreekt wereldwijd tot de verbeelding. Talloze toeristen verzamelen kroonkurken, bierviltjes, -glazen en -flesjes en brengen op die manier een stukje Belgische trots over de grenzen. Liefhebbers verenigen zich waar ook ter wereld en wisselen weetjes en proefnotities uit. In de Verenigde Staten en Japan verschijnt met regelmaat gespecialiseerde literatuur, waar we nauwelijks weet van hebben. Maar nooit eerder werd een dergelijk uitgebreide selectie verzameld als in dit referentiewerk. Het wordt zonder twijfel uw persoonlijke 'proefbijbel', een onmisbare leidraad in het uitgestrekte Belgische bierlandschap.

➤ pg 10

The *All Belgian Beers* book offers an alphabetical overview of the beers, brewed by the recognised Belgian (contract) brewers for their own assortment or for other beer companies.

The brewers are divided into four categories (see the overview on page 1560) according to Filip Geerts' website www.belgianbeerboard.be:

- Brewers who have their own brewery infrastructure.
- Gueuze blenders who buy lambic from different brewers and blend it according to their own recipes.
- "Brewery renters", as they are called in Belgium, who do not possess a (complete) brewing infrastructure and brew part or all of their beer at the facilities of fellow brewers.
- Contract brewers, individuals or companies, who commercialise beers with an original recipe as their main product, without brewing the beers themselves. They hire a brewery to produce their beers – in part or all of it – according to their guidelines.

This beer catalogue features both beers from big, industrial companies and from smaller craft breweries, microbreweries or home breweries, as long as they are bottled and sold outside the brewery or a local pub.

Own-label beers brewed for supermarkets, private-label beers or occasional beers have deliberately not been included in this publication. The reason has nothing to do with their taste or quality, but rather with the almost infinite number of these beers that exist in the Belgian market. Many occasional beers are created to give a personal or festive touch to some regional event. Almost any association or village has its own beer, which is not really a surprise: after all, we are talking about Belgium...

Publications like these are only a snapshot of the country at a certain moment in time. Not all Christmas and summer beers were available during the production phase of this book. Therefore, the list of seasonal beers described here is certainly not exhaustive. Some small breweries did not have certain beers in stock because they were temporarily sold out. On the other hand, there are undoubtedly already new beers available today, while others may have disappeared all together.

The editors of this book deliberately chose to provide only objective information, leaving assessments and ratings to the beer lovers and experts. Only facts and figures, provided by the brewers themselves, have been included: fermenting and beer style, composition, alcohol content, colour, brightness, how to serve and temperatures. The brewers also give their personal description of the character and taste of their beers, but in the end it is up to the individual tasters to write down their findings in their tasting notebook and to indicate their preferences.

We wish you a cheerful—or should we say: "beerful"—discovery!

Hilde Deweer
Compilator

Vous trouverez en effet dans *Toutes les bières belges* un aperçu alphabétique des bières brassées par les brasseurs (ou brasseurs locataires) belges, qu'ils soient reconnus pour leur propre assortiment ou par les firmes brassicoles.

Selon le site internet www.belgianbeerboard.be de Filip Geerts, l'on y distingue quatre catégories (voir aperçu à la page 1560)

- Les brasseurs qui disposent de leur propre infrastructure brassicole.
- Les coupeurs de gueuze qui achètent du lambic à différents brasseurs et les mélangent selon leur goût.
- Les brasserie locataires – à savoir les brasseurs qui ne disposent pas d'une installation de brassage (complète) et qui brassent partiellement ou totalement chez un collègue brasseur.
- Les sociétés brassicoles – en l'occurrence les personnes ou entreprises qui ont pour activité principale la commercialisation de bières de recette originale mais qu'ils ne brassent pas eux-mêmes. Ils les font produire (entièrement ou partiellement) 'à façon' par une brasserie.

Tant les bières de grands industriels que celles des brasseries familiales sont prises en compte dans ce catalogue. Et ce, pour autant qu'elles soient mises en bouteille et mises en vente en dehors de la brasserie ou de la taverne locale.

Les bières brassées et distribuées sous des marques mandatées par des supermarchés, bières à étiquette, bières de circonstance ou bières occasionnelles ne sont pas, et c'est un choix, prises en considération. Ce parti pris n'est pas dicté par des critères de goût ou de qualité, mais par la quantité énorme de bières que cela représenterait. En effet, de nombreuses bières occasionnelles résultent d'une touche personnelle ou festive dans le cadre d'un événement ou happening régional. Chaque association et village possèdent sa propre bière. Comment pourrait-il en être autrement en Belgique !

Une publication dans ce domaine est par nature un instantané partiel. Ainsi, lors de l'élaboration de ce livre, toutes les bières de Noël et d'été n'étaient pas disponibles. Ce dernier ne présente donc pas la liste exhaustive de toutes les bières de saison. Des brasseries de plus petite taille ne possédaient parfois plus certaines bières en réserve car elles étaient temporairement épuisées. Par ailleurs, de nouvelles bières seront entre-temps apparues sur le marché alors que d'autres auront peut-être disparu.

Un autre parti pris pour cette édition a été de ne donner que des informations objectives. Les appréciations et les cotations sont laissées aux papilles gustatives des fans et experts de bières. Seules les fiches signalétiques fournies par les brasseurs eux-mêmes sont reprises ici : nature de la fermentation et style de bière, composition et pourcentage d'alcool, couleur et clarté, méthode de servir et température idéale. L'occasion a été donnée à chaque brasseur de décrire le caractère et le goût de ses bières. En fin de compte toutefois, il revient au goûteur individuel de noter ses appréciations dans sa 'bible de la bière' et de pointer ses préférences.

Nous vous souhaitons une belle ballade riche en saveurs et découvertes !

Hilde Deweer
Compositeur

Alle Belgische Bieren biedt een alfabetisch overzicht van de bieren die worden gebrouwen door de erkende Belgische (huur)brouwers voor het eigen assortiment of voor dat van de bierfirma's.

Er wordt hierbij een onderscheid gemaakt tussen vier categorieën (zie overzicht op pagina 1560) volgens de website www.belgianbeerboard.be van Filip Geerts:

- De brouwers met een eigen brouwerij-infrastructuur.
- De geuzestekers: kopen lambiek aan bij verschillende brouwers en gaan die mengen volgens eigen smaak.
- De brouwerijhuurders: brouwers die niet zelf beschikken over een (volledige) brouwinstallatie en die gedeeltelijk of volledig gaan brouwen bij een collega-brouwer.
- De bierfirma's: personen of firma's die bieren met een origineel recept als hoofdactiviteit commercialiseren maar niet zelf brouwen. Zij laten hun bieren (volledig of gedeeltelijk) 'à façon' produceren door een brouwerij.

Zowel de bieren van grote industriële concerns als die van artisanale micro- of huisbrouwerijen komen in deze biercatalogus aan bod, voor zover ze gebotteld zijn en ze buiten de brouwerij of de lokale kroeg te koop worden aangeboden.

Distributiemerken gebrouwen in opdracht van supermarkten, etiketbieren, gelegenheidsbieren, of occasionele bieren worden in deze publicatie bewust buiten beschouwing gelaten. Deze keuze is niet ingegeven door smaak- of kwaliteitsnormen, maar heeft veeleer te maken met de haast onoverzienbare hoeveelheid aan bieren die deze oefening zou opleveren. Veel gelegenheidsbieren zijn immers het resultaat van een persoonlijke of feestelijke toets die aan een evenement of regionale happening wordt gegeven. Bijna iedere vereniging, quasi elk dorp heeft – hoe kan het ook anders in België – zijn eigen biertje.

Elke publicatie is een momentopname. Niet alle kerst- en zomerbieren waren beschikbaar tijdens de productiefase van dit boek. Het totale geregistreerde aanbod aan seizoensbieren is dus zeker geen exhaustieve lijst. Enkele kleinere brouwerijen hadden ook hier of daar een bier niet op voorraad omdat het tijdelijk was uitverkocht. Daarnaast zullen er intussen ongetwijfeld ook al nieuwe bieren hun opwachting maken, terwijl andere misschien alweer verdwenen zijn.

Bij de samenstelling van deze uitgave werd bewust gekozen om enkel objectieve informatie te geven. Beoordelingen en quoteringen worden overgelaten aan de geoefende smaakpapillen van de bierfanaten en -experten. Enkel de beschikbare facts en figures, verschaft door de brouwers zelf, zijn hier aan de orde: gisting en bierstijl, samenstelling en alcoholpercentage, kleur en helderheid, schenkmethode en -temperatuur. De brouwer is ook zelf aan het woord bij de omschrijving van het karakter en de smaak van zijn bieren, maar uiteindelijk is het aan de individuele proever om zijn bevindingen in 'zijn'of 'haar' bierbijbel te noteren en eventuele voorkeuren aan te stippen.

We wensen u een geestrijke ontdekkingstocht!

Hilde Deweer
Samensteller

	Fermentation	Fermentation	Gisting
	Beer style	Style de bière	Bierstijl
	Brewery / Brewery renter / Contract brewer	Brasserie / Brasseur locataire/ Société brassicole	Brouwerij / Brouwerijhuurder / Bierfirma
	Ingredients	Ingrédients	Ingrediënten
	Alcohol by volume percentage / ° plato	Pourcentage d'alcool / ° plato	Alcoholgehalte / ° plato
	Colour and transparency	Couleur et clarté	Kleur en helderheid
	How to serve	Méthode de servir	Schenkmethode
°C	Temperature	Température	Schenktemperatuur
	Character, taste and flavour	Caractère, goût et saveur	Karakter, smaak en aroma
i	Tips and facts	Conseils et détails intéressants	Tips en weetjes
	Comments	Notes	Notities

Aardmonnik

	top-fermentation, mixed unpasteurised	haute fermentation mixte non pasteurisée	hoge gisting gemengd niet gepasteuriseerd
	Flemish old brown	vieille brune flamande	Vlaams oud bruin
	at Brouwerij Deca De Struise Brouwers De Panne	chez Brouwerij Deca De Struise Brouwers La Panne	bij Brouwerij Deca De Struise Brouwers De Panne
	Pilsner, caramel malt, carafa, corn, wheat malt, candy sugar, yeast, water, hops (Bramling Cross, Hallertau Mittelfrueh), herbs (cinnamon, sweet orange rind, thyme, coriander), matures in oak barrels for 18 months.	Malt de pils et de caramel, carafa, maïs, malt de froment, sucre candi, levure, eau, houblon (Bramling Cross, Hallertau Mittelfrueh), herbes (cannelle, écorce d'orange doux, thym, coriandre). Mûrit en fûts de chêne pendant 18 mois.	pilsmout, karamelmout, carafa, maiskorn, tarwemout, kandijsuiker, gist, water, hop (Bramling Cross, Hallertau Mittelfrueh), kruiden (kaneel, zoete sinaasschil, tijm, koriander). Rijpt 18 maand op eikenhouten vaten.
%	8%	8%	8%
	(91 EBC) dark brown unfiltered creamy foam head	brun foncé (91 EBC) non filtrée faux col crémeux	donkerbruin (91 EBC) ongefilterd romige schuimkraag
	–	–	–
°C	–	–	–
	Complex, earthy aroma with a wine-like elegance.	Arôme terreux complexe avec une élégance de vin.	Complex aards aroma met een wijnachtige elegantie.
i	The name of the beer refers to its earthy character. It is a blend of 2 top-fermenting beers with an identical method of preparation.	Le nom de la bière renvoie à son caractère terreux. La bière est un mélange de 2 bières à fermentation haute qui se préparent de la même façon.	De naam verwijst naar het aardachtig karakter. Het bier is een blend van 2 bovengistende bieren van identieke receptuur.

AARDMONNIK - EARTHMONK
DSB
Struisebrouwers.be

Abbaye de Forest

	top-fermentation re-fermented in the bottle	fermentation haute refermentation en bou-teille	hoge gisting hergisting in de fles
	Tripel regional beer	triple bière régionale	tripel streekbier
	Brasserie de Silly Silly	Brasserie de Silly Silly	Brasserie de Silly Silly
	pale malt, sugar, yeast, Kent and Hallertau hops, water	malt pâle, sucre, levure, houblon Kent et Hallertau, eau	bleke mout, suiker, gist, Kent en Hallertauhop, water
%	6,50% 14° plato	6,50% 14° plato	6,50% 14° plato
	(9,8 EBC) blonde	blonde (9,8 EBC)	blond (9,8 EBC)
	–	–	–
°C	41 - 46 °F	5 - 8 °C	5 - 8 °C
	Slighty perfumed character beer with a fine bitter taste, and a subtle fruitiness of dry grapes which provides a refreshing bitter in the throat.	Bière de caractère légèrement parfumée avec un goût amer raffiné. Laisse une saveur fruitée subtile de raisins secs aboutissant en un goût amer rafraîchissant dans la gorge.	Licht geparfumeerd karakterbier met fijnbittere smaak. Laat een subtiele fruitigheid van droge druiven na die uitmondt in een opkikkerend bitter in de keel.
i	Provision beer brewed with respect for the abbey beer tradition.	Bière de conservation brassée en respectant la tradition des bières d'abbaye.	Bewaarbier gebrouwen met respect voor de traditie van het abdijbier.

BIERE BLONDE
BLOND BIER
Abbaye de Forest
Abbaye de
Forest
BLONDE
BLOND
alc. 6.5 % vol.
33cl
Abbaye de
Forest

Abbaye de Saint-Martin blonde

	top-fermentation re-fermented in the bottle	fermentation haute refermentation en bouteille	hoge gisting hergisting op de fles
	abbey beer	bière d'abbaye	abdijbier
	Brasserie de Brunehaut Rongy-Brunehaut	Brasserie de Brunehaut Rongy-Brunehaut	Brasserie de Brunehaut Rongy-Brunehaut
	3 malt varieties, hops, yeast, herbs, water	3 sortes de malt, houblon, levure, herbes, eau	3 moutsoorten, hop, gist, kruiden, water
%	7%	7%	7%
	blond slightly cloudy	blonde légèrement trouble	blond licht troebel
	–	–	–
°C	50 °F	10 °C	10 °C
	Round and perfumed. Spicy, slightly bitter.	Rond et aromatisé. Fruité et un peu amer.	Rond en geparfumeerd. Kruidig, licht bitter.
i	–	–	–

blonde
blond
Abdij
van
Abbaye
de
Saint-
Martin
Blonde - Blond

Saint - Martin

Abbaye de Saint Martin brune

	top-fermentation re-fermented in the bottle	fermentation haute refermentation en bouteille	hoge gisting hergisting op de fles
	dark abbey beer	bière d'abbaye brune	abdijbier donker
	Brasserie de Brunehaut Rongy-Brunehaut	Brasserie de Brunehaut Rongy-Brunehaut	Brasserie de Brunehaut Rongy-Brunehaut
	malt, wheat, yeast, herbs, water	malt, froment, levure, herbes, eau	mout, tarwe, gist, kruiden, water
%	8%	8%	8%
	brown and slightly misty	brune et légèrement voilée	bruin en licht wazig
	–	–	–
°C	50 °F	10 °C	10 °C
	Powerful and strong-bodied.	Fort et corsé.	Krachtig en gecorseerd.
i	–	–	–

brune
bruin
Abdij
van
Abbaye
de
Saint-
Martin
Brune - Bruin

Abbaye des Rocs blonde

	top-fermentation	fermentation haute	hoge gisting
	Belgian abbey beer blond	bière d'abbaye belge blonde	Belgisch abdijbier blond
	Abbaye des Rocs Montignies-sur-Rocs	Abbaye des Rocs Montignies-sur-Rocs	Abbaye des Rocs Montignies-sur-Rocs
	malt (Pilsner), hops (Hallertau, Brewers Gold), well water from a rocky subsoil	malt (pils), houblon (Hallertau, Brewers Gold), eau de puits d'un sous-sol rocailleux	mout (pilsen), hop (Hallertau, Brewers Gold), boorputwater uit een rotsrijke ondergrond
%	7,5% (16° plato)	7,5% (16° plato)	7,5% (16° plato)
	blonde	blonde	blond
	Savour in a balloon glas.	A déguster dans un verre ballon.	Degusteren in een ballonvormig glas.
°C	43 °F	6 °C	6 °C
	White flowers and vanilla aromas. No herbs added. Rich flavour palette with a pronounced bitter taste.	Arômes de fleurs blanches et de vanille. Sans adjonction d'herbes. Riche en saveurs avec une amertume prononcée.	Aroma's van witte bloemen en vanille. Zonder toevoeging van kruiden. Rijk smakenpalet met uitgesproken bitterheid.
i	The abbey 'L'Abbaye des Rocs' dates back from the 12th century. The beer keeps for about a year in a dark room.	'L'Abbaye des Rocs' date du 12ième siècle. La bière se conserve environ un an à l'abri de la lumière.	De abdij 'L'Abbaye des Rocs' dateert uit de 12e eeuw. Het bier is ongeveer een jaar houdbaar in een donkere ruimte.

Brasserie de
l'Abbaye des Rocs
Blond

Abbaye des Rocs brune

	top-fermentation	fermentation haute	hoge gisting
	Belgian abbey beer dark - ale	bière d'abbaye belge foncée - ale	Belgisch abdijbier donker - ale
	Abbaye des Rocs Montignies-sur-Rocs	Abbaye des Rocs Montignies-sur-Rocs	Abbaye des Rocs Montignies-sur-Rocs
	malt (pale, Munich, biscuit, roasted, caramel, aromatic), hops (Hallertau, Styrie, Brewers Gold), well water from a rocky subsoil.	malt (pâle, Munich, biscuit, brûlé, caramélisé, aromatique), houblon (Hallertau, Styrie, Brewers Gold), eau de puits d'un sous-sol rocailleux	mout (bleek, Munich, biscuit, gebrand, karamel, aromatisch), hop (Hallertau, Styrie, Brewers Gold), boorputwater uit een rotsrijke ondergrond
%	9% (18° plato)	9% (18° plato)	9% (18° plato)
	Brown-red like the volcano stone from the region.	Brun rouge comme la pierre de volcan de la région.	Bruinrood zoals de vulkaansteen uit de regio.
	Savour in a balloon glass.	A déguster dans un verre ballon.	Degusteren uit een ballonvormig glas.
	54 °F	12 °C	12 °C
	Full-bodied bitterness, balanced by a fruity flavour. Touches of roasty wood and a very long aftertaste.	Saveur amère corsée, équilibrée par un certain goût fruité. Touches de bois brûlé et arrière-bouche prolongée.	Gecorseerde bitterheid in evenwicht gebracht door een zekere fruitigheid. Toetsen van gebrand hout en zeer lange nasmaak.
i	The abbey 'L'Abbaye des Rocs' dates back from the 12th century. The beer keeps for about a year in a dark room.	'L'Abbaye des Rocs' date du 12ième siècle. La bière se conserve environ un an à l'abri de la lumière.	De abdij 'L'Abbaye des Rocs' dateert uit de 12e eeuw. Het bier bewaart ongeveer een jaar in een donkere ruimte.

Brasserie de
l'Abbaye des Rocs
Abbaye des Rocs
Brune
9% vol.
Bruin

Abbaye des Rocs grand cru

	top-fermentation	fermentation haute	hoge gisting
	Belgian abbey beer dark - ale	Bière d'abbaye belge foncée - ale	Belgisch abdijbier-ale donker - ale
	Abbaye des Rocs Montignies-sur-Rocs	Abbaye des Rocs Montignies-sur-Rocs	Abbaye des Rocs Montignies-sur-Rocs
	malt (pale, (cara)Munich, biscuit, roasted, caramel, aromatic), hops (Hallertau, Styrie, Saaz, Brewers Gold), well water from a rocky subsoil	malt (pâle, (cara)Munich, biscuit, brûlé, caramélisé, aromatique), houblon (Hallertau, Styrie, Saaz, Brewers Gold), eau de puits d'un sous-sol rocailleux	mout (bleek, (cara)Munich, biscuit, gebrand, karamel, aromatisch), hop (Hallertau, Styrie, Saaz, Brewers Gold), boorputwater uit een rotsrijke ondergrond
%	10% (18° plato)	10% (18° plato)	10% (18° plato)
	dark red	rouge foncé	donkerrood
	Savour in a balloon glass.	A déguster dans un verre ballon.	Degusteren uit een ballonvormig glas.
°C	54 °F	12 °C	12 °C
	Complex but very powerful aroma, influenced by herbs and hops. Easy digestible in spite of its density.	Arôme complexe mais très corsé par les herbes et le houblon. Facilement digestible malgré sa densité.	Complex maar zeer krachtig aroma beïnvloed door kruiden en hop. Licht verteerbaar ondanks zijn densiteit.
i	The abbey 'L'Abbaye des Rocs' dates back from the 12th century. The beer keeps for about a year in a dark room. Originally created for the American market, now also available in Europe.	'L'Abbaye des Rocs' date du 12ième siècle. La bière se conserve environ un an à l'abri de la lumière. Fabriquée à l'origine pour le marché américain, maintenant également disponible en Europe.	De abdij 'L'Abbaye des Rocs' dateert uit de 12e eeuw. Het bier bewaart ongeveer een jaar in een donkere ruimte. Oorspronkelijk gemaakt voor de Amerikaanse markt, nu ook in Europa verkrijgbaar.

....

Brasserie de
l'Abbaye des Rocs
Brune
BELGIAN BROWN ALE

Abdis blond

	top-fermentation	fermentation haute	hoge gisting
	blond abbey beer	bière d'abbaye blonde	blond abdijbier
	Brouwerij Liefmans Oudenaarde/Dentergem	Brouwerij Liefmans Audenarde/Dentergem	Brouwerij Liefmans Oudenaarde/Dentergem
	barley malt, sugar, hops, yeast, water	malt d'orge, sucre, houblon, levure, eau	gerstemout, suiker, hop, gist, water
%	6,50%	6,50%	6,50%
	light blond	blond clair	lichtblond
	–	–	–
	43 - 50 °F	6 - 10 °C	6 - 10 °C
	Floral and yeasty flavour, round and full-bodied, fine bitterness in the aftertaste. Malty character.	Arômes de fleurs et de levure, rond et franc, goût amer raffiné de la fin de bouche. Caractère malté et franc.	Floraal en gistig aroma, rond en volmondig, fijne bitterheid in de afdronk. Volmondig en moutig karakter.
i	–	–	–

BLOND ABDIJBIER VAN HOGE GISTING
BIERE D'ABBAYE BLONDE DE HAUTE FERMENTATION
Liefmans
ABDIS
BLOND - BLONDE
ABDIS
Liefmans

Abdis bruin

	top-fermentation	fermentation haute	hoge gisting
	dark abbey beer	bière d'abbaye foncée	donker abdijbier
	Brouwerij Liefmans Oudenaarde/Dentergem	Brouwerij Liefmans Audenarde/Dentergem	Brouwerij Liefmans Oudenaarde/Dentergem
	barley malt, sugar, corn, hops, yeast, water	malt d'orge, sucre, maïs, houblon, levure, eau	gerstemout, suiker, mais, hop, gist, water
%	6,50%	6,50%	6,50%
	red-brown	brun rouge	roodbruin
	–	–	–
°C	46 - 54 °F	8 - 12 °C	8 - 12 °C
	Coffee aroma and roast- ed malt. Pleasantly sweet with curaçao and anise touches.	Arômes de café et de malt grillé. Agréablement doux avec des touches de curaçao et d'anis.	Koffie-aroma en geroostér- de mout. Aangenaam zoetig met toetsen van curaçao en anijs.
i	–	–	–

BRUIN ABDIJBIER VAN HOGE GISTING
ABDIS
BRUIN - BRUNE
ABDIS
Liefmans
BREWERIES

Abdis tripel

	top-fermentation re-fermented in the bottle	fermentation haute refermentation en bouteille	hoge gisting hergisting in de fles
	Tripel abbey beer	triple bière d'abbaye	tripel abdijbier
	Brouwerij Liefmans Oudenaarde/Dentergem	Brouwerij Liefmans Audenarde/Dentergem	Brouwerij Liefmans Oudenaarde/Dentergem
	barley malt, sugar, corn, hops, yeast, water	malt d'orge, sucre, maïs, houblon, levure, eau	gerstemout, suiker, mais, hop, gist, water
%	8,20%	8,20%	8,20%
	golden blond slightly cloudy	blond doré légèrement trouble	goudblond licht troebel
	–	–	–
°C	46 - 54 °F	8 - 12 °C	8 - 12 °C
	Malty, dry-bitter with a fruity aroma and complex, full-bodied mouthfeel with a touch of caramel. Pleasant dry-bitter aftertaste.	Malté et amer sec avec arôme fruité et goût franc complexe avec touche de caramel. Fin de bouche agréable et amère-sèche.	Moutig en droogbitter met fruitig aroma en complexe volmondigheid met toets van karamel. Aangename en droogbittere afdronk.
i	–	–	–

TRIPEL ABDIJBIER MET HERGISTING
BIERE D'ABBAYE TRIPLE AVEC REFERMENTATION
Liefmans
ABDIS
TRIPEL – TRIPLE
ABDIS
Liefmans

Achel blond

	top-fermentation	fermentation haute	hoge gisting
	Trappist	trappiste	trappist
	De Achelse Kluis Hamont-Achel	De Achelse Kluis Hamont-Achel	De Achelse Kluis Hamont-Achel
	malt, hops, yeast, water	malt, houblon, levure, eau	mout, hop, gist, water
%	8%	8%	8%
	golden blond slightly cloudy by re-fermentation in the bottle	blond doré légèrement trouble par la refermentation en bouteille	goudblond lichttroebel door hergisting op de fles
	Pour slowly and leave approx. 1 cm of sediment in the bottle.	Verser doucement et laisser environ 1 cm de lie dans la bouteille.	Zachtjes uitschenken en ca. 1 cm in de fles laten.
°C	46 °F	8 °C	8 °C
	Intense character. Hop flavour with a slight touch of caramel, typical yeast flavour. Bitter and a little fruity with some green banana. Dry aftertaste with some hoppy bitter.	Caractère intense. Arôme houblonné avec touche légèrement caramélisée, arôme de levure typique. Amer et un peu fruité avec un peu de banane verte. Arrière-bouche sèche et un peu amère de houblon.	Intens karakter. Hoppig aroma met lichte karameltoets, typisch gistaroma. Bitter en beetje fruitig met wat groene banaan. Nasmaak droog en wat hopbitter.
i	Brewed at Saint Benedict's Abbey	Brassée dans l'Abbaye de Saint-Benoît.	Gebrouwen in de Sint-Benedictusabdij.

BLOND BIER
BIERE BLONDE
AUTHENTIC
TRAPPIST
PRODUCT
Trappist
Achel
Alc. 8° Vol
e33cl

Trappist
Achel

Achel bruin

	top-fermentation	fermentation haute	hoge gisting
	Trappist	trappiste	trappist
	De Achelse Kluis Hamont-Achel	De Achelse Kluis Hamont-Achel	De Achelse Kluis Hamont-Achel
	barley malt, hops, yeast, water	malt d'orge, houblon, levure, eau	gerstemout, hop, gist, water
%	8%	8%	8%
	dark red-brown	brun rouge foncé	donker roodbruin
	Pour slowly. Leave approx. 1 cm of sediment in the bottle and pour the yeast sediment if desired.	Verser doucement et laisser environ 1 cm de lie dans la bouteille. Le dépôt de levure peut éventuellement être versé.	Zachtjes uitschenken en ca. 1 cm in de fles laten. Het gistdepot mag desgewenst uitgeschonken worden.
°C	46 °F	8 °C	8 °C
	Smooth but powerful. Flavour: candy, nuts, earth tones and some yeast. Taste: strong, full-bodied caramel taste. Aftertaste: hop and bitter.	Doux mais corsé. Arôme: candi, noix, tons terreux et un peu de levure. Saveur franche, caramélisée, prononcée. Arrière-bouche houblonnée et amère.	Zacht maar krachtig. Aroma: kandij, noten, aardse tonen en wat gist. Smaak: volmondig, flinke karamelsmaak. Nasmaak: hoppig en bitter.
i	Brewed at Saint Benedict's Abbey	Brassée dans l'Abbaye de Saint-Benoît.	Gebrouwen in de Sint-Benedictusabdij.

BRUIN BIER
BIERE BRUNE
AUTHENTIC
TRAPPIST
PRODUCT
Trappist
Achel
e33cl

Trappist
Achel

Achel bruin extra

	top-fermentation re-fermented in the bottle	fermentation haute refermentation en bouteille	hoge gisting hergisting op de fles
	Trappist	trappiste	trappist
	De Achelse Kluis Hamont-Achel	De Achelse Kluis Hamont-Achel	De Achelse Kluis Hamont-Achel
	barley malt, hops, yeast, dark candy sugar, water	malt d'orge, houblon, levure, sucre candi brun, eau	gerstemout, hop, gist, donkere kandijsuiker, water
%	10%	10%	10%
	red-brown	brun rouge	roodbruin
	Pour slowly and leave approx. 1 cm of sediment in the bottle.	Verser doucement et laisser environ 1 cm de lie dans la bouteille.	Zachtjes uitschenken en ca. 1 cm in de fles laten.
°C	46 °F	8 °C	8 °C
	Generous, frank character. Sweetish and full-bodied with a considerable alcohol taste. Slightly roasty with some chocolate touches. Strong and bitter with a caramel aftertaste.	Caractère royal et généreux. Douceâtre et franc avec un sérieux goût d'alcool. Un peu brûlé avec quelques touches de chocolat. Arrière-bouche fort amère et quelque peu caramélisée.	Royaal en gul karakter. Zoetig en volmondig met een serieuze streep alcohol. Beetje gebrand met wat chocoladetoetsen. Nadronk stevig bitter met karamelachtige nasmaak.
i	Brewed at Saint Benedict's Abbey.	Brassée dans l'Abbaye de Saint-Benoît.	Gebrouwen in de Sint-Benedictusabdij.

BRUIN BIER EXTRA
AUTHENTIC
TRAPPIST
PRODUCT
BIERE BRUNE EXTRA
Trappist
Achel
e75cl

Trappist
Achel

Ada Blonde des Pères 6°

	top-fermentation	fermentation haute	hoge gisting
	abbey beer	bière d'abbaye	abdijbier
	Brasserie Val de Sambre Gozée	Brasserie Val de Sambre Gozée	Brasserie Val de Sambre Gozée
	first quality malts and hops	malts et houblons de premier choix	mouten en hoppen van eerste keuze
%	6% 14° plato	6% 14° plato	6% 14° plato
	gold-coloured	dorée	goudkleurig
	–	–	–
°C	46 °F	8 °C	8 °C
	Subtle bitterness and pronounced round.	Goût amer subtil et rond prononcé.	Subtiele bitterheid en uitgesproken rond.
i	Produced in the ruins of the Cistercian abbey of Aulne. ADA is short for Abbaye d'Aulne.	Fabriquée dans la ruine de l'abbaye des Cisterciennes d' Aulne. ADA est l'abrégé de Abbaye d'Aulne.	Wordt gefabriceerd in de ruïne van de Cisterciënzerinnenabdij van Aulne. ADA is de afkorting van Abbaye d'Aulne.

Bière d'abbaye
ADA
Abdijbier
Abbaye d'Aulne
BLONDE DES PERES SUR LIE

ADA
Abbaye d'Aulne

Ada Brune des Pères 6°

	top-fermentation	fermentation haute	hoge gisting
	abbey beer	bière d'abbaye	abdijbier
	Brasserie Val de Sambre Gozée	Brasserie Val de Sambre Gozée	Brasserie Val de Sambre Gozée
	first quality malts and hops	malts et houblons de premier choix	mouten en hoppen van eerste keuze
%	6% 14° plato	6% 14° plato	6% 14° plato
	deep copper	cuivre intense	diepkoper
	–	–	–
°C	50 °F	10 °C	10 °C
	Rich, perfumed aroma and creamy mouthfeel.	Arôme riche, parfumé et sensation savoureuse dans la bouche.	Rijk, geparfumeerd aroma en smeuïg mondgevoel.
i	Produced in the ruins of the Cistercian abbey of Aulne. ADA is short for Abbaye d'Aulne.	Fabriquée dans la ruine de l'abbaye des Cisterciennes d' Aulne. ADA est l'abrégé de Abbaye d'Aulne.	Wordt gefabriceerd in de ruïne van de Cisterciënzerinnenabdij van Aulne. ADA is de afkorting van Abbaye d'Aulne.

Bière d'abbaye
Abdij bier
ADA
BRUNE DES PERES SUR

Ada Super Noël 9°

	top-fermentation	fermentation haute	hoge gisting
	Christmas beer cuvée spéciale	bière de Noël cuvée speciale	kerstbier cuvée speciale
	Brasserie Val de Sambre Gozée	Brasserie Val de Sambre Gozée	Brasserie Val de Sambre Gozée
	first quality malts and hops	malts et houblons de premier choix	mouten en hoppen van eerste keuze
%	9% 20° plato	9% 20° plato	9% 20° plato
	–	–	–
	Pour slowly.	Verser lentement.	Traag uitschenken.
°C	50 °F	10 °C	10 °C
	–	–	–
i	Produced in the ruins of the Cistercian abbey of Aulne. ADA is short for Abbaye d'Aulne.	Fabriquée dans la ruine de l'abbaye des Cisterciennes de Aulne. ADA est l'abrégé de Abbaye d'Aulne.	Wordt gefabriceerd in de ruïne van de Cisterciënzerinnenabdij van Aulne. ADA is de afkorting van Abbaye d'Aulne.

Bière
Abbaye d'Aulne
Super
Noël
Abbaye d'Aulne

Ada Triple blonde 9°

	top-fermentation	fermentation haute	hoge gisting
	abbey beer	bière d'abbaye	abdijbier
	Brasserie Val de Sambre Gozée	Brasserie Val de Sambre Gozée	Brasserie Val de Sambre Gozée
	first quality malts and hops	malts et houblons de premier choix	mouten en hoppen van eerste keuze
%	9% 18° plato	9% 18° plato	9% 18° plato
	warm gold colour	couleur dorée chaude	gulden warme kleur
	Pour slowly.	Verser lentement.	Traag uitschenken.
°C	50 °F	10 °C	10 °C
	Round, strong and subtle taste.	Saveur ronde, corsée et subtile.	Ronde, sterke en subtiele smaak.
i	Produced in the ruins of the Cistercian abbey of Aulne. ADA is short for Abbaye d'Aulne.	Fabriquée dans la ruine de l'abbaye des Cisterciennes d' Aulne. ADA est l'abrégé de Abbaye d'Aulne.	Wordt gefabriceerd in de ruïne van de Cisterciënzerinnenabdij van Aulne. ADA is de afkorting van Abbaye d'Aulne.

Bière d'abbaye
ADA
Abdij bier
Abbaye d'Aulne
TRIPLE BLONDE SUR LIE
Abbaye d'Aulne

Ada Triple brune 9°

	top-fermentation	fermentation haute	hoge gisting
	abbey beer	bière d'abbaye	abdijbier
	Brasserie Val de Sambre Gozée	Brasserie Val de Sambre Gozée	Brasserie Val de Sambre Gozée
	first quality malts and hops	malts et houblons de premier choix	mouten en hoppen van eerste keuze
%	9% 18° plato	9% 18° plato	9% 18° plato
	–	–	–
	Pour slowly.	Verser lentement.	Traag uitschenken.
	50 °F	10 °C	10 °C
	Powerful flavour.	Arôme corsé.	Krachtig aroma.
i	Produced in the ruins of the Cistercian abbey of Aulne. ADA is short for Abbaye d'Aulne.	Fabriquée dans la ruine de l'abbaye des Cisterciennes d' Aulne. ADA est l'abrégé de Abbaye d'Aulne.	Wordt gefabriceerd in de ruïne van de Cisterciënzerinnenabdij van Aulne. ADA is de afkorting van Abbaye d'Aulne.

Birra d'abbazia
Birra d'abbazia
TRIPLE BRUNE SUR LIE

Ada Val de Sambre 6° Ambrée

	top-fermentation	fermentation haute	hoge gisting
	abbey beer	bière d'abbaye	abdijbier
	Brasserie Val de Sambre Gozée	Brasserie Val de Sambre Gozée	Brasserie Val de Sambre Gozée
	first quality malts and hops	malts et houblons de premier choix	mouten en hoppen van eerste keuze
%	6% 14° plato	6% 14° plato	6% 14° plato
	amber	ambrée	amber
	–	–	–
°C	46 °F	8 °C	8 °C
	–	–	–
i	Produced in the ruins of the Cistercian abbey of Aulne. ADA is short for Abbaye d'Aulne.	Fabriquée dans la ruine de l'abbaye des Cisterciennes d' Aulne. ADA est l'abrégé de Abbaye d'Aulne.	Wordt gefabriceerd in de ruïne van de Cisterciënzerinnenabdij van Aulne. ADA is de afkorting van Abbaye d'Aulne.

Bière
DE SAMBRE AMBREE SUR

Adelardus Tripel

	top-fermentation re-fermented in the bottle	fermentation haute refermentation en bouteille	hoge gisting nagisting op de fles
	Tripel	triple	tripel
	Brouwerij Kerkom Sint-Truiden	Brouwerij Kerkom Saint-Trond	Brouwerij Kerkom Sint-Truiden
	2 malt varieties, 2 Belgian hop varieties, white candy sugar, gruut, yeast, brewing water	2 sortes de malt, 2 sortes belges de houblon, sucre candi blanc, gruyt, levure, eau de brassage	2 moutsoorten, 2 Belgische hopsoorten, witte kandijsuiker, gruut, gist, brouwwater
%	9%	9%	9%
	high blond to light orange, unfiltered	blond doré à orange clair non filtrée	hoogblond tot licht oranje, ongefilterd
	Gently pour into a degreased, dry glass without sloshing and leave a 1 cm yeast sediment in the bottle or add it at the end.	Verser tranquillement sans clapotage dans un verre dégraissé et sec. Laisser un dépôt de levure de 1 cm dans la bouteille ou ajouter par après.	Rustig inschenken zonder klokgeluid in een ontvet en droog glas. Een gistdepot van 1 cm in de fles laten of achteraf bijgieten.
°C	–	–	–
	Complex and full with vanilla and honey flavour. Beer with high alcohol content with a very long, slightly bitter and full aftertaste.	Complexe et plein avec un arôme de vanille et de miel. Bière de dégustation avec une arrière-bouche très longue légèrement amère et pleiné.	Complex en vol met aroma van vanille en honing. Degustatiebier met een zeer lange, licht bittere en volle nasmaak.
i	Brewed for the opening of the abbey tower in Sint-Truiden on May 1st, 2005.	Brassée à l'occasion de l'ouverture de la tour de l'abbaye à Saint-Trond le 1 ier mai 2005.	Gebrouwen ter gelegenheid van de opening van de Abdijtoren in Sint-Truiden op 1 mei 2005.

Adelardus
Trudoabdijbier
Haspengouwse Tripel
Met smaakevolutie.
brouwwater, mout, gist, hop, kandijsuiker
0495/38.12.14 Sint-Truiden
Trudoabdijbier

Adelardus Trudoabdijbier

	top-fermentation re-fermented in the bottle	fermentation haute refermentation en bouteille	hoge gisting nagisting op de fles
	abbey beer dubbel	bière d'abbaye double	abdijbier dubbel
	Brouwerij Kerkom Sint-Truiden	Brouwerij Kerkom Sint-Trond	Brouwerij Kerkom Sint-Truiden
	made with gruut (herbs), 5 malt varieties, 2 Belgian hop varieties, dark candy sugar, yeast, well water	fabriquée de gruyt (herbes), 5 sortes de malt, 2 sortes de houblon belges, sucre candi foncé, levure, eau de source	gemaakt met gruut (kruiden), 5 moutsoorten, 2 Belgische hopsoorten, donkere kandijsuiker, gist, bronwater
%	7%	7%	7%
	dark, unfiltered	foncée, non filtrée	donker, ongefilterd
	Gently pour into a degreased, dry glass without sloshing and leave 1 cm yeast sediment in the bottle or add it at the end.	Verser tranquillement sans clapotage dans un verre dégraissé et sec. Laisser un dépôt de levure de 1 cm dans la bouteille ou ajouter par après.	Rustig inschenken zonder klokgeluid in een ontvet en droog glas. Een gistdepot van 1 cm in de fles laten of achteraf bijgieten.
°C	–	–	–
	A full taste with a soft, slightly spicy nose and a light, bitter aftertaste.	Saveur pleine avec parfum moelleux légèrement relevé et une arrière-bouche légèrement amère.	Een volle smaak met zachte, licht kruidige neus en een licht bittere nasmaak.
i	In the past, groats were subject to taxes and the brewers had to buy it at the Gruuthuus, the groats house.	Le Gruyt était frappé d'impôts dans des siècles précédents et le brasseur devait se le procurer dans le 'Gruuthuus'.	Gruut werd in vroegere eeuwen belast en de brouwer moest het aankopen in het Gruuthuus.

Adelardus
Trudoabdijbier
in de fles. Met smaakevolutie.
brouwwater, mout, gist, hop, kandijsuiker,
Kerkom : 0495/38.12.14 Sint-Truiden

DUBBEL-TRIPEL

A

Adler

	bottom-fermentation	fermentation basse	lage gisting
	Dortmunder Pilsner	Pilsen Dortmunter	dortmunderpils
	Brouwerij Haacht Boortmeerbeek	Brouwerij Haacht Boortmeerbeek	Brouwerij Haacht Boortmeerbeek
	barley malt, maize, sugar, hops, water	malt d'orge, maïs, sucre, houblon, eau	gerstemout, mais, suiker, hop, water
%	6,50%	6,50%	6,50%
	gold-coloured clear	dorée claire	goudkleurig helder
	Pour carefully in one fluent gesture, and leave the yeast sediment in the bottle.	Verser prudemment d'un seul mouvement souple et laisser le dépôt de levure dans la bouteille.	In 1 vloeiende beweging voorzichtig uitschenken en het gistdepot in de fles laten.
°C	37 °F	3 °C	3 °C
	Lager beer with the full taste of special beer and the thirst-quenching character of pilsner. Fine flavour with a well-balanced, dry aftertaste.	Bière blonde avec la saveur pleine d'une bière spéciale et le caractère désaltérant d'une pils. Arôme raffiné avec une arrière-bouche sèche, equilibrée.	Lagerbier met de volle smaak van speciaalbier en het dorstlessende karakter van pils. Fijn aroma met een uitgebalanceerde droge afdronk.
i	–	–	–

Adler
Premium Luxus
Beer
Adler
Premium Luxus
Beer

Adriaen Brouwer

	top-fermentation	fermentation haute	hoge gisting
	Flemish brown Oudenaards	Brune flamande d'Audenarde	Vlaams bruin Oudenaards
	Brouwerij Roman nv Mater	Brouwerij Roman Mater	Brouwerij Roman Mater
	barley malt, maize, hops, candy sugar, yeast, well water	malt d'orge, maïs, houblon, sucre candi, levure, eau de source	gerstemout, mais, hop, kandijsuiker, gist, bronwater
%	5%	5%	5%
	red-brown clear creamy foam head	brun rouge claire faux col crémeux	roodbruin helder romige schuimkraag
	Slowly pour into a degreased, rinsed beer glass, forming a nice foam head.	Verser lentement dans un verre de bière dégraissé et rincé et former un faux col solide.	Langzaam uitschenken in een ontvet en gespoeld bierglas en een mooie schuimkraag vormen.
°C	43 °F	6 °C	6 °C
	Sipping beer with a thirst-quenching character. Caramel malt aroma. Caramel sweet bitter-ish taste.	Bière de dégustation avec un caractère désaltérant. Arôme caramel malté. Saveur douce caramélisée et amère.	Degustatiebier met een dorstlessend karakter. Karamelmoutig aroma. Karamelzoete bitterige smaak.
i	Store in a dark, cool room. Adriaen Brouwer was a famous painter from Oudenaarde.	Conserver à l'abri de la lumière et de la chaleur. Adriaen Brouwer était un peintre fameux d'Audenarde.	Donker en koel bewaren. Adriaen Brouwer was een bekende Oudenaardse schilder.

Adriaen
Brouwer
Audenaerds Bruyn
Adriaen
Brouwer

Affligem Blond

	top-fermentation re-fermented in the bottle	fermentation haute refermentation en bouteille	hoge gisting hergisting op de fles
	Recognised Belgian blond abbey beer	Bière d'abbeye belge reconnue, blonde	Erkend Belgisch abdijbier blond
	Brouwerij Affligem Opwijk	Brouwerij Affligem Opwijk	Brouwerij Affligem Opwijk
	barley malt, hops, yeast, water	malt d'orge, houblon, levure, eau	gerstemout, hop, gist, water
%	6,80%	6,80%	6,80%
	gold-coloured clear	dorée claire	goudkleurig helder
	Slowly pour, leaving the yeast in the bottle.	Verser lentement et laisser la levure dans la bouteille.	Langzaam uitschenken en de gist in de fles laten.
°C	46 - 50 °F	8 - 10 °C	8 - 10 °C
	Fresh, strong, aromatic smell. Malty, hoppy taste with pleasant, bitter aftertaste.	Parfum frais, très aromatisé. Saveur maltée, houblonnée avec fin de bouche amère agréable	Frisse, sterk aromatische geur. Moutige, hoppige smaak met aangename bitterheid in de afdronk.
i	The abbey of Affligem is located on the border of the provinces of Flemish-Brabant and East-Flanders. It was founded in 1074 as a Benedictine convent.	L'abbaye de Affligem est située à la frontière des provinces du Brabant flamand et de la Flandre orientale et a été fondée en 1074 comme monastère de bénédictins.	De abdij van Affligem ligt op de grens van de provincies Vlaams-Brabant en Oost-Vlaanderen en ontstond in 1074 als Benedictijnerklooster.

ABDIJ • ABBAYE
Affligem
ABDIJ • ABBAYE
Affligem
ANNO 1074
Blond
Blond
Blonde

Affligem

Affligem Dubbel

	top-fermentation re-fermented in the bottle	fermentation haute refermentation en bouteille	hoge gisting hergisting op de fles
	Recognised Belgian dark abbey beer	bière d'abbaye belge reconnue, brune	Erkend Belgisch abdijbier donker
	Brouwerij Affligem Opwijk	Brouwerij Affligem Opwijk	Brouwerij Affligem Opwijk
	barley malt, hops, yeast, water	malt d'orge, houblon, le- vure, eau	gerstemout, hop, gist, water
%	6,80%	6,80%	6,80%
	red-brown	brun rouge	roodbruin
	Slowly pour, leaving the yeast in the bottle.	Verser lentement et laisser la levure dans la bouteille.	Langzaam uitschenken en de gist in de fles laten.
°C	46 - 50 °F	8 - 10 °C	8 - 10 °C
	Mild, slightly spicy taste with slightly sweet and smooth aftertaste. Roasty candy flavour.	Saveur tendre, légère- ment relevée avec une fin de bouche légèrement douce et moelleuse. Parfum de candi brûlé.	Milde, licht kruidige smaak met lichtzoete en zachte af- dronk. Geur van gebrande kandij.
i	The abbey of Affligem is located on the border of the provinces of Flemish-Brabant and East-Flanders. It was founded in 1074 as a Benedictine convent.	L'abbaye de Affligem est située à la frontière des provinces du Brabant flamand et de la Flandre orientale et a été fondée en 1074 comme monastè- re de bénédictins.	De abdij van Affligem ligt op de grens van de provincies Vlaams-Brabant en Oost-Vlaanderen en ontstond in 1074 als Benedictijnerklooster.

ABDIJ • ABBAYE
Affligem
ANNO 1074
Dubbel
Dubbel
Double
Affligem
ANNO 1074

Affligem Tripel

	top-fermentation re-fermented in the bottle	fermentation haute refermentation en bouteille	hoge gisting hergisting op de fles
	Recognised Belgian tripel abbey beer	bière d'abbaye belge reconnue, triple	Erkend Belgisch abdijbier tripel
	Brouwerij Affligem Opwijk	Brouwerij Affligem Opwijk	Brouwerij Affligem Opwijk
	barley malt, blond candy sugar, hops, yeast, water	malt d'orge, sucre candi blanc, houblon, levure, eau	gerstemout, blonde kandijsuiker, hop, gist, water
%	9,50%	9,50%	9,50%
	deep golden very full foam head	doré intense faux col très solide	diepgoud zeer volle schuimkraag
	Slowly pour, leaving the yeast in the bottle.	Verser lentement et laisser la levure dans la bouteille.	Langzaam uitschenken en de gist in de fles laten.
°C	46 - 50 °F	8 - 10 °C	8 - 10 °C
	Spicy, bitter character. Full, complex taste with hop and malt flavour.	Corsé, caractère amer. Saveur pleine, complexe avec un arôme de houblon et de malt.	Pittig, bitter karakter. Volle, complexe smaak met aroma van hop en mout.
i	The abbey of Affligem is located on the border of the provinces of Flemish-Brabant and East-Flanders. It was founded in 1074 as a Benedictine convent.	L'abbaye de Affligem est située à la frontière des provinces du Brabant flamand et de la Flandre orientale et a été fondée en 1074 comme monastère de bénèdictins.	De abdij van Affligem ligt op de grens van de provincies Vlaams-Brabant en Oost-Vlaanderen en ontstond in 1074 als Benedictijnerklooster.

ABBAYE • ABDIJ
Affligem
ABDIJ • ABBAYE
Affligem
ANNO 1074
Tripel
Tripel
Triple

Affligem

Altitude 6

	top-fermentation	fermentation haute	hoge gisting
	Ale	ale	ale
	Abbaye des Rocs Montignies-sur-Rocs	Abbaye des Rocs Montignies-sur-Rocs	Abbaye des Rocs Montignies-sur-Rocs
	pale malt, hops (Hallertau, Brewers Gold), well water from a rocky subsoil	malt pâle, houblon (Hallertau, Brewers Gold), eau de puits d'un sous-sol rocailleux	bleke mout, hop (Hallertau, Brewers Gold), boorputwater uit een rotsrijke ondergrond
%	6% 12° plato	6% 12° plato	6% 12° plato
	blond	blonde	blond
	savour in a glass with a stem	À déguster dans un verre à pied.	Degusteren uit een glas met voet.
°C	43 °F	6 °C	6 °C
	Soft, refreshing flavour with a refined bitterness.	Rafraîchissant, arôme moelleux avec une amertume raffinée.	Verfrissend, zacht aroma met een geraffineerde bitterheid.
i	The abbey 'L'Abbaye des Rocs' dates back from the 12th century. The beer keeps for about a year in a dark room.	'L'Abbaye des Rocs' date du 12ième siècle. La bière se conserve environ un an à l'abri de la lumière.	De abdij 'L'Abbaye des Rocs' dateert uit de 12e eeuw. Het bier is ongeveer een jaar houdbaar in een donkere ruimte.

Altitude 6
Blonde 6% vol Blond
Brasserie de
l'Abbaye des Rocs

A

Alvinne Blond

	top-fermentation	fermentation haute	hoge gisting
	regional beer	bière régionale	streekbier
	Picobrouwerij Alvinne Ingelmunster	Picobrouwerij Alvinne Ingelmunster	Picobrouwerij Alvinne Ingelmunster
	malt (Pilsner, wheat) granulated sugar, hops, yeast, water	malt (pils, froment) sucre cristallisé, houblon, levure, eau	mout (pils, tarwe), kristalsuiker, hop, gist, water
%	6,50%	6,50%	6,50%
	gold-yellow slightly cloudy	jaune doré légèrement trouble	goudgeel licht troebel
	Pour into a tulip-shaped glass or goblet. Leave the yeast (approx. 1 cm) at the bottom of the bottle. Pour slowly to obtain a nice foam head.	Verser dans un verre tulipe ou un calice. Laisser la levure (environ 1 cm) au fond de la bouteille. Verser lentement de sorte qu'un faux col solide se forme.	Uitschenken in een tulp- of kelkvormig glas. De gist (ca. 1 cm) op de bodem van de fles laten. Langzaam schenken zodat er een mooie schuimkraag ontstaat.
°C	46 °F	8 °C	8 °
	Hop and malt flavour, slightly bitter taste. Full-bodied.	Arôme houblonné et malté, saveur légèrement amère. Franc.	Hop- en moutaroma, lichtbittere smaak. Volmondig.
i	–	–	–

2003
ALVINNE
Picobrouwerij
BLOND
INGELMUNSTER
2003
ALVINNE
Picobrouwerij

Alvinne Bruin

	top-fermentation	fermentation haute	hoge gisting
	regional beer	bière régionale	streekbier
	Picobrouwerij Alvinne Ingelmunster	Picobrouwerij Alvinne Ingelmunster	Picobrouwerij Alvinne Ingelmunster
	malt (Pilsner, wheat, amber, chocolate, aroma, Munich) candy sugar, hops, yeast, water	malt (pils, froment, ambre, chocolat, arôme, Munich), sucre candi, houblon, levure, eau	mout (pils, tarwe, amber, chocolade, aroma, munich), kandijsuiker, hop, gist, water
%	6,50%	6,50%	6,50%
	dark red slightly cloudy	rouge foncé légèrement trouble	donkerrood lichttroebel
	Pour into a tulip-shaped glass or goblet. Leave the yeast (approx. 1 cm) at the bottom of the bottle. Pour slowly to obtain a nice foam head.	Verser dans un verre tulipe ou calice. Laisser la levure (environ 1 cm) au fond de la bouteille. Verser lentement de sorte qu'un faux col solide se forme.	Uitschenken in een tulp- of kelkvormig glas. De gist (ca. 1 cm) op de bodem van de fles laten. Langzaam schenken zodat er een mooie schuimkraag ontstaat.
°C	46 °F	8 °C	8 °C
	Roasty sweetness. Full-bodied and distinctive.	Saveur sucrée brûlée. Franc et plein de caractère.	Gebrande zoetigheid. Volmondig en karaktervol.
i	–	–	–

2003
ALVINNE
Picobrouwerij
BRUIN
INGELMUNSTER

Alvinne extra

	top-fermentation	fermentation haute	hoge gisting
	regional beer	bière régionale	streekbier
	Picobrouwerij Alvinne Ingelmunster	Picobrouwerij Alvinne Ingelmunster	Picobrouwerij Alvinne Ingelmunster
	malt (Pilsner, wheat, amber), granulated sugar, hops, yeast, water. With dry-hopping.	malt (pils, froment, ambre), sucre candi, houblon, levure, eau. Avec dryhopping.	mout (pils, tarwe, amber), kristalsuiker, hop, gist, water. Met dryhopping.
%	7,10%	7,10%	7,10%
	dark gold-coloured slightly cloudy	doré foncé	donkergoud lichttroebel
	Pour into a tulip-shaped glass or goblet. Leave the yeast (approx. 1 cm) at the bottom of the bottle. Pour slowly to obtain a nice foam head.	Verser dans une verre tulipe ou un calice. Laisser la levure (environ 1 cm) au fond de la bouteille. Verser lentement de sorte qu'un faux col solide se forme.	Uitschenken in een tulp- of kelkvormig glas. De gist (ca. 1 cm) op de bodem van de fles laten. Langzaam schenken zodat er een mooie schuimkraag ontstaat.
°C	46 °F	8 °C	8 °C
	Strong hop and malt flavour. Full-bodied.	Arôme prononcé houblonné et malté. Franc.	Sterk hop- en moutaroma. Volmondig.
i	–	–	–

2003
ALVINNE
Picobrouwerij
EXTRA
INGELMUNSTER
Zythos
2003
ALVINNE

Alvinne Tripel

	top-fermentation	fermentation haute	hoge gisting
	regional beer Tripel	bière régionale Triple	streekbier tripel
	Picobrouwerij Alvinne Ingelmunster	Picobrouwerij Alvinne Ingelmunster	Picobrouwerij Alvinne Ingelmunster
	malt (Pilsner, wheat and Pale Ale), granulated sugar, hops, yeast, vanilla, water	malt (pils, froment et pale ale), sucre cristallisé, houblon, levure, vanille, eau	mout (pils, tarwe en pale ale), kristalsuiker, hop, gist, vanille, water
%	8,70%	8,70%	8,70%
	light amber slightly cloudy	ambré clair légèrement trouble	lichtamber lichttroebel
	Pour into a tulip-shaped glass or goblet. Leave the yeast (approx. 1 cm) at the bottom of the bottle. Pour slowly to obtain a nice foam head.	verser dans une verre tulipe ou un calice. Laisser la levure (environ 1 cm) au fond de la bouteille. Verser lentement de sorte qu'un faux col solide se forme.	Uitschenken in een tulp- of kelkvormig glas. De gist (ca. 1 cm) op de bodem van de fles laten. Langzaam schenken zodat er een mooie schuimkraag ontstaat.
°C	46 °F	8 °C	8 °C
	Full-bodied and slightly sweetish character. Sweetish flavour and malt taste.	Caractère franc et légèrement sucré. Arôme sucré et saveur maltée.	Volmondig en lichtzoetig karakter. Zoetig aroma en moutige smaak.
i	–	–	–

2003
ALVINNE
Picobrouwerij
tripel
INGELMUNSTER
Zythos
WWW.ALVINNE.
2003
ALVINNE
Picobrouwerij

Angelus Blonde

	top-fermentation	fermentation haute	hoge gisting
	specialty beer blond	bière spéciale blonde	speciaalbier blond
	Brasserie Brootcoorens Erquelinnes	Brasserie Brootcoorens Erquelinnes	Brasserie Brootcoorens Erquelinnes
	Pilsner and amber malt, home-grown aromatic hops, yeast, water	malt de pils et d'ambre, houblon aromatique de propre culture, levure, eau	pils- en ambermout, aromatische hop van eigen teelt, gist, water
%	7%	7%	7%
	light amber unfiltered	ambré clair non filtrée	licht amber niet gefilterd
	Take care not to agitate the bottle and pour carefully.	Prendre soin que la bouteille n'a pas été secouée et verser prudemment.	Zorgen dat de fles niet geschud is en voorzichtig uitschenken.
°C	39 °F or 57 °F	4 °C ou 14 °C	4 °C of 14 °C
	Lively, natural beer with hoppy taste and aroma.	Bière naturelle vive avec saveur et arôme houblonnés.	Levend natuurbier met hoppige smaak en aroma.
i	–	–	–

ANGELUS
Bière
Naturelle
non filtrée
pur malt
BLONDE
Ce breuvage est le fruit d'une préparation originale
d'éléments naturels tels que: malts d'orge, houblon,
levures et d'une précieuse dose de respect envers ces
matières premières issues du terroir.
Alc.
7%vol.
℮75cl
Verre
consigné

ANGELUS

Angelus Brune

	top-fermentation	fermentation haute	hoge gisting
	dubbel	double	dubbel
	Brasserie Brootcoorens Erquelinnes	Brasserie Brootcoorens Erquelinnes	Brasserie Brootcoorens Erquelinnes
	Pilsner and amber malt, chocolate malt, aromatic hops, a touch of carafa, yeast, water	malt de pils et d'ambre, malt de chocolat, houblon aromatique, une pointe de carafa, levure, eau	pils- en ambermout, chocolademout, aromatische hop, een vleugje carafa, gist, water
%	7%	7%	7%
	brown and transparent unfiltered	brune et transparente non filtrée	bruin en transparant niet gefilterd
	Take care not to agitate the bottle and pour carefully.	Prendre soin que la bouteille n'a pas été secouée et verser prudemment.	Zorgen dat de fles niet geschud is en voorzichtig uitschenken.
°C	46 °F or 57 °F	8 °C ou 14 °C	8 °C of 14 °C
	Pleasant, smooth and very accessible character. Subtle Carafa flavour and aromatic hop.	Caractère doux, agréable et très abordable. Saveur subtile de carafa et de houblon aromatique.	Aangenaam, zacht en zeer toegankelijk karakter. Subtiele smaak van carafa en aromatische hop.
i	–	–	–

Angelus Spéciale Noël

	top-fermentation	fermentation haute	hoge gisting
	Christmas beer	bière de Noël	kerstbier
	Brasserie Brootcoorens Erquelinnes	Brasserie Brootcoorens Erquelinnes	Brasserie Brootcoorens Erquelinnes
	Pilsner and amber malt, aromatic hops, yeast, water	malt de pils et d'ambre, houblon aromatique, levure, eau	pils- en ambermout, aromatische hop, gist, water
%	9%	9%	9%
	copper-blond	blond cuivré	koperblond
	Take care not to agitate the bottle and pour carefully.	Prendre soin que la bouteille n'a pas été secouée et verser prudemment.	Zorgen dat de fles niet geschud is en voorzichtig uitschenken.
°C	39 °F or 50 °F	4 °C ou 10 °C	4 °C of 10 °C
	Pleasant, round and original but very accessible creamy beer with vanilla flavour. Prepared on a open fire with extra malt.	Agréable, rond et original mais très abordable. Bière onctueuse avec saveur de vanille, cuisson à feu nu avec adjonction accrûe de malt.	Aangenaam, rond en origineel maar toch zeer toegankelijk zacht bier met vanillesmaak. Gekookt op open vuur met extra mout.
i	–	–	–

ANGELUS
Bière
Naturelle
non filtrée
pur malt
Spéciale Noël
Ce brouvage est le fruit d'une préparation originale
d'éléments naturels tels que: malts d'orge, houblon,
levures et d'une précieuse dose de
matières premières issues du terroir.
Alc.
9% vol.
℮75cl
Verre
consigné

ANGELUS

Anker bok

	top-fermentation	fermentation haute	hoge gisting
	specialty beer Bock style	bière spéciale type bock	speciaalbier type bock
	Brouwerij Het Anker Mechelen	Brouwerij Het Anker Malines	Brouwerij Het Anker Mechelen
	only Belgian hops	houblon exclusivement belge	uitsluitend Belgische hop
%	6,50%	6,50%	6,50%
	amber	ambrée	amber
	–	–	–
°C	43 - 48 °F	6 - 9 °C	6 - 9 °C
	warm and yet thirst-quenching	Chaleureux mais néanmoins désaltérant.	Warm maar toch dorstlessend.
i	Keeps alive the bock beer. In the past it was brewed as the first beer of autumn, preparing for the cold winter. This beer was originally brewed for and by the Mechelen beer club The Beer Brothers.	Maintient la tradition de la bière bock: était jadis brassée comme la première bière d'arrière-saison, un préambule des mois d'hiver froids. À l'origine, cette bière était brassée pour et par le club de bière malinois The Beer Brothers.	Houdt de traditie van het bockbier in ere: werd vroeger gebrouwen als eerste najaarsbier, een aanloop naar de koude wintermaanden. Dit bier werd oorspronkelijk gebrouwen voor en door de Mechelse bierclub The Beer Brothers.

Proef de nazomer in uw glas
ANKER-BOK
www.hetanker.be
BELGISCH BIER • BELGIAN BEER • BIERE BELGE

ANKER-BOK

Anker Boscoulis

	top-fermentation	fermentation haute	hoge gisting
	fruity boutique beer based on blond	bière artisanale fruitée à base de bière blonde	artisanaal fruitbier op basis van blond
	Brouwerij Het Anker Mechelen	Brouwerij Het Anker Malines	Brouwerij Het Anker Mechelen
	Margriet as a base with 25% natural fruit juice. Malt, wheat, hops, yeast, wood fruits juice, water	Margriet comme bière de base enrichie de jus de fruits naturels à 25%. Malt, froment, houblon, levure, jus de fruits des bois, eau	Margriet als basisbier verrijkt met 25 % natuurlijk vruchtensap. Mout, tarwe, hop, gist, bosvruchtensap, water.
%	6,50%	6,50%	6,50%
	burgundy brown	brun bordeaux	bordeauxbruin
	–	–	–
°C	41 - 46 °F	5 - 8 °C	5 - 8 °C
	Smooth and well-balanced	Doux et équilibré.	Zacht en uitgebalanceerd.
i	Refers to the culinary term 'coulis': a liquid substance of pureed fruits.	Renvoie au terme culinaire 'coulis': une substance liquide de fruits en purée.	Verwijst naar de culinaire term 'coulis': een vloeibare substantie van gepureerde vruchten.

ANKER
BOSCOULIS
ANKER
BOSCOULIS
ANKER
1369

Antiek blond

	top-fermentation fermentation in the bottle	fermentation haute refermentation en bouteille	hoge gisting hergisting op de fles
	Ale	ale	ale
	Brouwerij Deca Woesten-Vleteren	Brouwerij Deca Woesten-Vleteren	Brouwerij Deca Woesten-Vleteren
	barley malt, hops, candy sugar, yeast, water	malt d'orge, houblon, sucre candi, levure, eau	gerstemout, hop, kandijsuiker, gist, water
%	8%	8%	8%
	amber	ambré	amber
	Bottle can be emptied.	Peut être versée complètement.	Mag helemaal uitgeschonken worden.
°C	43 - 50 °F	6 - 10 °C	6 - 10 °C
	Full-bodied character. Slighty bitter.	Caractère franc, légèrement amer.	Volmondig karakter. Lichtbitter.
i	The brewery has existed since the 19th century.	La brasserie existe déjà depuis le 19 ième siècle.	De brouwerij bestaat al sinds de 19e eeuw.

Oud Sterk bier
Bière Forte
Oude Traditie gebrouwen
Brassée à l'ancienne
Antiek
BLOND
BEVAT ALLE VITAMINES VAN DE GIST.
CAT. S
Alc. 8% Vol.
Antiek

Antiek bruin

	top-fermentation fermentation in the bottle	fermentation haute refermentation en bouteille	hoge gisting hergisting op de fles
	Ale	ale	ale
	Brouwerij Deca Woesten-Vleteren	Brouwerij Deca Woesten-Vleteren	Brouwerij Deca Woesten-Vleteren
	barley malt, hops, candy sugar, yeast, water	malt d'orge, houblon, sucre candi, levure, eau	gerstemout, hop, kandijsuiker, gist, water
%	8%	8%	8%
	dark brown	brun foncé	donkerbruin
	Bottle can be emptied.	Peut être versée complètement.	Mag helemaal uitgeschonken worden.
°C	43 - 50 °F	6 - 10 °C	6 - 10 °C
	–	–	–
i	–	–	–

Oud Sterk bier
Oude Traditie gebrouwen
Bière Forte
Brassée à l'
Antiek
BRUIN
GISTING OP DE FLES, FERMENTATION EN
BEVAT ALLE VITAMINES VAN DE GIST
CONTIENT TOUTES LES VITAMINES DE LA
CAT. S
Alc. 8% Vol.

Antiek Super 5 blond

	top-fermentation fermentation in the bottle	fermentation haute refermentation en bouteille	hoge gisting hergisting op de fles
	Ale	ale	ale
	Brouwerij Deca Woesten-Vleteren	Brouwerij Deca Woesten-Vleteren	Brouwerij Deca Woesten-Vleteren
	barley malt, hops, candy sugar, yeast, water	malt d'orge, houblon, sucre candi, levure, eau	gerstemout, hop, kandijsuiker, gist, water
%	5%	5%	5%
	blond	blonde	blond
	Bottle can be emptied.	Peut être versée complètement.	Mag helemaal uitgeschonken worden.
°C	43 - 50 °F	6 - 10 °C	6 - 10 °C
	–	–	–
i	–	–	–

Tradition gebrouwen
Brassée à l'ancienne
Antiek
SUPER 5 BLON
GISTING OP DE FLES, FERMENTATION
BEVAT ALLE VITAMINES VAN DE GIST
CONTIENT TOUTES LES VITAMINES
744 003254
CAT. I
Alc. 5% Vol.
BIJ VOORKEUR TE GEBRUIKEN VOOR / A CONSOMMER
Antiek

Apple Lindemans

	spontaneous fermentation	fermentation spontanée	spontane gisting
	fruit beer based on Lambic	bière fruitée à base de lambic	fruitbier op basis van lambiek
	Brouwerij Lindemans Vlezenbeek	Brouwerij Lindemans Vlezenbeek	Brouwerij Lindemans Vlezenbeek
	malt, wheat, hop apple juice (25%), fructose, water	malt, froment, houblon, jus de pommes (25%), fructose, eau	mout, tarwe, hop, appelsap (25%), fructose, water
%	3,50%	3,50%	3,50%
	yellow slightly hazy	jaune légèrement voilée	geel licht gesluierd
	Pour into a flute glass.	A verser dans une flûte	In een fluitglas uitschenken.
°C	37 - 39 °F	3 - 4 °C	3 - 4 °C
	Fruity character. Lively and strong onset turning into a balance of sweet (fruit) and smooth sour (lambic).	Caractère fruité. Début vif et corsé passant à un équilibre entre le caractère doux (fruits) et légèrement acidulé (lambic).	Fruitig karakter. Levendige en sterke aanzet die overgaat in een evenwicht van zoet (fruit) en zacht zuur (lambiek).
i	Suitable as an aperitif and as a thirst-quencher.	Convient comme apéritif et comme boisson désaltérante.	Geschikt als aperitief en als dorstlesser.

LINDEMANS
APPLE
PECHERESSE
LINDEMANS

Applebocq

	top-fermentation	fermentation haute	hoge gisting
	fruit beer	bière fruitée	fruitbier
	Brasserie du Bocq Purnode-Yvoir	Brasserie du Bocq Purnode-Yvoir	Brasserie du Bocq Purnode-Yvoir
	barley malt, wheat, hop varieties, yeast, herbs, apple juice (30%), water, natural apple juice aromas	malt d'orge, froment, houblon, levure, herbes, jus de pommes (30%), eau, arômes naturels de jus de pommes	gerstemout, tarwe, hop, gist, kruiden, appelsap (30%), water, natuurlijke aroma's van appelsap
%	3,10%	3,10%	3,10%
	straw-yellow (4 EBC) naturally cloudy	jaune paille (4 EBC) trouble naturelle	strogeel (4 EBC) natuurlijk troebel
	Pour half of the bottle, then smoothly revolve it to loosen up the flavour palette and to enhance the cloudy effect.	Verser le verre à moitié plain, tourner la bouteille pour dégager la palette aromatique et maximaliser l'effet trouble, puis verser le reste de la bière.	Het glas halfvol inschenken, de fles rondwalsen om het aromapalet los te maken en het troebel effect te maximaliseren. De fles daarna uitschenken.
°C	36 - 39 °F	2 - 4 °C	2 - 4 °C
	Nose that swings between apple and cinnamon, on a coriander and bitter orange base. Slightly sour apple, sweet with a touch of wheat.	Bouquet entre pomme et cannelle sur une base de coriandre et d'orange amère. Pomme légèrement acidulée, doux avec une pointe de froment.	Neus die schommelt tussen appel en kaneel, op een basis van koriander en bittere sinaasappel. Lichtzure appel, zoet met een tintje tarwe.
i	–	–	–

applebocq
www.bocq.be

Arabier

	top-fermentation re-fermented in the bottle unfiltered or centrifuged	fermentation haute refermentation en bouteille; non filtrée, ni centrifugée	hoge gisting nagisting op de fles niet gefilterd of gecentrifugeerd
	strong blond	blonde forte	sterk blond
	De Dolle Brouwers Diksmuide	De Dolle Brouwers Dixmude	De Dolle Brouwers Diksmuide
	pale malt, nugget hops from Poperinge. Dry-hopping: part of the hops are submitted to lagering for a month.	malt pâle, cônes de houblon nugget de Poperinge. Dryhopping: une quantité de cônes de houblon est ajoutée pendant un mois.	bleke mout, nugget hopbellen uit Poperinge. Dryhopping: een hoeveelheid bellenhop gaat een maand in de lagering.
%	8%	8%	8%
	blond	blonde	blond
	Connoisseurs prefer drinking it straight from the bottle.	Les connaisseurs préfèrent boire cette bière à la bouteille.	Kenners verkiezen dit bier uit de fles te drinken.
°C	46 - 50 °F	8 - 10 °C	8 - 10 °C
	Bitter.	Amer.	Bitter.
i	Preferably drink one year before the best before date (see info on cap). The name refers to the Arabic desert, where a fresh thirst-quencher like this one must be very welcome.	Déguster de préférence 1 an avant la date de péremption (voir info capsule). Le nom se réfère au désert arabe où un désaltérant comme celui-ci doit être la bienvenue.	Bij voorkeur 1 jaar voor vervaldatum degusteren (zie info capsule). De naam refereert naar de Arabische woestijn waar een frisse dorstlesser als deze welkom moet zijn.

33 CL. e
BREWED & BOTTLED BY
DE DOLLE BROUWERS IN
8600 ESEN BELGIUM
DE
DOLLE
BROUWERS

Arend blond

	top-fermentation re-fermented in the bottle	fermentation haute refermentation en bouteille	hoge gisting nagisting op de fles
	blond	blonde	blond
	Brouwerij De Ryck Herzele	Brouwerij De Ryck Herzele	Brouwerij De Ryck Herzele
	malt, hops, yeast, sucrose, herbs, water	malt, houblon, levure, sucrose, herbes, eau	mout, hop, gist, sucrose, kruiden, water
%	6,50%	6,50%	6,50%
	gold-coloured slightly hazy	dorée légèrement voilée	goud licht gesluierd
	Rinse the glass with cold water, take it by the stem and hold it slightly tilted. Pour slowly in a single movement, avoiding contact between bottle and glass or foam. Either leave the 1 cm yeast sediment in the bottle or pour it along with the beer.	Rincer le verre à l'eau froide, le tenir par le pied et légèrement en oblique. Verser la bière lentement et en un seul mouvement sans que la bouteille touche le verre ou l'écume. Laisser un dépôt de levure de 1 cm dans la bouteille ou la vider.	Het glas koud spoelen, bij de voet vastnemen en licht schuin houden. Het bier traag en in 1 beweging inschenken zonder dat de fles het glas of schuim raakt. Het gistdepot van 1 cm in de fles laten ofwel uitschenken.
°C	43 °F	6 °C	6 °C
	Rich, spicy, warming. Smooth, slighty sweet and spicy taste with fresh yeast and hop aromas.	Riche, relevé, réchauffant. Saveur douce, légèrement sucrée et fruitée avec des parfums frais de levure et de houblon.	Rijk, kruidig, verwarmend. Zachte, licht zoete en kruidige smaak met frisse gist- en hopgeuren.
i	The draught version of this beer is clear (filtered).	La bière au fût est claire (filtrée).	Van het vat is het bier helder (gefilterd).

Arend
Arend
blond
6.5 vol.% alc.
℮ 330ml
Arend

Arend dubbel

	top-fermentation re-fermented in the bottle	fermentation haute refermentation en bouteille	hoge gisting nagisting op de fles
	dubbel	double	dubbel
	Brouwerij De Ryck Herzele	Brouwerij De Ryck Herzele	Brouwerij De Ryck Herzele
	malt, hops, yeast, sucrose, herbs, water	malt, houblon, levure, sucrose, herbes, eau	mout, hop, gist, sucrose, kruiden, water
	6,50%	6,50%	6,50%
	brown slightly hazy	brune légèrement voilée	bruin licht gesluierd
	Rinse the glass with cold water, take it by the stem and hold it slightly tilted. Pour slowly in a single movement, avoiding contact between bottle and glass or foam. Either leave the 1 cm sediment in the bottle or pour it out along with the beer.	Rincer le verre à l'eau froide, le tenir par le pied et légèrement en oblique. verser la bière lentement et en un seul mouvement sans que la bouteille touche le verre ou l'écume. Laisser un dépôt de levure de 1 cm dans la bouteille ou la vider.	Het glas koud spoelen, bij de voet vastnemen en licht schuin houden. Het bier traag en in 1 beweging inschenken zonder dat de fles het glas of schuim raakt. Het gistdepot van 1 cm in de fles laten ofwel uitschenken.
	43 °F	6 °C	6 °C
	Rich and warming. Sweet caramel taste and flavour, combined with smooth hop bitterness.	Riche et réchauffant. Saveur caramélisée douce en combinaison avec le goût amer moelleux houblonné.	Rijk en verwarmend. Zoete karamelsmaak en -aroma in combinatie met zachte hopbitterheid.
	The draught version of this beer is clear (filtered).	La bière au fût est claire (filtrée).	Van het vat is het bier helder (gefilterd).

Arend
Arend
dubbel
6.5 vol. % alc.
330ml
Arend

Augrenoise

	top-fermentation	fermentation haute	hoge gisting
	cloudy blond	trouble blonde	troebel blond
	Augrenoise Acis Casteau	Augrenoise Acis Casteau	Augrenoise Acis Casteau
	barley malt, wheat malt, unmalted wheat, oat, Styrian Golding hops, brewed following the infusion method with yeast from the Orval brewery	malt d'orge, malt de froment, froment non malté, avoine, houblon Styrian Golding. Brassée selon la méthode d'infusion avec levure de la brasserie d'Orval.	gerstemout, tarwemout, niet gemoute tarwe, haver, Styrian Golding hop, gebrouwen volgens infusiemethode met gist van brouwerij Orval
%	6,50%	6,50%	6,50%
	blond and cloudy (13,4 EBC)	blonde trouble (13,4 EBC)	blond troebel (13,4 EBC)
	–	–	–
°C	39 °F	4 °C	4 °C
	Slighty sour and very refreshing. Flavours of sweetwood and lime with a touch of honey. Low bitterness: 9,7 EBU.	Légèrement acidulé et très rafraîchissant. Arômes de réglisse et de tilleul avec une touche de miel. Goût amer limité de 9,7 EBU.	Lichtzuur en zeer verfrissend. Aroma's van zoethout en linde met een toets honing. Beperkte bitterheid: 9,7 EBU.
i	Brewed under the supervision of the Orval engineer-brewer. Brewed in the framework of an educational integration project for handicapped people.	Brassée sous la supervision de l'ingénieur de brassage d'Orval. Brassée dans le cadre d'un projet pédagogique d'intégration pour handicapés.	Gebrouwen onder supervisie van de ingenieur-brouwer van Orval. Gebrouwen in het kader van een pedagogisch integratieproject voor gehandicapten.

Augrenoise
Augrenoise

Augrenoise blonde de Noël

	top-fermentation	fermentation haute	hoge gisting
	cloudy blond	blonde trouble	troebel blond
	Augrenoise Acis Casteau	Augrenoise Acis Casteau	Augrenoise Acis Casteau
	barley malt, wheat malt, unmalted wheat, oat, Styrian Golding hop. An extra portion of barley malt is added to increase the alcohol volume.	malt d'orge, malt de froment, froment non malté, avoine, houblon Styrian Golding. Une portion supplémentaire de malt d'orge est ajoutée pour une teneur d'alcool plus élevée.	gerstemout, tarwemout, niet gemoute tarwe, haver, Styrian Golding hop. Een extra portie gerstemout wordt toegevoegd voor een hoger alcoholvolume.
%	10%	10%	10%
	blond and cloudy (13,4 EBC)	blonde trouble (13,4 EBC)	blond troebel (13,4 EBC)
	–	–	–
°C	39 °F	4 °C	4 °C
	Refreshing. Aroma of lime and liquorice with a honey taste. Bitterness: 8,8 EBU.	Rafraîchissant. Arôme de tilleul et de réglisse avec une saveur de miel. Goût amer de 8,8 EBU.	Verfrissend. Aroma van linde en zoethout met een honingsmaak. Bitterheid 8,8 EBU.
i	Brewed under the supervision of the Orval engineer-brewer. Brewed in the framework of an educational integration project for handicapped people.	Brassée sous la supervision de l'ingénieur de brassage d'Orval. Brassée dans le cadre d'un projet pédagogique d'intégration pour handicapés.	Gebrouwen onder supervisie van de ingenieur-brouwer van Orval. Gebrouwen in het kader van een pedagogisch integratieproject voor gehandicapten.

Augrenoise
Blonde de Noël

Augrenoise

Augustijn

	top-fermentation re-fermented in the bottle	fermentation haute refermentation en bouteille	hoge gisting hergisting in de fles
	abbey beer blond	bière d'abbaye blonde	abdijbier blond
	Brouwerij Van Steenberge Ertvelde	Brouwerij Van Steenberge Ertvelde	Brouwerij Van Steenberge Ertvelde
	barley malt, hops, yeast, water	malt d'orge, houblon, levure, eau	gerstemout, hop, gist, water
	8% 16° plato	8% 16° plato	8% 16° plato
	light amber	ambré clair	licht amber
	Pour in a single, fluent and smooth movement, leaving 1 cm of yeast sediment in the bottle. The yeast sediment can be poured, making the beer cloudy.	Verser en un seul mouvement fluide et doux et laisser 1 cm de dépôt dans la bouteille. Le depôt de levure peut être versé et rend la bière trouble.	Uitschenken in 1 vloeiende, zachte beweging en 1 cm gistdepot in de fles laten. De gistfond kan worden uitgeschonken en maakt het bier troebel.
	50 - 54 °F	10 - 12 °C	10 - 12 °C
	Hoppy taste with a malt background with a round, ripe evolution. Light, fruity vanilla taste.	Saveur houblonnée avec un arrière-fond malté évoluant en plus rond et plus mûr. Légère saveur fruitée de vanille.	Hoppige smaak met een moutige achtergrond die ronder en rijper evolueert. Lichte, fruitachtige vanillesmaak.
i	Also available in a Grand Cru version (9%, a little heavier and drier)	Existe aussi en une version Grand Cru (9%, un peu plus forte et plus sèche)	Bestaat ook in een Grand Cru-versie (9%, iets zwaarder en iets droger)

Augustijn
Augustijn
echte bier
la vraie bière

Authentique 621

	top-fermentation	fermentation haute	hoge gisting
	traditionally brewed beer dubbel	bière artisanale double	artisanaal dubbel
	Authentique Brasserie Blaton	Authentique Brasserie Blaton	Authentique Brasserie Blaton
	yeast, sugar, six malt varieties, hops, corn, wheat, water	levure, sucre, 6 sortes de malt, houblon, maïs, froment, eau	gist, suiker, 6 moutsoorten, hop, maïs, tarwe, water
%	7,50%	7,50%	7,50%
	brown	brune	bruin
	Serve in a thoroughly rinsed and dried glass.	Verser dans un verre suffisamment rincé et séché.	Uitschenken in voldoende gespoeld en gedroogd glas.
°C	44 °F	6,5 °C	6,5 °C
	Slighty sugared and easily digestible beer with a pleasant bitterness.	Bière peu sucrée et facilement digestible avec un goût amer agréable.	Weinig gesuikerd en licht verteerbaar bier met een aangename bitterheid.
i	Boutique beer. Store the bottles upright.	Bière brassée de façon artisanale. Conserver les bouteilles en position verticale.	Artisanaal gebrouwen bier. Flesjes rechtopstaand bewaren.

62

Authentique Ambrée

	top-fermentation	fermentation haute	hoge gisting
	amber	ambrée	amber
	Authentique Brasserie Blaton	Authentique Brasserie Blaton	Authentique Brasserie Blaton
	yeast, malt, hops, brown sugar, water	levure, malt, houblon, sucre cassonade, eau	gist, mout, hop, bruine suiker, water
%	5%	5%	5%
	transparent copper	cuivre transparent	transparant koper
	Serve in a thoroughly rinsed and dried glass.	Verser dans un verre suffisamment rincé et séché.	Uitschenken in voldoende gespoeld en gedroogd glas.
°C	44 °F	6,5 °C	6,5 °C
	Accessible and refreshing taste with noble bitterness. Varied flavours of nuts and brown sugar	Saveur accessible et rafraîchissante avec un goût amer noble. Arômes variés de noix et de cassonade.	Toegankelijk en verfrissende smaak met nobele bitterheid. Gevarieerde aroma's van nootjes en bruine suiker.
i	Boutique beer. Store the bottles upright.	Bière brassée de façon artisanale. Conserver les bouteilles en position verticale.	Artisanaal gebrouwen bier. Flesjes rechtopstaand bewaren.

Authentique ambrée
Authentique Brasserie

Authentique Blonde

	top-fermentation	fermentation haute	hoge gisting
	blond	blonde	blond
	Authentique Brasserie Blaton	Authentique Brasserie Blaton	Authentique Brasserie Blaton
	yeast, malt, sugar, hops, white pepper, coriander, water	levure, malt, sucre, houblon, poivre blanc, coriandre, eau	gist, mout, suiker, hop, witte peper, koriander, water
%	6,50%	6,50%	6,50%
	transparent blonde	blonde transparente	transparant blond
	Serve in a thoroughly rinsed and dried glass.	Verser dans un verre suffisamment rincé et séché.	Uitschenken in voldoende gespoeld en gedroogd glas.
°C	44 °F	6,5 °C	6,5 °C
	Luxury beer with a lively, powerful character. Touches of white pepper and coriander.	Bière de luxe avec un caractère vif et corsé. Touches de poivre blanc et de coriandre.	Luxebier met een levendig en krachtig karakter. Toetsen van witte peper en koriander.
i	Boutique beer. Store the bottles upright.	Bière brassée de façon artisanale. Conserver les bouteilles en position verticale.	Artisanaal gebrouwen bier. Flesjes rechtopstaand bewaren.

Authentique blonde
Alc. 6,5%
33cl e
Authentique Brasserie

Authentique Blonde de Noël

	top-fermentation	fermentation haute	hoge gisting
	winter beer	bière hivernale	winterbier
	Authentique Brasserie Blaton	Authentique Brasserie Blaton	Authentique Brasserie Blaton
	yeast, sugar, malt, hops, star anise, juniper berry, water	levure, sucre, malt, houblon, anis, baie de genièvre, eau	gist, suiker, mout, hop, steranijs, jeneverbes, water
%	9%	9%	9%
	transparent blond	blonde transparente	transparant blond
	Serve in a thoroughly rinsed and dried glass.	Verser dans un verre suffisamment rincé et séché.	Uitschenken in een voldoende gespoeld en gedroogd glas.
°C	44 °F	6,5 °C	6,5 °C
	Dessert beer with light sour taste.	Bière de dessert avec un goût légèrement acidulé.	Dessertbier met lichtzure smaak.
i	Boutique beer. Store the bottles upright.	Bière brassée de façon artisanale. Conserver les bouteilles en position verticale.	Artisanaal gebrouwen bier. Flesjes rechtopstaand bewaren.

Blonde de Noël
Alc. 9%vol
33cl
Authentique Brasserie

Authentique Triple

	top-fermentation	fermentation haute	hoge gisting
	Tripel	triple	tripel
	Authentique Brasserie Blaton	Authentique Brasserie Blaton	Authentique Brasserie Blaton
	yeast, sugar, hops, malt, water	levure, sucre, houblon, malt, eau	gist, suiker, hop, mout, water
%	9,50%	9,50%	9,50%
	transparent amber	ambre transparente	transparant amber
	Serve in a thoroughly rinsed and dried glass.	Verser dans un verre suffisamment rincé et séché.	Uitschenken in een voldoende gespoeld en gedroogd glas.
°C	44 °F	6,5 °C	6,5 °C
	Sipping beer that excels with cheese. Smooth and bitter taste, sugared and naturally alcoholised.	Bière de dégustation qui s'accorde parfaitement avec le fromage. Saveur moelleuse et amère, sucrée et alcoolisée par voie naturelle.	Degustatiebier dat uitstekend past bij kaas. Zachte en bittere smaak, gesuikerd en natuurlijk gealcoholiseerd.
i	Boutique beer. Store the bottles upright.	Bière brassée de façon artisanale. Conserver les bouteilles en position verticale.	Artisanaal gebrouwen bier. Flesjes rechtopstaand bewaren.

Authentique triple
Alc. 9,5%
Authentique

Autruche Bière des Gilles

	top-fermentation re-fermented in the bottle	fermentation haute refermentation en bouteille	hoge gisting nagisting op de fles
	specialty beer	bière spéciale	speciaalbier
	Brasserie de Silenrieux Silenrieux	Brasserie de Silenrieux Silenrieux	Brasserie de Silenrieux Silenrieux
	malt, hops, herbs, water	malt, houblon, herbes, eau	mout, hop, kruiden, water
%	7%	7%	7%
	blond cloudy (unfiltered)	blonde trouble (non filtrée)	blond troebel (niet gefilterd)
	Gently revolve or shake the bottle before opening to obtain a cloudy beer.	Tourner légèrement ou secouer la bouteille avant de l'ouvrir pour obtenir une bière trouble.	De fles licht draaien of schudden voor het openen om een troebel bier te bekomen.
°C	45 - 50 °F	7 - 10 °C	7 - 10 °C
	Malty taste. Refreshing.	Saveur maltée. Rafraîchissant.	Moutsmaak. Verfrissend.
i	–	–	–

L'autruche
bière des Gilles
l'autruche

Bacchus

	mixed fermentation	fermentation mixte	gemengde gisting
	Flemish red	rouge flamande	Vlaams rood
	Castle Brewery Van Honsebrouck Ingelmunster	Castle Brewery Van Honsebrouck Ingelmunster	Castle Brewery Van Honsebrouck Ingelmunster
	malt, sugar, hops, water	malt, sucre, houblon, eau	mout, suiker, hop, water
%	4,50%	4,50%	4,50%
	red-brown clear	brun rouge claire	roodbruin helder
	Pour into a newly rinsed glass keeping it upright near the end.	Verser dans un verre récemment rincé d'abord tenu en oblique et à la fin en position verticale.	Uitschenken in een vers gespoeld glas dat eerst schuin gehouden wordt en op het einde verticaal gehouden wordt.
°C	41 °F	5 °C	5 °C
	Refreshing. Smoothly sourish with a fruity aftertaste. The taste is influenced by the temporary storage in oak-wood barrels.	Rafraîchissant. Acidulé moelleux avec une fin de bouche fruitée. La saveur est influencée par une conservation partielle en fûts de chêne.	Verfrissend. Zachtzurig met een fruitige afdronk. De smaak wordt beïnvloed door gedeeltelijke bewaring in eikenhouten vaten.
i	The brewery classifies this beer as old-brown.	La brasserie classe cette bière parmi les vieilles brunes.	De brouwerij catalogeert het als oud bruin.

BIERE BELGE
BELGIAN BEER
Bacchus
BREWED AND BOTTLED BY VAN HONSEBROUCK
INGELMUNSTER BELGIUM

Bacchus

Balthazar

	top-fermentation	fermentation haute	hoge gisting
	regional beer winter beer	bière régionale, bière hi- vernale	streekbier winterbier
	Picobrouwerij Alvinne Ingelmunster	Picobrouwerij Alvinne Ingelmunster	Picobrouwerij Alvinne Ingelmunster
	malt (Pilsner, wheat, amber, chocolate, flavour, Munich), candy sugar, granulated sugar, hops, yeast, ginger, coriander, cardemom, water	malt (pils, froment, ambre, chocolat, arôme, Munich), sucre candi, sucre cristallisé, houblon, levure, gingembre, coriandre, cardamome, eau	mout (pils, tarwe, amber, chocolade, aroma, munich), kandijsuiker, kristalsuiker, hop, gist, gember, koriander, kardemom, water
%	9%	9%	9%
	black	noire	zwart
	Pour into a tulip-shaped glass or goblet and leave the yeast (approx. 1 cm) at the bottom of the bottle. Pour slowly to obtain a nice foam head.	Verser dans un verrre tulipe ou calice. Laisser la levure (environ 1 cm) au fond de la bouteille. Verser lentement de sorte qu'un faux col solide se forme.	Uitschenken in een tulp- of kelkvormig glas. De gist (ca. 1 cm) op de bodem van de fles laten. Langzaam schenken zodat een mooie schuimkraag ontstaat.
°C	46 °F	8 °C	8 °C
	Spicy aroma and taste. Full-bodied.	Arôme et saveur relevés. Goût franc.	Kruidig aroma en smaak. Volmondig.
i	–	–	–

ALTHAZAR
WWW.ALVINNE.BE
INFO@ALVINNE.BE
STATIEGELD 10 CENT
2003
ALVINNE

Barbãr

	top-fermentation	fermentation haute	hoge gisting
	strong blond	blonde forte	sterk blond
	Brasserie Lefebvre Quenast	Brasserie Lefebvre Quenast	Brasserie Lefebvre Quenast
	barley malt, wheat, honey, hops, sugar, curaçao orange, yeast, water	malt d'orge, froment, miel, houblon, sucre, orange curaçao, levure, eau	gerstemout, tarwe, honing, hop, suiker, curaçaosinaasappel, gist, water
%	8%	8%	8%
	amber blond	blond ambré	amberblond
	Pour into a pint-pot.	Verser dans une chope.	Uitschenken in een pintglas.
°C	41 °F	5 °C	5 °C
	Smooth and slightly bitter.	Moelleux et légèrement amer.	Zacht en licht bitter.
i	–	–	–

Barbãr
Blond met Honing
Blonde au Miel
FORTE BLONDE AU MIEL - SPECIAAL
Barbãr
DOPPIO MALTO - STRONG ALE MADE
Barbãr

Barbãr winter bok

	top-fermentation	fermentation haute	hoge gisting
	specialty beer strong dark	bière spéciale très foncée	speciaalbier sterk donker
	Brasserie Lefebvre Quenast	Brasserie Lefebvre Quenast	Brasserie Lefebvre Quenast
	barley malt, wheat, honey, hops, sugar, curaçao orange, yeast, water	malt d'orge, froment, miel, houblon, sucre, orange curaçao, levure, eau	gerstemout, tarwe, honing, hop, suiker, curaçaosinaas-appel, gist, water
%	8%	8%	8%
	–	–	–
	Pour into a pint-pot.	Verser dans une chope.	Uitschenken in een pint-glas.
°C	41 °F	5 °C	5 °C
	–	–	–
i	–	–	–

Barbãr
Winter Bok
Barbãr
Winter Bok
Barbãr

Bavik premium pils

	bottom-fermentation	fermentation basse	lage gisting
	Pilsner	pils	pils
	Brouwerij Bavik Bavikhove	Brouwerij Bavik Bavikhove	Brouwerij Bavik Bavikhove
	barley malt, hops, yeast, fine herbs, pure spring water	malt d'orge, houblon, levure, fines herbes, eau de source pure	gerstemout, hop, gist, fijne kruiden, zuiver bronwater
%	5,20%	5,20%	5,20%
	blond clear	blonde claire	blond helder
	Pour into a degreased, rinsed and wet glass, avoiding any contact between the bottle and the foam.	Verser dans un verre dégraissé, rincé et mouillé sans que la bouteille touche le faux col.	Uitschenken in een ontvet, gespoeld en nat glas zonder dat de fles het schuim raakt.
°C	36 - 39 °F	2 - 4 °C	2 - 4 °C
	Crispy, pleasant and smooth taste, created by the fine hop species. Full-bodied character with a fresh bitterness.	Picotant et agréablement doux par les variétés délicates de houblon. Caractère franc avec un goût amer frais.	Knisperig en aangenaam zacht door de fijne hopsoorten. Volmondig karakter met een frisse bitterheid.
i	Proclaimed Belgium's Best Pilsner by the consumers' magazine Testaankoop in 2005.	Couronnée en 2005 meilleure pils de Belgique par Test-Achats.	In 2005 door Testaankoop bekroond als beste pils van België.

Premium Pils
BELGIAN PREMIUM PILS
BAVIK
FIRST QUALITY BEER
BAVIK
Anno 1894

Beersel biologisch

	top-fermentation re-fermented in the bottle	fermentation haute refermentation en bouteille	hoge gisting hergisting op de fles
	blond organic beer	bière blonde biologique	blond biologisch bier
	Brouwerij 3 fonteinen Beersel	Brouwerij 3 fonteinen Beersel	Brouwerij 3 fonteinen Beersel
	malt, wheat, hops, beet sugar, water	malt, froment, houblon, sucre de betterave, eau	mout, tarwe, hop, bietsuiker, water
%	7%	7%	7%
	blond unfiltered	blonde non filtrée	blond ongefilterd
	–	–	–
°C	–	–	–
	Slightly sweetish taste, evolving into full-bodiedness with a fine bitter aftertaste.	Saveur légèrement douce évoluant vers un goût franc avec une arrière-bouche amère raffinée.	Lichtzoetige smaak die overgaat in een volmondigheid met een fijne bittere afdronk.
i	–	–	–

BIOLOGISCH BIER VAN HOGE GISTING
Beersel
BIERE BIOLOGIQUE DE HAUTE FERMENTATION

Beersel blond

	top-fermentation re-fermented in the bottle	fermentation haute refermentation en bouteille	hoge gisting hergisting op de fles
	blond	blonde	blond
	Brouwerij 3 fonteinen Beersel	Brouwerij 3 fonteinen Beersel	Brouwerij 3 fonteinen Beersel
	lager malt, 10% wheat, hops, water	malt de conservation, 10% froment, houblon, eau	lagermout, 10% tarwe, hop, water
%	7%	7%	7%
	blond	blonde	blond
	–	–	–
°C	–	–	–
	Slightly sweetish taste, fine bitter thirst-quencher.	Saveur légèrement douce, désaltérante amère raffinée.	Lichtzoetige smaak, fijnbittere dorstlesser.
i	–	–	–

BLOND BIER VAN HOGE GISTING
Beersel
BIERE BLONDE DE HAUTE FERMENTATION

Beersel lager

	bottom-fermentation re-fermented in the bottle	fermentation basse refermentation en bouteille	lage gisting hergisting op de fles
	full-malt Lager	lager maltée complète	lager volmout
	Brouwerij 3 fonteinen Beersel	Brouwerij 3 fonteinen Beersel	Brouwerij 3 fonteinen Beersel
	barley malt, Saaz hops, lager yeast, sugar, water	malt d'orge, houblon Saaz, levure de conservation, sucre, eau	gerstemout, Saaz hop, lagergist, suiker, water
%	5,20%	5,20%	5,20%
	blond unfiltered	blonde non filtrée	blond ongefilterd
	–	–	–
°C	–	–	–
	Finely hopped with a pleasant bitterness.	Houblonné raffiné avec un goût amer agréable	Fijn gehopt met een aangename bitterheid.
i	–	–	–

BIER VAN LAGE GISTING
Beersel
LAGER
BIERE DE FERMENTATION BASSE

Beersel tarwebier

	top-fermentation re-fermented in the bottle	fermentation haute refermentation en bouteille	hoge gisting hergisting op de fles
	Witbier	bière blanche	witbier
	Brouwerij 3 fonteinen Beersel	Brouwerij 3 fonteinen Beersel	Brouwerij 3 fonteinen Beersel
	composition of Lambic: 60% malt, 40% wheat, hops, water	composition du lambic: 60% malt, 40% froment, houblon, eau	samenstelling van lambiek: 60% mout, 40% tarwe, hop, water
%	6%	6%	6%
	blond	blonde	blond
	–	–	–
°C	–	–	–
	–	–	–
i	–	–	–

....

....

....

....

....

TARWEBIER VAN HOGE GISTING
Beersel
BIERE DE FROMENT DE HAUTE FERMENTATION

Bel Pils

	bottom-fermentation	fermentation basse	lage gisting
	typically Belgian Pilsner	pils typiquement belge	typisch Belgische pils
	Duvel Moortgat Corp. Puurs	Duvel Moortgat Corp. Puurs	Duvel Moortgat Corp. Puurs
	barley malt, sugar, fine hop varieties, yeast, water	malt d'orge, sucre, variétés fines de houblon, levure, eau	gerstemout, suiker, fijne hopsoorten, gist, water
%	5%	5%	5%
	blond	blonde	blond
	Pour in a single movement into a cool glass, previously rinsed with pure, cold water. Let the foam run over the rim of the glass and skim off the excess foam and big bubbles with a spatula or knife (big carbon dioxide bubbles cause the foam head to disappear more quickly).	Verser d'un seul trait dans un verre rincé à l'eau froide et propre. Laisser dépasser l'écume et enlever l'écume débordante ainsi que les grosses bulles avec une spatule ou un couteau du bord du verre (de grandes bulles d'oxyde carbonique font disparaître l'écume).	In 1 keer uitschenken in een koel glas dat vooraf gespoeld is met koud, zuiver water. Laten overschuimen en het overtollige schuim en grove bellen met een spatel of mes van de rand van het glas afhalen (grote koolzuurbellen doen het schuim verdwijnen).
°C	37 - 39 °F	3 - 4 °C	3 - 4 °C
	Pure, dry and well-hopped pilsner with a slightly bitter touch. Typical taste of Saaz hop and lager yeast.	Pils pure, sèche et bien houblonnée avec une touche légèrement amère. Goût typique de houblon Saaz et de levure de conservation.	Zuivere, droge en welgehopte pils met een lichtbittere toets. Typische smaak van Saazhop en lagergist.
i	–	–	–

BIER · BIÈRE
BEL
PILS
ANNO
1871
BEL
PILS

Belgian Angel Stout

	top-fermentation	fermentation haute	hoge gisting
	Stout	stout	stout
	Brasserie Brootcoorens Erquelinnes	Brasserie Brootcoorens Erquelinnes	Brasserie Brootcoorens Erquelinnes
	Pilsner, roasted and amber malt, home-grown hops, yeast, water	malt de pils, malt brûlé et ambré, houblon aromatique de propre culture, levure, eau	pils-, gebrande en ambermout, aromatische hop van eigen teelt, gist, water
%	5,20%	5,20%	5,20%
	dark brown	brun foncé	donkerbruin
	Pour slowly.	Verser lentement.	Langzaam uitschenken.
°C	37 °F or 46 °F	3 °C ou 8 °C	3 °C of 8 °C
	Creamy, pronounced although not aggressive malt taste. Prepared on a open fire, with extra malt added.	Onctueuse avec bonne présence de malt torréfié mais sans agressivité. Cuisson à feu nu et adjonction accrûe de malt.	Zacht met uitgesproken gebrande mout zonder agressief te zijn. Gekookt op open vuur met extra toevoeging van mout.
i	This beer is brewed for the hop feast, every second weekend of September.	Brassée à l'occasion de la fête du houblon chaque deuxième weekend de septembre.	Wordt gebrouwen naar aanleiding van het hoppefeest elk tweede weekend van september.

Belgian Angel Stout

Belgian framboises

	top-fermentation	fermentation haute	hoge gisting
	fruit beer	bière fruitée	fruitbier
	Brasserie Lefebvre Quenast	Brasserie Lefebvre Quenast	Brasserie Lefebvre Quenast
	barley malt, wheat, hops, raspberry juice (10%), sugar, yeast, flavouring, acesulfame K, water	malt d'orge, froment, houblon, jus de framboise (10%), sucre, levure, arômes, acesulfam. K, eau	gerstemout, tarwe, hop, frambozensap (10%), suiker, gist, aroma's, acesulfam. K, water
%	3,50%	3,50%	3,50%
	ruby red transparent or cloudy if very cold	rouge rubis transparente ou trouble si très froide	robijnrood transparant of troebel indien zeer koud
	Pour into a glass with a stem.	Verser dans un verre à pied.	Uitschenken in een glas met voet.
°C	36 - 39 °F	2 - 4 °C	2 - 4 °C
	Very sugared. Raspberry taste and aroma.	Très sucré. Saveur et arôme de framboises.	Zeer gesuikerd. Smaak en aroma van frambozen.
i	–	–	–

BELGIAN
FRAMBOISES
Bière aux
framboises
Raspberry
beer
BELGIAN
FRAMBOISES
BELGIAN
FRAMBOISES

Belgian kriek

Fermentation	top-fermentation	fermentation haute	hoge gisting
Type	fruit beer	bière fruitée	fruitbier
Brewery	Brasserie Lefebvre Quenast	Brasserie Lefebvre Quenast	Brasserie Lefebvre Quenast
Ingredients	malt, wheat, hop varieties, cherry juice (20%), sugar, yeast, flavourings, acesulfame K, water	malt, froment, houblon, jus de cerises (20%), sucre, levure, arômes, acesulfam. K, eau.	mout, tarwe, hop, kersensap (20%), suiker, gist, aroma's, acesulfam. K, water
%	3,50%	3,50%	3,50%
Colour	cherry red clear	rouge cerise claire	kersenrood helder
Glass	–	–	–
°C	36 - 39 °F	2 - 4 °C	2 - 4 °C
Taste	Sugared and very fruity beer. Cherry and almond taste and aroma.	Bière sucrée et très fruitée. Saveur et arôme de cerise et d'amande.	Gesuikerd en zeer fruitig bier. Smaak en aroma van kers en amandel.
i	–	–	–

BELGIAN
KRIEK
Bière
aux cerises
Cherry
beer
BELGIAN
KRIEK

Belgian Pêches

	top-fermentation	fermentation haute	hoge gisting
	fruit beer	bière fruitée	fruitbier
	Brasserie Lefebvre Quenast	Brasserie Lefebvre Quenast	Brasserie Lefebvre Quenast
	barley malt, wheat, hop varieties, peach juice (15%), sugar, yeast, flavourings, acesulfame.K, water.	malt d'orge, froment, houblon, jus de pêches (15%), sucre, levure, arômes, acesulfam. K, eau.	gerstemout, tarwe, hop, perzikensap (15%), suiker, gist, aroma's, acesulfam.K, water.
%	3,50%	3,50%	3,50%
	yellow peach cloudy if served very cold	pêche jaune trouble si très froide	gele perzik troebel indien zeer koud
	Pour into a glass with a stem.	Verser dans un verre à pied.	Uitschenken in een glas met voet.
°C	36 - 39 °F	2 - 4 °C	2 - 4 °C
	Taste and aroma of peaches, apricots and mango.	Saveur et arôme de pêche, abricot et de mangue.	Smaak en aroma van perziken, abrikozen en mango.
i	–	–	–

Bière aux pêches
Peach beer
BELGIAN PÊCHES
alc./vol.

Bella Mère

	top-fermentation	fermentation haute	hoge gisting
	Ale	ale	ale
	Brasserie Artisanale Millevertus Toernich	Brasserie Artisanale Millevertus Toernich	Brasserie Artisanale Millevertus Toernich
	different malt, hop and yeast varieties, water	Différentes sortes de malt, de houblon et de levure, eau	verschillende mout-, hop- en gistsoorten, water
%	6,50%	6,50%	6,50%
	amber blond	blond ambré	amberblond
	–	–	–
	45 °F	7 °C	7 °C
	Overall bitterness.	Amer sur toute la ligne.	Bitter over de hele lijn.
i	–	–	–

Brasserie Artisanale
MMMH!!
MILLEVERTUS

B

Bellegems Bruin

	bottom-fermentation	fermentation basse	lage gisting
	Flemish red	Rouge flamande	Vlaams rood
	Brouwerij Bockor Bellegem	Brouwerij Bockor Bellegem	Brouwerij Bockor Bellegem
	barley malt, wheat, hops, yeast, water	malt d'orge, froment, houblon, levure, eau	gerstemout, tarwe, hop, gist, water
%	5,50%	5,50%	5,50%
	burgundy colour	couleur bourgogne	bourgognekleur
	Rinse the glass with cold water, tilt it a little, pour carefully half of the bottle then keep the glass upright and pour the rest of the bottle in a single movement.	Rincer le verre à l'eau froide, le tenir légèrement incliné et verser la bière prudemment à moitié. Puis relever le verre et vider la bouteille d'un seul trait.	Het glas koud spoelen, licht schuin houden en voorzichtig half inschenken. Daarna het glas recht houden en de rest in 1 beweging inschenken.
°C	41 - 46 °F	5 - 8 °C	5 - 8 °C
	Sharp and thirst-quenching with a pleasant sourness. Well-balanced sweet-and-sour taste with a slightly fruity aroma.	Âpre et désaltérant avec une agréable acidité. Saveur aigre-douce équilibrée et arôme fruité léger.	Scherp en dorstlessend met een aangename wrangheid. Evenwichtige zoetzure smaak en licht fruitig aroma.
i	–	–	–

Brouwerij
Bockor
Bellegems bruin
Bellegems bruin

Belle-Vue Extra Appel-Kers

	spontaneous fermentation	fermentation spontanée	spontane gisting
	fruit beer	bière fruitée	fruitbier
	Inbev Belgium Brewsite Belle-Vue	Inbev Belgium Brewsite Belle-Vue	Inbev Belgium Brewsite Belle-Vue
	wheat, malt, hops, apples and cherries, brewing water	froment, malt, houblon, pommes et cerises, eau de brassage	tarwe, mout, hop, appels en kersen, brouwwater
%	2,40%	2,40%	2,40%
	red clear	rouge claire	rood helder
	Pour into a degreased, rinsed glass in a single, smooth movement. Skim off in a 45° angle. A 3 cm foam head is perfect.	Verser d'un seul mouvement dans un verre dégraissé, rincé. Ecumer sous un angle de 45°. Un faux col de 3 cm est parfait.	In 1 beweging vlot uitschenken in een vetvrij, gespoeld glas. Afschuimen onder een hoek van 45°. Een schuimkraag van 3 cm is perfect.
°C	37 °F	3 °C	3 °C
	Pronounced fruity and sweet taste.	Saveur fruitée et douce prononcée.	Uitgesproken fruitige en zoete smaak.
i	–	–	–

BELLE-VUE
Extra
&
POMME
CERISE
BELLE-VUE
Extra
KRIEK

Belle-Vue Extra Kriek

	spontaneous fermentation	fermentation spontanée	spontane gisting
	fruit beer	bière fruitée	fruitbier
	Inbev Belgium Brewsite Belle-Vue	Inbev Belgium Brewsite Belle-Vue	Inbev Belgium Brewsite Belle-Vue
	wheat, malt, hops, extra quantity of cherries, brewing water based on young Lambic.	froment, malt, houblon, cerises en extra grande quantité, eau de brassage, lambic jeune.	tarwe, mout, hop, extra veel krieken, brouwwater, jonge lambiek.
%	4,30%	4,30%	4,30%
	ruby red	rouge rubis	robijnrood
	Pour into a degreased, rinsed glass in a single, smooth movement. Skim off in a 45° angle. A 3 cm foam head is perfect.	Verser d'un seul mouvement dans un verre dégraissé, rincé. Ecumer sous un angle de 45°. Un faux col de 3 cm est parfait.	In 1 beweging vlot uitschenken in een vetvrij, gespoeld glas. Afschuimen onder een hoek van 45°. Een schuimkraag van 3 cm is perfect.
°C	37 °F	3 °C	3 °C
	Pronounced fruity and sweet taste.	Saveur fruitée et douce prononcée.	Uitgesproken fruitige en zoete smaak.
i	–	–	–

Extra
KRIEK
BELLE-VUE
Extra
KRIEK
Extra fruitig en fris
Extra fruité et frais
BELLE-VUE
Extra
KRIEK

B

Belle-Vue Kriek

	spontaneous fermentation	fermentation spontanée	spontane gisting
	fruit beer	bière fruitée	fruitbier
	Inbev Belgium Brewsite Belle-Vue	Inbev Belgium Brewsite Belle-Vue	Inbev Belgium Brewsite Belle-Vue
	wheat, malt, more than one year old hops, wild yeasts, cherries, water	froment, malt, houblon suranné, levures sauvages, cerises, eau	tarwe, mout, overjaarse hop, wilde gisten, krieken, water
%	5,10%	5,10%	5,10%
	ruby red	rouge rubis	robijnrood
	Pour into a degreased, rinsed glass in a single, smooth movement. Skim off in a 45° angle. A 3 cm foam head is perfect.	Verser d'un seul mouvement dans un verre dégraissé, rincé. Ecumer sous un angle de 45°. Un faux col de 3 cm est parfait.	In 1 beweging vlot uitschenken in een vetvrij, gespoeld glas. Afschuimen onder een hoek van 45°. Een schuimkraag van 3 cm is perfect.
°C	37 °F	3 °C	3 °C
	Traditional cherry Lambic with fruity, sweet-and-sour aftertaste.	Saveur traditionnelle du lambic de cerises avec fin de bouché fruitée, aigre-douce.	Traditionele smaak van kriekenlambiek met fruitige, zoetzure afdronk.
i	Suitable as an aperitif.	Convient comme apéritif.	Geschikt als aperitief.

BELLE-VUE
KRIEK
P.H. VANDENSTOCK
BELLE-VUE
KRIEK

BELLE-VUE
KRIEK

Bersalis

	top-fermentation re-fermented in the bottle	fermentation haute refermentation en bouteille	hoge gisting nagisting op de fles
	Tripel	triple	tripel
	Geuzestekerij Oud Beersel Beersel	Geuzestekerij Oud Beersel Beersel	Geuzestekerij Oud Beersel Beersel
	wheat malt, barley malt, hops, yeast, herbs, water	malt de froment et d'orge, houblon, levure, herbes, eau	tarwemout, gerstemout, hop, gist, kruiden, water
%	9,50%	9,50%	9,50%
	gold-yellow	jaune doré	goudgeel
	Pour swiftly to make the beer whirl in a degreased, dry glass. Avoid contact between bottle and foam. Leave the yeast in the bottle.	Verser agilement de sorte que la bière tourne dans le verre dégraissé et séché sans que la bouteille touche l'écume. Laisser la levure dans la bouteille.	Gezwind uitschenken zodat het bier ronddraait in het ontvette, droge glas zonder dat de fles het schuim raakt. De gist in de fles laten.
°C	46 - 54 °F	8 - 12 °C	8 - 12 °C
	Rich, spicy, full round and intriguing. Refreshing aroma of citrus and malt. Full taste of wheat mout, first fruity bitter, then roundish and sweet. Pleasant, spicy aftertaste.	Riche, corsé, plein rond et intrigant. Arôme rafraîchissant d'agrumes de malt. Saveur pleine de froment malté, d'abord amer fruité, par la suite rond et doux. Arrière-bouche agréable d'herbes.	Rijk, pittig, volrond en intrigerend. Verfrissend aroma van citrus en mout. Volle smaak van tarwemout, eerst fruitig bitter, daarna rondig en zoet. Aangename nasmaak van kruiden.
i	Wort is not (yet) brewed in their own brewery.	Le moût n'est pas (encore) brassée dans la brasserie propre.	Wort wordt (nog) niet in de eigen brouwerij gebrouwen.

Bersalis

Bieken

	top-fermentation re-fermented in the bottle	fermentation haute refermentation en bouteille	hoge gisting hergisting op de fles
	Tripel blond	triple blonde	tripel blond
	Huisbrouwerij Boelens Belsele	Huisbrouwerij Boelens Belsele	Huisbrouwerij Boelens Belsele
	water, malt, honey	eau, malt, miel	water, mout, honing
%	8,50%	8,50%	8,50%
	blond clear	blonde claire	blond helder
	Pour carefully so that the yeast sediment stays at the bottom of the bottle.	Verser prudemment pour laisser le dépôt de levure dans la bouteille.	Voorzichtig uitschenken om het gistbezinksel op de bodem te laten.
°C	46 °F	8 °C	8 °C
	Very malty and full flavour with flowery aftertaste.	Très malté et plein avec une fin de bouche fleurie.	Zeer moutig en vol met bloemige afdronk.
i	The name refers to the spice cake factory the Biekens in Sint-Niklaas. In this region, Bieke is also a popular woman's pet name.	Le nom de cette bière renvoie à l'usine de pain d'épices Biekens à Sint-Niklaas. Bieke est dans cette région aussi une appellation affectueuse pour une femme.	De naam verwijst naar de peperkoekfabriek De Biekens in Sint-Niklaas. Bieke is in deze streek ook de koosnaam voor een vrouw.

....

....

....

BIEKEN
BIEKEN
Gebrouwen door • Brassée par • Brewed by
Brouwerij Boelens
Kerkstraat 7 • B-9111 Belsele

Bière Brut

	top-fermentation 3x re-fermented in the bottle	fermentation haute triple refermentation en bouteille	hoge gisting 3 x hergist in de fles
	Brut beer	bière brute	brutbier
	Brouwerij Malheur Buggenhout	Brouwerij Malheur Buggenhout	Brouwerij Malheur Buggenhout
	Malt, barley, hops, yeast, water. The yeast is removed from the bottle by special procedures (riddling and disgorging).	Malt, orge, houblon, levure, eau. La levure est enlevée de la bouteille par des procédés spéciaux (remuage et dégorgement).	Mout, gerst, hop, gist, water. Via speciale procédés (remuage en dégorgement) wordt de gist uit de fles verwijderd.
%	11%	11%	11%
	blond	blonde	blond
	–	–	–
°C	refrigerated	température de réfrigérateur	frigofris
	Refined and sparkling with a lively foam head and an elegant aftertaste.	Raffiné et pétillant avec un faux col corsé et une arrière-bouche élégante.	Verfijnd en sprankelend met een pittige schuimkraag en een elegante nasmaak.
i	Can be drunk as an aperitif or as a dessert beer. For the 175th aniversary of Belgium, a Malheur Cuvée Royale was brewed: a 9% blond beer.	Convient comme apéritif et digestif ou en accompagnement du dessert. A l'occasion du 175ième anniversaire de la Belgique, une Malheur Cuvée Royale, une bière blonde de 9 % également a été brassée.	Geschikt als aperitief en digestief of dessertbier. Ter gelegenheid van 175 jaar België werd ook een Malheur Cuvée Royale gebrouwen, een blond bier van 9 %.

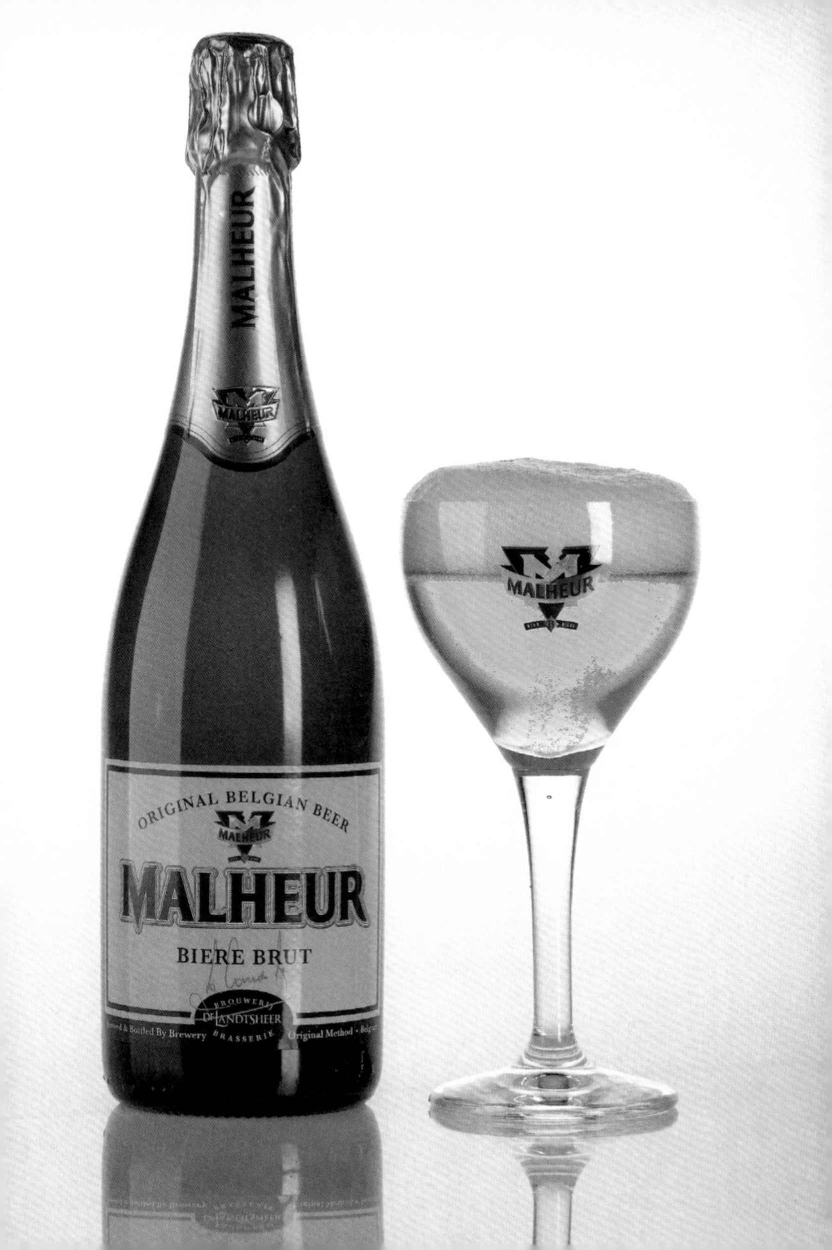

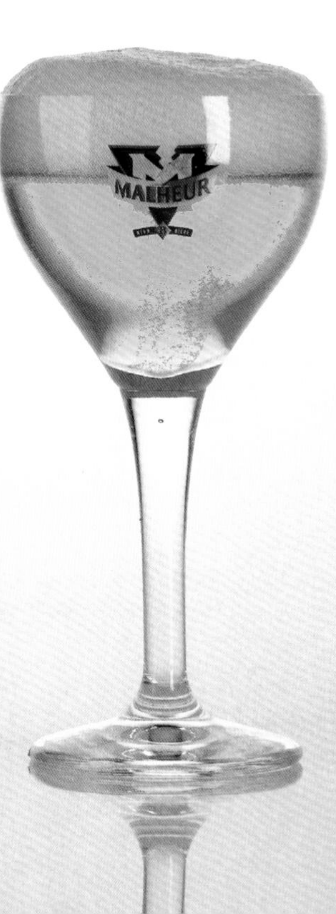

MALHEUR
MALHEUR
ORIGINAL BELGIAN BEER
MALHEUR
MALHEUR
BIERE BRUT
BROUWERIJ
DE LANDTSHEER
BRASSERIE
Bottled By Brewery
Original Method
MALHEUR

Bière Darbyste

	top-fermentation re-fermented in the bottle	fermentation haute refermentation en bouteille	hoge gisting hergisting in de fles
	specialty beer	bière spéciale	speciaalbier
	Brasserie de Blaugies Blaugies-Dour	Brasserie de Blaugies Blaugies-Dour	Brasserie de Blaugies Blaugies-Dour
	malt, wheat, hops, fig juice, yeast, water. Boutique beer without herbs or additives.	malt, froment, houblon, jus de figues, levure, eau. Produit artisanal sans herbes ou additifs.	mout, tarwe, hop, vijgensap, gist, water. Artisanaal product zonder kruiden of additieven.
%	5,80%	5,80%	5,80%
	gold-coloured unfiltered	doré non filtrée	goudkleurig niet gefilterd
	–	–	–
°C	43 - 46 °F	6 - 8 °C	6 - 8 °C
	Digestive and refreshing. Fine bitterness, fruity but not sugared.	Digestif et rafraîchissant. Saveur amère raffinée, fruitée mais non sucrée.	Digestief en verfrissend. Fijne bitterheid, fruitig maar niet gesuikerd.
i	The name refers to an ancient, typical dish of the region. The Darbystes are the disciples of priest Darby, who gather in the region of Mons-Borinage.	Le nom de cette bière renvoie à un plat ancien régional. Les Darbystes sont les adeptes du Curé Darby qui se réunissent dans la région de Mons-Borinage.	De naam verwijst naar een oud streekgerecht. De Darbystes zijn de leerlingen van Pastoor Darby die samenkomen in de streek van Mons-Borinage.

La Moneuse
BLA GES
Blaugies
Bière
Darbyste
BIERE - BÆR
Bière Artisanale Belge
non filtrée, refermentée en bouteille.
Cette bière traditionnelle à base de malt,
de froment et de figues se conserve couchée -
se boit très fraîche.
5 410557 000029
e75 cl.
Brasserie de Blaugies. Tél. 065/65 03 60
435, rue de la Frontière - B 7370 Blaugies
5,8% vol alc

Bière de Beloeil

	top-fermentation re-fermented in the bottle	fermentation haute refermentation en bouteille	hoge gisting nagisting in de fles
	amber	ambrée	amber
	Brasserie Dupont Tourpes-Leuze	Brasserie Dupont Tourpes-Leuze	Brasserie Dupont Tourpes-Leuze
	based on 5 different malt varieties and fine hop varieties	À base de 5 sortes différentes de malt et de variétés de houblon fines	op basis van 5 verschillende moutsoorten en fijne hopsoorten
%	8,50%	8,50%	8,50%
	amber-coloured	ambrée	amberkleurig
	–	–	–
°C	cellar temperature (54 °F) or slightly cooled	température de cave (12°C) ou légèrement rafraîchie	keldertemperatuur (12 °C) of lichtgekoeld
	Fairly complex with malt and hop flavours.	Assez complexe avec des arômes de malt et de houblon.	Vrij complex met aroma's van mout en hop.
i	Brewed since 1988 by order of the municipality of Beloeil, famous for its castle.	Brassée depuis 1988 à la demande de la commune de Beloeil, fameuse pour son château.	Gebrouwen sinds 1988 op aanvraag van de gemeente Beloeil, vermaard om zijn kasteel.

BELGIQUE
Alc. 8,5 % Vol.
La Bière de Belœil
e75cl
Brassée à la brasserie DUPONT à TOURPES
avec du malt provenant de la malterie de Belœil.

Bière de Miel bio

	top-fermentation re-fermented in the bottle	fermentation haute refermentation en bouteille	hoge gisting nagisting in de fles
	honey beer	bière de miel	honingbier
	Brasserie Dupont Tourpes-Leuze	Brasserie Dupont Tourpes-Leuze	Brasserie Dupont Tourpes-Leuze
	Based on organic honey, with a very particular taste.	À base de miel biologique avec un goût particulier.	Op basis van biologische honing, met aparte smaak.
%	8%	8%	8%
	amber-coloured	ambrée	amberkleurig
	–	–	–
	cellar temperature (54 °F) or slightly cooled	température de cave (12°C) ou légèrement rafraîchie	keldertemperatuur (12 °C) of lichtgekoeld
	Prominent honey taste and aroma but not sweet due to the re-fermentation of the honey. Complex beer because of secondary fermentation in the cellar.	Saveur et arôme de miel dominants mais pas sucrés par la fermentation secondaire du miel. Bière complexe par la refermentation évoluant encore dans la cave.	Dominerende honingsmaak en -aroma maar niet zoet door de hergisting van de honing. Complex bier door de nagisting dat verder evolueert in de kelder.
i	Has a "Biogarantie label". The label on the bottle is a reproduction of the original one from 1880, when the honey beer was a specialty of the farm brewery Rimaux-Deridder.	Avec le label Biogarantie®. L'étiquette est une reproduction de l'étiquette originale de 1880 au moment où la bière de miel était une spécialité de la brasserie de ferme Rimaux-Deridder.	Met label Biogarantie®. Het etiket is een reproductie van het oorspronkelijke etiket uit 1880 toen het honingbier een specialiteit was van hoevebrouwerij Rimaux-Deridder.

Bière de Miel
℮ 25 cl
Biologique · Biologisch
Bière de Miel

Bière des Ours

	top-fermentation re-fermented in the bottle	fermentation haute refermentation en bouteille	hoge gisting hergisting in de fles
	honey beer	bière de miel	honingbier
	Brasserie La Binchoise Binche	Brasserie La Binchoise Binche	Brasserie La Binchoise Binche
	before the main fermentation, honey is added	ajout de miel avant la fermentation principale	voor de hoofdgisting wordt honing toegevoegd
%	8,40%	8,40%	8,40%
	–	–	–
	blond	blonde	blond
°C	–	–	–
	Smooth and aromatic sipping or aperitif beer.	Bière de dégustation ou d'apéritif douce et aromatisée.	Zacht en aromatisch degustatie- of aperitiefbier.
i	The high alcohol content is the result of the yeast sugars in the honey.	La teneur élevée en alcool est le résultat des sucres de levure dans le miel.	Het hoge alcoholgehalte is het resultaat van de gistsuikers in de honing.

LA BINCHOISE
BIÈRE BELGE
REFERMENTÉE EN BOUTEILLE
Bière des Ours
BIÈRE AU MIEL
LA BINCHOISE
SINCE 1987

Bière du Corsaire Cuvée Spéciale

	top-fermentation re-fermented in the bottle	fermentation haute refermentation en bouteille	hoge gisting hergisting in de fles
	Belgian Ale - double-malt strong blond	Belgian ale - maltée double, blonde forte	Belgian ale - dubbelmoutig sterk blond
	Brouwerij Huyghe Melle	Brouwerij Huyghe Melle	Brouwerij Huyghe Melle
	barley malt, hops, yeast, candy sugar, water	malt d'orge, houblon, levure, eau, sucre candi	gerstemout, hop, gist, kandijsuiker, water
%	9,40%	9,40%	9,40%
	blond	blonde	blond
	–	–	–
°C	–	–	–
	Sipping beer with a light roasted bitter aftertaste and a touch of roasted caramel.	Bière de dégustation avec une fin de bouche fumée légèrement amère et une touche de caramélisé brûlé.	Degustatiebier met lichtgerookte bittere afdronk, toets van gebrande karamel.
i	Heavy brother of Delirium, pirate beer.	Le frère plus fort de delirium, bière pirate.	Zwaardere broer van delirium, piratenbier.

BELGIAN ALE

Bière Spéciale Belge

	top-fermentation re-fermented in the bottle unpasteurised	fermentation haute refermentation en bouteille non pasteurisée	hoge gisting hergisting in de fles niet gepasteuriseerd
	Spéciale Belge	spéciale belge	spéciale belge
	Brasserie La Binchoise Binche	Brasserie La Binchoise Binche	Brasserie La Binchoise Binche
	–	–	–
%	5%	5%	5%
	amber	ambrée	amber
	–	–	–
°C	–	–	–
	Fine bitterness.	Saveur amère raffinée.	Fijne bitterheid.
i	–	–	–

BIERE SPECIALE
BELGE
5% vol. alc.
0,25 L
BRASSERIE
LA BINCHOISE
BELGE
LA BINCHOISE

Big Bavik

	bottom-fermentation	fermentation basse	lage gisting
	Pilsner	pils	pilsbier
	Brouwerij Bavik Bavikhove	Brouwerij Bavik Bavikhove	Brouwerij Bavik Bavikhove
	barley malt, hops, yeast, pure spring water	malt d'orge, houblon, levure, eau de source pure	gerstemout, hop, gist, zuiver bronwater
%	5%	5%	5%
	clear gold-yellow	jaune doré vif	helder goudgeel
	Pour into a degreased, rinsed and wet glass, avoiding contact between bottle and foam.	Verser dans un verre dégraissé, rincé et mouillé sans que la bouteille touche le faux col.	Uitschenken in een ontvet, gespoeld en nat glas zonder dat de fles het schuim raakt.
°C	36 - 39 °F	2 - 4 °C	2 - 4 °C
	Slightly spicy with sweet malt. Fresh, light, crispy and hoppy character.	Légèrement relevé avec un goût sucré malté. Caractère frais, léger, picotant et houblonné.	Licht kruidig met een moutige zoetheid. Fris, licht, knisperig en hoppig karakter.
i	–	–	–

BELGIAN PREMIUM EXPORT
BAVIK
FIRST QUALITY BEER
BAVIK
Anno 1894

B

Bink blond

	top-fermentation re-fermented in the bottle	fermentation haute refermentation en bouteille	hoge gisting nagisting op de fles
	blond	blonde	blond
	Brouwerij Kerkom Sint-Truiden	Brouwerij Kerkom Saint-Trond	Brouwerij Kerkom Sint-Truiden
	2 malt varieties, 3 Belgian hop varieties (Challenger, Saaz, East-Kent Goldings), yeast, brewing water	2 sortes de malt, 3 variétés belges de houblon (Challenger, Saaz, East-Kent Goldings), levure, eau de brassage	2 moutsoorten, 3 Belgische hopsoorten (Challenger, Saaz, East-Kent Goldings), gist, brouwwater
%	5,50%	5,50%	5,50%
	copper-coloured unfiltered	cuivrée non filtrée	koperkleurig ongefilterd
	Gently pour into a degreased, dry glass without sloshing. Leave 1 cm yeast sediment in the bottle or add it at the end.	Verser tranquillement sans clapotage dans un verre dégraissé et sec. Laisser un dépôt de levure de 1 cm dans la bouteille ou l'ajouter par après.	Rustig inschenken zonder klokgeluid in een ontvet en droog glas. Een gistdepot van 1 cm in de fles laten of achteraf bijgieten.
°C	–	–	–
	Exceptional character beer: bitter, hoppy thirst-quencher with a low alcohol content, not taking part in the sweetening trend of Belgian beers. Fresh and easily digestible, fruity taste, hoppy nose, bitterish aftertaste.	Bière de caractère rare: désaltérant amer et houblonné avec une teneur basse en alcool, par laquelle elle s'écarte de la tendance de l'adoucissement des bières belges. Frais et facilement digestible, goût fruité, parfum houblonné, arrière-goût amer.	Zeldzaam karakterbier: bittere, hoppige dorstlesser met laag alcoholgehalte, waarmee het afwijkt van de trend van de verzoeting van de Belgische bieren. Fris en licht verteerbaar, fruitige smaak, hoppige neus, bitterige nasmaak.
i	–	–	–

BINK
blond
gebrouwen streekbier van hoge gisting uit
Met smaakevolutie. Ingrediënten: brouwwater,
Kerkom : 0495/38.12.14 Sint-Truiden

BINK
Brouwerij
Kerkom

Bink Bloesem

	top-fermentation re-fermented in the bottle unpasteurised	fermentation haute refermentation en bouteille; non pasteurisée	hoge gisting nagisting op de fles niet gepasteuriseerd
	blond	blonde	blond
	Brouwerij Kerkom Sint-Truiden	Brouwerij Kerkom Saint-Trond	Brouwerij Kerkom Sint-Truiden
	5 malt varieties, 1 hop variety, yeast, honey from Sint-Truiden, pear syrup from Vrolingen, brewing water	5 sortes de malt, 1 variété de houblon, levure, miel de Saint-Trond, sirop de poire de Vrolingen, eau de brassage	5 moutsoorten, 1 hopsoort, gist, honing van Sint-Truiden, perenstroop van Vrolingen, brouwwater
%	7,10%	7,10%	7,10%
	dark amber with red hues unfiltered	ambre foncé avec des teintes rouges; non filtrée	donker amber met rode tint ongefilterd
	Gently pour into a degreased, dry glass without sloshing. Leave 1 cm yeast sediment in the bottle or add it at the end.	Verser tranquillement sans clapotage dans un verre dégraissé et sec. Laisser un dépôt de levure de 1 cm dans la bouteille ou l'ajouter par après.	Rustig inschenken zonder klokgeluid in een ontvet en droog glas. Een gistdepot van 1 cm in de fles laten of achteraf bijgieten.
°C	–	–	–
	Fruity with a light sweet tone and a long, fruity, smoothly bitter aftertaste.	Fruité avec un teint légèrement doux et une fin de bouche longue, fruitée et douce-amère.	Fruitig met een lichtzoete tint en een lange fruitige, zacht bittere afdronk.
i	–	–	–

BINK
Ambachtelijk gebrouwen speciaalbier,
met honing en perensiroop uit
Nagisting in de fles. Met smaakevolutie.
Ingrediënten: brouwwater, mout, gist, hop.
0495/38.12.14 Sint-Truiden
BINK

Bink bruin

	top-fermentation re-fermented in the bottle unpasteurised	fermentation haute refermentation en bouteille; non pasteurisée	hoge gisting nagisting op de fles niet gepasteuriseerd
	Scottish style type	type scotch	scotchtype
	Brouwerij Kerkom Sint-Truiden	Brouwerij Kerkom Sint-Trond	Brouwerij Kerkom Sint-Truiden
	4 malt varieties, 1 Belgian hop variety, yeast, brewing water	4 sortes de malt, 1 variété belge de houblon, levure, eau de brassage	4 moutsoorten, 1 Belgische hopsoort, gist, brouwwater
%	5,50%	5,50%	5,50%
	dark brown unfiltered	brun foncé non filtrée	donkerbruin ongefilterd
	Gently pour into a degreased, dry glass without sloshing. Leave 1 cm yeast sediment in the bottle or add it at the end.	Verser tranquillement sans clapotage dans un verre dégraissé et sec. Laisser un dépôt de levure de 1 cm dans la bouteille ou l'ajouter par après.	Rustig inschenken zonder klokgeluid in een ontvet en droog glas. Een gistdepot van 1 cm in de fles laten of achteraf bijgieten.
°C	–	–	–
	Full-bodied and smoothly bitter with a sweetish malt aftertaste.	Franc et légèrement amer avec une fin de bouche douce maltée.	Volmondig en zacht bitter met een zoetig moutige afdronk.
i	–	–	–

BINK
bruin
BINK
Brouwerij
Kerkom

B

Biolégère

	top-fermentation re-fermented in the bottle	fermentation haute refermentation en bouteille	hoge gisting nagisting in de fles
	Saisons	bière de saison	saison
	Brasserie Dupont Tourpes-Leuze	Brasserie Dupont Tourpes-Leuze	Brasserie Dupont Tourpes-Leuze
	–	–	–
%	3,50%	3,50%	3,50%
	blond	blonde	blond
	–	–	–
	slightly cooled	légèrement rafraîchie	licht gekoeld
	Light and refreshing, well-balanced and relatively complex, distinctive despite the low alcohol content. Taste and aromas of malt and citrus fruits.	Léger et rafraîchissant, équilibré et relativement complexe, plein de caractère malgré la basse teneur d'alcool. Saveur et arômes de malt et de fruits de citron.	Licht en verfrissend, evenwichtig en relatief complex, karaktervol ondanks het laag alcoholgehalte. Smaak en aroma's van mout en citrusvruchten.
i	The production is supervised by Ecocert®, with a 'Biogarantie' -label.	La production est contrôlée par Ecocert®. Avec le label Biogarantie®.	De productie wordt gecontroleerd door Ecocert®. Met label Biogarantie®.

....

....

....

....

....

Biolégère
À BASE DE MALT ET DE HOUBLON ISSUS DE CULTURE BIOLOGIQUE
e25cl
Alc.3,5%Vol.
bière non filtrée
ongefilterd bier
L07039A
03/2009
DUPONT

Black Hole

	bottom-fermentation	fermentation basse	lage gisting
	premium Lager	premium lager	premium lager
	Brouwerij Roman Mater	Brouwerij Roman Mater	Brouwerij Roman Mater
	barley malt, hops, corn, yeast, well water	malt d'orge, houblon, maïs, levure, eau de source	gerstemout, hop, mais, gist, bronwater
%	5,60%	5,60%	5,60%
	light-yellow clear	jaune clair claire	lichtgeel helder
	Pour slowly into a degreased, rinsed beer glass.	Verser lentement dans un verre de bière dégraissé et rincé.	Langzaam uitschenken in een ontvet en gespoeld bierglas.
°C	37 °F	3 °C	3 °C
	Distinctive thirst-quencher. Fruity hop taste of Czech aroma hop and dry bitter aftertaste.	Désaltérant de caractère. Saveur houblonnée fruitée de houblon aromatique Tchèque et fin de bouche amère sèche.	Karaktervolle dorstlesser. Fruitige hopsmaak van Tsjechische aromahop en droge bittere afdronk.
i	Store in a dark, cool room.	Conserver à l'abri de la lumière et de la chaleur.	Donker en koel bewaren.

BLACK
HOLE
PREMIUM LAGER BEER
BLACK
HOLE

Black Mortal

	top-fermentation re-fermented in the bottle	fermentation haute refermentation en bouteille	hoge gisting hergisting op de fles
	strong dark	bière foncée forte	sterk donker
	Mortal's Beers Jamagne	Mortal's Beers Jamagne	Mortal's Beers Jamagne
	malt, sugar, hops, oak bark, yeast, water	malt, sucre, houblon, écorce de chêne, levure, eau	mout, suiker, hop, eikenschors, gist, water
%	8%	8%	8%
	brown	brune	bruin
	–	–	–
°C	39 - 43 °F	4 - 6 °C	4 - 6 °C
	Soft, with oak and candy touches.	Moelleux avec une touche de chêne et de candi.	Zacht met een toets van eik en kandij.
i	–	–	–

WWW.MORTALSBEERS.BE
Black Mortal
Alc. 8,0% vol.
33 cl
MORTALS BEERS

Blanche de Bruxelles

	top-fermentation	fermentation haute	hoge gisting
	Witbier	bière blanche	witbier
	Brasserie Lefebvre Quenast	Brasserie Lefebvre Quenast	Brasserie Lefebvre Quenast
	barley malt, wheat (40%), hop varieties, sugar, yeast, coriander, curaçao, water	malt d'orge, froment (40%), sortes de houblon, sucre, levure, coriandre, curaçao, eau	gerstemout, tarwe (40%), hopsoorten, suiker, gist, koriander, curaçao, water
%	4,50%	4,50%	4,50%
	very pale cloudy	très pâle trouble	zeer bleek troebel
	Pour into a yard glass.	Verser dans un verre conique.	Uitschenken in een konisch glas.
°C	36 - 41 °F	2 - 5 °C	2 - 5 °C
	Harmonious taste of malt, wheat and orange rind.	Saveur harmonieuse de malt, de froment et de zeste d'orange.	Harmonische smaak van mout, tarwe en sinaasappelschil.
i	–	–	–

BLANCHE DE
Bière Blanche
White Beer
BRUXELLES
330 ml e
4.5% alc/vol
BLANCHE DE
Bière Blanche
White Beer
BRUXELLES

B Blanche de Namur

	top-fermentation re-fermented in the bottle	fermentation haute refermentation en bouteille	hoge gisting met hergisting in de fles
	Witbier	bière blanche	witbier
	Brasserie du Bocq Purnode-Yvoir	Brasserie du Bocq Purnode-Yvoir	Brasserie du Bocq Purnode-Yvoir
	barley malt, wheat, hop varieties, yeast, herbs, water	malt d'orge, froment, sortes de houblon, levure, herbes, eau	gerstemout, tarwe, hoppesoorten, gist, kruiden, water
%	4,50%	4,50%	4,50%
	blonde (5 EBC) cloudy and milky	blonde (5 EBC) trouble et laiteuse	blond (5 EBC) troebel en melkachtig
	Pour half of the bottle, then smoothly revolve it to loosen up the flavour palette and to enhance the cloudy effect.	Remplir le verre à moitié, tourner la bouteille pour dégager la palette aromatique et maximaliser l'effet trouble. Vider la bouteille.	Het glas halfvol inschenken, de fles rondwalsen om het aromapalet los te maken en het troebel effect te maximaliseren. De fles daarna uitschenken.
°C	36 - 39 °F	2 - 4 °C	2 - 4 °C
	Fine, fruity nose with coriander and bitter orange rind flavours (12EBU). Smooth, fine and thirst-quenching beer, slightly sour, not bitter (12 EBU).	Bouquet fin et fruité avec des arômes de coriandre et de zeste d'orange amer. Bière moelleuse raffinée et désaltérante, légèrement acidulée, et non amère (12EBU).	Fijne en fruitige neus met aroma's van koriander en bittere sinaasappelschil. Zacht, fijn en dorstlessend bier, lichtjes zuur, niet bitter (12EBU).
i	–	–	–

....

....

Blanche
de Namur
~ Bière sur Lie ~
Blanche
de Namur
Une tradition de brasseurs depuis 1858
Een brouwerstraditie sinds 1858

WITBIER
Blanche
de Namur

Blanche des Honnelles

	top-fermentation	fermentation haute	hoge gisting
	Witbier	bière blanche	witbier
	Abbaye des Rocs Montignies-sur-Rocs	Abbaye des Rocs Montignies-sur-Rocs	Abbaye des Rocs Montignies-sur-Rocs
	malt (of wheat, oat, barley), hops (Hallertau, Brewers Gold), well water from a rocky subsoil.	malt (de froment, avoine, orge), houblon (Hallertau, Brewers Gold), eau de puits d'un sous-sol rocailleux	mout (van tarwe, haver, gerst), hop (Hallertau, Brewers Gold), boorputwater uit een rotsrijke ondergrond
%	6% (16° plato)	6% (16° plato)	6% (16° plato)
	cloudy blond beer	bière blonde trouble	troebel blond bier
	Savour in a flute-glass.	À déguster dans une flûte.	Degusteren uit een fluitglas.
	43 °F	6 °C	6 °C
	Smooth and refreshing.	Doux et rafraîchissant.	Zacht en verfrissend.
	The abbey 'L'Abbaye des Rocs' dates back from the 12th century. The beer keeps for about a year in a dark room.	'L'Abbaye des Rocs' date du 12ième siècle. La bière se conserve environ un an à l'abri de la lumière.	De abdij 'L'Abbaye des Rocs' dateert uit de 12e eeuw. Het bier bewaart ongeveer een jaar in een donkere ruimte.

Blanche
des Honnelles
Blanche double
Dubbel wit
6% vol.
Brasserie de
l'Abbaye des Rocs

Blanche des Neiges

top-fermentation natural re-fermentation	fermentation haute refermentation naturelle	hoge gisting natuurlijke hergisting
Witbier	bière blanche	witbier
Brouwerij Huyghe Melle	Brouwerij Huyghe Melle	Brouwerij Huyghe Melle
60% barley malt, 40% wheat, re-fermentation sugar, hops, yeast, aroma, water, coriander, orange rind	60% malt d'orge, 40% froment, sucre de refermentation, houblon, levure, arômes, eau, coriandre, écorce d'orange	60% gerstemout, 40% tarwe, hergistingssuiker, hop, gist, aroma, water, koriander, sinaasschil
5%	5%	5%
light-yellow cloudy	jaune clair trouble	lichtgeel troebel
–	–	–
39 °F	4 °C	4 °C
Fruity Witbier.	Bière blanche fruitée	Fruitig witbier.
This is the same beer as Floris Witbier, but for the Belgian market.	Bière identique à la blanche Floris; destinée au marché belge.	Is hetzelfde bier als Floris witbier; bestemd voor de Belgische markt.

Blanche des Neiges
Wit Bier
e33 cl.
Blanche des Neiges

Blanche des Saisis

	top-fermentation re-fermented in the bottle	fermentation haute refermentation en bouteille	hoge gisting nagisting in de fles
	Witbier	bière blanche	witbier
	Brasserie des Légendes Brewsite Quintine Ellezelles	Brasserie des Légendes Brewsite Quintine Ellezelles	Brasserie des Légendes Brewsite Quintine Ellezelles
	60% barley malt, 40% wheat, hops, yeast, water	60% malt d'orge, 40% froment, houblon, levure, eau	60% gerstemout, 40% tarwe, hop, gist, water
%	5,90%	5,90%	5,90%
	yellow-blond cloudy	blond jaune trouble	geelblond troebel
	–	–	–
	41 - 46 °F	5 - 8 °C	5 - 8 °C
	Bitterness caused by the hops (no coriander or orange rind added), fruity aroma and wheat taste. Dry thirst-quencher with pronounced hoppy character.	Goût amer provenant uniquement du houblon (aucune adjonction de coriandre ou de zeste d'orange), arôme fruité et saveur de froment. Désaltérant sec avec caractère houblonné prononcé.	Bitterheid die enkel uit de hop ontstaat (geen toevoeging van koriander of sinaasappelschil), fruitig aroma en smaak van tarwe. Droge dorstlesser met uitgesproken hopkarakter.
i	–	–	–

La Bière des Collines
Tarwebier Bière de Froment
van des
SAISIS
Brasserie Ellezelloise
Alc. 5,9% vol.
℮ 33 cl
S.P.R.L.
P.V.B.A.
Bière Belge • Belgisch Bier • Belgian Beer • Cervezza Extra

La Bière des Collines
Witbier Bière Blanche
van des
SAISIS
Brasserie Ellezelloise

Blanche du Hainaut bio

	top-fermentation re-fermented in the bottle	fermentation haute refermentation en bouteille	hoge gisting nagisting in de fles
	Witbier	bière blanche	witbier
	Brasserie Dupont Tourpes-Leuze	Brasserie Dupont Tourpes-Leuze	Brasserie Dupont Tourpes-Leuze
	Based on organic barley and wheat malt, organic hops, coriander and orange rind.	À base de malt d'orge et de froment biologique, houblon biologique, coriandre et zeste d'orange.	Op basis van biologische gerst- en tarwemout, biologische hop, koriander en sinaasschil.
%	5,50%	5,50%	5,50%
	yellow	jaune	geel
	–	–	–
°C	slightly cooled	légèrement rafraîchie	lichtgekoeld
	Light and smooth with a touch of bitterness. Refreshing owing to the combination of sour, coriander and orange.	Léger et doux avec une pointe d'amertume. Désaltérant par une combinaison d'acidité et d'une touche de coriandre et d'orange.	Licht en zacht met een vleugje bitterheid. Verfrissend door de combinatie van zuurheid met een snuifje koriander en sinaas.
i	The production is supervised by Ecocert® and has the 'Biogarantie label'.	La production est contrôlée par Ecocert®. Avec le label Biogarantie®.	De productie wordt gecontroleerd door Ecocert®. Met label Biogarantie®.

TOURPES
BLANCHE
DU
HAINAUT
Biologique
e25cl
Alc.5,5%Vol.
bière non filtrée
ongefilterd bier
04/2009

DUPONT

Blanchette de Lorraine

	top-fermentation re-fermented in the bottle	fermentation haute refermentation en bouteille	hoge gisting hergisting op de fles
	fruit beer based on Witbier	bière fruitée à base de bière blanche	fruitbier op basis van witbier
	Brasserie Artisanale Millevertus Toernich	Brasserie Artisanale Millevertus Toernich	Brasserie Artisanale Millevertus Toernich
	different malt and hop varieties, wheat, yeast, mashed mirabelles, coriander, orange rind, water	différentes sortes de malt et de houblon; froment, levure, purée de mirabelles, coriandre, écorce d'orange, eau	verschillende mout- en hopsoorten, tarwe, gist, mirabellenpuree, koriander, sinaasschil, water
%	5%	5%	5%
	orange cloudy	orange trouble	oranje troebel
	Serve in a frozen glass.	Verser dans un verre gelé.	Uitschenken in een bevroren glas.
°C	39 °F	4 °C	4 °C
	Fresh and fruity.	Frais et fruité.	Fris en fruitig.
i	Brewed in Belgian Lorraine with Lorraine mirabelles, which are French mirabelles with 'appellation contrôlée'.	Brassée en Lorraine Belge avec des mirabelles françaises 'appellation contrôlée' mirabelle de Lorraine'.	Gebrouwen in Belgisch Lotharingen met mirabelles de Lorraine, Franse mirabellen met 'appellation contrôlée'.

BLANCHETTE de LORRAINE
Brasserie Artisanale
MMMH!!
MILLEVERTUS

B

Blanchette de Toernich

	top-fermentation re-fermented in the bottle	fermentation haute refermentation en bouteille	hoge gisting hergisting op de fles
	Witbier special	bière blanche spéciale	witbier speciaal
	Brasserie Artisanale Millevertus Toernich	Brasserie Artisanale Millevertus Toernich	Brasserie Artisanale Millevertus Toernich
	different malt varieties, wheat, hops, coriander, orange rind, yeast, water	différentes sortes de malt, froment, houblon, coriandre, écorce d'orange, levure, eau	verschillende moutsoorten, tarwe, hop, koriander, sinaasappelschil, gist, water
%	6%	6%	6%
	blond cloudy	blonde trouble	blond troebel
	Serve in a witbier glass.	Verser dans un verre de bière blanche.	Uitschenken in het witbierglas.
°C	39°F	4°C	4°C
	Fresh and thirstquenching.	Frais et rafraîchissant.	Fris en dorstlessend.
i	–	–	–

BLANCHETTE
de Tœrnich
Brasserie Artisanale
MMMH!!
MILLEVERTUS

Bloemenbier

	top-fermentation re-fermented in the bottle	fermentation haute refermentation en bouteille	hoge gisting hergisting in de fles
	Belgian strong Ale	Belgian strong Ale	Belgian strong ale
	De Proefbrouwerij/Andelot Lochristi	De Proefbrouwerij/Andelot Lochristi	De Proefbrouwerij/Andelot Lochristi
	Malt, hops, yeast, flowers, spring water. Fortified with flowers and plants.	Malt, houblon, levure, eau de source. Enrichie de fleurs et plantes	Mout, hop, gist, bronwater. Verrijkt met bloemen en planten.
%	7%	7%	7%
	amber	ambrée	amber
	–	–	–
°C	–	–	–
	–	–	–
i	–	–	–

BLOEMEN

B

Blonde Bie

	top-fermentation	fermentation haute	hoge gisting
	blond	blonde	blond
	Brouwerij De Bie Loker	Brouwerij De Bie Loker	Brouwerij De Bie Loker
	malt, hops, sugar, yeast, herbs, water	malt, houblon, sucre, levure, herbes, eau	mout, hop, suiker, gist, kruiden, water
%	8%	8%	8%
	blond clear	blonde claire	blond helder
	–	–	–
°C	–	–	–
	–	–	–
i	–	–	–

Blonde Bie
De Bie

Blonde tradition

	top-fermentation re-fermented in the bottle unpasteurised	fermentation haute refermentation en bouteille; non pasteurisée	hoge gisting hergisting in de fles niet gepasteuriseerd
	blond	blonde	blond
	Brasserie La Binchoise Binche	Brasserie La Binchoise Binche	Brasserie La Binchoise Binche
	aromatic hop varieties, coriander, orange rind, malt	variétés de houblon aromatiques, coriandre, écorce d'orange, malt	aromatische hopsoorten, koriander, sinaasschil, mout
%	6,20%	6,20%	6,20%
	gold-yellow slightly cloudy, unfiltered. White, fine and creamy foam head.	jaune doré légèrement trouble, non filtrée avec un faux col fin et crémeux	goudgeel licht troebel, niet gefilterd. Witte, fijne en romige schuimkraag.
	–	–	–
°C	–	–	–
	Fine bitterness and round mouthfeel.	Goût amer raffiné et rond en bouche.	Fijne bitterheid en rond in de mond.
i	–	–	–

BELGISCH BIER MET NAGISTING IN DE FLES Cat S
LA BINCHOISE
BIÈRE BELGE
REFERMENTÉE EN BOUTEILLE
BLONDE
TRADITION
6,5%vol alc

LA BINCHOISE
SINCE 1987

Blusser

	bottom-fermentation	fermentation basse	lage gisting
	Pilsner	pils	pils
	Brouwerij Het Anker Mechelen	Brouwerij Het Anker Malines	Brouwerij Het Anker Mechelen
	only Belgian hops	houblon exclusivement belge	uitsluitend Belgische hop
%	5,20%	5,20%	5,20%
	gold-yellow	jaune doré	goudgeel
	–	–	–
	39 - 41 °F	4 - 5 °C	4 - 5 °C
	–	–	–
i	Only available in the region of Mechelen. Brewed in honour of the inhabitants of Mechelen who tried to extinguish the moon.	Seulement disponible dans la région de Malines et brassée en l'honneur des Malinois qui essayaient d'éteindre la lune.	Enkel verkrijgbaar in de regio Mechelen en gebrouwen ter ere van de Mechelaars die de maan probeerden te blussen.

....

....

....

....

....

Brouwerij Het Anker
ANNO 1369
BLUSSER
Belgian Premium Pils
BELGISCH BIER • BELGIAN BEER • BIERE BELGE
Brouwerij Het Anker
ANNO 1369
BLUSSER
Belgian Premium Pils

Bock

	bottom-fermentation	fermentation basse	lage gisting
	table beer	bière de table	tafelbier
	Brouwerij Leroy Boezinge	Brouwerij Leroy Boezinge	Brouwerij Leroy Boezinge
	malt, rice, hops, water	malt, riz, houblon, eau	mout, rijst, hop, water
%	1,80%	1,80%	1,80%
	blond clear	blonde claire	blond helder
	Pour slowly in a single, smooth movement in a degreased glass. Keep the glass tilted and avoid sloshing the beer. Skim off the foam.	Verser lentement en un seul mouvement fluide dans un verre dégraissé tenu en oblique. Ne pas laisser la bière clapoter. Ecumer le verre.	Traag en in 1 vloeiende beweging uitschenken in een vetvrij glas dat wordt schuin gehouden. Het bier niet laten klotsen. Het glas afschuimen.
°C	37 °F	3 °C	3 °C
	Sweet and slightly alcoholic thirst-quencher. Sweet and fruity.	Désaltérant doux et légèrement alcoolisé. Doux et fruité.	Zoete en licht alcoholische dorstlesser. Zoet en fruitig.
i	–	–	–

BOCK
LEROY
KUNSTMATIG GEZOET

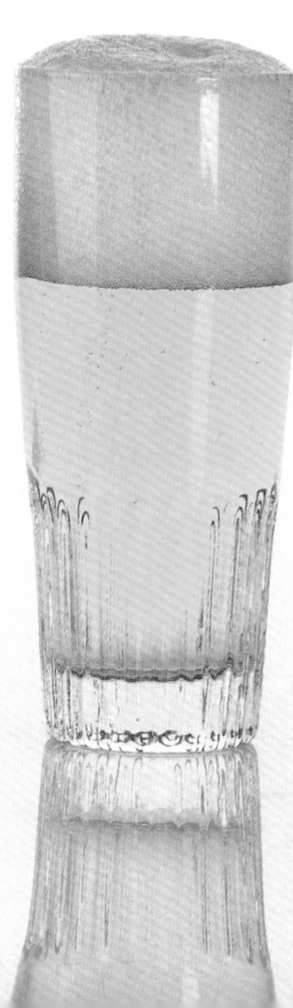

B

Bock Pils

	bottom-fermentation	fermentation basse	lage gisting
	Pilsner	pils	pils
	Palm Breweries Site Palm Steenhuffel	Palm Breweries Site Palm Steenhuffel	Palm Breweries Site Palm Steenhuffel
	Pilsner malts, 100% Czech Saaz hop, yeast, water	malts de pils, houblon 100% Saaz tchèque, levure, eau	pilsmouten, 100% Saaz hop uit Tsjechië, gist, water
%	5,20%	5,20%	5,20%
	blond	blonde	blond
	Can be emptied in a pilsner glass.	Peut être complètement versé dans un verre pils.	Mag helemaal uitgeschonken worden in een pilsglas.
°C	37 °F	3 °C	3 °C
	Pleasantly bitter with a dry aftertaste. Hoppy and slightly spiced.	Goût amer agréable avec une fin de bouche sèche. Houblonné et légèrement aromatisé.	Aangenaam bitter met droge afdronk. Hoppig en licht gekruid.
i	–	–	–

BOCK
BOCK
PILS
BOCK

Bockor

	bottom-fermentation	fermentation basse	lage gisting
	Pilsner	pils	pilsbier
	Brouwerij Bockor Bellegem	Brouwerij Bockor Bellegem	Brouwerij Bockor Bellegem
	barley malt, corn, hops, yeast, water	malt d'orge, maïs, houblon, levure, eau	gerstemout, maïs, hop, gist, water
%	5,20%	5,20%	5,20%
	blond clear	blonde claire	blond helder
	Rinse the glass with cold water, tilt it a little and pour half of the bottle carefully. Then keep the glass upright and pour the rest of the bottle in a single movement.	Rincer le verre à l'eau froide, le tenir légèrement incliné et le remplir prudemment à moitié. Relever le verre et vider la bouteille en un seul mouvement.	Het glas koud spoelen, licht schuin houden en voorzichtig half inschenken. Daarna het glas recht houden en de rest in 1 beweging inschenken.
°C	39 - 43 °F	4 - 6 °C	4 - 6 °C
	Session beer with modest bitterness. Dry, neutral taste with a bitter aftertaste.	Pils facilement buvable avec un goût amer restreint. Saveur sèche et neutre, puis amère.	Vlot drinkbare pils met ingetoomde bitterheid. Droge, neutrale smaak die bitterig uitvloeit.
i	–	–	–

....

....

....

....

BOCKOR
VANDERGHINSTE
ANNO 1892
BOCKOR
Pils
BELLEGEM

ANNO 1892
BOCKOR

Bockor blauw

	bottom-fermentation	fermentation basse	lage gisting
	export	export	export
	Brouwerij Bockor Bellegem	Brouwerij Bockor Bellegem	Brouwerij Bockor Bellegem
	barley malt, corn, hops, yeast, water	malt d'orge, maïs, houblon, levure, eau	gerstemout, maïs, hop, gist, water
%	5,20%	5,20%	5,20%
	blond clear	blonde claire	blond helder
	Can be drunk from the bottle.	Peut être bue à la bouteille.	Mag uit de fles gedronken worden.
°C	39 - 43 °F	4 - 6 °C	4 - 6 °C
	Smooth texture. Pure and light in the mouth.	Texture douce. Pur et léger dans la bouche.	Zachte textuur. Zuiver en licht in de mond.
i	–	–	–

BOCKOR
BLAUW
Meesterbrouwers · Maîtres-Brasseurs
ANNO 1892
BOCKOR
BLAUW
BROUWERIJ
BRASSERIE
VANDER GHINSTE

ANNO 1892
BOCKOR

Boerke blond

	top-fermentation re-fermented in the bottle	fermentation haute refermentation en bouteille	hoge gisting hergisting op de fles
	blond	blonde	blond
	Brouwerij Angerik Dilbeek	Brouwerij Angerik Dilbeek	Brouwerij Angerik Dilbeek
	malt, hops, herbs (coriander), yeast, water	malt, houblon, herbes (coriandre), levure, eau	mout, hop, kruiden (koriander), gist, water
%	6,80%	6,80%	6,80%
	blond-amber unfiltered, cloudy	blond-ambré non filtrée, trouble	blond-amber ongefilterd, troebel
	–	–	–
°C	–	–	–
	Robust beer with a rich flavour palette, aftertaste with hop touch.	Bière forte avec une palette de saveurs riche, fin de bouche avec touche de houblon.	Robuust bier met een rijk smakenpalet, afdronk met hoppetoets.
i	The name Angerik is a contraction of Angelo and Erik, the founders' names. This beer is only brewed with Belgian hop and malt. In the summer a Kriek Boerken is brewed with cherries from Schaarbeek.	Le nom Angerik provient de la contraction d'Angelo et d'Erik, les prénoms des fondateurs. Cette bière est brassée uniquement avec des houblons et malts belges. En été, une Kriek Boerken est brassée avec des cerises de Schaarbeek.	De naam Angerik is een samenvoeging van Angelo en Erik, de namen van de stichters. Dit bier wordt enkel met Belgische hop en mout gebrouwen. In de zomer wordt ook een Kriek Boerken gebrouwen met Schaarbeekse krieken.

Boerke
Brouwerij Angerik
Boerke
Brouwerij Angerik

Boerke donker

	top-fermentation re-fermented in the bottle	fermentation haute refermentation en bouteille	hoge gisting hergisting op de fles
	dark	foncée	donker
	Brouwerij Angerik Dilbeek	Brouwerij Angerik Dilbeek	Brouwerij Angerik Dilbeek
	roasted malt, hops, herbs, yeast, water	malt brûlé, houblon, herbes, levure, eau	gebrande mout, hop, kruiden, gist, water
%	6,80%	6,80%	6,80%
	dark red	rouge foncé	donkerrood
	–	–	–
°C	–	–	–
	Smooth with powerful aftertaste.	Doux avec fin de bouche corsée.	Zacht met krachtige afdronk.
i	The name Angerik is a contraction of Angelo and Erik, the founders' names. This beer is only brewed with Belgian hop and malt.	Le nom Angerik provient de la contraction d'Angelo et d'Erik, les prénoms des fondateurs. Cette bière est brassée uniquement avec des houblons et malts belges.	De naam Angerik is een samenvoeging van Angelo en Erik, de namen van de stichters. Dit bier wordt enkel met Belgische hop en mout gebrouwen.

Boerke
Boerke

Bokkereyer

	top-fermentation	fermentation haute	hoge gisting
	amber	ambrée	amber
	Brouwerij Sint-Jozef Opitter	Brouwerij Sint-Jozef Opitter	Brouwerij Sint-Jozef Opitter
	malt, hops, sugar, herbs, starch, caramel sugar, water	malt, houblon, sucre, herbes, fécule, sucre caramel, eau	mout, hop, suiker, kruiden, zetmeel, karamelsuiker, water
%	6%	6%	6%
	light brownish	brun clair	lichtbruinig
	Pour into a clean, degreased glass, avoiding contact between the bottle and the foam.	Verser dans un verre propre, dégraissé sans que la bouteille touche l'écume.	Uitschenken in een zuiver, ontvet glas zonder dat de fles het schuim raakt.
°C	36 - 39 °F	2 - 4 °C	2 - 4 °C
	Rich beer with soft aromas and a gentle aftertaste.	Biere riche avec des arômes moelleux et une fin de bouche moelleuse.	Rijk bier met zachte aroma's en zachte afdronk.
i	–	–	–

BOKKEREYER
BROUWERIJ SINT JOZEF - B 3690 BREE
BOKKEREYER
LUXE BIER
CAT. 1
BOKKEREYER

Bokrijks Kruikenbier

	EN	FR	NL
	top-fermentation re-fermented in the bottle	fermentation haute refermentation en bouteille	hoge gisting hergisting in de fles
	blond abbey beer	bière d'abbaye blonde	blond abdijbier
	Collega-brouwers for Brouwerij Sterkens Meer	Collega-brouwers pour Brouwerij Sterkens Meer	Collega-brouwers voor Brouwerij Sterkens Meer
	malt, hops, yeast, water	malt, houblon, levure, eau	mout, hop, gist, water
%	7,20%	7,20%	7,20%
	light blond, filtered	blond clair, filtrée	lichtblond, gefilterd
	Carefully serve in the sipping glass, with a generous foam head.	Verser prudemment dans le verre de dégustation avec faux col solide.	Voorzichtig uitschenken in het degustatieglas met een ruime schuimkraag.
°C	43 - 50 °F	6 - 10 °C	6 - 10 °C
	Solid and heavy. Citrus and honey flavours. Powerful taste of alcohol and herbs. Mild bitterness.	Solide et lourd. Arôme d'agrumes et de miel. Saveur forte d'alcool et d'herbes, goût amer moelleux.	Stevig en zwaar. Aroma van citrus en honing. Krachtige smaak van alcohol, kruiden en milde bitterheid.
i	Over 90% of the production is exported. Production and bottling are temporarily taking place at Du Bocq and other breweries.	Plus de 90% est destiné à l'exportation. La production et la mise en bouteilles sont (provisoirement) réalisées par la brasserie Du Bocq et d'autres brasseries.	Meer dan 90% is bestemd voor export. Productie en bottelen gebeurt (voorlopig) bij Du Bocq en andere brouwerijen.

BELGIAN GOLDEN ALE
Bokrijks kruikenbier
e75 cl PRODUCT OF BELGIUM

B

Bons Vœux

	top-fermentation re-fermented in the bottle	fermentation haute refermentation en bouteille	hoge gisting nagisting in de fles
	blond	blonde	blond
	Brasserie Dupont Tourpes-Leuze	Brasserie Dupont Tourpes-Leuze	Brasserie Dupont Tourpes-Leuze
	Long maturation phase. With dry-hopping.	Longue période de mûrissement. Avec dry hopping.	Lange rijpingsfase. Met dry hopping.
%	9,50%	9,50%	9,50%
	copper-blond	blond cuivre	koperblond
	–	–	–
°C	cellar temperature (54 °F) or slightly cooled	température de cave (12 °C) ou légèrement rafraîchie	keldertemperatuur (12 °C) of lichtgekoeld
	Complex aroma and flavour owing to the fine hop and yeast types used. Smooth, bitter and fruity.	Arôme et saveur complexes par le houblon fin et les sortes de levure. Doux, amer et fruité.	Complex aroma en smaak door de fijne hop en gistsoorten. Zacht, bitter en fruitig.
i	Offered to the customers as a New Year's present from 1970 onwards, it was also introduced to the market because of its great success. Store at cellar temperature for an optimal taste evolution.	Offerte aux clients à partir de 1970 comme cadeau de fin d'année et suite au grand intérêt commercialisée par la suite. Conserver à température de cave pour une évolution optimale du goût.	Werd vanaf 1970 aangeboden als nieuwjaarsgeschenk voor de klanten en door de grote belangstelling later ook gecommercialiseerd. Bewaren op keldertemperatuur voor een optimale smaakevolutie.

Brasserie Dupont
Tourpes • Belgique
AVEC LES
Bons Vœux
DE LA BRASSERIE DUPONT
℮75cl
Alc. 9,5% vol.

AVEC LES
Bons Vœux
DE LA BRASSERIE DUPONT

Bon Secours ambrée

	top-fermentation	fermentation haute	hoge gisting
	amber	ambrée	amber
	Brasserie Caulier Peruwelz	Brasserie Caulier Peruwelz	Brasserie Caulier Peruwelz
	malt, hops, yeast, candy sugar, water	malt, houblon, levure, sucre candi, eau	mout, hop, gist, kandijsuiker, water
%	8%	8%	8%
	amber	ambrée	amber
	Slowly pour half of the bottle in order to obtain a nice foam head.	Verser doucement la moitié de la bouteille de sorte qu'un faux col solide se forme.	De helft van de fles zachtjes uitschenken zodat er zich een mooie schuimkraag vormt.
°C	43 - 50 °F	6 - 10 °C	6 - 10 °C
	Round, malt and hoppy with a bitter aftertaste.	Rond, malté et houblonné avec une arrière-bouche amère.	Rond, moutig en hoppig met een bittere nasmaak.
i	–	–	–

Alc. 8% Vol.
BRASSERIE CAULIER
Ambrée
Bon Secours
Bière Vivante!!
BELGIAN BEER
BIERE ARTISANALE A FERMENTATION HAUTE
Bon Secours

Bon Secours blonde

	top-fermentation	fermentation haute	hoge gisting
	blond	blonde	blond
	Brasserie Caulier Peruwelz	Brasserie Caulier Peruwelz	Brasserie Caulier Peruwelz
	malt, hops, yeast, candy sugar, water	malt, houblon, levure, sucre candi, eau	mout, hop, gist, kandijsuiker, water
%	8%	8%	8%
	blond	blonde	blond
	Slowly pour half of the bottle in order to obtain a nice foam head.	Verser doucement la moitié de la bouteille de sorte qu'un faux col solide se forme.	De helft van de fles zachtjes uitschenken zodat er zich een mooie schuimkraag vormt.
	43 - 50 °F	6 - 10 °C	6 - 10 °C
	Round and well-balanced, light bitterness and malt taste, hoppy.	Rond et équilibré, saveur légèrement amère et maltée, houblonnée.	Rond en evenwichtig, lichte bitterheid en moutsmaak, hoppig.
i	–	–	–

Alc.
8%
Vol.
BRASSERIE
CAULIER
Blonde
Bon Secours
Bière Vivante!!
BELGIAN
BEER
BIERE ARTISANALE A FERMENTATION HAUTE
Bon Secours
Bière Vivante!!

Bon Secours brune

(fermentation)	top-fermentation	fermentation haute	hoge gisting
(type)	dubbel	double	dubbel
(brewery)	Brasserie Caulier Peruwelz	Brasserie Caulier Peruwelz	Brasserie Caulier Peruwelz
(ingredients)	malt, hops, yeast, candy sugar, water	malt, houblon, levure, sucre candi, eau	mout, hop, gist, kandijsuiker, water
%	8%	8%	8%
(colour)	brown	brune	bruin
(serving)	Slowly pour half of the bottle in order to obtain a nice foam head.	Verser doucement la moitié de la bouteille de sorte qu'un faux col solide se forme.	De helft van de fles zachtjes uitschenken zodat er zich een mooie schuimkraag vormt.
(temperature)	43 - 50 °F	6 - 10 °C	6 - 10 °C
(taste)	Smooth and perfumed character. Flavour of mocca, anise and roasty touch. Bitter aftertaste.	Caractère doux et parfumé. Arôme de moka, d'anis et de brûlé. Arrière-bouche amère.	Zacht en geparfumeerd karakter. Aroma van moka, anijs en gebrand. Bittere nasmaak.
i	–	–	–

Alc.
8%
Vol.
BRASSERIE
CAULIER
Brune
Bon Secours
Bière Vivante !!
BELGIAN
BEER
Alc.
8%
Vol.
BIÈRE ARTISANALE A FERMENTATION HAUTE
Bon Secours
Bière Vivante !!

Bon Secours Framboise

	top-fermentation	fermentation haute	hoge gisting
	fruit beer	bière fruitée	fruitbier
	Brasserie Caulier Peruwelz	Brasserie Caulier Peruwelz	Brasserie Caulier Peruwelz
	malt, hops, yeast, raspberry juice, water	malt, houblon, levure, jus de framboises, eau	mout, hop, gist, frambozensap, water
%	7%	7%	7%
	red	rouge	rood
	Slowly pour half of the bottle in order to obtain a nice foam head.	Verser doucement la moitié de la bouteille de sorte qu'un faux col solide se forme.	De helft van de fles zachtjes uitschenken zodat er zich een mooie schuimkraag vormt.
°C	43 - 50 °F	6 - 10 °C	6 - 10 °C
	Forest fruit.	Fruits des bois.	Bosvruchten.
i	Sugar-free.	Sans sucres.	Suikervrij.

FRAMBOISE
Bon Secours
FRAMBOISE
Secours
0,33l
Bon Secours
FRAMBOISE
BIERE ARTISANALE A FERMENTATION HAUTE 100%
ARTISANAAL GEBROUWEN BIER MET HOGE GISTING 100%

Bon Secours Myrtille

	top-fermentation	fermentation haute	hoge gisting
	fruit beer	bière fruitée	fruitbier
	Brasserie Caulier Peruwelz	Brasserie Caulier Peruwelz	Brasserie Caulier Peruwelz
	malt, hops, yeast, myrtil juice, water	malt, houblon, levure, jus de myrtilles, eau	mout, hop, gist, myrtillen-sap, water
%	7%	7%	7%
	dark red	rouge foncé	donkerrood
	Slowly pour half of the bottle in order to obtain a nice foam head.	Verser doucement la moitié de la bouteille de sorte qu'un faux col solide se forme.	De helft van de fles zachtjes uitschenken zodat er zich een mooie schuimkraag vormt.
°C	43 - 50 °F	6 - 10 °C	6 - 10 °C
	Forest fruit.	Fruits des bois.	Bosvruchten.
i	Sugar-free.	Sans sucres.	Suikervrij.

Bon Secours
MYRTILLE
Bon Secours
MYRTILLE
0,33l
Bon Secours
MYRTILLE
Bon Secours
Bière Vivante !!

Bon Secours Blonde de Noël

	top-fermentation	fermentation haute	hoge gisting
	winter beer	bière hivernale	winterbier
	Brasserie Caulier Peruwelz	Brasserie Caulier Peruwelz	Brasserie Caulier Peruwelz
	malt, hops, yeast, candy sugar, water	malt, houblon, levure, sucre candi, eau	mout, hop, gist, kandijsuiker, water
%	10%	10%	10%
	blond	blonde	blond
	Slowly pour half of the bottle in order to obtain a nice foam head.	Verser doucement la moitié de la bouteille de sorte qu'un faux col solide se forme	De helft van de fles zachtjes uitschenken zodat er zich een mooie schuimkraag vormt.
°C	43 - 50 °F	6 - 10 °C	6 - 10 °C
	Powerful with a strong taste, caramel.	Corsé avec une saveur prononcée, caramélisée.	Krachtig met sterke smaak, karamel.
i	–	–	–

BLONDE
Alc. 10% Vol.
Blonde de Noël
EN BOUTEILLE
0,33L
Bon Secours
Bière Vivante !!

Bornem dubbel

	top-fermentation re-fermented in the bottle	fermentation haute refermentation en bouteille	hoge gisting hergisting in de fles
	Recognised Belgian abbey beer	Bière d'abbaye belge reconnue	Erkend Belgisch abdijbier
	Brouwerij Van Steenberge Ertvelde	Brouwerij Van Steenberge Ertvelde	Brouwerij Van Steenberge Ertvelde
	barley malt, hops, yeast, water	malt d'orge, houblon, levure, eau	gerstemout, hop, gist, water
%	8% 16° plato	8% 16° plato	8% 16° plato
	Dark brown with burgundy-red undertone. Creamy, rich foam head.	Brun foncé avec une nuance rouge bordeaux. Faux col crémeux et riche.	Donkerbruin met bordeauxrode ondertoon. Romige, rijke schuimkraag.
	Pour in a single, fluent and smooth movement, leaving 1 cm of yeast sediment in the bottle.	Verser en un seul mouvement fluide et doux et laisser 1 cm de dépôt de levure dans la bouteille.	Uitschenken in 1 vloeiende, zachte beweging en 1 cm gistdepot in de fles laten.
°C	50 - 54 °F	10 - 12 °C	10 - 12 °C
	Fruity taste with a light touch of grain.	Saveur fruitée avec une légère touche de céréales.	Fruitige smaak met lichte toets van graan.
i	A living abbey beer brewed by order of the Saint Bernard abbey in Bornem.	Une bière d'abbaye vive brassée à la demande de l'abbaye de Saint-Benoît à Bornem.	Een levend abdijbier gebrouwen in opdracht van de Sint-Bernardusabdij in Bornem.

Dubbel
Double
Anno
1784
Bornem
Belgisch Abdijbier - Bière Belge d'Abbaye

Bornem

Bornem tripel

	top-fermentation re-fermented in the bottle	fermentation haute refermentation en bouteille	hoge gisting hergisting in de fles
	Recognised Belgian abbey beer	Bière d'abbaye belge reconnue	Erkend Belgisch abdijbier
	Brouwerij Van Steenberge Ertvelde	Brouwerij Van Steenberge Ertvelde	Brouwerij Van Steenberge Ertvelde
	barley malt, hops, yeast, water	malt d'orge, houblon, levure, eau	gerstemout, hop, gist, water
%	9% - 18,5° plato	9% - 18,5° plato	9% - 18,5° plato
	blond nice foam head	blonde faux col solide	blond mooie schuimkraag
	Pour in a single, fluent and smooth movement, leaving 1 cm of yeast sediment in the bottle. The sediment can be poured, for a cloudy beer.	Verser en un seul mouvement fluide et doux et laisser 1 cm de dépôt de levure dans la bouteille. Le depôt peut être versé et rend la bière trouble.	Uitschenken in 1 vloeiende, zachte beweging en 1 cm gistdepot in de fles laten. De gistfond kan worden uitgeschonken en maakt het bier troebel.
°C	50 - 54 °F	10 - 12 °C	10 - 12 °C
	Smooth mouthfeel, hoppy and full of taste, excellent sweet bitter balance, pleasant aroma and long-lasting aftertaste.	Doux dans la bouche, goût houblonné et plein, équilibre doux-amer excellent, parfum agréable et arrière-bouche longue.	Zacht in de mond, hoppig en vol van smaak, uitstekende zoetbitter balans, aangename geur en lange nasmaak.
i	A living abbey beer brewed by order of the Saint Bernard abbey in Bornem.	Une bière d'abbaye vivante brassée à la demande de l'abbaye de Saint-Benoît à Bornem.	Een levend abdijbier gebrouwen in opdracht van de Sint-Bernardusabdij in Bornem.

Tripel
Triple
Anno
1784
Bornem
Belgisch Abdijbier - Bière Belge d'Abbaye
Bornem

Bosbier

	bottom-fermentation	fermentation basse	lage gisting
	Local beer Pilsner with fruit	bière régionale pils avec jus de fruits	streekbier pils met vruchtensap
	Brouwerij Sint Jozef Opitter	Brouwerij Sint Jozef Opitter	Brouwerij Sint Jozef Opitter
	malt, hops, starch, bilberry juice, water	malt, houblon, amidon, jus de myrtilles, eau	mout, hop, zetmeel, bosbessensap, water
%	4%	4%	4%
	bilberry	myrtilles	bosbessen
	Pour into a clean, degreased glass, avoiding contact between bottle and foam.	Verser dans un verre propre et dégraissé sans que la bouteille touche l'écume.	Uitschenken in een zuiver, ontvet glas zonder dat de fles het schuim raakt.
°C	36 - 39 °F	2 - 4 °C	2 - 4 °C
	Fruity and refreshing. Full-bodied bilberry taste and aroma.	Fruité et rafraîchissant. Goût et parfum francs de groseilles.	Fruitig en verfrissend. Volmondige bosbessensmaak en -geur.
i	–	–	–

Streekbier
BOSBIER
BIERE DE PAYS
Streekbier
BOSBIER
OP BASIS VAN BOSBESSEN
A BASE DE MYRTILLES
BROUWERIJ St. JOZEF
3960 BREE-OPITTER
e 25cl
Streekbier
BOSBIER

B Boskeun

	top-fermentation re-fermented in the bottle unfiltered or centrifuged	fermentation haute refermentation en bouteille non filtrée, ni centrifugée	hoge gisting nagisting op de fles niet gefilterd of gecentrifugeerd
	Tripel Easter beer	triple Bière de Pâques	tripel Paasbier
	De Dolle Brouwers Diksmuide	De Dolle Brouwers Dixmude	De Dolle Brouwers Diksmuide
	With cane sugar and Golding hops.	On utilise le sucre de canne et le houblon Golding.	Er wordt gebruik gemaakt van rietsuiker en Golding hop.
%	10%	10%	10%
	pale to amber	blanc touchant l'ambré	bleek tot amber
	Serve in an Oerbeer glass or wine glass.	À verser dans un verre oerbier ou un verre de vin.	In een oerbierglas of wijnglas.
°C	50 - 54 °F	10 - 12 °C	10 - 12 °C
	Smooth.	Doux.	Zacht.
i	Easter beer. The name refers to the nickname of one of the 'Dolle Brouwers' (mad brewers).	Bière de Pâques dont le nom se réfère au sobriquet d'un des 'Dolle Brouwers'.	Paasbier waarvan de naam refereert aan de spotnaam van een van de 'Dolle Brouwers'.

Bos
keun
CAT.S 33CL
SPECIAAL PAASBIER
BREWED & BOTTLED
BELGIUM

ANNO 1980
oerbier
NAT EN

Bosprotter

	top-fermentation	fermentation haute	hoge gisting
	Tripel	triple	tripel
	't Hofbrouwerijke Beerzel	't Hofbrouwerijke Beerzel	't Hofbrouwerijke Beerzel
	malt, hops, yeast, herbs, water	malt, houblon, levure, herbes, eau	mout, hop, gist, kruiden, water
%	8,50%	8,50%	8,50%
	corn-gold blond slightly cloudy, unfiltered	jaune blé doré légèrement trouble (non filtrée)	korengoudblond licht troebel, ongefilterd
	Pour carefully, leaving 1 cm in the bottle.	Verser prudemment et laisser 1 cm dans la bouteille.	Voorzichtig uitschenken en 1 cm in het flesje laten.
°C	50 - 54 °F	10 - 12 °C	10 - 12 °C
	Full-bodied malt taste with a light caramel touch and a refreshing, bitter aftertaste.	Saveur maltée franche avec une légère touche de caramel et une fin de bouche rafraîchissante, amère.	Volmondige moutsmaak met lichte karameltoets en een verfrissende bittere afdronk.
i	Can be stored for a very long time.	Peut se conserver longtemps.	Kan lang bewaard worden.

't Hofbrouwerijke
bosprotter

't Hofbrouwerijke

Bourgogne des Flandres

	mixed fermentation	fermentation mixte	gemengde gisting
	specialty beer brown	bière spéciale brune	speciaalbier bruin
	Brouwerij Timmermans Itterbeek	Brouwerij Timmermans Itterbeek	Brouwerij Timmermans Itterbeek
	barley malt, sugar, corn, roasted barley, wheat, hops, flavouring, water	malt d'orge, sucre, maïs, orge brûlé, froment, houblon, arômes, eau	gerstemout, suiker, mais, gebrande gerst, tarwe, hop, aroma's, water
%	5%	5%	5%
	brown	brune	bruin
	–	–	–
°C	37 - 43 °F	3 - 6 °C	3 - 6 °C
	Similar to the taste of Flemish bruinbier but less sour. Balance of sweet tones with dry bitterness.	Proche de la saveur de la bière brune flamande mais moins acidulé. Équilibre entre tons doux et goût amer sec.	Benadert de smaak van Vlaams bruinbier maar is minder zuur. Evenwicht van zoete tonen met droge bitterheid.
i	–	–	–

Bourgogne
des
Flandres
des
Flandres

Brasserie de Bellevaux black

	top-fermentation unpasteurised	fermentation haute non pasteurisée	hoge gisting niet gepasteuriseerd
	dark Ale	ale foncée	donkere ale
	Brasserie de Bellevaux Malmédy	Brasserie de Bellevaux Malmédy	Brasserie de Bellevaux Malmédy
	barley malt, hops, water	malt d'orge, houblon, eau	gerstemout, hop, water
%	6,50%	6,50%	6,50%
	almost black, solid, cream-coloured foam head; unfiltered	presque noir, faux col de couleur crème prononcée; non filtrée	bijna zwart, stevige crèmekleurige schuimkraag; niet gefilterd
	Pour into a tall glass that has been rinsed with cold water.	Verser dans un verre haut rincé à l'eau froide.	Uitschenken in een met koud water gespoeld hoog glas.
°C	46 - 54 °F	8 - 12 °C	8 - 12 °C
	Strong and full-bodied character. Taste and aroma of butterscotch, roasted malt, bitter aftertaste.	Caractère corsé et plein. Saveur et arôme de butterscotch, malt grillé, fin de bouche amère.	Krachtig en vol karakter. Smaak en aroma van butterscotch, geroosterde mout, bittere afdronk.
i	Very recently founded brewery.	Brasserie récemment ouverte.	Zeer recent opgestarte brouwerij.

BRASSERIE DE
BELLEVAUX
MALMEDY
BLACK
6,3
33 CL

B

Brasserie de Bellevaux blanche

	top-fermentation unpasteurised	fermentation haute non pasteurisée	hoge gisting niet gepasteuriseerd
	Witbier	bière blanche	witbier
	Brasserie de Bellevaux Malmédy	Brasserie de Bellevaux Malmédy	Brasserie de Bellevaux Malmédy
	barley malt, wheat malt, hops, herbs, well water	malt d'orge, malt de froment, houblon, herbes, eau de source	gerstemout, tarwemout, hop, kruiden, bronwater
%	4,80%	4,80%	4,80%
	pale yellow fine, white foam unfiltered	jaune pâle écume blanche fine non filtrée	bleekgeel fijn wit schuim ongefilterd
	Pour into a tall glass, rinsed with cold water.	Verser dans un verre haut rincé à l'eau froide.	Uitschenken in een met koud water gespoeld hoog glas.
°C	41 - 46 °F	5 - 8 °C	5 - 8 °C
	Refreshing and thirst-quenching character. Taste and aroma of citrus fruit, sourish with light bitter aftertaste.	Rafraîchissant et de caractère désaltérant. Saveur et arôme d'agrumes, rance avec fin de bouche légèrement amère.	Verfrissend en dorstlessend karakter. Smaak en aroma van citrusfruit, ranzig met licht bittere afdronk.
i	Suitable as an aperitif. Very recently founded brewery.	Convient comme apéritif. Brasserie récemment ouverte.	Geschikt als aperitief. Zeer recent opgestarte brouwerij.

BRASSERIE DE
BELLEVAUX
MALMEDY
BLANCHE
4,8% VOL 33cl
BRASSERIE DE
BELLEVAUX

Brasserie de Bellevaux blonde

	top-fermentation unpasteurised	fermentation haute non pasteurisée	hoge gisting niet gepasteuriseerd
	abbey beer	bière d'abbaye	abdijbier
	Brasserie de Bellevaux Malmédy	Brasserie de Bellevaux Malmédy	Brasserie de Bellevaux Malmédy
	barley malt, hops, candy sugar, well water	malt d'orge, houblon, sucre candi, eau de source	gerstemout, hop, kandijsuiker, bronwater
%	7%	7%	7%
	Dark blond with white foam head. Clear to slightly cloudy, unfiltered.	Blond foncé avec faux col blanc. Claire à légèrement trouble, non filtrée.	Donkerblond met witte schuimkraag. Helder tot licht troebel, ongefilterd.
	Pour into a degreased goblet. Leave the yeast sediment in the bottle.	Verser tranquillement dans un verre calice dégraissé et laisser le dépôt de levure dans la bouteille.	Rustig uitschenken in een vetvrij kelkglas en het gistdepot in de fles laten.
°C	43 - 50 °F	6 - 10 °C	6 - 10 °C
	Rich and spicy character. Fruity and slightly sweet with a bitter aftertaste.	Caractère riche et relevé. Fruité et légèrement doux avec fin de bouche amère.	Rijk en kruidig karakter. Fruitig en licht zoet met bittere afdronk.
i	Very recently founded brewery.	Brasserie récemment ouverte.	Zeer recent opgestarte brouwerij.

BRASSERIE DE
BELLEVAUX
MALMEDY
BLONDE
7,0% VOL 33CL
BRASSERIE DE
BELLEVAUX

Brasserie de Bellevaux brune

	top-fermentation unpasteurised	fermentation haute non pasteurisée	hoge gisting niet gepasteuriseerd
	abbey beer	bière d'abbaye	abdijbier
	Brasserie de Bellevaux Malmédy	Brasserie de Bellevaux Malmédy	Brasserie de Bellevaux Malmédy
	barley malt, hops, candy sugar, well water	malt d'orge, houblon, sucre candi, eau de source	gerstemout, hop, kandijsuiker, bronwater
%	6,80%	6,80%	6,80%
	hazelnut unfiltered	noisette non filtrée	hazelnoot niet gefilterd
	Pour slowly in a degreased goblet, leaving the yeast sediment in the bottle.	Verser tranquillement dans un verre calice dégraissé et laisser le dépôt de levure dans la bouteille.	Rustig uitschenken in een vetvrij kelkglas en het gistdepot in de fles laten.
°C	46 - 54 °F	8 - 12 °C	8 - 12 °C
	Full and smooth character. Full-bodied, slightly malty sweet, smooth aftertaste.	Caractère plein et doux. Franc, légèrement malté-doux, fin de bouche douce.	Vol en zacht karakter. Volmondig, licht moutig zoet, zachte nasmaak.
i	Very recently founded brewery.	Brasserie récemment ouverte.	Zeer recente opgestarte brouwerij.

BRASSERIE DE
BELLEVAUX
MALMEDY
BRUNE
6,8% VOL 33CL

B

Brice

	top-fermentation re-fermented in the bottle	fermentation haute refermentation en bouteille	hoge gisting hergisting in de fles
	local beer	bière régionale	streekbier
	Brasserie Grain d'Orge Hombourt-Plombières	Brasserie Grain d'Orge Hombourt-Plombières	Brasserie Grain d'Orge Hombourt-Plombières
	malt, hops, yeast, sugar, herbs, water	malt, houblon, sucre, levure, herbes, eau	mout, hop, gist, suiker, kruiden, water
%	7,50%	7,50%	7,50%
	deep blond transparent	blond soutenu transparente	krachtig blond transparant
	Pour in a single movement, leaving the yeast sediment (ca. 5 mm) in the bottle.	Verser en un seul mouvement et laisser le dépôt de levure (environ 5 mm) dans la bouteille.	In 1 beweging uitschenken en het gistdepot (ca. 5 mm) in de fles laten.
°C	39 - 43 °F	4 - 6 °C	4 - 6 °C
	Fresh, fruity session beer. Fresh nose with touches of spices and smooth hop.	Bière fraîche, facilement buvable. Parfum frais avec des touches d'herbes et de houblon moelleux.	Fris, fruitig doordrinkbier. Frisse neus met toetsen van kruiden en zachte hop.
i	–	–	–

Brice & Joup
blonde & brune
Bière blonde artisanale
Brice
du Pays de Herve
* Aubel *

Brigand

	top-fermentation	fermentation haute refermentation en bouteille	hoge gisting nagisting op de fles
	regional beer re-fermented in the bottle	bière régionale blonde	streekbier blond
	Castle Brewery Van Honsebrouck Ingelmunster	Castle Brewery Van Honsebrouck Ingelmunster	Castle Brewery Van Honsebrouck Ingelmunster
	barley malt, wheat malt, hops, yeast, sugar, water	malt d'orge, malt de froment, houblon, levure, sucre, eau	gerstemout, tarwemout, hop, gist, suiker, water
%	9%	9%	9%
	dark blond clear	blond foncé claire	donkerblond helder
	Pour into a newly rinsed glass. Tilt it first, then straighten. Yeast can be poured, according to taste.	Verser dans un verre récemment rincé d'abord tenu en oblique et à la fin en position verticale. La levure est versée selon le goût.	Uitschenken in een vers gespoeld glas dat eerst schuin gehouden wordt en op het einde verticaal gehouden wordt. De gist wordt volgens eigen smaak al dan niet uitgeschonken.
°C	46 °F	8 °C	8 °C
	Hoppy and spicy. Full taste with wheat malt influences. Bitter aftertaste.	Houblonné et aromatisé. Saveur pleine avec influence de froment malté. Fin de bouche amère.	Hoppig en kruidig. Volle smaak met invloed van tarwemout. Bittere afdronk.
i	–	–	–

Bière
Belge
Belgisch
Bier
BRIGAND
1798
BRIGAND

Brugge Blond

	top-fermentation	fermentation haute	hoge gisting
	city beer heavy blond	bière citadine blonde forte	stadsbier zwaar blond
	Palm Breweries Site Palm Steenhuffel	Palm Breweries Site Palm Steenhuffel	Palm Breweries Site Palm Steenhuffel
	special malts, fine aromatic hops, yeast, herbs, water	malts spéciaux, cônes aromatiques fins, levure, herbes, eau	speciale mouten, fijne aromahoppen, gist, kruiden, water
%	6,60%	6,60%	6,60%
	blond	blonde	blond
	Serve in a goblet with stem	Servir dans un verre calice à pied.	Serveren in een kelkglas met voet.
°C	43 °F	6 °C	6 °C
	Spicy and fruity. Ends with a fine, bitter hop touch.	Aromatisé et fruité. Se termine par une touche raffinée de houblon.	Kruidig en fruitig. Eindigt met een fijne bittertoets van hop.
i	–	–	–

BRUGGE
Anno 1872
BRUGGE
Blond
33 cl
Anno 1872
BRUGGE
Blond

Brugs

	top-fermentation	fermentation haute	hoge gisting
	Witbier	bière blanche	witbier
	Alken Maes corporation Alken	Alken Maes corporation Alken	Alken Maes corporation Alken
	–	–	–
%	4,80%	4,80%	4,80%
	light-yellow naturally cloudy	jaune clair aspect trouble naturel	lichtgeel natuurlijke troebelheid
	Empty in a degreased, rinsed and wet glass. Let overflow and skim off the foam.	Verser complètement dans un verre dégraissé, rincé et mouillé. Laisser déborder et écumer.	Helemaal uitschenken in een ontvet, gespoeld en nat glas. Laten overlopen en afschuimen.
	36 - 39 °F	2 - 4 °C	2 - 4 °C
	Well-balanced sweet-and-sour, fresh and fruity with a rich character. Touches of wheat, hop, orange, apple peel and coriander.	Aigre-doux équilibré, frais et fruité avec un caractère riche. Saveur de froment, houblon, zeste d'orange et peau de pomme, coriandre.	Evenwichtig zuurzoet, fris en fruitig met een rijk karakter. Smaak van tarwe, hop, sinaas- en appelschil, koriander.
i	–	–	–

Brugs
Brugs
4.8 %
Brugs

Brugse Straffe Hendrik blond

	top-fermentation re-fermented in the bottle	fermentation haute refermentation en bouteille	hoge gisting nagisting in de fles
	blond	blonde	blond
	Brouwerij Liefmans Oudenaarde/Dentergem	Brouwerij Liefmans Audenarde/Dentergem	Brouwerij Liefmans Oudenaarde/Dentergem
	barley malt, corn, sugar, English hops, yeast, water.	malt d'orge, maïs, sucre, houblon anglais, levure, eau	gerstemout, mais, suiker, Engelse hop, gist, water.
%	6%	6%	6%
	straw-yellow slightly cloudy	jaune paille légèrement trouble	strogeel licht troebel
	Leave the yeast in the bottle.	Laisser la levure dans la bouteille.	De gist in het flesje laten.
°C	43 - 50 °F	6 - 10 °C	6 - 10 °C
	Malty and hoppy character. Fresh onset with dry aftertaste and a fruity hop aroma.	Caractère malté et houblonné. Début frais avec fin de bouche sèche et arôme houblonné fruité.	Moutig en hoppig karakter. Frisse aanhef met droge afdronk en fruitig hoparoma.
i	This beer was created for the Halve Maan in Bruges in 1981, for the inauguration of the Saint Arnold statue. Saint Arnold is the saint of the brewers.	Cette bière a fait ses débuts en 1981 auprès de 'De Halve Maan' à Bruges, à l'occasion de l'inauguration de la statue de Saint-Arnould (patron des brasseurs).	Dit bier ontstond bij De Halve Maan in Brugge in 1981, n.a.v. de inhuldiging van het Sint-Arnoldusbeeld (patroonheilige van de brouwers).

BELGISCH BIER - BIERE BELGE
Brugse
Straffe Hendrik
ALC. 6% VOL
25 cl
5406 2092

Brugse Straffe Hendrik bruin

	top-fermentation re-fermented in the bottle	fermentation haute refermentation en bouteille	hoge gisting nagisting in de fles
	heavy dark brown Ale	ale brune double foncée	zware donkere bruine ale
	Brouwerij Liefmans Oudenaarde/Dentergem	Brouwerij Liefmans Audenarde/Dentergem	Brouwerij Liefmans Oudenaarde/Dentergem
	barley malt, roasted malt, corn, sugar, hops, yeast, herbs, water	malt d'orge, malt grillé, maïs, sucre, houblon, levure, herbes, eau	gerstemout, geroosterde mout, mais, suiker, hop, gist, kruiden, water
%	8,50%	8,50%	8,50%
	dark brown slightly cloudy	brun foncé légèrement trouble	donkerbruin licht troebel
	Leave the yeast in the bottle.	Laisser la levure dans la bouteille.	De gist in het flesje laten.
°C	46 - 50 °F	8 - 10 °C	8 - 10 °C
	Spicy, malty sipping beer. Soft taste with a touch of liquorice, malt and herbs, caramel-like aroma.	Bière de dégustation relevée et maltée. Goût moelleux avec des touches de réglisse, de malt et d'herbes. Arômes de caramel.	Kruidig en moutig degustatiebier. Zachte smaak met toets van zoethout, mout en kruiden. Karamelachtig aroma.
i	–	–	–

BELGISCH BIER - BIERE BELGE
BRUIN
ALC. 8,5% VOL
BLOND
5°
"Straffe Hendrik"
8,5°

Brugse Tripel

	top-fermentation re-fermented in the bottle	fermentation haute refermentation en bouteille	hoge gisting nagisting op de fles
	city beer heavy blond	bière citadine blonde forte	stadsbier zwaar blond
	Palm Breweries Site Palm Steenhuffel	Palm Breweries Site Palm Steenhuffel	Palm Breweries Site Palm Steenhuffel
	special malts, fine aromatic hops, yeast, water	malts spéciaux, houblons aromatiques fins, levure, eau	speciale mouten, fijne aromahoppen, gist, water
%	8,70%	8,70%	8,70%
	blond	blonde	blond
	Serve in a very tall glass.	Servir dans un verre très haut.	Serveren in een heel hoog glas.
°C	43 °F	6 °C	6 °C
	Spicy and roasty bouquet. Very full taste and malty character. Dry fruitiness in the aftertaste.	Bouquet aromatisé et fumé. Saveur très pleine et caractère malté. Goût fruité sec en fin de bouche.	Kruidig en gerookt boeket. Zeer volle smaak en moutkarakter. Droge fruitigheid in de afdronk.
i	–	–	–

BRUGGE
Tripel
DE GOUDEN
BOOM
BRUGGE
Tripel
BRUGGE
Tripel

Brugse Zot blond

	top-fermentation re-fermented in the bottle	fermentation haute refermentation en bouteille	hoge gisting hergisting op de fles
	Ale	ale	ale
	Brouwerij De Halve Maan Brugge	Brouwerij De Halve Maan Bruges	Brouwerij De Halve Maan Brugge
	4 malt varieties and 2 aromatic hop varieties, candy sugar, yeast, water	4 sortes de malt et 2 variétés de houblon aromatique, sucre candi, levure, eau	4 moutsoorten en 2 aromatische hopvariëteiten, kandijsuiker, gist, water
%	6%	6%	6%
	golden blond rich foam head clear	blond doré faux col riche claire	goudblond rijke schuimkraag helder
	Pour carefully, leaving 1 cm of yeast sediment in the bottle.	Verser prudemment et laisser un dépôt de levure de 1 cm dans la bouteille.	Voorzichtig uitschenken en 1 cm gistdepot in de fles laten.
°C	45 °F	7 °C	7 °C
	Dry, light bitter, fruity aroma with citrus touches. Hoppy character ending in a tasteful dryness with a fruity effect.	Arôme fruité, sec, légèrement amer avec des touches d'agrumes. Caractère houblonné aboutissant en un goût sec savoureux se présentant fruité.	Fruitig, droog, licht bitter aroma met toetsen van citrus. Hoppig karakter eindigend in een smakelijke droogheid die fruitig overkomt.
i	The name of the beer refers to the nickname of the inhabitants of Bruges (a legend from the times of Maximilian of Austria).	Le nom de la bière renvoie au sobriquet des Brugeois (légende qui date du temps de Maximilien d'Autriche).	De naam van het bier refereert aan de bijnaam van de Bruggelingen (legende uit de tijd van Maximiliaan van Oostenrijk).

brugse Zot
brugse Zot

Brugse Zot dubbel

	top-fermentation re-fermented in the bottle	fermentation haute refermentation en bouteille	hoge gisting hergisting op de fles
	dubbel Ale	ale double	ale dubbel
	Brouwerij De Halve Maan Brugge	Brouwerij De Halve Maan Bruges	Brouwerij De Halve Maan Brugge
	6 special malt varieties and Saaz hops, candy sugar, yeast, water	6 sortes de malt et houblon Saaz, sucre candi, levure, eau	6 speciale moutsoorten en Saaz hop, kandijsuiker, gist, water
%	7,50%	7,50%	7,50%
	ruby red	rouge rubis	robijnrood
	Pour carefully, leaving 1 cm of yeast sediment in the bottle.	Verser prudemment et laisser un dépôt de levure de 1 cm dans la bouteille.	Traag uitschenken en 1 cm gistdepot in de fles laten.
°C	46 °F	8 °C	8 °C
	Rich aroma and bitter hop touch. Taste of roasted malt with a bitter touch of Czech Saaz hop.	Arôme riche et touche houblonnée amère. Saveur de malt grillé avec une touche amère du houblon Saaz tchèque.	Rijk aroma en bittere hoptoets. Smaak van geroosterde mout met een bittere toets van de Tjechische Saaz hop.
i	The name of the beer refers to the nickname of the inhabitants of Bruges, a legend that dates back from the time of Maximilian of Austria.	Le nom de la bière renvoie au sobriquet des Brugeois (légende qui date du temps de Maximilien d'Autriche).	De naam van het bier refereert aan de bijnaam van de Bruggelingen (legende uit de tijd van Maximiliaan van Oostenrijk).

brugse
Zot
DUBBEL
Brouwerij De Halve Maan
brugse
Zot

Bruin Leroy

	bottom-fermentation	fermentation basse	lage gisting
	table beer	bière de table	tafelbier
	Brouwerij Leroy Boezinge	Brouwerij Leroy Boezinge	Brouwerij Leroy Boezinge
	malt, rice, hops, caramel, artificial sweetener, water	malt, riz, houblon, caramel, édulcorant artificiel, eau	mout, rijst, hop, karamel, kunstmatige zoetstof, water
%	1,80%	1,80%	1,80%
	dark brown	brun foncé	donkerbruin
	Pour slowly in a single, smooth movement in a degreased glass. Keep the glass tilted and avoid sloshing the beer. Skim off the foam.	Verser lentement en un seul mouvement fluide dans un verre dégraissé tenu en oblique. Ne pas laisser la bière clapoter. Ecumer le verre.	Traag en in 1 vloeiende beweging uitschenken in een vetvrij glas dat wordt schuingehouden. Het bier niet laten klotsen. Het glas afschuimen.
°C	37 °F	3 °C	3 °C
	Sweet and slightly alcoholic thirst-quencher. Sweet and fruity.	Désaltérant doux et légèrement alcoolisé. Doux et fruité.	Zoete en licht alcoholische dorstlesser. Zoet en fruitig.
i	–	–	–

BRUIN
LEROY
KUNSTMATIG GEZOET

Brune tradition

	top-fermentation re-fermented in the bottle unpasteurised	fermentation haute refermentation en bouteille non pasteurisée	hoge gisting hergisting in de fles niet gepasteuriseerd
	dubbel	double	dubbel
	Brasserie La Binchoise Binche	Brasserie La Binchoise Binche	Brasserie La Binchoise Binche
	Based on 3 malt varieties of which 1 roasted, aromatic hop varieties.	Brassée à base de 3 sortes de malt dont 1 brûlé, variétés de houblon aromatiques.	Gebrouwen op basis van 3 moutsoorten waarvan 1 gebrand, aromatische hopsoorten.
%	8,20%	8,20%	8,20%
	Very dark brown. Exuberant, light amber-coloured foam head.	Brun très foncé. Faux col excessif, écume légèrement ambrée.	Zeer donkerbruin. Uitbundige, licht amberkleurige schuimkraag.
	–	–	–
°C	–	–	–
	Easily digestible with a malty character. Long-lasting and dry aftertaste influenced by the aromatic hop species.	Facile à digérer avec un caractère malté. Arrière-bouche longue et fin de bouche sèche renvoyant aux diverses sortes de houblon aromatisé.	Licht verteerbaar met een moutig karakter. Lange nasmaak en droge afdronk die verwijst naar de aromatische hopsoorten.
i	–	–	–

PRODUCT OF BELGIUM
LA BINCHOISE
ARTISANAL BROWN ALE
BRUNE
LA BINCHOISE

Brunehaut Terroir

	top-fermentation re-fermented in the bottle	fermentation haute refermentation en bouteille	hoge gisting hergisting op de fles
	Witbier organic	bière blanche biologique	witbier biologisch
	Brasserie de Brunehaut Rongy-Brunehaut	Brasserie de Brunehaut Rongy-Brunehaut	Brasserie de Brunehaut Rongy-Brunehaut
	malt, wheat, hops, yeast, herbs, water	malt, froment, houblon, levure, herbes, eau	mout, tarwe, hop, gist, kruiden, water
%	5%	5%	5%
	whitish and misty	blancheâtre et voilée	witachtig en wazig
	–	–	–
	41 - 43 °F	5 - 6 °C	5 - 6 °C
	Refreshing and perfumed. Fruity with a touch of bitterness.	Rafraîchissant et parfumé. Fruité et un peu amer.	Verfrissend en geparfumeerd. Fruitig en een vleugje bitter.
i	–	–	–

Brunehaut
Terroir

Brunehaut

Brunehaut Tradition

	top-fermentation re-fermented in the bottle	fermentation haute refermentation en bouteille	hoge gisting hergisting op de fles
	amber	ambrée	amber
	Brasserie de Brunehaut Rongy-Brunehaut	Brasserie de Brunehaut Rongy-Brunehaut	Brasserie de Brunehaut Rongy-Brunehaut
	malt, hops, yeast, water	malt, houblon, levure, eau	mout, hop, gist, water
%	6,50%	6,50%	6,50%
	amber	ambrée	amber
	–	–	–
°C	41 - 46 °F	5 - 8 °C	5 - 8 °C
	Round and perfumed.	Rond et parfumé.	Rond en geparfumeerd.
i	–	–	–

Brunehaut
Brunehaut tradition

Brunehaut

Brunehaut Village

	top-fermentation re-fermented in the bottle	fermentation haute refermentation en bouteille	hoge gisting hergisting op de fles
	blond	blonde	blond
	Brasserie de Brunehaut Rongy-Brunehaut	Brasserie de Brunehaut Rongy-Brunehaut	Brasserie de Brunehaut Rongy-Brunehaut
	malt, hops, yeast, water	malt, houblon, levure, eau	mout, hop, gist, water
%	6,50%	6,50%	6,50%
	blond	blonde	blond
	–	–	–
°C	41 - 46 °F	5 - 8 °C	5 - 8 °C
	Light and refreshing.	Léger et rafraîchissant.	Licht en verfrissend.
i	–	–	–

Brunehaut
Brunehaut villages

Brunehaut

Buffalo

	top-fermentation re-fermented in the bottle	fermentation haute refermentation en bouteille	hoge gisting hergisting op de fles
	regional beer	bière régionale	streekbier
	Brouwerij Van Den Bossche St-Lievens-Esse	Brouwerij Van Den Bossche St-Lievens-Esse	Brouwerij Van Den Bossche St-Lievens-Esse
	Hops, yeast, fermentable sugar, water. Malt varieties: Pilsner, Pale Ale, caramel, roast.	Houblon, levure, sucre de fermentation, eau. Sortes de malt: pils, pale ale, caramélisé, grillé.	Hop, gist, vergistbare suiker, water. Moutsoorten: pils, pale ale, karamel, roast.
%	6%	6%	6%
	dark	foncée	donker
	Pour slowly for a nice foam head with hat. Leave a small amount in the bottle (it can be served afterwards) and present the bottle with the glass.	Verser lentement pour obtenir un faux col solide avec chapeau. Laisser un peu de biére dans la bouteille (peut être versé par la suite) et offrir aussi la bouteille.	Langzaam inschenken voor een mooie schuimkraag en schuimhoed. Een restje in de fles laten (kan achteraf bijgeschonken worden) en de fles mee aanbieden.
°C	43 - 46 °F	6 - 8 °C	6 - 8 °C
	–	–	–
i	Has existed since 1907 and is the brewery's oldest beer. The name refers to the Buffalo Bill circus.	Existe depuis 1907 et est la bière la plus ancienne de la brasserie. Le nom se réfère au cirque Buffalo Bill.	Bestaat sedert 1907 en is het oudste bier van de brouwerij. De naam verwijst naar het circus Buffalo Bill.

Bière de fermentation haute
Buffalo
25 cl.
5 412215 367017
Buffalo

Buffalo Belgian Stout

	top-fermentation re-fermented in the bottle	fermentation haute refermentation en bouteille	hoge gisting hergisting op de fles
	Stout	stout	stout
	Brouwerij Van Den Bossche St-Lievens-Esse	Brouwerij Van Den Bossche St-Lievens-Esse	Brouwerij Van Den Bossche St-Lievens-Esse
	Hops, yeast, fermentable sugar, water. Malt varieties: Pilsner, Pale Ale, caramel, roast.	Malt, houblon, sucre de fermentation, eau. Sortes de malt: pils, pale ale, caramélisé, grillé.	Hop, gist, vergistbare suiker, water. Moutsoorten: pils, pale ale, karamel, roast.
%	9%	9%	9%
	dark brown to black beige creamy foam head	brun foncé-noire faux col beige, crémeux	donkerbruin tot zwart beige, romige schuimkraag
	Pour slowly for a nice foam head. Leave a small amount in the bottle and present the bottle with the glass.	Verser lentement pour obtenir un faux col solide. Laisser un peu de bière dans la bouteille et offrir aussi la bouteille.	Langzaam inschenken voor een mooie schuimkraag. Een restje in de fles laten en de fles mee aanbieden.
°C	43 - 46 °F	6 - 8 °C	6 - 8 °C
	Nose of roasted malt with alcohol and chocolate touches. Taste: first sweet with a chocolate and roasted coffee flavour, then dry and bitter.	Parfum de malt brûlé avec des touches d'alcool et de chocolat. Goût: début doux avec des arômes de chocolat et de café brûlé. Fin de bouche sèche et amère.	Neus van gebrande mout met toetsen van alcohol en chocolade. Smaak: zoete aanhef met chocolade en gebrande koffie. Droge en bittere afdronk.
i	New beer for the 100th anniversary of the Buffalo beer.	Nouvelle bière créée à l'occasion du centenaire de la bière Buffalo.	Nieuw bier ter gelegenheid van de 100e verjaardag van het bier Buffalo.

PRODUCT OF BELGI
Buffalo
Belgian Stout
Buffalo

Buitenlust dubbel blond

	top-fermentation re-fermented in the bottle	fermentation haute refermentation en bouteille	hoge gisting hergisting op de fles
	strong blond	blonde forte	sterk blond
	Proefbrouwerij Lochristi for Buitenlust, Zulte	Proefbrouwerij Lochristi pour Buitenlust, Zulte	Proefbrouwerij Lochristi voor Buitenlust, Zulte
	barley malt, hops, yeast, water	malt d'orge, houblon, levure, eau	gerstemout, hop, gist, water
%	8,50%	8,50%	8,50%
	Dark blond because of the concentration of the ingredients (18 °plato).	Blond foncé par la concentration des matières premières (18 ° plato).	Donkerblond door de concentratie van de grondstoffen (18 ° plato).
	Pour smoothly in a single movement, leaving the sediment in the bottle. Do not serve too cold so as to fully appreciate the aroma.	Verser doucement en un seul mouvement et laisser le dépôt dans la bouteille. Ne pas servir trop froide, sinon l'odeur disparaît.	Zacht uitschenken in 1 beweging en het bezinksel in de fles laten. Niet te koud schenken, anders is de geur weg.
°C	46 - 50 °F or 57 - 59 °F	8 - 10 °C ou 14 - 15 °C	8 - 10 °C of 14 - 15 °C
	Provision beer with taste evolution. Alcohol, malt and hop are well-balanced and blur each other. The bitternes (30 EBU) is compensated by the malt sugar.	Bière de conservation avec saveur évolutive. L'alcool, le malt et le houblon sont bien équilibrés et se cachent l'un l'autre: le goût amer (30 EBU) est compensé par le sucre malté.	Bewaarbier met smaakevolutie. Alcohol, mout en hop zijn mooi in balans en verdoezelen elkaar: bitter (30 EBU) wordt gecompenseerd door de moutsuiker.
i	The label is an old, original family picture.	L'étiquette est une vieille photo de la famille.	Het etiket is een oude, originele familiefoto.

DUBBEL
BUITENLUST
BUITENLUST

Bush Ambrée

	top-fermentation	fermentation haute	hoge gisting
	strong blond	blonde forte	sterk blond
	Brasserie Dubuisson Pipaix-Leuze	Brasserie Dubuisson Pipaix-Leuze	Brasserie Dubuisson Pipaix-Leuze
	malt, hops, natural sugar, yeast, water	malt, houblon, sucre naturel, levure, eau	mout, hop, natuurlijke suiker, gist, water
%	12%	12%	12%
	red-copper 100% filtered	cuivre rouge 100 % filtrée	roodkoper 100 % gefilterd
	–	–	–
	50 °F	10 °C	10 °C
	Digestive, typical bitter-sweet taste, powerful aroma of roasty nuts.	Digestif, saveur typiquement amère-douce, arôme corsé de noix brûlés.	Digestief, typische bitterzoete smaak, krachtig aroma van gebrande noten.
i	–	–	–

Dubuisson
Bush
THE STRONGEST BELGIAN BEER
12%
AMBREE
AMBER
Bush

Bush Blonde

	top-fermentation	fermentation haute	hoge gisting
	strong blond	blonde forte	sterk blond
	Brasserie Dubuisson Pipaix-Leuze	Brasserie Dubuisson Pipaix-Leuze	Brasserie Dubuisson Pipaix-Leuze
	malt, hops (Saaz), sugar, yeast, water	malt, houblon (Saaz), sucre, levure, eau	mout, hop (Saaz), suiker, gist, water
%	10,50%	10,50%	10,50%
	amber blond 100% filtered	blond ambré 100% filtrée	amberblond 100% gefilterd
	–	–	–
°C	50 °F	10 °C	10 °C
	Very easily digestible beer with well-balanced flavours, smooth and round.	Bière facile à digérer avec des arômes équilibrés, doux et ronds.	Zeer licht verteerbaar bier met evenwichtige aroma's, zacht en rond.
i	–	–	–

Dubuisson
Bush
BLONDE • BLOND
10,5%
Bush

Bush de Noël

	top-fermentation	fermentation haute	hoge gisting
	strong blond winter beer	blonde forte bière hivernale	sterk blond winterbier
	Brasserie Dubuisson Pipaix-Leuze	Brasserie Dubuisson Pipaix-Leuze	Brasserie Dubuisson Pipaix-Leuze
	malt, caramel malt, yeast, sugar, hops, water	malt, malt caramélisé, levure, sucre, houblon, eau	mout, karamelmout, gist, suiker, hop, water
%	12%	12%	12%
	red-copper 100% filtered	cuivre rouge 100 % filtrée	roodkoper 100 % gefilterd
	–	–	–
°C	50 °F	10 °C	10 °C
	Well-balanced fruit taste with a slightly hoppy flavour.	Saveur fruitée équilibrée avec un arôme légèrement houblonné.	Evenwichtige fruitsmaak met een licht hoppig aroma.
i	–	–	–

1769
Bush de Noël
Spéciale Noël
Bush

Bush de Noël premium

	top-fermentation re-fermented in the bottle (75 cl)	fermentation haute refermentation en bouteille (75 cl)	hoge gisting nagisting op de fles (75 cl)
	strong blond winter beer	blonde forte bière hivernale	sterk blond winterbier
	Brasserie Dubuisson Pipaix-Leuze	Brasserie Dubuisson Pipaix-Leuze	Brasserie Dubuisson Pipaix-Leuze
	malt, caramel malt, hops, sugar, yeast, water	malt, malt caramélisé, houblon, sucre, levure, eau	mout, karamelmout, hop, suiker, gist, water
%	13%	13%	13%
	copper slightly cloudy	cuivre légèrement trouble	koper licht troebel
	–	–	–
°C	–	–	–
	–	–	–
i	–	–	–

1769
Bush de Noël
Premium
Bush

Bush prestige

	top-fermentation in oak barrels re-fermented in the bottle (75 cl)	fermentation haute en fûts de chêne refermentation en bouteille (75 cl)	hoge gisting op eikenhouten vaten nagisting op de fles (75 cl)
	strong blond	blonde forte	sterk blond
	Brasserie Dubuisson Pipaix-Leuze	Brasserie Dubuisson Pipaix-Leuze	Brasserie Dubuisson Pipaix-Leuze
	malt, sugar, hops, yeast, water	malt, sucre, houblon, levure, eau	mout, suiker, hop, gist, water
%	13%	13%	13%
	amber naturally cloudy by the refermentation in the bottle	ambrée trouble naturel par refermentation en bouteille	amber natuurlijk troebel door hergisting in de fles
	–	–	–
°C	50 °F	10 °C	10 °C
	Typical character owing to the tannin of the oakwood barrels. Forest flavours and a powerful, round taste.	Caractère typique par les tannins des fûts de chêne. Arômes boisés, saveur corsée et ronde.	Typisch karakter door de tannine van de eikenhouten vaten. Bosaroma's, krachtige en ronde smaak.
i	Store in the drawer of the refrigerator at 6 to 7 °C.	Conserver dans le tiroir du réfrigérateur à 6 à 7 °C.	Bewaren in de frigolade op 6 à 7 °C.

Cuvée Spéciale
Dubuisson
Bush
Prestige
Mûrie à l'ancienne

Bush

Cambrinus

	top-fermentation	fermentation haute	hoge gisting
	Belgian Ale	ale belge	Belgische ale
	Brouwerij Verhaeghe Vichte	Brouwerij Verhaeghe Vichte	Brouwerij Verhaeghe Vichte
	malt, hops, yeast, water	malt, houblon, levure, eau	mout, hop, gist, water
%	5,10%	5,10%	5,10%
	amber filtered	ambrée filtrée	amber gefilterd
	Pour in a dry bulb jar with stem.	Verser dans un verre ballon sec à pied.	Uitschenken in een droog bolglas met voet.
°C	37 °F	3 °C	3 °C
	Malty with a fruity yeast touch.	Malté avec une touche fruitée de levure.	Moutig met een fruitige gisttoets.
i	–	–	–

Cam
Cambrinus
brinus
amber bier - bière ambrée
hoge gisting
bière de haute

Cam
brinus

Campus

	top-fermentation re-fermented in the bottle	fermentation haute refermentation en bouteille	hoge gisting hergisting op de fles
	strong dark	foncée forte	sterk donker
	Brouwerij Huyghe Melle	Brouwerij Huyghe Melle	Brouwerij Huyghe Melle
	roasted malt varieties, hops, yeast, herbs, water	variétes de malt brûlé, houblon, levure, herbes, eau	gebrande moutsoorten, hop, gist, kruiden, water
%	7%	7%	7%
	red-brown	brun rouge	roodbruin
	Serve in a bulb jar.	Verser dans un verre ballon.	Uitschenken in een bolglas.
°C	–	–	–
	Rich amber beer with a honey touch in harmony with a discrete fruity flavour and pronounced maltiness. Aftertaste: dry and bitter caramel.	Bière ambrée riche avec des touches de miel en harmonie avec un goût fruité discret et un goût malté prononcé. Fin de bouche sèche et amère caramélisée.	Rijk amberbier met honingtoets in harmonie met een discrete fruitigheid en een duidelijke moutigheid. Afdronk droog en bitter karamel.
i	–	–	–

Campus
ambachtelijk bier
bière artisanale
BIERTOREN
KAMPENHOUT
ALC 7% VOL
Campus

C

Campus gold

	top-fermentation re-fermented in the bottle	fermentation haute refermentation en bouteille	hoge gisting hergisting in de fles
	blond	blonde	blond
	Brouwerij Huyghe Melle	Brouwerij Huyghe Melle	Brouwerij Huyghe Melle
	roasted malt varieties, hops, yeast, herbs, water	variétés de malt brûlé, houblon, levure, herbes, eau	gebrande moutsoorten, hop, gist, kruiden, water
%	6,20%	6,20%	6,20%
	blond	blonde	blond
	Serve in a bulb jar.	Verser dans un verre ballon.	Uitschenken in een bolglas.
°C	–	–	–
	Fresh taste, less bitter than Campus.	Goût frais, moins amer que la Campus.	Frisse smaak, minder bitter dan de Campus.
i	Originally brewed by the former Brabant brewery De Biertoren.	A l'origine brassée par l'ancienne brasserie du Brabant De Biertoren.	Oorspronkelijk gebrouwen door de toenmalige Brabantse brouwerij De Biertoren.

Campus
CAT. SUP
Gold
e 33cl
Campus

Canaster

	top-fermentation re-fermented in the bottle	fermentation haute refermentation en bouteille	hoge gisting nagisting op de fles
	winter scotch	scotch hivernal	winterscotch
	Brouwerij De Glazen Toren Erpe-Mere	Brouwerij De Glazen Toren Erpe-Mere	Brouwerij De Glazen Toren Erpe-Mere
	barley malt, wheat malt, caramel malts, dark candy sugar, hops, yeast, water	malt d'orge, malt de froment, malts caramélisés, sucre candi brun, houblon, levure, eau	gerstemout, tarwemout, karamelmouten, donkere kandijsuiker, hop, gist, water
%	8,70%	8,70%	8,70%
	Dark red to brown, with fine bubbles. Clear with solid foam head.	Rouge foncé à brun, finement pétillante. Claire avec faux col solide.	Donkerrood tot bruin, fijnparelend. Helder met stevige schuimkraag.
	Pour carefully into a dry, long glass (e.g. tulip glass).	Verser prudemment dans un verre sec, oblong (p. ex. tulipe).	Voorzichtig uitschenken in een droog, langwerpig (bv. tulpvormig) glas.
°C	45 - 46 °F	7 - 8 °C	7 - 8 °C
	Dry character. Flavour of roasty malt, fruity esters, light caramel and candy and a little liquorice.	Caractère sec. Arôme de malt brûlé, esters fruités, caramel léger, candi et un peu de réglisse.	Droog karakter. Aroma van gebrande mout, fruitige esters, lichte karamel, kandij en drop.
i	–	–	–

CANASTER
WINTERSCOTCH
DE GLAZEN TOREN

Caracole

	top-fermentation	fermentation haute	hoge gisting
	amber	ambrée	amber
	La Brasserie Caracole Falmignoul	La Brasserie Caracole Falmignoul	La Brasserie Caracole Falmignoul
	5 malt varieties, 2 hop varieties, yeast, orange rind, water	5 variétés de malt, 2 sortes de houblon, levure, écorce d'orange, eau	5 moutsoorten, 2 hopsoorten, gist, sinaasschil, water
%	7,50%	7,50%	7,50%
	amber	ambrée	amber
	–	–	–
	Cellar temperature.	Température de cave.	Keldertemperatuur.
	Round (cara malt and orange rind) and fruity with rich aroma's and a very distinctive taste.	Rond (malt cara et zeste d'orange) et fruité avec arômes riches et saveur très spécifique.	Rond (caramout en sinaasschil) en fruitig met rijke aroma's en een zeer specifieke smaak.
i	–	–	–

Caracole
Bière • Bier • Beer
Cerveza • Birra doppio malto

Caracole

Cassis Lindemans

	spontaneous fermentation	fermentation spontanée	spontane gisting
	fruit beer based on Lambic	bière fruitée à base de lambic	fruitbier op basis van lambiek
	Brouwerij Lindemans Vlezenbeek	Brouwerij Lindemans Vlezenbeek	Brouwerij Lindemans Vlezenbeek
	malt, wheat, hops, blackberry juice (25%), fructose, water	malt, froment, houblon, jus de baies noires (25%), fructose, eau	mout, tarwe, hop, zwarte-bessensap (25%), fructose, water
%	3,50%	3,50%	3,50%
	dark red slightly hazy	rouge foncé légèrement voilée	donkerrood licht gesluierd
	Pour into a flute glass.	Verser dans une flûte.	In een fluitglas uitschenken.
°C	37 - 39 °F	3 - 4 °C	3 - 4 °C
	Fruity character. Lively and strong onset turning into a balance of sweet (fruit) and slightly sour (lambic).	Caractère fruité. Début vif et corsé passant à un équilibre de douceur (fruits) et d'acidité légère (lambic).	Fruitig karakter. Levendige en sterke aanzet die overgaat in een evenwicht van zoet (fruit) en zacht zuur (lambiek).
i	Suitable as an aperitif and as a thirst-quencher.	Convient comme apéritif et comme boisson désaltérante.	Geschikt als aperitief en als dorstlesser.

LINDEMANS
CASSIS
3,5%
37,5cl
PECHERESSE

Celis White

	top-fermentation	fermentation haute	hoge gisting
	Witbier	bière blanche	witbier
	Brouwerij Van Steenberge Ertvelde	Brouwerij Van Steenberge Ertvelde	Brouwerij Van Steenberge Ertvelde
	barley malt, hops, yeast, wheat flour, water	malt d'orge, houblon, levure, farine de froment, eau	gerstemout, hop, gist, tarwemeel, water
%	5% 12° plato	5% 12° plato	5% 12° plato
	blond cloudy, misty white veil	blonde trouble, voile blanc fade	blond troebel, wazigwitte sluier
	Pour till there is 4 cm beer left in the bottle. Revolve the bottle and pour the rest for a nice glass of cloudy beer.	Verser jusqu'à ce qu'il reste 4 cm de bière dans la bouteille. Secouer la bouteille et la vider pour avoir un joli verre de bière bien trouble.	Uitschenken tot er nog 4 cm bier in de fles is. De fles even rondwalsen en de rest van het bier uitschenken tot het mooi troebel het glas vult.
°C	43 °F	6 °C	6 °C
	Touch of fruit and spices. Refreshing and light.	Touches de fruits et d'herbes. Rafraîchissant et léger.	Toets van fruit en kruiden. Verfrissend en licht.
i	Brewed under licence following the original recipe of Pierre Celis (brewer of the Hoegaarden witbier). Sales are allowed in all countries except the USA.	Fabriquée sous licence d'après la recette originale de Pierre Celis (brasseur de la Bière Blanche de Hoegaarden) acceptée pour commercialisation dans tous les pays, sauf aux Etats-Unis.	Wordt gemaakt onder licentie volgens het originele recept van Pierre Celis (brouwer van het Witbier van Hoegaarden) en mag in alle landen, behalve USA, worden gecommercialiseerd.

Celis Brewery
CELIS WHITE
BELGIAN WHITE BEER
WIT BIER
BIERE BLANCHE

Celtic Angel

	top-fermentation re-fermented in the bottle	fermentation haute refermentation en bouteille	hoge gisting met hergisting op de fles
	amber	ambrée	amber
	Microbrouwerij Achilles Itegem	Microbrouwerij Achilles Itegem	Microbrouwerij Achilles Itegem
	coloured malt, aromatic hops, yeast, water	malt coloré, houblon aromatique, levure, eau	kleurmout, aromatische hop, gist, water
%	6,20%	6,20%	6,20%
	deep warm amber	ambré intense chaud	diepwarm amber
	–	–	–
°C	–	–	–
	Distinctive, round and spicy flavour, created by the malt. Slight touch of natural bitterness.	Goût relevé arrondi et de caractère par l'utilisation de malts. Touche légère d'amertume naturelle.	Karaktervolle en afgeronde kruidigheid door het gebruik van mouten. Lichte toets van natuurlijke bitterheid.
i	–	–	–

CELTIC ANGEL
Celtic Angel
SERAFIJN
BIER VAN HOGE GISTING • FLASCHENGÄRUNG
BIÈRE DE FERMENTATION HAUTE
Serafijn

Cervesia

	top-fermentation re-fermented in the bottle	fermentation haute refermentation en bouteille	hoge gisting nagisting in de fles
	blond	blonde	blond
	Brasserie Dupont Tourpes-Leuze	Brasserie Dupont Tourpes-Leuze	Brasserie Dupont Tourpes-Leuze
	barley and wheat malt, hops, herbs and spices	malt d'orge et de froment, houblon, herbes et condiments	gerst- en tarwemout, hop, kruiden en specerijen
%	8%	8%	8%
	blond	blonde	blond
	–	–	–
°C	Slightly cooled.	Légèrement rafraîchie.	Licht gekoeld.
	Unusual taste and aroma of flowers and herbs. Refreshing and thirst-quenching.	Saveur inhabituelle, arômes de fleurs et d'herbes. Frais et désaltérant.	Ongewone smaak en aroma's van bloemen en kruiden. Fris en dorstlessend.
i	Brewed since 1983 upon the initiative of the Archéosite d'Aubechies, an archeological site near the brewery.	Brassée depuis 1983 à l'initiative de l'Archéosite d'Aubechies, un site archéologique dans les alentours de la brasserie.	Gebrouwen sinds 1983 op initiatief van de Archéosite d'Aubechies, een archeologische site in de omgeving van de brouwerij.

CERVESIA
ARCHEOSITE
AUBECHIES - BLICQUY
L07008A 12:47
02/2009
75 cl

Chapeau Abricot

	spontaneous fermentation	fermentation spontanée	spontane gisting
	fruit beer based on Lambic	bière fruitée à base de lambic	fruitbier op basis van lambiek
	Brouwerij De Troch Wambeek-Ternat	Brouwerij De Troch Wambeek-Ternat	Brouwerij De Troch Wambeek-Ternat
	Lambic mixed with apricot juice.	Mélange de lambic et de jus d'abricots.	Lambiek gemengd met abrikozensap.
%	3,50%	3,50%	3,50%
	blond	blonde	blond
	–	–	–
°C	43 °F	6 °C	6 °C
	Refreshingly sweet.	Doux, rafraîchissant.	Verfrissend zoet.
i	–	–	–

abricot
CHAPEAU
CHAPEAU
abricot
LAMBIC
PRODUCT OF BELGIUM

CHAPEAU
LAMBIC DE TROCH

Chapeau Banana

	spontaneous fermentation	fermentation spontanée	spontane gisting
	fruit beer based on Lambic	bière fruitée à base de lambic	fruitbier op basis van lambiek
	Brouwerij De Troch Wambeek-Ternat	Brouwerij De Troch Wambeek-Ternat	Brouwerij De Troch Wambeek-Ternat
	Lambic mixed with banana juice.	Mélange de lambic et de jus de bananes.	Lambiek gemengd met bananensap.
%	3,50%	3,50%	3,50%
	blond cloudy	blonde trouble	blond troebel
	–	–	–
°C	43 °F	6 °C	6 °C
	Refreshingly sweet with banana flavour.	Doux, rafraîchissant avec un arôme de banane.	Verfrissend zoet met aroma van banaan.
i	First banana beer in Europe. Originally brewed under the name Leopard de Troch.	Première bière de banane en Europe, commercialisée à l'origine sous le nom de Leopard De Troch.	Eerste bananenbier in Europa. Oorspronkelijk gecommercialiseerd onder de naam Leopard De Troch.

CHAPEAU
CHAPEAU
banana
LAMBIC
PRODUCT OF BELGIUM

CHAPEAU
LAMBIC DE TROCH

Chapeau Cuvee oude gueuze

	spontaneous fermentation	fermentation spontanée	spontane gisting
	Gueuze Lambic	gueuze lambic	geuze lambiek
	Brouwerij De Troch Wambeek-Ternat	Brouwerij De Troch Wambeek-Ternat	Brouwerij De Troch Wambeek-Ternat
	Lambic, hops, barley malt, wheat, water	lambic, houblon, malt d'orge, froment, eau	lambiek, hop, gerstemout, tarwe, water
%	5,50%	5,50%	5,50%
	–	–	–
	Pour gently while revolving the glass.	Verser doucement en tournant le verre.	Zacht inschenken en ondertussen het glas draaien.
	45 °F	7 °C	7 °C
	Refreshing and spontaneous. Sour taste and aroma.	Rafraîchissant et spontané. Saveur et arôme acidulés.	Verfrissend en spontaan. Zure smaak en aroma.
i	Recognised regional product as first old gueuze.	Produit régional reconnu en tant que première Vieille Gueuze.	Erkend streekproduct als eerste oude geuze.

CUVEE
Chapeau
CUVEE
Chapeau
LAMBIC
Oude Gueuze
PRODUCT OF BELGIUM

CHAPEAU
LAMBIC DE TROCH

Chapeau Exotic (ananas)

	spontaneous fermentation	fermentation spontanée	spontane gisting
	fruit beer based on Lambic	bière fruitée à base de lambic	fruitbier op basis van lambiek
	Brouwerij De Troch Wambeek-Ternat	Brouwerij De Troch Wambeek-Ternat	Brouwerij De Troch Wambeek-Ternat
	Lambic mixed with pine-apple juice.	Mélange de lambic et de jus d'ananas.	Lambiek gemengd met ananassap.
%	3,50%	3,50%	3,50%
	blond	blonde	blond
	–	–	–
°C	43 °F	6 °C	6 °C
	Refreshingly sweet.	Doux, rafraîchissant.	Verfrissend zoet.
i	Particularly appreciated in Ghana.	Surtout apprécié sur le marché ghanéen.	Vooral in trek op de Ghanese markt.

exotic
CHAPEAU
CHAPEAU
exotic
LAMBIC
PRODUCT OF BELGIUM
CHAPEAU
LAMBIC DE TROCH

Chapeau Faro

	spontaneous fermentation	fermentation spontanée	spontane gisting
	sweetened Gueuze	gueuze adoucie	aangezoete geuze
	Brouwerij De Troch Wambeek-Ternat	Brouwerij De Troch Wambeek-Ternat	Brouwerij De Troch Wambeek-Ternat
	Sweetened with candy sugar.	Edulcoré au sucre candi.	Aangezoet met kandijsuiker.
%	4,75%	4,75%	4,75%
	very dark amber	ambré très foncé	zeer donker amber
	–	–	–
°C	43 °F	6 °C	6 °C
	Refreshingly sweet.	Doux, rafraîchissant.	Verfrissend zoet.
i	–	–	–

faro
CHAPEAU
CHAPEAU
faro
LAMBIC
PRODUCT OF BELGIUM
CHAPEAU

Chapeau Fraises

	spontaneous fermentation	fermentation spontanée	spontane gisting
	fruit beer based on Lambic	bière fruitée à base de lambic	fruitbier op basis van lambiek
	Brouwerij De Troch Wambeek-Ternat	Brouwerij De Troch Wambeek-Ternat	Brouwerij De Troch Wambeek-Ternat
	Lambic mixed with straw-berry juice.	Mélange de lambic et de jus de fraises.	Lambiek gemengd met aardbeiensap.
%	3,50%	3,50%	3,50%
	red	rouge	rood
	–	–	–
°C	43 °F	6 °C	6 °C
	Refreshingly sweet.	Doux, rafraîchissant.	Verfrissend zoet.
i	–	–	–

fraises
CHAPEAU
CHAPEAU
fraises
LAMBIC
PRODUCT OF BELGIUM

Chapeau Framboise

	spontaneous fermentation	fermentation spontanée	spontane gisting
	fruit beer based on Lambic	bière fruitée à base de lambic	fruitbier op basis van lambiek
	Brouwerij De Troch Wambeek-Ternat	Brouwerij De Troch Wambeek-Ternat	Brouwerij De Troch Wambeek-Ternat
	Lambic mixed with raspberry juice.	Mélange de lambic et de jus de framboises.	Lambiek gemengd met frambozensap.
%	3,50%	3,50%	3,50%
	red	rouge	rood
	–	–	–
°C	43 °F	6 °C	6 °C
	Refreshingly sweet.	Doux, rafraîchissant.	Verfrissend zoet.
i	–	–	–

framboise
CHAPEAU
CHAPEAU
framboise
LAMBIC
PRODUCT OF BELGIUM
CHAPEAU

Chapeau gueuze

	spontaneous fermentation	fermentation spontanée	spontane gisting
	Gueuze	gueuze	geuze
	Brouwerij De Troch Wambeek-Ternat	Brouwerij De Troch Wambeek-Ternat	Brouwerij De Troch Wambeek-Ternat
	yeast, hops, malt, wheat, sugar, water	levure, houblon, malt, froment, sucre, eau	gist, hop, mout, tarwe, suiker, water
%	5,50%	5,50%	5,50%
	dark amber	ambré foncé	donker amber
	–	–	–
	–	–	–
	Sweet-and-sour.	Aigre-doux.	Zoetzurig.
	–	–	–

gueuze
CHAPEAU
CHAPEAU
gueuze
LAMBIC
PRODUCT OF BELGIUM
CHAPEAU

Chapeau Kriek

	spontaneous fermentation	fermentation spontanée	spontane gisting
	fruit beer based on Lambic	bière fruitée à base de lambic	fruitbier op basis van lambiek
	Brouwerij De Troch Wambeek-Ternat	Brouwerij De Troch Wambeek-Ternat	Brouwerij De Troch Wambeek-Ternat
	Lambic mixed with cherries.	Mélange de lambic et de cerises.	Lambiek gemengd met krieken.
%	3,50%	3,50%	3,50%
	red	rouge	rood
	–	–	–
°C	43 °F	6 °C	6 °C
	Refreshingly sweet.	Doux, rafraîchissant.	Verfrissend zoet.
i	–	–	–

kriek
CHAPEAU
CHAPEAU
kriek
LAMBIC
PRODUCT OF BELGIUM

Chapeau Lemon

	spontaneous fermentation	fermentation spontanée	spontane gisting
	fruit beer based on Lambic	bière fruitée à base de lambic	fruitbier op basis van lambiek
	Brouwerij De Troch Wambeek-Ternat	Brouwerij De Troch Wambeek-Ternat	Brouwerij De Troch Wambeek-Ternat
	Lambic mixed with lemon juice.	Mélange de lambic et de jus de citron.	Lambiek gemengd met citroensap.
%	3,50%	3,50%	3,50%
	blond	blonde	blond
	–	–	–
°C	43 °F	6 °C	6 °C
	Very refreshing. Sweet-and-sour.	Très rafraîchissant. Aigre-doux.	Zeer verfrissend. Zuurzoet.
i	Particularly appreciated in Thailand.	Surtout appréciée sur le marché thailandais.	Vooral in trek op de Thaise markt.

lemon
CHAPEAU
CHAPEAU
lemon
LAMBIC
PRODUCT OF BELGIUM

CHAPEAU
LAMBIC DE TROCH

Chapeau Mirabelle

	spontaneous fermentation	fermentation spontanée	spontane gisting
	fruit beer based on Lambic	bière fruitée à base de lambic	fruitbier op basis van lambiek
	Brouwerij De Troch Wambeek-Ternat	Brouwerij De Troch Wambeek-Ternat	Brouwerij De Troch Wambeek-Ternat
	Lambic mixed with pressed mirabelle juice.	Mélange de lambic et de jus pressé de mirabelles.	Lambiek gemengd met geperst mirabellensap.
%	3,50%	3,50%	3,50%
	blond cloudy	blonde trouble	blond troebel
	–	–	–
°C	43 °F	6 °C	6 °C
	Refreshingly sweet.	Doux, rafraîchissant.	Verfrissend zoet.
i	Particularly appreciated in France.	Surtout en faveur sur le marché français.	Vooral in trek op de Franse markt.

mirabelle
CHAPEAU
CHAPEAU
mirabelle
LAMBIC
PRODUCT OF BELGIUM
CHAPEAU
LAMBIC DE TROCH

Chapeau Pêche

	spontaneous fermentation	fermentation spontanée	spontane gisting
	fruit beer based on Lambic	bière fruitée à base de lambic	fruitbier op basis van lambiek
	Brouwerij De Troch Wambeek-Ternat	Brouwerij De Troch Wambeek-Ternat	Brouwerij De Troch Wambeek-Ternat
	Lambic mixed with peach juice.	Mélange de lambic et de jus de pêche.	Lambiek gemengd met perzikensap.
%	3,50%	3,50%	3,50%
	blond cloudy	blonde trouble	blond troebel
	–	–	–
°C	43 °F	6 °C	6 °C
	Refreshingly sweet.	Doux, rafraîchissant.	Verfrissend zoet.
i	–	–	–

pêche
CHAPEAU
CHAPEAU
pêche
LAMBIC
PRODUCT OF BELGIUM
CHAPEAU
LAMBIC DE TROCH

Chapeau winter gueuze

	spontaneous fermentation	fermentation spontanée	spontane gisting
	Gueuze Christmas beer	gueuze bière de Noël	geuze kerstbier
	Brouwerij De Troch Wambeek-Ternat	Brouwerij De Troch Wambeek-Ternat	Brouwerij De Troch Wambeek-Ternat
	yeast, hops, malt, wheat, sugar, aroma, water	levure, houblon, malt, froment, sucre, arôme, eau	gist, hop, mout, tarwe, suiker, aroma, water
%	5,60%	5,60%	5,60%
	–	–	–
	Pour gently, revolving the glass whilst pouring.	Verser doucement en tournant le verre.	Zacht inschenken en ondertussen het glas draaien.
°C	45 °F	7 °C	7 °C
	–	–	–
i	–	–	–

CHAPEAU
CHAPEAU
LAMBIC
PRODUCT OF BELGIUM
CHAPEAU

Chimay Bleue

	top-fermentation re-fermented in the bottle	fermentation haute refermentation en bouteille	hoge gisting hergisting op de fles
	Trappist	trappiste	trappist
	Abbaye de Scourmont Forges-Les-Chimay	Abbaye de Scourmont Forges-Les-Chimay	Abbaye de Scourmont Forges-Les-Chimay
	barley malt, wheat, sugar, yeast, hops, water	malt d'orge, froment, sucre, levure, houblon, eau	gerstemout, tarwe, suiker, gist, hop, water
%	9%	9%	9%
	Dark brown, unfiltered. Thick, brown creamy foam head.	Brun foncé, non filtré. Faux col épais, brun crémeux.	Donkerbruin, niet gefilterd. Dikke, bruincrèmige schuimkraag.
	Degrease the glass and avoid fingerprints. Hold the glass by its stem, slightly tilted, and slowly pour the beer, avoiding contact between bottle and glass or foam.	Dégraisser le verre complètement et éviter des empreintes de doigts. Tenir le verre légèrement incliné par le pied et verser lentement la bière sans que la bouteille touche le verre ou l'écume.	Het glas helemaal ontvetten en vingerafdrukken vermijden. Het glas bij de voet licht schuin houden en het bier langzaam inschenken zonder dat de fles het glas of het schuim raakt.
°C	50 - 54 °F	10 - 12 °C	10 - 12 °C
	Powerful and complex. Bouquet of fine spices with a shade of caramel.	Corsé et complexe. Bouquet d'herbes fines, pointe de caramel.	Krachtig en complex. Boeket van fijne kruiden, vleugje karamel.
i	Becomes more complex with age. Keep upright.	Devient plus complexe en mûrissant. Se conserve en position verticale.	Wordt complexer met verouderen. Verticaal bewaren.

20 06
CHIMAY
CHIMAY
Pères Trappistes
BIERE BRASSEE A L'ABBAYE DE SCOURMONT
BIER GEBROUWEN IN DE ABDIJ VAN SCOURMONT

CHIMAY

Chimay rouge

	top-fermentation re-fermented in the bottle	fermentation haute refermentation en bouteille	hoge gisting hergisting op de fles
	Trappist	trappiste	trappist
	Abbaye de Scourmont Forges-Les-Chimay	Abbaye de Scourmont Forges-Les-Chimay	Abbaye de Scourmont Forges-Les-Chimay
	barley malt, wheat, sugar, yeast, hops, water	malt d'orge, froment, sucre, levure, houblon, eau	gerstemout, tarwe, suiker, gist, hop, water
%	7%	7%	7%
	Red-copper, unfiltered. Compact, creamy foam head.	Cuivre rouge, non filtré. Faux col compact et crémeux.	Roodkoper, niet gefilterd. Dichte en romige schuimkraag.
	Degrease the glass and avoid fingerprints. Hold the glass by its stem, slightly tilted, and slowly pour the beer, avoiding contact between bottle and glass or foam.	Dégraisser le verre complètement et éviter des empreintes de doigts. Tenir le verre légèrement incliné par le pied et verser lentement la bière sans que la bouteille touche le verre ou l'écume.	Het glas helemaal ontvetten en vingerafdrukken vermijden. Het glas bij de voet licht schuin houden en het bier langzaam inschenken zonder dat de fles het glas of het schuim raakt.
	46 °F or room temperature	8 °C ou température ambiante	8 °C of kamertemperatuur
	Smooth but solid aroma. Apricot-like fruit, matured by fermentation. Silky smoothness with a slightly bitter touch.	Doux mais solide. Parfum fruité d'abricot par la fermentation. Soyeuse en bouche avec une touche légèrement amère.	Zacht maar stevig. Abrikoosachtige fruitgeur gerijpt door de gisting. Zijdezacht met een lichte bittere toets.
i	Store upright at cellar temperature.	Conserver en position verticale à température de cave.	Verticaal bewaren op keldertemperatuur.

BRUNE
CHIMAY
BRUIN
CHIMAY
Pères Trappistes
BIERE BRASSEE A L'ABBAYE DE SCOURMONT
GEBROUWEN IN DE ABDIJ VAN SCOURMONT

CHIMAY

Chimay Tripel

	top-fermentation re-fermented in the bottle	fermentation haute refermentation en bouteille	hoge gisting hergisting op de fles
	Trappist	trappiste	trappist
	Abbaye de Scourmont Forges-Les-Chimay	Abbaye de Scourmont Forges-Les-Chimay	Abbaye de Scourmont Forges-Les-Chimay
	barley malt, wheat, sugar, yeast, hops, water	malt d'orge, froment, sucre, levure, houblon, eau	gerstemout, tarwe, suiker, gist, hop, water
%	8%	8%	8%
	Blond amber, slightly hazy, unfiltered.	Blond ambré, légèrement voilée, non filtrée.	Blond amber, licht gesluierd, niet gefilterd.
	Degrease the glass and avoid fingerprints. Hold the glass by its stem, slightly tilted, and slowly pour the beer, avoiding contact between bottle and glass or foam.	Dégraisser le verre complètement et éviter des empreintes de doigts. Tenir le verre légèrement incliné par le pied et verser lentement la bière sans que la bouteille touche le verre ou l'écume.	Het glas helemaal ontvetten en vingerafdrukken vermijden. Het glas bij de voet licht schuin houden en het bier langzaam inschenken zonder dat de fles het glas of het schuim raakt.
°C	43 - 46 °F	6 - 8 °C	6 - 8 °C
	Silky smoothness with a fine, bitter aftertaste. Hoppy flavour with a dominating touch of fruity muscat and dry grapes.	Soyeuse avec une fin de bouche amère raffinée. Arôme houblonné avec une dominance de touches fruitées de muscadet et de raisin séché.	Zijdezacht met fijne bitterheid in de afdronk. Hoppig aroma met dominantie van fruitige muscattoets en droge-druiftoets.
i	Drink the beer when it is young and fresh.	Déguster la bière jeune et fraîche.	Jong en fris degusteren.

TRIPLE
CHIMAY
TRIPEL
CHIMAY
BIERE BRASSEE A L'ABBAYE DE SCOURMONT
BIER GEBROUWEN IN DE ABDIJ VAN SCOURMONT

CHIMAY

Christmas Ale Corsendonk

	top-fermentation re-fermented in the bottle	fermentation haute refermentation en bouteille	hoge gisting hergisting op de fles
	Christmas beer	bière de Noël	kerstbier
	Brasserie du Bocq for Brouwerij Corsendonk Oud-Turnhout	Brasserie du Bocq pour Brouwerij Corsendonk Oud-Turnhout	Brasserie du Bocq voor Brouwerij Corsendonk Oud-Turnhout
	special malts, hops, yeast, coriander, water	malts spéciaux, houblon, levure, coriandre, eau	speciale mouten, hop, gist, koriander, water
%	8,50%	8,50%	8,50%
	red-brown	brun rouge	roodbruin
	Pour carefully, avoid the beer sloshing and leave 1 cm of the yeast in the bottle. Never store in the fridge: serve the bottle in an ice-bucket if you want to drink it chilled.	Verser lentement dans un verre incliné sans que la bière clapote et laisser 1 cm de levure dans la bouteille. Ne jamais conserver au réfrigérateur: servir la bière dans un seau à glaces si on veut la boire rafraîchie.	Traag uitschenken in een schuingehouden glas zonder dat het bier klokt en 1 cm gist op de bodem van de fles laten. Nooit in de frigo bewaren: het bier in een ijsemmer serveren als je het gekoeld wil drinken.
°C	43 - 46 °F	6 - 8 °C	6 - 8 °C
	Fine, malty nose. Round, well-balanced taste with a dry and refined aftertaste.	Parfum fin, malté. Saveur ronde équilibrée avec une fin de bouche sèche et raffinée.	Fijne, moutige neus. Ronde, evenwichtige smaak met een droge en verfijnde afdronk.
i	Store the bottles upright in a cool, dark cellar (10 to 14 °C).	A conserver en position verticale dans une cave fraîche et à l'abri de la lumière (10 à 14 °C).	Flessen verticaal bewaren in een koele, donkere kelder (10 à 14 °C).

Corsendonk
Christmas Ale
BIERE BELGE
Corsendonk
Christmas Ale
Corsendonk
Christmas Ale

Christmas Leroy

	top-fermentation re-fermented in the bottle	fermentation haute refermentation en bouteille	hoge gisting nagisting op de fles
	specialty beer winter beer	bière spéciale bière hivernale	speciaalbier winterbier
	Brouwerij Leroy Boezinge	Brouwerij Leroy Boezinge	Brouwerij Leroy Boezinge
	malt, sugar, spices, sweet-ener, yeast, water	malt, sucre, condiments, édulcorant, levure, eau	mout, suiker, specerijen, zoetstof, gist, water
%	7,50%	7,50%	7,50%
	dark red-brown	brun rouge foncé	donker roodbruin
	Pour slowly in a single, smooth movement in a degreased glass. Keep the glass tilted and avoid sloshing. Skim off the foam.	Verser lentement en un seul mouvement fluide dans un verre dégraissé tenu en oblique. Ne pas laisser la bière clapoter. Ecumer le verre.	Traag en in 1 vloeiende beweging uitschenken in een vetvrij glas dat wordt schuingehouden. Het bier niet laten klotsen. Het glas afschuimen.
°C	46 - 50 °F	8 - 10 °C	8 - 10 °C
	Spicy and wintry. Pronounced spicy touch (cherry, curaçao).	Relevé et hivernal. Touche d'herbes prononcée (réglise, cerises, curaçao).	Kruidig en winters. Uitgesproken kruidige toets (zoethout, kers, curaçao).
i	–	–	–

Christmas
Christmas
Christmas
Leroy

Christmas pale ale

	top-fermentation re-fermented in the bottle	fermentation haute refermentation en bouteille	hoge gisting nagisting op de fles
	Ale - amber beer	ale - bière ambrée	ale - amberbier
	Brouwerij De Ryck Herzele	Brouwerij De Ryck Herzele	Brouwerij De Ryck Herzele
	malt, hops, yeast, sucrose, herbs, water	malt, houblon, levure, sucrose, herbes, eau	mout, hop, gist, sucrose, kruiden, water
%	6,30%	6,30%	6,30%
	dark amber slightly hazy	ambré foncé légèrement voilée	donker amber licht gesluierd
	Rinse the glass with cold water, take it by the stem and hold it slightly tilted. Slowly pour in a single movement, avoiding contact between bottle and glass or foam. Either leave the 1 cm yeast sediment in the bottle or pour it out along with the beer.	Rincer le verre à l'eau froide, le prendre par le pied et le tenir légèrement en oblique. Verser lentement en un seul mouvement sans que la bouteille touche le verre ou l'écume. Laisser un dépôt de levure de 1 cm dans la bouteille ou le verser.	Het glas koud spoelen, bij de voet vastnemen en licht schuin houden. Het bier traag en in 1 beweging inschenken zonder dat de fles het glas of schuim raakt. Het gistdepot van 1 cm in de fles laten ofwel uitschenken.
°C	43 °F	6 °C	6 °C
	Typical warming winter beer. Rich malt caramel taste, hoppy touches, long-lasting aftertaste.	Bière hivernale typique réchauffante. Goût riche de malt caramélisé et de houblon, fin de bouche longue.	Typisch verwarmend winterbier. Rijke moutkaramelsmaak, hoppige toetsen, lange afdronk.
i	The draught version of this beer is clear (filtered).	La bière au fût est claire (filtrée).	Van het vat is het bier helder (gefilterd).

CHRISTMAS
PALE-ALE
Christmas Pale-Ale
De Ryck

Christmas Verhaeghe

	top-fermentation	fermentation haute	hoge gisting
	winter beer	bière hivernale	winterbier
	Brouwerij Verhaeghe Vichte	Brouwerij Verhaeghe Vichte	Brouwerij Verhaeghe Vichte
	malt, hops, yeast, water	malt, houblon, levure, eau	mout, hop, gist, water
%	7,20%	7,20%	7,20%
	blond filtered	blonde filtrée	blond gefilterd
	Serve in a dry beer snifter with foot.	Verser dans un verre ballon sec à pied.	Uitschenken in een droog bolglas met voet.
°C	37 °F	3 °C	3 °C
	Hoppy and bitter, which is quite unique for a winter beer.	Houblonné et amer, ce qui est plutôt unique pour une bière hivernale.	Hoppig en bitter wat vrij uniek is voor een winterbier.
i	–	–	–

Alc. 7,2% Vol.
Noël
Christmas
Weihnacht
BROUW. VERHAEGHE VICHTE

Christmas
VICHTE

Ciney blond

	top-fermentation	fermentation haute	hoge gisting
	specialty beer	bière spéciale	speciaalbier
	Alken Maes corporation Alken	Alken Maes corporation Alken	Alken Maes corporation Alken
	–	–	–
%	7%	7%	7%
	gold blond clear	dorée claire	goudblond helder
	Pour carefully into a de-greased, dry glass. Pour slowly to obtain a nice foam head.	Verser soigneusement dans un verre dégraissé et sec. Verser lentement de sorte qu'un faux col solide se forme.	Zorgvuldig uitschenken in een ontvet, droog glas. Langzaam schenken zodat er een mooie schuimkraag ontstaat.
°C	43 °F	6 °C	6 °C
	Soft, fruity taste with a well-balanced, pleasant bitterness.	Saveur douce, fruitée avec un goût amer équilibré et agréable.	Zacht. Fruitige smaak met evenwichtige, aangename bitterheid.
i	–	–	–

Alc. 7 Vol.
BLONDE • BLOND
CINEY
'De Grande Tradition
Van Aloude Traditie
CINEY

C

Ciney bruin

	top-fermentation	fermentation haute	hoge gisting
	specialty beer	bière spéciale	speciaalbier
	Alken Maes corporation Alken	Alken Maes corporation Alken	Alken Maes corporation Alken
	–	–	–
%	7%	7%	7%
	dark brown with red shades	brun foncé avec des teintes rouges	donkerbruin met rode tinten
	Pour carefully into a degreased, dry glass. Pour slowly to obtain a nice foam head.	Verser soigneusement dans un verre dégraissé et sec. Verser lentement de sorte qu'un faux col solide se forme.	Zorgvuldig uitschenken in een ontvet, droog glas. Langzaam schenken zodat er een mooie schuimkraag ontstaat.
°C	43 °F	6 °C	6 °C
	Distinctive, fruity taste. Full-bodied with a smooth aftertaste.	Saveur fruitée de caractère. Fin de bouche franche et douce.	Karaktervolle, fruitige smaak. Volmondig en zacht in de afdronk.
i	–	–	–

CUVÉ
Alc. 7
BRUNE · BRUIN
CINEY
De Grande Tradition
Van Aloude Traditie
CINEY

Cnudde

	top-fermentation	fermentation haute	hoge gisting
	Oudenaards brown	brune d'Audenarde	Oudenaards bruin
	Brouwerij Cnudde Eine-Oudenaarde	Brouwerij Cnudde Eine-Audenarde	Brouwerij Cnudde Eine-Oudenaarde
	barley malt, sugar, hops, yeast, water	malt d'orge, sucre, houblon, levure, eau	gerstemout, suiker, hop, gist, water
%	5%	5%	5%
	amber brown clear	brun ambré claire	amberbruin helder
	–	–	–
°C	39 - 41 °F	4 - 5 °C	4 - 5 °C
	–	–	–
i	Also called 'graveyard beer', because the wells from which the water is pumped, are located near a graveyard. Hard to find today in a bottled version. Almost exclusively sold as a draught beer.	Est aussi appelée bière de cimetière parce que les puits dont l'eau est tirée sont situés près du cimetière. Actuellement difficile à trouver en bouteilles, presque exclusivement livrée au fût.	Wordt ook kerkhofbier genoemd omdat de boorputten waaruit het water wordt gehaald in de buurt van het kerkhof gesitueerd zijn. Momenteel nog moeilijk gebotteld te vinden, quasi uitsluitend op vat geleverd.

CNUDDE
CNUDDE

Cochonette

	top-fermentation re-fermented in the bottle unpasteurised	fermentation haute refermentation en bouteille non pasteurisée	hoge gisting hergisting op de fles niet gepasteuriseerd
	amber	ambrée	amber
	Brasserie à Vapeur Pipaix	Brasserie à Vapeur Pipaix	Brasserie à Vapeur Pipaix
	barley malt, hops, yeast, herbs, water	malt d'orge, houblon, levure, herbes, eau	gerstemout, hop, gist, kruiden, water
%	9%	9%	9%
	amber unfiltered	ambrée non filtrée	amber niet gefilterd
	–	–	–
°C	55 - 64 °F	13 - 18 °C	13 - 18 °C
	Very strong. Delicate and fruity nose. Smooth and full-bodied, slightly hopped but well-balanced. Spicy (roasted chicory, coriander, orange skin).	Très corsé. Parfum délicat et fruité. Doux et franc. Houblon doux mais relevé harmonieusement (chicorée brûlée, coriandre, zeste d'orange).	Zeer sterk. Delicate en fruitige neus. Zacht en volmondig, zachte hop maar evenwichtig gekruid (gebrande cichorei, koriander, sinaasappelschil).
i	Traditionally brewed natural beer that can be stored for a long time.	Bière naturelle brassée de façon naturelle, se conserve longtemps.	Op traditionele wijze gebrouwen natuurbier dat lang houdbaar is.

COCHONNETTE
Artisanal Belgian Amber Ale
Bière Belge Artisanale Ambrée
Brasserie à Vapeur
BIERE EXTRA FORTE . EXTRA STRONG BEER
Cochonn
peur

Contra Pils

	bottom-fermentation	fermentation basse	lage gisting
	Pilsner	pils	pilsbier
	Brouwerij Contreras Gavere	Brouwerij Contreras Gavere	Brouwerij Contreras Gavere
	barley malt, hop (Saaz), bottom-fermenting yeast, water	malt d'orge, houblon (Saaz), levure de fermentation basse, eau	gerstemout, hop (Saaz), lagegistingsgist, water
%	5%	5%	5%
	gold-yellow crystal-clear	jaune doré claire comme du cristal	goudgeel kristalhelder
	Empty in a degreased, rinsed and wet glass. Tilt the glass about 45° and pour the beer, avoiding contact between bottle and foam. Provide a foam head of approx. 2 cm.	Verser complètement dans un verre dégraissé, rincé et mouillé. Tenir le verre incliné à 45°, verser la bière sans que la bouteille touche l'écume. Prévoir un faux col de 2 cm environ.	Helemaal uitschenken in een ontvet, gespoeld en nat glas. Het glas 45° schuin houden, het bier uitschenken zonder dat de fles het schuim raakt. Een schuimkraag van ca. 2 cm voorzien.
°C	36 - 39 °F	2 - 4 °C	2 - 4 °C
	Fresh and distinctive. Smooth bitterness, hoppy aroma.	Frais et plein de caractère. Goût amer moelleux, arôme houblonné.	Fris en karaktervol. Zachte bitterheid, hoppig aroma.
i	–	–	–

Contra Pils
Brij. CONTRERAS
B 9890
GAVERE

PILS
CONTRERAS

Contreras' Especial Mars

	top-fermentation re-fermented in the bottle	fermentation haute refermentation en bouteille	hoge gisting hergisting op de fles
	season beer	bière de saison	seizoensbier
	Brouwerij Contreras Gavere	Brouwerij Contreras Gavere	Brouwerij Contreras Gavere
	barley malt, hop (Hallertau, Styrian, Brewers gold), sugar (for re-fermentation), top-fermenting yeast, water	malt d'orge, houblon (Hallertau, Styrian, Brewers gold), sucre (pour refermentation), levure de fermentation haute, eau	gerstemout, hop (Hallertau, Styrian, Brewers gold), suiker (voor hergisting), hogegistingsgist, water
%	6,50%	6,50%	6,50%
	amber blond, clear	blond ambré, claire	amberblond, helder
	Empty in a degreased, rinsed and dry glass. Tilt the glass about 45° and gently pour the beer, avoiding contact between bottle and foam. Provide a foam head of approx. 5 cm.	Verser complètement dans un verre dégraissé, rincé et sec. Tenir le verre incliné à 45°, verser la bière sans que la bouteille touche l'écume. Prévoir un faux col de 5 cm environ.	Helemaal uitschenken in een ontvet, gespoeld en droog glas. Het glas 45° schuin houden, uitschenken zonder dat de fles het schuim raakt. Een schuimkraag van ca. 5 cm voorzien.
°C	45 °F	7 °C	7 °C
	Malty, slightly sour.	Malté, légèrement acidulé.	Moutig, licht zurig.
i	Store upright. Most breweries used to make a spring beer. Contreras is one of the few that holds on to this tradition.	Conserver en position verticale. La plupart des brasseries fabriquaient autrefois une bière de printemps; Contreras fait honneur à cette tradition.	Verticaal bewaren. De meeste brouwerijen maakten vroeger een lentebier. Contreras is een van weinige brouwerijen die deze traditie in ere houdt.

CONTRERAS
Mars
ESPECIAL
CONTRERAS
Mars
ESPECIAL

Cookie beer

	top-fermentation re-fermented in the bottle	fermentation haute refermentation en bouteille	hoge gisting hergisting in de fles
	city or regional beer	bière citadine ou régionale	stads- of streekbier
	Brasserie d'Ecaussinnes Ecaussinnes d'Enghien	Brasserie d'Ecaussinnes Ecaussinnes d'Enghien	Brasserie d'Ecaussinnes Ecaussinnes d'Enghien
	malt, hops, candy sugar, cinnamon, ginger, yeast, well water	malt, houblon, sucre candi, cannelle, gingembre, levure, eau de source	mout, hop, kandijsuiker, kaneel, gember, gist, bronwater
%	8%	8%	8%
	blond	blonde	blond
	–	–	–
	37 °F	3 °C	3 °C
	Tastes like cinnamon and spiced biscuits with a malty onset.	Saveur de cannelle et de spéculos avec début houblonné.	Smaakt naar kaneel en speculoos. De introductie is moutig.
	–	–	–

BELGIAN ALE
Cookie Beer
33cl
Ultra
des
Ecaussinnes

Corsendonk Agnus

	top-fermentation re-fermented in the bottle	fermentation haute refermentation en bouteille	hoge gisting hergisting op de fles
	Tripel	triple	tripel
	Brasserie du Bocq for Brouwerij Corsendonk Oud-Turnhout	Brasserie du Bocq pour Brouwerij Corsendonk Oud-Turnhout	Brasserie du Bocq voor Brouwerij Corsendonk Oud-Turnhout
	–	–	–
%	7,50%	7,50%	7,50%
	golden-yellow, clear	jaune doré, claire	goudgeel, helder
	Pour carefully, avoid the beer sloshing. Leave 1 cm yeast in the bottle. Never store in the fridge. Serve the bottle in an ice-bucket if you want to drink it chilled.	Verser lentement dans un verre incliné sans que la bière clapote. Laisser 1 cm de levure dans la bouteille. À ne jamais conserver au réfrigérateur: servir la bière dans un seau à glaces si on veut la boire rafraîchie.	Traag uitschenken in een schuingehouden glas zonder dat het bier klokt. 1 cm gist op de bodem van de fles laten. Nooit in de frigo bewaren: het bier in een ijsemmer serveren als je het gekoeld wilt drinken.
°C	43 - 46 °F	6 - 8 °C	6 - 8 °C
	A fresh and lively beer with a spicy taste that evolves into a hoppy aftertaste.	Bière fraîche et vive avec une saveur corsée aboutissant en une fin de bouche houblonnée.	Een fris en levendig bier met een pittige smaak die evolueert in een gehopte afdronk.
i	Store the bottles upright in a cool, dark cellar (10 to 14 °C).	Bouteilles à conserver en position verticale dans une cave fraîche et à l'abri de la lumière (10 à 14 °C).	Flessen verticaal bewaren in een koele, donkere kelder (10 à 14 °C).
	....		

SIGILLVM MONASTERY B. MARIE DE CORSSENDONC
Corsendonk®
Corsendonk®

Corsendonk Pater

	top-fermentation re-fermented in the bottle	fermentation haute refermentation en bouteille	hoge gisting hergisting op de fles
	dubbel	double	dubbel
	Brasserie du Bocq for Brouwerij Corsendonk Oud-Turnhout	Brasserie du Bocq pour Brouwerij Corsendonk Oud-Turnhout	Brasserie du Bocq voor Brouwerij Corsendonk Oud-Turnhout
	malt, hops, yeast, water	malt, houblon, levure, eau	mout, hop, gist, water
%	7,50%	7,50%	7,50%
	deep brown-red	brun rouge intense	diepbruin rood
	Pour carefully, avoid the beer sloshing. Leave 1 cm yeast in the bottle. Never store in the fridge. Serve the bottle in an ice-bucket if you want to drink it chilled.	Verser lentement dans un verre incliné sans que la bière clapote. Laisser 1 cm de levure au fond de la bouteille. À ne jamais conserver au réfrigérateur: servir la bière dans un seau à glaces si on veut la boire rafraîchie.	Traag uitschenken in een schuingehouden glas zonder dat het bier klokt. 1 cm gist op de bodem van de fles laten. Nooit in de frigo bewaren: het bier op ijs serveren in een ijsemmer als je het gekoeld wil drinken.
°C	43 - 46 °F	6 - 8 °C	6 - 8 °C
	A fresh and lively beer with a smooth and round taste.	Bière fraîche et vive avec une saveur douce et ronde.	Een fris en levendig bier met een zachte en ronde smaak.
i	Store the bottles upright in a cool, dark cellar (10 to 14 °C).	Bouteilles à conserver en position verticale dans une cave fraîche et à l'abri de la lumière (10 à 14 °C).	Flessen verticaal bewaren in een koele, donkere kelder (10 à 14 °C).

SIGILLVM · MONASTERY · B · MARIE · DE · CORSSENDONC
Corsendonk®
SIGILLVM · MONASTERY · B · MARIE · DE · CORSSENDONC
Corsendonk®

Cré Tonnerre

	top-fermentation refermented with rum	fermentation haute refermentation au rhum	hoge gisting hergisting met rum
	Tripel	triple	tripel
	Brasserie de Silly Silly	Brasserie de Silly Silly	Brasserie de Silly Silly
	pale barley malt, sugar, yeast, Kent and Hallertau hops, brown Mayarum, water	malt d'orge pâle, sucre, levure, houblon Kent et Hallertau, rhum maya brun, eau	bleke gerstemout, suiker, gist, Kent en Hallertauhop, bruine Mayarum, water
%	7% 14° plato	7% 14° plato	7% 14° plato
	blond (9,8 EBC) shiny, clear	blonde (9,8 EBC) brillante, claire	blond (9,8 EBC) briljant, helder
	–	–	–
°C	39 - 45 °F	4 - 7 °C	4 - 7 °C
	Smooth and round with a Caribbean touch.	Moelleux et rond avec des touches caraïbes.	Zacht en rond met Caribische toets.
i	The name refers to a French music band.	Le nom renvoie à un groupe de musiciens français.	De naam verwijst naar een Franse muziekgroep.

LA
CRÉ TONNERRE
LA CRÉ TONNERRE

Cristal

	bottom-fermentation	fermentation basse	lage gisting
	Pilsner	pils	pils
	Alken Maes corporation Alken	Alken Maes corporation Alken	Alken Maes corporation Alken
	–	–	–
	4,80%	4,80%	4,80%
	pure, blond Pilsener	pils pure, blonde	zuivere, blonde pils
	Empty in a degreased, rinsed and wet glass. Let overflow and skim off the foam.	Verser complètement dans un verre dégraissé, rincé et mouillé. Laisser déborder et écumer.	Helemaal uitschenken in een ontvet, gespoeld en nat glas. Laten overlopen en afschuimen.
	37 °F	3 °C	3 °C
	Distinctive taste. Refreshingly bitter aftertaste.	Saveur de caractère. Fin de bouche rafraîchissante et amère.	Karaktervolle smaak. Verfrissende bitterheid in de afdronk.
	–	–	–

Cristal
Cristal

Cristal

Cuvée de Bouillon

	top-fermentation re-fermented in the bottle unpasteurised	fermentation haute refermentation en bouteille non pasteurisée	hoge gisting hergisting op de fles ongepasteuriseerd
	abbey beer blond	bière d'abbaye blonde	abdijbier blond
	Brasserie de Bouillon Bouillon	Brasserie de Bouillon Bouillon	Brasserie de Bouillon Bouillon
	barley malt, hops, Orval yeast, nut extract, citrus and orange rind, water	malt d'orge, houblon, levure d'Orval, extrait de noix, écorce d'oranges et d'agrumes, eau	gerstemout, hop, Orvalgist, notenextract, citrus- en sinaasschil, water
%	6,50%	6,50%	6,50%
	blond unfiltered	blonde non filtrée	blond niet gefilterd
	Hold the glass slightly tilted while pouring the beer.	Tenir le verre légèrement incliné et verser.	Het glas licht schuin houden en inschenken.
°C	46 - 54 °F	8 - 12 °C	8 - 12 °C
	Slightly soury, traditionally brewed sipping beer. Refreshing, lively beer with taste evolution.	Bière de dégustation légèrement acidulée. Bière rafraîchissante et vive avec saveur évolutive.	Licht zurig ambachtelijk degustatiebier. Verfrissend en levend bier met smaakevolutie.
i	–	–	–

BIÈRE ARTISANALE
Cuvée de Bouillon
Blonde
33 cle
CUVEE DE
BOUILLON

Cuvée des trolls

	top-fermentation	fermentation haute	hoge gisting
	blond	blonde	blond
	Brasserie Dubuisson Pipaix-Leuze	Brasserie Dubuisson Pipaix-Leuze	Brasserie Dubuisson Pipaix-Leuze
	malt, hops, sugar, yeast, dried orange rind, water	malt, houblon, sucre, levure, écorce d'orange séché, eau	mout, hop, suiker, gist, gedroogde sinaasappelschil, water
%	7%	7%	7%
	blond and filtered	blonde et filtrée	blond en gefilterd
	–	–	–
	50 °F	10 °C	10 °C
	Fine, well-balanced fruit flavour.	Arôme fruité équilibré et raffiné.	Evenwichtig en fijn fruitaroma.
i	–	–	–

Cuvée des
TROLLS

Cuvée Ermesinde

	top-fermentation	fermentation haute	hoge gisting
	specialty beer boutique beer	bière spéciale artisanale	speciaalbier artisanaal
	Brasserie Saint-Monon for Arelbières Arlon	Brasserie Saint-Monon pour Arelbières Arlon	Brasserie Saint-Monon voor Arelbières Arlon
	malt varieties, hop varieties, honey, herbs, yeast, water	variétés de malt, variétés de houblon, miel, herbes, levure, eau	moutsoorten, hopsoorten, honing, kruiden, gist, water
%	7,80%	7,80%	7,80%
	amber slightly cloudy	ambrée légèrement trouble	amber licht troebel
	Serve in a 38 cl Cervoise glass.	Dans un verre type Cervoise de 38 cl.	In een glas type Cervoise van 38 cl.
°C	46 °F	8 °C	8 °C
	Flowery character. Liquorice, fig and honey flavours. Aroma of ripe fruits with some flowery touches.	Caractère fleuri. Saveur de réglisse, figue et miel. Arôme de fruits mûrs avec quelques touches fleuries.	Bloemig karakter. Smaak van zoethout, vijg en honing. Aroma van rijpe vruchten met enkele bloemige toetsen.
i	–	–	–

Cuvée
Ermesind
Ambrée du pays d'Arlon
De donkel gellen Beier vum Areierland
Cuvée
Ermesinde

Cuvée St Antoine blonde

	top-fermentation re-fermented in the bottle unpasteurised	fermentation haute refermentation en bouteille non pasteurisée	hoge gisting hergisting in de fles niet gepasteuriseerd
	abbey beer	bière d'abbaye	abdijbier
	Brasserie du Flo Blehen-Hannut	Brasserie du Flo Blehen-Hannut	Brasserie du Flo Blehen-Hannut
	Pilsener malt, sugar, hop varieties, herbs, yeast, water	malt de pils, sucre, sortes de houblon, herbes, levure, eau	pilsmout, suiker, hopsoorten, kruiden, gist, water
%	7,50%	7,50%	7,50%
	blond to rusty	blond rouille	blond tot roest
	Pour carefully tilting the rinsed, dry glass.	Verser prudemment dans un verre rincé et séché tenu en oblique.	Voorzichtig uitschenken in een gespoeld en gedroogd glas dat schuingehouden wordt.
°C	45 - 46 °F	7 - 8 °C	7 - 8 °C
	Slightly fruity character. Flowery taste with pronounced bitterness.	Caractère légèrement fruité. Saveur fleurie avec goût amer prononcé.	Licht fruitig karakter. Bloemensmaak met uitgesproken bitterheid.
i	–	–	–

Cuvée St Antoine
Cuvée
St.Antoine

Cuvée St Antoine brune

	top-fermentation re-fermented in the bottle unpasteurised	fermentation haute refermentation en bouteille non pasteurisée	hoge gisting hergisting in de fles niet gepasteuriseerd
	Scotch	scotch	scotch
	Brasserie du Flo Blehen-Hannut	Brasserie du Flo Blehen-Hannut	Brasserie du Flo Blehen-Hannut
	Pilsener malt, crystal malt, sugar, hops, herbs, yeast, water	malt de pils, malt de cristal, sucre, houblon, herbes, levure, eau	pilsmout, cristalmout, suiker, hop, kruiden, gist, water
%	9%	9%	9%
	brown to black	brune à noire	bruin tot zwart
	Pour carefully into a rinsed, dry glass, holding the glass tilted.	Verser prudemment dans un verre rincé et séché tenu en oblique.	Voorzichtig uitschenken in een gespoeld en gedroogd glas dat schuin gehouden wordt.
°C	45 - 46 °F	7 - 8 °C	7 - 8 °C
	Light fruity character. Flowery taste with pronounced bitterness.	Caractère légèrement fruité. Saveur fleurie avec un goût amer prononcé.	Licht fruitig karakter. Bloemensmaak met uitgesproken bitterheid.
i	–	–	–

Cuvée
St.Antoine
Cuvée St Antoine

Dark Brut Malheur Dark Reserve

	top-fermentation 3x re-fermented in the bottle	fermentation haute triple refermentation en bouteille	hoge gisting 3 x hergist in de fles
	Brut beer	bière brute	brutbier
	Brouwerij Malheur Buggenhout	Brouwerij Malheur Buggenhout	Brouwerij Malheur Buggenhout
	Malt, barley, hops, yeast, water. The yeast is removed from the bottle by special procedures (riddling and disgorging).	Malt, orge, houblon, levure, eau. La levure est enlevée de la bouteille par des procédés spéciaux (remuage et dégorgement).	Mout, gerst, hop, gist, water. Via speciale procédés (remuage en dégorgement) wordt de gist uit de fles verwijderd.
%	12%	12%	12%
	dark brown with a brown, creamy and generous foam	brun foncé avec écume brune, crémeuse et abondante	donkerbruin; bruin, romig en overvloedig schuim
	–	–	–
°C	refrigerated	température de réfrigérateur	frigofris
	Well-balanced, oak dry brut taste by lagering in young American oak barrels, roasted especially for this beer. Complex aroma.	Saveur brute, equilibrée de chêne sec par la conservation en chêne américain jeune spécialement brûlé pour cette bière. Parfum complexe.	Evenwichtige, eikdroge brut-smaak door lagering op jonge Amerikaanse eik die speciaal voor dit bier gebrand werd. Complexe geur.
i	The first dark brut beer in the world.	La première bière brute foncée au monde.	Het eerste donkere brutbier ter wereld.

MALHEUR
MALHEUR
DARK RESERVE
MALHEUR

D

Dark Leireken

	top-fermentation	fermentation haute	hoge gisting
	dubbel	double	dubbel
	Brouwerij Silenrieux for Guldenboot Opwijk	Brouwerij Silenrieux pour Guldenboot Opwijk	Brouwerij Silenrieux voor Guldenboot Opwijk
	organic barley malt, organic buckwheat, organic cane sugar, hops, yeast, water	malt d'orge biologique, sarrasin biologique, sucre de canne biologique, houblon, levure, eau	biogerstemout, bioboekweit, biorietsuiker, hop, gist, water
%	6%	6%	6%
	40 EBC cloudy	40 EBC trouble	40 EBC troebel
	Hold the glass tilted (45°) whilst pouring.	Tenir le verre incliné (45 °) au moment de verser.	Het glas schuin houden (45 °) bij het inschenken.
°C	37 °F	3 °C	3 °C
	Full-bodied with caramel taste.	Franc avec saveur caramélisée.	Volmondig met karamelsmaak.
i	Label is about to change.	L'étiquette va bientôt changer.	Het etiket wijzigt binnenkort.

DARK
Leireken
2008
0,10 €
25cl - 6%

De Graal blond

	top-fermentation re-fermented in the bottle	fermentation haute refermentation en bouteille	hoge of bovengisting nagisting op de fles
	specialty beer, blond	bière spéciale, blonde	speciaalbier, blond
	Brouwerij De Graal Brakel	Brouwerij De Graal Brakel	Brouwerij De Graal Brakel
	Malt, yeast, sugar, hops, water. Dry-hopping for natural hop flavours.	Malt, levure, sucre, houblon, eau. Dryhopping pour les arômes naturels.	Mout, gist, suiker, hop, water. Dryhopping voor natuurlijke hoparoma's.
%	6,50%	6,50%	6,50%
	gold blond, clear	blond doré, claire	goudblond, helder
	Pour carefully in a single, smooth movement and leave the yeast sediment in the bottle.	Verser prudemment en un seul mouvement fluide et laisser le dépôt de levure dans la bouteille.	In 1 vloeiende beweging voorzichtig uitschenken en het gistdepot in de fles laten.
°C	46 - 50 °F	8 - 10 °C	8 - 10 °C
	Soft, not bitter beer. Malty, citrus-like aroma. Spicy, flowery taste, nuts and vanilla. Touch of alcohol in the aftertaste.	Bière douce et pas amère. Arôme malté et d'agrumes. Saveur relevée, fleurie, de noix et de vanille. Touche d'alcool en fin de bouche	Zacht, niet bitter bier. Moutig en citrusachtig aroma. Kruidige, bloemige smaak, noten en vanille. Milde alcoholtoets in de afdronk.
i	Store the bottle upright in a dark, cool room.	Conserver la bouteille en position verticale, à l'abri de la lumière et de la chaleur.	Fles verticaal bewaren op een donkere, koele plaats.

de graal
Blond
Alc 6,5% Vol
de graal

De Graal dubbel

	top-fermentation re-fermented in the bottle	fermentation haute refermentation en bouteille	hoge of bovengisting nagisting op de fles
	specialty beer, dubbel	bière spéciale, double	speciaalbier, dubbel
	Brouwerij De Graal Brakel	Brouwerij De Graal Brakel	Brouwerij De Graal Brakel
	malt, yeast, brown candy sugar, hops, water	malt, houblon, sucre de candi brun, levure, eau	mout, gist, bruine kandij-suiker, hop, water
%	6,50%	6,50%	6,50%
	red-brown clear	brun rouge claire	roodbruin helder
	Pour carefully in a single, smooth movement and leave the yeast sediment in the bottle.	Verser prudemment en un seul mouvement fluide et laisser le dépôt de levure dans la bouteille.	In 1 vloeiende beweging voorzichtig uitschenken en het gistdepot in de fles laten.
°C	46 - 50 °F	8 - 10 °C	8 - 10 °C
	Smooth beer with a spicy undertone. Aroma of malt and spices. Slightly sweet taste of sweet chocolate, caramel and raisin with a touch of bitterness.	Bière douce avec un arrière-fond relevé. Arômes de malt et d'herbes. Saveur légèrement douce de chocolat, de caramel et de raisins avec un goût légèrement amer.	Zacht bier met een kruidige ondertoon. Aroma van mout en kruiden. Lichtzoete chocolade-, karamel- en rozijnensmaak met lichte bitterheid.
i	Store the bottle upright in a dark, cool room.	Conserver la bouteille en position verticale, à l'abri de la lumière et de la chaleur.	Fles verticaal bewaren op een donkere, koele plaats.

de graal
Dubbel
6,5%
de graal

De Graal gember

	top-fermentation re-fermented in the bottle	fermentation haute refermentation en bouteille	hoge of bovengisting nagisting op de fles
	specialty beer blond	bière spéciale blonde	speciaalbier blond
	Brouwerij De Graal Brakel	Brouwerij De Graal Brakel	Brouwerij De Graal Brakel
	malt, yeast, ginger, hops, water	malt, levure, gingembre, houblon, eau	mout, gist, gember, hop, water
%	8%	8%	8%
	blond clear	blonde claire	blond helder
	Pour carefully in a single, smooth movement and leave the yeast sediment in the bottle.	Verser prudemment en un seul mouvement fluide et laisser le dépôt de levure dans la bouteille.	In 1 vloeiende beweging voorzichtig uitschenken en het gistdepot in de fles laten.
°C	46 - 50 °F	8 - 10 °C	8 - 10 °C
	Fresh thirst-quencher. Sweet, bitter and spicy beer with pronounced though not dominating ginger touch.	Désaltérant frais. Bière douce, amère et relevée avec un goût de gingembre prononcé, non dominant.	Frisse dorstlesser. Zoet, bitter en kruidig bier met geprononceerde gember die niet overheerst.
i	Store the bottle upright in a dark, cool room.	Conserver la bouteille en position verticale, à l'abri de la lumière et de la chaleur.	Fles verticaal bewaren op een donkere, koele plaats.

de
graal
Gember
de
graal

De Graal Speciale

	top-fermentation re-fermented in the bottle	fermentation haute refermentation en bouteille	hoge of bovengisting nagisting op de fles
	specialty beer dark	bière spéciale foncée	speciaalbier donker
	Brouwerij De Graal Brakel	Brouwerij De Graal Brakel	Brouwerij De Graal Brakel
	malt, hops, yeast, brown candy sugar, water	malt, houblon, sucre de candi brun, levure, eau	mout, hop, gist, bruine kandijsuiker, water
%	8%	8%	8%
	dark clear	foncée claire	donker helder
	Pour carefully in a single, smooth movement and leave the yeast sediment in the bottle.	Verser prudemment en un seul mouvement fluide et laisser le dépôt de levure dans la bouteille.	In 1 vloeiende beweging voorzichtig uitschenken en het gistdepot in de fles laten.
°C	46 - 50 °F	8 - 10 °C	8 - 10 °C
	Heavy and smooth roasted taste. Pleasant, fruity aroma. Malty, slightly sweetish, bitter taste with touches of candy.	Corsé et légèrement grillé. Arôme fruité agréable. Goût malté, légèrement sucré, amer avec des touches de candi.	Zwaar en zacht geroosterd. Aangenaam fruitig aroma. Moutig, licht zoetig, bittere smaak met toetsen van kandij.
i	Store the bottle upright in a dark, cool room.	Conserver la bouteille en position verticale, à l'abri de la lumière et de la chaleur.	Fles verticaal bewaren op een donkere, koele plaats.

....

....

....

de graal
Speciale
Alc 8% Vol
de graal

De Graal tripel

	top-fermentation re-fermented in the bottle	fermentation haute refermentation en bouteille	hoge of bovengisting nagisting op de fles
	specialty beer Tripel	bière spéciale triple	speciaalbier tripel
	Brouwerij De Graal Brakel	Brouwerij De Graal Brakel	Brouwerij De Graal Brakel
	malt, German hops, yeast, water	malt, houblon allemand, levure, eau	mout, Duitse hop, gist, water
%	9%	9%	9%
	blond clear	blonde claire	blond helder
	Pour carefully in a single, smooth movement and leave the yeast sediment in the bottle.	Verser prudemment en un seul mouvement fluide et laisser le dépôt de levure dans la bouteille.	In 1 vloeiende beweging voorzichtig uitschenken en het gistdepot in de fles laten.
°C	46 - 50 °F	8 - 10 °C	8 - 10 °C
	Bitter and richly hopped heavy beer. Powerfully sweet, spicy, fruity and alcoholic aroma. The sweet taste is at the same time fruity (peaches) and spicy.	Bière forte amère et richement houblonnée. Arôme corsé doux, relevé, fruité et alcoolisé. Saveur douce et en même temps fruitée (pêches) et aromatisée.	Bitter en rijkelijk gehopt zwaar bier. Krachtig zoet, kruidig, fruitig en alcoholisch aroma. Zoete smaak die tegelijk fruitig (perziken) en kruidig is.
i	Store the bottle upright in a dark, cool room.	Conserver la bouteille en position verticale, à l'abri de la lumière et de la chaleur.	Fles verticaal bewaren op een donkere, koele plaats.

de
graal
Tripel
Alc 9% Vol
de
graal

De Koninck amber

	top-fermentation	fermentation haute	hoge gisting
	amber	ambrée	amber
	Brouwerij De Koninck Antwerpen	Brouwerij De Koninck Antwerpen	Brouwerij De Koninck Antwerpen
	malt, hops, yeast, water	malt, houblon, levure, eau	mout, hop, gist, water
%	5%	5%	5%
	amber clear	ambrée claire	amber helder
	Hold the bottle high to start with and pour in one movement until the bottle is empty.	Tenir la bouteille haut au début et continuer à verser jusqu'à ce qu'elle soit vide.	De fles hoog houden bij de start en doorschenken tot de fles leeg is.
°C	43 - 46 °F	6 - 8 °C	6 - 8 °C
	Malty character. Fresh, hop-bitter taste with an aromatic, hop-bitter finish.	Caractère malté. Saveur fraîche, amère et houblonnée avec finition relevée, amère et houblonnée.	Moutig karakter. Frisse, hopbittere smaak met aromatische, hopbittere finish.
i	–	–	–

DE KONINCK
1833
DE KONINCK
1833
AMBER • HOGE GISTING
ALC. 5% VOL.
BELGISCH BIER - BIERE BELGE

De Koninck blond

	top-fermentation	fermentation haute	hoge gisting
	blond	blonde	blond
	Brouwerij De Koninck Antwerpen	Brouwerij De Koninck Antwerpen	Brouwerij De Koninck Antwerpen
	malt, hops, yeast, organic cane sugar, water	malt, houblon, levure, sucre de canne biologique, eau	mout, hop, gist, biologische rietsuiker, water
%	6%	6%	6%
	gold-yellow clear	jaune doré claire	goudgeel helder
	Hold the bottle high to start with and pour in one movement until the bottle is empty.	Tenir la bouteille haut au début et continuer à verser jusqu'à ce qu'elle soit vide.	De fles hoog houden bij de start en doorschenken tot de fles leeg is.
	43 - 46 °F	6 - 8 °C	6 - 8 °C
	Fresh thirst-quencher. Starts with touches of citrus and malt, aromatic aftertaste evoking the Saaz hop.	Désaltérant frais. Touches initiales d'agrumes et de malt, fin de bouche aromatique évoquant le houblon Saaz.	Frisse dorstlesser. Start met toetsen van citrus en mout, aromatische afdronk die refereert aan de Saaz hop.
i	–	–	–

BLOND BLONDE
DE KONINCK
BELGISCH BIER
BIERE BELGE
DE KONINCK
1833
BLOND·BLONDE

DE KONINCK
1833

De Koninck tripel

	top-fermentation	fermentation haute	hoge gisting
	Tripel	triple	tripel
	Brouwerij De Koninck Antwerpen	Brouwerij De Koninck Anvers	Brouwerij De Koninck Antwerpen
	malt, hops, yeast, organic cane sugar, water	malt, houblon, levure, sucre de canne biologique, eau	mout, hop, gist, biologische rietsuiker, water
%	8%	8%	8%
	bronze, clear	bronze, claire	brons, helder
	Hold the bottle high to start with and slowly lower until a nice foam head is formed.	Tenir la bouteille haut au début et baisser lentement jusqu'à la formation d'un faux col solide.	De fles hoog houden bij de start, en langzaam zakken tot een mooie schuimkraag is gevormd.
°C	46 - 50 °F	8 - 10 °C	8 - 10 °C
	Warm alcoholic character and a refreshing session beer. Soft, sweet onset with a full-bodied climax of fruity esters. Aftertaste: aromatic hop bitter (Saaz)	Caractère alcoolisé chaleureux et simultanément désaltérant, facilement buvable. Début moelleux, doux avec un sommet franc d'esters fruités. Fin de bouche aromatique, amère, houblonnée (Saaz).	Warm alcoholisch karakter en tegelijk verfrissende doordrinker. Zachte, zoete start met een volmondig hoogtepunt van fruitige esters. Afdronk: aromatisch hopbitter (Saaz).
i	–	–	–

TRIPEL TRIPLE
DE KONINCK
BELGISCH BIER
BIERE BELGE
DE KONINCK
1833
TRIPEL · TRIPLE
ALC. 8% VOL.
HOGE GISTING · FERMENTATION HAUTE
DE KONINCK
1833

Deinze Export

	bottom-fermentation	fermentation basse	lage gisting
	export	export	export
	De Proefbrouwerij for Huisbrouwerij St Canarus Gottem	De Proefbrouwerij pour Huisbrouwerij St Canarus Gottem	De Proefbrouwerij voor Huisbrouwerij St Canarus Gottem
	Pilsner malt, aromatic hops, water	malt de pils, houblon aromatique, eau	pilsmout, aromahop, water
%	6%	6%	6%
	crystal-blond clear	blond cristal claire	kristalblond helder
	A beer to be drunk straight from the bottle.	Se boit à la bouteille.	Wordt uit de fles gedronken.
°C	43 - 46 °F	6 - 8 °C	6 - 8 °C
	Easily digestible. Pure, well-balanced bitterness.	Se digère facilement. Amertume pure et équilibrée.	Licht verteerbaar. Zuivere, evenwichtige bitterheid.
i	Initially brewed at the request of the 'Young Chamber' of Deinze.	A l'origine brassée à la demande de la Jonge Kamer de Deinze.	Initieel gebrouwen op verzoek van de Jonge Kamer van Deinze.

Deinze & Leiestreek
bevat gerstemout
DEINZE
EXPORT

Delirium nocturnum

	top-fermentation re-fermented in the bottle	fermentation haute refermentation en bouteille	hoge gisting hergisting in de fles
	strong dark	forte foncée	sterk donker
	Brouwerij Huyghe Melle	Brouwerij Huyghe Melle	Brouwerij Huyghe Melle
	malt (including roast-ed malt varieties), hops, yeast, herbs, water	malt (e.a. des variétés de malt brûlées), houblon, levure, herbes, eau	mout (o.a. gebrande moutsoorten), hop, gist, kruiden, water
%	8,50%	8,50%	8,50%
	deep brown	brun intense	diepbruin
	Serve in a goblet.	Verser dans un verre ballon.	Uitschenken in een bolglas.
°C	–	–	–
	More robust and harder than the Delirium tremens. Warm, velvety soft character beer with a very strong taste: tones of alcohol, hops and bitter rind. Long-lasting, bitter aftertaste.	Plus corsé et fort que le Delirium tremens. Bière de caractère chaude, moelleuse et veloutée avec un goût corsé: touches d'alcool, houblon et zeste amer. Fin de bouche amère longue.	Meer gecorseerd en harder dan de Delirium tremens. Warm en fluweelzacht karakterbier met een zeer sterke smaak: tonen van alcohol, hop en bittere schil. Lange bittere afdronk.
i	–	–	–

DELIRIUM
DELIRIUM
nocturnum

Delirium tremens

	top-fermentation re-fermented in the bottle	fermentation haute refermentation en bouteille	hoge gisting hergisting in de fles
	Tripel	triple	tripel
	Brouwerij Huyghe Melle	Brouwerij Huyghe Melle	Brouwerij Huyghe Melle
	malt, hops, yeast, herbs, water	malt, houblon, levure, herbes, eau	mout, hop, gist, kruiden, water
%	8,50%	8,50%	8,50%
	blond clear	blonde claire	blond helder
	Serve in a goblet.	Verser dans un verre ballon.	Uitschenken in een bolglas.
°C	–	–	–
	Malty nose with bitter tones. Aftertaste: peppery and bitter, but never aggressive.	Parfum malté avec des touches amères. Fin de bouche poivrée et amère sans agressivité.	Moutige neus met bittere tonen. Afdronk: peper en bitter zonder agressiviteit.
i	–	–	–

DELIRIUM
DELIRIUM
tremens
FAMILY BREWERY
BRASSERIE FAMILIALE
HUYGHE
SINCE / DEPUIS 1654

DELIRIUM
tremens

Dentergems wit bier

	top-fermentation re-fermented in the bottle	fermentation haute refermentation en bouteille	hoge gisting nagisting in de fles
	Witbier	bière blanche	witbier
	Brouwerij Liefmans Oudenaarde/Dentergem	Brouwerij Liefmans Audenarde/Dentergem	Brouwerij Liefmans Oudenaarde/Dentergem
	barley malt, wheat malt, wheat, corn, hops, coriander, curaçao, yeast, water	malt d'orge et de froment, froment, maïs, houblon, coriandre, curaçao, levure, eau	gerstemout, tarwemout, tarwe, mais, hop, koriander, curaçao, gist, water
%	5%	5%	5%
	white-yellow slightly cloudy (unfiltered)	blanc-jaune légèrement trouble (non filtrée)	witgeel licht troebel (ongefilterd)
	Pour half of the bottle, loosen the yeast with a revolving movement and then continue serving.	Verser la moitié de la bouteille, dégager la levure en tournant la bouteille et la vider.	De helft van de fles uitschenken, de gist losmaken met een ronddraaiende beweging en daarna verder uitschenken.
°C	39 - 43 °F	4 - 6 °C	4 - 6 °C
	Soft, spicy thirst-quencher. Soft, spicy and refreshing taste with a slightly spicy aroma.	Désaltérant doux, relevé. Saveur moelleuse et relevée, goût rafraîchissant avec un arôme légèrement relevé.	Zachte, kruidige dorstlesser. Zachte, kruidige en verfrissende smaak met licht kruidig aroma.
i	Winner of the International Press Award 2003 as Best Belgian Beer.	International Press Award 2003 comme Best Belgian Beer.	International Press Award 2003 als Best Belgian Beer.

BELGISCH BIER - BIERE BELGE
WIT BIER
25 cl e
Dentergems
alc. 5% vol
Bier hergist in de fles
Bière refermentée en bouteille
BIERE BLANCHE
WIT
Dentergems
BLANCHE

D DeuS, Brut des Flandres

	first top-fermentation bottom re-fermented in the bottle	fermentation haute refermentation basse en bouteille	hoge eerste gisting lage hergisting op de fles
	brut beer	bière brute	brut bier
	Brouwerij Bosteels Buggenhout	Brouwerij Bosteels Buggenhout	Brouwerij Bosteels Buggenhout
	barley malts, hops, water	malt d'orge, houblon, eau	gerstemouten, hop, water
%	11,50%	11,50%	11,50%
	Light blond, pale golden, clear saturation with extremely small bubbles. Fine, very white, merengue-like foam head.	Blond clair, saturation claire légèrement dorée avec des bulles minuscules. Faux col fin, blanc, comme de la meringue.	Lichtblond, bleekgouden, heldere saturatie met uiterst minuscule belletjes. Fijne, spierwitte, merengueachtige schuimkraag.
	Chill in the refrigerator for 6 to 12 hours and lay in an ice bucket before serving. Gently pour into a cooled flute-glass.	Mettre au réfrigérateur pendant 6 à 12 heures et ensuite dans un seau à glace. Verser doucement dans des flûtes rafraîchies.	6 à 12 uur op temperatuur brengen in de koelkast en voor het uitschenken in een ijsemmer leggen. Zacht uitschenken in gekoelde fluitglazen.
°C	36 - 39 °F	2 - 4 °C	2 - 4 °C
	Delicate and complex: aromas of fresh apples, enhanced by mint, thyme, ginger, lemon skin, malt, pear, hops, allspice and cloves. Creamy and sparkling, light and airy, sweet and fruity, with dry finishing touch.	Délicat et complexe: arômes de pomme, menthe, thym, gingembre, zeste de citron, malt, poire, houblon, poivre de la Jamaïque et girofle. Crémeux et pétillant, léger, doux et fruité avec finition sèche.	Delicaat en complex: aroma's van verse appels versterkt door munt, tijm, gember, citroenschil, mout, peer, hop, allspice en kruidnagel. Romig en sprankelend, licht en luchtig, zoet en fruitig, met droge afwerking.
i	–	–	–

CB
BEYOND THE BEST OF
DEUS
Brut des Flandres
Cuvée Prestige
BELGIAN ALE

Dikke Mathile

	top-fermentation	fermentation haute	hoge gisting
	amber	ambrée	amber
	Brouwerij Strubbe Ichtegem	Brouwerij Strubbe Ichtegem	Brouwerij Strubbe Ichtegem
	Ambrée malt, cara Munich, hops, herbs, yeast, water	malt ambré, cara Munich, houblon, herbes, levure, eau	ambermout, caramunich, hop, kruiden, gist, water
%	6,50%	6,50%	6,50%
	amber by the malt varieties used filtered	ambrée par les variétés de malt utilisées filtrée	amber door de gebruikte moutsoorten gefilterd
	–	–	–
	43 °F	6 °C	6 °C
	Malty, hoppy.	Malté, houblonné.	Moutig, hoppig.
i	Originally brewed by order of a group of Ostend beer lovers. The name refers to the popular name of a statue in Ostend. The label features a sculpture by Constant Permeke's grandson.	A l'origine brassée à la demande d'un groupe d'amateurs de bière d'Ostende. Le nom de la bière renvoie à la dénomination populaire d'une statue à Ostende. L'étiquette représente cette statue de la main du petit-fils de Constant Permeke.	Oorspronkelijk gebrouwen in opdracht van een groep Oostendse bierliefhebbers. De naam verwijst naar de volkse benaming van een standbeeld uit Oostende. Op het etiket staat een beeld van de kleinzoon van Constant Permeke.

Dikke Mathile
Ostens bier van hoge gisting,
ambachtelijk gebrouwen naar aloude traditie.

Dominus Double

	top-fermentation	fermentation haute	hoge gisting
	abbey beer	bière d'abbaye	abdijbier
	Brouwerij Timmermans/ Koningshoeven Itterbeek	Brouwerij Timmermans/ Koningshoeven Itterbeek	Brouwerij Timmermans/ Koningshoeven Itterbeek
	barley malt, sugar, hops, water	malt d'orge, sucre, houblon, eau	gerstemout, suiker, hop, water
%	6,50%	6,50%	6,50%
	brown	brune	bruin
	–	–	–
	43 - 46 °F	6 - 8 °C	6 - 8 °C
	Dry bitterness from the first moment, obtained by the typical Pale Ale malts and the aromatised hop.	Saveur amère sèche dès la première gorgée par les malts pale ale typiques et le houblon aromatisé.	Droge bitterheid vanaf de eerste slok door de typische pale ale mouten en de gearomatiseerde hop.
i	–	–	–

Dominus®
DOUBLE
Bière monastique
-Brune-

Dominus

Dominus Triple

	top-fermentation	fermentation haute	hoge gisting
	abbey beer	bière d'abbaye	abdijbier
	Brouwerij Timmermans/ Koningshoeven Itterbeek	Brouwerij Timmermans/ Koningshoeven Itterbeek	Brouwerij Timmermans/ Koningshoeven Itterbeek
	barley malt, sugar, hops, water	malt d'orge, sucre, houblon, eau	gerstemout, suiker, hop, water
%	8%	8%	8%
	blond/amber	blond/ambré	blond/amber
	–	–	–
°C	43 - 46 °F	6 - 8 °C	6 - 8 °C
	Bitter with exotic smoothness (white raisin sugar). Dry bitter but at the same time fruity aftertaste.	Goût amer avec une douceur exotique (sucre de raisins secs blancs). Arrière-bouche sèche, amère mais aussi fruitée.	Bitter met exotische zachtheid (suiker van witte rozijnen). Droogbittere maar ook fruitige nasmaak.
i	–	–	–

Dominus
TRIPLE
Bière monastique
Blonde

Dominus

Double Bie

	top-fermentation	fermentation haute	hoge gisting
	dubbel	double	dubbel
	Brouwerij De Bie Loker	Brouwerij De Bie Loker	Brouwerij De Bie Loker
	–	–	–
%	6%	6%	6%
	dark brown	brun foncé	donkerbruin
	–	–	–
°C	–	–	–
	Sweet and fairly bitter.	Doux et assez amer.	Zoet en vrij bitter.
i	–	–	–

Double Bie
Brouwerij De Bie
B-8958 Loker
Tel.: 0475 23 47 95
www.brijdebie.be
DB

Double Enghien blonde

	top-fermentation	fermentation haute	hoge gisting
	regional beer	bière régionale	streekbier
	Brasserie de Silly Silly	Brasserie de Silly Silly	Brasserie de Silly Silly
	pale malt, sugar, Kent and Hallertau hops, yeast, water	malt pâle, sucre, houblon Kent et Hallertau, levure, eau	bleke mout, suiker, Kent en Hallertau hop, gist, water
%	7,50% 16,5° plato	7,50% 16,5° plato	7,50% 16,5° plato
	blond (9,5 EBC)	blonde (9,5 EBC)	blond (9,5 EBC)
	Pour carefully into a narrow goblet.	Verser tranquillement dans un verre calice large.	Rustig uitschenken in een breed kelkglas.
°C	39 - 46 °F	4 - 8 °C	4 - 8 °C
	Well-balanced bitter in the middle and round in the aftertaste.	Goût central amer équilibré, rond en fin de bouche.	Evenwichtig bitter in het midden en rond in de afdronk.
i	Boutique beer. Brewed by Tennstedt Decroes in Enghien till 1975.	Brassée de façon artisanale. Brassée jusqu'à 1975 par la Brasserie Tennstedt Decroes à Enghien.	Artisanaal gebrouwen. Werd tot 1975 gebrouwen door Brouwerij Tennstedt Decroes in Enghien.

Blonde
DOUBLE ENGHIEN
Blonde
AMBACHTELIJK BELGISCH BIER
Alc. 7,5 % vol e33cl

Double Enghien brune

	top-fermentation	fermentation haute	hoge gisting
	regional beer	bière régionale	streekbier
	Brasserie de Silly Silly	Brasserie de Silly Silly	Brasserie de Silly Silly
	pale malt, caramelised malt, aromatic malt, sugar, Kent and Hallertau hops, yeast, water	malt pâle, malt caraméli-sé, malt aromatisé, sucre, houblon Kent et Hallertau, levure, eau	bleke mout, gekaramelli-seerde mout, aromatische mout, suiker, Kent en Hal-lertau hop, gist, water
%	8% 17,5° plato	8% 17,5° plato	8% 17,5° plato
	amber (24 EBC)	ambrée (24 EBC)	amber (24 EBC)
	Pour carefully into a goblet.	Verser tranquillement dans un verre calice large.	Rustig uitschenken in een breed kelkglas.
	41 - 48 °F	5 - 9 °C	5 - 9 °C
	Unique flavour obtained by the different malt types used.	Arôme unique par les va-riétés de malt utilisées.	Uniek aroma door de gebruikte moutsoorten.
i	Boutique beer. Until 1975 brewed by Brouwerij Tennstedt Decroes in Enghien.	Brassée de façon artisanale. Brassée jusqu'à 1975 par la Brasserie Tennstedt Decroes à Enghien.	Artisanaal gebrouwen. Werd tot 1975 gebrouwen door Brouwerij Tennstedt Decroes in Enghien.

Brune
DOUBLE
ENGHIEN
Brune

Double export

	bottom-fermentation	fermentation basse	lage gisting
	export	export	export
	Brasserie L'Imprimerie Brussels	Brasserie L'Imprimerie Bruxelles	Brasserie L'Imprimerie Brussel
	100% malt	100 % malt	100 % mout
%	6,40%	6,40%	6,40%
	amber	ambrée	amber
	–	–	–
	–	–	–
	–	–	–
	–	–	–

Double Export
Vandenheuvel
Since 1850
Double Export
VANDENHEUVEL

Douce Brunette

	top-fermentation	fermentation haute	hoge gisting
	Ale	ale	ale
	Brasserie Artisanale Millevertus Toernich	Brasserie Artisanale Millevertus Toernich	Brasserie Artisanale Millevertus Toernich
	different malt, hop and yeast varieties, water	différentes variétés de malt, de houblon et de levure, eau	verschillende mout-, hop- en gistsoorten, water
%	7 °C	7 °C	7 °C
	amber, gold-coloured	ambrée, dorée	amber, goudkleurig
	–	–	–
	54 °F	12 °C	12 °C
	Smooth malty character beer. Bitter background taste.	Bière de caractère douce, maltée. Amertume en retrait.	Zacht moutig karakterbier. Bitter op de achtergrond.
i	–	–	–

DOUCE BRUNETTE
Brasserie Artisanale
MMMH!!
MILLEVERTUS

Druïde blond

	top-fermentation re-fermented in the bottle	fermentation haute refermentation en bouteille	hoge gisting hergisting op de fles
	blond specialty beer	bière spéciale blonde	blond speciaalbier
	at De Proefbrouwerij Brouwerij Druïde Deerlijk	chez De Proefbrouwerij Brouwerij Druïde Deerlijk	bij De Proefbrouwerij Brouwerij Druïde Deerlijk
	4 malt varieties, sugar, 2 hop varieties, yeast, water	4 variétés de malt, sucre, 2 sortes de houblon, levure, eau	4 moutsoorten, suiker, 2 hopsoorten, gist, water
%	6,50%	6,50%	6,50%
	golden blond brilliantly clear, filtered; fine carbon dioxide bubbles and big, white foam head.	blond doré claire, brillante, filtrée, pétillement léger de gaz carbonique et grand faux col blanc.	goudblond briljant helder, gefilterd; fijne koolzuurpareling en grote, witte schuimkraag.
	Serve in the appropriate glass, with a solid foam head. The ideal thirst-quencher when served cold. At room temperature, a pleasant hop flavour with a light, spicy touch.	Verser dans le verre approprié avec un faux col solide. Rafraîchie, cette bière est un désaltérant idéal. A température de chambre, elle a un arôme houblonné agréable avec une touche légère, relevée.	Uitschenken in het bijhorende glas en voorzien van een stevige schuimkraag. Koud geschonken: ideale dorstlesser. Kamertemperatuur: aangenaam hoparoma met lichte, kruidige toets.
°C	46 - 54 °F	8 - 12 °C	8 - 12 °C
	Full taste with pleasant bitterness and a slightly fruity aftertaste. Fresh with a hoppy character, obtained by the dry-hopping.	Saveur pleine avec un goût amer agréable et une fin de bouche légèrement fruitée. Frais avec caractère houblonné par le dryhopping.	Volle smaak met aangename bitterheid en licht fruitige afdronk. Fris met een hoppig karakter door dryhopping.
i	Store vertically in a cool, dark room (12°C).	Conserver en position verticale à l'abri de la chaleur et de la lumière.	Verticaal bewaren op een koele en donkere plaats (12 °C).

Druide
Blond
Druide

Druïde bruin

	top-fermentation re-fermented in the bottle	fermentation haute refermentation en bouteille	hoge gisting hergisting op de fles
	dubbel specialty beer	bière spéciale double	dubbel speciaalbier
	at De Proefbrouwerij, Brouwerij Druïde Deerlijk	chez De Proefbrouwerij Brouwerij Druïde Deerlijk	bij De Proefbrouwerij Brouwerij Druïde Deerlijk
	4 malt varieties, sugar, 2 hop varieties, yeast, water	4 variétés de malt, sucre, 2 sortes de houblon, levure, eau	4 moutsoorten, suiker, 2 hopsoorten, gist, water
%	6,50%	6,50%	6,50%
	clear ruby red filtered creamy foam head	rouge rubis clair filtrée faux col crémeux	helder robijnrood gefilterd romige schuimkraag
	Serve in the corresponding glass, with a solid foam head.	Verser dans le verre approprié avec un faux col solide.	Uitschenken in het bijhorende glas en voorzien van een stevige schuimkraag.
°C	50 - 55 °F	10 - 13 °C	10 - 13 °C
	Full-bodied with a bitter aftertaste. Slightly sweet with roasted malt, bitter and dry near the end. Malt and caramel aroma.	Franc avec une fin de bouche amère. Goût légèrement doux, malt brûlé, amer et sec en fin de bouche. Arômes de malt et de caramel.	Volmondig met een bittere afdronk. Een lichte zoetigheid, gebrande mout, bitter en droog op het einde. Aroma van mout en karamel.
i	Store vertically in a cool, dark room (12 °C).	Conserver en position verticale à l'abri de la chaleur et de la lumière.	Verticaal bewaren op een koele en donkere plaats (12 °C).

Druide
Bruin

Ducassis

	top-fermentation re-fermented in the bottle	fermentation haute refermentation en bouteille	hoge gisting nagisting in de fles
	fruit beer	bière fruitée	fruitbier
	Brasserie des Légendes Brewsite Gouyasse Irchonwelz (Ath)	Brasserie des Légendes Brewsite Gouyasse Irchonwelz (Ath)	Brasserie des Légendes Brewsite Gouyasse Irchonwelz (Ath)
	with 30% blackcurrant, malt, hops, yeast, fructose, water	adjonction de 30 % de baies de cassis, malt, houblon, levure, fructose, eau	met toevoeging van 30 % zwarte cassisbessen, mout, hop, gist, fructose, water
%	3%	3%	3%
	ruby red	rouge rubis	robijnrood
	Degrease the glass, rinse thoroughly with hot water and dry. With yeast sediment: revolve the bottle before serving the last third. Without yeast sediment: pour carefully and leave the sediment in the bottle.	Dégraisser les verres, bien les rincer à l'eau chaude et sécher. Avec dépôt de levure: tourner le dernier tiers de la bière avant de verser. Dans dépôt: laisser le fond dans la bouteille.	Het glas ontvetten, spoelen met warm water en drogen. Met gistbezinkel: het laatste derde van de fles walsen voor het uitschenken. Zonder gistbezinksel: voorzichtig uitschenken en de fond in de fles laten.
°C	41 - 46 °F	5 - 8 °C	5 - 8 °C
	Smooth, refreshing, sourish. Pronounced aroma of blackcurrant and red fruits.	Doux, rafraîchissant, acidulé. Arômes prononcés de cassis et de fruits rouges.	Zacht, verfrissend, lichtzurig. Uitgesproken aroma van cassis en rode vruchten.
i	First top-fermenting beer with real blackcurrant. Made in collaboration with 2 farmers from Nuits Saint-Georges.	Première bière de haute fermentation avec du vrai cassis en collaboration avec 2 cultivateurs de Nuits-Saint-Georges.	Eerste bier van hoge gisting met echte cassis, in samenwerking met 2 telers uit Nuits Saint-Georges.

BRASSERIE DES GÉANTS
Château-Brasserie
DUCASSIS
La fruitée des Géants
Belgisch Bier - Bière Belge - Belgian Beer
DUCASSIS

Duchesse de Bourgogne

	mixed fermentation	fermentation mixte	gemengde gisting
	West-Flanders red-brown	brune rouge de la Flandre Occidentale	Westvlaams roodbruin
	Brouwerij Verhaeghe Vichte	Brouwerij Verhaeghe Vichte	Brouwerij Verhaeghe Vichte
	Different malt varieties, wheat, more than one year old hops, water. Lagered in oak barrels.	Différentes variétés de malt, froment, houblon suranné, eau. Conservée en fûts de chêne.	Verschillende moutsoorten, tarwe, overjaarse hop, water. Gelagerd op eikenhouten vaten.
%	6,20%	6,20%	6,20%
	red-brown filtered	brun rouge filtrée	roodbruin gefilterd
	Pour in one movement in a dry bulb jar with stem.	Verser en un seul mouvement dans un verre ballon sec sur pied.	Uitschenken in 1 beweging in een droog bolglas op voet.
°C	39 °F or 46 - 54 °F	4 °C ou 8 - 12 °C	4 °C of 8 - 12 °C
	Sweet and fresh sipping beer. Fruity character, obtained by the tannins in the oakwood barrels.	Bière de dégustation douce et fraîche. Caractère fruité par les tannins des fûts de chêne.	Zoet en fris degustatiebier. Fruitig karakter door de looistoffen van de eikenhouten vaten.
i	–	–	–

DUCHESSE
DE BOURGOGNE
DUCHESSE
DE BOURGOGNE

DUCHESSE
DE BOURGOGNE

Duivelsbier

	top-fermentation re-fermented in the bottle	fermentation haute refermentation en bouteille	hoge gisting hergisting op de fles
	dark specialty beer	bière spéciale foncée	donker speciaalbier
	Brouwerij Boon Lembeek	Brouwerij Boon Lembeek	Brouwerij Boon Lembeek
	3 varieties of barley malt, candy sugar, leaf hops, yeast, water	3 variétés de malt d'orge, sucre candi, feuilles de houblon, levure, eau	3 soorten gerstemout, kandijsuiker, bladhop, gist, water
%	5%	5%	5%
	dark brown	brun foncé	donkerbruin
	–	–	–
	max. 14° C	max. 14° C	max. 14° C
	–	–	–
i	Specialty beer from the city of Halle since 1833.	Bière spéciale de la ville de Halle depuis 1833.	Speciaalbier van de stad Halle sinds 1833.

DONKER
1883
Duivels
Bier
FONCÉ - DARK
Met nagisting op de fles - Refermentée
en bouteille - Bottle conditioned
8°

Dulle Teve

	top-fermentation re-fermented in the bottle unfiltered nor centrifuged	fermentation haute refermentation en bouteille non filtrée, ni centrifugée	hoge gisting nagisting op de fles niet gefilterd of gecentrifugeerd
	Tripel	triple	tripel
	De Dolle Brouwers Diksmuide	De Dolle Brouwers Dixmude	De Dolle Brouwers Diksmuide
	malt, white candy sugar, Golding hops	malt, sucre candi blanc, houblon Golding	mout, witte kandijsuiker, Golding hop
%	10%	10%	10%
	light amber	légèrement ambrée	licht amber
	Serve in an Oerbeer glass or wine glass.	Dans un verre oerbier ou un verre de vin.	In een oerbierglas of wijnglas.
°C	50 - 54 °F	10 - 12 °C	10 - 12 °C
	Stubborn, a little smoother than Arabier but fairly treacherous.	Capiteux, un peu plus moelleux que la bière 'arabier' mais très traître!	Koppig, iets zachter dan arabier maar vrij verraderlijk!
i	The original English translation 'mad bitch' was rejected by the US FDA. In that country, it is sold under the name 'triple'. The label was designed by the Bruges artist Peter Six and redesigned by Kris Herteleer.	La traduction anglaise originale 'mad bitch' a été refusée par l'Agence Fédérale Alimentaire des Etats-Unis. La bière y est vendue sous le nom 'triple'. L'étiquette a été conçue par l'artiste brugeois Peter Six et redessinée par Kris Herteleer.	De oorspronkelijke Engelse vertaling 'mad bitch' werd geweigerd door het US Federaal Voedselagentschap. Het bier wordt in USA verkocht onder de naam tripel. Het etiket werd ontworpen door de Brugse kunstenaar Peter Six en hertekend door Kris Herteleer.

10°
DULLE TEVE
TRIPLE
ANNO 1980
oerbier
NAT EN STRAF

Duvel

	top-fermentation re-fermented in the bottle	fermentation haute refermentation en bouteille	hoge gisting hergisting in de fles
	specialty beer	bière spéciale	speciaalbier
	Duvel Moortgat Corporation Puurs	Duvel Moortgat Corporation Puurs	Duvel Moortgat Corporation Puurs
	barley malt, sugar, fine hop varieties, yeast, water	malt d'orge, sucre, variétés fines de houblon, levure, eau	gerstemout, suiker, fijne hopsoorten, gist, water
%	8,50%	8,50%	8,50%
	golden blond	blond doré	goudblond
	Pour carefully into a dry tulip-shaped glass and leave 1 cm of beer (the yeast sediment) in the bottle, as it makes the beer cloudy.	Verser prudemment dans un verre tulipe sec et laisser un 1 cm de fond de levure dans la bouteille (rend la bière trouble).	Voorzichtig uitschenken in een droog tulpvormig glas. 1cm bier (gistfond) in de fles laten (maakt het bier troebel).
°C	43 - 50 °F	6 - 10 °C	6 - 10 °C
	Slightly malty, sweetish flavour that turns into a hoppy taste, ending with a touch of bitterness.	Saveur initiale légèrement douce-maltée, puis houblonnée et amère en fin de bouche.	Licht moutzoetige smaakaanzet die hoppig wordt en uitvloeit in bitterheid.
i	–	–	–

Duvel

Duvel

Duvel gefilterd

	top-fermentation	fermentation haute	hoge gisting
	specialty beer	bière spéciale	speciaalbier
	Duvel Moortgat Corporation Puurs	Duvel Moortgat Corporation Puurs	Duvel Moortgat Corporation Puurs
	barley malt, sugar, fine hop varieties, yeast, water	malt d'orge, sucre, variétés fines de houblon, levure, eau	gerstemout, suiker, fijne hopsoorten, gist, water
%	7,50%	7,50%	7,50%
	golden blond	blond doré	goudblond
	Pour into a dry glass.	Verser dans un verre sec.	Uitschenken in een droog glas.
°C	43 - 50 °F	6 - 10 °C	6 - 10 °C
	Light, fruity and dry aroma. Slightly alcoholic-sweet taste, thirst-quencher with a pronounced hoppy character.	Arôme léger, fruité, sec. Saveur légèrement alcoolisée, douce, désaltérante avec un caractère de houblon prononcé.	Licht, fruitig, droog aroma. Licht alcoholzoete smaak, dorstlesser met een uitgesproken hopkarakter.
i	–	–	–

Duvel
Anno
1871
Duvel
Gefilterd speciaalbier van hoge gisting
met de fijnste mout en hop gebrouwen
Bière spéciale filtrée, avec les malts et
les houblons les plus fins
Duvel

Echt Kriekenbier

	mixed fermentation	fermentation mixte	gemengde gisting
	fruit beer based on red-brown	bière fruitée à base de brune rouge	fruitbier op basis van roodbruin
	Brouwerij Verhaeghe Vichte	Brouwerij Verhaeghe Vichte	Brouwerij Verhaeghe Vichte
	malt, wheat, hops, full Limburg cherries, water. Brewed with red-brown Ale. Matured in oak barrels for approximately 8 months.	Malt, froment, houblon, cerises limbourgeoises, eau. Brassée à base de ale brune-rouge. Mûrie en moyenne 8 mois en fûts de chêne.	mout, tarwe, hop, volle Limburgse krieken, water. Gebrouwen op basis van roodbruine ale. Gemiddeld 8 maanden gerijpt op eikenhouten vaten.
%	6,80%	6,80%	6,80%
	red filtered	rouge filtrée	rood gefilterd
	A tall glass with foot is recommended. Pour slowly into a tilted glass in one smooth movement, avoiding contact between bottle and glass or foam head.	Verser prudemment et en oblique en un seul mouvement fluide sans que la bouteille touche le verre ou le faux col. Un verre haut à pied est recommandé.	Voorzichtig en schuin uitschenken in 1 vlotte beweging zonder dat de fles het glas of de schuimkraag raakt. Een hoog glas op voet is aangewezen.
°C	43 °F	6 °C	6 °C
	Sweet, refreshing and fruity thirst-quencher.	Désaltérant doux-frais et fruité.	Zoetfrisse en fruitige dorstlesser.
i	–	–	–

Echt Kriekenbier
Echt
Kriekenbier

Echt
Kriekenbier

Egmont

	top-fermentation	fermentation haute	hoge gisting
	blond Tripel	triple blonde	blonde tripel
	Brouwerij Strubbe for Brouwerij Crombé Zottegem	Brouwerij Strubbe pour Brouwerij Crombé Zottegem	Brouwerij Strubbe voor Brouwerij Crombé Zottegem
	–	–	–
%	7%	7%	7%
	amber	ambrée	amber
	–	–	–
°C	–	–	–
	Zottegem triple, beer with taste evolution.	Bière triple de Zottegem avec saveur évolutive.	Zottegemse tripel, bier met smaakevolutie.
i	Brewed by Brouwerij Strubbe in Ichtegem following an ancient, original recipe of Crombé.	Brassée par la Brasserie Strubbe de Ichtegem d'après une recette originale de Crombé.	Gebrouwen door Brouwerij Strubbe uit Ichtegem naar een oud, origineel recept van Crombé.

Egmont

E

Ekla super pils

top-fermentation	fermentation haute	hoge gisting
Pilsner	pils	pils
Brasserie L'Imprimerie Brussels	Brasserie L'Imprimerie Bruxelles	Brasserie L'Imprimerie Brussel
–	–	–
4,80%	4,80%	4,80%
blond	blonde	blond
–	–	–
–	–	–
Refreshing and slightly bitter. Smooth beer with a fruity touch.	Rafraîchissant et légèrement amer. Bière douce avec une touche fruitée.	Verfrissend en licht bitter. Zacht bier met een fruitige toets.
The Belgian beer par excellence at the 1958 World Exhibition.	La bière belge par excellence à l'exposition universelle de 1958.	Het Belgische bier bij uitstek op de wereldtentoonstelling van 1958.

EKLA
SUPER PILS
Vandenheuvel
Since 1850
EKLA
VANDENHEUVEL

Ename Blond

	top-fermentation re-fermented in the bottle	fermentation haute refermentation en bouteille	hoge gisting nagisting op de fles
	recognised Belgian abbey beer	Bière d'abbaye belge reconnue	Erkend Belgisch abdijbier
	Brouwerij Roman Mater	Brouwerij Roman Mater	Brouwerij Roman Mater
	barley malt, hops, sugars, yeast, well water	malt d'orge, houblon, sucres, levure, eau de source	gerstemout, hop, suikers, gist, bronwater
%	6,50%	6,50%	6,50%
	blond	blonde	blond
	Pour carefully in a single, smooth movement and leave the yeast sediment in the bottle.	Verser prudemment en un mouvement fluide et laisser le dépôt de levure dans la bouteille.	Voorzichtig uitschenken in 1 vlotte beweging en de gistfond in de fles laten.
°C	43 °F	6 °C	6 °C
	Strong alcoholic yet thirst-quenching. Malt-sweetish, fruity and slightly hoppy aroma. Well-balanced taste with pronounced, pleasant hoppy bitterness.	Très alcoolisé mais rafraîchissant. Doux-malté, fruité et arôme légèrement houblonné. Saveur équilibrée avec un accent sur l'amertume houblonnée agréable.	Sterk alcoholisch maar toch dorstlessend. Moutzoetig, fruitig en licht hoppig aroma. Uitgebalanceerde smaak met nadruk op aangename hopbitterheid.
i	Store in a dark, cool room.	Conserver à l'abri de la lumière et de la chaleur.	Donker en koel bewaren.

BLOND
ENAME
ABDIJBIER/BIERE D'ABBAYE

ENAME

Ename Cuvée 974

	top-fermentation re-fermented in the bottle	fermentation haute refermentation en bouteille	hoge gisting nagisting op de fles
	recognised Belgian abbey beer	Bière d'abbaye belge reconnue	Erkend Belgisch abdijbier
	Brouwerij Roman Mater	Brouwerij Roman Mater	Brouwerij Roman Mater
	barley malt, hops, sugars, yeast, herbs, well water	malt d'orge, houblon, sucres, levure, eau de source	gerstemout, hop, suikers, gist, kruiden, bronwater
%	7%	7%	7%
	amber-red	rouge ambré	amberrood
	Pour carefully in a single, smooth movement and leave the yeast sediment in the bottle.	Verser prudemment en un mouvement fluide et laisser le dépôt de levure dans la bouteille.	Voorzichtig uitschenken in 1 vlotte beweging en de gistfond in de fles laten.
°C	43 °F	6 °C	6 °C
	Winter beer with an aroma of malt, vanilla and berries. Fruity taste of sweetish caramel and smooth bitterness.	Bière hivernale avec un arôme de malt, de vanille et de groseilles. Saveur fruitée de caramel doux, amertume douce.	Winterbier met een aroma van mout, vanille en bessen. Fruitige smaak van zoetig karamel en zachte bitterheid.
i	Store in a dark, cool room.	Conserver à l'abri de la lumière et de la chaleur.	Donker en koel bewaren.

CUVEE 974
ENAME
ABDIJBIER/BIERE D'ABBAYE
ENAME
ABDIJBIER/BIERE D'ABBAYE

Ename Dubbel

	top-fermentation re-fermented in the bottle	fermentation haute refermentation en bouteille	hoge gisting nagisting op de fles
	recognised Belgian abbey beer	Bière d'abbaye belge reconnue	Erkend Belgisch abdijbier
	Brouwerij Roman Mater	Brouwerij Roman Mater	Brouwerij Roman Mater
	barley malt, hops, candy sugar, yeast, well water	malt d'orge, houblon, sucre candi, levure, eau de source	gerstemout, hop, kandijsuiker, gist, bronwater
%	6,50%	6,50%	6,50%
	dark red-brown	brun rouge foncé	donkerrood bruin
	Pour carefully, avoiding contact between bottle and foam head. Leave the yeast sediment in the bottle.	Verser prudemment sans que la bouteille touche le faux col et laisser le dépôt de levure dans la bouteille.	Voorzichtig uitschenken zonder dat de fles de schuimkraag raakt en de gistfond in de fles laten.
°C	43 °F	6 °C	6 °C
	Aroma of caramelized malt and sweetened fruit. Caramel taste of roasted malt and smooth, hoppy bitterness	Arôme de malt caramélisé et de fruit sucré. Goût caramélisé de malt grillé et goût amer doux, houblonné.	Aroma van gekaramelliseerde mout en gezoet fruit. Karamelsmaak van geroosterde mout en zachte, hoppige bitterheid.
i	Store in a dark, cool room.	Conserver à l'abri de la lumière et de la chaleur.	Donker en koel bewaren.

DUBBEL
ENAME
ABDIJBIER/BIERE D'ABBAYE

ENAME
ABDIJBIER/BIERE D'ABBAYE

Ename Tripel

	top-fermentation re-fermented in the bottle	fermentation haute refermentation en bouteille	hoge gisting nagisting op de fles
	recognised Belgian abbey beer	Bière belge d'abbaye reconnue	Erkend Belgisch abdijbier
	Brouwerij Roman Mater	Brouwerij Roman Mater	Brouwerij Roman Mater
	barley malt, hops, sugars, yeast, well water	malt d'orge, houblon, sucres, levure, eau de source	gerstemout, hop, suikers, gist, bronwater
%	8,50%	8,50%	8,50%
	blond	blonde	blond
	Pour carefully in one, smooth movement and leave the yeast sediment in the bottle.	Verser prudemment en un mouvement fluide et laisser le dépôt de levure dans la bouteille.	Voorzichtig uitschenken in 1 vlotte beweging en de gistfond in de fles laten.
°C	43 °F	6 °C	6 °C
	Smoothly malty, slightly spicy, fruity and alcoholic flavour. Spicy, malty taste with smoothly bitter, alcoholic aftertaste.	Houblonné-doux, légèrement relevé, arôme fruité et alcoolisé. Goût relevé, malté avec une fin de bouche moelleuse-amère alcoolisée.	Zacht moutig, licht kruidig, fruitig en alcoholisch aroma. Pittige, moutige smaak met zachtbittere alcoholische afdronk.
i	Store in a dark, cool room.	Conserver à l'abri de la lumière et de la chaleur.	Donker en koel bewaren.

TRIPEL
ENAME
ABDIJBIER/BIERE D'ABBAYE

ENAME

Enghien Noël

	top-fermentation re-fermented in the bottle	fermentation haute refermentation en bouteille	hoge gisting hergisting in de fles
	Tripel regional beer christmas beer	bière régionale triple bière de Noël	tripel streekbier kerstbier
	Brasserie de Silly Silly	Brasserie de Silly Silly	Brasserie de Silly Silly
	pale malt, sugar, yeast, Kent and Hallertau hops, water	malt pâle, sucre, levure, houblon Kent et Hallertau, eau	bleke mout, suiker, gist, Kent en Hallertauhop, water
%	9% 20° plato	9% 20° plato	9% 20° plato
	blond (10,2 EBC)	blonde (10,2 EBC)	blond (10,2 EBC)
	–	–	–
°C	41 - 46 °F	5 - 8 °C	5 - 8 °C
	A combination of freshness, warmth and pleasant bitterness. Covers the palate from the first sip, developing a refreshing vanilla flavour with a touch of pepper.	Une combinaison de fraîcheur et de chaleur avec une amertume agréable. Recouvre le palais dès la première gorgée et déploie un goût de vanille rafraîchissant avec une pointe de poivre.	Een combinatie van frisheid en warmte met aangename bitterheid. Bedekt het gehemelte vanaf de eerste slok en ontplooit een verfrissende vanillesmaak met een vleugje peper.
i	Provision beer.	Bière à conserver.	Bewaarbier.

Noël
ENGHIEN
Noël
TRIPLE BLONDE
TRIPEL BLOND
alc. 9% vol 33 cl.e

Eupener Bier

	bottom-fermentation	fermentation basse	lage gisting
	premium Pilsner	pils premium	premium pils
	Brouwerij Haacht Boortmeerbeek	Brouwerij Haacht Boortmeerbeek	Brouwerij Haacht Boortmeerbeek
	barley malt, hops, water	malt d'orge, houblon, eau	gerstemout, hop, water
%	5%	5%	5%
	clear and light blond; foam head with fine bubbles	blond clair, limpide; faux col avec des bulles fines	helder en lichtblond; schuimkraag met fijne bellen
	Pour carefully into a rinsed, wet bulb jar avoiding contact between bottle and foam head.	Verser prudemment dans un verre mouillé sans que la bouteille touche l'écume.	Voorzichtig uitschenken in een gespoeld, nat kogelglas zonder dat de fles het schuim raakt.
°C	37 °F	3 °C	3 °C
	–	–	–
i	Typical Eupener Bier brewed following the German Reinheitsgebot. This is a regulation from 1516 stating that only pure malt, noble hops, yeast and water must be used in the brewing process.	Bière typique d'Eupen brassée selon le 'Reinheitsgebot' allemand (ordonnance de 1516) prévoyant que seulement du malt pur, du houblon sélectionné, de la levure et de l'eau peuvent être utilisés pendant le brassage.	Typisch Eupener Bier gebrouwen volgens het Duitse Reinheitsgebot (verordening uit 1516) waarbij alleen zuivere mout, edele hop, gist en water mogen worden gebruikt tijdens het brouwproces.

Anno 1834
BIERE PILS BIER
Eupener
Bier
Rein Gerstenmalz und Edelhopfen

Eupener Bier
SEIT 1834
Rein Malz
und Edelhopfen

Extra special Export Stout

	top-fermentation	fermentation haute	hoge gisting
	Stout	stout	stout
	De Dolle Brouwers Esen	De Dolle Brouwers Esen	De Dolle Brouwers Esen
	malt (roasted, pale, cara), Nugget hops, yeast, water	malt (grillé, pâle, cara), houblon Nugget, levure, eau	mout (geroosterd, bleek, cara), Nugget hop, gist, water
%	9%	9%	9%
	pitch-black with beige foam head	noir foncé avec faux col beige	pikzwart met beige schuimkraag
	Serve in a big, robust glass as for Guinness.	Dans un verre solide et robuste tel que pour Guinness.	In een kloek en robuust glas zoals voor Guinness.
°C	50 - 54 °F	10 - 12 °C	10 - 12 °C
	Much appreciated by Anglo-Saxon beer drinkers. Heavy, bitter, a little sour and very solid.	Apprécié auprès du public anglo-saxon. Fort, amer, un peu acidulé et très solide.	Geliefd bij een Angelsaksisch publiek. Zwaar, bitter, een beetje zuur en zeer kloek.
i	Brewed since 2004 at the request of the American distributor. Stout used to be recommended in revalidation therapies, because it increases the hematocrit level in the blood.	Brassée depuis 2004 à la demande de l'importateur américain. Le stout était jadis recommandé pour la rééducation et augmente la valeur de l'hématocrite dans le sang.	Wordt sedert 2004 gebrouwen op aanvraag van de Amerikaanse invoerder. Stout werd vroeger aangeraden voor revalidatie. Het verhoogt het hematocrietgehalte in het bloed.

33cl.
11.2 FL.OZ
SPECIAL EXTRA EXPORT STOUT
BREWED & BOTTLED BY DE DOLLE BROUWERS
REFERMENTED IN THE BOTTLE
ESEN BELGIUM
9% ALC/VOL
DE DOLLE BROUWERS

Ezel bruin

	top-fermentation	fermentation haute	hoge gisting
	dark amber	ambré foncé	donker amber
	Brouwerij Bavik Bavikhove	Brouwerij Bavik Bavikhove	Brouwerij Bavik Bavikhove
	barley malt, hops, yeast, fine herbs, pure well water	malt d'orge, houblon, levure, fines herbes, eau de source pure	gerstemout, hop, gist, fijne kruiden, zuiver bronwater
%	6,50%	6,50%	6,50%
	light brown slightly cloudy	brun clair légèrement trouble	lichtbruin licht troebel
	Pour into a degreased, rinsed and wet glass, avoiding any contact between bottle and foam.	Verser dans un verre dégraissé, rincé et mouillé sans que la bouteille touche le faux col.	Uitschenken in een ontvet, gespoeld en nat glas zonder dat de fles het schuim raakt.
°C	43 - 46 °F	6 - 8 °C	6 - 8 °C
	Solid with a pronounced fruity aroma. Full-bodied and fruity character.	Solide avec un arôme fruité prononcé. Caractère franc et fruité.	Stevig met een uitgesproken fruitig aroma. Volmondig en fruitig karakter.
i	–	–	–

EZEL
bier / Biere brune / Brown beer
EZEL

Ezel wit

	top-fermentation	fermentation haute	hoge gisting
	Witbier amber-coloured	bière blanche ambrée	witbier amberkleurig
	Brouwerij Bavik Bavikhove	Brouwerij Bavik Bavikhove	Brouwerij Bavik Bavikhove
	barley malt, hops, yeast, wheat, pure well water	malt d'orge, houblon, levure, froment, eau de source pure	gerstemout, hop, gist, tarwe, zuiver bronwater
%	5,80%	5,80%	5,80%
	pale-yellow amber slightly cloudy	ambré jaune pâle légèrement trouble	bleekgeel amber licht troebel
	Pour into a degreased, rinsed and wet glass avoiding contact between bottle and foam.	Verser dans un verre dégraissé, rincé et mouillé sans que la bouteille touche le faux col.	Uitschenken in een ontvet, gespoeld en nat glas zonder dat de fles het schuim raakt.
°C	39 - 43 °F	4 - 6 °C	4 - 6 °C
	Creamy and smooth, but with a spicy aftertaste. Full and solid character.	Crémeux et doux mais corsé en fin de bouche. Caractère plein et solide.	Romig en zacht maar toch pittig in de afdronk. Vol en stevig karakter.
i	–	–	–

EZEL
EZEL

Fantôme BBB Dark white

	top-fermentation	fermentation haute	hoge gisting
	Belgian Ale	ale belge	Belgian ale
	Brasserie Fantôme Soy	Brasserie Fantôme Soy	Brasserie Fantôme Soy
	with herbs (including black pepper)	contient des herbes (e.a. du poivre noir)	bevat kruiden (o.a. zwarte peper)
%	4,50%	4,50%	4,50%
	–	–	–
	Serve in a Trappist or tulip-shaped glass.	Verser dans un verre trappiste ou tulipe.	Uitschenken in een trappist- of tulpglas.
°C	–	–	–
	–	–	–
i	BBB refers to the website www.babblebelt.com, of The Burgundian Babble Belt, an international community of Belgian beer lovers.	BBB fait référence au site web www.babblebelt.com du Burgundian Babble Belt, une communauté internationale d'amateurs de bières belges.	BBB verwijst naar de website www.babblebelt.com van The Burgundian Babble Belt, een internationale community van Belgisch-bierfanaten.

DARK
WHITE
BELGIAN ALE
BREWED WITH SPICES
BBB
www.babblebelt.com

Fantôme Black Ghost

	top-fermentation	fermentation haute	hoge gisting
	Belgian strong Ale	Belgian strong Ale	Belgian strong ale
	Brasserie Fantôme Soy	Brasserie Fantôme Soy	Brasserie Fantôme Soy
	barley malt, hops, yeast, water	malt d'orge, houblon, levure, eau	gerstemout, hop, gist, water
%	8%	8%	8%
	–	–	–
	Serve in a Trappist or tulip-shaped glass.	Verser dans un verre trappiste ou tulipe.	Uitschenken in een trappist- of tulpglas.
°C	–	–	–
	–	–	–
i	The Fantôme beers are hard to come by in Belguim. Even the brewer heardly has them in stock.	Les bières de la brasserie Fantôme sont difficiles à trouver en Belgique, même le brasseur a peu de stock.	De bieren van Fantôme zijn in België heel moeilijk te vinden, zelfs de brouwer heeft weinig op voorraad.

Black Ghost

Fantôme été

fermentation	top-fermentation	fermentation haute	hoge gisting
type	Saisons	bière de saison	saison
brewery	Brasserie Fantôme Soy	Brasserie Fantôme Soy	Brasserie Fantôme Soy
ingredients	barley malt, hops, yeast, water and herbs	malt d'orge, houblon, levure, eau et herbes	gerstemout, hop, gist, water en kruiden
%	8%	8%	8%
colour	light-yellow with a solid foam head	jaune claire avec faux col solide	lichtgeel heeft een stevige schuimkraag
glass	Serve in a tulip-shaped glass (cfr. Duvel).	Verser dans un verre tulipe (voir Duvel).	Uitschenken in een tulpglas (cfr. Duvel).
°C	–	–	–
taste	Aroma of fruity esters. Complex fruit and citrus taste owing to the herbs.	Arômes d'esters fruités. Saveur complexe de fruits et d'agrumes par la présence d'herbes.	Aroma van fruitige esters. Complexe fruit- en citrussmaak door de kruiden.
i	–	–	–

été
Fantôme

Faro Lindemans

	spontaneous fermentation	fermentation spontanée	spontane gisting
	Faro Lambic	faro lambic	faro lambiek
	Brouwerij Lindemans Vlezenbeek	Brouwerij Lindemans Vlezenbeek	Brouwerij Lindemans Vlezenbeek
	malt, wheat, hops, candy sugar, water	malt, froment, houblon, sucre candi, eau	mout, tarwe, hop, kandij-suiker, water
%	4,50%	4,50%	4,50%
	pearl-brown clear	brun perlé claire	parelbruin helder
	Pour into a pint jug.	Verser dans une chope.	In een pintglas uitschenken.
°C	37 - 39 °F	3 - 4 °C	3 - 4 °C
	Sweet-and-sour and thirst-quenching. Sweet taste of candy with slightly sourish aftertaste.	Aigre-doux et désaltérant. Saveur douce de candi avec une fin de bouche douce, acidulée.	Zoetzuur en dorstlessend. Zoete smaak van kandij met zachtzurige afdronk.
i	Goes nicely with many desserts.	Convient avec beaucoup de desserts.	Past bij vele desserts.

FARO
Lambic
Lindemans
Oud Streek-Bier
Bière Régionale et Artisanale

Lindemans

Fasso blond

	top-fermentation re-fermented in the bottle	fermentation haute refermentation en bouteille	hoge gisting hergisting op de fles
	blond	blonde	blond
	Brouwerij Vissenaken Vissenaken-Tienen	Brouwerij Vissenaken Vissenaken-Tienen	Brouwerij Vissenaken Vissenaken-Tienen
	barley malt, wheat malt, hops, sugar, yeast, brewing water. Boutique beer.	malt d'orge et de froment, houblon, sucre, levure, eau de brassage. Brassage artisanal.	gerstemout, tarwemout, hop, suiker, gist, brouwwater. Ambachtelijk gebrouwen.
%	6,50%	6,50%	6,50%
	blond cloudy (unfiltered)	blonde trouble (non filtrée)	blond troebel (ongefilterd)
	Pour slowly into a bulb jar, with or without yeast sediment.	Verser lentement dans un verre ballon, avec ou sans dépôt de levure.	Langzaam inschenken in een bolvormig glas, met of zonder gist.
°C	46 - 54 °F	8 - 12 °C	8 - 12 °C
	Savoury thirst-quencher. Bitter beer with a full malt taste and an exotic, fruity aroma.	Désaltérant savoureux. Bière plutôt amère avec un goût malté plein et un arôme fruité exotique.	Smaakvolle dorstlesser. Bitterig bier met een volle moutsmaak en een exotisch-fruitig aroma.
i	Store upright at cellar temperature. The taste is at its best three months after the bottling date.	Conserver en position verticale à température de cave. Ce n'est que 3 mois après la mise en bouteilles que la saveur arrive à son sommet.	Rechtop bewaren op keldertemperatuur. Pas 3 maanden na botteldatum is de smaak geëvolueerd tot op zijn best.

Blond
FASSO

Felix Kriekbier

	top-fermentation	fermentation haute	hoge gisting
	Oudenaards Kriek beer - Flemish sour Ale	bière Kriek d'Audenarde - Flemish sour ale	Oudenaards kriekbier - Flemish sour ale
	Brouwerij Verhaeghe for Brouwerij Clarysse Oudenaarde	Brouwerij Verhaeghe pour Brouwerij Clarysse Oudenaarde	Brouwerij Verhaeghe voor Brouwerij Clarysse Oudenaarde
	Boutique beer with taste evolution	Bière brassée de façon artisanale avec évolution de saveur.	artisanaal gebrouwen bier met smaakevolutie
%	3,50%	3,50%	3,50%
	–	–	–
	–	–	–
°C	–	–	–
	–	–	–
	–	–	–

Felix
KRIEKBIER
Felix
KRIEKBIER

Floreffe blonde

	top-fermentation	fermentation haute	hoge gisting
	recognised Belgian abbey beer blond	Bière d'abbaye belge reconnue blonde	Erkend Belgisch abdijbier blond
	Brasserie Lefebvre Quenast	Brasserie Lefebvre Quenast	Brasserie Lefebvre Quenast
	barley malt, hops, candy sugar, yeast, water	malt d'orge, sucre candi, houblon, levure, eau	gerstemout, hop, kandijsuiker, gist, water
%	6,30%	6,30%	6,30%
	clear	claire	helder
	Pour into a goblet.	Verser dans un verre ballon.	Uitschenken in een ballonglas.
°C	39 - 50 °F	4 - 10 °C	4 - 10 °C
	Malty beer with a well-balanced bitterness. Hoppy flavour.	Bière maltée avec un goût amer équilibré. Arôme de cônes de houblon.	Moutig bier met een evenwichtige bitterheid. Aroma van hopbellen.
i	–	–	–

FLOREFFE
Blonde-Blond
FLOREFFE
BIÈRE D' ABBAYE - ABDIJBIER
Blonde
Blond

Bière
d'Abbaye
Abdij
Bier
FLOREFFE

Floreffe double

	top-fermentation	fermentation haute	hoge gisting
	recognised Belgian abbey beer brown	Bière d'abbaye belge reconnue brune	Erkend Belgisch abdijbier bruin
	Brasserie Lefebvre Quenast	Brasserie Lefebvre Quenast	Brasserie Lefebvre Quenast
	barley malt, hops, candy sugar, yeast, water	malt d'orge, houblon, sucre candi, levure, eau	gerstemout, hop, kandijsuiker, gist, water
%	6,30%	6,30%	6,30%
	brown	brune	bruin
	Pour into a goblet.	Verser dans un verre ballon.	Uitschenken in een ballonglas.
°C	46 - 54 °F	8 - 12 °C	8 - 12 °C
	–	–	–
i	–	–	–

FLOREFFE
Double-Dubbel
Bière d'Abbaye
Abdij Bier
FLOREFFE
FLOREFFE
BIÈRE D' ABBAYE - ABDIJBIER
Double
Dubbel

Floreffe Prima Melior

	top-fermentation	fermentation haute	hoge gisting
	recognised Belgian abbey beer	Bière d'abbaye belge reconnue	Erkend Belgisch abdijbier
	Brasserie Lefebvre Quenast	Brasserie Lefebvre Quenast	Brasserie Lefebvre Quenast
	barley malt, roasted malt, candy sugar, yeast, flavourings, water	malt d'orge, malt brûlé, sucre candi, levure, arômes, eau	gerstemout, gebrande mout, kandijsuiker, gist, aroma's, water
%	8%	8%	8%
	very dark brown	brun très foncé	zeer donkerbruin
	Place the bottle upright 48 hours before serving. Pour into a glass with a stem.	Mettre la bouteille en position verticale 48 heures avant la dégustation. Verser dans un verre à pied.	De fles 48 uren voor het degusteren verticaal zetten. Uitschenken in een glas met voet.
°C	39 - 45 °F	4 - 7 °C	4 - 7 °C
	Smooth and slightly bitter. Changing, deep taste influenced by the special malt types and spices. Flavour of anise and spices.	Moelleux et légèrement amer. Saveur évolutive et profonde renvoyant aux variétés spéciales de malt et d'herbes. Arôme d'anis et d'herbes.	Zacht en licht bitter. Evoluerende, diepe smaak die refereert naar de speciale moutsoorten en de kruiden. Aroma van anijs en kruiden
i	–	–	–

FLOREFFE
Prima Melior
FLOREFFE
BIÈRE D' ABBAYE - ABDIJBIER
Prima
Melior

Bière
d'Abbaye
Abdij
Bier
FLOREFFE

Floreffe tripel

	top-fermentation	fermentation haute	hoge gisting
	Tripel	triple	tripel
	Brasserie Lefebvre Quenast	Brasserie Lefebvre Quenast	Brasserie Lefebvre Quenast
	barley malt, hops, candy sugar, yeast, water	malt d'orge, houblon, sucre candi, levure, eau	gerstemout, hop, kandij-suiker, gist, water
%	8%	8%	8%
	slightly hazy if served cold	légèrement voilée si servie froide	licht gesluierd indien koud geserveerd
	Pour into a glass with a stem and leave the yeast sediment in the bottle.	Verser dans un verre à pied et laisser le dépôt de levure dans la bouteille.	Uitschenken in een glas met voet en het gistdepot in de fles laten.
°C	39 - 46 °F	4 - 8 °C	4 - 8 °C
	Bitter and smooth.	Amer et doux.	Bitter en zacht.
i	Store the bottles upright.	Conserver les bouteilles en position verticale.	De flessen verticaal bewaren.

FLOREFFE
Triple - Tripel
FLOREFFE
BIÈRE D' ABBAYE - ABDIJBIER
Triple
Tripel

Bière
d'Abbaye
Abdij
Bier
FLOREFFE

Floris Apple

	top-fermentation	fermentation haute	hoge gisting
	Witbier with fruit	bière blanche fruitée	witbier met fruit
	Brouwerij Huyghe Melle	Brouwerij Huyghe Melle	Brouwerij Huyghe Melle
	60% barley malt, 40% wheat, apple juice (30%), hops, yeast, natural fruit flavouring, water, coriander, orange rind.	60% malt d'orge, 40% froment, jus de pommes (30%), houblon, levure, arôme naturel de fruits, eau, coriandre, écorce d'orange	60 % gerstemout, 40 % tarwe, appelsap (30%), hop, gist, natuurlijk fruitaroma, water, koriander, sinaasschil.
%	3,60%	3,60%	3,60%
	yellow	jaune	geel
	Serve in a fluteglass.	Verser dans une flûte.	Uitschenken in een fluitglas.
°C	39 °F	4 °C	4 °C
	–	–	–
	–	–	–

FLORIS
FLORIS
Apple
1654
Beer brewed
with spices and juice
of apple

WITTE FRUITBIEREN
FLORIS
WITBIER · HUYGHE · BLANCHE

Floris cactus

top-fermentation	fermentation haute	hoge gisting
Witbier with fruit	bière blanche fruitée	witbier met fruit
Brouwerij Huyghe Melle	Brouwerij Huyghe Melle	Brouwerij Huyghe Melle
60% barley malt, 40% wheat, lime juice, hops, yeast, natural fruit flavour, water, coriander, orange rind	60% malt d'orge, 40% froment, jus de citron vert, houblon, levure, arôme naturel de fruits, eau, coriandre, écorce d'orange	60 % gerstemout, 40 % tarwe, limoensap, hop, gist, natuurlijk fruitaroma, water, koriander, sinaasschil
4,20%	4,20%	4,20%
lime-yellow green cloudy	jaune citron vert trouble	limoengeel/groen troebel
Serve in a flute-glass.	Verser dans une flûte.	Uitschenken in een fluitgla
39 °F	4 °C	4 °C
Thirst-quencher with a touch of lime and a very fresh aftertaste.	Désaltérant avec touche de citron vert et fin de bouche très fraîche.	Dorstlesser met limoentoets en zeer frisse afdron
–	–	–

FLORIS
Cactus
1654
WHITE FRUITSBEERS
FLORIS
WITBIER · HUYGHE · BLANCHE

Floris chocolat

	top-fermentation	fermentation haute	hoge gisting
	Witbier with chocolate	bière blanche au chocolat	witbier met chocolade
	Brouwerij Huyghe Melle	Brouwerij Huyghe Melle	Brouwerij Huyghe Melle
	60% barley malt, 40% wheat, chocolate, hops, yeast, aroma, water, coriander, orange rind	60% malt d'orge, 40% froment, chocolat, houblon, levure, arômes, eau, coriandre, écorce d'orange	60 % gerstemout, 40 % tarwe, chocolade, hop, gist, aroma, water, koriander, sinaasschil
%	4,20%	4,20%	4,20%
	chestnut cloudy	marron trouble	kastanjebruin troebel
	Serve in a flute-glass.	Verser dans une flûte.	Uitschenken in een fluitglas.
°C	39 °F	4 °C	4 °C
	Bitter with a pronounced fondant flavour. Slightly dry aftertaste, rounded off by the chocolate.	Amer avec goût fondant prononcé. Fin de bouche légèrement amère arrondie par le chocolat.	Bitter met uitgesproken fondantsmaak. Lichtdroge afdronk die wordt afgerond door de chocolade.
i	–	–	–

Belgian
FLORIS
FLORIS
Chocolat
1654
WITTE FRUITBIEREN
FLORIS
WITBIER · HUYGHE · BLANCHE

Floris fraise

	top-fermentation	fermentation haute	hoge gisting
	Witbier with fruit	bière blanche fruitée	witbier met fruit
	Brouwerij Huyghe Melle	Brouwerij Huyghe Melle	Brouwerij Huyghe Melle
	60% barley malt, 40% wheat, strawberry juice (30%), hops, yeast, natural fruit aroma, water, coriander, orange rind	60% malt d'orge, 40% froment, jus de fraises (30%), houblon, levure, arôme naturel de fruits, eau, coriandre, écorce d'orange	60 % gerstemout, 40 % tar-we, aardbeiensap (30%), hop, gist, natuurlijk fruitaroma, water, koriander, sinaasschil
	3,60%	3,60%	3,60%
	dark pink cloudy	rose foncé trouble	donkerroze troebel
	Serve in a flute-glass.	Verser dans une flûte.	Uitschenken in een fluitgla
	39 °F	4 °C	4 °C
	Strawberry flavour and aroma. Sweet with a slightly bitter touch.	Arôme et saveur de fraise. Doux avec une touche légèrement amère.	Aroma en smaak van aardbei. Zoet met lichtbittere toets.
	–	–	–

Belgian
FLORIS
FLORIS
Fraise
1654
BLANCHE AUX FRUITS
FLORIS
WITBIER · HUYGHE · BLANCHE

Floris Honey

	top-fermentation	fermentation haute	hoge gisting
	Witbier with honey	bière blanche au miel	witbier met honing
	Brouwerij Huyghe Melle	Brouwerij Huyghe Melle	Brouwerij Huyghe Melle
	60% barley malt, 40% wheat, honey (15%), hops, yeast, aroma, water, coriander, orange rind	60% malt d'orge, 40% froment, miel (15%), houblon, levure, arômes, eau, coriandre, écorce d'orange	60 % gerstemout, 40 % tarwe, honing (15%), hop, gist, aroma, water, koriander, sinaasschil
%	4,50%	4,50%	4,50%
	yellow cloudy	jaune trouble	geel troebel
	Serve in a flute-glass.	Verser dans une flûte.	Uitschenken in een fluitglas
	39 °F	4 °C	4 °C
	First sweet and slightly bitter, then honey. Honey aroma. Atertaste: honey and dry, bitter orange rind.	Doux et légèrement amer cédant au miel. Arôme de miel. Fin de bouche: miel et zeste d'orange sec et amer.	Zoet en lichtbitter die plaatsmaken voor honing. Honingaroma. Afdronk: honing en droge, bittere sinaasschil.
i	–	–	–

FLORIS
Honey
1654
WITTE FRUITBIEREN
FLORIS
WITBIER-HUYGHE-BLANCHE

Floris Kriek

	top-fermentation	fermentation haute	hoge gisting
	Witbier with fruit	bière blanche fruitée	witbier met fruit
	Brouwerij Huyghe Melle	Brouwerij Huyghe Melle	Brouwerij Huyghe Melle
	60% barley malt, 40% wheat, sour cherry juice (30%), hops, yeast, natural fruit flavouring, water, coriander, orange rind.	60% malt d'orge, 40% froment, jus de cerises griottes (30%), houblon, levure, arôme naturel de fruits, eau, coriandre, écorce d'orange.	60 % gerstemout, 40 % tarwe, kriekensap van griotte (30%), hop, gist, natuurlijk fruitaroma, water, koriander, sinaasschil.
%	3,60%	3,60%	3,60%
	cherry red	rouge cerise	kersenrood
	Serve in a flute-glass.	Verser dans une flûte.	Uitschenken in een fluitgla
°C	39 °F	4 °C	4 °C
	Sweet cherry taste with a bitter touch in the middle of the palate.	Saveur douce de cerises avec une touche amère au milieu du palais.	Zoete kersensmaak met ee bittere toets in het midder van het gehemelte.
i	–	–	–

Belgian
FLORIS
FLORIS
Kriek
1654
FRUITBIEREN
FLORIS
WITBIER - HUYGHE - BLANCHE

Floris Ninkeberry

	top-fermentation	fermentation haute	hoge gisting
	Witbier with fruit	bière blanche fruitée	witbier met fruit
	Brouwerij Huyghe Melle	Brouwerij Huyghe Melle	Brouwerij Huyghe Melle
	60% barley malt, 40% wheat, hops, yeast, natural fruit aroma, coriander, orange rind, water, fruit juices (mango, apricot, passion fruits, peach)	60% malt d'orge, 40% froment, houblon, levure, arôme naturel de fruits, coriandre, écorce d'orange, eau, jus de fruits (mangue, abricot, pêche, fruit de la passion)	60 % gerstemout, 40 % tarwe, hop, gist, natuurlijk fruitaroma, koriander, sinaasschil, water, fruitsappen (mango, abrikoos, passievruchten, perzik)
	3,60%	3,60%	3,60%
	yellow, cloudy	jaune, trouble	geel, troebel
	Serve in a flute-glass.	Verser dans une flûte.	Schenken in een fluitglas.
	39 °F	4 °C	4 °C
	Special, deep aroma, less perfumed than other Floris beers. Progressive freshness of exotic fruits with in the middle the bitterness of nuts. Overall fruity flavour.	Arôme spécial et profond moins parfumé que celui des autres bières Floris. Fraîcheur progressive de fruits exotiques avec au milieu un goût amer de noix. Fruité sur toute la ligne.	Speciaal en diep aroma dat minder geparfumeerd is dan dat van de andere Florisbieren. Progressieve frisheid van exotische vruchten met in het midden een bitterheid van noten. Fruitig over de hele lijn.
	Floris and Ninke are the children of one of the key people involved in the development of Floris beers.	Floris et Ninke sont les prénoms des enfants d'un des promoteurs du développement des bières Floris.	Floris en Ninke zijn de namen van de kinderen van een van de drijvende krachten bij de ontwikkeling van de Florisbieren.

FLORIS
Ninkeberry
1654
WITTE FRUITBIEREN
FLORIS
WITBIER - HUYGHE - BLANCHE

Floris Passion

	top-fermentation	fermentation haute	hoge gisting
	Witbier with fruit	bière blanche fruitée	witbier met fruit
	Brouwerij Huyghe Melle	Brouwerij Huyghe Melle	Brouwerij Huyghe Melle
	60% barley malt, 40% wheat, passion fruit juice (30%), hops, yeast, natural fruit flavouring, water, coriander, orange rind	60% malt d'orge, 40% froment, jus de fruits de la passion (30%), houblon, levure, arôme naturel de fruits, eau, coriandre, écorce d'orange	60 % gerstemout, 40 % tarwe, passievruchtensap (30%), hop, gist, natuurlijk fruitaroma, water, koriander, sinaasschil
%	3,60%	3,60%	3,60%
	dark-yellow	jaune foncée	donkergeel
	Serve in a flute-glass.	Verser dans une flûte.	Uitschenken in een fluitglas.
°C	39 °F	4 °C	4 °C
	Warm, rich beer with a perfect harmony between aroma and taste.	Bière chaude et riche avec une harmonie parfaite d'arôme et de saveur.	Een warm en rijk bier waar aroma en smaak perfect harmoniëren.
i	–	–	–

Belgian
FLORIS
FLORIS
Passion
1654
WITTE FRUITBIEREN
FLORIS
WITBIER-HUYGHE-BLANCHE

Floris wit

	top-fermentation	fermentation haute	hoge gisting
	Witbier	bière blanche	witbier
	Brouwerij Huyghe Melle	Brouwerij Huyghe Melle	Brouwerij Huyghe Melle
	60% barley malt, 40% wheat, re-fermentation sugar, hops, yeast, aroma, water, coriander, orange rind	60% malt d'orge, 40% froment, sucre de refermentation, houblon, levure, arômes, eau, coriandre, écorce d'orange	60 % gerstemout, 40 % tarwe, hergistingssuiker, hop, gist, aroma, water, koriander, sinaasschil
%	5%	5%	5,%
	light-yellow cloudy	jaune clair trouble	lichtgeel troebel
	Serve in a flute glass.	Verser dans une flûte.	Uitschenken in een fluitglas.
	39 °F	4 °C	4 °C
	Fruity Witbier.	Bière blanche fruitée.	Fruitig witbier.
	This beer is equal to Blanche des Neiges and is intended for export.	La même bière que Blanche des Neiges; destinée au marché étranger.	Is hetzelfde bier als Blanche des Neiges; bestemd voor de buitenlandse markt.

Belgian
FLORIS
BELGIAN
FLORIS
Wit-Blanche
WITTE FRUITBIEREN
FLORIS
WITBIER - HUYGHE - BLANCHE

Forestinne

	top-fermentation	fermentation haute	hoge gisting
	Tripel	triple	tripel
	at Brasserie La Caracole B.G.V., Haillot	chez Brasserie La Caracole B.G.V., Haillot	bij Brasserie La Caracole B.G.V., Haillot
	different malt varieties, hops, yeast varieties, water	différentes variétés de malt, houblon, sortes de levure, eau	verschillende moutsoorten, hop, gistsoorten, water
%	7,50%	7,50%	7,50%
	copper-blond clear	blond cuivre claire	koperblond helder
	Leave the yeast sediment in the bottle and pour 3/4 of the bottle.	Verser 3/4 de la bière et laisser le dépôt de levure dans la bouteille.	Het gistdepot in de fles laten en de fles voor 3/4 uitschenken.
°C	50 - 54 °F	10 - 12 °C	10 - 12 °C
	Woody beer with malt touches. Not very sweet and no pronounced bitterness.	Bière à goût boisé avec des touches maltées. Pas trop doux, ni amer prononcé.	Houtsmaak met toetsen van mout. Niet te zoet en ook niet uitgesproken bitter.
i	–	–	–

Forestinne
Forestinne

Framboise Girardin

	spontaneous fermentation (no yeast added)	fermentation spontanée (sans adjonction de levure)	spontane gisting (geen toevoeging van gist)
	fruit beer Lambic beer	bière fruitée bière lambic	fruitbier lambiekbier
	Brouwerij Girardin Sint-Ulriks-Kapelle	Brouwerij Girardin Sint-Ulriks-Kapelle	Brouwerij Girardin Sint-Ulriks-Kapelle
	wheat, barley malt, more than one year old hops, raspberries, water	froment, malt d'orge, houblon suranné, framboises, eau	tarwe, gerstemout, overjaarse hop, frambozen, water
%	5%	5%	5%
	raspberry colour clear	couleur framboise claire	frambozenkleur helder
	In a bulb jar or in a flute-glass like champagne.	Comme le champagne. Dans des flûtes.	In een bol glas of, zoals champagne, in fluitglazen.
°C	Slightly cooled.	Légèrement rafraîchie.	Licht gekoeld.
	Fresh beer, great aperitif. Sweet-sour raspberry taste. The bitter substances are reduced by the fully-fermented hops.	Bière fraîche, convient comme apéritif. Saveur de framboise moelleuse, aigre-douce. Les substances amères sont réduites par les cônes de houblon séchés.	Fris, geschikt als aperitiefbier. Malse, zoetzure frambozensmaak. Door de belegen gedroogde hopbellen zijn de bitterstoffen gereduceerd.
i	Made with real raspberries, which is fairly unique. Store horizontally in a dark, cool room (max. 15 °C).	Fabriquée avec de vraies framboises, ce qui est assez unique. Conserver en position horizontale, à l'abri de la lumière et de la chaleur (max. 15 °C).	Gemaakt met echte frambozen, wat vrij uniek is. Horizontaal, donker en koel (max. 15 °C) bewaren.

SPONTANE GISTING
FERMENTATION SPONTANÉE
FRAMBOISE
GIRARDIN
1882
e 37,5 CL

GIRARDIN
SINT-ULRIKS-KAPELLE

Framboise Boon

	spontaneous fermentation	fermentation spontanée	spontane gisting
	fruit beer	bière fruitée	fruitbier
	Brouwerij Boon Lembeek	Brouwerij Boon Lembeek	Brouwerij Boon Lembeek
	Blend of young and old Lambic, matured in oak barrels. With real raspberries (25%).	Mélange de lambic jeune et vieux mûri en fûts de chêne. Contient de vraies framboises (25%).	Versnijding van jonge en oude lambiek gerijpt op eikenhouten vaten. Met echte frambozen (25%)
%	5%	5%	5%
	raspberry red	rouge framboise	frambozenrood
	–	–	–
	–	–	–
	Sweet-and-sour raspberry taste.	Saveur de framboise aigre-douce.	Zuurzoete frambozensmaak.
i	Kriek has existed since the 19th century, raspberry lambic was created in the early 20th century and has known a revival since the 1970's.	La kriek existe déjà depuis le 19ième siècle, le lambic de framboise est apparu au début du 20 ème siècle et connaît un renouveau depuis les années 1970.	Kriek bestaat al sinds de 19e eeuw, frambozenlambiek is ontstaan in het begin van de 20e eeuw en kent een revival sedert de jaren 1970.

2005
FRAMBOISE
BOON
LAMBIEK 100% LAMBIC

Framboise
Boon

Framboise Lindemans

	spontaneous fermentation	fermentation spontanée	spontane gisting
	fruit beer based on Lambic	bière fruitée à base de lambic	fruitbier op basis van lambiek
	Brouwerij Lindemans Vlezenbeek	Brouwerij Lindemans Vlezenbeek	Brouwerij Lindemans Vlezenbeek
	malt, wheat, hops, rasp-berry juice (25%), fruc-tose, water	malt, froment, houblon, jus de framboises (25%), fructose, eau	mout, tarwe, hop, frambozensap (25%), fructose, water
%	2,50%	2,50%	2,50%
	red slightly hazy	rouge légèrement voilée	rood licht gesluierd
	Pour into a flute-glass.	Verser dans une flûte.	In een fluitglas uitschenken.
°C	37 - 39 °F	3 - 4 °C	3 - 4 °C
	Fruity character. Lively and strong onset turning into a balance of sweet (fruit) and slightly sour (lambic).	Caractère fruité. Début vif et corsé passant à un équilibre de douceur (fruits) et de légère acidulité (lambic).	Fruitig karakter. Levendige en sterke aanzet die overgaat in een evenwicht van zoet (fruit) en zacht zuur (lambiek).
i	Suitable as an aperitif and as a thirst-quencher.	Convient comme apéritif et comme désaltérant.	Geschikt als aperitief en als dorstlesser.

Lindemans
FRAMBOISE
37,5cl
25 cl
FRAMBOISE

Framboise max

	spontaneous fermentation	fermentation spontanée	spontane gisting
	fruit beer	bière fruitée	fruitbier
	Brouwerij Bockor Bellegem	Brouwerij Bockor Bellegem	Brouwerij Bockor Bellegem
	barley malt, wheat, hops, yeast, nature-identical aromas, water	malt d'orge, froment, houblon, arômes naturels, eau	gerstemout, tarwe, hop, gist, natuuridentische aroma's, water
%	3%	3%	3%
	glowing red	rouge intense	gloedrood
	Rinse the glass with cold water, tilt it a little and pour carefully half of the bottle. Then keep the glass upright and pour the rest of the bottle in one single movement.	Rincer le verre à l'eau froide, le tenir légèrement incliné et le remplir prudemment à moitié. Puis relever le verre et vider la bouteille d'un seul trait.	Het glas koud spoelen, licht schuin houden en voorzichtig half inschenken. Daarna het glas recht houden en de rest in 1 beweging inschenken.
°C	41 - 46 °F	5 - 8 °C	5 - 8 °C
	Fruity and fresh. Sweet-and-sour with a clear raspberry aroma.	Fruité et frais. Aigre-doux avec un arôme prononcé de framboises.	Fruitig en fris. Zoetzurig met een duidelijk frambozenaroma.
i	–	–	–

framboise
MAX
framboise
MAX
MEER SMAAK - PLUS DE GOÛT
Jacobins

MAX

Frasnoise Givrée

	top-fermentation re-fermented in the bottle	fermentation haute refermentation en bouteille	hoge gisting hergisting in de fles
	amber	ambrée	amber
	Brasserie Artisanale La Frasnoise Frasnes-lez-Buissenal	Brasserie Artisanale La Frasnoise Frasnes-lez-Buissenal	Brasserie Artisanale La Frasnoise Frasnes-lez-Buissenal
	barley malt, yeasts, hop varieties, sugars, herbs, water	malt d'orge, levures, variétés de houblon, sucres, herbes, eau	gerstemout, gisten, hopsoorten, suikers, kruiden, water
%	6,30%	6,30%	6,30%
	copper-coloured clear and transparent unfiltered	couleur cuivre claire et transparente non filtrée	koperkleurig helder en transparant niet gefilterd
	Pour in a single movement to obtain a nice foam head.	Verser en un seul mouvement de sorte qu'un faux col solide se forme.	In 1 beweging uitschenken zodat er een mooie schuimkraag ontstaat.
°C	41 - 45 °F	5 - 7 °C	5 - 7 °C
	Complex taste, noticeable bitterness in the back of the mouth. Mixture of roundness and spices with a long-lasting effect. Wide range of generous, perfumed aromas, rich in essences.	Goût complexe, amertume en fin de bouche, avec un mélange de rondeur et d'épices qui se libèrent lentement. Arômes nombreux, riches et parfumés.	Complexe smaak, bitterheid in de afdronk, met een mengeling van rondheid en kruiden die zich langzaam manifesteren. Talrijke, rijke, geparfumeerde aroma's.
i	Natural, lively beer brewed following an ancient recipe.	Bière naturelle et vive basée sur une vieille recette.	Natuurlijk en levend bier op basis van een oud recept

Bière Belge
Frasnoise
Cuivrée Brassée avec
La Frasnoise - 5, rue basse B-7911
Frasnoise

Fruitesse appel

	top-fermentation	fermentation haute	hoge gisting
	fruit beer	bière fruitée	fruitbier
	Brouwerij Liefmans Oudenaarde/Dentergem	Brouwerij Liefmans Audenarde/Dentergem	Brouwerij Liefmans Oudenaarde/Dentergem
	Based on soured blonde beer. Barley malt, wheat malt, apple juice, sugar, aroma, maize, hops, yeast, water.	A base de bière blonde acidulée. Malt d'orge et de froment, jus de pommes, sucre, arômes, maïs, houblon, levure, eau.	Op basis van verzuurd blond bier. Gerstemout, tarwemout, appelsap, suiker, aroma, mais, hop, gist, water.
%	3,50%	3,50%	3,50%
	blond-yellow clear	jaune blond claire	blondgeel helder
	–	–	–
°C	43 - 46 °F	6 - 8 °C	6 - 8 °C
	Fruity, sweet and intense.	Fruité, doux et intense.	Fruitig, zoet en intens.
i	–	–	–

Liefmans
Fruitesse
Fruitesse
Appel-Pomme
Liefmans
Fruitesse
Appel-Pomme

Fruitesse framboos

	top-fermentation	fermentation haute	hoge gisting
	fruit beer	bière fruitée	fruitbier
	Brouwerij Liefmans Oudenaarde/Dentergem	Brouwerij Liefmans Audenarde/Dentergem	Brouwerij Liefmans Oudenaarde/Dentergem
	Based on soured blond beer. Barley malt, wheat malt, raspberry juice, sugar, aroma, maize, hops, yeast, water.	A base de bière blonde acidulée. Malt d'orge et de froment, jus de framboises, sucre, arômes, maïs, houblon, levure, eau.	Op basis van verzuurd blond bier. Gerstemout, tarwemout, frambozensap, suiker, aroma, mais, hop, gist, water.
%	3,50%	3,50%	3,50%
	raspberry red clear	rouge framboise claire	frambozenrood helder
	–	–	–
°C	43 - 46 °F	6 - 8 °C	6 - 8 °C
	Fruity, sweet and intense.	Fruité, doux et intense.	Fruitig, zoet en intens.
i	–	–	–

Fruitesse
BIÈRE BELGE
Liefmans
Fruitesse
3,5% vol
Liefmans
Fruitesse

Fruitesse kriekbier

	top-fermentation	fermentation haute	hoge gisting
	fruit beer/Kriek beer	bière fruitée/bière kriek	fruitbier/kriekbier
	Brouwerij Liefmans Oudenaarde/Dentergem	Brouwerij Liefmans Oudenaarde/Dentergem	Brouwerij Liefmans Oudenaarde/Dentergem
	Based on soured blond beer. Barley malt, wheat malt, cherry juice, sugar, aroma, corn, hops, yeast, water.	A base de bière blonde acidulée. Malt d'orge et de froment, jus de cerises, sucre, arômes, maïs, houblon, levure, eau.	Op basis van verzuurd blond bier. Gerstemout, tarwemout, kriekensap, suiker, aroma, mais, hop, gist, water.
%	3,50%	3,50%	3,50%
	clear red	rouge vif	helderrood
	–	–	–
	43 - 46 °F	6 - 8 °C	6 - 8 °C
	Fruity, sweet and intense	Fruité, doux et intense.	Fruitig, zoet en intens.
i	–	–	–

Liefmans
Fruitesse
Kriekbier
Liefmans
Fruitesse

Fruitesse perzik

	top-fermentation	fermentation haute	hoge gisting
	fruit beer	bière fruitée	fruitbier
	Brouwerij Liefmans Oudenaarde/Dentergem	Brouwerij Liefmans Oudenaarde/Dentergem	Brouwerij Liefmans Oudenaarde/Dentergem
	Based on soured blond beer. Barley malt, wheat malt, peach juice, sugar, aroma, maize, hops, yeast, water.	A base de bière blonde acidulée. Malt d'orge et de froment, jus de pêche, sucre, arômes, maïs, houblon, levure, eau.	Op basis van verzuurd blond bier. Gerstemout, tarwemout, perziksap, suiker, aroma, mais, hop, gist, water.
%	3,50%	3,50%	3,50%
	straw-yellow clear	jaune paille claire	strogeel helder
	–	–	–
°C	43 - 46 °F	6 - 8 °C	6 - 8 °C
	Fruity, sweet and intense.	Fruité, doux et intense.	Fruitig, zoet en intens.
i	–	–	–

Fruitesse
Perzik-Pêche
Liefmans
Fruitesse
Perzik-Pêche
Liefmans
Fruitesse

Gaspar

	top-fermentation	fermentation haute	hoge gisting
	regional beer winter beer	bière régionale bière hivernale	streekbier winterbier
	Picobrouwerij Alvinne Ingelmunster	Picobrouwerij Alvinne Ingelmunster	Picobrouwerij Alvinne Ingelmunster
	malt (Pilsner, wheat, amber), granulated sugar, hops, yeast, water	malt (pils, froment, ambre), sucre cristallisé, houblon, levure, eau.	mout (pils, tarwe, amber) kristalsuiker, hop, gist, water.
%	8%	8%	8%
	dark blond	blond foncé	donkerblond
	Pour into a tulip-glass or goblet. Leave the yeast (approx. 1 cm) at the bottom of the bottle. Pour slowly to obtain a nice foam head.	Verser dans un verre tulipe ou calice. Laisser la levure (environ 1 cm) au fond de la bouteille. Verser lentement de sorte qu'un faux col solide se forme.	Uitschenken in een tulp- of kelkvormig glas. De gist (ca. 1 cm) op de bodem van de fles laten. Langzaam schenken zodat er een mooie schuimkraag ontstaat.
°C	46 °F	8 °C	8 °C
	Dominating hoppy taste and aroma, bitter.	Saveur et arômes houblonnés dominants, goût amer.	Een en al hoppigheid in smaak en aroma. Bitter.
i	–	–	–

ALVINNE
2003
ALVINNE

’t Gaverhopke den blonde

	top-fermentation	fermentation haute	hoge gisting
	specialty beer super	bière spéciale super	speciaalbier super
	Brouwerij ’t Gaverhopke Harelbeke	Brouwerij ’t Gaverhopke Harelbeke	Brouwerij ’t Gaverhopke Harelbeke
	malt, hops, yeast, herbs, water	malt, houblon, levure, herbes, eau	mout, hop, gist, kruiden, water
%	8%	8%	8%
	blond clear	ambrée claire	blond helder
	Pour smoothly.	Verser doucement.	Zacht inschenken.
°C	52 °F	11 °C	11 °C
	Bittersweet, fruity and hop-bitter aroma. Bitter aftertaste. Full mouthfeel.	Doux-amer, fruité et arôme houblonné amer. Fin de bouche amère.	Zoetbitter, fruitig en hopbitter aroma, bittere nasmaak. Vloeit uit in de mond.
i	–	–	–

Ambachtelijke Brouwerij met proefzaal
'T GAVERHOPKE
Ambachtelijk bier van hoge gisting
Blond 8°
33cl
Gebrouwen en gebotteld : Ambachtelijke brouwerij 'T GAVERHOPKE
Steenbrugstraat 187 - 8530 Stasegem - www.tgaverhopke.be
Tel & Fax 056/258670 - GSM 0497/760412 - info@tgaverhopke.be

’t Gaverhopke den bruine

	top-fermentation	fermentation haute	hoge gisting
	specialty beer super	bière spéciale super	speciaalbier super
	Brouwerij ’t Gaverhopke Harelbeke	Brouwerij ’t Gaverhopke Harelbeke	Brouwerij ’t Gaverhopke Harelbeke
	malt, hops, yeast, herbs, water	malt, houblon, levure, herbes, eau	mout, hop, gist, kruiden, water
%	8%	8%	8%
	brown	brune	bruin
	Pour quickly and firmly.	Verser rapidement et vigoureusement.	Snel en krachtig inschenken.
°C	52°F	11°C	11°C
	Half pearly, full-bodied. Sweetish specialty beer with a spicy, fruity caramel aroma.	Mi-perlant, fluide dans la bouche. Bière spéciale douce avec un arôme de caramel relevé et fruité.	Half parelend, vloeit uit in de mond. Zoetig speciaalbier met een kruidig en fruitig karamelaroma.
i	–	–	–

'T GAVERHOPKE
Ambachtelijke Brouwerij met proefzaal
'T GAVERHOPKE
Ambachtelijk bier van hoge gisting
Bruin 8°
33cl
Gebrouwen en gebotteld : Ambachtelijke brouwerij 'T GAVERHOPKE
Steenbrugstraat 187 - 8530 Stasegem - www.tgaverhopke.be
Tel & Fax 056/258670 - GSM 0497/760412 - info@tgaverhopke.be

’t Gaverhopke den twaalf

	top-fermentation	fermentation haute	hoge gisting
	specialty beer super	bière spéciale super	speciaalbier super
	Brouwerij ’t Gaverhopke Harelbeke	Brouwerij ’t Gaverhopke Harelbeke	Brouwerij ’t Gaverhopke Harelbeke
	malt, hops, yeast, herbs, water	malt, houblon, levure, herbes, eau	mout, hop, gist, kruiden, water
%	12%	12%	12%
	dark brown clear	brun foncé claire	donkerbruin helder
	Pour firmly.	Verser vigoureusement.	Krachtig inschenken.
°C	52°F	11°C	11°C
	Full-bodied and with a familiar aftertaste. Caramel aroma.	Fluide dans la bouche avec une arrière-bouche familière. Arôme caramélisé.	Vloeit uit in de mond en heeft een vertrouwde nasmaak. Karamelaroma.
i	–	–	–

Ambachtelijke Brouwerij met proefzaal
'T GAVERHOPKE
Ambachtelijk bier van hoge gisting
Bruin 12°
33cl
Gebrouwen op basis van natuurlijke ingrediënten : Water, Gerst, Hoppe, Gist & Kruiden
Gebrouwen en gebotteld : Ambachtelijke brouwerij 'T GAVERHOPKE
Steenbrugstraat 187 - 8530 Stasegem - www.tgaverhopke.be
Tel & Fax 056/258670 - GSM 0497/760412 - info@tgaverhopke.be
'T GAVERHOPKE

't Gaverhopke Kerstbier

	top-fermentation	fermentation haute	hoge gisting
	specialty beer super	bière spéciale super	speciaalbier super
	Brouwerij 't Gaverhopke Harelbeke	Brouwerij 't Gaverhopke Harelbeke	Brouwerij 't Gaverhopke Harelbeke
	malt, hops, yeast, herbs, water	malt, houblon, levure, herbes, eau	mout, hop, gist, kruiden, water
%	8%	8%	8%
	brown	brune	bruin
	Pour gently.	Verser doucement.	Zacht inschenken.
°C	52°F	11°C	11°C
	Half pearly, sweetish specialty beer with a hop-bitter, fruity aroma.	Bière spéciale douce mi-perlante avec un arôme amer houblonné et fruité.	Half parelend zoetig speciaalbier met een hopbitter en fruitig aroma.
i	–	–	–

Ambachtelijke Brouwerij met proefzaal
'T GAVERHOPKE
Ambachtelijk bier van hoge gisting
Kerstbier 8°
33cl
Gebrouwen en gebotteld : Ambachtelijke brouwerij 'T GAVERHOPKE
Steenbrugstraat 187 - 8530 Stasegem - www.tgaverhopke.be
Tel & Fax 056/258670 - GSM 0497/760412 - info@tgaverhopke.be
'T GAVERHOPKE

't Gaverhopke Kriek

	top-fermentation	fermentation haute	hoge gisting
	specialty beer super	bière spéciale super	speciaalbier super
	Brouwerij 't Gaverhopke Harelbeke	Brouwerij 't Gaverhopke Harelbeke	Brouwerij 't Gaverhopke Harelbeke
	malt, hops, yeast, herbs, water	malt, houblon, levure, herbes, eau	mout, hop, gist, kruiden, water
%	7%	7%	7%
	dark pink-red	rose foncé-rouge	donkerroze-rood
	Pour slowly.	Verser lentement.	Langzaam inschenken.
	52°F	11°C	11°C
	Half pearly, sweetish specialty beer with a hop-bitter, fruity aroma.	Bière spéciale douce mi-perlante avec un arôme amer houblonné et fruité.	Half parelend zoetig speciaalbier met een hopbitter en fruitig aroma.
i	–	–	–

Ambachtelijke Brouwerij met proefzaal
'T GAVERHOPKE
Ambachtelijk bier van hoge gisting
Kriek 7°
33cl
Gebrouwen en gebotteld : Ambachtelijke brouwerij 'T GAVERHOPKE
Steenbrugstraat 187 - 8530 Stasegem - www.tgaverhopke.be
Tel & Fax 056/258670 - GSM 0497/760412 - info@tgaverhopke.be
'T GAVERHOPKE

’t Gaverhopke Paasbier

	top-fermentation	fermentation haute	hoge gisting
	specialty beer super	bière spéciale super	speciaalbier super
	Brouwerij ’t Gaverhopke Harelbeke	Brouwerij ’t Gaverhopke Harelbeke	Brouwerij ’t Gaverhopke Harelbeke
	malt, hops, yeast, herbs, water	malt, houblon, levure, herbes, eau	mout, hop, gist, kruiden, water
%	8%	8%	8%
	blond clear	blonde claire	blond helder
	Pour gently.	Verser doucement.	Zacht inschenken.
°C	52°F	11°C	11°C
	Half pearly, sweetish specialty beer with a hop-bitter, fruity aroma.	Bière spéciale douce mi-perlante avec un arôme amer houblonné et fruité.	Half parelend zoetig speciaalbier met een hopbitter en fruitig aroma.
i	–	–	–

Ambachtelijke Brouwerij met proefzaal
'T GAVERHOPKE
Ambachtelijk bier van hoge gisting
Paasbier 8°
33cl
Gebrouwen op basis van natuurlijke ingrediënten : Water, Gerst, Hoppe, Gist & Kruiden
Gebrouwen en gebotteld : Ambachtelijke brouwerij 'T GAVERHOPKE
Steenbrugstraat 187 - 8530 Stasegem - www.tgaverhopke.be
Tel & Fax 056/258670 - GSM 0497/760412 - info@tgaverhopke.be
'T GAVERHOPKE

Geuze Cantillon

	spontaneous fermentation naturally re-fermented in the bottle	fermentation spontanée refermentation naturelle en bouteille	spontane gisting natuurlijke hergisting op de fles
	Gueuze Lambic	gueuze lambic	geuze lambiek
	Brouwerij Cantillon Brussels	Brouwerij Cantillon Bruxelles	Brouwerij Cantillon Brussel
	barley malt, wheat, more than one year old hops	malt d'orge, froment, houblon suranné	gerstemout, tarwe, overjaarse hop
%	5%	5%	5%
	gold-coloured	dorée	goudkleurig
	The use of a wine basket is recommended if the bottle was stored horizontally. Place the bottle in an upright position 48 hours before serving, so as to decant the sediment.	Un panier verseur est recommandé si la bouteille a été conservée en position horizontale. Mettre la bouteille 48 heures avant de servir en position verticale pour faire descendre le dépôt.	Een schenkmandje is aangewezen wanneer de fles horizontaal bewaard werd. De fles 48 uur voor het uitschenken verticaal plaasten om het bezinksel te decanteren.
°C	cellar temperature (54 - 61 °F)	température de cave (12 - 16 °C)	keldertemperatuur (12 - 16 °C)
	Strong-bodied, pronounced sour but smooth taste. Aroma: a touch of natural cider	Saveur corsée, acidulée prononcée mais moelleuse. Arôme: une pointe de cidre naturel.	Gecorseerd, uitgesproken zure maar zachte smaak. Aroma: een vleugje natuurcider.
i	–	–	–

CANTILLON
Brewers of Belgium's Most Authentic Lambic
Gueuze 100% Lambic Bio
The Brussels' Gueuze

CANTILLON

Geuze fond Girardin

	spontaneous fermentation re-fermentation in the bottle	fermentation spontanée refermentation en bouteille	spontane gisting hergisting op de fles
	Gueuze, lambic beer	gueuze, bière lambic	geuze lambiekbier
	Brouwerij Girardin Sint-Ulriks-Kapelle	Brouwerij Girardin Sint-Ulriks-Kapelle	Brouwerij Girardin Sint-Ulriks-Kapelle
	wheat, barley malt, more than 1 year old hops, water	froment, malt d'orge, houblon suranné, eau	tarwe, gerstemout, overjaarse hop, water
%	5%	5%	5%
	Gold-yellow. Clarity depends on way of serving. The yeast sits at the bottom and makes the beer cloudy.	Jaune doré. La limpidité dépend de la méthode de verser. La levure se trouve dans le fond et rend la bière trouble.	Goudgeel. De helderheid hangt af van de schenkmethode: de biergist zit in de fond en maakt het bier troebel.
	Rinse the glass with pure, tepid water. Tilt the bottle, stop the cork and pour the glass in one movement. Leave the sediment in the bottle for a clear beer.	Rincer le verre à l'eau tiède propre, tenir la bouteille bien en oblique, retenir le bouchon et verser d'un seul mouvement. Ne pas verser la levure pour avoir une bière claire.	Het glas spoelen met lauw zuiver water. Drogen naar wens. De fles goed schuin houden, het kurk tegenhouden en in 1 beweging schenken. De fond niet meegieten voor een heldere pint.
°C	cellar temperature (50 - 59 °F)	température de cave (10 - 15 °C)	keldertemperatuur (10 - 15 °C)
	Excellent aperitif. Fresh, sour, solid, fruity and dry.	Apéritif excellent. Frais, acidulé, solide, fruité, sec.	Geschikt als aperitief. Fris, zuur, stevig, fruitig, droog.
i	Store horizontally in a dark, cool place.	Conserver en position horizontale à l'abri de la lumière et de la chaleur.	Donker, koel en horizontaal bewaren.

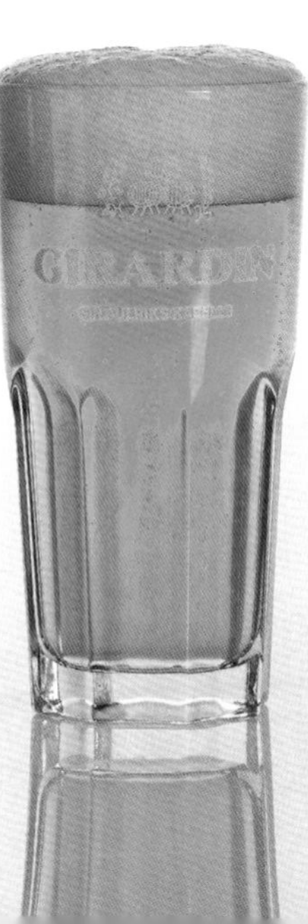
GUEUZE
GIRARDIN
1882
e 75 CL
GIRARDIN

Geuze Fond Tradition

	spontaneous fermentation re-fermented in the bottle	fermentation spontanée refermentation en bouteille	spontane gisting nagisting op de fles
	Gueuze Lambic	gueuze lambic	geuze lambiek
	Castle Brewery Van Honsebrouck Ingelmunster	Castle Brewery Van Honsebrouck Ingelmunster	Castle Brewery Van Honsebrouck Ingelmunster
	malt, hops, wheat, water, 100% old lambic.	malt, houblon, froment, eau, 100% vieux lambic.	mout, hop, tarwe, water 100% oude lambiek.
%	5%	5%	5%
	blond slightly cloudy, unfiltered	blonde légèrement trouble, non filtrée	blond licht troebel, niet gefilterd
	Slowly pour into a newly rinsed glass. Tilt the glass first, then put it in a vertical position. Leave the yeast sediment in the bottle.	Verser lentement dans un verre rincé tenu d'abord en oblique et à la fin en position verticale. Laisser le dépôt de levure dans la bouteille.	Langzaam uitschenken in een vers gespoeld glas dat eerst schuin en op het einde verticaal gehouden wordt. Het gistdepot in de fles laten.
°C	41 °F	5 °C	5 °C
	Very fresh. Sourish with strong noticeable influence of wheat, wild yeast and the storage in oakwood barrels.	Très frais. Acidulé avec une influence perceptible de froment, levures sauvages. Conservation en fûts de chêne.	Zeer fris. Zurig met sterk waarneembare invloed van tarwe, wildgisten en bewaring op eikenhouten vaten.
i	This is the Gueuze for connoisseurs.	C'est la gueuze des vrais amateurs.	Dit is de geuze voor de echte liefhebbers.

GUEUZE
FOND
TRADITION
Lambic
NIET GEFILTERD NON FILTRÉ

- CASSIS - FARO -
PREMIUM

Geuze gefilterd Girardin

	spontaneous fermentation	fermentation spontanée	spontane gisting
	Gueuze Lambic beer	bière gueuze lambic	geuze lambiekbier
	Brouwerij Girardin Sint-Ulriks-Kapelle	Brouwerij Girardin Sint-Ulriks-Kapelle	Brouwerij Girardin Sint-Ulriks-Kapelle
	wheat, barley malt, more than 1 year old hops, water	froment, malt d'orge, houblon suranné, eau	tarwe, gerstemout, overjaarse hop, water
%	5%	5%	5%
	clear gold-yellow	jaune doré clair	helder goudgeel
	Rinse the glass with pure, tepid water and dry. Tilt the bottle, stop the cork and pour the beer in one movement. Do not pour the sediment so as to have a clear pint of beer.	Rincer le verre à l'eau tiède propre et sécher. Tenir la bouteille bien en oblique, retenir le bouchon et verser d'un seul mouvement. Ne pas verser la levure pour une pinte claire.	Het glas spoelen met lauw zuiver water en afdrogen. De fles goed schuin houden, het kurk tegenhouden en in 1 beweging schenken. De fond niet meegieten voor een heldere pint.
°C	cooled	rafraîchie	gekoeld
	Slightly sour with a touch of sherry.	Légèrement acidulé, touche de xéres.	Licht zurig, sherrytoets.
i	A mix of Lambic beers of different ages. Re-fermentation happens in a reservoir and the beer is filtered before bottling.	Un mélange de bières lambics de différents âges. La refermentation se produit dans un réservoir et la bière est filtrée avant d'être mise en bouteille.	Een mengeling van lambiek van verschillende leeftijden. De hergisting gebeurt op een tank en het bier is gefilterd voor het op de fles komt.

GUEUZE
GIRARDIN
1882
Gebrouwen en gebotteld door - Brassée et soutirée par
Sint-Ulriks-Kapelle - Belgium
e 37,5CL

GIRARDIN
SINT-ULRIKS-KAPELLE

Geuze Jacobins

	spontaneous fermentation	fermentation spontanée	spontane gisting
	Gueuze	gueuze	geuze
	Brouwerij Bockor Bellegem	Brouwerij Bockor Bellegem	Brouwerij Bockor Bellegem
	wheat, barley malt, hops, water	froment, malt d'orge, houblon, eau	tarwe, gerstemout, hop, water
%	5,50%	5,50%	5,50%
	amber	ambrée	amber
	Rinse the glass with cold water, tilt it a little and pour carefully half of the bottle. Next, keep the glass upright and pour the rest of the bottle in one single movement.	Rincer le verre à l'eau froide, le tenir légèrement incliné et le remplir prudemment à moitié. Puis relever le verre et verser la bière qui reste d'un seul trait.	Het glas koud spoelen, licht schuin houden en voorzichtig half inschenken. Daarna het glas recht houden en de rest van het bier in 1 beweging uitschenken.
°C	41 - 46 °F	5 - 8 °C	5 - 8 °C
	Basic taste sweet-and-sour.	Saveur de base aigre-douce.	Zoetzurige basissmaak.
i	–	–	–

Jacobins
GUEUZE
Lambic
Jacobins
GUEUZE
Lambic

Jacobins
gueuze lambic

Geuze Lindemans

	spontaneous fermentation filtered	fermentation spontanée filtrée	spontane gisting gefilterd
	Gueuze Lambic	gueuze lambic	geuze lambiek
	Brouwerij Lindemans Vlezenbeek	Brouwerij Lindemans Vlezenbeek	Brouwerij Lindemans Vlezenbeek
	malt, wheat, hops, fructose, water	malt, froment, houblon, fructose, eau	mout, tarwe, hop, fructose, water
%	5,50%	5,50%	5,50%
	gold blond clear	blond doré claire	goudblond helder
	Pour into a Gueuze glass.	Verser dans un verre gueuze.	In een geuzeglas uitschenken.
°C	37 - 39 °F	3 - 4 °C	3 - 4 °C
	Slightly sourish. Smooth gueuze with a slightly sweet onset and fresh sourish aftertaste.	Moelleux acidulé. Gueuze douce avec un début légèrement sucré et une fin de bouche fraîche, acidulée.	Zacht zurig. Zachte geuze met een lichtzoete aanzet en fris zurige afdronk.
i	–	–	–

LINDEMANS
GUEUZE
Lindemans

Geuze mariage parfait
Oude geuze Boon

	Spontaneous fermentation. Re-fermented in the bottle by the young Lambic which contains fermentable sugars.	Fermentation spontanée. Refermentation en bouteille par le lambic jeune contentant des sucres commutables en levure.	Spontane gisting. Nagisting op de fles door de jonge lambiek die vergistbare suikers bevat.
	Old Gueuze	Vieille gueuze	Oude geuze
	Brouwerij Boon Lembeek	Brouwerij Boon Lembeek	Brouwerij Boon Lembeek
	a selected blend of 90% mellow Lambic (at least 18 months), 5% distinctive 3 year-old beer and 5% very young Lambic	mélange sélectionné de 90% de lambic doux (au moins 18 mois), 5% de bière de caractère de 3 ans et 5% de lambic très jeune	geselecteerde mengeling van 90% malse lambiek (minstens 18 maand oud), 5% karaktervol bier van 3 jaar en 5% heel jonge lambiek
%	8%	8%	8%
	–	–	–
	–	–	–
°C	Cellar temperature.	Température de cave.	Keldertempertuur.
	–	–	–
i	Only champagne bottles are suitable for gueuze because of the high pressure.	Seules les bouteilles de champagne résistent à la haute pression de la gueuze.	Enkel champagneflessen kunnen weerstaan aan de hoge druk van de geuze.

8
Alc / Vol
OUDE
GEUZE
BOON
Mariage Parfait

Geuze
Boon
LEMBEEK

Geuze St Louis

	spontaneous fermentation	fermentation spontanée	spontane gisting
	Gueuze	gueuze	geuze
	Castle Brewery Van Honsebrouck Ingelmunster	Castle Brewery Van Honsebrouck Ingelmunster	Castle Brewery Van Honsebrouck Ingelmunster
	malt, hops, wheat, sugar, water	malt, houblon, froment, sucre, eau	mout, hop, tarwe, suiker, water
%	4,50%	4,50%	4,50%
	light amber cloudy	ambré clair trouble	licht amber troebel
	Pour slowly into a newly rinsed glass. tilt the glass to start with, and keep it upright near the end.	Verser lentement dans un verre rincé d'abord tenu en oblique et à la fin en position verticale.	Langzaam uitschenken in een vers gespoeld glas dat eerst schuin en op het einde verticaal gehouden wordt.
°C	41 °F	5 °C	5 °C
	Refreshing. Sweet-and-sour with a clear wheat taste and an influence of wild yeasts and oak barrels.	Rafraîchissant. Aigre-doux avec une saveur de froment prononcée, influence des levures sauvages et des fûts de chêne.	Verfrissend. Zuurzoet met duidelijke tarwesmaak, invloed van wildgisten en eiken vaten.
i	–	–	–

Bière Belge
Belgisch Bier
St Louis
GUEUZE
Lambic
- CASSIS - FARO -
PREMIUM
St Louis

Gigi speciale

	bottom-fermentation	fermentation basse	lage gisting
	table beer/Pilsner	bière de table/pils	tafelbier/pils
	Brouwerij Gigi Gérouville	Brouwerij Gigi Gérouville	Brouwerij Gigi Gérouville
	Pilsner malt, yeast, hops, sugar, sweetener, water	malt de pils, levure, houblon, sucre, édulcorant, eau	pilsmout, gist, hop, suiker, zoetstof, water
%	2,50%	2,50%	2,50%
	dark blond	blond foncé	donkerblond
	Pour like a Pilsner.	Verser comme une pils.	Uitschenken als een pilsbier.
°C	Fridge temperature.	Température de réfrigérateur.	Koelkasttemperatuur.
	Light thirst-quencher.	Désaltérant léger.	Lichte dorstlesser.
i	Boutique beer from the region Gaume.	Bière de la région de la Gaume brassée de façon artisanale.	Streekbier uit de Gaume-regio dat artisanaal gebrouwen wordt.

GEROUVILLE
1888
Fabrication
SPECIALE
Gigi
GEROUVILLE - TEL: 063/57 75 15

Gildenbier

	top-fermentation	fermentation haute	hoge gisting
	specialty beer	bière spéciale	speciaalbier
	Brouwerij Haacht Boortmeerbeek	Brouwerij Haacht Boortmeerbeek	Brouwerij Haacht Boortmeerbeek
	barley malt, maize, sugar, hops, water	malt d'orge, maïs, sucre,houblon, eau	gerstemout, mais, suiker, hop, water
%	7%	7%	7%
	dark and filtered creamy foam	foncée, filtrée écume crémeuse	donker en gefilterd romig schuim
	Pour carefully into a rinsed, wet mug, avoiding contact between bottle and foam head.	Verser prudemment dans un verre mouillé sans que la bouteille touche l'écume.	Voorzichtig uitschenken in een gespoeld, nat glas zonder dat de fles het schuim raakt.
°C	46 - 50 °F	8 - 10 °C	8 - 10 °C
	First mild and sweet. Aftertaste fairly strong but soft and sweet with a slightly bitter aftertaste.	Initialement mi-doux, arrière-bouche plutôt corsée mais douce, fin de bouche légèrement amère.	Eerst mildzoet. Afdronk behoorlijk fors maar zachtzoet met een licht bittere nasmaak.
i	Perfect to accompany a chocolate dessert. Forever linked with the guild's ball of the Diest archers' guild. At midnight, candidate members had to drink a litre of beer, standing on one leg, to become a member.	Accompagne parfaitement un dessert au chocolat. Depuis longtemps liée au bal de la guilde des tireurs de Diest, où les candidats-membres devaient boire à minuit un litre de bière en s'appuyant sur une jambe pour devenir membre.	Past uitstekend bij een chocoladedessert. Van oudsher verbonden met het gildenbal van de Diestse schuttersgilde. Vroeger moesten kandidaat-leden om 12 u op één been 1 liter bier uitdrinken om lid te worden.

Gildenbier
diest

Gildenbier

Glühkriek

	mixed fermentation	fermentation mixte	gemengde gisting
	soury Kriek beer	bière kriek acidulée	zurig kriekbier
	Brouwerij Liefmans Oudenaarde/Dentergem	Brouwerij Liefmans Audenarde/Dentergem	Brouwerij Liefmans Oudenaarde/Dentergem
	Brewed like a regular Kriek, with addition at the end of herbs and candy sugar. Cherries, wheat malt, sugar, corn, hops, herbs, yeast, water.	Est brassée comme la Kriek ordinaire, avec adjonction d'herbes et de sucre candi à la fin. Cerises, malt d'orge, sucre, maïs, houblon, herbes, levure, eau.	Wordt gebrouwen zoals gewone kriek, met toevoeging van kruiden en kandijsuiker op het einde. Krieken, gerstemout, suiker, mais, hop, kruiden gist, water.
	6%	6%	6%
	brown-red slightly cloudy	brun rouge légèrement trouble	bruinrood licht troebel
	–	–	–
	Heat up at 70°C like glühwein.	Chauffer la bière comme du glühwein jusqu'à 70 °C.	Het bier als glühwein opwarmen tot 70 °C.
	Spicy, wintry Kriek beer. Sweet-and-sour with the natural taste of cherries and cherry aroma.	Bière kriek hivernale relevée, aigre-douce avec des arômes naturels de cerises.	Kruidig, winters kriekbier. Zuurzoet met natuurlijke smaak van krieken en krie kenaroma.
	–.	–	–

Liefmans
Liefmans

Gordon Finest Gold

	bottom-fermentation	fermentation basse	lage gisting
	blond	blonde	blond
	Brouwerij Timmermans/ John Martin Itterbeek	Brouwerij Timmermans/ John Martin Itterbeek	Brouwerij Timmermans/ John Martin Itterbeek
	barley malt, sugar, hops, water	malt d'orge, sucre, houblon, eau	gerstemout, suiker, hop, water
%	10%	10%	10%
	blond	blonde	blond
	–	–	–
°C	37 - 43 °F	3 - 6 °C	3 - 6 °C
	Strong and silky. Round taste, obtained by the high alcohol volume, which is toned down by the pale malts.	Forte et soyeuse. Saveur arrondie par la haute teneur en alcool adoucie par les malts pâles.	Sterk en zijdeachtig. Afgeronde smaak door het hoge alcoholvolume die verzacht wordt door de bleke mouten.
i	–	–	–

GORDON
1909
FINEST GOLD
BEER
ALC 10 % VOL

GORDON
FINEST BEERS

Gordon Finest Platinum

	bottom-fermentation	fermentation basse	lage gisting
	strong blond	blonde forte	sterk blond
	Brouwerij Timmermans/ John Martin Itterbeek	Brouwerij Timmermans/ John Martin Itterbeek	Brouwerij Timmermans/ John Martin Itterbeek
	barley malt, sugar, hops, water	malt d'orge, sucre, houblon, eau	gerstemout, suiker, hop, water
%	12%	12%	12%
	blond	blonde	blond
	–	–	–
°C	37 - 43 °F	3 - 6 °C	3 - 6 °C
	Soft, silky texture with a bitter touch. Full and slightly prickly on the tongue.	Velouté avec une touche amère. Plein et légèrement pétillant sur la langue.	Fluweelzacht met bittere toets. Vol en licht prikkelend op de tong.
i	–	–	–

GORDON
FINEST
PLATINUM

Gordon Finest Red

	bottom-fermentation	fermentation basse	lage gisting
	strong red	rouge forte	sterk rood
	Brouwerij Timmermans/ John Martin Itterbeek	Brouwerij Timmermans/ John Martin Itterbeek	Brouwerij Timmermans/ John Martin Itterbeek
	barley malt, sugar, hops, water	malt d'orge, sucre, houblon, eau	gerstemout, suiker, hop, water
%	8,40%	8,40%	8,40%
	dark amber	ambré foncé	donker amber
	–	–	–
	43 - 46 °F	6 - 8 °C	6 - 8 °C
	Dry, spicy touches. Smooth bitterness turning into an alcohol and peppery aftertaste.	Touches sèches, relevées. Goût amer moelleux aboutissant en une fin de bouche d'alcool et de poivre.	Droge, kruidige toetsen. Zachte bitterheid die overgaat in een nasmaak van alcohol en peper.
i	–	–	–

GORDON
ESTD
1909
FINEST RED
BEER
ALC 8,4 % VOL

GORDON
FINEST BEERS

Gordon Finest Scotch

	top-fermentation	fermentation haute	hoge gisting
	Scottish Ale	scottish ale	scottish ale
	Brouwerij Timmermans/ John Martin Itterbeek	Brouwerij Timmermans/ John Martin Itterbeek	Brouwerij Timmermans/ John Martin Itterbeek
	barley malt, sugar, corn, roasted barley, hops, malt, water	malt d'orge, sucre, maïs, orge brûlé, houblon, malt, eau	gerstemout, suiker, mais, gebrande gerst, hop, mout, water
%	8,60%	8,60%	8,60%
	dark ruby red	rouge rubis foncé	donker robijnrood
	–	–	–
°C	43 - 46 °F	6 - 8 °C	6 - 8 °C
	Smooth and full-bodied. Bitterness (aromatic hop) combined with sweet and roasty malt.	Doux et corsé. Saveur amère (houblon aromatisé) avec des touches de malt doux et brûlé.	Zacht en gecorseerd. Bitterheid (aromatische hop) gecombineerd met zoet en gebrande mout.
i	–	–	–

GORDON
FINEST SCOTCH
HIGHLAND
ALE

GORDON
FINEST BEERS

Gordon Finest Silver

	bottom-fermentation	fermentation basse	lage gisting
	strong blond	blonde forte	sterk blond
	Brouwerij Timmermans/ John Martin Itterbeek	Brouwerij Timmermans/ John Martin Itterbeek	Brouwerij Timmermans/ John Martin Itterbeek
	barley malt, sugar, hops, water	malt d'orge, houblon, sucre, eau	gerstemout, suiker, hop, water
%	7,70%	7,70%	7,70%
	blond	blonde	blond
	–	–	–
	37 - 43 °F	3 - 6 °C	3 - 6 °C
	Round with a refined hop taste.	Rond avec une saveur houblonnée raffinée.	Rond met verfijnde hopsmaak.
	–	–	–

strong blond bee
GORDON
ESTD
1909
FINEST SILVER
BEER
ALC 7,7 % VOL
GORDON
FINEST BEERS

Gordon Xmas

	top-fermentation	fermentation haute	hoge gisting
	Scottish style Ale Christmas beer	scotch ale bière de Noël	scotch ale kerstbier
	Brouwerij Timmermans/ John Martin Itterbeek	Brouwerij Timmermans/ John Martin Itterbeek	Brouwerij Timmermans/ John Martin Itterbeek
	barley malt, corn, malt, roasted barley, sugar, hops, water	malt d'orge, maïs, malt, orge brûlé, sucre, houblon, eau	gerstemout, mais, mout, gebrande gerst, suiker, hop, water
%	8,80%	8,80%	8,80%
	dark ruby red	rouge rubis foncé	donker robijnrood
	–	–	–
°C	43 - 46 °F	6 - 8 °C	6 - 8 °C
	–	–	–
i	–	–	–

GORDON
Xmas

GORDON
FINEST BEERS

Gouden Carolus Cuvée van de keizer

	top-fermentation re-fermented in the bottle	fermentation haute refermentation en bouteille	hoge gisting hergisting op de fles
	specialty beer	bière spéciale	speciaalbier
	Brouwerij Het Anker Mechelen	Brouwerij Het Anker Malines	Brouwerij Het Anker Mechelen
	barley malt, corn, sugar, hops, yeast, water	malt d'orge, maïs, sucre, houblon, levure, eau	gerstemout, mais, suiker, hop, gist, water
%	11%	11%	11%
	ruby red	rouge rubis	robijnrood
	Take a degreased goblet by the stem and hold it slightly tilted. Pour the beer slowly and in a single movement, avoiding contact with the glass or the foam.	Prendre un verre calice dégraissé par le pied et le tenir légèrement incliné. Verser la bière en un seul mouvement sans toucher le verre ou l'écume.	Een vetvrij kelkglas bij de voet vastnemen en licht schuin houden. Het bier traag en in 1 beweging uitschenken zonder het glas of schuim te raken.
°C	43 - 48 °F	6 - 9 °C	6 - 9 °C
	Perfect harmony between the soft warmth of wine and the freshness of beer. Sipping beer with a very refined taste and mysterious aromas.	Harmonie parfaite entre la chaleur moelleuse de vin et la fraîcheur de bière. Bière de dégustation avec un goût très raffiné et des arômes mystérieux.	Perfecte harmonie tussen de zachte warmte van wijn en de frisheid van bier. Degustatiebier met een zeer geraffineerde smaak en mysterieuze aroma's.
i	An ideal stock beer.	Bière idéale à conserver.	Ideaal bewaarbier.

2006
CUVEE VAN DE KEIZER
CAROLUS D'OR

Gouden Carolus Ambrio

	top-fermentation re-fermented in the bottle	fermentation haute refermentation en bouteille	hoge gisting hergisting op de fles
	amber	ambrée	amber
	Brouwerij Het Anker Mechelen	Brouwerij Het Anker Malines	Brouwerij Het Anker Mechelen
	different malt varieties, Belgian hop varieties and herbs	diférentes sortes de malt, sortes de houblon belge et herbes	verscheidene moutsoorten, Belgische hopsoorten en kruiden
%	7%	7%	7%
	light amber	ambré clair	licht amber
	Hold a degreased goblet by the stem and tilt it a little. Pour the beer in one single movement avoiding contact with glass or foam.	Prendre un verre calice dégraissé par le pied et le tenir incliné. Verser la bière lentement en un seul mouvement sans toucher le verre ni l'écume.	Een vetvrij kelkglas bij de voet vastnemen en licht schuin houden. Het bier traag en in 1 beweging uitschenken zonder het glas of schuim te raken.
°C	43 - 48 °F	6 - 9 °C	6 - 9 °C
	Combines the full-bodied character of brown beer with the freshness of blond beer. Aromatised and spicy.	Combine le goût franc de la bière brune avec la fraîcheur de la bière blonde. Aromatisé et corsé.	Combineert de volmondigheid van bruin bier met de frisheid van blond bier. Gearomatiseerd en pittig.
i	Brewed following the old recipe of Mechelsen Bruynen, a beer Charles Quint sent by ship to Spain. The original recipe goes back to 1421.	Brassée selon la recette séculaire de la Mechelsen Bruynen (la recette de base date de 1421), une bière exportée en Espagne par Charles Quint.	Gebrouwen volgens het recept van Mechelsen Bruynen (het basisrecept dateert van 1421), bier dat door Keizer Karel naar Spanje werd verscheept.

AMBRIO
GOUDEN
CAROLUS
AMBRIO
BELGIAN BEER
GOUDEN CAROLUS
CAROLUS D'OR

Gouden Carolus Christmas

	top-fermentation re-fermented in the bottle	fermentation haute refermentation en bouteille	hoge gisting hergisting op de fles
	specialty beer heavy Christmas beer	bière spéciale bière de Noël forte	speciaalbier zwaar kerstbier
	Brouwerij Het Anker Mechelen	Brouwerij Het Anker Malines	Brouwerij Het Anker Mechelen
	Specific seasoning (six species) in three phases of the brewing process, 3 varieties of Belgian hop	assaisonnement spécifique (6 sortes) en 3 phases du brassage, 3 sortes de houblon belge	specifieke kruiding (6 soorten) bij 3 fasen van het brouwproces, 3 soorten Belgische hop
%	10,50%	10,50%	10,50%
	brown-red	rouge brun	bruinrood
	–	–	–
°C	48 - 54 °F	9 - 12 °C	9 - 12 °C
	Spicy sipping beer with a very refined flavour that gives a warm feeling on cold winter evenings.	Bière de dégustation relevée avec un arôme très raffiné donnant un sentiment chaleureux lors des soirées hivernales froides.	Kruidig degustatiebier met een zeer geraffineerd aroma dat een warm gevoel geeft tijdens koude winteravonden.
i	Is brewed at the end of August and then matures for a few months in order to obtain the best possible flavour balance.	Est brassée fin août et mûrit par la suite quelques mois pour obtenir un équilibre de saveur optimal.	Wordt eind augustus gebrouwen en rijpt daarna een paar maanden voor een optimaal smaakevenwicht.

BELGISCH BIER • BELGIAN BEER

CAROLUS D'OR

Gouden Carolus Classic

	top-fermentation re-fermented in the bottle	fermentation haute refermentation en bouteille	hoge gisting hergisting op de fles
	dark specialty beer	bière spéciale foncée	donker speciaalbier
	Brouwerij Het Anker Mechelen	Brouwerij Het Anker Malines	Brouwerij Het Anker Mechelen
	Brewed following the classical infusion method with Belgian hops, dark and aromatic malt varieties and caramel.	Brassée selon la méthode classique d'infusion avec du houblon belge, des variétés foncées et aromatisées de malt et du caramel.	Gebrouwen volgens de klassieke infusiemethode met Belgische hop, donker en aromatische moutsoorten en karamel.
%	8,50%	8,50%	8,50%
	ruby red	rouge rubis	robijnrood
	Hold a degreased goblet by the stem and tilt it a little. Pour the beer in a single movement avoiding contact with the glass or the foam.	Prendre un verre calice dégraissé par le pied et le tenir légèrement incliné. Verser la bière lentement en un seul mouvement sans toucher le verre ni l'écume.	Een vetvrij kelkglas bij de voet vastnemen en licht schuin houden. Het bier traag en in 1 beweging uitschenken zonder het glas of schuim te raken.
°C	43 - 48 °F	6 - 9 °C	6 - 9 °C
	Beer with a high density that combines the warmth of wine with the freshness of beer.	Bière de haute densité englobant la chaleur du vin et la fraîcheur de la bière.	Bier met een hoge densiteit dat de warmte van wijn en de frisheid van bier verenigt.
i	Mechels Keizersbier is named after the gold coins in the time of Charlemagne.	Mechels Keizersbier dont le nom provient des pièces de monnaie d'or au temps de Charles Quint.	Mechels Keizersbier genoemd naar de gouden muntstukken ten tijde van Keizer Karel.

8,5
CLASSIC
GOUDEN
CAROLUS
CLASSIC
BELGISCH BIER • BELGIAN BEER

CAROLUS D'OR

Gouden Carolus Easter Beer

	top-fermentation	fermentation haute	hoge gisting
	specialty beer blond	bière spéciale blonde	speciaalbier blond
	Brouwerij Het Anker Mechelen	Brouwerij Het Anker Malines	Brouwerij Het Anker Mechelen
	based on Belgian hops exclusively	exclusivement à base de houblon belge	op basis van uitsluitend Belgische hop
%	10%	10%	10%
	ruby red	rouge rubis	robijnrood
	–	–	–
°C	48 - 54 °F	9 - 12 °C	9 - 12 °C
	Spicy spring beer, full-bodied and at the same time thirst-quenching. Smooth taste in spite of the high alcohol content.	Bière de printemps relevée à la fois franche et désaltérante. Malgré sa haute teneur en alcool, elle a une saveur moelleuse.	Kruidig voorjaarsbier dat tegelijk volmondig en dorst lessend is. Ondanks het hoge alcoholvolume heeft het toch een zachte smaak.
i	–	–	–

GOUDEN
CAROLUS
Easter Beer
BELGIAN BEER

CAROLUS
CAROLUS D'OR

Gouden Carolus Tripel

	top-fermentation re-fermented in the bottle	fermentation haute refermentation en bouteille	hoge gisting hergisting op de fles
	specialty beer Tripel	bière spéciale triple	speciaalbier tripel
	Brouwerij Het Anker Mechelen	Brouwerij Het Anker Malines	Brouwerij Het Anker Mechelen
	Brewed following an ancient tradition: ripe barley, Belgian hop varieties including some cultivated for the aroma, pale malt.	Brassée suivant l'ancienne tradition: orge mûr, variétés de houblon belges dont une partie mise à tremper pour l'arôme, malt pâle.	Volgens oude traditie gebrouwen: rijpe gerst, Belgische hopsoorten waarvan een deel geweekt voor het aroma, bleke mout.
%	9%	9%	9%
	gold-yellow	jaune doré	goudgeel
	Hold a degreased goblet by the stem and tilt it a little. Pour the beer in a single movement, avoiding contact with glass or foam.	Prendre un verre calice dégraissé par le pied et le tenir légèrement incliné. Verser la bière lentement en un seul mouvement sans toucher le verre ni l'écume.	Een vetvrij kelkglas bij de voet vastnemen en licht schuin houden. Het bier traag en in 1 beweging uitschenken zonder het glas of schuim te raken.
°C	48 - 54 °F	9 - 12 °C	9 - 12 °C
	Tender with a pure taste, full-bodied yet thirst-quenching. Heavy, refreshing and a little spicy.	Tendre avec une saveur pure, franche et néanmoins désaltérante. Fort, rafraîchissant et quelque peu relevé.	Teder met een zuivere smaak, volmondig en toch dorstlessend. Zwaar, verfrissend en ietwat kruidig.
i	Winner of a Gold Award at the 'World Beer Cup' in 2002, category 'Triple'.	A gagné en 2002 le Gold Award au 'World Beer Cup', catégorie 'triple'.	Won in 2002 de Gold Award op de 'World Beer Cup', categorie 'tripel'.

TRIPLE
GOUDEN
CAROLUS
TRIPLE

GOUDEN CAROLUS
CAROLUS D'OR

Gouyasse tradition

	top-fermentation re-fermented in the bottle	fermentation haute refermentation en bouteille	hoge gisting nagisting in de fles
	specialty beer	bière spéciale	speciaalbier
	Brasserie des Légendes Brewsite Gouyasse Irchonwelz (Ath)	Brasserie des Légendes Brewsite Gouyasse Irchonwelz (Ath)	Brasserie des Légendes Brewsite Gouyasse Irchonwelz (Ath)
	malt, hop, yeast, pure water	malt, houblon, levure, eau pure	mout, hop, gist, zuiver water
%	6%	6%	6%
	light-yellow, pearly foam	jaune clair, écume perlée	lichtgeel, gepareld schuim
	Degrease the glass, rinse thoroughly with hot water and dry. With yeast sediment: revolve the bottle before serving the last third. Without yeast sediment: pour carefully and leave sediment in the bottle.	Dégraisser le verre, le rincer bien à l'eau chaude et le sécher. Avec dépôt de levure: tourner le dernier tiers de bière avant de le verser. Sans dépôt de levure: verser prudemment et laisser la levure dans la bouteille.	Het glas ontvetten, goed spoelen met warm water en drogen. Met gistbezinkel: het laatste derde van het bier walsen voor het uitschenken. Zonder gistbezinksel: voorzichtig schenken en de fond in de fles laten.
°C	41 - 46 °F	5 - 8 °C	5 - 8 °C
	Aroma of malt and fruit with some lemon. Perfect balance between dry bitterness and malt, weakening the hop taste.	Arôme de malt et de fruits avec une touche d'agrumes légère. Equilibre parfait entre le goût amer sec et le malt qui réduit l'effet du houblon.	Aroma van mout en fruit met lichte toets van citroen. Perfect evenwicht tussen droge bitterheid en mout die de hoptoets verzwakt.
i	Store upright in the cellar or in the refrigerator.	Conserver en position verticale tant dans la cave qu'au réfrigérateur.	Verticaal bewaren zowel in de kelder als in de frigo.

BRASSERIE DES GÉANTS
Château-Brasserie
GOUYASSE
Bière Belge

GOUYASSE

Gouyasse tripel

	top-fermentation re-fermented in the bottle	fermentation haute refermentation en bouteille	hoge gisting nagisting in de fles
	Tripel special	triple spéciale	tripel speciaal
	Brasserie des Légendes Brewsite Gouyasse Irchonwelz (Ath)	Brasserie des Légendes Brewsite Gouyasse Irchonwelz (Ath)	Brasserie des Légendes Brewsite Gouyasse Irchonwelz (Ath)
	malt, hops, yeast, water	malt, houblon, levure, eau	mout, hop, gist, water
%	9%	9%	9%
	golden blond	blond doré	goudblond
	Degrease the glass, rinse thoroughly with hot water and dry. With yeast sediment: smoothly revolve the bottle before serving the last third. Without yeast sediment: pour carefully and leave sediment in the bottle.	Dégraisser le verre, bien rincer à l'eau chaude et sécher. Avec dépôt de levure: tourner le dernier tiers de bière avant de le verser. Sans dépôt de levure: verser prudemment et laisser la levure dans la bouteille.	Het glas ontvetten, goed spoelen met warm water en drogen. Met gistbezinkel: het laatste derde van het bier walsen voor het uitschenken. Zonder gistbezinksel: voorzichtig schenken en de fond in de fles laten.
°C	46 - 54 °F	8 - 12 °C	8 - 12 °C
	Fruity and spicy, round in the mouth. Well-balanced taste of hop and long-lasting bitterness.	Fruité et relevé, rond dans la bouche. Saveur équilibrée de houblon et goût amer prolongé.	Fruitig en kruidig, rond in de mond. Evenwichtige smaak van hop en lange bitterheid.
i	–	–	–

GOUYASSE

Grand cru Bruocsella

	spontaneous fermentation	fermentation spontanée	spontane gisting
	Lambic (3 years)	lambic (3 ans)	lambiek (3 jaar)
	Brouwerij Cantillon Brussels	Brouwerij Cantillon Bruxelles	Brouwerij Cantillon Brussel
	barley malt, wheat, more than one year old hops	malt d'orge, froment, houblon suranné	gerstemout, tarwe, overjaarse hop
%	5%	5%	5%
	gold-coloured	dorée	goudkleurig
	The use of a wine basket is recommended if the bottle was stored horizontally. Place the bottle in upright position 48 hours before serving.	Un panier verseur est recommandé si la bouteille a été conservée en position horizontale. Mettre la bouteille 48 heures avant de servir en position verticale pour faire descendre la levure.	Een schenkmandje is aangewezen wanneer de fles horizontaal bewaard werd. De fles 48 uur voor het uitschenken verticaal plaaste[illegible] om het bezinksel te decanteren.
°C	cellar temperature 54 - 61 °F	température de cave 12 - 16 °C	keldertemperatuur 12 - 16 °C
	Very powerful. Fine sourish taste, aromas of great oxidized wines (yellow wine, sherry...).	Très corsé. Saveur raffinée acidulée, arômes de grands vins oxydés (vin jaune, xéres...).	Zeer krachtig. Fijnzurige smaak, aroma's van grote geoxideerde wijnen (gele wijn, sherry...).
i	–	–	–

Grand Cru
Lambic Bio

Greut Lawauitj

	top-fermentation naturally re-fermented in the bottle	fermentation haute refermentation naturelle en bouteille	hoge gisting natuurlijke hergisting op de fles
	Spéciale Belge	spéciale belge	speciale belge
	Brouwerij Slaghmuylder Ninove	Brouwerij Slaghmuylder Ninove	Brouwerij Slaghmuylder Ninove
	barley malt, yeast, water hop varieties: Belgian Hallertau, Czech Styrie	malt d'orge, levure, eau variétés de houblon: Hallertau belge, Styrie tchèque	gerstemout, gist, water hopsoorten: Belgische Hallertau, Tsjechische Styrie
%	5,50%	5,50%	5,50%
	amber	ambrée	amber
	Pour in a single, fluent and smooth movement. Leave the sediment in the bottle.	Verser prudemment en un seul mouvement fluide et laisser le dépôt de levure dans la bouteille.	Voorzichtig uitschenken in 1 vloeiende, zachte beweging. Het gistdepot in de fles laten.
°C	46 - 54 °F	8 - 12 °C	8 - 12 °C
	Lively beer with taste evolution. Nice session beer. Fruity esters (banana) of the yeast.	Bière vive facilement buvable avec saveur évolutive. Esters fruités (banane) de la levure.	Levend bier met smaakevolutie, vlot doordrinkbier. Fruitige esters (banaan) van de gist.
i	The only amber beer that is re-fermented in the bottle or the barrel. Brewed for the 2004 European Town Criers' Championship. The name of this beer is a dialect expression meaning "a lot of noise".	La seule bière ambrée avec refermentation en bouteille ou au fût. Brassée à l'occasion du Championnat Européen des 'Bellemannen' en 2004. Le nom de la bière est l'expression dialectale de 'beaucoup de bruit'.	Het enige amberbier dat hergist is op fles of vat. Gebrouwen t.g.v. van het Europees Kampioenschap van de Bellemannen in 2004. De naam van het bier is een dialectuitdrukking voor 'veel lawaai'.

Greut
Lawauitj
EKB
2004
NINOVE
Greut
Lawauitj
EKB

Grimbergen blond

	top-fermentation	fermentation haute	hoge gisting
	recognised Belgian abbey beer	Bière d'abbaye belge reconnue	Erkend Belgisch abdijbier
	Alken Maes corporation Alken	Alken Maes corporation Alken	Alken Maes corporation Alken
	–	–	–
%	7,70%	7,70%	7,70%
	ochre-blond	blond ocre	okerblond
	Pour carefully into a degreased, dry glass. Pour slowly to obtain a nice foam head.	Verser soigneusement dans un verre dégraissé sec. Verser lentement de sorte qu'un faux col solide se forme.	Zorgvuldig uitschenken in een ontvet, droog glas. Langzaam schenken zodat er een mooie schuimkraag ontstaat.
°C	43 °F	6 °C	6 °C
	Slightly fruity, bittersweet and full beer with caramel touches.	Bière légèrement fruitée, douce-amère et pleine aux touches caramélisées.	Lichtfruitig, zoetbitter vol bier met toetsen van karamel.
i	Authentic abbey beer, excellent to accompany a meal.	Cette authentique bière d'abbaye convient parfaitement aux repas.	Authentiek abdijbier uitstekend geschikt voor bij de maaltijd.

ABDIJBIER BIÈRE D'ABBAYE
ANNO 1128
GRIMBERGEN
ARDET NEC CONSUMITUR
Blond Blonde

ABDIJBIER BIÈRE D'ABBAYE
GRIMBERGEN
ARDET NEC CONSUMITUR

Grimbergen Cuvée de l'Ermitage

	top-fermentation	fermentation haute	hoge gisting
	Recognised Belgian abbey beer	Bière d'abbaye belge reconnue	Erkend Belgisch abdijbier
	Alken Maes corporation Alken	Alken Maes corporation Alken	Alken Maes corporation Alken
	–	–	–
%	7,50%	7,50%	7,50%
	light and warm, red-brown colour clear	couleur brune-rouge claire et chaude claire	lichte en warme, roodbruine kleur helder
	Pour carefully into a degreased, dry glass. Pour slowly to obtain a nice foam head.	Verser soigneusement dans un verre dégraissé sec. Verser lentement de sorte qu'un faux col solide se forme.	Zorgvuldig uitschenken in een ontvet, droog glas. Langzaam schenken zodat er een mooie schuimkraag ontstaat.
°C	43 °F	6 °C	6 °C
	Round taste, emphasized by a strong, pleasant bitterness.	Saveur ronde accentuée par un goût amer prononcé et agréable.	Ronde smaak geaccentueerd door een sterke, aangename bitterheid.
i	Authentic abbey beer.	Authentique bière d'abbaye.	Authentiek abdijbier.

ABDIJBIER BIÈRE D'ABBAYE
ANNO 1128
GRIMBERGEN
ARDET NEC CONSUMITUR
Cuvée de l'Ermitage

ABDIJBIER BIÈRE D'ABBAYE
ANNO 1128
GRIMBERGEN
ARDET NEC CONSUMITUR

Grimbergen dubbel

	top-fermentation	fermentation haute	hoge gisting
	Recognised Belgian abbey beer	Bière d'abbaye belge reconnue	Erkend Belgisch abdijbier
	Alken Maes corporation Alken	Alken Maes corporation Alken	Alken Maes corporation Alken
	–	–	–
%	6,50%	6,50%	6,50%
	deep red burgundy colour	couleur bourgogne rouge intense	dieprode bourgognekleur
	Pour carefully into a degreased, dry glass. Pour slowly to obtain a nice foam head.	Verser soigneusement dans un verre dégraissé sec. Verser lentement de sorte qu'un faux col solide se forme.	Zorgvuldig uitschenken in een ontvet, droog glas. Langzaam schenken zodat er een mooie schuimkraag ontstaat.
°C	43 °F	6 °C	6 °C
	Bittersweet, full beer with caramel touches.	Doux-amer avec beaucoup de plénitude et des touches caramélisées.	Zoetbitter, vol bier met toetsen van karamel.
i	Authentic abbey beer, excellent to accompany a meal.	Cette authentique bière d'abbaye convient parfaitement aux repas.	Authentiek abdijbier uitstekend geschikt voor bij de maaltijd.

GRIMBERGEN
ABDIJBIER BIÈRE D'ABBAYE
ANNO 1128
GRIMBERGEN
ARDET NEC CONSUMITUR
Dubbel Double

ABDIJBIER BIÈRE D'ABBAYE
ANNO 1128
GRIMBERGEN
ARDET NEC CONSUMITUR

Grimbergen Optimo Bruno

	top-fermentation	fermentation haute	hoge gisting
	Recognised Belgian abbey beer	Bière d'abbaye belge reconnue	Erkend Belgisch abdijbier
	Alken Maes corporation Alken	Alken Maes corporation Alken	Alken Maes corporation Alken
	–	–	–
%	10%	10%	10%
	dark amber-coloured	ambré foncé	donker amberkleurig
	Pour carefully into a de-greased, dry glass. Pour slowly to obtain a nice foam head.	Verser soigneusement dans un verre dégraissé et sec. Verser lentement de sorte qu'un faux col solide se forme.	Zorgvuldig uitschenken in een ontvet, droog glas. Langzaam schenken zodat er een mooie schuimkraag ontstaat.
°C	43 °F	6 °C	6 °C
	Bittersweet with a pronounced, powerful alcoholic aftertaste. Good balance between hop and malt owing to the double fermentation.	Doux-amer avec une fin de bouche prononcée, alcoolisée corsée. La double fermentation assure un équilibre entre le houblon et le malt.	Zoetbitter met uitgesproken en krachtige alcoholische afdronk. De dubbele gisting zorgt voor balans tussen hop en mout.
i	Authentic abbey beer.	Authentique bière d'abbaye.	Authentiek abdijbier.

ABDIJBIER BIÈRE D'ABBAYE
ANNO 1128
GRIMBERGEN
ARDET NEC CONSUMITUR
Optimo Bruno

Grimbergen tripel

	top-fermentation re-fermented in the bottle	fermentation haute refermentation en bouteille	hoge gisting hergisting op fles
	Recognised Belgian abbey beer	Bière belge d'abbaye reconnue	Erkend Belgisch abdijbier
	Alken Maes corporation Alken	Alken Maes corporation Alken	Alken Maes corporation Alken
	–	–	–
%	9%	9%	9%
	amber-blond	blond ambré	amberblond
	Pour carefully into a degreased, dry glass. Pour slowly for a nice foam head.	Verser soigneusement dans un verre dégraissé et sec. Laisser la levure au fond de la bouteille.	Zorgvuldig uitschenken in een ontvet, droog glas. Langzaam schenken zodat er een mooie schuimkraag ontstaat.
°C	43 - 50 °F	6 - 10 °C	6 - 10 °C
	Bittersweet, spicy, full-bodied with a warm aftertaste.	Amer-doux, corsé, plein rond avec fin de bouche chaleureuse.	Bitterzoet, pittig, volrond met warme afdronk.
i	Authentic abbey beer.	Authentique bière d'abbaye.	Authentiek abdijbier.

ABDIJBIER BIÈRE D'ABBAYE
ANNO 1128
GRIMBERGEN
ARDET NEC CONSUMITUR
Tripel Triple

ABDIJBIER BIÈRE D'ABBAYE
GRIMBERGEN
ARDET NEC CONSUMITUR

Grisette Blanche

	top-fermentation re-fermented in the bottle	fermentation haute refermentation en bouteille	hoge gisting hergisting in de fles
	Witbier	bière blanche	witbier
	Brasserie Saint-Feuillien Le Roeulx	Brasserie Saint-Feuillien Le Roeulx	Brasserie Saint-Feuillien Le Roeulx
	barley malt, sugar, hops, yeast, vitamine C, brewing water	malt d'orge, sucre, houblon, levure, vitamine C, eau de brassage	gerstemout, suiker, hop, gist, vitamine C, brouwwater
%	5%	5%	5%
	blond and pearly veiled, unfiltered	blonde et perlante voilée, non filtrée	blond en parelend gesluierd, niet gefilterd
	–	–	–
	39 °F	4 °C	4 °C
	Light character beer with smooth taste and aroma.	Bière de caractère légère, saveur et arôme moelleux.	Licht karakterbier, zachte smaak en aroma.
	–	–	–

BLANCHE
grisette
WITBIER
Licht bier van hoge gisting

grisette

Grisette Blonde

	top-fermentation re-fermented in the bottle	fermentation haute refermentation en bouteille	hoge gisting hergisting in de fles
	Belgian specialty beer	bière spéciale belge	Belgisch speciaalbier
	Brasserie Saint-Feuillien Le Roeulx	Brasserie Saint-Feuillien Le Roeulx	Brasserie Saint-Feuillien Le Roeulx
	barley malt, sugar, hops, yeast, vitamine C, brewing water	malt d'orge, sucre, houblon, levure, vitamine C, eau de brassage	gerstemout, suiker, hop, gist, vitamine C, brouwwater
%	5%	5%	5%
	straw-yellow	jaune paille	strogeel
	–	–	–
°C	39 °F	4 °C	4 °C
	Refreshing summer beer. Rich perfumes when served at room temperature.	Bière d'été rafraîchissante. Parfums riches lors de la dégustation à température de chambre.	Verfrissend zomerbier. Rijke parfums bij degustatie op kamertemperatuur.
i	–	–	–

BLONDE
grisette
BLOND
Bière légère de haute fermentation
Licht bier van hoge gisting
grisette

Grisette Country cool

	top-fermentation	fermentation haute	hoge gisting
	fruit beer	bière fruitée	fruitbier
	Brasserie Saint-Feuillien Le Roeulx	Brasserie Saint-Feuillien Le Roeulx	Brasserie Saint-Feuillien Le Roeulx
	barley malt, sugar, hops, yeast, vitamine C, brewing water	malt d'orge, sucre, houblon, levure, vitamine C, eau de brassage	gerstemout, suiker, hop, gist, vitamine C, brouwwater
%	3,50%	3,50%	3,50%
	light pink evokes the subtle, warm effect of amber	rose clair évoque la subtilité et la chaleur de l'ambré	lichtroze warm en subtiel amber
	–	–	–
°C	39 °F	4 °C	4 °C
	Smooth, fresh and slightly perfumed. Flavour of apples, quinces and prunes.	Moelleux, frais et légèrement parfumé. Saveur de pommes, coings et prunes.	Zacht, fris en licht geparfumeerd. Smaak van appels, kweeperen en pruimen.
i	–	–	–

3,5°
grisette
Country
Cool
grisette

Grisette Fruits des bois

	top-fermentation	fermentation haute	hoge gisting
	fruit beer	bière fruitée	fruitbier
	Brasserie Saint-Feuillien Le Roeulx	Brasserie Saint-Feuillien Le Roeulx	Brasserie Saint-Feuillien Le Roeulx
	barley malt, wheat malt, fructose/glucose syrup, hops, natural juice of forest fruits, natural flavouring of red fruits, sweetener, vitamine C, ascorbine acid, brewing water	malt d'orge, malt de froment, sirop de fructose/glucose, houblon, jus naturel de fruits des bois, arôme naturel de fruits rouges, édulcorant, vitamine C, acide ascorbine, eau de brassage	gerstemout, tarwemout, fructose/glucosesiroop, hop, natuurlijk bosvruchtensap, natuurlijk aroma van rode vruchten, zoetstof, vitamine C, ascorbinezuur, brouwwater
%	3,50%	3,50%	3,50%
	purple-red, like a young burgundy wine	rouge violet, fait penser à un Bourgogne jeune	purperrood, doet denken aan een jonge Bourgogne
	–	–	–
°C	39 °F	4 °C	4 °C
	Contrast of sweet and sourish flavours, like a delicious fruit cocktail. Red fruit flavours.	Contraste de goûts doux et acidulés comme une coupe de fruits délicieuse. Arômes de fruits rouges.	Contrast van zoete en zurige smaken zoals een schitterende fruitcoupe. Aroma's van rood fruit.
i	–	–	–

3,5°
ALC % VOL
bosvruchten
grisette
fruits des bois
Bière légère de haute fermentation
Licht bier van hoge gisting

grisette

Grotten Flemish Ale

	top-fermentation	fermentation haute	hoge gisting
	Belgian strong Ale	Belgian strong ale	Belgian strong ale
	Brouwerij Sint-Bernardus Watou	Brouwerij Sint-Bernardus Watou	Brouwerij Sint-Bernardus Watou
	–	–	–
%	7,7%	7,7%	7,7%
	apricot-coloured firm foam head	couleur abricot faux col solide	abrikozenkleur stevige schuimkraag
	–	–	–
°C	–	–	–
	Mild flavour of yeast, with touches of citrus and coriander. Taste: sweet evolving in coriander, lemon rind and pepper. Aftertase: pepper, hops and a warm alcohol touch.	Arôme doux de houblon avec des touches d'agrumes et de coriandre. Goût: doux évoluant vers le coriandre, l'écorce de citron et le poivre. Fin de bouche: poivre, houblon et touche d'alcool.	Mild aroma van gist met toetsen van citrus en koriander. Smaak: zoet dat evolueert naar koriander, citroenschil en peper. Afdronk: peper, hop en warme alcoholtoets.
i	Product for the USA.	Brassée pour les Etats-Unis.	Gebrouwen voor de USA.

PIERRE CELIS SIGNATURE SELECTION
GROTTEN
Flemish Ale
KANNE (B) - VALKENBURG (NL)
UNIQUE BELGIAN ALE
Product of Belgium
1 PT. 9.4FL. OZ.
GROTTENBIER
BIERE DES GROTTES

Grottenbier/Grotten brown

	top-fermentation re-fermented in the bottle	fermentation haute refermentation en bouteille	hoge gisting hergisting op de fles
	regional beer	bière régionale	streekbier
	Brouwerij St-Bernardus Watou	Brouwerij St-Bernardus Watou	Brouwerij St-Bernardus Watou
	Different malt varieties, hops, sugar, yeast, water. The beer matures in the marl caves of Kanne and Valkenburg, where air humidity is very high.	Différentes variétés de malt, houblon, sucre, levure, eau. La bière mûrit dans les cavernes calcaires de Kanne et Valkenburg, où l'air est très humide.	Verschillende moutsoorten, hop, suiker, gist, water. Het bier rijpt in de mergelgrotten van Kanne en Valkenburg waar de lucht zeer vochtig is.
%	6,50%	6,50%	6,50%
	dark brown unfiltered	brun foncé non filtrée	donkerbruin ongefilterd
	Pour into a glass, rinsed with cold water. Leave the glass upright and pour the beer carefully in one single, fluent movement. The yeast sediment is left in the bottle.	Verser dans un verre rincé à l'eau froide. Laisser le verre en position verticale et verser la bière prudemment en un seul mouvement fluide. Laisser le dépôt de levure dans la bouteille.	Uitschenken in een met koud water gespoeld glas. Het glas rechtop laten staan en het bier in 1 vloeiende beweging voorzichtig schenken. Het gistdepot in de fles laten.
°C	43 - 50 °F	6 - 10 °C	6 - 10 °C
	Pleasant fruity aroma, balanced between bitter and sweet.	Arôme fruité agréable avec un équilibre entre amertume et douceur.	Aangenaam fruitig aroma met een evenwicht tussen bitter en zoet.
i	Created by the master-brewer Pierre Celis.	Créée par maître brasseur Pierre Celis.	Gecreëerd door Meesterbrouwer Pierre Celis.

GROTTENBIER
BIERE DES GROTTES
BRUIN - BRUNE
GROTTENBIER
BRUIN
BRUNE
KANNE (B)-VALKENBURG (NL)
BIERE DES GROTTES
GROTTENBIER
BIERE DES GROTTES
KANNE (B)
VALKENBURG (NL)

Guido

	top-fermentation re-fermented in the bottle unpasteurised	fermentation haute refermentation en bouteille non pasteurisée	hoge gisting hergisting op de fles niet gepasteuriseerd
	strong dubbel	double forte	sterk dubbel
	Brouwerij De Regenboog Brugge	Brouwerij De Regenboog Bruges	Brouwerij De Regenboog Brugge
	3 malt varieties (Pilsner, cara, roasted), Hallertau hops, dark candy, raisins, honey, yeast, water	3 variétés de malt (pils, cara, brûlé), houblon Hallertau, candi foncé, raisins secs, miel, levure, eau	3 moutsoorten (pils, cara, gebrande), Hallertau hop, donkere kandij, rozijnen, honing, gist, water
%	8%	8%	8%
	dark unfiltered	foncée non filtrée	donker niet gefilterd
	–	–	–
°C	50 °F	10 °C	10 °C
	Sweet and wine-like, with full-bodied, fruity flavour.	Doux et viticole, franche, arôme fruité.	Zoet en wijnachtig, volmondig, fruitig aroma.
i	Boutique beer that can be kept up to two years after the bottling date. Brewed for the Guido Gezelle Year in 1999.	Bière artisanale qui peut se conserver 2 ans après la date de la mise en bouteilles. Brassée à l'occasion de l'année de Guido Gezelle en 1999	Artisanaal bier, 2 jaar houdbaar na botteldatum. Gebrouwen n.a.v. het Guido Gezelle-jaar in 1999.

Guido
Guido is een donker bruin bier,
gebrouwen met mout, hop, kandij,
rozijnen, honing, gist en water.
33 cl ℮ Cat S 8% vol
5 425004 256010

Guido

Gulden Draak

	top-fermentation re-fermented in the bottle	fermentation haute refermentation en bouteille	hoge gisting hergisting in de fles
	strong dark	foncée forte	sterk donker
	Brouwerij Van Steenberge Ertvelde	Brouwerij Van Steenberge Ertvelde	Brouwerij Van Steenberge Ertvelde
	barley malt, hops, yeast, water	malt d'orge, houblon, levure, eau	gerstemout, hop, gist, water
%	10,50% 23° plato	10,50% 23° plato	10,50% 23° plato
	dark red	rouge foncé	donkerrood
	Pour in a single, fluent and smooth movement, leaving 1 cm of yeast sediment in the bottle. The sediment can be poured, making the beer cloudy.	Verser en un seul mouvement fluide et doux et laisser 1 cm de dépôt de levure dans la bouteille. Le depôt peut être versé et rend la bière trouble.	Uitschenken in 1 vloeiende, zachte beweging en 1 cm gistdepot in de fles laten. De gistfond kan worden uitgeschonken en maakt het bier troebel.
°C	50 - 54 °F	10 - 12 °C	10 - 12 °C
	typical, rich, glowing taste with a coffee or chocolate touch.	Saveur typique, riche, ardente qui fait penser au café ou au chocolat.	Typische, rijke, gloeiende smaak die doet denken aan koffie, of aan chocolade.
i	Named after the gold statue on top of the Ghent belfry.	Son nom renvoie à la statue en or au sommet du Beffroi de Gand.	Genoemd naar het gouden beeld bovenop het Gentse Belfort.

Gulden Draak
Gulden Draak

Guldenberg

	top-fermentation	fermentation haute	hoge gisting
	Tripel	triple	tripel
	Brouwerij De Ranke Wevelgem	Brouwerij De Ranke Wevelgem	Brouwerij De Ranke Wevelgem
	Pale malt, hop flowers, industrial yeast. With dry-hopping.	Malt pâle, fleurs de houblon, levure de culture. Avec dry hopping.	Bleekmout, hopbloemen, cultuurgist. Met dry hopping.
%	8,50%	8,50%	8,50%
	dark blond slightly cloudy	blond foncé légèrement trouble	donkerblond licht troebel
	–	–	–
°C	Moderately cooled.	Rafraîchie modérément.	Medium koel.
	Hoppy and bittersweet.	Houblonné et amer-doux.	Hoppig en zoetbitter.
i	–	–	–

Guldenberg®
33 cl℮
Alc. 8,5% vol
Abdijbier • Bière d'Abbaye

Hapkin

	top-fermentation re-fermented in the bottle	fermentation haute refermentation en bouteille	hoge gisting hergisting op de fles
	strong blond	blonde forte	sterk blond
	Alken Maes corporation Alken	Alken Maes corporation Alken	Alken Maes corporation Alken
	–	–	–
	8,50%	8,50%	8,50%
	blond unique, imposing, creamy foam head	blonde faux col unique, imposant et crémeux	blond unieke, imposante en romige kraag
	Pour carefully into a degreased, dry glass. Fill the glass in one smooth movement for a nice, big foam head.	Verser soigneusement dans un verre dégraissé et sec. Remplir le verre doucement d'un seul trait pour obtenir un faux col solide.	Zorgvuldig uitschenken in een ontvet, droog glas. Het glas in 1 beweging zachtjes vullen voor een grote schuimkraag.
	46 °F	8 °C	8 °C
	Flowery Saaz hop flavour. Smooth malty character. Sparkling, perfumed fruit flavour.	Arôme fleuri de houblon Saaz. Caractère houblonné moelleux. Goût fruité, parfumé, pétillant.	Bloemrijk aroma van Saazhop. Zacht moutig karakter. Sprankelende, gepar fumeerde fruitigheid.
	–	–	–

HAPKIN
ANNO 1877
HAPKIN
ANNO 1877
Het blonde bier
uit het Houtland
L603
HAPKIN
ANNO 1877

Hector Amber

	top-fermentation re-fermented in the bottle unpasteurised	fermentation haute refermentation en bouteille non pasteurisée	hoge gisting hergisting op de fles niet gepasteuriseerd
	amber	ambrée	amber
	Brouwerij De Graal for Brouwerij Sublim, Leuven	Brouwerij De Graal pour Brouwerij Sublim, Louvain	Brouwerij De Graal voor Brouwerij Sublim, Leuven
	malt, hops, yeast, water	malt, houblon, levure, eau	mout, hop, gist, water
%	7,70%	7,70%	7,70%
	dark amber-coloured cloudy, unfiltered fine, creamy foam	ambré foncé trouble, non filtrée écume fine et crémeuse	donker amberkleurig troebel, ongefilterd fijn, romig schuim
	Pour slowly in a tulip-shaped glass. The yeast sediment can be poured or left in the bottle.	Verser lentement dans un verre tulipe. Verser également la levure ou la laisser dans la bouteille.	Traag inschenken in een tulpglas. De gistbodem mee inschenken of in de fles laten.
°C	46 - 54 °F	8 - 12 °C	8 - 12 °C
	Aroma: mainly fruity-yeasty (apricot), some caramel malt and a touch of smokiness. Also warm alcohol and aromatic hop. Malty at the onset, evolving to fruity. Aftertaste: hoppy bitter and peppery spicy, finishing the malt flavour.	Parfum fruité-houblonné (abricot), un peu de malt caramélisé et un trait de fumée. Parfum d'alcool et de houblon aromatisé. Saveur initiale maltée aboutissant en arômes fruités. Fin de bouche amère, houblonnée et surtout relevée de poivre arrondissant le goût malté.	Geur: vooral fruitig-gistig (abrikoos), wat karamelmout en wat rokerigheid. Ook warme alcohol en aromatische hop. Smaak: begint moutig en mondt uit in fruitige aroma's. Afdronk: hopbitter en vooral peperige kruidigheid die de moutsmaak afrondt.
i	–	–	–

HECTOR
AMBER
Bier - Biere Alc. 7.7 % vol Cat S - ℮33cl
HECTOR

Hector Tripel

	top-fermentation re-fermented in the bottle unpasteurised	fermentation haute refermentation en bouteille non pasteurisée	hoge gisting hergisting op de fles niet gepasteuriseerd
	Tripel	triple	tripel
	Brouwerij De Graal for Brouwerij Sublim, Leuven	Brouwerij De Graal pour Brouwerij Sublim, Louvain	Brouwerij De Graal voor Brouwerij Sublim, Leuven
	malt, hops, yeast, water	malt, houblon, levure, eau	mout, hop, gist, water
%	8,20%	8,20%	8,20%
	dark blond cloudy, unfiltered	blond foncé trouble, non filtrée	donkerblond troebel, ongefilterd
	Pour slowly in a tulip-shaped glass. The yeast sediment can be poured or left in the bottle.	Verser lentement dans un verre tulipe. Verser le dépôt de levure ou le laisser dans la bouteille.	Traag inschenken in een tulpglas. De gistbodem mee inschenken of in de fles laten.
°C	46 - 54 °F	8 - 12 °C	8 - 12 °C
	Pleasant, spicy and round hoppy nose with citrus touches, robust and fine bitter at the same time. Full and creamy mouthfeel. The malt aroma turns into a strong, dry and grainy malt aroma. Aftertaste extra hoppy bitter with a peppery spiciness.	Agréable, relevé et rond. Parfum houblonné avec des touches d'agrumes à la fois solides et amères, raffinées. Sensation de bouche pleine et crémeuse. Parfum malté aboutissant en des arômes plus forts, secs et céréales. Fin de bouche extra amère-houblonnée avec une saveur relevée, poivrée.	Aangenaam, kruidig en rond. Hoppige neus met citrustoetsen, tegelijk robuust en fijnbitter. Vol en romig mondgevoel. De moutgeur evolueert naar een sterker, droog en grani moutaroma. Afdronk: extra hopbitter met peperige kruidigheid.
i	–	–	–

HECTOR
TRIPEL
Bier - Bière Alc. 8.2 % vol Cat.S - ℮33cl
HECTOR

Hellekapelle

	top-fermentation re-fermented in the bottle	fermentation haute refermentation en bouteille	hoge gisting hergisting in de fles
	blond	blonde	blond
	Brouwerij De Bie Loker	Brouwerij De Bie Loker	Brouwerij De Bie Loker
	hops, yeast, malt, water	malt, houblon, levure, eau	hop, gist, mout, water
%	5%	5%	5%
	blond slightly cloudy draught beer	blonde un peu trouble au fût	blond iets troebel van het vat
	–	–	–
°C	43 °F	6 °C	6 °C
	Spicy hop taste.	Saveur houblonnée corsée.	Pittige hopsmaak.
i	Hellekapelle is the name of the brasserie near the brewery. Loker-Heuvelland is a region, known for its stories about witches.	Hellekapelle est le nom du café situé près de la brasserie. Loker-Heuvelland est une région de contes de sorcières.	Hellekapelle is de naam van de brasserie bij de brouwerij. Loker-Heuvelland is de streek van de heksenverhalen.

Brouwerij De Bie
B-8958 Loker
Tel 0475 23 47 95
Hellekapelle

Helleketelbier

	top-fermentation	fermentation haute	hoge gisting
	amber	ambrée	amber
	Brouwerij De Bie Loker	Brouwerij De Bie Loker	Brouwerij De Bie Loker
	malt, hops, wheat, candy sugar, yeast, herbs, water	malt, houblon, froment, sucre candi, levure, herbes, eau	mout, hop, tarwe, kandijsuiker, gist, kruiden, water
	7%	7%	7%
	amber	ambrée	amber
	–	–	–
	43 °F	6 °C	6 °C
	Spicy.	Epicé.	Kruidig.
	–	–	–

Helleketelbier
Brouwerij De Bie • B-8958 Loker
tel. 0475 23 47 95
Helleketelbier

Hercule Stout

	top-fermentation re-fermented in the bottle	fermentation haute refermentation en bouteille	hoge gisting nagisting in de fles
	Stout	stout	stout
	Brasserie des Légendes Brewsite Quintine Ellezelles	Brasserie des Légendes Brewsite Quintine Ellezelles	Brasserie des Légendes Brewsite Quintine Ellezelles
	pale malt, roasted malt, hops, yeast, water	malt pâle, malt brûlé, houblon, levure, eau	bleke mout, gebrande mout, hop, gist, water
%	9%	9%	9%
	black	noire	zwart
	–	–	–
°C	46 - 54 °F	8 - 12 °C	8 - 12 °C
	Robust and smooth. Creamy, mocca, spicy touch.	Solide et doux. Crémeux, goût de moka, touche aromatique.	Robuust en zacht. Romig, mokka, kruidige toets.
i	–	–	–

La Bière des Collines
HERCULE
STOUT
Brasserie Ellezelloise
Alc. 8,4% vol.
e 33 cl
S.P.R.L.
B.V.B.A.
Bière Belge • Belgisch Bier • Belgian Beer • Cerveza Extra
Fabriquée et embouteillée par • Gebrouwen en gebotteld te • Brewed and bottled by
Guinaumont 75 • B-7890 ELLEZELLES • +32 (0)68 54 31 60

Hervoise

	top-fermentation re-fermented in the bottle	fermentation haute refermentation en bouteille	hoge gisting hergisting in de fles
	regional beer	bière régionale	streekbier
	Brasserie Grain d'Orge Hombourt-Plombières	Brasserie Grain d'Orge Hombourt-Plombières	Brasserie Grain d'Orge Hombourt-Plombières
	malt varieties, yeast, hops, sugar, pure sugar-free apple and pear syrup (14 kg/800 l), herbs, water	variétés de malt, levure, houblon, sucre, sirop pur sans sucre de pommes et de poires (14 kg/800 l), herbes, eau	moutsoorten, gist, hop, suiker, pure suikervrije siroop van appels en peren (14 kg/800 l), kruiden, water
%	8,20%	8,20%	8,20%
	red-brown	brun rouge	roodbruin
	Leave the yeast sediment in the bottle.	Laisser le dépôt de levure dans la bouteille.	Het gistdepot in de fles laten.
°C	43 - 46 °F	6 - 8 °C	6 - 8 °C
	Fresh, fruity (apple and pear), spicy and above all sourish.	Frais, fruité (pommes et poires), relevé et surtout acidulé.	Fris, fruitig (appel en peer), kruidig en vooral zurig.
i	–	–	–

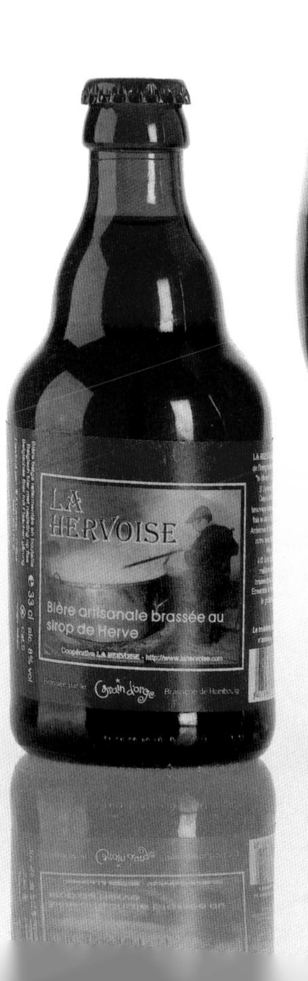
LA HERVOISE
Bière artisanale brassée au sirop de Herve
Brassée par le
Brasserie de Hombourg

LA HERVOISE
Bière au sirop

Het Kapittel Abt

	top-fermentation re-fermented in the bottle	fermentation haute refermentation en bouteille	hoge gisting nagisting op de fles
	abbey beer	bière d'abbaye	abdijbier
	Brouwerij Van Eecke Watou	Brouwerij Van Eecke Watou	Brouwerij Van Eecke Watou
	malt, spices, yeast, sweetener, water	malt, condiments, levure, édulcorant, eau	mout, specerijen, gist, zoetstof, water
%	10%	10%	10%
	light amber - ochre	ambré clair - ocre	licht amber - oker
	Hold the glass by the stem and tilt it slightly. Slowly pour in a single movement. Leave 1 cm of beer (sediment) in the bottle.	Tenir le verre en oblique par le pied et verser lentement en un seul mouvement. Laisser 1 cm de bière (levure) dans la bouteille.	Het glas bij de voet schuin houden en het bier traag in 1 beweging uitschenken. 1 cm bier (depot) in het flesje laten.
°C	46 - 55 °F	8 - 13 °C	8 - 13 °C
	Tripel with spicy, full round taste with warm chocolate touch.	Triple avec saveur corsée, pleine et ronde et une touche chaude de chocolat.	Tripel met pittige, volronde smaak met warme chocoladetoets.
i	–	–	–

Het Kapittel Blond

	top-fermentation re-fermented in the bottle	fermentation haute refermentation en bouteille	hoge gisting nagisting op de fles
	abbey beer	bière d'abbaye	abdijbier
	Brouwerij Van Eecke Watou	Brouwerij Van Eecke Watou	Brouwerij Van Eecke Watou
	malt, spices, yeast, sweet-ener, water	malt, condiments, levure, édulcorant, eau	mout, specerijen, gist, zoetstof, water
%	6,50%	6,50%	6,50%
	blond	blonde	blond
	Hold the glass by the stem and tilt it slightly. Slowly pour in a single movement. Leave 1 cm of beer (sediment) in the bottle.	Tenir le verre en oblique par le pied et verser lentement en un seul mouvement. Laisser 1 cm de bière (levure) dans la bouteille.	Het glas bij de voet schuin houden en het bier traag in 1 beweging uitschenken. 1 cm bier (depot) in het flesje laten.
°C	46 - 55 °F	8 - 13 °C	8 - 13 °C
	Session beer. Sweet, slightly malty flavour.	Bière qui se boit facilement. Arôme doux, légèrement malté.	Doordrinkbier. Zoet, licht moutaroma.
i	–	–	–

Kapittel
Kapittel

Kapittel
Watou

Het Kapittel Dubbel

	top-fermentation re-fermented in the bottle	fermentation haute refermentation en bouteille	hoge gisting nagisting op de fles
	abbey beer	bière d'abbaye	abdijbier
	Brouwerij Van Eecke Watou	Brouwerij Van Eecke Watou	Brouwerij Van Eecke Watou
	malt, caramel, spices, yeast, sweetener, water	malt, caramel, condiments, levure, édulcorant, eau	mout, karamel, specerijen, gist, zoetstof, water
%	7,50%	7,50%	7,50%
	dark brown	brun foncé	donkerbruin
	Hold the glass by the stem and tilt it slightly. Slowly pour in a single movement. Leave 1 cm of beer (sediment) in the bottle.	Tenir le verre en oblique par le pied et verser la bière lentement en un seul mouvement. Laisser 1 cm de bière (levure) dans la bouteille.	Het glas bij de voet schuin houden en het bier traag in 1 beweging uitschenken. 1 cm bier (depot) in het flesje laten.
°C	46 - 55 °F	8 - 13 °C	8 - 13 °C
	Sweet and fruity. Light malt flavour with hoppy aftertaste.	Doux et fruité. Arôme légèrement malté avec une fin de bouche houblonnée.	Zoet en fruitig. Licht moutaroma met hoppige afdronk.
i	Originally a blended beer. Today it is brewed as a separate top-fermenting beer.	A l'origine une bière coupée, actuellement brassée comme bière séparée de fermentation haute.	Oorspronkelijk een versnijbier dat vandaag als een apart hogegistingsbier wordt gebrouwen.

Kapittel
Kapittel
Watou
Dubbel
Kapittel
Watou

Het Kapittel Pater

	top-fermentation re-fermented in the bottle	fermentation haute refermentation en bouteille	hoge gisting nagisting op de fles
	abbey beer	bière d'abbaye	abdijbier
	Brouwerij Van Eecke Watou	Brouwerij Van Eecke Watou	Brouwerij Van Eecke Watou
	malt, caramel, spices, yeast, sweetener, water	malt, caramel, condiments, levure, édulcorant, eau	mout, karamel, specerijen, gist, zoetstof, water
%	6%	6%	6%
	dark brown	brun foncé	donkerbruin
	Hold the glass by the stem and tilt it slightly. Slowly pour in a single movement. Leave 1 cm of beer (sediment) in the bottle.	Tenir le verre en oblique par le pied et verser la bière lentement en un seul mouvement. Laisser 1 cm de bière (levure) dans la bouteille.	Het glas bij de voet schuin houden en het bier traag in 1 beweging uitschenken. 1 cm bier (depot) in het flesje laten.
°C	46 - 55 °F	8 - 13 °C	8 - 13 °C
	Session beer. Light sweet malt flavour, slightly bitter, caramel and liquorice.	Bière qui se boit facilement. Arôme malté légèrement doux, légèrement amer de caramel et réglisse.	Doordrinkbier. Licht zoet moutaroma, lichtjes bitter, karamel en zoethout.
i	The term "kapittel" (chapter) refers to a hierarchic structure in an abbey or convent.	Le terme 'kapittel' renvoie à la hiérarchie au sein d'une abbaye ou d'une monastère.	De term kapittel staat voor de hiërarchie binnen een abdij of klooster.

Kapittel
Watou

Het Kapittel Prior

	top-fermentation re-fermented in the bottle	fermentation haute refermentation en bouteille	hoge gisting nagisting op de fles
	abbey beer	bière d'abbaye	abdijbier
	Brouwerij Van Eecke Watou	Brouwerij Van Eecke Watou	Brouwerij Van Eecke Watou
	malt, caramel, spices, yeast, sweetener, water	malt, caramel, condiments, levure, édulcorant, eau	mout, karamel, specerijen, gist, zoetstof, water
%	9%	9%	9%
	dark brown	brun foncé	donkerbruin
	Hold the glass by its stem and tilt slightly. Slowly pour in a single movement. Leave 1 cm of beer (sediment) in the bottle.	Tenir le verre légèrement en oblique par le pied et verser la bière lentement en un seul mouvement. Laisser 1 cm de bière (levure) dans la bouteille.	Het glas bij de voet schuin houden en het bier traag in 1 beweging uitschenken. 1 cm bier (depot) in het flesje laten.
°C	46 - 55 °F	8 - 13 °C	8 - 13 °C
	Full-bodied and solid with an impressive aromatic palette. Alcohol, chocolate, spices, slightly roasted malts. Light bitter aftertaste with a sweet touch near the end.	Franc et corsé avec une palette de parfums impressionnante. Alcool, chocolat, épices, malts légèrement brûlés. Fin de bouche légèrement amère avec une touche finale douce.	Volmondig en stevig met een indrukwekkend geurenpalet. Alcohol, chocolade, specerijen, licht gebrande mouten. Licht bittere afdronk met zoete toets op het einde.
i	–	–	–

Kapittel
Kapittel
Watou
Prior
Kapittel
Watou

Hik blond

	top-fermentation re-fermented in the bottle	fermentation haute refermentation en bouteille	hoge gisting hergisting op de fles
	Ale unpasteurised	ale non pasteurisée	ale niet gepasteuriseerd
	at Picobrouwerij Alvinne het Alternatief Izegem	chez Picobrouwerij Alvinne het Alternatief Izegem	bij Picobrouwerij Alvinne Het Alternatief Izegem
	three malt varieties (Pilsener, Munich, wheat), three hop varieties, yeast, herbs, brewing water. No additives.	3 variétés de malt (pils, Munich, froment), 3 sortes de houblon, levure, herbes, eau de brassage. Pas d'additifs.	3 soorten mout (pils, munich, tarwe), 3 hopsoorten, gist, kruiden, brouwwater. Geen additieven.
%	6,50%	6,50%	6,50%
	blond (11 EBC) unfiltered	blonde (11 EBC) non filtrée	blond (11 EBC) niet gefilterd
	Pour carefully in the Alternatief glass.	Verser prudemment dans le verre Alternatief.	Voorzichtig uitschenken in het Alternatiefglas.
°C	43 - 46 °F	6 - 8 °C	6 - 8 °C
	A lively full-malt beer with a full-bodied, fruity and bitter character. Taste and aroma: citrus, fruity, bitterness.	Une bière vive pleinement maltée avec un caractère franc fruité et amer. Saveur et arôme: agrumes, fruits, amertume.	Een levend volmoutbier met een volmondig fruitig en bitter karakter. Smaak en aroma: citrus, fruitig, bitterheid.
i	–	–	–

....

....

....

HiK
BiER
Het alternatief

Hik bruin

	top-fermentation re-fermented in the bottle	fermentation haute refermentation en bouteille	hoge gisting hergisting op de fles
	between dubbel and Stout unpasteurised	entre double et stout non pasteurisée	tussen dubbel en stout niet gepasteuriseerd
	at Picobrouwerij Alvinne Het Alternatief Izegem	chez Picobrouwerij Alvinne Het Alternatief Izegem	bij Picobrouwerij Alvinne Het Alternatief Izegem
	6 malt varieties (including Pilsner and chocolate malt), 3 hop varieties, yeast, candy sugar, brewing water, no additives	6 variétés de malt (e.a. malt de pils et de chocolat), 3 sortes de houblon, levure, sucre candi, eau de brassage, pas d'additifs	6 soorten mout (o.a. pils- en chocolademout), 3 hopsoorten, gist, kandijsuiker, brouwwater, geen additieven
%	6,50%	6,50%	6,50%
	dark brown (165 EBC) unfiltered	brun foncé (165 EBC) non filtrée	donkerbruin (165 EBC) niet gefilterd
	Pour carefully in the Alternatief glass.	Verser prudemment dans le verre Alternatief.	Voorzichtig uitschenken in het Alternatiefglas.
°C	46 - 50 °F	8 - 10 °C	8 - 10 °C
	A lively, unsweetened beer, full-bodied and dry. Many flavour nuances, including hop bitter and chocolate bitter.	Une bière vive non sucrée franche et sèche. Beaucoup de nuances de saveur dont amer-houblon et amer-chocolat.	Een levend, niet zoet bier dat volmondig en droog is. Veel smaaknuances waaronder hopbitter en chocoladebitter.
i	–	–	–

HiK
BiER
BRUiN

Himelein

	top-fermentation re-fermented in the bottle	fermentation haute refermentation en bouteille	hoge gisting hergisting op de fles
	dark	foncée	donker
	Brouwerij Vissenaken Vissenaken-Tienen	Brouwerij Vissenaken Vissenaken-Tienen	Brouwerij Vissenaken Vissenaken-Tienen
	barley malt, hops, sugar, yeast, brewing water. Boutique beer.	malt d'orge, houblon, sucre, levure, eau de brassage. Brassage artisanal.	gerstemout, hop, suiker, gist, brouwwater. Ambachtelijk gebrouwen.
%	6%	6%	6%
	dark brown unfiltered	brun foncé non filtrée	donkerbruin ongefilterd
	Slowly pour into a bulb jar, with or without yeast.	Verser lentement dans un verre ballon, avec ou sans levure.	Langzaam inschenken in een bolvormig glas, met of zonder gist.
°C	46 - 54 °F	8 - 12 °C	8 - 12 °C
	Savoury thirst-quencher. Sweet but not sticky, full malt taste with a bitter nuance and a fruity touch.	Désaltérant savoureux. Doux mais pas collant, goût malté plein avec une nuance amère et une touche fruitée.	Smaakvolle dorstlesser. Zoet maar niet plakkerig, volle moutsmaak met een bittere nuance en fruitige toets.
i	Store upright at cellar temperature. The taste evolution is at its best from three months after the bottling date onwards.	Conserver en position verticale à température de cave. Ce n'est que 3 mois après la date de la mise en bouteilles que la saveur arrive à son sommet.	Rechtop bewaren op keldertemperatuur. Pas 3 maanden na botteldatum is de smaak geëvolueerd tot op zijn best.

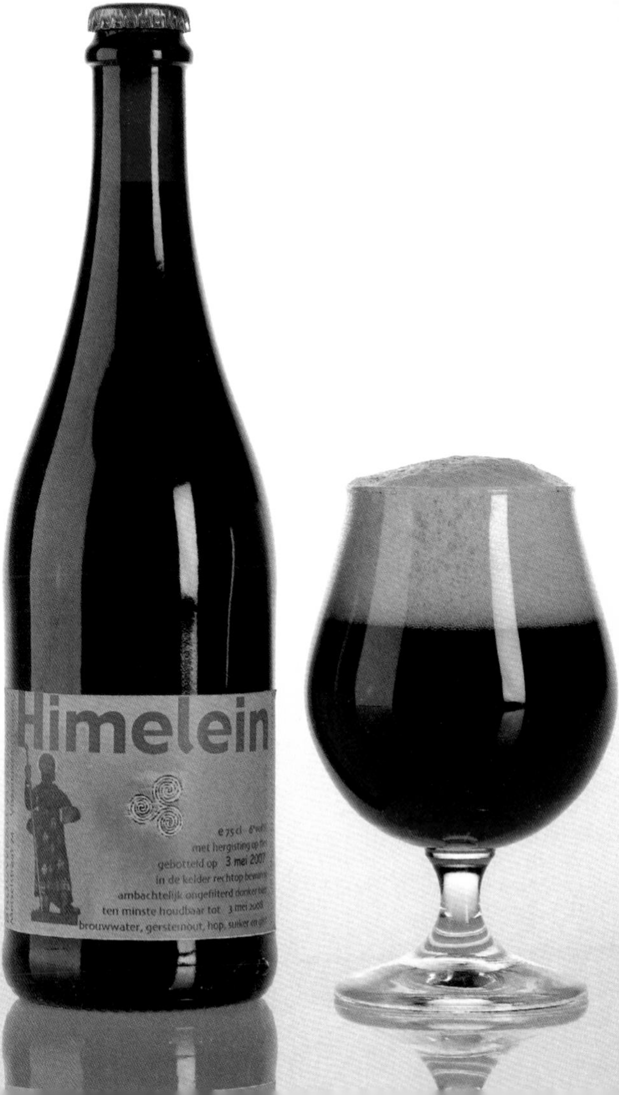

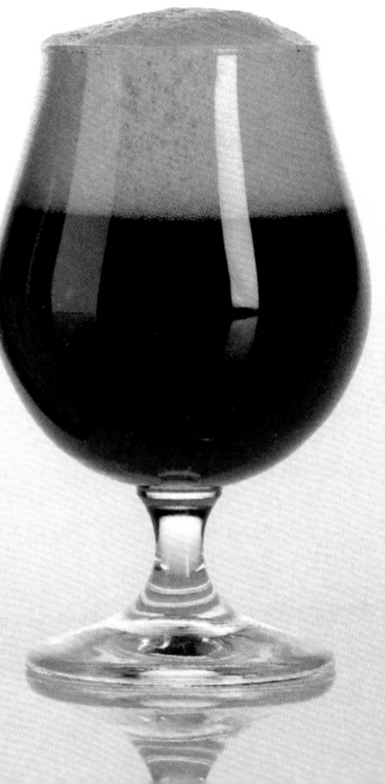

Himelein
e 75 cl
met hergisting op
gebotteld op 3 mei 2007
in de kelder rechtop
ambachtelijk ongefilterd donker
ten minste houdbaar tot 3 mei 2008
brouwwater, gerstemout, hop, suiker en

Hoegaarden Grand Cru

	top-fermentation re-fermented in the bottle	fermentation haute refermentation en bouteille	hoge gisting hergisting op de fles
	strong blond	blonde forte	sterk blond
	Inbev Belgium Brewsite Jupiler	Inbev Belgium Brewsite Jupiler	Inbev Belgium Brewsite Jupiler
	wheat, malt, hops, yeast, coriander, orange rind, water	froment, malt, houblon, levure, coriandre, écorce d'orange, eau	tarwe, mout, hop, gist, koriander, sinaasappelschil water
%	8,70%	8,70%	8,70%
	peach-yellow cloudy yeast veil	jaune pêche voile de levure trouble	perzikgeel troebele gistsluier
	Rinse the glass in cold water, tilt it and smoothly pour the beer. Skim off if desired	Rincer le verre à l'eau froide, le tenir incliné et verser la bière doucement. Ecumer selon le goût.	Het glas onder koud water spoelen, schuin houden en het bier zacht uitschenken. Desgewenst afschuimen.
°C	41 °F	5 °C	5 °C
	Fruity aroma and taste bouquet, warm aftertaste. Subtle and complex beer with a high alcohol content.	Arômes et bouquet de saveurs fruités, fin de bouche chaleureuse. Bière de dégustation subtile et complexe.	Fruitig aroma en smaakboeket, warme afdronk. Subtiel en complex degustatiebier.
i	In the near future, this beer wil be brewed in Hoegaarden again.	Bientôt, cette bière sera à nouveau brassée à Hoegaarden.	Binnenkort wordt dit bier terug in Hoegaarden gebrouwen.

Hoegaarden
Grand Cru

Hoegaarden
Grand Cru

Hoegaarden Rosée

	top-fermentation re-fermented in the bottle	fermentation haute refermentation en bouteille	hoge gisting hergisting op de fles
	Witbier aromatised	bière blanche aromatisée	witbier gearomatiseerd
	Inbev Belgium Brewsite Jupiler	Inbev Belgium Brewsite Jupiler	Inbev Belgium Brewsite Jupiler
	wheat, pale malt, corn, hops, yeast, coriander, orange rind, water, seasoned with herbs and natural raspberry flavour, sugar, minimum 10% fruit.	froment, malt pâle, maïs, houblon, levure, coriandre, écorce d'orange, eau, aromatisé aux herbes et à l'arôme naturel de framboises, sucre, 10% fruits minimum	tarwe, bleekmout, mais, hop, gist, koriander, sinaasschil, water, gearomatiseerd met kruiden en natuurlijk frambozenaroma, suiker, 10% fruit minimum
%	4,50%	4,50%	4,50%
	light pink, cloudy	rose clair trouble	lichtroze troebel
	Rinse the glass with cold water. Tilt it and pour half of the beer with sufficient foam. Loosen the yeast sediment from the bottom by firmly spinning the bottle and continue pouring until the creamy foam head reaches the edge of the glass. Skim off if desired.	Rincer le verre à l'eau froide, le tenir en oblique et verser la moitié de la bière avec suffisamment d'écume. Dégager le dépôt de levure en tournant fort et continuer à verser jusqu'à ce que le faux col crémeux arrive au bord du verre. Ecumer selon le goût.	Het glas onder koud water spoelen, schuin houden en het bier half uitschenken met voldoende schuim. De gistbodem losmaken door de fles krachtig rond te walsen en verder uitschenken tot de romige kraag aan de glasrand komt. Desgewenst afschuimen.
°C	36 - 37 °F	2 - 3 °C	2 - 3 °C
	–	–	–
i	In the near future, this beer will be brewed in Hoegaarden again.	Bientôt, cette bière sera à nouveau brassée à Hoegaarden.	Binnenkort wordt dit bier terug in Hoegaarden gebrouwen.
	....		

Hoegaarden
Rosée
Hoegaarden

Hoegaarden speciale

	top-fermentation re-fermented in the bottle	fermentation haute refermentation en bouteille	hoge gisting hergisting op de fles
	strong blond beer	bière blonde forte	sterk blond bier
	Inbev Belgium Brewsite Jupiler	Inbev Belgium Brewsite Jupiler	Inbev Belgium Brewsite Jupiler
	wheat, light roasted malts, hops, yeast, coriander, orange rind, water	froment, malt légèrement brûlé, houblon, levure, coriandre, écorce d'orange, eau	tarwe, licht gebrande mouten, hop, gist, koriander, sinaasappelschil, water
%	5,50%	5,50%	5,50%
	golden blond cloudy yeast veil	blond doré voile de levure trouble	goudblond troebele gistsluier
	Rinse the glass in cold water, tilt it and smoothly pour the beer. Skim off if desired.	Rincer le verre à l'eau froide, le tenir incliné et verser la bière doucement. Ecumer selon le goût.	Het glas onder koud water spoelen, schuin houden en het bier zacht uitschenken. Desgewenst afschuimen.
°C	36 - 37 °F	2 - 3 °C	2 - 3 °C
	Sweeter and warmer than the common Hoegaarden witbier. Ample and deep nose with malt and fine hops. Bitter, long-lasting taste that covers the spiciness.	Plus doux et chaleureux que la Hoegaarden Blanche ordinaire. Parfum large et profond de malt et de houblon raffiné. Saveur amère qui reste longtemps en bouche et qui couvre le goût relevé.	Zoeter en warmer dan het gewone Hoegaarden Witbier. Ruime en diepe neus met mout en fijne hop. Bittere smaak die lang in de mond blijft en de kruidigheid toedekt.
i	In the near future, this beer will be brewed in Hoegaarden again.	Bientôt, cette bière sera à nouveau brassée à Hoegaarden.	Binnenkort wordt dit bier terug in Hoegaarden gebrouwen.

Hoegaarden
SPECIALE
Hoegaarden
SPECIALE
Goudblond Witbier • Bière Blanche Dorée
25cl
Hoegaarden
SPECIALE

Hoegaarden Verboden Vrucht

	top-fermentation re-fermented in the bottle	fermentation haute refermentation en bouteille	hoge gisting hergisting op de fles
	strong dark	foncée forte	sterk donker
	Inbev Belgium Brewsite Jupiler	Inbev Belgium Brewsite Jupiler	Inbev Belgium Brewsite Jupiler
	dark malt, hops, yeast, coriander, water	malt foncé, houblon, levure, coriandre, eau	donkere mout, hop, gist, koriander, water
%	8,80%	8,80%	8,80%
	brown-red very compact foam head	brun rouge faux col très épais	bruinrood zeer dichte schuimkraag
	Rinse the glass in cold water, tilt it and smoothly pour the beer. Skim off if desired.	Rincer le verre à l'eau froide, le tenir incliné et verser la bière doucement. Ecumer selon le goût.	Het glas onder koud water spoelen, schuin houden en het bier zacht uitschenken. Desgewenst afschuimen.
°C	41 °F	5 °C	5 °C
	Assertive onset with a very smooth, gratifying end. Spicy plant flavour, sweet but especially dry with a coriander accent, full in the mouth.	Début assertif, fin très douce et caressante. Arôme de plantes relevé, doux mais surtout sec avec un accent de coriandre plein dans la bouche.	Assertieve start maar zeer zacht en strelend einde. Kruidig plantenaroma, zoet maar vooral droog met korianderaccent, vol in de mond.
i	In the near future, this beer will be brewed in Hoegaarden again.	Bientôt, cette bière sera à nouveau brassée à Hoegaarden.	Binnenkort wordt dit bier terug in Hoegaarden gebrouwen.

DE VERBODEN VRUCHT
bier op gist
bière sur levure
LE FRUIT DEFENDU
DE VERBODEN VRUCHT · LE FRUIT DEFENDU
Br HOEGAARDEN

Hoegaarden wit

	top-fermentation re-fermented in the bottle	fermentation haute refermentation en bouteille	hoge gisting hergisting op de fles
	Witbier	bière blanche	witbier
	Inbev Belgium Brewsite Jupiler	Inbev Belgium Brewsite Jupiler	Inbev Belgium Brewsite Jupiler
	wheat, pale malt, corn, hops, yeast, coriander, orange rind, water	froment, malt pâle, maïs, houblon, levure, coriandre, écorce d'orange, eau	tarwe, bleekmout, maïs, hop, gist, koriander, sinaasappelschil, water
	4,90%	4,90%	4,90%
	white-yellow with cloudy yeast veil	blanc jaune avec une voile de levure trouble	witgeel met troebele gistsluier
	Rinse the glass in cold water, tilt it and pour half of the bottle creating sufficient foam. Loosen the yeast sediment by firmly revolving the bottle and continue filling the glass until the creamy head reaches the rim of the glass. Skim off if desired	Rincer le verre à l'eau froide, le tenir incliné et verser la moitié de la bière avec suffisamment d'écume. Dégager le dépôt de levure en secouant fort la bouteille et continuer à verser jusqu'à ce que le col crémeux atteigne le bord du verre. Ecumer selon le goût.	Het glas onder koud water spoelen, schuin houden en het bier half uitschenken met voldoende schuim. De gistbodem losmaken door de fles krachtig rond te walsen en verder uitschenken tot de romige kraag aan de glasrand komt. Desgewenst afschuimen.
	36 - 37 °F	2 - 3 °C	2 - 3 °C
	Spicy, fresh aroma and taste with a strong coriander accent.	Arôme relevé et frais avec accent de coriandre prononcé.	Kruidig en fris aroma met sterk korianderaccent.
	In the near future, this beer will be brewed in Hoegaarden again.	Bientôt, cette bière sera à nouveau brassée à Hoegaarden.	Binnenkort wordt dit bier terug in Hoegaarden gebrouwen.

ORIGINEEL BELGISCH WITBIER
Hoegaarden
witbier-bière blanche
BIÈRE BLANCHE BELGE ORIGINALE

Hoegaarden

Hofblues

	top-fermentation	fermentation haute	hoge gisting
	Stout	stout	stout
	't Hofbrouwerijke Beerzel	't Hofbrouwerijke Beerzel	't Hofbrouwerijke Beerzel
	malt, hops, yeast, water	malt, houblon, levure, eau	mout, hop, gist, water
	5,50%	5,50%	5,50%
	dark to black dark foam head	foncée à noire faux col foncé	donker tot zwart donkere schuimkraag
	Pour carefully, leaving 1 cm in the bottle.	Verser prudemment et laisser 1 cm de bière dans la bouteille.	Voorzichtig uitschenken en 1 cm in het flesje laten.
	50 °F	10 °C	10 °C
	Spicy and hoppy. Nose of mocca, a well-balanced bitterness and a slightly roasty taste.	Corsé et houblonné. Parfum de moka, saveur amère équilibrée et touche de goût légèrement brûlée.	Pittig en hoppig. Neus van mokka, een evenwichtige bitterheid en een lichtgebrande smaaktoets.
	–	–	–

't Hofbrouwerijke
hofblues

't Hofbrouwerijke

Hofdraak

	top-fermentation	fermentation haute	hoge gisting
	Dubbel	double	dubbel
	't Hofbrouwerijke Beerzel	't Hofbrouwerijke Beerzel	't Hofbrouwerijke Beerzel
	malt, hops, yeast, herbs, water	malt, houblon, levure, herbes, eau	mout, hop, gist, kruiden, water
%	6,20%	6,20%	6,20%
	dark clear	foncée, claire	donker helder
	Pour carefully, leaving 1 cm in the bottle.	Verser prudemment et laisser 1 cm de bière dans la bouteille.	Voorzichtig uitschenken en 1 cm in het flesje laten.
°C	50 - 54 °F	10 - 12 °C	10 - 12 °C
	Full and spicy. Full-bodied with a malty touch and a slightly bitter finish with a spicy aftertaste.	Plein et relevé. Franc avec une touche maltée et une note finale légèrement amère, fin de bouche relevée.	Vol kruidig. Volmondig met een moutige toets en een licht bittere eindnoot die kruidig uitvloeit.
i	–	–	–

't Hofbrouwerijke
hofdraak

Hofelf

	top-fermentation	fermentation haute	hoge gisting
	wheat Tripel	triple de froment	tarwetripel
	't Hofbrouwerijke Beerzel	't Hofbrouwerijke Beerzel	't Hofbrouwerijke Beerzel
	malt, hops, yeast, herbs, water	malt, houblon, levure, herbes, eau	mout, hop, gist, kruiden, water
	7,50%	7,50%	7,50%
	blond cloudy Witbier creamy foam head	blonde bière blanche trouble faux col crémeux	blond troebel witbier romige schuimkraag
	Pour carefully, leaving 1 cm in the bottle.	Verser prudemment et laisser 1 cm de bière dans la bouteille.	Voorzichtig uitschenken en 1 cm in het flesje laten.
	50 - 54 °F	10 - 12 °C	10 - 12 °C
	Slightly sourish but with a sweet touch of wheat malt. Full-bodied.	Légèrement acidulé avec une touche douce de froment malté. Franc.	Zachtzurig maar met zoete toets van tarwemout. Volmondig.
	–	–	–

't Hofbrouwerijke
hofelf

't Hofbrouwerijke

Hoftrol

	top-fermentation	fermentation haute	hoge gisting
	Ale	ale	ale
	't Hofbrouwerijke Beerzel	't Hofbrouwerijke Beerzel	't Hofbrouwerijke Beerzel
	malt, hops, yeast, herbs, water	malt, houblon, levure, herbes, eau	mout, hop, gist, kruiden, water
%	6,50%	6,50%	6,50%
	amber slightly cloudy, unfiltered	ambrée légèrement trouble, non filtrée	amber licht troebel, ongefilterd
	Pour carefully, leaving 1 cm in the bottle.	Verser prudemment et laisser 1 cm de bière dans la bouteille.	Voorzichtig uitschenken en 1 cm in het flesje laten.
°C	43 - 54 °F	6 - 12 °C	6 - 12 °C
	Bitter and hoppy character. Dry beer with a fresh slightly sourish flavour (owing to the special yeast stem). Wood flavour and a refreshing, bitter aftertaste.	Caractère amer et houblonné. Bière sèche avec un goût frais légèrement acidulé (type de levure spéciale). Arôme boisé et fin de bouche amère et rafraîchissante.	Bitter en hoppig karakter. Droog biertje met een frisse lichtzurigheid (speciale giststam). Houtaroma en verfrissend bittere afdronk.
i	–	–	–

't Hofbrouwerijke
hoftrol

't Hofbrouwerijke

Hommelbier

	top-fermentation re-fermented in the bottle	fermentation haute refermentation en bouteille	hoge gisting nagisting op de fles
	regional beer	bière régionale	streekbier
	Brouwerij Van Eecke Watou	Brouwerij Van Eecke Watou	Brouwerij Van Eecke Watou
	malt, spices, hops, yeast, water, 3 types of regional hops, including 1 used for dry-hopping	malt, condiments, houblon, levure, eau, 3 types de houblon régional dont un utilisé pour dryhopping	mout, specerijen, hop, gist, water, 3 types regionale hop waarvan 1 gebruikt voor dryhopping
%	7,50%	7,50%	7,50%
	light bronze	couleur bronze claire	licht bronskleurig
	Hold the glass by the stem and tilt it. Pour slowly in a single movement. Either pour the yeast sediment or leave it in the bottle.	Tenir le verre en oblique par le pied et verser la bière lentement en un seul mouvement. Verser le dépôt de levure selon le goût.	Het glas bij de voet schuin houden en het bier traag in 1 beweging uitschenken. Het gistdepot kan naar keuze al dan niet worden uitgeschonken.
°C	43 - 46 °F	6 - 8 °C	6 - 8 °C
	Very refreshing hop character. Very bitter with flowery hop flavours.	Caractère houblonné très rafraîchissant. Goût amer prononcé et arômes houblonnés fleuris.	Zeer verfrissend hopkarakter. Hoge bitterheid en bloemige hoparoma's.
i	–	–	–

5 412896 000012
poperings
hommel
bier
Belgian beer
poperings
hommel
bier

poperings
hommel
bier

Hoogstraten Poorter

	top-fermentation re-fermented in the bottle	fermentation haute refermentation en bouteille	hoge gisting hergisting in de fles
	Dubbel abbey beer	bière d'abbaye double	dubbel abdijbier
	Collega-brouwers for Brouwerij Sterkens Meer	Collega-brouwers pour Brouwerij Sterkens Meer	Collega-brouwers voor Brouwerij Sterkens Meer
	malt, hops, yeast, water	malt, houblon, levure, eau	mout, hop, gist, water
%	6,50%	6,50%	6,50%
	dark brown, filtered	brun foncé, filtrée	donkerbruin, gefilterd
	Carefully serve in the sipping glass, with a generous foam head.	Verser prudemment dans un verre de dégustation avec un faux col solide.	Voorzichtig uitschenken in het degustatieglas met een ruime schuimkraag.
°C	43 - 50 °F	6 - 10 °C	6 - 10 °C
	Solid and powerful. Slightly sweet with caramel touches. Taste: alcohol and hops with a touch of chocolate and roasted malt. Dry aftertaste.	Solide et fort. Légèrement doux avec des touches caramélisées. Saveur: alcool et houblon avec une touche de chocolat et de malt brûlée. Fin de bouche sèche.	Stevig en krachtig. Lichtzoetig met toetsen van karamel. Smaak: alcohol en hop met een vleugje chocolade en gebrande mout. Droge afdronk.
i	More than 90% is destined for export. For four years, production and bottling have been taking place temporarily at Du Bocq and other breweries.	Plus de 90% de la production est exporté. Depuis quatre ans, la production et la mise en bouteilles se font provisoirement chez du Bocq et d'autres brasseries.	Meer dan 90% is bestemd voor export. Productie en bottelen gebeurt sinds een viertal jaar (voorlopig) bij Du Bocq en andere brouwerijen.

1210 - POORTER - 1985
℮75 CL - 1 Pt. 9.4 Fl.Oz.
1210 - POORTER - 1985
HOOGSTRATEN
PORTER - PRODUCT OF BELGIUM

Ichtegem's Grand Cru

	mixed top-fermentation centrifuged	fermentation haute mixte centrifugée	gemengde hoge gisting gecentrifugeerd
	West-Flanders red-brown	brune-rouge de la Flandre-Occidentale	Westvlaams roodbruin
	Brouwerij Strubbe Ichtegem	Brouwerij Strubbe Ichtegem	Brouwerij Strubbe Ichtegem
	80% Pilsner malt, 10% caramel malt, 10% Munich malt, corn, sugar, yeast, water, more than one year old Poperinge hops, English Kent Golding, Styrian, Saaz Zatec. After two years' lagering the beer is blended with a young, sweet beer (40%).	80% malt de pils, 10% malt caramélisé, 10% malt Munich, maïs, sucre, levure, eau, houblon suranné de Poperinge, Kent Golding anglais, Styrian, Saaz Zatec. Après 2 ans de conservation, la bière est mélangée à une bière jeune et douce (40%).	80% pilsmout, 10% karamelmout, 10% munichmout, mais, suiker, gist, water, hop (overjaarse Poperingse hop, Engelse Kent Golding, Styrian, Saaz Zatec). Na 2 jaar lagering wordt het bier gemengd met een jong en zoet bier (40%).
%	6,50%, 15° plato	6,50%, 15° plato	6,50%, 15° plato
	red-brown, filtered	brun rouge, filtrée	roodbruin, gefilterd
	–	–	–
°C	43 °F	6 °C	6 °C
	Refreshing wood taste (18 months' lagering in oak barrels).	Goût boisé et rafraîchissant (conservée 18 mois en fûts de chêne).	Verfrissend, houtsmaak (18 maand gelagerd op eikenhout).
i	The oak barrels come from the Bordeaux region, where they were used once to store wine.	Les fûts en bois de chêne proviennent de la région de Bordeaux et ont été utilisés une fois pour le vin.	De eikenhouten vaten komen uit de regio van Bordeaux en werden 1 maal voor wijn gebruikt.

175
STRUBBE
Ichtegem's
Grand Cru
Flemish Red Ale
matured in oak barrels
Oud Bruin gerijpt in eiken vaten
Product of Belgium
ingr: water, malt, caramalt, rice, hops, yeast

STRUBBE
Ichtegem

Ichtegem's Oud Bruin

	mixed and top-fermentation	fermentation haute et mixte	gemengde en hoge gisting
	West-Flanders red-brown	brune-rouge de la Flandre-Occidentale	Westvlaams roodbruin
	Brouwerij Strubbe Ichtegem	Brouwerij Strubbe Ichtegem	Brouwerij Strubbe Ichtegem
	75% Pilsner malt, 20% amber malt, 5% caramel malt, corn, yeast, water. More than one year old hops from Poperinge. Matured in oak barrels for 12 months	75% malt de pils, 20% malt ambré, 5% malt caramélisé, maïs, levure, eau. Houblon suranné de Poperinge. Mûrie en fûts de chêne pendant 12 mois.	75% pilsmout, 20% ambermout, 5% karamelmout, mais, gist, water. Overjaarse hop uit Poperinge. 12 maanden gerijpt op eiken vaten.
	5,50%	5,50%	5,50%
	red-brown filtered	brun rouge filtrée	roodbruin gefilterd
	–	–	–
	43 °F	6 °C	6 °C
	Sweet-and-sour, refreshing.	Aigre-doux, rafraîchissant.	Zoetzuur, verfrissend.
	After the primary fermentation, 80% of the beer is stored for lagering for about two months. The rest undergoes a spontaneous lactic acid fermentation. This process can last up to 18 months.	Après la fermentation principale, 80% de la bière est stocké pour environ 2 mois. Le reste subit une fermentation spontanée d'acide lactique dans des réservoirs. Ce processus peut durer 18 mois.	Na de hoofdgisting gaat 80% in lagering voor ca. 2 maanden. De rest ondergaat een spontane melkzure gisting in de bewaartanks. Dit proces kan tot 18 maanden duren.

Ichtegem's
gerijpt in eiken vaten
Alc. vol 5,5 %
OUD BRUIN
NATUURLIJK BIER VAN HOGE GISTING
GEBROUWEN NAAR OUDE TRADITIE

OUD BRUIN

Iris

	spontaneous fermentation re-fermented in the bottle by adding liqueur.	fermentation spontanée refermentation en bouteille par adjonction de liqueur	spontane gisting hergisting op de fles door toevoeging van likeur
	Lambic unblended	lambic non coupé	lambiek, onversneden
	Brouwerij Cantillon Brussels	Brouwerij Cantillon Bruxelles	Brouwerij Cantillon Brussel
	barley malt, Pale Ale type, 50% more than one year old hops, 50% fresh hops	malt d'orge type pale ale, 50% houblon suranné, 50% houblon frais	gerstemout type pale ale, 50% overjaarse hop, 50% verse hop
%	6%	6%	6%
	amber by the Pale Ale malt	ambré par le malt pale ale	amber door de pale ale-mou[t]
	The use of a wine basket is recommended if the bottle was stored horizontally. Place the bottle in upright position 48 hours before serving to decant the sediment.	Un panier verseur est recommandé si la bouteille a été conservée en position horizontale. Mettre la bouteille 48 heures avant de servir dans une position verticale pour faire descendre la levure.	Een schenkmandje is aangewezen wanneer de fles horizontaal bewaard werd. De fles 48 uur voor het uitschenken verticaal plaatse[n] om het bezinksel te decanteren.
°C	cellar temp. (54 - 61 °F)	temp. de cave (12 - 16 °C)	keldertemp. (12 - 16 °C)
	Well-balanced taste of sour and bitter, like wine. Bitter caramel owing to the malt and fruity because of the hops.	Saveur équilibrée acide et amère approchant le vin. Goût caramel amer par le malt et fruité par le houblon.	Evenwichtige smaak van zuur en bitter. De smaak neigt naar wijn. Bittere karamel door de mout en fru[i]tig door de hop.
i	The brewery has a bond with the city of Brussels, of which the iris is the symbol.	La brasserie a un lien étroit avec la ville de Bruxelles dont l'iris est le symbole.	De brouwerij heeft een nauwe band met Brussel, waarvan de iris het symbool is.

CANTILLON
Iris 2004

CANTILLON

Jan De Lichte 4-granen dubbel wit

	top-fermentation re-fermented in the bottle	fermentation haute refermentation en bouteille	hoge gisting nagisting op de fles
	Witbier	bière blanche	witbier
	Brouwerij De Glazen Toren Erpe-Mere	Brouwerij De Glazen Toren Erpe-Mere	Brouwerij De Glazen Toren Erpe-Mere
	barley malt, wheat malt, oat, buckwheat, water	malt d'orge, malt de froment, avoine, sarrasin, eau	gerstemout, tarwemout, haver, boekweit, water
%	7%	7%	7%
	hazy straw-yellow very sparkling	jaune paille voilé très pétillant	strogeel gesluierd sterk parelend
	Pour carefully into a dry, long glass (e.g. a tulip-shaped glass)	Verser prudemment dans un verre sec, oblong (par exemple tulipe).	Voorzichtig uitschenken in een droog, langwerpig (bijv. tulpvormig) glas.
°C	41 - 43 °F	5 - 6 °C	5 - 6 °C
	Spicy and slightly bitter. Grapefruit flavour and a velvety, dry aftertaste.	Aromatisé et légèrement amer. Arôme de pamplemousse et fin de bouche veloutée, sèche.	Kruidig en licht bitter. Aroma van pompelmoes en fluwelige, droge afdronk.
i	–	–	–

JAN
DE LICHTE
KLEINBROUWERIJ
DE GLAZEN TOREN
Dubbel wit

KLEINBROUWERIJ
DE GLAZEN TOREN

Jan van Gent

	top-fermentation unpasteurised	fermentation haute non pasteurisée	hoge gisting ongepasteuriseerd
	Spéciale Belge	spéciale belge	spéciale belge
	Brouwerij Liefmans Oudenaarde/Dentergem	Brouwerij Liefmans Audenarde/Dentergem	Brouwerij Liefmans Oudenaarde/Dentergem
	barley malt, corn, sugar, hops, yeast, water	malt d'orge, maïs, sucre, houblon, levure, eau	gerstemout, mais, suiker, hop, gist, water
%	5,50%	5,50%	5,50%
	amber-coloured slightly cloudy	ambrée légèrement trouble	amberkleurig licht troebel
	–	–	–
°C	43 - 50 °F	6 - 10 °C	6 - 10 °C
	Smooth taste of typical Liefmans yeast. Bittersweet taste with malty character. Roasted malt aroma.	Saveur douce de levure Liefmans typique. Goût doux-amer avec un caractère malté, arôme de malt grillé.	Zachte smaak van typische Liefmansgist. Bitterzoete smaak met moutkarakter, aroma van geroosterde mout.
i	–	–	–

Lifmans brouwsel
Jan van Gent
OUDENAARDE · BELGIUM

Jan van Gent

Jessenhofke

	top-fermentation re-fermented in the bottle	fermentation haute refermentation en bouteille	hoge gisting hergisting op de fles
	Belgian strong Ale	Belgian strong ale	Belgian strong ale
	De Proefbrouwerij for Jessenhofke Hasselt	De Proefbrouwerij pour Jessenhofke Hasselt	De Proefbrouwerij voor Jessenhofke Hasselt
	pilsner malt, crude wheat, 1 bitter hop variety, 2 varieties of aromatic hops, unrefined cane sugar, garlic, yeast, water	malt de pils, froment cru, 1 sorte de houblon amer, 2 sortes de houblon aromatiques, sucre de canne non raffiné, ail, levure, eau.	pilsmout, ruwe tarwe, 1 soort bitterhop, 2 soorten aromahop, ongeraffineerde rietsuiker, knoflook, gist, water
%	8%	8%	8%
	clear blond with a red shine	blond clair avec reflets rouges	helder blond met rode schij
	Pour into a bulb jar in a single movement, with or without yeast.	Verser en un seul mouvement dans un verre ballon avec ou sans levure.	In 1 beweging inschenken in een bolvormig glas, met of zonder gist.
°C	45 - 52 °F	7 - 11 °C	7 - 11 °C
	Perfectly well-balanced beer with unique taste sensation and full-bodied character. Spicy and dry with a light sweet touch.	Bière parfaitement équilibrée avec une sensation de goût unique et un caractère franc. Relevé, corsé, sec avec une touche légèrement douce.	Perfect evenwichtig bier met unieke smaaksensatie en volmondig karakter. Kruidig, pittig, droog met een lichtzoete toets.
i	Proclaimed "Best Amateur Beer" by the Limburgse Biervrienden (Zythos) in 2002.	Déclarée en 2002 meilleur brassage d'amateurs par les Limburgse Biervrienden (Zythos).	In 2002 uitgeroepen tot bes te amateurbrouwsel door de Limburgse Biervrienden (Zythos).

Jessenhofke
Jessenhofke
drink matig, doch regelmatig

Joseph

	top-fermentation re-fermented in the bottle	fermentation haute refermentation en bouteille	hoge gisting nagisting op de fles
	specialty beer spelt beer	bière spéciale bière d'épeautre	speciaalbier speltbier
	Brasserie de Silenrieux Silenrieux	Brasserie de Silenrieux Silenrieux	Brasserie de Silenrieux Silenrieux
	barley, spelt, hops, herbs, water	orge, épeautre, houblon, herbes, eau	gerst, spelt, hop, kruiden, water
%	5,40%	5,40%	5,40%
	blond cloudy (unfiltered) white, shiny foam head	blonde trouble (non filtrée) faux col blanc, brillant	blond troebel (niet gefilterd) witte, blinkende schuimkraag
	Softly revolve or shake the bottle before opening to obtain a cloudy beer.	Tourner légèrement ou secouer la bouteille avant de l'ouvrir pour obtenir une bière trouble.	De fles licht draaien of schudden voor het openen om een troebel bier te bekomen.
°C	45 - 50 °F	7 - 10 °C	7 - 10 °C
	Slightly fruity and smooth. Refreshing session beer.	Légèrement fruité et doux. Bière rafraîchissante qui se boit facilement.	Licht fruitig en zacht. Verfrissend doordrinkbier.
i	Also has an organic version. Spelt is an ancient grain and a predecessor of wheat. It is easy to grow.	Existe également en version BIO. L'épeautre est une vieille culture, prédécesseur du froment, dont la culture demande peu d'attention.	Bestaat ook in BIO-versie. Spelt is een oud gewas, de voorganger van tarwe. De teelt ervan vraagt weinig zorg.

JOSEPH
BRASSERIE
SILENRIEUX
Bière artisanale refermentée en bouteille.
Ambachtelijk bier met nagisting op fles.
Beer secondary fermentation in the bottle.
JOSEPH
Bière . Bier
Bière d'épeautre

Joup

	top-fermentation re-fermented in the bottle	fermentation haute refermentation en bouteille	hoge gisting hergisting in de fles
	regional beer	bière régionale	streekbier
	Brasserie Grain d'Orge Hombourt-Plombières	Brasserie Grain d'Orge Hombourt-Plombières	Brasserie Grain d'Orge Hombourt-Plombières
	malt varieties, hop varieties, yeast, sugar, herbs, water	variétés de malt et de houblon, levure, sucre, herbes, eau	moutsoorten, hopsoorten, gist, suiker, kruiden, water
%	7,50%	7,50%	7,50%
	brown with red hues	brune avec tintes rouges	bruin met rode tinten
	Leave the yeast sediment in the bottle.	Laisser le dépôt de levure dans la bouteille.	Het gistdepot in de fles laten.
°C	43 - 46 °F	6 - 8 °C	6 - 8 °C
	Smooth and round. Well-balanced hop taste with a variety of spices and caramel touches.	Doux et rond. Saveur houblonnée équilibrée avec une variété d'herbes et de touches caramélisées.	Zacht en rond. Evenwichtige hopsmaak met een variëteit aan kruiden en toetsen van karamel.
i	–	–	–

Bière brune artisanale
Joup
du Pays de Herve
* Aubel *

Brice & Joup
blonde & brune

Judas

	top-fermentation re-fermented in the bottle	fermentation haute refermentation en bouteille	hoge gisting hergisting op de fles
	strong blond	blonde forte	sterk blond
	Alken Maes corporation Alken	Alken Maes corporation Alken	Alken Maes corporation Alken
	–	–	–
%	8,50%	8,50%	8,50%
	ochre-blond	blond ocre	okerblond
	Pour carefully into a de-greased, dry glass. Fill the glass in one smooth movement for a nice, big foam head. Leave the yeast at the bottom of the bottle.	Verser soigneusement dans un verre dégraissé, sec. Remplir doucement le verre d'un seul trait pour obtenir un faux col solide. Laisser la levure au fond de la bouteille.	Zorgvuldig uitschenken in een ontvet, droog glas. Het glas in 1 beweging zachtjes vullen voor een grote schuimkraag. De gist op de bodem van de fles laten.
°C	43 - 50 °F	6 - 10 °C	6 - 10 °C
	Bittersweet, smooth and full-bodied.	Amer-doux, moelleux et franc.	Bitterzoet, zacht en volmondig.
i	–	–	–

Judas

Jules de Bananes

	top-fermentation re-fermented in the bottle	fermentation haute refermentation en bouteille	hoge gisting nagisting op de fles
	fruit beer	bière fruitée	fruitbier
	Brouwerij De Ryck Herzele	Brouwerij De Ryck Herzele	Brouwerij De Ryck Herzele
	malt, hops, yeast, sucrose, natural banana flavours, milk base, sweeteners, water	malt, houblon, levure, sucrose, saveurs naturelles de banane, base de lait, édulcorants, eau	mout, hop, gist, sucrose, natuurlijke bananenflavors, melkbasis, zoetstoffen, water
%	4,90%	4,90%	4,90%
	white banana colour	couleur banane blanche	witte bananenkleur
	Rinse the glass with cold water, take it by the stem and tilt it slightly. Pour slowly in a single movement, avoiding contact between bottle and glass or foam. Empty the bottle.	Rincer le verre à l'eau froide et le tenir légèrement en oblique par le pied. Verser la bière lentement et complètement, en un seul mouvement sans que la bouteille touche le verre ou l'écume.	Het glas koud spoelen, bij de voet vastnemen en licht schuin houden. Het bier traag en in 1 beweging inschenken zonder dat de fles het glas of schuim raakt. Het flesje volledig uitschenken.
°C	37 - 39 °F	3 - 4 °C	3 - 4 °C
	Refreshing and summery. Overwhelmingly sweet fruity banana flavour, with a clear and beer-like aftertaste.	Rafraîchissant et estival. Arôme dominant, fruité et doux de bananes, fin de bouche avec saveur de bière.	Verfrissend en zomers. Overweldigend zoetfruitig bananenaroma, duidelijke en bierige afdronk.
i	–	–	–

Jules
de
bananes
banana beer
brewery DE RYCK
DE RYCK

Jules de Kriek

	top-fermentation re-fermented in the bottle	fermentation haute refermentation en bouteille	hoge gisting nagisting op de fles
	fruit beer	bière fruitée	fruitbier
	Brouwerij De Ryck Herzele	Brouwerij De Ryck Herzele	Brouwerij De Ryck Herzele
	malt, hops, yeast, sucrose, natural cherry flavours, milk base, sweeteners, water	malt, houblon, levure, sucrose, goûts naturels de cerises, lait, édulcorants, eau	mout, hop, gist, sucrose, natuurlijke kriekenflavors, melkbasis, zoetstoffen, water
%	4,90%	4,90%	4,90%
	pink-red	rouge rose	rozerood
	Rinse the glass with cold water, take it by the stem and tilt it slightly. Pour slowly in a single movement, avoiding contact between bottle and glass or foam. Either leave the 1 cm yeast sediment in the bottle or pour it out along with the beer.	Rincer le verre à l'eau froide et le tenir légèrement en oblique par le pied. Verser la bière lentement et en un seul mouvement sans que la bouteille touche le verre ou l'écume. Laisser un dépôt de levure de 1 cm dans la bouteille ou la vider.	Het glas koud spoelen, bij de voet vastnemen en licht schuin houden. Het bier traag en in 1 beweging inschenken zonder dat de fles het glas of schuim raakt. Het gistdepot van 1 cm in de fles laten ofwel uitschenken.
°C	37 - 39 °F	3 - 4 °C	3 - 4 °C
	Refreshing and summery. Pronounced cherry aroma and taste, sweet and full-bodied. The fruity character does not take away the taste of beer.	Rafraîchissant et estival. Parfum et saveur prononcés de cerise avec un goût franc doux. La saveur de bière reste malgré le caractère fruité.	Verfrissend en zomers. Geprononceerde kriekengeur en -smaak met zoete volmondigheid. De biersmaak blijft ondanks het fruitige karakter.
i	–	–	–

Jules
de kriek
kriek beer
brewery DE RYCK
KRIEK
DE RYCK

Jupiler

	bottom-fermentation	fermentation basse	lage gisting
	Pilsner	pils	pilsbier
	Inbev Belgium Brewsite Jupiler	Inbev Belgium Brewsite Jupiler	Inbev Belgium Brewsite Jupiler
	pale malt, corn, hops, yeast, water	malt pâle, maïs, houblon, levure, eau	bleekmout, maïs, hop, gist, water
%	5,20%	5,20%	5,20%
	gold-coloured	dorée	goudkleurig
	Rinse the glass in cold water, tilt it and smoothly pour the beer. Skim off if desired.	Rincer le verre à l'eau froide, le tenir incliné et verser la bière doucement. Ecumer selon le goût.	Het glas onder koud water spoelen, schuin houden en het bier zacht uitschenken. Desgewenst afschuimen.
°C	37 °F	3 °C	3 °C
	Light taste but with a full malt mouthfeel. Fresh and slightly fruity (a touch of cherry and nut), with a smooth aftertaste.	Saveur légère avec une sensation maltée pleine dans la bouche. Frais et légèrement fruité (un peu de cerise et de noix), fin de bouche douce.	Licht van smaak maar met een vol moutig mondgevoel Fris en licht fruitig (tikkeltje kers en noot), zachte afdronk.
i	–	–	–

SERVIR FRAIS
KOEL SCHENKEN
BRASSERIE
BROUWERIJ
Jupiler
BREWED AND BOTTLED IN BELGIUM
BIERE • BIER • BEER
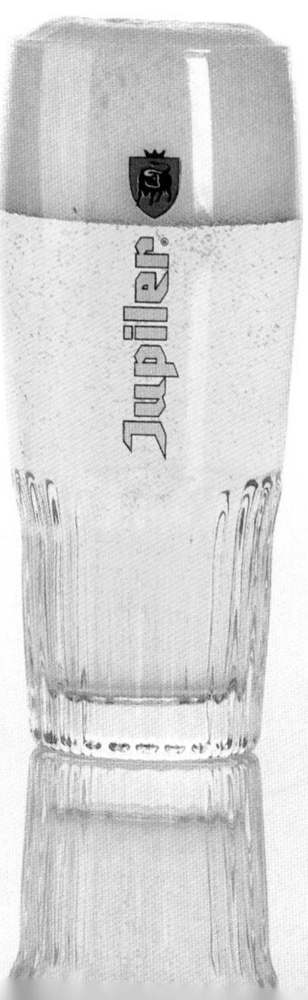
Jupiler

Jupiler blue

	bottom-fermentation	fermentation basse	lage gisting
	Pilsner	pils	pilsbier
	Inbev Belgium Brewsite Jupiler	Inbev Belgium Brewsite Jupiler	Inbev Belgium Brewsite Jupiler
	malt, corn, hops, brew-ing water	malt, maïs, houblon, eau de brassage	mout, maïs, hop, brouw-water
%	3,30%	3,30%	3,30%
	gold-coloured	dorée	goudkleurig
	Rinse the glass in cold wa-ter, tilt it and smoothly pour the beer. Skim off if desired.	Rincer le verre à l'eau froi-de, le tenir incliné et verser la bière doucement. Ecu-mer selon le goût.	Het glas onder koud water spoelen, schuin houden en het bier zacht uitschenken. Desgewenst afschuimen.
°C	37 °F	3 °C	3 °C
	Light taste but with a full malt mouthfeel. Refresh-ing, smooth and slight-ly fruity.	Saveur légère avec une sensation maltée pleine dans la bouche. Rafraî-chissant, doux et légère-ment fruité.	Licht van smaak maar met een vol moutig mondge-voel. Verfrissend, zacht en licht gefruit.
i	–	–	–

Jupiler
BLUE
BRASSERIE
Jupiler
BLUE
BIERE BLONDE
BLOND BIER
25 cl
ALC. 3.3% Vol.

Jupiler
BLUE

Kameleon amber

	top-fermentation re-fermented in the bottle	fermentation haute refermentation en bouteille	hoge gisting hergisting op de fles
	amber	ambrée	amber
	Brouwerij Den Hopperd Westmeerbeek	Brouwerij Den Hopperd Westmeerbeek	Brouwerij Den Hopperd Westmeerbeek
	malt, hops, yeast, sugar, water	malt, houblon, levure, sucre, eau	mout, hop, gist, suiker, water
%	6,5%	6,5%	6,5%
	amber slightly cloudy	ambrée légèrement troublée	amber lichttroebel
	–	–	–
°C	5° C	5°C	5° C
	Fruity, slightly bitter.	Fruité, légèrement amer.	Fruitig, licht bitter
i	Organic beer.	Bière biologique.	Biologisch bier.

BIER - BIERE BIOLOGIQUE
KAMELEON

Kameleon ginseng

	top-fermentation re-fermented in the bottle	fermentation haute refermentation en bouteille	hoge gisting hergisting op de fles
	herbal beer	bière aux épices	kruidenbier
	Brouwerij Den Hopperd Westmeerbeek	Brouwerij Den Hopperd Westmeerbeek	Brouwerij Den Hopperd Westmeerbeek
	barley malt, hops, yeast, sugar, ginseng, water	malt d'orge, houblon, levure, sucre, racine de ginseng, eau	gerstemout, hop, gist, suiker, ginsengwortel, water
%	6,50%	6,50%	6,50%
	blond cloudy	blonde légèrement trouble	blond lichttroebel
	–	–	–
°C	5° C	5° C	5° C
	Fruity, slightly bitter, ginseng flavour.	Fruité, légèrement amer, arôme de ginseng.	Fruitig, licht bitter, ginsengaroma.
i	Organic boutique bier.	Bière biologique brassée de façon artisanale.	Ambachtelijk gebrouwen biologisch bier.

BIOLOGISCH BIER - BIERE BIOLOGIQUE
KAMELEON
GINSENG
hergist op fles
refermentée en bouteille
bevat gerstemout
contient du malt d'orge
33 cl ℮ • 6,5 % vol. alc • cat.5

Kameleon Tripel

	top-fermentation re-fermented in the bottle	fermentation haute refermentation en bouteille	hoge gisting hergisting op de fles
	Tripel	triple	tripel
	Brouwerij Den Hopperd Westmeerbeek	Brouwerij Den Hopperd Westmeerbeek	Brouwerij Den Hopperd Westmeerbeek
	malt, hops, yeast, sugar, water	malt, houblon, levure, sucre, eau	mout, hop, gist, suiker, water
%	8,50%	8,50%	8,50%
	blond slightly cloudy	blonde légèrement trouble	blond lichttroebel
	–	–	–
°C	5° C	5° C	5° C
	Fruity with bitter after-taste.	Fruité avec une fin de bouche amère.	Fruitig met bittere nasmaak.
i	Organic beer.	Bière biologique.	Biologisch bier.

KAMELEON
TRIPEL

Kastaar

	top-fermentation unpasteurised	fermentation haute non pasteurisée	hoge gisting niet gepasteuriseerd
	blond	blonde	blond
	Brouwerij De Block Peizegem-Merchtem	Brouwerij De Block Peizegem-Merchtem	Brouwerij De Block Peizegem-Merchtem
	wheat, malt, hops, yeast, sugar, water	froment, malt, houblon, levure, sucre, eau	tarwe, mout, hop, gist, suiker, water
%	6%	6%	6%
	blond to copper clear with a full, round, creamy foam head	blonde à cuivre claire avec un faux col solide, rond et crémeux	blond tot koper helder met volle, ronde, romige schuimkraag
	cfr. Chimay	voir chimay	cfr. chimay
	43 - 46 °F	6 - 8 °C	6 - 8 °C
	Refreshing, deeply malty character. Pleasant touch of fresh yeast.	Caractère frais et malté profond. Touche agréable de levure fraîche.	Fris en diepmoutig karakter. Aangename toets van verse gist.
i	–	–	–

Old Style
K-STAR K-STAR
HOGE GISTING
ALTA FERMENTAZIONE
HAUTE FERMENTATION
HIGH FERMENTATION
oude stijl
in ere sinds
1887
Kastaar
Alc. vol 6%
33cl e
BELGISCH BIER - BIERE BELGE
BELGIAN ALE
BIRRA SPECIALE - CERVEZA BELGA
PRODOTTA E IMBOTTIGLIATA DALLA BIRRERIA

Kastaar

Kasteel bruin

	top-fermentation	fermentation haute	hoge gisting
	regional brown beer	bière régionale brune	bruin streekbier
	Castle Brewery Van Honsebrouck Ingelmunster	Castle Brewery Van Honsebrouck Ingelmunster	Castle Brewery Van Honsebrouck Ingelmunster
	malt, sugar, hops, yeast, water	malt, houblon, sucre, levure, eau	mout, suiker, hop, gist, water
%	11%	11%	11%
	dark brown clear	brun foncé claire	donkerbruin helder
	Pour into a degreased, dry glass. Hold the glass vertically and fill in a single, fast movement.	Verser dans un verre dégraissé et sec. Tenir le verre en position verticale et verser rapidement d'un seul trait.	Uitschenken in een ontvet droog glas. Het glas verticaal houden en in 1 beweging snel inschenken.
°C	54 °F	12 °C	12 °C
	Smooth and fully round. Strong influence of special malts and dark sugars.	Doux, plein et rond. Forte influence des malts spéciaux et des sucres foncés.	Zacht en volrond. Sterke invloed van speciale mouten en donkere suikers.
i	There will soon be an 8% vol.alc. Kasteel Rouge, a cherry beer based on Kasteel Bruin. This beer is already available in the USA and in the Netherlands.	Prochainement une Kasteel rouge de 8% vol. sera créée, une bière cerise à base de Kasteel brune. Cette bière est déjà disponible à l'étranger (Etats-Unis et Pays-Bas).	Binnenkort komt er ook een Kasteel rouge van 8% vol. alc., een kersenbier op basis van Kasteel bruin. Dit bier is al beschikbaar in het buitenland (USA en Nederland)

....

....

....

KASTEEL bier
INGELMUNSTER
Brewed anno 2005
KASTEEL bier
11°
Bruin-Brune

Kasteel tripel

	top-fermentation re-fermented in the bottle	fermentation haute refermentation en bouteille	hoge gisting nagisting op de fles
	regional beer Tripel	bière régionale triple	streekbier tripel
	Castle Brewery Van Honsebrouck Ingelmunster	Castle Brewery Van Honsebrouck Ingelmunster	Castle Brewery Van Honsebrouck Ingelmunster
	malt, corn, sugar, hops, yeast, water	malt, maïs, sucre, houblon, levure, eau	mout, mais, suiker, hop, gist, water
%	11%	11%	11%
	blond clear	blonde claire	blond helder
	Pour into a degreased, dry glass. Hold the glass vertically and fill in a single, fast movement. The yeast is either poured in the glass or left in the bottle.	Verser dans un verre dégraissé et sec. Tenir le verre dans une position verticale et verser rapidement d'un seul trait. La levure est versée selon le goût.	Uitschenken in een ontvet droog glas. Het glas verticaal houden en in 1 beweging snel inschenken. De gist wordt volgens eigen smaak al dan niet uitgeschonken.
°C	48 °F	9 °C	9 °C
	Powerful and fully round. Full taste, fruity with smooth aftertaste.	Corsé, plein et rond. Goût plein, fruité avec une fin de bouche douce.	Krachtig en volrond. Volle smaak, fruitig met zachte afdronk.
i	–	–	–

INGELMUNSTER
KASTEEL bier
11°
Triple
KASTEEL bier

Katje Special

	bottom-fermentation	fermentation basse	lage gisting
	dark Ale	ale foncée	donker ale
	Brouwerij Leroy Boezinge	Brouwerij Leroy Boezinge	Brouwerij Leroy Boezinge
	malt, spices, sweetener, caramel, hops, water	malt, condiments, édulcorant, caramel, houblon, eau	mout, specerijen, zoetstof, karamel, hop, water
%	6%	6%	6%
	blond clear	blonde claire	blond helder
	Pour slowly in a single, smooth movement, into a degreased glass. Keep the glass tilted and avoid sloshing the beer. Skim off the foam.	Verser lentement en un seul mouvement fluide dans un verre dégraissé tenu en oblique. Ne pas laisser la bière clapoter. Ecumer le verre.	Traag en in 1 vloeiende beweging uitschenken in een vetvrij glas dat wordt schuingehouden. Het bier niet laten klotsen. Het glas afschuimen.
°C	41 - 43 °F	5 - 6 °C	5 - 6 °C
	Well-rounded but powerful. Slightly sweet with prominent malt flavour.	Arrondi mais corsé. Légèrement doux avec arôme de malt prononcé.	Afgerond maar krachtig. Licht zoet met prominent moutaroma.
i	Launched in May 1954 for the Ypres Kattenfeesten, which still take place every year.	Lancée en mai 1954 à l'occasion des fêtes du chat à Ypres qui ont toujours lieu chaque année.	Gelanceerd in mei 1954 ter gelegenheid van de Ieperse Kattenfeesten die jaarlijks nog plaatsvinden.

KATJE
SPECIAL
KATJE
LEROY BOEZINGE
25cl

SPECIAL
LEROY
KATJE
BOEZINGE

Keizer Karel goudblond

	top-fermentation	fermentation haute	hoge gisting
	specialty beer	bière spéciale	speciaalbier
	Brouwerij Haacht Boortmeerbeek	Brouwerij Haacht Boortmeerbeek	Brouwerij Haacht Boortmeerbeek
	barley malt, corn, sugar, hops, water	malt d'orge, mais, sucre, houblon, eau	gerstemout, mais, suiker, hop, water
%	8,50%	8,50%	8,50%
	golden blond filtered	blond doré filtrée	goudblond gefilterd
	Pour carefully into a rinsed, wet Charles Quint glass, avoiding contact between bottle and foam.	Verser prudemment dans un verre Keizer Karel rincé mouillé sans que la bouteille touche l'écume.	Voorzichtig uitschenken in een gespoeld, nat Keizer-Karelglas zonder dat de fles het schuim raakt.
°C	45 °F	7 °C	7 °C
	Spicy hop aroma, sweet taste and a pleasant, dry bitter aftertaste.	Arôme de houblon relevé, saveur douce et fin de bouche sèche, amère.	Kruidig hoparoma, zoete smaak en een aangenaam droge bittere afdronk.
i	Refers to the legend of Charles Quint in Olen. To allow the emperor to enjoy sunrise and sunset in summer, two beers were brewed. One was golden blond like the pure morning light, the other ruby red like the warm twilight.	Renvoie à la légende de Charles Quint à Olen. Pour permettre à l'empereur de profiter de la montée et de la descente du soleil de l'été, deux bières ont été fabriquées: l'une blonde comme de l'or représentant la lumière pure du matin, l'autre rouge rubis représentant le crépuscule chaud.	Verwijst naar de legende van Keizer Karel in Olen. Om de keizer te laten genieten van het rijzen en dalen van de zomerzon, werden 2 bieren gebrouwen: 'het ene goudblond als het zuivere ochtendlicht, het andere robijnrood als de warme avondschemering'.

1500 1558
Keizer Karel
Goud Blond
Blonde Dorée
Charles Quint

Keizer Karel

Keizer Karel robijnrood

	top-fermentation	fermentation haute	hoge gisting
	specialty beer	bière spéciale	speciaalbier
	Brouwerij Haacht Boortmeerbeek	Brouwerij Haacht Boortmeerbeek	Brouwerij Haacht Boortmeerbeek
	barley malt, herbs, sugar, hops, water	malt d'orge, herbes, sucre, houblon, eau	gerstemout, kruiden, suiker, hop, water
%	8,50%	8,50%	8,50%
	dark filtered	foncée, filtrée	donker gefilterd
	Pour carefully into a rinsed, wet Charles Quint glass, avoiding contact between bottle and foam.	Verser prudemment dans un verre Keizer Karel rincé et mouillé sans que la bouteille touche l'écume.	Voorzichtig uitschenken in een gespoeld, nat Keizer-Karelglas zonder dat de fles het schuim raakt.
°C	46 - 50 °F	8 - 10 °C	8 - 10 °C
	Sweetish and fruity aroma, a smooth, full taste and a sweet hoppy aftertaste.	Arôme doux et fruité, goût doux plein et fin de bouche douce, houblonnée.	Zoetig en fruitig aroma, een zachte volle smaak en een zoethoppige afdronk.
i	Cfr. Keizer Karel goudblond.	Voir Keizer Karel goudblond.	Cfr. Keizer Karel goudblond.

1500
Keizer Karel
Robijn
Rood
Charles Quint

Keizer Karel

Kempisch Vuur driedubbel

top-fermentation re-fermented in the bottle	fermentation haute refermentation en bouteille	hoge gisting hergisting op de fles
Scottish style	scotch	scotch
De Proefbrouwerij for Bieren Pirlot Pulderbos	De Proefbrouwerij pour Bieren Pirlot Pulderbos	De Proefbrouwerij voor Bieren Pirlot Pulderbos
malt (Pilsener Munich, cara, roast), hops (Tomahawk), herbs, yeast, spring water	malt (pils, Munich, cara, roast), houblon (Tomahawk), herbes, levure, eau de source	mout (pils, munich, ca-ra, roast), hop (Tomahawk), kruiden, gist, bronwater
7,50%	7,50%	7,50%
The proteins of the wheat malt create a solid, stable foam head. 55 EBC.	Les protéines du malt de froment assurent un faux col solide stable. 55 EBC.	De eiwitten van het tarwe-mout zorgen voor een stevi ge schuimkraag. 55 EBC.
Pour in a single, slow movement in degreased, dry glasses. The yeast can be poured.	Verser lentement en un seul mouvement dans des verres dégraissés secs. Ver-ser la levure selon le goût.	Traag en in 1 beweging schenken in ontvette, drog glazen. De gist naar keuze mee uitschenken.
46 - 50 °F	8 - 10 °C	8 - 10 °C
Pleasantly full-bodied by the large quantity of Cara 120 malt. Fruity, full taste, followed by a com-plex aftertaste which be-comes well-rounded with a pleasant roasty touch. Bitterness: 26 EBU.	Agréable et franc par la grande quantité de malt cara-120. Saveur fruitée, pleine suivie d'une fin de bouche complexe arron-die par une touche brûlée agréable. Amertume de 26 EBU.	Aangenaam volmondig doo de grote hoeveelheid cara-120-mout. Fruitige, volle smaak onmiddellijk gevolg door een complexe afdronk die wordt afgerond met een aangenaam gebrande toets. Bitterheid van 26 EBU.
Store in a dark, cool room.	Conserver à l'abri de la chaleur et de la lumière.	Donker en koel bewaren.

3-Dubbel
Kempisch Vuur
7,5
Kempisch Vuur

Kempisch Vuur tripel

	top-fermentation re-fermented in the bottle	fermentation haute refermentation en bouteille	hoge gisting hergisting op de fles
	abbey beer Tripel	bière d'abbaye triple	abdijbier tripel
	De Proefbrouwerij for Bieren Pirlot, Pulderbos	De Proefbrouwerij pour Bieren Pirlot, Pulderbos	De Proefbrouwerij voor Bieren Pirlot, Pulderbos
	malt (Pilsner, wheat, oat, maize), hops (Brewers Gold, Styrian), herbs, yeast, well water	malt (pils, froment, avoine, maïs), houblon (Brewers Gold, Styrian), herbes, levure, eau de source	mout (pils, tarwe, haver, mais), hop (Brewers Gold, Styrian), kruiden, gist, bronwater
%	7,50%	7,50%	7,50%
	The proteins of the wheat malt create a solid, stable foam head. 11 EBC.	Les protéines du malt de froment assurent un faux col solide stable. 11 EBC.	De eiwitten van het tarwemout zorgen voor een stevi ge, schuimkraag. 11 EBC.
	Pour in a single, slow movement in degreased, dry glasses. The yeast can be poured.	Verser lentement en un seul mouvement dans des verres dégraissés secs. Verser la levure selon le goût.	Traag en in 1 beweging schenken in ontvette, drog glazen. De gist naar keuze mee uitschenken.
°C	46 - 50 °F	8 - 10 °C	8 - 10 °C
	Pleasantly full-bodied, fruity, full taste followed by a complex, harmonious and spicy aftertaste. Bitterness: 32 EBU.	Franc, agréable. Saveur fruitée et pleine suivie d'une fin de bouche complexe, harmonieuse et relevée. Amertume: 32 EBU.	Aangenaam volmondig. Fruitige, volle smaak gevolgd door een complexe, harmonieuze en kruidige afdronk. Bitterheid: 32 EBU
i	Store in a dark, cool room.	Conserver à l'abri de la chaleur et de la lumière	Donker en koel bewaren. Bier met smaakevolutie.

Tripel
Kempisch Vuur
7,5

Kempisch Vuur

Kerkomse Tripel

	top-fermentation re-fermented in the bottle	fermentation haute refermentation en bouteille	hoge gisting hergisting op de fles
	regional beer Tripel	bière régionale triple	streekbier tripel
	Brouwerij Kerkom Sint-Truiden	Brouwerij Kerkom Saint-Trond	Brouwerij Kerkom Sint-Truiden
	2 Belgian hop varieties, barley malt, yeast, water	2 sortes de houblon belge, malt d'orge, levure, eau	2 Belgische hopsoorten, gerstemout, gist, water
%	9%	9%	9%
	–	–	–
	–	–	–
°C	–	–	–
	Beer with taste evolution.	Bière avec saveur évolutive.	Bier met smaakevolutie.
i	100% Haspengouwen regional boutique beer.	Bière régionale 100% artisanale de Haspengouw.	100% ambachtelijk Haspengouws streekbier.

Kerkomse
Tripel
Alc. 9% vol
75cl
BINK
Brouwerij
Kerkom

Kerstbie

	top-fermentation	fermentation haute	hoge gisting
	winter beer	bière hivernale	winterbier
	Brouwerij De Bie Loker	Brouwerij De Bie Loker	Brouwerij De Bie Loker
	malt, hops, yeast, candy sugar, honey, herbs, water	malt, houblon, levure, sucre candi, miel, herbes, eau	mout, hop, gist, kandijsuiker, honing, kruiden, water
%	8%	8%	8%
	dark	foncée	donker
	–	–	–
°C	43 °F	6 °C	6 °C
	Spicy with a smooth honey taste.	Goût relevé avec une saveur moelleuse de miel.	Kruidig met een zachte honingsmaak.
i	–	–	–

Kerstbie
De Bie, B-8958 Loker
ALC. 8% VOL.

Kerstvuur

	top-fermentation re-fermented in the bottle	fermentation haute refermentation en bouteille	hoge gisting hergisting op de fles
	blond winter beer	bière blonde hivernale	blond winterbier
	De Proefbrouwerij for Bieren Pirlot, Pulderbos	De Proefbrouwerij pour Bieren Pirlot, Pulderbos	De Proefbrouwerij voor Bieren Pirlot, Pulderbos
	malt (Pilsner Munich, wheat, oat, corn), hops (Brewers Gold, Styrian), herbs, yeast, spring water	malt (pils, Munich, froment, avoine, maïs), houblon (Brewers Gold, Styrian), herbes, levure, eau de source	mout (pils, munich, tarwe, haver, mais), hop (Brewers Gold, Styrian), kruiden, gist, bronwater
%	9%	9%	9%
	The proteins of the wheat malt create a solid, stable foam head. 16 EBC.	Les protéines du malt de froment assurent un faux col solide stable. 16 EBC.	De tarwemouteiwitten zorgen voor een stevige, stabiele schuimkraag. 16 EBC.
	Pour in a single, slow movement in degreased, dry glasses. The yeast can be poured.	Verser lentement en un seul mouvement dans des verres dégraissés secs. Verser la levure selon le goût.	Traag en in 1 beweging schenken in ontvette, droge glazen. De gist naar keuze mee uitschenken.
°C	46 - 50 °F	8 - 10 °C	8 - 10 °C
	Pleasantly full-bodied. Extra malty owing to the Munich, which does not allow an alcohol flavour. Harmonious, spicy aftertaste. Bitterness: 32 EBU	Franc et agréable. Extra malté (le malt Munich ne permet pas de goût alcoolisé). Fin de bouche harmonieuse, relevée. Amertume de 32 EBU.	Aangenaam volmondig. Extra moutigheid door de munich die geen alcoholsmaak toelaat. Harmonieuze, kruidige afdronk. Bitterheid van 32 EBU.
i	Store in a dark, cool room. Beer with taste evolution.	Conserver à l'abri de la chaleur et de la lumière. Bière avec saveur évolutive.	Donker en koel bewaren. Bier met smaakevolutie.
	....		

Kempisch Vuur
2006
Kerstvuur
e 33 cl
Alc 9% Vol

Keyte

	top-fermentation re-fermented in the bottle	fermentation haute refermentation en bouteille	hoge gisting nagisting op de fles
	Tripel blond	triple blonde	tripel blond
	Brouwerij Strubbe Ichtegem	Brouwerij Strubbe Ichtegem	Brouwerij Strubbe Ichtegem
	Pilsner malt, Munich malt, clear candy sugar, hops, fresh yeast, spring water	malt de pils, malt Munich, sucre candi clair, houblon, levure fraîche, eau de source	pilsmout, munichmout, heldere kandijsuiker, hoppellets, verse gist, bronwater
%	7,70%	7,70%	7,70%
	–	–	–
	–	–	–
°C	46 °F	8 °C	8 °C
	Full, bittersweet.	Plein, doux-amer.	Vol, bitterzoet.
i	Beer with taste evolution, made by order of the Ostend Bierjutters in 2004.	Bière avec saveur évolutive fabriquée à la demande des 'Oostendse Bierjutters' en 2004.	Bier met smaakevolutie gemaakt in opdracht van de Oostendse Bierjutters in 2004.

Ostenda
Keyte
OSTENS BELEGERINGSBIER
Keyte
OSTENS BELEGERINGSBIER

Kloeke blonde

	top-fermentation unpasteurised	fermentation haute non pasteurisée	hoge gisting niet gepasteuriseerd
	Belgian blond Ale	Belgian blond ale	Belgian blond ale
	at Brouwerij Deca De Struise Brouwers De Panne	chez Brouwerij Deca De Struise Brouwers La Panne	bij Brouwerij Deca De Struise Brouwers De Panne
	Pilsner malt, Munich malt, yeast, water, hops: Challenger, Hallertauer Mittelfrueh, herbs: sweet orange rind, thyme	malt de pils, malt Munich, levure, eau, houblon: Challenger, Hallertauer Mittelfrueh, herbes: écorces d'orange doux, thym	pilsmout, munichmout, gist, water, hop: Challenger, Hallertauer Mittelfrueh, kruiden: zoete sinaasschillen, tijm
%	5%	5%	5%
	(11 EBC) golden blonde soft and cloudy unfiltered	blond doré (11 EBC) légèrement trouble non filtrée	goudblond (11 EBC) zacht troebel ongefilterd
	–	–	–
°C	–	–	–
	Aroma: dry malt with a soft, spicy character. Taste: medium dry, refreshing with a fine, hoppy aftertaste. 24 IBU (soft bitter).	Arôme: malt sec avec un caractère moelleux fruité. Saveur: sec moyen, rafraîchissant avec une fin de bouche fine houblonnée. 24 IBU (légèrement amer).	Aroma: droge mout met een zacht kruidig karakter. Smaak: mediumdroog, verfrissend met een fijn hoppige afdronk. 24 IBU (zacht bitter).
i	The name referes to one of the Struise Brouwers' wife.	Le nom renvoie à l'épouse d'un des Struise Brouwers.	De naam refereert aan de vrouw van een van de Struise Brouwers.

AUTHENTIC
KLOEKE
BLONDE
Medium Dry
at Vleteren by De Struise Brouwers for Vdaco bvba
DSB
Struisebrouwers.be

Koekelaring

	top-fermentation re-fermented in the bottle	fermentation haute refermentation en bouteille	hoge gisting hergisting op de fles
	specialty beer	bière spéciale	speciaalbier
	at De Graal De Hoevebrouwers Zottegem	chez De Graal De Hoevebrouwers Zottegem	bij De Graal De Hoevebrouwers Zottegem
	malt (Pilsner, wheat, cara red, cara aroma, chocolate without bitter), hops (EK Goldings, Hallertau), yeast (T58), water	malt (pils, froment, cara red, arôme cara, chocolat pas amer), houblon (EK Goldings, Hallertau), levure (T58), eau	mout (pils, tarwe, cara red, cara aroma, ontbitterde chocolade), hop (EK Goldings, Hallertau), gist (T58), water
	6,50%	6,50%	6,50%
	red-brown clear	brun rouge claire	roodbruin helder
	Pour into a degreased goblet in a single movement, avoiding contact with glass or foam. Leave approx. 1 cm of beer in the bottle.	Verser en un seul mouvement dans un verre calice dégraissé sans toucher le verre et l'écume. Laisser environ 1 cm de bière dans la bouteille.	In 1 beweging in een vetvrij kelkglas gieten zonder het glas en het schuim te raken. Ongeveer 1 cm bier in de fles laten.
	43 - 50 °F	6 - 10 °C	6 - 10 °C
	Full-bodied and rich. Sweet malty onset with a hoppy aftertaste.	Franc et riche. Début doux malté avec une fin de bouche houblonnée.	Volmondig en rijk. Zoetmoutige aanhef met een hoppige afdronk.
	Koekelaring is a bakery product from Zottegem, available from November to February.	Koekelaring est une spécialité pâtissière de Zottegem disponible de novembre à février.	Koekelaring is een Zottegemse bakkerijspecialiteit die verkrijgbaar is tussen november en februari.

6,5 % vol.alc
Koekelaring
Info@dehoevebrouwers.be

Kool Mortal

top-fermentation re-fermented in the bottle	fermentation haute refermentation en bouteille	hoge gisting hergisting op de fles
herb spice beer lavender	bière aux épices lavande	kruidenbier lavendel
Mortal's Beers Jamagne	Mortal's Beers Jamagne	Mortal's Beers Jamagne
malt, sugar, tradition- al honey, hops, lavender, yeast, water	malt, sucre, miel artisanal, houblon, lavande, levure, eau	mout, suiker, artisanale honing, hop, lavendel, gist, water
5,20%	5,20%	5,20%
–	–	–
–	–	–
39 - 43 °F	4 - 6 °C	4 - 6 °C
Hoppy, lavender. Fruity character beer.	Houblonné, lavande. Bière de caractère fruitée.	Hoppig, lavendel. Fruitig karakterbier.
–	–	–

WWW.MORTALSBEERS.BE
MORTALS BEERS

Kriek Girardin

	spontaneous fermentation	fermentation spontanée	spontane gisting
	fruit beer Lambic beer	bière fruitée bière lambic	fruitbier lambiekbier
	Brouwerij Girardin Sint-Ulriks-Kapelle	Brouwerij Girardin Sint-Ulriks-Kapelle	Brouwerij Girardin Sint-Ulriks-Kapelle
	wheat, barley malt, more than 1 year old hops, cherries, water	froment, malt d'orge, houblon suranné, cerises, eau	tarwe, gerstemout, overjaarse hop, krieken, water
%	5%	5%	5%
	clear ruby-red	rouge rubis clair	helder robijnrood
	Like champagne. In a flute-glass.	Comme le champagne. Dans des flûtes.	Zoals champagne. In fluitglazen.
°C	cool	frais	fris
	Fruity, cherry, sourish.	Fruité, cerise, acidulé.	Fruitig, krieken, zurig.
i	Made with real cherries still containing their stone (instead of with cherry juice).	Fabriquée à partir de vraies cerises avec noyau (au lieu de jus de cerises).	Gemaakt met echte krieken die nog hun pit bevatten (in plaats van kriekensap).

SPONTANE GISTING
FERMENTATION SPONTANÉE
KRIEK
GIRARDIN
1882
Gebrouwen en gebotteld door - Brassée et soutirée par
Brouwerij Girardin, Lindenberg 10-12, Sint-Ulriks-Kapelle - Belgium
e 75 CL
GIRARDIN
SINT-ULRIKS-KAPELLE

Kriek Cantillon

	spontaneous fermentation naturally re-fermented in the bottle	fermentation spontanée refermentation naturelle en bouteille	spontane gisting natuurlijke hergisting op de fles
	fruit beer Lambic	bière fruitée lambic	fruitbier lambiek
	Brouwerij Cantillon Brussels	Brouwerij Cantillon Bruxelles	Brouwerij Cantillon Brussel
	barley malt, wheat, more than one year old hops, fresh cherries	malt d'orge, froment, houblon suranné, cerises fraîches	gerstemout, tarwe, overjaarse hop, verse kersen
%	5,50%	5,50%	5,50%
	ruby-red	rouge rubis	robijnrood
	The use of a wine basket is recommended if the bottle was stored horizontally. Place the bottle in an upright position 48 hours before serving.	Un panier verseur est recommandé si la bouteille a été conservée en position horizontale. Mettre la bouteille 48 heures avant de servir dans une position verticale pour faire descendre la levure.	Een schenkmandje is aangewezen wanneer de fles horizontaal bewaard werd. De fles 48 uur voor het uitschenken verticaal plaasten om het bezinksel te decanteren.
°C	cellar temperature (54 - 61 °F)	température de cave (12 - 16 °C)	keldertemperatuur (12 - 16 °C)
	Intensely fruity, sourish taste and pronounced cherry aroma with a touch of kirsch.	Goût fruité intense, saveur acidulée et arôme de cerises prononcé, pointe de kirsch.	Intense fruitigheid, zurige smaak en uitgesproken kersenaroma, vleugje kirsch.
i	–	–	–

CANTILLON
Kriek 100% Lambic

CANTILLON

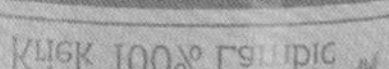

Kriek Boon

	spontaneous fermentation	fermentation spontanée	spontane gisting
	fruit beer	bière fruitée	fruitbier
	Brouwerij Boon Lembeek	Brouwerij Boon Lembeek	Brouwerij Boon Lembeek
	Blend of young and old Lambic, matured in oak barrels. Real cherries (25%).	Mélange de jeune et vieux lambic mûri en fûts en bois de chêne. Vraies cerises (25%).	Versnijding van jonge en oude lambiek gerijpt op eikenhouten vaten. Echte krieken (25%).
%	4,50%	4,50%	4,50%
	red	rouge	rood
	–	–	–
°C	–	–	–
	Refreshing, non-foaming. Sweet-and-sour cherry taste.	Frais, sans écume. Saveur de cerise aigre-douce.	Fris, niet schuimend. Zuurzoete kriekensmaak.
i	Originally created with Schaarbeek cherries, now especially with Noord cherries and lambic that is at least six months old. Many taverns that had lambic, used to make their own kriek, tapping it from the typical stone bottles.	A l'origine fabriquée avec des cerises de Schaerbeek, maintenant principalement avec des cerises du nord et du lambic de minimum 6 mois. Beaucoup de brasseries qui avaient le lambic en stock fabriquaient autrefois leur propre kriek et la servaient dans des cruches en pierre typiques.	Oorspronkelijk gemaakt met Schaarbeekse krieken, nu vooral met Noordkrieken, en lambiek van minimum 6 maanden oud. Vroeger maakten veel herbergen die lambiek hadden liggen zelf hun kriek. Ze tapten hem in de typische stenen kruiken.

2005
KRIEK
BOON
LAMBIEK 100% LAMBIC

Kriek De Ranke

	mixed fermentation	fermentation mixte	gemengde gisting
	fruit beer	bière fruitée	fruitbier
	Brouwerij De Ranke Wevelgem	Brouwerij De Ranke Wevelgem	Brouwerij De Ranke Wevelgem
	malt, wheat, hop flowers, wild yeasts, cherries blended with Lambic	malt, froment, fleurs de houblon, levures sauvages, cerises, coupée avec le lambic	mout, tarwe, hopbloemen, wilde gisten, krieken, versneden met lambiek
%	7%	7%	7%
	red slightly cloudy	rouge légèrement trouble	rood licht troebel
	–	–	–
°C	moderately cooled	rafraîchie modérément	medium koel
	Sourish cherry taste and aroma.	Acidulé, saveur et arôme de cerises.	Zurig, kriekensmaak en -aroma.
i	–	–	–

BROUWERIJ - BRASSERIE
DE RANKE
KRIEK
DE RANKE
7% Vol. Alc.

Kriek Fantastiek

	top-fermentation re-fermented in the bottle	fermentation haute refermentation en bouteille	hoge gisting nagisting op de fles
	bitter-and-sour Kriek based on Ale	kriek amère-acidulée à base d'ale	zuurbittere kriek op basis van ale
	Brouwerij De Ryck Herzele	Brouwerij De Ryck Herzele	Brouwerij De Ryck Herzele
	malt, hops, yeast, sucrose, cherry extract, water. Based on Christmas Pale Ale.	malt, houblon, levure, sucrose, extrait de cerises, eau. A base de Christmas pale ale.	mout, hop, gist, sucrose, kriekenextract, water. Op basis van Christmas pale ale.
%	4,90%	4,90%	4,90%
	brown-red	brun rouge	bruinrood
	Rinse the glass with cold water, take it by the stem and hold it slightly tilted. Slowly pour in a single movement, avoiding contact between bottle and glass or foam. Leave 1 cm yeast sediment in the bottle or pour it along.	Rincer le verre à l'eau froide, le tenir légèrement en oblique par le pied. Verser la bière lentement et en un seul mouvement sans que la bouteille touche le verre ou l'écume. Laisser 1 cm de levure dans la bouteille ou la verser.	Het glas koud spoelen, bij de voet vastnemen en licht schuin houden. Het bier traag en in 1 beweging inschenken zonder dat de fles het glas of schuim raakt. Het gistdepot van 1 cm in de fles laten ofwel uitschenken.
°C	39 - 43 °F	4 - 6 °C	4 - 6 °C
	Refreshing and summery, bitter-and-sour. Unusual combination of fruit flavours and aromas with typical malt and hop bitterness.	Rafraîchissant et estival, amer-acidulé. Combinaison obstinée de goûts et de parfums fruités, amertume typique de malt et de houblon.	Verfrissend en zomers, zuurbitter. Eigenzinnige combinatie van fruitsmaken en -geuren met typisch mout en hopbitterheid.
i	–	–	–

....

DE RYCK
Kriek Fantastiek
bvba Brouwerij DE RYCK - Kerkstraat 24 - 9550 Herzele
tel: 0032/(0)53/62 23 02 - fax: 0032/(0)53/63 15 41
brouwerij.de.ryck@skynet.be - www.brouwerijderyck.be
DE RYCK

Kriek Jacobins

	spontaneous fermentation	fermentation spontanée	spontane gisting
	fruit beer	bière fruitée	fruitbier
	Brouwerij Bockor Bellegem	Brouwerij Bockor Bellegem	Brouwerij Bockor Bellegem
	barley malt, wheat, hops, yeast, cherry juices, natural flavours, water	malt d'orge, froment, houblon, levure, jus de cerises, arômes naturels, eau	gerstemout, tarwe, hop, gist, kriekensappen, natuurlijke aroma's, water
%	4,50%	4,50%	4,50%
	clear red	rouge clair	helderrood
	Rinse the glass with cold water, tilt it a little and pour carefully half of the bottle. Next keep the glass upright and pour the rest of the bottle in a single movement.	Rincer le verre à l'eau froide, le tenir légèrement incliné et le remplir à moitié. Puis relever le verre et verser la bière qui reste d'un seul trait.	Het glas koud spoelen, lich schuin houden en voorzichtig half inschenken. Daarna het glas recht houden en de rest in 1 bewegin inschenken.
°C	41 - 46 °F	5 - 8 °C	5 - 8 °C
	Fresh fruity character. sweet-and-sour taste.	Caractère fruité et frais. Saveur aigre-douce.	Frisfruitig karakter. Zoetzure smaak.
i	–	–	–

Jacobins
KRIEK
Lambic
Jacobins
KRIEK
Lambic

Jacobins
KRIEK LAMBIC

Kriek Lindemans

	spontaneous fermentation	fermentation spontanée	spontane gisting
	fruit beer based on Lambic	bière fruitée à base de lambic	fruitbier op basis van lambiek
	Brouwerij Lindemans Vlezenbeek	Brouwerij Lindemans Vlezenbeek	Brouwerij Lindemans Vlezenbeek
	malt, wheat, hops, cherry juice (25%), fructose, water	malt, froment, houblon, jus de cerises (25%), fructose, eau	mout, tarwe, hop, kriekensap (25%), fructose, water
%	3,50%	3,50%	3,50%
	red slightly hazy	rouge légèrement voilée	rood licht gesluierd
	Pour into a flute-glass or beer snifter.	Verser dans une flûte ou un verre ballon.	In een fluitglas of bolglas uitschenken.
°C	37 - 39 °F	3 - 4 °C	3 - 4 °C
	Fruity character. Lively and strong onset turning into a balance of sweet (fruit) and smooth sour (lambic).	Caractère fruité. Début vif et corsé passant à un équilibre de douceur (fruits) et d'acidité légère (lambic).	Fruitig karakter. Levendige en sterke aanzet die overgaat in een evenwicht van zoet (fruit) en zacht zuur (lambiek).
i	Suitable as an aperitif and as a thirst-quencher.	Convient comme apéritif et comme boisson désaltérante.	Geschikt als aperitief en als dorstlesser.

....

....

....

....

Lindemans
KRIEK
KRIEK

Kriek Max

	spontaneous fermentation	fermentation spontanée	spontane gisting
	fruit beer	bière fruitée	fruitbier
	Brouwerij Bockor Bellegem	Brouwerij Bockor Bellegem	Brouwerij Bockor Bellegem
	barley malt, wheat, hops, yeast, cherry juices, natural flavouring, water	malt d'orge, froment, houblon, levure, jus de cerises, arômes naturels, eau	gerstemout, tarwe, hop, gist, kriekensappen, natuurlijke aroma's, water
%	3,20%	3,20%	3,20%
	clear red	rouge clair	helderrood
	Rinse the glass with cold water, tilt it a little and pour carefully half of the bottle. Next keep the glass upright and pour the rest of the bottle in a single movement.	Rincer le verre à l'eau froide, le tenir légèrement incliné et le remplir prudemment à moitié. Puis relever le verre et verser le reste de la bière d'un seul trait.	Het glas koud spoelen, licht schuin houden en voorzichtig half inschenken. Daarna het glas recht houden en de rest in 1 beweging inschenken.
°C	41 - 46 °F	5 - 8 °C	5 - 8 °C
	Fresh fruity character. Sweet-and-sour taste.	Caractère fruité et frais. Saveur aigre-douce.	Frisfruitig karakter. Zoetzure smaak.
i	–	–	–

kriek
MAX
MEER SMAAK - PLUS DE GOÛT
Jacobins

kriek
MAX

Kriek St Louis

	spontaneous fermentation	fermentation spontanée	spontane gisting
	fruit beer based on Gueuze Lambic	bière fruitée à base de gueuze lambic	fruitbier op basis van geuze lambiek
	Castle Brewery Van Honsebrouck Ingelmunster	Castle Brewery Van Honsebrouck Ingelmunster	Castle Brewery Van Honsebrouck Ingelmunster
	malt, wheat, sugar, hops, cherries, flavouring, water. The sour cherries are immersed in Geuze Lambic during 6 monts.	malt, froment, sucre, houblon, cerises, arôme, eau. Les cérises acidulées restent au minimum 6 mois dans la gueuze lambic.	mout, tarwe, suiker, hop, krieken, aroma, water. De zure krieken liggen minimum 6 maanden in geuze lambiek.
%	4%	4%	4%
	deep red clear	rouge intense claire	dieprood helder
	Pour into a newly rinsed glass. Keep it tilted first, in a vertical position next.	Verser dans un verre rincé tenu d'abord en oblique et à la fin en position verticale.	Uitschenken in een vers gespoeld glas dat eerst schui en op het einde verticaal gehouden wordt.
°C	41 °F	5 °C	5 °C
	Refreshing and fruity. Cherry taste and aroma with discrete pip touch.	Frais et fruité. Saveur et arôme de cerises avec une touche discrète de noyaux.	Fris en fruitig. Kriekensmaak en -aroma met discrete pittentoets.
i	–	–	–

....

....

St Louis
KRIEK
Lambic
Bière
Belge
Belgisch
Bier
St Louis
KRIEK
Lambic
St Louis
KRIEK

Kriekedebie

	top-fermentation	fermentation haute	hoge gisting
	fruit beer	bière fruitée	fruitbier
	Brouwerij De Bie Loker	Brouwerij De Bie Loker	Brouwerij De Bie Loker
	malt, hops, yeast, cherry extract, water	malt, houblon, levure, extrait de cerises, eau	mout, hop, gist, krieken-extract, water
%	6%	6%	6%
	ruby red	rouge rubis	robijnrood
	–	–	–
	43 °F	6 °C	6 °C
	Slightly sour.	Légèrement acidulé.	Zachtzuur.
i	–	–	–

Kriekedebie
Kriekedebie

Kriekenbier

	bottom-fermentation	fermentation basse	lage gisting
	Witbier with fruit juice	bière blanche avec jus de fruits	witbier met vruchtensap
	Brouwerij Sint-Jozef Opitter	Brouwerij Sint-Jozef Opitter	Brouwerij Sint-Jozef Opitter
	malt, hops, wheat, oat, herbs, sugar, juice, water	malt, houblon, froment, avoine, herbes, sucre, jus, eau	mout, hop, tarwe, haver, kruiden, suiker, sap, water
%	3,50%	3,50%	3,50%
	red	rouge	rood
	Pour into a clean, degreased glass, avoiding contact between bottle and foam.	Verser dans un verre propre et dégraissé sans que la bouteille touche l'écume.	Uitschenken in een zuiver, ontvet glas zonder dat de fles het schuim raakt.
°C	36 - 39 °F	2 - 4 °C	2 - 4 °C
	Sweet, fruity and refreshing. Overwhelming cherry taste.	Doux, fruité et rafraîchissant. Goût dominant de cerises.	Zoet fruitig en verfrissend. Overweldigende kriekensmaak.
i	–	–	–

Morel
NIEUW!
KRIEKEN BIER
NIEUW!
KRIEKEN BIER
BROUWERIJ St. JOZEF
KRIEKEN BIER

La Barbiot ambrée
La bière des Connaisseurs

	top-fermentation	fermentation haute	hoge gisting
	amber	ambrée	amber
	Brasserie La Barbiot Ville-sur-Haine	Brasserie La Barbiot Ville-sur-Haine	Brasserie La Barbiot Ville-sur-Haine
	barley malt, wilde hops, yeast, water	malt d'orge, houblon sauvage, levure, eau	gerstemout, wilde hop, gist, water
%	9,50%	9,50%	9,50%
	amber	ambrée	amber
	Serve in a balloon glass.	Verser dans un verre ballon.	Uitschenken in een ballonglas.
	Cellar temperature.	Température de cave.	Keldertemperatuur.
	–	–	–
i	–	–	–

Barbiot
bière ambrée
BARBIOT

La Barbiot blonde
La bière des Connaisseurs

	top-fermentation	fermentation haute	hoge gisting
	blond	blonde	blond
	Brasserie La Barbiot Ville-sur-Haine	Brasserie La Barbiot Ville-sur-Haine	Brasserie La Barbiot Ville-sur-Haine
	barley malt, wild hops, yeast, water	malt d'orge, houblon sauvage, levure, eau	gerstemout, wilde hop, gist, water
%	8%	8%	8%
	blond	blonde	blond
	Serve in a balloon glass.	Verser dans un verre ballon.	Uitschenken in een ballonglas.
°C	Cellar temperature.	Température de cave.	Keldertemperatuur.
	–	–	–
i	–	–	–

bière blonde
BARBIOT

La Botteresse Ambrée

	top-fermentation triple fermentation	fermentation haute triple fermentation	hoge gisting driedubbele gisting
	specialty beer boutique beer	bière spéciale artisanale	speciaalbier artisanaal
	Brasserie La Botteresse de Sur-Les-Bois Saint-Georges	Brasserie La Botteresse de Sur-Les-Bois Saint-Georges	Brasserie La Botteresse de Sur-Les-Bois Saint-Georges
	aromatic malts and herbs	malts aromatiques et herbes	aromatische mouten en kruiden
%	8,50%	8,50%	8,50%
	dark amber unfiltered	ambré foncé non filtrée	donker amber ongefilterd
	Pour into a degreased, dry glass, leaving 1 cm of yeast sediment in the bottle.	Verser dans un verre dégraissé, sec et laisser un dépôt de levure de 1 cm dans la bouteille.	Uitschenken in een ontvet, droog glas en 1 cm gistdepot in de fles laten.
°C	50 °F	10 °C	10 °C
	Sipping beer. Powerful, well-balanced taste of spices and aromatic hops and malt.	Bière de dégustation. Saveur corsée et équilibrée par les herbes, le houblon aromatique et le malt.	Degustatiebier. Krachtige en evenwichtige smaak door de kruiden en de aromatische hop en mout.
i	Also exists in a honey version, which is smooth, round and fruity, with a lighter colour and a honey flavour based on spices.	Existe aussi en version Miel qui est moelleuse, ronde et fruitée, de couleur plus claire et avec un arôme de miel à base d'herbes.	Bestaat ook in een honingversie die zacht, rond en fruitig is, en lichter van kleur, met een aroma van honing op een kruidige basis.

La Botteresse
ambrée
ARTISANALE DES BRUYÈRES
JUPILLE - BELGIQUE
La Botteresse

La Botteresse blonde

	top-fermentation triple fermentation	fermentation haute triple fermentation	hoge gisting driedubbele gisting
	specialty beer boutique beer	bière spéciale artisanale	speciaalbier artisanaal
	Brasserie La Botteresse de Sur-Les-Bois Saint-Georges	Brasserie La Botteresse de Sur-Les-Bois Saint-Georges	Brasserie La Botteresse de Sur-Les-Bois Saint-Georges
	aromatic malts, malted grain varieties, unmalted wheat and oat	malts aromatiques, sortes de blé malté, froment non malté et avoine	aromatische mouten, gemoute graansoorten, ongemoute tarwe en haver
%	7,50%	7,50%	7,50%
	blond hazy (unfiltered)	blonde voilée (non filtrée)	blond gesluierd (ongefilterd)
	Pour into a degreased, dry glass, leaving 1 cm of yeast sediment in the bottle.	Verser dans un verre dégraissé, sec avec ou sans dépôt de levure.	Uitschenken in een ontvet, droog glas met of zonder gistdepot.
°C	46 °F	8 °C	8 °C
	Refreshing, round and well-balanced. Flower and fruit aromas, taste and aroma of wheat and oat.	Rafraîchissant, rond et équilibré. Arômes de fleurs et de fruits, saveur et arômes de froment et d'avoine.	Verfrissend, rond en evenwichtig. Aroma's van bloemen en fruit, smaak en aroma van tarwe en haver.
i	–	–	–

....

....

....

La Botteresse
Blonde
BRASSERIE ARTISANALE DES BRUYÈRES
JUPILLE - BELGIQUE
E-mail : bruyeres@belgique.com
La Botteresse

La Botteresse Brune

	top-fermentation triple fermentation	fermentation haute triple fermentation	hoge gisting driedubbele gisting
	specialty beer boutique beer	bière spéciale artisanale	speciaalbier artisanaal
	Brasserie La Botteresse de Sur-Les-Bois Saint-Georges	Brasserie La Botteresse de Sur-Les-Bois Saint-Georges	Brasserie La Botteresse de Sur-Les-Bois Saint-Georges
	aromatic and roasted malt varieties, herbs	malts aromatiques et brûlés, herbes	aromatische en gebrande moutsoorten, kruiden
%	9,50%	9,50%	9,50%
	brown to black unfiltered	brune à noire non filtrée	bruin tot zwart ongefilterd
	Pour into a degreased, dry glass, leaving 1 cm of yeast sediment in the bottle.	Verser dans un verre dégraissé, sec et laisser un dépôt de levure de 1 cm dans la bouteille.	Uitschenken in een ontvet, droog glas en 1 cm gistdepot in de fles laten.
°C	50 °F	10 °C	10 °C
	Powerful but round and well-balanced sipping beer. Fruity, spicy taste with liquorice and roasty malt.	Bière de dégustation corsée mais ronde et équilibrée. Saveur fruitée et aromatisée de réglisse et de malt brûlé.	Krachtig maar rond en evenwichtig degustatiebier. De smaak is fruitig en kruidig met zoethout en gebrande mout.
i	–	–	–

....

....

....

La Botteresse
Brune
ARTISANALE DES BRUYÈRES
BELGIQUE
La Botteresse

La Chérie

	top-fermentation	fermentation haute	hoge gisting
	fruit beer	bière fruitée	fruitbier
	Brasserie Val de Sambre Gozée	Brasserie Val de Sambre Gozée	Brasserie Val de Sambre Gozée
	witbier with barley and wheat, aromatised with sour cherries	bière blanche d'orge et froment aromatisée avec des cerises griottes	witbier van gerst en tarwe gearomatiseerd met griotte kersen
%	5% 12° plato	5 % 12° plato	5 % 12° plato
	pink hazy	rose voilée	roze gesluierd
	–	–	–
°C	46 °F	8 °C	8 °C
	Smooth and refreshing taste of sour cherries.	Saveur douce et rafraîchis-sante de cerises griottes.	Zachte en verfrissende smaak van griottekersen.
i	–	–	–

La Chérie
La Chérie
La bière
ALC. 5% VOL
à la cerise
Kersen Bier

La Chérie

La Chèvenis

	top-fermentation re-fermented in the bottle unpasteurised	fermentation haute refermentation en bouteille non pasteurisée	hoge gisting hergisting op de fles ongepasteuriseerd
	specialty beer blond	bière spéciale blonde	speciaalbier blond
	Brasserie de Bouillon Bouillon	Brasserie de Bouillon Bouillon	Brasserie de Bouillon Bouillon
	barley malt, hop varieties, Orval yeast, hemp grains, herbs, water	malt d'orge, variétés de houblon, levure Orval, graines de chanvre, herbes, eau	gerstemout, hopsoorten, Orvalgist, hennepkorrels, kruiden, water
%	6%	6%	6%
	blond unfiltered	blonde non filtrée	blond niet gefilterd
	Hold the glass slightly tilted while pouring the beer.	Tenir le verre légèrement incliné et verser.	Het glas licht schuin houden en inschenken.
°C	46 - 54 °F	8 - 12 °C	8 - 12 °C
	Sipping beer with hemp flavour and aroma.	Bière de dégustation avec saveur et arômes de chanvre.	Degustatiebier met hennepsmaak en -aroma.
i	–	–	–

....

....

....

....

....

alc. 6% vol.
Bière au Chanvre et Houblon
La Chèvenis
Produite par la www.brasseriedebouillon.be

CUVEE DE
BOUILLON

La Chouffe

	top-fermentation re-fermented in the bottle	fermentation haute refermentation en bouteille	hoge gisting hergisting op de fles
	regional beer	bière régionale	streekbier
	Duvel Moortgat corporation Brasserie d'Achouffe Achouffe-Wibrin	Duvel Moortgat corporation Brasserie d'Achouffe Achouffe-Wibrin	Duvel Moortgat corporatio Brasserie d'Achouffe Achouffe-Wibrin
	malt, hops, coriander, sugar, yeast, water	malt, houblon, coriandre, sucre, levure, eau	mout, hop, koriander, suiker, gist, water
%	8%	8%	8%
	golden blond unfiltered	blond doré non filtrée	goudblond ongefilterd
	–	–	–
°C	46 - 54 °F	8 - 12 °C	8 - 12 °C
	Sparkling, strong, fruity, spicy beer with flavour evolution. Without additives and not pasteurised.	Bière pétillante, corsée, fruitée, arômatisée avec évolution de la saveur. Sans additifs et non pasteurisée.	Bruisend, sterk, fruitig, kruidig bier met smaakevolutie. Zonder additieven en ongepasteuriseerd.
i	Store upright in a dark, cool room. A layer of yeast sediment at the bottom of the bottle is normal.	A conserver verticalement à l'abri de la lumière et de la chaleur. Un dépôt de levure au fond de la bouteille est normal.	Verticaal bewaren in een donkere, koele ruimte. Een gistlaagje op de bodem van de fles is normaal.

....

....

....

....

BIÈRE
BLONDE
BLOND BIER
LA
CHOUFFE
BIÈRE BLONDE D'ARDENNE - ARDENS BLOND BIER
Brasserie d'Achouffe - 6666 Achouffe - Belgique
e75cl

La Crianza

	mixed top-fermentation with Lambic	mixte fermentation haute avec lambic	gemengd hoge gisting met lambiek
	Blended beer with Lambic. Matured in oak barrels for nine months.	Bière mixte avec lambic. Mûrie en fûts de chêne pendant 9 mois.	Mengbier met lambiek. 9 maanden gerijpt op eikenhout.
	at De Ranke Brasserie de la Senne Brussels	chez De Ranke Brasserie de la Senne Bruxelles	bij De Ranke Brasserie de la Senne Brussel
	malt, hops, barley, yeast, water	malt, houblon, orge, levure, eau	mout, hop, gerst, gist, water
%	7%	7%	7%
	–	–	–
	Serve in the corresponding glass.	Verser dans le verre approprié.	Uitschenken in het bijpassende glas.
°C	41 °F	5 °C	5 °C
	A touch of sherry on a pleasant sourish undertone.	Pointe de xéres sur un arrière-fond acidulé agréable.	Vleugje sherry op een aangenaam zurige ondertoon.
i	Boutique beer. The old micro-brewery Sint Pieters in Sint-Pieters-Leeuw was getting too small. Whilst a new brewery is built in Brussels (opening in 2008), beers are produced at brouwerij De Ranke.	Brassée de façon traditionnelle. L'ancienne micro-brasserie Sint-Pieters à Sint-Pieters-Leeuw devenait trop petite; en attendant l'ouverture d'une nouvelle brasserie à Bruxelles (2008) la production se fait chez brasserie De Ranke.	Op traditionele wijze gebrouwen. De oude microbrouwerij Sint Pieters in Sint-Pieters-Leeuw werd te klein; in afwachting van de opening van een nieuwe brouwerij in Brussel (2008) is de productie naar brouwerij De Ranke verhuisd.

CRIANZA
www.brasseriedelasenne.be
BRASSERIE DE LA SENNE

La Divine

	top-fermentation	fermentation haute	hoge gisting
	abbey beer	bière d'abbaye	abdijbier
	Brasserie de Silly Silly	Brasserie de Silly Silly	Brasserie de Silly Silly
	pale malt, caramelized malt, aromatic malt, sugar, Kent and Hallertau hops, yeast, water	malt pâle, malt caramélisé, malt aromatique, sucre, houblon Kent et Hallertau, levure, eau	bleke mout, gekaramelliseerde mout, aromatische mout, suiker, Kent en Hallertau hop, gist, water
%	9,50% 19° plato	9,50% 19° plato	9,50% 19° plato
	amber (35 EBC)	ambrée (35 EBC)	amber (35 EBC)
	Pour carefully into a goblet.	Verser tranquillement dans un verre calice large.	Rustig uitschenken in een breed kelkglas.
	45 - 50 °F	7 - 10 °C	7 - 10 °C
	Extra strong beer with a velvety smooth flavour and a pleasant hop and wood taste. Very fine, bitter, smoky aftertaste with alcohol flavour.	Bière extra forte avec un arôme velouté et un goût agréable de houblon et de bois. Fin de bouche très raffinée, amère, fumée avec un goût d'alcool.	Extra sterk bier met een flu weelzacht aroma en een aangename hop- en houtsmaak. Heel fijne, bittere, gerookte afdronk met alcoholsmaak
	Boutique beer.	Brassée de façon artisanale.	Artisanaal gebrouwen.

La Divine
La Divine
AMBACHTELIJK BELGISCH BIER
BIERE BELGE ARTISANALE

La Divine

La Djean d'Mady Bière gaumaise de Virton

	top-fermentation re-fermented in the bottle	fermentation haute refermentation en bouteille	hoge gisting hergisting op de fles
	amber	ambrée	amber
	Microbrasserie Ste Hélène Ethe	Microbrasserie Ste Hélène Ethe	Microbrasserie Ste Hélène Ethe
	–	–	–
%	5,50%	5,50%	5,50%
	–	–	–
	–	–	–
°C	50 - 54 °F	10 - 12 °C	10 - 12 °C
	Slightly bitter session beer with a biscuit-like touch.	Bière légèrement amère avec une touche de biscuit, se boit facilement.	Lichtbitter doordrinkbier met een toets van biscuit.
i	Boutique beer. The label was designed by the artist Palix.	Brassée de façon artisanale. L'étiquette est conçue par le dessinateur Palix.	Artisanaal gebrouwen. Het etiket is ontworpen door tekenaar Palix.

AMBRÉE
5,5%
LA
DJEAN
D'
MADY
BIERE GAUMAISE
DE VIRTON

La Djean Triple
Bière gaumaise de Virton

	top-fermentation re-fermented in the bottle	fermentation haute refermentation en bouteille	hoge gisting hergisting op de fles
	amber	ambrée	amber
	Microbrasserie Ste Hélène Ethe	Microbrasserie Ste Hélène Ethe	Microbrasserie Ste Hélène Ethe
	Pale Ale malt, Elzas hops, yeast, sugar, water	malt pale ale, houblon d'Al-sace, levure, sucre, eau	pale ale mout, Elzas hop, gist, suiker, water
%	9%	9%	9%
	unfiltered	non filtrée	ongefilterd
	–	–	–
	46 - 50 °F	8 - 10 °C	8 - 10 °C
	Powerful with pure malt and hop flavours.	Corsé avec des arômes purs maltés et houblonnés.	Krachtig met pure mout- en hoparoma's.
i	Boutique beer. The label was designed by the artist Palix.	Brassée de façon artisanale. L'étiquette est conçue par le dessinateur Palix.	Artisanaal gebrouwen. Het etiket is ontworpen door tekenaar Palix.

AMBRÉE
9%
LA
DJEAN
TRIPLE
BIERE GAUMAISE DE VIRTON

La gauloise ambrée

	top-fermentation re-fermented in the bottle	fermentation haute refermentation en bouteille	hoge gisting met hergisting in de fles
	specialty beer amber	bière spéciale ambrée	speciaalbier amber
	Brasserie du Bocq Purnode-Yvoir	Brasserie du Bocq Purnode-Yvoir	Brasserie du Bocq Purnode-Yvoir
	barley malt, wheat starch, hop varieties, yeast, herbs, water	malt d'orge, fécule de froment, sortes de houblon, levure, herbes, eau	gerstemout, tarwezetme hoppesoorten, gist, kruiden, water
%	5,50%	5,50%	5,50%
	amber-coloured (30 EBC), clear and gently sparkling; fine, generous foam head	couleur ambrée (30 EBC), claire et finement pétillante; faux col fin, ample	amberkleurig (30 EBC), helder, fijn sprankelend; fijne, gulle schuimkraag
	Gently pour into a perfectly degreased glass. Leave the yeast sediment (natural re-fermenting) in the bottle.	Verser doucement dans un verre parfaitement dégraissé. Laisser le dépôt de levure (refermentation naturelle) dans la bouteille.	Zacht uitschenken in een perfect ontvet glas. Het gis bezinksel (natuurlijke hergisting) in de fles laten.
°C	41 - 54 °F	5 - 12 °C	5 - 12 °C
	Pleasant mixture of hop flavours and a light touch of liquorice. Clear bitterness (30 EBU), smooth and thirst-quenching beer.	Mélange agréable d'arômes de houblon et touche légère de réglisse. Saveur amère prononcée (30 EBU), bière douce et désaltérante.	Aangename mengeling v hoparoma's en lichte toe van zoethout. Duidelijke bitterheid (30 EBU), zacht en dorstlessend bier.
i	–	–	–

AMBREE
LAGAULOISE
Une tradition de brasseurs depuis 1858
Een brouwerstraditie sinds 1858

LAGAULOISE

La gauloise blonde

	top-fermentation re-fermented in the bottle	fermentation haute refermentation en bouteille	hoge gisting met hergisting in de fles
	blond specialty beer	bière spéciale blonde	speciaalbier blond
	Brasserie du Bocq Purnode-Yvoir	Brasserie du Bocq Purnode-Yvoir	Brasserie du Bocq Purnode-Yvoir
	barley malt, hop varieties, yeast, water	malt d'orge, sortes de houblon, levure, eau	gerstemout, hoppesoorten, gist, water
%	6,30%	6,30%	6,30%
	blond (10,5 EBC), shiny, sparkling fine, creamy foam head	blonde (10,5 EBC), brillante, pétillante faux col fin, crémeux	blond (10,5 EBC), glanzend, sprankelend fijne, roomachtige kraag
	Gently pour into a perfectly degreased glass. Leave the yeast sediment (natural re-fermenting) in the bottle.	Verser doucement dans un verre parfaitement dégraissé. Laisser le dépôt de levure (refermentation naturelle) dans la bouteille.	Zacht uitschenken in een perfect ontvet glas. Het gistbezinksel (natuurlijke hergisting) in de fles laten.
°C	41 - 54 °F	5 - 12 °C	5 - 12 °C
	Delicious nose, created by a trace of fine hops. Mild, smooth taste, great aperitif. 22EBU.	Bouquet exquis par une pointe de houblon fin. Saveur généreuse, douce, convient comme apéritif. 22 EBU.	Heerlijke neus door een zweem van fijne hop. Milde, zachte smaak, geschikt als aperitief. 22 EBU.
i	–	–	–

BLONDE
LAGAULOISE
Une tradition de brasseurs depuis 1858
Een brouwerstraditie sinds 1858

LAGAULOISE

La gauloise brune

	top-fermentation re-fermentation in the bottle	fermentation haute refermentation en bouteille	hoge gisting hergisting in de fles
	specialty beer strong brown	bière spéciale brune forte	speciaalbier sterk bruin
	Brasserie du Bocq Purnode-Yvoir	Brasserie du Bocq Purnode-Yvoir	Brasserie du Bocq Purnode-Yvoir
	barley malt, hop varieties, yeast, herbs, water	malt d'orge, sortes de houblon, levure, herbes, eau	gerstemout, hoppesoorten, gist, kruiden, water
%	8,10%	8,10%	8,10%
	dark ruby red (70 EBC) clear and lively fine, full, white foam head	rouge rubis foncé (70 EBC) claire et vive faux col fin, ample, blanc	donker robijnrood (70 EBC) helder en levendig fijne, volle, witte kraag
	Gently pour into a perfectly degreased glass. Leave the yeast sediment (natural re-fermenting) in the bottle.	Verser doucement dans un verre parfaitement dégraissé. Laisser le dépôt de levure (refermentation naturelle) dans la bouteille.	Zacht uitschenken in een perfect ontvet glas. Het gistbezinksel (natuurlijke hergisting) in de fles laten.
°C	46 - 54 °F	8 - 12 °C	8 - 12 °C
	The nose is typical, rich, well-balanced and with a light coriander smell. Taste of special malts, full-bodied, well-balanced, with a slightly bitter aftertaste (32 EBU).	Bouquet typique, riche, équilibré avec un parfum léger de coriandre. Saveur de malts spéciaux, franche, équilibrée, avec une arrière-bouche légèrement amère (32 EBU).	De neus is typisch, rijk, evenwichtig met een lichte koriandergeur. Smaak van speciale mouten, volmondig, evenwichtig, met licht bittere nasmaak (32 EBU).
i	–	–	–

BRUNE
LAGAULOISE
Une tradition de brasseurs depuis 1858
Een brouwerstraditie sinds 1858

LAGAULOISE

La Grognarde
Bière de Virton

	top-fermentation re-fermented in the bottle	fermentation haute refermentation en bouteille	hoge gisting hergisting op de fles
	blond	blonde	blond
	Microbrasserie Ste Hélène Ethe	Microbrasserie Ste Hélène Ethe	Microbrasserie Ste Hélène Ethe
	malt, hops, yeast, sugar, water	malt, houblon, levure, sucre, eau	mout, hop, gist, suiker, water
%	5,50%	5,50%	5,50%
	blond unfiltered	blonde non filtrée	blond ongefilterd
	–	–	–
°C	50 - 54 °F	10 - 12 °C	10 - 12 °C
	Smooth and bitter.	Moelleux et amer.	Zacht en bitter.
i	Boutique beer. The label was designed by the artist Palix.	Brassée de façon artisanale. L'étiquette est conçue par le dessinateur Palix.	Artisanaal gebrouwen. Het etiket is ontworpen door tekenaar Palix.

LA
GROGNARDE
BIERE DE VIRTON

SH
Sainte Hélène

La Guillotine

	top-fermentation re-fermented in the bottle	fermentation haute refermentation en bouteille	hoge gisting hergisting in de fles
	strong blond	blonde forte	sterk blond
	Brouwerij Huyghe Melle	Brouwerij Huyghe Melle	Brouwerij Huyghe Melle
	barley malt, hops, yeast, water	malt d'orge, houblon, levure, eau	gerstemout, hop, gist, wate
%	8,50%	8,50%	8,50%
	blond clear	blonde claire	blond helder
	Serve in a goblet.	Verser dans un verre ballon.	Uitschenken in een bolglas
°C	–	–	–
	Nose of aromatic hops and powerful flavour and aftertaste.	Parfum de houblon aromatique. Goût et fin de bouche corsés.	Neus van aromatische hop. Krachtige smaak en afdronk.
i	Made for the French market, for the national day celebrations on July 14th.	Fabriquée pour le marché français, spécialement pour la fête nationale (14 juillet).	Gemaakt voor de Franse markt, speciaal voor de viering van de nationale feestdag (14 juli).

La Guillotine

La Marquise du Pont d'Oye Bière gaumaise de Virton

	top-fermentation re-fermented in the bottle	fermentation haute refermentation en bouteille	hoge gisting hergisting op de fles
	dubbel	double	dubbel
	Microbrasserie Ste Hélène Ethe	Microbrasserie Ste Hélène Ethe	Microbrasserie Ste Hélène Ethe
	lager malt	malt de lager	lager mout
%	6%	6%	6%
	–	–	–
	–	–	–
	50 - 54 °F	10 - 12 °C	10 - 12 °C
	Fine hops and malt flavour. Biscuit, chocolate and a touch of coffee.	Arômes raffinés de houblon et de malt. Biscuit, chocolat et une pointe de café.	Fijn aroma van hop en mout. Biscuit, chocolade en een vleugje koffie.
i	Boutique beer. The label was designed by the artist Palix.	Brassée de façon artisanale. L'étiquette est conçue par le dessinateur Palix.	Artisanaal gebrouwen. Het etiket is ontworpen door tekenaar Palix.

6%
BRUNE
La Marquise du Pont d'Oye
Gaumaise de Virton

La Médiévale

	top-fermentation re-fermented in the bottle unpasteurised	fermentation haute refermentation en bouteille non pasteurisée	hoge gisting hergisting op de fles ongepasteuriseerd
	abbey beer amber	bière d'abbaye ambrée	abdijbier amber
	Brasserie de Bouillon Bouillon	Brasserie de Bouillon Bouillon	Brasserie de Bouillon Bouillon
	barley malt, cara malt, hops, Orval yeast, water	malt d'orge, malt cara, houblon, levure Orval, eau	gerstemout, caramout, hop Orvalgist, water
%	6%	6%	6%
	amber unfiltered	ambrée non filtrée	amber niet gefilterd
	Hold the glass slightly tilt- ed while pouring the beer.	Tenir le verre légèrement incliné et verser.	Het glas licht schuin houden en inschenken.
°C	46 - 54 °F	8 - 12 °C	8 - 12 °C
	Traditionally brewed, round sipping beer.	Bière de dégustation artisanale ronde.	Ambachtelijk rond degus- tatiebier.
i	–	–	–

alc. 6% vol.
Belgian Beer
La Médiévale
Ambrée
PUR MALT, NON FILTREE REFERMENTEE EN BOUTEILLE
BIER, NIET GEFILTERD, NAGISTING IN DE FLES
CUVEE DE
BOUILLON

La Moneuse

	top-fermentation re-fermented in the bottle	fermentation haute refermentation en bouteille	hoge gisting hergisting in de fles
	specialty beer boutique beer	bière spéciale artisanale	speciaalbier artisanaal
	Brasserie de Blaugies Blaugies-Dour	Brasserie de Blaugies Blaugies-Dour	Brasserie de Blaugies Blaugies-Dour
	Malt, hops, yeast, water. Boutique beer without herbs or additives.	Malt, houblon, levure, eau. Produit artisanal sans herbes ou additifs.	Mout, hop, gist, water. Artisanaal product zonder kruiden of additieven.
%	8%	8%	8%
	amber unfiltered	ambrée non filtrée	amber niet gefilterd
	–	–	–
°C	43 - 46 °F	6 - 8 °C	6 - 8 °C
	Digestive and refreshing. Fine bitterness and long-lasting aftertaste.	Digestif et rafraîchissant. Saveur amère raffinée et arrière-bouche longue.	Digestief en verfrissend. Fijne bitterheid en lange nasmaak.
i	The brewer is a descendant of Antoine Joseph Moneuse, the leader of the gang of thieves 'Chauffeurs du Nord', who put their victims with their feet in the furnace until they confessed where their money was hidden.	La femme brasseur est une descendante d'Antoine Joseph Moneuse, le chef de la bande de voleurs 'Chauffeurs du Nord' qui mettaient les pieds de leurs victimes dans le feu à jusqu'à ce qu'elles révèlent où elles avaient caché leur argent.	De vrouwelijke brouwer is een afstammeling van Antoine Joseph Moneuse, de leider van de dievenbende 'Chauffeurs du Nord' die hun slachtoffers met de voeten in de stookplaats staken tot ze vertelden waar ze hun geld verborgen.

Blaugies

La Moneuse

BIERE - BIER

Brasserie de Blaugies

Bière Artisanale Belge
non filtrée. Brassée à l'ancienne
et refermentée en bouteille
Conserver couchée et servir frais

5 410557 000012

e75 cl.

8%

La Poiluchette blonde Cuvée du château

	top-fermentation re-fermented in the bottle	fermentation haute refermentation en bouteille	hoge gisting hergisting in de fles
	regional beer	bière régionale	streekbier
	Brouwerij Huyghe Melle	Brouwerij Huyghe Melle	Brouwerij Huyghe Melle
	malt, hops, yeast, water	malt, houblon, levure, eau	mout, hop, gist, water
	7,50%	7,50%	7,50%
	blonde clear	blonde claire	blond helder
	Serve in a flute-glass.	Verser dans une flûte.	Uitschenken in een fluitglas.
	refrigerated	température de réfrigérateur	frigofris
	Boutique beer. Sipping beer.	Bière de dégustation artisanale.	Artisanaal degustatiebier
	Originally brewed for the carnival celebrations in the region of Charleroi. Today it is a best-seller on the international market.	Brassée à l'origine lors des fêtes de carnaval dans la région de Charleroi mais la bière s'est développée entre-temps et a obtenu un réel succès sur les marchés étrangers.	Werd origineel gebrouwen voor de carnavalsfeesten in de regio Charleroi maar is ondertussen uitgegroeid tot een commercieel succes op de buitenlandse markt.

La Poiluchette
Blonde
CUVÉE DU CHÂTEAU
ALC 7,5% VOL
412186 001521
La Poiluchette

La Quenast

	bottom-fermentation	fermentation basse	lage gisting
	Pilsner	pils	pils
	Brasserie Lefebvre Quenast	Brasserie Lefebvre Quenast	Brasserie Lefebvre Quenast
	barley malt, corn, hops, yeast, water	malt d'orge, maïs, houblon, levure, eau	gerstemout, mais, hop, gist, water
%	5,20%	5,20%	5,20%
	blond clear	blonde claire	blond helder
	–	–	–
°C	39 - 43 °F	4 - 6 °C	4 - 6 °C
	–	–	–
i	–	–	–

TRADITION &
EXCELLENCE
LAQUENAST
BELGIAN PREMIUM PILS

La Rulles Blonde Bière de Gaume

top-fermentation re-fermented in the bottle unpasteurised	fermentation haute refermentation en bouteille non pasteurisée	hoge gisting hergisting op de fles ongepasteuriseerd
blond	blonde	blond
Brasserie Artisanale de Rulles Rulles	Brasserie Artisanale de Rulles Rulles	Brasserie Artisanale de Rulles Rulles
Pilsner and amber malt	malt de pils et malt ambré	pilsmout en ambermout
7%	7%	7%
golden blond unfiltered	blond doré non filtrée	goudblond niet gefilterd
–	–	–
–	–	–
Light biscuit taste, both smooth and bitter.	Saveur légère de biscuit, douce et amère à la fois.	Lichte biscuitsmaak, zacht en bitter tegelijk.
–	–	–

Bière de Gaume
La Rulles
Blonde
La Rulles

La Rulles Brune
Bière de Gaume

	top-fermentation re-fermented in the bottle unpasteurised	fermentation haute refermentation en bouteille non pasteurisée	hoge gisting hergisting op de fles ongepasteuriseerd
	dubbel	double	dubbel
	Brasserie Artisanale de Rulles Rulles	Brasserie Artisanale de Rulles Rulles	Brasserie Artisanale de Rulles Rulles
	Pilsner malt, amber malt, caramel and roasted malt, hops, yeast, water	malt de pils et malt ambré, malt caramélisé et brûlé, houblon, levure, eau	pilsmout, ambermout, karamel- en gebrande mout, hop, gist, water
%	6,50%	6,50%	6,50%
	brown unfiltered	brune non filtrée	bruin niet gefilterd
	–	–	–
°C	46 - 50 °F	8 - 10 °C	8 - 10 °C
	Prominent malt flavour with a touch of fruit and bitterness.	Dominance de malt avec une touche de fruits et d'amertume.	Moutdominantie met een toets van fruit en bitterheid.
i	–	–	–

Bière de Gaume
Rulles
Brune

La Rulles

La Rulles Estivale
Bière de Gaume

	top-fermentation re-fermented in the bottle unpasteurised	fermentation haute refermentation en bouteille non pasteurisée	hoge gisting hergisting op de fles ongepasteuriseerd
	blond	blonde	blond
	Brasserie Artisanale de Rulles Rulles	Brasserie Artisanale de Rulles Rulles	Brasserie Artisanale de Rulles Rulles
	pure malt	malt pur	pure mout
%	5,20%	5,20%	5,20%
	blond	blonde	blond
	–	–	–
°C	46 - 50 °F	8 - 10 °C	8 - 10 °C
	Refreshing and bitter.	Rafraîchissant et amer.	Verfrissend en bitter.
i	Beside the summer beer exists also a winter beer, 'La Rulles Cuvée Meilleurs Voeux'.	Outre la bière estivale, il existe aussi une bière hivernale: 'La Rulles Cuvée Meilleurs Voeux'.	Naast het zomerbier bestaat er ook een winterbier 'La Rulles Cuvée Meilleurs Voeux'.

....

....

....

....

....

de Gaume
Rulles
La Rulles

La Rulles Triple Bière de Gaume

	top-fermentation re-fermented in the bottle unpasteurised	fermentation haute refermentation en bouteille non pasteurisée	hoge gisting hergisting op de fles ongepasteuriseerd
	Tripel	triple	tripel
	Brasserie Artisanale de Rulles Rulles	Brasserie Artisanale de Rulles Rulles	Brasserie Artisanale de Rulles Rulles
	–	–	–
%	8,40%	8,40%	8,40%
	unfiltered	non filtrée	niet gefilterd
	–	–	–
°C	46 - 50 °F	8 - 10 °C	8 - 10 °C
	Sipping beer, full and bitter.	Bière de dégustation pleine et amère.	Degustatiebier, vol en bitter.
i	–	–	–

La Rulles

La Sainte Hélène ambrée
Brasserie Gaumaise

	top-fermentation re-fermented in the bottle	fermentation haute refermentation en bouteille	hoge gisting hergisting op de fles
	amber	ambrée	amber
	Microbrasserie Ste Hélène Ethe	Microbrasserie Ste Hélène Ethe	Microbrasserie Ste Hélène Ethe
	malt, hops, yeast, sugar, water	malt, houblon, levure, sucre, eau	mout, hop, gist, suiker, water
%	8,50%	8,50%	8,50%
	unfiltered	non filtrée	ongefilterd
	–	–	–
°C	cool or room temperature	rafraîchie ou à température ambiante	fris of kamertemperatuur
	Smooth and full with taste evolution, caramel and fruit flavour.	Moelleux et plein avec évolution de la saveur. Saveur de caramel et de fruits.	Zacht en vol met smaakevolutie. Smaak van karamel en fruit.
i	Boutique beer. The label was designed by the artist Palix.	Brassée de façon artisanale. L'étiquette est conçue par le dessinateur Palix.	Artisanaal gebrouwen. Het etiket is ontworpen door tekenaar Palix.

8,5%
Ambrée
Brasserie Gaumaise
La
Sainte Hélène

La Sainte Hélène blonde
Brasserie Gaumaise

top-fermentation re-fermented in the bottle	fermentation haute refermentation en bouteille	hoge gisting hergisting op de fles
blond	blonde	blond
Microbrasserie Ste Hélène Ethe	Microbrasserie Ste Hélène Ethe	Microbrasserie Ste Hélène Ethe
English and German hops	houblon anglais et allemand	Engelse en Duitse hop
6,50%	6,50%	6,50%
dark blond	blond foncé	donkerblond
Pour carefully in a tulip-shaped glass and leave the sediment in the bottle.	Verser prudemment dans un verre tulipe et laisser la lie dans la bouteille.	Voorzichtig uitschenken in een tulpglas en de droesem op de bodem van de fles laten.
50 - 54 °F	10 - 12 °C	10 - 12 °C
Smooth bitter provision beer with a hoppy flavour.	Bière de conservation amère-moelleuse avec un arôme houblonné.	Zacht bitter bewaarbier met een hoppig aroma.
Boutique beer. The label was designed by the artist Palix.	Brassée de façon artisanale. L'étiquette est conçue par le dessinateur Palix.	Artisanaal gebrouwen. Het etiket is ontworpen door tekenaar Palix.

6,5%
Blonde
Brasserie Gaumaise
La
Sainte Hélène
Sainte Hélène

La Sambresse

	top-fermentation	fermentation haute	hoge gisting
	blond	blonde	blond
	Brasserie Brootcoorens Erquelinnes	Brasserie Brootcoorens Erquelinnes	Brasserie Brootcoorens Erquelinnes
	Pilsner and amber malt, aromatic hops, orange rind, juniper-berry, coriander, yeast, water	malt de pils et malt ambré, houblon aromatique, écorce d'orange, baie de genièvre, coriandre, levure, eau	pils- en ambermout, aroma tische hop, sinaasschil, jeneverbes, koriander, gist water
%	8%	8%	8%
	blond unfiltered yet transparent	blonde non filtrée mais transparente	blond ongefilterd maar transparant
	Do not shake the bottle and pour carefully.	Prendre soin que la bouteille n'a pas été secouée et verser prudemment.	Zorgen dat de fles niet geschud is en voorzichtig uitschenken.
	39 °F or 50 °F	4 °C ou 10 °C	4 °C of 10 °C
	Pleasant, round and original but very accessible natural beer. Well-balanced taste evolution and an aroma with hoppy and spicy touch.	Bière naturelle agréable, ronde et originale mais très abordable. Saveur évolutive équilibrée et arôme avec touche de houblon et d'herbes.	Aangenaam, rond en origineel maar toch zeer toegankelijk natuurbier. Evenwichtige evoluerende smaak en aroma met hoptoets en kruidentoets.
i	–	–	–

LA SAMBRESSE
BLONDE
Bière
Naturelle
Pur malt
Non filtrée
Alc.
8% vol.
℮ 75 cl
Verre
consigné
BIÈRE DE SAMBRE ET DE TENDRESSE

La Sur-Les-Bois Ambrée

	top-fermentation triple fermentation	fermentation haute triple fermentation	hoge gisting driedubbele gisting
	specialty beer boutique beer	bière spéciale artisanale	speciaalbier artisanaal
	Brasserie La Botteresse de Sur-Les-Bois Saint-Georges	Brasserie La Botteresse de Sur-Les-Bois Saint-Georges	Brasserie La Botteresse de Sur-Les-Bois Saint-Georges
	traditional and roasted malt varieties, herbs	malts traditionnels et brûlés, herbes	traditionele en gebrande moutsoorten, kruiden
	8%	8%	8%
	amber unfiltered	ambrée non filtrée	amber ongefilterd
	Pour into a degreased, dry glass, leaving 1 cm of yeast sediment in the bottle.	Verser dans un verre dégraissé, sec et laisser un dépôt de levure de 1 cm dans la bouteille.	Uitschenken in een ontve droog glas en 1 cm gistdepot in de fles laten.
	43 - 45 °F	6 - 7 °C	6 - 7 °C
	Refreshing, digestive, smooth and slightly hopped. Slightly fruity and spicy taste and aroma.	Rafraîchissant, digestif, doux et légèrement houblonné. Saveur et arômes légèrement fruités et relevés.	Verfrissend, digestief, zach en licht gehopt. Licht fruitige en kruidige smaak en aroma.
	–	–	–

Sur-les-Bois
Alc. 8% Vol.
33cl.
Bière
artisanale
Ambrée
Brasserie Artisanale "La Botteresse de Sur-les-Bois" - 4470 Saint-Georges
Bière Artisanale

La Sur-Les-Bois Blonde

top-fermentation triple fermentation	fermentation haute triple fermentation	hoge gisting driedubbele gisting
specialty beer boutique beer	bière spéciale artisanale	speciaalbier artisanaal
Brasserie La Botteresse de Sur-Les-Bois Saint-Georges	Brasserie La Botteresse de Sur-Les-Bois Saint-Georges	Brasserie La Botteresse de Sur-Les-Bois Saint-Georges
traditional malt varieties and orange rind	variétés traditionnelles de malt et écorce d'orange	traditionele moutsoorten en sinaasappelschil
7%	7%	7%
blond unfiltered	blonde non filtrée	blond ongefilterd
Pour into a degreased, dry glass, leaving 1 cm of yeast sediment in the bottle.	Verser dans un verre dégraissé, sec et laisser un dépôt de levure de 1 cm dans la bouteille.	Uitschenken in een ontvet, droog glas en 1 cm gistdepot in de fles laten.
43 - 45 °F	6 - 7 °C	6 - 7 °C
Refreshing and fruity with a fine hoppy taste and aroma.	Rafraîchissant et fruité avec saveur et arômes houblonnés raffinés.	Verfrissend en fruitig met fijne hopsmaak en -aroma.
–	–	–

Sur-les-Bois
Alc. 7% Vol.
33cl.
Bière artisanale
Blonde
"La Botteresse de Sur-les-Bois" - 4470 Saint-Georges
Sur-les-Bois
Bière Artisanale

La Sur-Les-Bois Brune

	top-fermentation triple fermentation	fermentation haute triple fermentation	hoge gisting driedubbele gisting
	specialty beer boutique beer	bière spéciale artisanale	speciaalbier artisanaal
	Brasserie La Botteresse de Sur-Les-Bois Saint-Georges	Brasserie La Botteresse de Sur-Les-Bois Saint-Georges	Brasserie La Botteresse de Sur-Les-Bois Saint-Georges
	traditional malt varieties, aromatic malt varieties, chocolate malt	variétés traditionnelles et aromatiques de malt, malt chocolat	traditionele moutsoorten, aromatische moutsoorten, chocolademout
%	9%	9%	9%
	brown unfiltered	brune non filtrée	bruin ongefilterd
	Pour into a degreased, dry glass and leave 1 cm yeast sediment in the bottle.	Verser dans un verre dégraissé, sec et laisser un dépôt de levure de 1 cm dans la bouteille.	Uitschenken in een ontvet, droog glas en 1 cm gistdepot in de fles laten.
°C	50 °F	10 °C	10 °C
	Round and well-balanced sipping beer. Fruity with a taste of roasty malt, liquorice and coffee.	Bière de dégustation ronde et équilibrée. Goût fruité avec des touches de malt brûlé, réglisse et café.	Rond en evenwichtig degustatiebier. Fruitig met smaaktoetsen van gebrande mout, zoethout en koffie.
i	–	–	–

Sur-les-Bois
8,5% Vol.
33cl.
Bièré
artisanale
Brune
"La Botteresse de Sur-les-Bois" - 4470 Saint-Georges

La Vauban 1707-2007

	top-fermentation re-fermented in the bottle unpasteurised	fermentation haute refermentation en bouteille non pasteurisée	hoge gisting hergisting op de fles ongepasteuriseerd
	abbey beer	bière d'abbaye	abdijbier
	Brasserie de Bouillon Bouillon	Brasserie de Bouillon Bouillon	Brasserie de Bouillon Bouillon
	barley malt, hops, Orval yeast, herbs, water	malt d'orge, houblon, levure Orval, herbes, eau	gerstemout, hop, Orvalgist kruiden, water
%	6%	6%	6%
	blond unfiltered	blonde non filtrée	blond niet gefilterd
	Hold the glass slightly tilted while pouring.	Tenir le verre légèrement incliné et verser.	Het glas licht schuin houden en inschenken.
°C	46 - 54 °F	8 - 12 °C	8 - 12 °C
	Light and slightly bitter sipping beer.	Bière de dégustation légère et légèrement amère.	Licht en lichtbitter degustatiebier.
i	Brewed for the 300th anniversary of Maréchal Vauban's death. The label features the Castle of Bouillon on the background.	Brassée à l'occasion du 300ième anniversaire du décès du Maréchal Vauban. L'étiquette représente le Château de Bouillon.	Gebrouwen n.a.v. de 300e verjaardag van het overlijden van Maréchal Vauban. Op het etiket staat op de achtergrond Het Kasteel van Bouillon.

CUVEE DE
BOUILLON
Maréchal Vauban

Lam Gods

	top-fermentation re-fermented in the bottle	fermentation haute refermentation en bouteille	hoge gisting met nagisting in de fles
	dubbel	double	dubbel
	Brouwerij Van Steenberge for Microbrouwerij Paele-man, Wetteren	Brouwerij Van Steenberge pour Microbrouwerij Pae-leman, Wetteren	Brouwerij Van Steenberge voor Microbrouwerij Paele-man, Wetteren
	–	–	–
%	6,20%	6,20%	6,20%
	dark unfiltered	foncée non filtrée	donker ongefilterd
	–	–	–
	–	–	–
	Traditional, soft beer with a touch of star anise and caramelized malt.	Bière artisanale moelleu-se avec une pointe d'anis et une touche maltée caramélisée.	Ambachtelijk zacht bier met een vleugje steranijs en gekaramelliseerde mouttoets.
i	Sipping beer with taste evolution. Store in a cool, dark room.	Bière de dégustation avec évolution de saveur. Conserver à l'abri de la chaleur et de la lumière.	Degustatiebier met smaak-evolutie. Bewaren op een koele donkere plaats.

Lam Gods
alc. 6,2% vol. e 33 cl. cat. S.
02/11/08 02KF 13:39
Lam Gods

Lamoral degmont

top-fermentation re-fermented in the bottle	fermentation haute refermentation en bouteille	hoge gisting hergisting op de fles
regional beer	bière régionale	streekbier tripel
Brouwerij Van Den Bossche St-Lievens-Esse	Brouwerij Van Den Bossche St-Lievens-Esse	Brouwerij Van Den Bossch St-Lievens-Esse
hops, yeast, fermentable sugar, water. Malt varieties: Pilsner, caramel, Pale Ale.	malt, houblon, sucre de fermentation, eau. Variétés de malt: pils, caramélisé, pale ale.	hop, gist, vergistbare suiker, water. Moutsoorten: pils, karame pale ale.
8%	8%	8%
amber blond nice, white foam head	blond ambré faux col solide, blanc	amberblond mooie, witte schuimkraag
Pour slowly for a nice foam head with hat. Leave a small amount in the bottle (it can be served afterwards) and present the bottle with the glass.	Verser lentement pour obtenir un faux col solide avec chapeau. Laisser un peu de bière dans la bouteille (peut être versé par la suite) et offrir aussi la bouteille.	Langzaam inschenken voo een mooie schuimkraag en schuimhoed. Een restje in de fles laten (kan achteraf bijgeschonken worden) en de fles mee aanbieden.
43 - 46 °F	6 - 8 °C	6 - 8 °C
Aroma: mainly fruit and spices. Flavour: first spicy touches, then a fast evolution toward an intense, bitter aftertaste.	Parfum: dominance de fruits et d'herbes. Saveur: touches relevées aboutissant très rapidement à une fin de bouche amère intense.	Geur: overheersend fruitig en kruidig. Smaak: eerst kruidige toetsen die vrij snel evolueren naar een intens bittere afdronk.
–	–	–

LAMORAL
TRIPEL
LAMORAL
degmont

Leffe 9°

	top-fermentation	fermentation haute	hoge gisting
	recognised Belgian abbey beer	Bière d'abbaye belge reconnue	Erkend Belgisch abdijbier
	Inbev Belgium Leuven	Inbev Belgium Louvain	Inbev Belgium Leuven
	barley malt, corn, hops, yeast, water	malt d'orge, maïs, houblon, levure, eau	gerstemout, maïs, hop, gist water
%	9%	9%	9%
	–	–	–
	Rinse the glass in cold water, tilt it and carefully pour the beer. Skim off if desired.	Rincer le verre à l'eau froide, le tenir incliné et verser la bière doucement. Ecumer selon le goût.	Het glas in koud water spoelen, schuin houden en het bier zacht uitschenken. Desgewenst afschuimen.
°C	43 - 46 °F	6 - 8 °C	6 - 8 °C
	Powerful full taste. Strong fruity and spicy flavour (cloves, vanilla) with a slightly roasty touch, that reminds of cognac or whisky. Long aromatic and warm aftertaste.	Saveur pleine, corsée. Arôme très fruité et relevé (girofle, vanille) avec une touche légèrement fumée qui fait penser au cognac ou au whisky. Fin de bouche aromatique, longue et chaude.	Krachtige volle smaak. Sterk fruitig en kruidig (kruidnagel, vanille) aroma met licht gerookte toets die aan cognac of whisky doet denken. Lange aromatische en warme afdronk.
i	–	–	–

Bière d'Abbaye
9°
9°
Leffe
Leffe
Bier
Abbaye de Abdij van
Leffe
9°

Leffe

Leffe blond

	top-fermentation	fermentation haute	hoge gisting
	recognised Belgian abbey beer	Bière belge d'abbaye reconnue	Erkend Belgisch abdijbier blond
	Inbev Belgium Leuven	Inbev Belgium Louvain	Inbev Belgium Leuven
	pale malt, corn, hops, yeast, water	malt pâle, maïs, houblon, levure, eau	bleekmout, maïs, hop, gist, water
%	6,60%	6,60%	6,60%
	nice golden colour	joli doré	fraai goud
	Rinse the glass in cold water, tilt it and carefully pour the beer. Skim off if desired.	Rincer le verre à l'eau froide, le tenir incliné et verser la bière doucement. Ecumer selon le goût.	Het glas in koud water spoelen, schuin houden en het bier zacht uitschenken. Desgewenst afschuimen.
°C	41 - 43 °F	5 - 6 °C	5 - 6 °C
	Orange-like palette with a nut-like and creamy structure. Smooth, full and spicy taste, powerful aftertaste and spicy undertone.	Palette d'orange avec une structure crémeuse de noix. Saveur moelleuse, pleine et relevée, fin de bouche solide et arrière-fond corsé.	Sinaasachtig palet met een nootachtige en romige structuur. Zachte, volle en kruidige smaak, krachtige afdronk en pittige ondertoon.
i	–	–	–

Leffe
BLONDE
BLOND
Abbaye de
Abdij van
Leffe
BLONDE · BLOND

Abbaye de
Abdij van
Leffe

Leffe bruin

	top-fermentation	fermentation haute	hoge gisting
	recognised brown Belgian abbey beer	Bière d'abbaye belge brune reconnue	Erkend Belgisch abdijbi bruin
	Inbev Belgium Leuven	Inbev Belgium Louvain	Inbev Belgium Leuven
	dark roasted malt, corn, hops, yeast, water	malt brûlé, maïs, houblon, levure, eau	donkergebrande mout, maïs, hop, gist, water
%	6,50%	6,50%	6,50%
	deep autumn-brown	brun d'automne intense	diep herfstbruin
	Rinse the glass in cold water, tilt it and carefully pour the beer. Skim off if desired.	Rincer le verre à l'eau froide, le tenir incliné et verser la bière doucement. Ecumer selon le goût.	Het glas in koud water spoelen, schuin houden het bier zacht uitschen Desgewenst afschuimen
°C	41 - 43 °F	5 - 6 °C	5 - 6 °C
	Full taste. A trace of dessert apple in the bouquet. Fruity sweet and brown sugar with caramel and toffee. Dry, spicy aftertaste.	Saveur pleine. Touche de pomme de dessert dans le bouquet. Doux et fruité, cassonade et caramel. Fin de bouche sèche et relevée.	Volle smaak. Zweem van dessertappe het boeket. Fruitig zoet tot bruine s ker met karamel en toff Droge en kruidige afdrc
i	Store at cellar temperature.	Conserver à température de cave.	Bewaren op keldertempe ratuur.

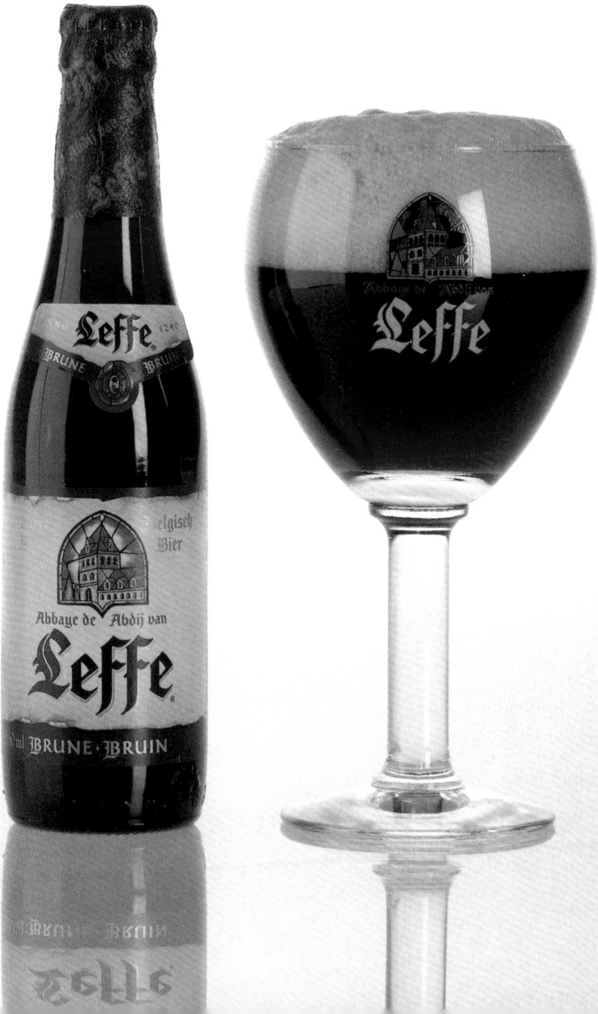

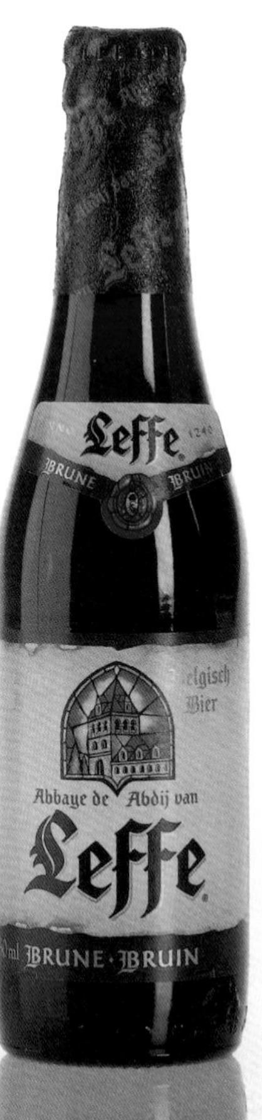

Leffe
BRUNE
BRUIN
Bier
Abbaye de Abdij van
Leffe
BRUNE · BRUIN
Abbaye de Abdij van
Leffe

Leireken amber

	top-fermentation	fermentation haute	hoge gisting
	amber	ambrée	amber
	Brouwerij Silenrieux for Guldenboot Opwijk	Brouwerij Silenrieux pour Guldenboot Opwijk	Brouwerij Silenrieux voor Guldenboot Opwijk
	organic barley malt, organic buckwheat, biosucrose, hops, yeast, water	malt d'orge bio, sarrasin bio, sucrose bio, houblon, levure, eau	biogerstemout, bioboe[illegible] weit, biosucrose, hop, [illegible] water
%	6%	6%	6%
	7 EBC cloudy	7 EBC trouble	7 EBC troebel
	Hold the glass tilted (45°) whilst pouring.	Tenir le verre incliné (45 °) au moment de verser.	Het glas schuin houden bij het inschenken.
	37 °F	3 °C	3 °C
	Full-bodied refreshening, round fruity.	Franc et frais, rond et fruité.	Volmondig fris, rond fruitig.
i	–	–	–

AMBER
Leireken
2010
0,10 €

Leutebok

	top-fermentation re-fermented in the bottle	fermentation haute refermentation en bouteille	hoge gisting hergisting in de fles
	regional beer dark	bière régionale foncée	streekbier donker
	Brouwerij Van Steenberge Ertvelde	Brouwerij Van Steenberge Ertvelde	Brouwerij Van Steenbe Ertvelde
	barley malt, hops, yeast, water	malt d'orge, houblon, levure, eau	gerstemout, hop, gist,
%	7,50% 16° plato	7,50% 16° plato	7,50% 16° plato
	dark red	rouge foncé	donkerrood
	Pour in a single, fluent and careful movement, leaving 1 cm of yeast sediment in the bottle. Typical tumbler in a wooden holder.	Verser en un seul mouvement fluide et doux et laisser 1 cm de dépôt de levure dans la bouteille. Verre typique inversable avec support en bois.	Uitschenken in 1 vloei zachte beweging en 1 c gistdepot in de fles late Heeft een typisch tuim glas met houten voet.
°C	50 - 54 °F	10 - 12 °C	10 - 12 °C
	Aromatic, not too pronounced, but full and with a mild mouthfeel.	Aromatique, pas trop prononcé, mais plein et doux dans la bouche.	Aromatisch, niet te ui sproken, maar vol en n in de mond.
i	'Leute' means 'fun' in Flemish. The goat and the hops in the logo refer to the brewery and the neighbouring hop fields when the production of the bok beer started in 1927.	'Leute' est flamand pour 'plaisir'. Le bouc et le vrille de houblon renvoient aux activités agricoles dans la brasserie et aux champs de houblon adjacents lors de la création de la bokbier en 1927.	'Leute' is Vlaams voor ' zier'. De bok en hoppe in het logo verwijzen n de agrarische activiteit op de brouwerij en de palende hoppevelden b de opstart van het bok in 1927.
	....		

LEUTE
BOKBIER
LEUTE
ANNO
1927
BOKBIER

LEUTE
ANNO
1927
BOKBIER
LEUTE BOKBIER®

Liefmans Framboos

	mixed fermentation	fermentation mixte	gemengde gisting
	soury raspberry beer	bière de framboises acidulée	zurig frambozenbier
	Brouwerij Liefmans Oudenaarde/Dentergem	Brouwerij Liefmans Audenarde/Dentergem	Brouwerij Liefmans Oudenaarde/Denterge
	Blend of brown and Goudenband with mashed raspberries. Barley malt, corn, sugar, raspberry juice, flavouring, hops, yeast, water.	Mélange de brune et de Goudenband avec adjonction de framboises pressées. Malt d'orge, maïs, sucre, jus de framboises, arômes, houblon, levure, eau.	Mengeling van bruin e Goudenband met toevo ging van geperste fram bozen. Gerstemout, mais, suik frambozensap, aroma, gist, water.
	4,50%	4,50%	4,50%
	raspberry red slightly cloudy	rouge framboise légèrement trouble	frambozenrood licht troebel
	–	–	–
°C	43 - 50 °F	6 - 10 °C	6 - 10 °C
	Sourish and fruity. Sweet-and-sour with a natural raspberry flavour and aroma.	Acidulé et fruité. Aigre-doux avec un goût naturel et des arômes de framboises.	Zurig en fruitig. Zuurzoet met natuurlij smaak van frambozen e frambozenaroma.
	–	–	–

Liefmans
FRAMBOZENBIER
Liefmans
CHAMPION BEER 2004

Liefmans 'Goudenband' Provision beer

	top-fermentation	fermentation haute	hoge gisting
	soury dark-brown Ale	ale brun foncé acidulé	zurige donkerbruine al
	Brouwerij Liefmans Oudenaarde/Dentergem	Brouwerij Liefmans Audenarde/Dentergem	Brouwerij Liefmans Oudenaarde/Dentergen
	Special malts, sugar, corn, hops, yeast, water. Matures four to eight months in lager cellars.	Malts spéciaux, sucre, maïs, houblon, levure, eau. Mûrit 4 à 8 mois dans des caves.	Speciale mouten, suike mais, hop, gist, water. Rijpt 4 à 8 maanden in lagerkelders.
%	8%	8%	8%
	dark brown slightly cloudy	brun foncé légèrement trouble	donkerbruin licht troebel
	–	–	–
°C	46 - 54 °F	8 - 12 °C	8 - 12 °C
	Sourish character. Sweet-and-sour, malty and caramel-like aroma.	Caractère acidulé. Aigre-doux, houblonné et arôme caramélisé.	Zurig karakter. Zuurzoet, moutig en ka melachtig aroma.
i	Can be kept for a long time. Positive taste evolution when stored horizontally at cellar temperature.	Se conserve longtemps, évolution de la saveur positive en position horizontale à température de cave.	Lang houdbaar en posit smaakevolutie bij horiz tale bewaring op keldeı peratuur.

Gold Medal
Certified by
Member of
PROVISION BEER
"GOUDENBAND"
Liefmans
Oudenaarde
BELGIUM

Liefmans
GOUDENBAND

Liefmans Kriekbier

	mixed fermentation	fermentation mixte	gemengde gisting
	soury Kriek beer	bière kriek acidulée	zurig kriekbier
	Brouwerij Liefmans Oudenaarde/Dentergem	Brouwerij Liefmans Audenarde/Dentergem	Brouwerij Liefmans Oudenaarde/Denterg
	A blend of brown and Goudenband (min. six months old) with cherries (pips included) added. Lagering: six months to two years. Cherries with pip, barley malt, sugar, corn, hops, yeast, flavouring, water.	Mélange de brune et de Goudenband (min. 6 mois d'âge) avec adjonction de cerises (avec noyau). Conservation de 6 mois à 2 ans. Cerises avec noyau, malt d'orge, sucre, maïs, houblon, levure, arômes, eau.	Mengeling van bruin Goudenband (min. 6 den oud) met toevoeg van krieken (met pit). Lagering van 6 maan tot 2 jaar. Krieken met pit, gerst mout, suiker, mais, h gist, aroma, water.
	6%	6%	6%
	brown-red slightly cloudy	brun rouge légèrement trouble	bruinrood licht troebel
	–	–	–
	43 - 50 °F	6 - 10 °C	6 - 10 °C
	Sourish and fruity. Sweet-and-sour with a natural cherry flavour and aroma.	Acidulé et fruité. Aigre-doux avec un goût naturel et des arômes de cerises.	Zurig en fruitig. Zuurzoet met natuur smaak van krieken en kriekenaroma.
	–	–	–

KRIEKBIER
Liefmans
OUDENAARDE - BELGIUM

Liefmans Oud Bruin

	mixed fermentation	fermentation mixte	gemengde gisting
	dark brown soury Ale	brun foncé ale acidulé	donkerbruine zurige ale
	Brouwerij Liefmans Oudenaarde/Dentergem	Brouwerij Liefmans Audenarde/Dentergem	Brouwerij Liefmans Oudenaarde/Dentergem
	Barley malt, sugar, hops, yeast, water. Matures four to eight months in lagering.	Malt d'orge, sucre, houblon, levure, eau. Mûrit 4 à 8 mois.	Gerstemout, suiker, ho gist, water. Rijpt 4 à 8 maanden in gering
%	5%	5%	5%
	dark brown slightly cloudy	brun foncé légèrement trouble	donkerbruin licht troebel
	–	–	–
	43 - 50 °F	6 - 10 °C	6 - 10 °C
	Sourish character. Sweet-and-sour, malty and caramel-like flavour.	Caractère acidulé. Aigre-doux avec un arôme caramélisé.	Zurig karakter. Zuurzo moutig en karamelach aroma.
i	–	–	–

OUDENAARDS BRUIN BIER
1679
OUD BRUIN
Liefmans
BIÈRE BRUNE DES FLANDRES
25cl e
Liefmans

Limburgse Witte

	top-fermentation unfiltered	fermentation haute non filtrée	hoge gisting ongefilterd
	Witbier	bière blanche	witbier
	Brouwerij Martens, Bocholt and Brouwerij Sint-Jozef, Opitter	Brouwerij Martens, Bocholt et Brouwerij Sint-Jozef, Opitter	Brouwerij Martens, Boc en Brouwerij Sint-Jozef Opitter
	wheat, hops, yeast, lemon pulp, water	froment, houblon, levure, pulpe de citron, eau	tarwe, hop, gist, citro pulp, water
%	5%	5%	5%
	cloudy nice, solid foam head	trouble faux col beau et solide	troebel mooie, vaste schuimk
	Pour half of the bottle, stop, revolve the bottle in your hand, then pour the rest.	Verser la bouteille à moitié, faire une pause, tourner la bouteille dans la main et puis continuer à verser.	De fles half uitschenk eventjes stoppen, de fl draaien in de hand en na verder schenken.
°C	36 °F	2 °C	2 °C
	Full and well-rounded.	Plein et rond.	Vol en afgerond.
i	Joint product from the Martens and Sint-Jozef breweries.	Produit commun des brasseries Martens et Sint-Jozef.	Gezamenlijk product de brouwerijen Marte Sint-Jozef.

Limburgse
Witte
ROCHOLT
SINT-JOZEF
ANNO 1993
WIT BIER · BIERE BLANCHE
Limburgse
Witte
DUO-BROUW
ANNO 1993
25cl ALC 5% vol
Witte
DUO - BROUW

Livinus

	top-fermentation	fermentation haute	hoge gisting
	regional beer	bière régionale	streekbier
	Brouwerij Van Den Bossche Sint-Lievens-Esse	Brouwerij Van Den Bossche Sint-Lievens-Esse	Brouwerij Van Den Bos Sint-Lievens-Esse
	Pilsner malt, cara malt, fermentable sugar, yeast, hops, water	malt de pils, malt cara, sucre fermentable, levure, houblon, eau	pilsmout, caramout, v gistbare suiker, gist, h water
%	5,20%	5,20%	5,20%
	golden blond	blond doré	goudblond
	Pour the beer slowly without sloshing. Make a nice foam head and hat.	Verser la bière lentement sans la laisser glouglouter. Former un beau faux col avec chapeau.	Het bier langzaam uit- schenken zonder het t ten klokken. Een mooie schuimkra schuimhoed vormen.
°C	37 - 43 °F	3 - 6 °C	3 - 6 °C
	Full taste with a slightly bitter aftertaste.	Goût plein avec une fin de bouche légèrement amère.	Volle smaak met een l bittere afdronk.
i	The beer was brewed for the first time for the Saint-Livinus celebrations in Sint-Lievens-Esse in 2007.	La bière a été brassée pour la première fois en 2007 à l'occasion des fêtes St Livinus à Sint-Lievens-Esse.	Het bier werd voor het gebrouwen ter geleger van de Sint-Livinusfee in Sint-Lievens-Esse in

BLOND BIER VAN HOGE GISTING
BR VAN DEN BOSSCHE
BIERE BLONDE DE FERMENTATION HAUTE

Pater
Lieven

Loterbol

top-fermentation re-fermented in the bottle	fermentation haute refermentation en bouteille	hoge gisting hergisting op de fles
blond	blonde	blond
Brouwerij Duysters Diest	Brouwerij Duysters Diest	Brouwerij Duysters Diest
Malt, hops, yeast, water. Dry-hopping.	Malt, houblon, levu- re, eau. Dry hopping.	Mout, hop, gist, water Dry hopping.
8%	8%	8%
blond unfiltered	blonde non filtrée	blond niet gefilterd
–	–	–
–	–	–
Bitter, fruity flavour, with a dry aftertaste.	Amer, arôme fruité, arrière-bouche sèche.	Bitter, fruitig aroma, d afdronk.
Also has an 8% brown version. Tuverbol (11%) is a blend of blond with 3 Fontein-en Lambik.	Existe aussi dans une version brune de 8%. Tuverbol (11%) est un mélange de blonde et de 3 Fontaines Lambic.	Bestaat ook in een bru versie van 8%. Tuverbol (11%) is een r geling van blond met teinen Lambik.

Loterbol
Alc. 8% Vol ℮ 33 cl/330 ml
5 425006 980609
MICHEL THEYSSTRAAT 58A B-3290 DIEST
Loterbol

Loubecoise

top-fermentation re-fermented in the bottle	fermentation haute refermentation en bouteille	hoge gisting hergisting in de fles
regional beer	bière citadine ou régionale	stads- of streekbier
Brasserie d'Ecaussinnes Ecaussinnes d'Enghien	Brasserie d'Ecaussinnes Ecaussinnes d'Enghien	Brasserie d'Ecaussinne Ecaussinnes d'Enghie
malts, hops, candy sugar, maple syrup, yeast, spring water	malts, houblon, sucre candi, sirop d'érable, levure, eau de source	mouten, hop, kandijs esdoornsiroop, gist, br water
8%	8%	8%
burgundy	bordeaux	bordeaux
–	–	–
46 °F	8 °C	8 °C
Flavour of brown sugar. Strong taste of Québec maple syrup.	Arôme de cassonade. Goût fort de sirop d'érable du Québec.	Aroma van bruine sui Sterke smaak van aho siroop uit Québec.
–	–	–

LA LOUBÉCOISE
Bière Forte - Strong Beer
Bière brune Belge artisanale au sirop d'érable Québécois
Ultra
des
Ecaussinnes

Lucifer

	top-fermentation re-fermented in the bottle	fermentation haute refermentation en bouteille	hoge gisting nagisting in de fles
	strong blond	blonde forte	sterk blond
	Brouwerij Liefmans Oudenaarde/Dentergem	Brouwerij Liefmans Audenarde/Dentergem	Brouwerij Liefmans Oudenaarde/Dentergem
	barley malt, corn, pale candy sugar, hops, yeast, water	malt d'orge, maïs, sucre candi blanc, houblon, levure, eau	gerstemout, mais, bleke kandijsuiker, hop, gist, water
%	8,50%	8,50%	8,50%
	gold-yellow clear	jaune doré claire	goudgeel helder
	Leave the yeast in the bottle.	Laisser la levure dans la bouteille.	De gist in het flesje lat
°C	43 - 50 °F	6 - 10 °C	6 - 10 °C
	Sipping beer with a delicate flavour. Dry, hoppy start and full-bodied taste and after-taste.	Bière de dégustation avec un arôme délicat. Saveur initiale houblonnée et sèche, goût et fin de bouche francs.	Degustatiebier met de aroma. Droge, hoppige aanvar volmondige smaak en dronk.
i	Winner of the World Beer Cup 2004 Gold Award.	World Beer Cup 2004 Gold Award.	World Beer Cup 2004 (Award.

Lucifer
SPECIAALBIER OP GIST
BIÈRE SPÉCIALE SUR LIE
BELGIAN GOLDEN ALE ON LEES
Lucifer

Maes

	bottom-fermentation	fermentation basse	lage gisting
	Pilsner	pils	pils
	Alken Maes corporation Alken	Alken Maes corporation Alken	Alken Maes corporatio Alken
	–	–	–
	4,90%	4,90%	4,90%
	gold-yellow	jaune doré	goudgeel
	Empty in a degreased, rinsed and wet glass. Let overflow and skim off the foam.	Verser complètement dans un verre dégraissé, rincé et mouillé. Laisser déborder et écumer.	Helemaal uitschenken een ontvet, gespoeld e nat glas. Laten overlopen en afs men.
	37 °F	3 °C	3 °C
	Refreshing and thirst-quenching. Fruity, pure, light flavour with a pleasant bitterness.	Rafraîchissant et désaltérant. Fruité, pur, léger avec un goût amer agréable.	Verfrissend en dorstles Fruitig, zuiver, licht va smaak met een aangen bitterheid.
	–	–	–

ANNO 1880
MAES
BIER BIERE
BROUWERIJEN ALKEN-MAES BRASSERIES
ANNO 1880
MAES
BIER BIERE
BROUWERIJEN ALKEN-MAES BRASSERIES

Malheur 6°

	top-fermentation re-fermented in the bottle	fermentation haute refermentation en bouteille	hoge gisting hergisting op de fles
	blond	blonde	blond
	Brouwerij Malheur Buggenhout	Brouwerij Malheur Buggenhout	Brouwerij Malheur Buggenhout
	malt, hops, sugar, yeast, water	malt, houblon, sucre, levure, eau	mout, hop, suiker, gist, water
	6%	6%	6%
	golden blond	blond doré	goudblond
	–	–	–
	46 - 50 °F	8 - 10 °C	8 - 10 °C
	Session beer with the powerful taste of a specialty beer. Accessible bitterness.	Facilement buvable avec la saveur corsée d'une bière spéciale. Goût amer accessible.	Doordrinkbier met de smaakkracht van een speciaalbier. Toegankelijke bitterhei
	–	–	–

MALHEUR
BIER 6 BIERE
MALHEUR 6 MALHEUR 6 MALHEUR
MALHEUR
BIER BIERE

Malheur 10°

	top-fermentation re-fermented in the bottle	fermentation haute refermentation en bouteille	hoge gisting hergisting op de fles
	special blond	blonde spéciale	speciaal blond
	Brouwerij Malheur Buggenhout	Brouwerij Malheur Buggenhout	Brouwerij Malheur Buggenhout
	malt, hops, sugar, yeast, water	malt, houblon, sucre, levure, eau	mout, hop, suiker, gist, water
%	10%	10%	10%
	sunny yellow	jaune soleil	zonnegeel
	–	–	–
°C	46 - 50 °F	8 - 10 °C	8 - 10 °C
	Rose-like peach flavour with a touch of lemon and orange rind. A touch of bitter-sour and a warm aftertaste.	Arômes de pêches et de roses avec une touche d'écorce de citron et d'orange. Une pointe amère-acidulée et une fin de bouche chaleureuse.	Rozenachtig perzikaroma met toets van citroen- en sinaasappelschil. Een vleugje bitterzuur en een warme afdronk.
i	–	–	–

MALHEUR 10 MALHEUR 10
10
MALHEUR
BIER 10 BIERE
MALHEUR 10 MALHEUR 10
MALHEUR
BIER 10 BIERE

Malheur 12°

	top-fermentation re-fermented in the bottle	fermentation haute refermentation en bouteille	hoge gisting hergisting op de fles
	strong brown as opposed to strong blond	brune forte contrepartie de blonde forte	sterk donker als tegenhanger van sterk blond
	Brouwerij Malheur Buggenhout	Brouwerij Malheur Buggenhout	Brouwerij Malheur Buggenhout
	malt, hops, sugar, yeast, water	malt, houblon, sucre, levure, eau	mout, hop, suiker, gist, water
%	12%	12%	12%
	red-brown	brun rouge	roodbruin
	–	–	–
	46 - 50 °F	8 - 10 °C	8 - 10 °C
	Bouquet of hop flowers. Round, full taste, very drinkable.	Bouquet de fleurs de houblon. Goût rond et plein, se boit facilement.	Boeket van hopbloemen. Ronde en volle smaak, drinkbaar.
i	–	–	–

12
MALHEUR
MALHEUR

Mandarin Mortal

	top-fermentation re-fermented in the bottle	fermentation haute refermentation en bouteille	hoge gisting hergisting op de fles
	fruit beer	bière fruitée	fruitbier
	Mortal's Beers Jamagne	Mortal's Beers Jamagne	Mortal's Beers Jamagne
	malt, sugar, hops, mandarin rind, yeast, water	malt, sucre, houblon, écorce de mandarine, levure, eau	mout, suiker, hop, mar nenschil, gist, water
%	5,20%	5,20%	5,20%
	–	–	–
	–	–	–
	39 - 43 °F	4 - 6 °C	4 - 6 °C
	Light and fruity beer.	Bière légère et fruitée.	Licht en fruitig bier.
i	–	–	–

WWW.MORTALSBEERS.BE
Alc. 5,2 % vol.
33 cl e

MORTALS BEERS

Marckloff

	top-fermentation	fermentation haute	hoge gisting
	specialty beer	bière spéciale	speciaalbier
	Brasserie La Ferme au Chêne Durbuy	Brasserie La Ferme au Chêne Durbuy	Brasserie La Ferme au Chêne Durbuy
	malt, hops, sugar, herbs, yeast, water	malt, houblon, sucre, herbes, levure, eau	mout, hop, suiker, krui gist, water
%	6,50%	6,50%	6,50%
	amber slightly cloudy	ambrée légèrement trouble	amber licht troebel
	Pour carefully so as to leave the yeast sediment in the bottle.	Verser prudemment de sorte que le dépôt de levure reste dans la bouteille.	Voorzichtig uitschenke zodat het gistbezinksel de fles blijft.
°C	46 °F	8 °C	8 °C
	Smooth and slightly bitter.	Doux et légèrement amer.	Zacht en lichtbitter.
i	Micro-brewery. The beer is bottled and sold almost exclusively in the brewery.	Microbrasserie. Les bières y sont mises en bouteilles et vendues sur place.	Microbrasserie: de biere worden gebotteld maar beperkt beschikbaar bu de brouwerij.

Brassée à
La Ferme
au Chêne
à Durbuy
Goût évolutif
Refermentation en
Marckloff
1331
Cat. S
086/21.10.67
0,75L 6,5% Vol.
Marckloff
DURBUY

Maredsous 6°

	top-fermentation re-fermented in the bottle	fermentation haute refermentation en bouteille	hoge gisting hergisting in de fles
	recognised Belgian abbey beer	Bière belge d'abbaye reconnue	Erkend Belgisch abdijbi blond
	Duvel Moortgat Corp. Puurs	Duvel Moortgat Corp. Puurs	Duvel Moortgat Corp. Puurs
	barley malt, sugar, fine hop varieties, yeast, water	malt d'orge, sucre, sortes fines de houblon, levure, eau	gerstemout, suiker, fijn hopsoorten, gist, water
	6%	6%	6%
	blond	blonde	blond
	Pour carefully into a dry tulip-shaped glass. Leave 1 cm of beer (the yeast sediment) in the bottle, as it makes the beer cloudy.	Verser prudemment dans un verre tulipe sec. Laisser un 1 cm de bière (fond de levure) dans la bouteille; il rend la bière trouble.	Voorzichtig uitschenke een droog tulpvormig g 1 cm bier (gistfond) in d fles laten (maakt het bi troebel).
	43 - 50 °F	6 - 10 °C	6 - 10 °C
	The ideal thirst-quencher. Chiefly refreshing, slightly bitter aftertaste with a touch of fruit flavours.	Désaltérant idéal. Fin de bouche principalement fraîche, légèrement amère avec une touche fruitée.	Ideale dorstlesser. Overwegend frisse, lich tere afdronk met een to fruitigheid.
	The draught version (without re-fermenting) is served in a wet glass.	Pour la version au fût (sans refermentation), on utilise un verre mouillé.	Voor de versie op vat (ze der hergisting) wordt e nat glas gebruikt.

BIERE BELGE D'ABBAYE
BELGISCH ABDIJBIER
MAREDSOUS
BLONDE 6° BLOND
MAREDSOUS

Maredsous 8°

	top-fermentation re-fermented in the bottle	fermentation haute refermentation en bouteille	hoge gisting hergisting in de fles
	recognised Belgian abbey beer	Bière d'abbaye belge reconnue	Erkend Belgisch abdij bruin
	Duvel Moortgat Corp. Puurs	Duvel Moortgat Corp. Puurs	Duvel Moortgat Corp. Puurs
	barley malt, sugar, fine hop varieties, yeast, water	malt d'orge, sucre, sortes fines de houblon, levure, eau	gerstemout, suiker, fij hopsoorten, gist, wate
%	8%	8%	8%
	deep-brown burgundy colour	couleur bourgogne brun intense	diepbruine bourgogn
	Pour carefully into a dry tulip-shaped glass. Leave 1 cm of beer (the yeast sediment) in the bottle, as it makes the beer cloudy.	Verser prudemment dans un verre tulipe sec. Laisser un 1 cm de bière (fond de levure) dans la bouteille; il rend la bière trouble.	Voorzichtig uitschenk een droog tulpvormig 1cm bier (gistfond) in fles laten (maakt het b troebel).
	46 - 54 °F	8 - 12 °C	8 - 12 °C
	Generous caramel bouquet with an expert blend of fruit touches.	Un bouquet caramélisé royal avec des touches fruitées magistralement dosées.	Een royaal karamelbo met meesterlijk gedos fruittoetsen.
i	The draught version (without re-fermenting) is served in a wet glass.	Pour la version au fût (sans refermentation), on utilise un verre mouillé.	Voor de versie op vat (der hergisting) wordt nat glas gebruikt.

BIÈRE BELGE D'ABBAYE ◆ BELGISCH ABDIJBIER
MAREDSOUS
BRUNE 8° BRUIN
MAREDSOUS

Maredsous 10°

	top-fermentation re-fermented in the bottle	fermentation haute refermentation en bouteille	hoge gisting hergisting in de fles
	recognised Belgian abbey beer	Bière d'abbaye belge reconnue	Erkend Belgisch abdijb tripel
	Duvel Moortgat Corp. Puurs	Duvel Moortgat Corp. Puurs	Duvel Moortgat Corp. Puurs
	barley malt, sugar, fine hop varieties, yeast, water	malt d'orge, sucre, sortes fines de houblon, levure, eau	gerstemout, suiker, fijn hopsoorten, gist, water
	10%	10%	10%
	deep-blond Tripel with very fine bubbles	triple blond intense avec des bulles très fines	diepblonde tripel met fijne pareling
	Pour carefully into a dry tulip-shaped glass. Leave 1 cm of beer (the yeast sediment) in the bottle, as it makes the beer cloudy.	Verser prudemment dans un verre tulipe sec. Laisser un 1 cm de bière (fond de levure) dans la bouteille; il rend la bière trouble.	Voorzichtig uitschenke een droog tulpvormig 1 cm bier (gistfond) in fles laten (maakt het b troebel).
	43 - 50 °F	6 - 10 °C	6 - 10 °C
	Harmonious, full taste of sour, sweet and bitter. Heartwarming aftertaste.	Saveur pleine harmonieuse acidulée, douce et amère. Fin de bouche chaleureuse.	Harmonieuze volle sm van zuur, zoet en bitte Hartverwarmende afd
	The draught version (without re-fermenting) is served in a wet glass.	Pour la version au fût (sans refermentation), on utilise un verre mouillé.	Voor de versie op vat (z der hergisting) wordt e nat glas gebruikt.

BIERE BELGE D'ABBAYE ◆ BELGISCH ABDIJBIER
MAREDSOUS
TRIPLE 10° TRIPEL
REFERMENTÉE EN BOUTEILLE - HERGIST IN DE FLES

BIERE BELGE D'ABBAYE ◆ BELGISCH ABDIJBIER
MAREDSOUS

Margriet

	top-fermentation	fermentation haute	hoge gisting
	blond	blonde	blond
	Brouwerij Het Anker Mechelen	Brouwerij Het Anker Malines	Brouwerij Het Anker Mechelen
	four-grain beer with a unique use of rosebuds	bière aux quatre grains avec une utilisation unique de boutons de roses	viergranenbier met un gebruik van rozenkno
	6,50%	6,50%	6,50%
	blond	blonde	blond
	–	–	–
	41- 46 °F	5- 8 °C	5- 8 °C
	Ideal thirst-quencher for the summer with a strong, saturated sparkling effect.	Désaltérant idéal en été ayant un effet perlant fort saturé.	Ideale dorstlesser in de mer die een sterk gesat reerd, parelend effect h
	Named after Margareth of Austria. This beer is also sold under the name 'Anker Blond'.	Son nom est emprunté à Marguerite d'Autriche. Cette bière se vend également sous le nom 'Anker Blond'.	Genoemd naar Margar van Oostenrijk. Dit bie wordt ook verkocht on de naam Anker blond.

margriet
margriet
feestelijk cultuurbier

margriet
feestelijk cultuurbier

Martens Pils

bottom-fermentation	fermentation basse	lage gisting
Pilsner	pils	pils
Brouwerij Martens Bocholt	Brouwerij Martens Bocholt	Brouwerij Martens Bocholt
–	–	–
5%	5%	5%
blond clear	blonde claire	blond helder
cfr. Pilsner	voir pils	cfr. pils
36 °F	2 °C	2 °C
Refreshing and full-bodied.	Frais et relevé.	Fris en pittig.
–	–	–

Kenners kennen geen beter.
BELGISCH BIER • BIERE BELGE • BELGIAN BEER
BIRRA BELGA • CERVEZA BELGA • CERVEJA BELGA
anno 1758
MARTENS PILS
ANNO 1758
MARTENS PILS

Martin's pale ale

	top-fermentation	fermentation haute	hoge gisting
	Pale Ale	pale ale	pale ale
	Brouwerij Timmermans/ John Martin Itterbeek	Brouwerij Timmermans/ John Martin Itterbeek	Brouwerij Timmermar John Martin Itterbeek
	barley malt, sugar, corn, roasted barley, hops, water	malt d'orge, sucre, maïs, orge brûlé, houblon, eau	gerstemout, suiker, ma gebrande gerst, hop, w
	5,50%	5,50%	5,50%
	amber	ambrée	amber
	–	–	–
	43 - 46 °F	6 - 8 °C	6 - 8 °C
	The typical malt and aromatised hop give a dry bitterness from the onset.	Malt typique et houblon aromatisé se traduisant en un goût amer dès le début.	Typische mout en gear tiseerde hop vertalen z in een droge bitterheic af het begin.
	–	–	–

MARTIN'S
PALE ALE
MARTIN'S
PALE ALE
MARTIN'S
BLOND & PALE ALE

Mater Witbier

	top-fermentation	fermentation haute	hoge gisting
	Witbier	bière blanche	witbier
	Brouwerij Roman Mater	Brouwerij Roman Mater	Brouwerij Roman Mater
	barley malt, wheat, hops, herbs, yeast, spring water	malt d'orge, froment, houblon, herbes, levure, eau de source	gerstemout, tarwe, ho kruiden, gist, bronwat
%	5%	5%	5%
	light-yellow cloudy, unfiltered	jaune clair trouble, non filtrée	lichtgeel troebel, niet gefilterd
	Swiftly pour into a degreased, chilled and rinsed beer glass. Pour the sediment along with the beer.	Verser rapidement dans un verre de bière dégraissé, rafraîchi et rincé. Verser également le dépôt de levure.	Vlot uitschenken in ee ontvet, gekoeld en ges bierglas. De fond mee uitschen
°C	37 °F	3 °C	3 °C
	Refreshing with flavours of citrus fruits and coriander. Well-balanced sweet-and-sour taste.	Rafraîchissant avec des arômes d'agrumes et de coriandre. Saveur aigre-douce équilibrée.	Verfrissend met aroma van citrusvruchten en riander. Uitgebalanceerde zoet re smaak.
i	Store in a dark, cool room.	Conserver à l'abri de la lumière et de la chaleur.	Donker en koel beware

MATER
WIT BIER
MATER
BIERE BLANCHE
MATER

Maurootje Lauwse Saison

	top-fermentation	fermentation haute	hoge gisting
	regional beer Saisons	bière régionale saison	streekbier saison
	Picobrouwerij Alvinne Ingelmunster	Picobrouwerij Alvinne Ingelmunster	Picobrouwerij Alvinne Ingelmunster
	malt (Pilsner, wheat, rye) granulated sugar, hops, yeast, coriander, juniper berries, water	malt (pils, froment, seigle), sucre cristallisé, houblon, levure, coriandre, baies de genièvre, eau	mout (pils, tarwe, rogg kristalsuiker, hop, gist ander, jeneverbessen,
	7%	7%	7%
	blond	blonde	blond
	Pour into a tulip-shaped glass or goblet. Leave the yeast (approx. 1 cm) at the bottom of the bottle. Pour slowly to obtain a nice foam head.	Verser dans un verre tulipe ou calice. Laisser la levure (environ 1 cm) au fond de la bouteille. Verser lentement de sorte qu'un beau faux col se forme.	Uitschenken in een tu kelkvormig glas. De gist (ca. 1 cm) op de dem van de fles laten. Langzaam schenken z er een mooie schuimk ontstaat.
	46 °F	8 °C	8 °C
	Spicy taste and aroma. Full-bodied.	Saveur et arômes relevés. Franc.	Kruidige smaak en aro Volmondig.
	–	–	–

n Maurootje
Lauwse Saison
ALVINNE

Mc Chouffe

	top-fermentation	fermentation haute	hoge gisting
	regional beer	bière régionale	streekbier
	Duvel Moortgat Corp. Brewsite Brass. d'Achouffe Achouffe-Wibrin	Duvel Moortgat Corp. Brewsite Brass. d'Achouffe Achouffe-Wibrin	Duvel Moortgat Corp. Brewsite Brass. d'Acho Achouffe-Wibrin
	malt, hops, sugar, yeast, water	malt, houblon, sucre, levure, eau	mout, hop, suiker, gist water
	8%	8%	8%
	dark unfiltered	foncée non filtrée	donker ongefilterd
	–	–	–
	46 - 54 °F	8 - 12 °C	8 - 12 °C
	Scottish style beer from the Ardennes.	Une 'Scotch' ardennaise	Een Ardense 'Scotch'.
	Store upright in a dark, cool room. A layer of yeast sediment at the bottom of the bottle is normal.	A conserver verticalement à l'abri de la lumière et de la chaleur. Un dépôt de levure au fond de la bouteille est normal.	Verticaal bewaren in ee donkere, koele ruimte. Een gistlaagje op de bo van de fles is normaal.

BIÈRE
BRUNE
BRUIN BIER
Mc
CHOUFFE
BIÈRE BRUNE D'ARDENNE - ARDENS BRUIN BIER
Brasserie d'Achouffe - 6666 Achouffe - Belgique

Mc CHOUFFE

Melchior

	top-fermentation	fermentation haute	hoge gisting
	barley wine regional beer winter beer	vin d'orge bière régionale bière hivernale	gerstewijn streekbier winterbier
	Picobrouwerij Alvinne Ingelmunster	Picobrouwerij Alvinne Ingelmunster	Picobrouwerij Alvinne Ingelmunster
	malt (Pilsner, wheat, amber), granulated sugar, hops, yeast, musterd seeds, water	malt (pils, froment, ambré), sucre cristallisé, houblon, levure, graines de moutarde, eau	mout (pils, tarwe, amb kristalsuiker, hop, gist, terdzaden, water
%	11%	11%	11%
	amber	ambrée	amber
	Pour into a tulip-shaped glass or goblet. Leave the yeast (approx. 1 cm) at the bottom of the bottle. Pour slowly to obtain a nice foam head.	Verser dans un verre tulipe ou calice. Laisser la levure (environ 1 cm) au fond de la bouteille. Verser lentement de sorte qu'un beau faux col se forme.	Uitschenken in een tul kelkvormig glas. De gist (ca. 1 cm) op de dem van de fles laten. Langzaam schenken zo er een mooie schuimkr ontstaat.
°C	46 °F	8 °C	8 °C
	Spicy and alcoholic taste and aroma. Strong alcoholic 'barley wine'.	Saveur et arôme relevés et alcoolisés. 'Barley wine' fortement alcoolisé.	Kruidige en alcoholisch smaak en aroma. Sterk alcoholische 'bar wine'.
i	–	–	–

MELCHIO
ALVINNE
2003
ALVINNE
vzw

Moeder Overste

	top-fermentation	fermentation haute	hoge gisting
	Tripel	triple	tripel
	Brasserie Lefebvre Quenast	Brasserie Lefebvre Quenast	Brasserie Lefebvre Quenast
	barley malt, hops, candy sugar, yeast, water	malt d'orge, houblon, sucre candi, levure, eau	gerstemout, hop, kand ker, gist, water
	8%	8%	8%
	slightly hazy if served cold	légèrement voilée si servie froide	licht gesluierd indien geschonken
	Pour into a glass with a stem and leave the yeast sediment in the bottle.	Verser dans un verre à pied et laisser le dépôt de levure dans la bouteille.	Uitschenken in een gla met voet en het gistbez sel in de fles laten.
	39 - 46 °F	4 - 8 °C	4 - 8 °C
	Bitter and smooth.	Amer et moelleux.	Bitter en zacht.
	Store the bottles upright.	Conserver les bouteilles en position verticale.	De flessen verticaal bewaren.

Tripel
Moeder Overste
Tripel
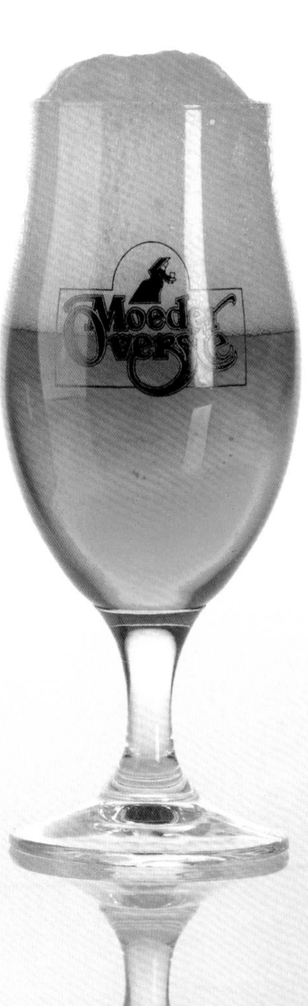
Moeder Overste

Moinette biologique

	top-fermentation re-fermented in the bottle	fermentation haute refermentation en bouteille	hoge gisting nagisting in de fles
	blond	blonde	blond
	Brasserie Dupont Tourpes-Leuze	Brasserie Dupont Tourpes-Leuze	Brasserie Dupont Tourpes-Leuze
	–	–	–
	7,50%	7,50%	7,50%
	blond unfiltered	blonde non filtrée	blond ongefilterd
	–	–	–
	cellar temperature (54 °F) or slightly cooled	température de cave (12 °C) ou légèrement rafraîchie	keldertemperatuur (12 ° of lichtgekoeld
	Flavours of malt, fruit and fine hop. Thirst-quenching owing to the combination of smoothness, bitterness and fruitiness.	Arômes de malt, de fruits et de houblon fin. Désaltérant par la combinaison des goûts moelleux, amers et fruités.	Aroma's van mout, fru fijne hop. Dorstlessend door de c binatie van zachtheid, terheid en fruitigheid.
	The production is supervised by Ecocert®. The beer carries the label of Biogarantie®.	La production est contrôlée par Ecocert®. Avec le label Biogarantie®.	De productie wordt gec troleerd door Ecocert®. Met label Biogarantie®.

Moinette
Moinette
Biologique
À BASE DE MALT ET DE HOUBLON ISSUS DE CULTURE BIOLOGIQUE
e 25cl
Alc.7,5%Vol.
bière non filtrée
ongefilterd bier
L06183B
12/2008

Moinette blonde

	top-fermentation re-fermented in the bottle	fermentation haute refermentation en bouteille	hoge gisting nagisting in de fles
	blond	blonde	blond
	Brasserie Dupont Tourpes-Leuze	Brasserie Dupont Tourpes-Leuze	Brasserie Dupont Tourpes-Leuze
	–	–	–
	8,50%	8,50%	8,50%
	copper-coloured	couleur cuivre	koperkleurig
	–	–	–
	cellar temperature (54 °F) or slightly cooled	température de cave (12 °C) ou légèrement rafraîchie	keldertemperatuur (12 ° of lichtgekoeld
	Fine hop and yeast flavours. Refreshing owing to the balance between sweet, bitter and fruity. Complex and harmonious owing to re-fermentation in the bottle.	Arômes raffinés de houblon et de levure. Rafraîchissant par l'équilibre de goûts doux, amers et fruités. Complexe et harmonieux par la refermentation en bouteille.	Fijne hop- en gistaroma Verfrissend door evenw van zoet, bitter en fruit Complex en harmonieu door hergisting in de fl
	The original name was 'Abbaye de la Moinette'. Moinette refers to the word 'moëne', meaning 'swamp'. The beer has the same name because the area around the brewery is rather swampy.	Le nom d'origine était 'Abbaye de la Moinette'. Moinette renvoie au vocable 'moëne' qui signifie marais; le nom de la bière y est relié parce que la région autour de brasserie est assez marécageuse.	De oorspronkelijke naa was 'Abbaye de la Moin Moinette verwijst naar woord 'moëne' wat mo betekent. De naam van bier is hieraan gelinkt dat de streek rond de b werij vrij moerassig is.
	....		

Tourpes • Belgique
Moinette
BLONDE • BLOND
relementée en bouteille • Bier met nagisting in de fles
33cl
Alc. 8,5%

Moinette

Moinette brune

top-fermentation re-fermented in the bottle	fermentation haute refermentation en bouteille	hoge gisting nagisting in de fles
dubbel	double	dubbel
Brasserie Dupont Tourpes-Leuze	Brasserie Dupont Tourpes-Leuze	Brasserie Dupont Tourpes-Leuze
based on a blend of 4 special malts	A base d'un mélange de 4 malts spéciaux.	Op basis van een menge van 4 speciale mouten.
8,50%	8,50%	8,50%
Light dark-brown to rusty with scarlet hues	Brun foncé clair à roux avec des teintes rouges vives.	Licht donkerbruin tot rc sig met vuurrode tinten
–	–	–
cellar temperature	température de cave	keldertemperatuur
Dominating hop and malt aroma and taste. Smoothly bitter and slightly fruity. Complex and harmonious taste evolution owing to re-fermentation in the bottle.	Saveur dominante, arômes de houblon et de malt. Légèrement amer en combinaison avec le goût légèrement fruité. Evolution de la saveur complexe et harmonieuse par la refermentation en bouteille.	Dominerende smaak en aroma's van hop en mou Zacht bitter in combina met licht fruitig. Complexe en harmonie smaakevolutie door nag ting in de fles.
Store at cellar temperature for an optimal taste evolution.	Conserver à température de cave pour une évolution optimale de la saveur.	Bewaren op keldertempe ratuur voor een optimal smaakevolutie.

Moinette
BRUNE • BRUIN

Moinette

Mongozo banana

	top-fermentation	fermentation haute	hoge gisting
	exotic fruit beer	bière fruitée exotique	exotisch fruitbier
	Brouwerij Huyghe Melle	Brouwerij Huyghe Melle	Brouwerij Huyghe Melle
	barley malt, fair trade organic bananas and quinoa, yeast, hops, sugar, water. Made with mangozo quinoa and banana.	malt d'orge, bananes biologiques fairtrade, quinoa, levure, houblon, sucre, eau. Faite à base de mangozo quinoa et de bananes.	Gerstemout, fairtrade b logische bananen en qu gist, hop, suiker, water. Gemaakt op basis van mangozo quinoa waara banaan is toegevoegd.
%	4,50%	4,50%	4,50%
	dark-yellow cloudy	jaune foncée trouble	donkergeel troebel
	Serve in a flute-glass.	Verser dans une flûte.	Uitschenken in een flu glas.
°C	39 °F	4 °C	4 °C
	Banana flavour and aroma.	Saveur et arômes de banane.	Smaak en aroma van banaan.
i	–	–	–

Banana
ONGOZO
FAIRTRADE
so Fair so Good!

MONGOZO

Mongozo coconut

	top-fermentation	fermentation haute	hoge gisting
	exotic fruit beer	bière fruitée exotique	exotisch fruitbier
	Brouwerij Huyghe Melle	Brouwerij Huyghe Melle	Brouwerij Huyghe Melle
	Barley malt, fair trade organic quinoa (African grain species), coconut, yeast, hops, flavouring, water. Made with mangozo quinoa and natural coconut juice.	Malt d'orge, quinoa biologique fairtrade (type de blé africain), noix de coco, levure, houblon,arômes, eau. Faite à base de mangozo quinoa et de jus naturel de noix de coco.	Gerstemout, fairtrade b[illegible] logische quinoa (Afrika[illegible] graansoort), kokosnoot, hop, aroma's, water. Gemaakt op basis van m[illegible] gozo quinoa waaraan n[illegible] lijk kokosvruchtvleessa[illegible] toegevoegd.
	3,50%	3,50%	3,50%
	yellow-white cloudy	blanc jaune trouble	geelwit troebel
	Serve in a flute-glass.	Verser dans une flûte.	Uitschenken in een flu[illegible] glas.
	39 °F	4 °C	4 °C
	Coconut flavour and aroma.	Saveur et arôme de noix de coco.	Smaak en aroma van kokosnoot.
	–	–	–

Coconut
NGOZO
FAIRTRADE
Fair so Good!

MONGOZO

Mongozo palmnut

	top-fermentation	fermentation haute	hoge gisting
	exotic fruit beer	bière fruitée exotique	exotisch fruitbier
	Brouwerij Huyghe Melle	Brouwerij Huyghe Melle	Brouwerij Huyghe Melle
	Barley malt, fair trade organic palm nuts and quinoa, yeast, hops, sugar, water. Made with mangozo quinoa and palm nut.	Malt d'orge, noix de palmier biologiques fairtrade, quinoa, levure, houblon, sucre, eau. Faite à base de mangozo quinoa et de noix de palmier.	Gerstemout, fairtrade b gische palmnoten en q gist, hop, suiker, water. Gemaakt op basis van r gozo quinoa waaraan p nut is toegevoegd.
	7%	7%	7%
	amber-coloured	ambrée	amberkleurig
	Serve in a flute-glass.	Verser dans une flûte.	Uitschenken in een flu glas.
	39 °F	4 °C	4 °C
	Palm nut flavour and aroma.	Saveur et arôme de noix de palmier.	Smaak en aroma van p nut.
	–	–	–

Fair so Good!

MONGOZO

Mongozo quinua

	top-fermentation	fermentation haute	hoge gisting
	exotic beer	bière exotique	exotisch bier
	Brouwerij Huyghe Melle	Brouwerij Huyghe Melle	Brouwerij Huyghe Melle
	malt, fair trade organic quinoa, yeast, hops, sugar, water	malt, quinoa biologique fairtrade, levure, houblon, sucre, eau	mout, fairtrade biologi quinoa, gist, hop, suike water
%	5,90%	5,90%	5,90%
	Pilsner colour clear	pils claire	pilskleur helder
	Serve in a flute-glass.	Verser dans une flûte.	Uitschenken in een flu glas.
	39 °F	4 °C	4 °C
	–	–	–
	–	–	–

Quinua
ONGOZO
FAIRTRADE
Fair so Good!

MONGOZO

Mont Saint-Aubert

	top-fermentation re-fermented in the bottle	fermentation haute refermentation en bouteille	hoge gisting hergisting op de fles
	blond	blonde	blond
	Brasserie de Brunehaut Rongy-Brunehaut	Brasserie de Brunehaut Rongy-Brunehaut	Brasserie de Brunehau Rongy-Brunehaut
	malt, hops, yeast, water	malt, houblon, levure, eau	mout, hop, gist, water
	8%	8%	8%
	blond	blonde	blond
	–	–	–
	43 - 50 °F	6 - 10 °C	6 - 10 °C
	Strong and full-bodied.	Fort et corsé.	Sterk en krachtig.
	–	–	–

BIÈRE DU MONT SAINT-AUBERT
FERMENTATION HAUTE
MONT SAINT AUBERT

Montagnarde

	top-fermentation	fermentation haute	hoge gisting
	Tripel	triple	tripel
	Abbaye des Rocs Montignies-sur-Rocs	Abbaye des Rocs Montignies-sur-Rocs	Abbaye des Rocs Montignies-sur-Rocs
	malt (pale, Munich) hops (Hallertau, Brewers Gold) well water from a rocky subsoil	malt (pâle, Munich) houblon (Hallertau, Brewers Gold) eau de puits d'un sous-sol rocailleux	mout (bleek, munich) hop (Hallertau, Brewe Gold) boorputwater uit een rijke ondergrond
%	9% 20° plato	9% 20° plato	9% 20° plato
	light amber	ambré clair	licht amber
	Savour in a bulb jar.	Déguster dans un verre ballon.	Degusteren uit een ba vormig glas.
°C	54 °F	12 °C	12 °C
	A touch of hops.	Touche de houblon.	Toets van hop.
i	The abbey 'L'Abbaye des Rocs' dates back from the 12th century. The beer keeps for about a year in a dark room. Montagnard is the name given to the inhabitants of the region.	'L'Abbaye des Rocs' date du 12ième siècle. La bière se conserve environ un an à l'abri de la lumière. Montagnard est le nom donné aux habitants de la région.	De abdij 'L'Abbaye des dateert uit de 12e eeu Het bier is ongeveer ee jaar houdbaar in een kere ruimte. Montagnard is de naa gegeven wordt aan de ners uit de regio.

erie de l'Abbaye de
Montagnarde
Ambrée
9% vol.
Amber
Brasserie de
l'Abbaye des Rocs

Mort subite Gueuze

	spontaneous fermentation re-fermented in the bottle	fermentation spontanée refermentation en bouteille	spontane gisting nagisting op de fles
	Gueuze	gueuze	geuze
	Alken Maes Corporation Brewsite Mort Subite Kobbegem	Alken Maes Corporation Brewsite Mort Subite Kobbegem	Alken Maes Corporati Brewsite Mort Subite Kobbegem
	–	–	–
	4,50%	4,50%	4,50%
	gold-yellow clear, filtered	jaune doré claire, filtrée	goudgeel helder, gefilterd
	Empty in a degreased, rinsed and wet glass. Let overflow and skim off the foam.	Verser complètement dans un verre dégraissé, rincé et mouillé. Laisser déborder et écumer.	Helemaal uitschenken een ontvet, gespoeld e nat glas. Laten overlopen en afs men.
	36 - 39 °F	2 - 4 °C	2 - 4 °C
	Spicy, sweet-and-sour and thirst-quenching.	Désaltérant corsé, aigre-doux.	Pittige, zuurzoete dors lesser.
	Matured in oak barrels.	Mûrit en fûts de chêne.	Gerijpt op eiken vaten

MORT
SUBITE

ANNO 1686
MORT
SUBITE
LAMBIC
Gueuze
TRADITIONNELLE

MORT
SUBITE

Mort subite Kriek

	spontaneous fermentation	fermentation spontanée	spontane gisting
	fruit beer	bière fruitée	fruitbier
	Alken Maes Corporation Brewsite Mort Subite Kobbegem	Alken Maes Corporation Brewsite Mort Subite Kobbegem	Alken Maes Corporat Brewsite Mort Subite Kobbegem
	–	–	–
	4,50%	4,50%	4,50%
	bright-red	rouge vif	helrood
	Empty in a degreased, rinsed and wet glass. Let overflow and skim off the foam.	Verser complètement dans un verre dégraissé, rincé et mouillé. Laisser déborder et écumer.	Helemaal uitschenke een ontvet, gespoeld nat glas. Laten overlopen en a men.
	36 - 39 °F	2 - 4 °C	2 - 4 °C
	Refreshing, sweet-and-sour with the taste of fresh cherries.	Frais et aigre-doux avec une saveur de cerises fraîches.	Fris zuurzoet met de van verse krieken.
	Authentic blend of old and young Lambic with Belgian cherries added.	Mélange authentique de vieux et de jeune lambic auxquels sont ajoutées des cerises belges.	Authentieke mengeli van oude en jonge la waaraan Belgische kr zijn toegevoegd.

MORT
SUBITE
Kriek
ANNO 1686
MORT
SUBITE
LAMBIC
Kriek

ANNO
MORT
SUBITE
LAMBIC

Mort subite Oude Gueuze

	spontaneous fermentation re-fermented in the bottle	fermentation spontanée refermentation en bouteille	spontane gisting nagisting op de fles
	Gueuze	gueuze	geuze
	Alken Maes Corporation Brewsite Mort Subite Kobbegem	Alken Maes Corporation Brewsite Mort Subite Kobbegem	Alken Maes Corporati Brewsite Mort Subite Kobbegem
	blend of old and young Lambic	mélange de vieux et de jeune lambic	mengeling van oude e ge lambiek
	7%	7%	7%
	unfiltered, 100% re-fermented in the bottle	non filtrée avec 100% de refermentation en bouteille	ongefilterd met 100% gisting op de fles
	Empty in a degreased, rinsed and wet glass. Let overflow and skim off the foam.	Verser complètement dans un verre dégraissé, rincé et mouillé. Laisser déborder et écumer.	Helemaal uitschenken een ontvet, gespoeld e nat glas. Laten overlopen en afs men.
	cellar temperature	température de cave	keldertemperatuur
	Fresh and spicy citric character, no sweetening.	Caractère d'agrumes frais et corsé. Sans sucres.	Fris en pittig citruska zonder zoet.
	–	–	–

MORT
SUBITE
LAMBIC
Oude Gueuze
A L'ANCIENNE
MORT
SUBITE

Mort subite Xtreme Framboi

	spontaneous fermentation	fermentation spontanée	spontane gisting
	fruit beer	bière fruitée	fruitbier
	Alken Maes Corporation Brewsite Mort Subite Kobbegem	Alken Maes Corporation Brewsite Mort Subite Kobbegem	Alken Maes Corporati Brewsite Mort Subite Kobbegem
	–	–	–
%	4,20%	4,20%	4,20%
	pink champagne	champagne rose	roze champagne
	Empty in a degreased, rinsed and wet glass. Let overflow and skim off the foam.	Verser complètement dans un verre dégraissé, rincé et mouillé. Laisser déborder et écumer.	Helemaal uitschenken een ontvet, gespoeld e nat glas. Laten overlopen en afs men.
°C	36 - 39 °F	2 - 4 °C	2 - 4 °C
	Extra fruity. Full-bodied sweet and fruity raspberry taste.	Extra fruité. Saveur de framboises franche, douce et fruitée.	Extra fruitig. Volmondig zoete en fr frambozensmaak.
i	Winner of the silver medal in the 'fruit beer' category of the Brewing Industry National Awards' 2005.	A gagné la médaille d'argent dans la catégorie des bières fruitées au 'Brewing Industry National Awards' 2005.	Won de zilveren meda in de categorie fruitbi op de 'Brewing Industr National Awards' 2005

MORT
SUBITE
(framboise)
BIER - BIERE
MORT
SUBITE

Mort subite Xtreme Kriek

	spontaneous fermentation	fermentation spontanée	spontane gisting
	fruit beer	bière fruitée	fruitbier
	Alken Maes Corporation Brewsite Mort Subite Kobbegem	Alken Maes Corporation Brewsite Mort Subite Kobbegem	Alken Maes Corporatic Brewsite Mort Subite Kobbegem
	–	–	–
	4,30%	4,30%	4,30%
	bright-red	rouge vif	felrood
	Empty in a degreased, rinsed and wet glass. Let overflow and skim off the foam.	Verser complètement dans un verre dégraissé, rincé et mouillé. Laisser déborder et écumer.	Helemaal uitschenken een ontvet, gespoeld e nat glas. Laten overlopen en afs men.
	36 - 39 °F	2 - 4 °C	2 - 4 °C
	Extra fruity. Full-bodied sweet and fruity cherry taste.	Extra fruité. Saveur de cerises franche, sucrée et fruitée.	Extra fruitig. Volmondig zoete en fr kriekensmaak.
	Winner of the gold medal in the 'fruit beer' category of the Brewing Industry National Awards' 2005.	Médaille d'or des bières fruitées 'Brewing Industry International Awards' 2005.	Gouden medaille fruit 'Brewing Industry Inte tional Awards' 2005.

ANNO
MORT
SUBITE
BIER - BIÈRE

ANNO
MORT
SUBITE
LAMBIC

Mousse de Toernich

	top-fermentation re-fermented in the bottle	fermentation haute refermentation en bouteille	hoge gisting hergisting op de fles
	Ale	ale	ale
	Brasserie Artisanale Millevertus Toernich	Brasserie Artisanale Millevertus Toernich	Brasserie Artisanale Millevertus Toernich
	different malt, hop and yeast varieties, water	différentes sortes de malt, de houblon et de levures, eau	verschillende mout-, gistsoorten, water
	6,50%	6,50%	6,50%
	blond, amber	blonde, ambré	blond, amber
	Serve at room temperature.	Verser à température ambiante.	Uitschenken op kame peratuur.
	45 - 54 °F	7 - 12 °C	7 - 12 °C
	Refreshing, aromatic owing to the hop species used, smooth owing to the malts used.	Rafraîchissant et aromatisé par les sortes de houblon utilisées, moelleux par les sortes de malt utilisées.	Verfrissend, aromatis door de gebruikte ho ten, zacht door de ge te moutsoorten.
	–	–	–

MOUSSE
de Tœrnich
Brasserie Artisanale
MMMH!!
MILLEVERTUS

Mystic witbier met krieken

	top-fermentation	fermentation haute	hoge gisting
	Witbier with fruit	bière blanche fruitée	witbier met fruit
	Brouwerij Haacht Boortmeerbeek	Brouwerij Haacht Boortmeerbeek	Brouwerij Haacht Boortmeerbeek
	barley malt, wheat malt, unmalted wheat, sugar, hops, herbs, yeast, fructose, cherry juice (25 %) water, acesulfame K (sweetener), natural flavouring	malt d'orge, malt de froment, froment non malté, sucre, houblon, herbes, levure, fructose, jus de cerises (25 %), eau, acesulfamide K (édulcorant), arômes naturels	gerstemout, tarwemou gemoute tarwe, suiker kruiden, gist, fructose, kriekensap (25 %), wat acesulfaam K (zoetstof tuurlijke aroma's
%	3,50%	3,50%	3,50%
	clear red	rouge vif	helder rood
	Pour carefully into a rinsed, wet Mystic glass, avoiding contact between bottle and foam.	Verser prudemment dans un verre Mystic rincé et mouillé sans que la bouteille touche l'écume.	Voorzichtig uitschenke een gespoeld, nat Myst zonder dat de fles het schuim raakt.
°C	37 °F	3 °C	3 °C
	Powerful taste of cherries, combined with the freshness of a Witbier. Fruity-sour onset, turning smoothly into a slightly sweet, non-sticky aftertaste.	Goût corsé de cerises avec la fraîcheur d'une bière blonde. Goût initial fruité, acidulé passant doucement à une fin de bouche légèrement douce, non collante.	Krachtige smaak van kr gecombineerd met de f heid van een witbier. Fruitzure aanzet die za overvloeit in een licht z niet kleverige afdronk.
i	–	–	–

Mystic
Mystic
Mystic
Witbier met krieken
Blanche aux cerises
BROUWERIJ HAACHT BRASSERIE

Mystic witbier met limoen

top-fermentation	fermentation haute	hoge gisting
Witbier with fruit	bière blanche fruitée	witbier met fruit
Brouwerij Haacht Boortmeerbeek	Brouwerij Haacht Boortmeerbeek	Brouwerij Haacht Boortmeerbeek
barley malt, wheat malt, unmalted wheat, sugar, hops, herbs, yeast, natural lime and lemon flavouring, citric acid (food acid), acesulfame K (sweetener), water	malt d'orge, malt de froment, froment non malté, sucre, houblon, herbes, levure, arômes naturels de citron et de citron vert, acide citrique (acide alimentaire), acesulfamide K, eau	gerstemou[t], tarwemou[t], ongemoute tarwe, suik[er], hop, kruiden, gist, nat[uur]lijk aroma van limoen [en] citroen, citroenzuur (v[oe]dingszuur), acesulfaam [K] (zoetstof), water
3,50%	3,50%	3,50%
slightly cloudy (unfiltered) foam head with fine bubbles	légèrement trouble (non filtrée) faux col avec des bulles fines	licht troebel (ongefilte[rd]) schuimkraag met fijne bellen
Pour carefully into a rinsed, wet Mystic glass, avoiding contact between bottle and foam.	Verser prudemment dans un verre Mystic rincé et mouillé sans que la bouteille touche l'écume.	Voorzichtig uitschenke[n in] een gespoeld, nat Myst[ic] glas zonder dat de fles schuim raakt.
37 °F	3 °C	3 °C
Spicy thirst-quencher, refreshing and fruity, based on spicy, unfiltered Witbier. Smooth tingling of citric fruits with a pleasant, sweet and refreshing aftertaste.	Désaltérant corsé, frais et fruité à base de bière blanche relevée, non filtrée. Léger picotement d'agrumes avec une fin de bouche douce, agréable et rafraîchissante.	Pittige dorstlesser, fris [en] fruitig, op basis van kr[uidig] ongefilterd witbier. Zachte prikkeling van [ci]trusvruchten met een [aan]genaam zoet en verfris[sende] de afdronk.
–	–	–

Mystic
Mystic
Witbier met limoen
Blanche au citron vert
BROUWERIJ HAACHT BRASSERIE
Mystic

Netebuk

	top-fermentation re-fermented in the bottle unpasteurised	fermentation haute refermentation en bou- teille non pasteurisée	hoge gisting hergisting op de fles niet gepasteuriseerd
	strong blond to amber	blonde à ambrée forte	sterk blond tot amber
	Huisbrouwerij 't Brouwkot Gullegem	Huisbrouwerij 't Brouwkot Gullegem	Huisbrouwerij 't Brouw Gullegem
	barley malt, wheat, hops, sugar, yeast, water	malt d'orge, froment, houblon, sucre, levu- re, eau	gerstemout, tarwe, ho ker, gist, water
%	6,50%	6,50%	6,50%
	golden blond slightly cloudy	blond doré légèrement trouble	goudblond licht troebel
	Degrease the glass and hold it slightly tilted whilst pouring. Pour the beer carefully in one single movement.	Dégraisser le verre et le tenir légèrement incliné au moment de verser. Verser la bière prudem- ment en un seul mouve- ment.	Het glas vetvrij maken licht schuin houden ti het inschenken. Het bier voorzichtig in beweging uitschenken.
°C	46 - 50 °F	8 - 10 °C	8 - 10 °C
	Full-bodied thirst- quencher. Full and mild mouthfeel with a lively hoppy touch and refreshing bitterness.	Désaltérant franc. Plein et tendre dans la bouche avec une touche de houblon corsée et un goût amer rafraîchissant.	Volmondige dorstlesse Vol en mild in de mon met een pittige toets v hop die de bitterheid f laat uitvloeien.
i	–	–	–

Netebuk
goudblond
natuurbier
Netebuk
75cl.
Belgian Beer

Newton

	top-fermentation	fermentation haute	hoge gisting
	fruit beer	bière fruitée	fruitbier
	Brasserie Lefebvre Quenast	Brasserie Lefebvre Quenast	Brasserie Lefebvre Quenast
	barley malt, wheat, hops, apple juice, sugar, yeast, flavouring, water	malt d'orge, froment, houblon, jus de pommes, sucre, levure, arômes, eau	gerstemout, tarwe, hop, appelsap, suiker, gist, aroma's, water
%	3,50%	3,50%	3,50%
	very pale slightly hazy	très pâle légèrement voilée	zeer bleek licht gesluierd
	Pour into a conic glass or drink straight from the bottle.	Verser dans un verre conique ou boire à la bouteille.	Uitschenken in een kon[illegible] glas of uit de fles drinke[illegible]
°C	34 - 39 °F	1 - 4 °C	1 - 4 °C
	Sugared taste, soured with green apples. Apple aroma and flavour.	Saveur sucrée acidulée par des pommes vertes. Parfum et saveur de pommes.	Gesuikerde smaak die is aangezuurd met groene appels. Appelgeur en -smaak.
i	–	–	–

Newton
Newton
bière à la pomme
appelbier:
apple beer:
birra con mela:
apfelbier:
æble øle :
cerveza:
con manzana:
alc./vol.
330 ml
Newton

N'Ice Chouffe

	top-fermentation	fermentation haute	hoge gisting
	regional beer winter beer	bière régionale bière hivernale	streekbier winterbier
	Duvel Moortgat Corp. Brewsite Brass. d'Achouffe Achouffe-Wibrin	Duvel Moortgat Corp. Brewsite Brass. d'Achouffe Achouffe-Wibrin	Duvel Moortgat Corp. Brewsite Brass. d'Achou Achouffe-Wibrin
	malt, hops, sugar, thyme, curaçao rind, yeast, water	malt, houblon, sucre, thym, écorce de curaçao, levure, eau	mout, hop, suiker, tijm, raçaoschil, gist, water
%	10%	10%	10%
	dark unfiltered	foncée non filtrée	donker ongefilterd
	–	–	–
°C	54 °F	12 °C	12 °C
	Warm character.	Caractère réchauffant.	Verwarmend karaker.
i	–	–	–

CHOUFFE
N'ICE
LA CHOUFFE

Noblesse

	top-fermentation re-fermented in the bottle	fermentation haute refermentation en bouteille	hoge gisting hergisting op de fles
	cross between Köllsch and Pale Ale	mélange de Köllsch et de pale ale	kruising van Köllsch en pale ale
	De Dochter van de Korenaar Baarle-Hertog	De Dochter van de Korenaar Baarle-Hertog	De Dochter van de Kore Baarle-Hertog
	barley malt, wheat malt, 3 hop varieties, brewer's yeast, water	malt d'orge, malt de froment, 3 sortes de houblon, levure de bière, eau	gerstemout, tarwemou soorten hop, biergist, w
%	5,50%	5,50%	5,50%
	blond clear but unfiltered	blonde claire mais non filtrée	blond helder maar ongefilter
	Leave the yeast sediment in the bottle.	Laisser le dépôt de levure dans la bouteille.	Het gistdepot in de fles ten.
°C	46 °F	8 °C	8 °C
	Firmly hopped beer with a good combination of spicy, bitter and sweet touches. A solid session beer as well as a sipping beer to be enjoyed at ease.	Bière fort houblonnée avec une bonne combinaison de nuances relevées, amères et légèrement douces. A la fois une bière facilement buvable que de dégustation dont on profite lentement.	Stevig gehopt bier met goede combinatie van dige/bittere en zachtzo nuances. Zowel een stevig doord bier als een degustatie- bier waar je langzaam geniet.
i	–	–	–

Brouwerij
De Dochter
van de Korenaar
— Baarle's bier op traditionele wijze gebrouwen —
Noblesse
Edel Blond bier van hoge gisting met hergisting op fles
Ingrediënten : Water, gerstemout, tarwemout, hop, biergist.
Gebrouwen door / Brassée par / Brewed by : Brouwerij / Brasserie / Brewery
De Dochter van de Korenaar - 2387 Baarle-Hertog Belgium
INH 330 mL ℮
ALC. 5,5% VOL

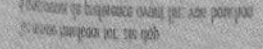

Nostradamus

	top-fermentation	fermentation haute	hoge gisting
	strong dubbel	double forte	sterk dubbel
	La Brasserie Caracole Falmignoul	La Brasserie Caracole Falmignoul	La Brasserie Caracole Falmignoul
	5 malt varieties, Hallertau hops, yeast, water	5 sortes de malt, houblon Hallertau, levure, eau	5 moutsoorten, Haller hop, gist, water
	9,00%	9,00%	9,00%
	brown	brune	bruin
	–	–	–
	cellar temperature	température de cave	keldertemperatuur
	Powerful, full-bodied sipping beer for cold winter nights with pear and chocolate flavours.	Bière de dégustation relevée et corsée pour les soirées hivernales avec arômes de poires et de chocolat.	Hartig en gecorseerd c tatiebier voor koude w avonden met aroma's peren en chocolade.
	–	–	–

Alc. 9 % vol.

Oeral

	top-fermentation re-fermented in the bottle unfiltered or centrifuged	fermentation haute refermentation en bou- teille non filtrée ni centrifugée	hoge gisting nagisting op de fles niet gefilterd of gecentr fugeerd
	strong blond	blonde forte	sterk blond
	De Dolle Brouwers Diksmuide	De Dolle Brouwers Dixmude	De Dolle Brouwers Diksmuide
	Lighter version of Arabi- er but without the dry- hopping. With Golding hops.	Version plus légère de ara- bier mais sans dryhop- ping. Avec houblon Golding.	Lichtere versie van Arab maar zonder dryhoppin Met Golding hop.
	7%	7%	7%
	Pale and clear if perfect- ly served.	Claire et limpide si parfai- tement versée.	Licht en helder indien fect uitgeschonken.
	–	–	–
	46 - 50 °F	8 - 10 °C	8 - 10 °C
	Fairly bitter summer beer (bitterness 50 EBU)	Bière d'été assez amère (50 EBU).	Vrij bitter (bitterheid 5 EBU) zomerbier.
	This beer is also sold un- der other brand names.	Est aussi vendue sous d'autres noms.	Wordt ook onder ander merknamen verkocht.

BREWED & BOTTLED BY
DE DOLLE BROUWERS BV
8600 ESEN BELGIUM
oerali
BIER

ANNO 1980
oerbier
NAT EN STRAF

Oerbier

	top-fermentation re-fermented in the bottle unfiltered or centrifuged	fermentation haute refermentation en bouteille non filtrée ni centrifugée	hoge gisting nagisting op de fles niet gefilterd of gecent. fugeerd
	strong dubbel	double forte	sterk dubbel
	De Dolle Brouwers Diksmuide	De Dolle Brouwers Dixmude	De Dolle Brouwers Diksmuide
	4 malt varieties, aromatic hops from Poperinge, no additives	4 sortes de malt, cônes de houblon aromatiques de Poperinge, aucun additif	4 moutsoorten, aromat hopbellen uit Popering geen additieven
	9%	9%	9%
	dark	foncée	donker
	The yeast sediment of approx. 2 cl is rich in vitamin B and can be drunk. Connoisseurs drink it separately. Serve in the typical 'Charente' glass.	Le dépôt de levure de 2 cl riche en vitamines B peut être bu. Les connaisseurs le boivent séparément. Verser dans un verre typique de vin de Charente.	Het vitaminerijke (vit. gistdepot van ca. 2 cl m gedronken worden. Ke drinken dit apart uit. Uitschenken in het typ 'Charenteglas'.
	54 °F	12 °C	12 °C
	Very full-bodied. Touches of hop and malt bitter, sweet and slightly sourish. Great character and long aftertaste.	Très franc, touches houblonnées et maltées amères et un peu acidulées. Beaucoup de caractère et une fin de bouche longue.	Zeer volmondig, toetse van hopbitter, moutbi zoet en een beetje zuri Veel karakter en lange dronk.
	When the glass is half-empty, the text 'wet and stiff' appears. Oerbier is the brewery's flagship.	Quand le verre est à moitié vide, le texte 'humide et forte' apparaît. Oerbier est le navire-amiral de la brasserie.	Wanneer het glas halfle is, lees je de bedrukkin en straf'. Oerbier is het geschip van de brouwe
	....		

ANNO 1980
oerbier
BREWED & BOTTLED IN ESEN (8600) BELGIUM
BY DE DOLLE BROUWERS 051/502781
ANNO 1980
oerbier

Okymore-Oxymore

	top-fermentation	fermentation haute	hoge gisting
	between Pilsner and Witbier	entre pils et bière blanche	tussen pils en witbier
	Périple en la Demeure Gouvy	Périple en la Demeure Gouvy	Périple en la Demeure Gouvy
	barley malt, wheat malt, wheat, spelt, oat	malt d'orge, malt de froment, froment, épeautre, avoine	gerstemout, tarwemou tarwe, spelt, haver
	5%	5%	5%
	light-yellow	doré clair	lichtgoud
	Preferably draught, poured into the appropriate glass.	De préférence du fût dans le verre approprié.	Bij voorkeur uit het vat het corresponderende
	36 - 39 °F	2 - 4 °C	2 - 4 °C
	Hoppy nose with citric touches. Bitter, mineral taste with a touch of roses, slightly malty with some bitterness near the end.	Parfum houblonné avec des touches d'agrumes. Goût amer, minéral avec des touches de roses, légèrement malté avec une arrière-bouche un peu amère.	Hoppige neus met toets van citrus. Bittere, mineralige sma met rozentoets, licht m tig met iets bitterheid het einde.
	–	–	–

oxymore
bière de fermentation haute
0,75cl
oxymore
bière de fermentation haute

Ondineke, Oilsjtersen tripel

top-fermentation re-fermented in the bottle	fermentation haute refermentation en bouteille	hoge gisting nagisting op de fles
Tripel	triple	tripel
Brouwerij De Glazen Toren Erpe-Mere	Brouwerij De Glazen Toren Erpe-Mere	Brouwerij De Glazen To Erpe-Mere
barley malt, candy sugar, hops, yeast, water	malt d'orge, sucre candi, houblon, levure, eau	gerstemout, kandijsuik hop, gist, water
8,50%	8,50%	8,50%
golden blond and slightly hazy, very sparkling with tiny bubbles, solid foam head	blond doré et légèrement voilée, pétillant fortement avec de petites bulles faux col solide	goudblond en lichtgesl erd, sterk en fijn parele stevige schuimkraag
Pour carefully into a dry, tall (e.g. a tulip-shaped) glass.	Verser prudemment dans un verre sec, oblong (p. ex. tulipe).	Voorzichtig uitschenke een droog, langwerpig tulpvormig) glas.
45 °F	7 °C	7 °C
Slightly bitter with hazy alcohol. Fruity, smoothly bitter with caramel malt in the aftertaste.	Légèrement amer avec de l'alcool voilé. Fruité, moelleux, amer avec une fin de bouche de malt caramélisé.	Licht bitter met geslui alcohol. Fruitig, zacht bitter me ramelmout in de afdro
–	–	–

KLEINBROUWERIJ
DE GLAZEN TOREN

Ops-Ale

bottom-fermentation	fermentation basse	lage gisting
premium Pilsner	pils de luxe	luxepils
Brouwerij Sint-Jozef Opitter	Brouwerij Sint-Jozef Opitter	Brouwerij Sint-Jozef Opitter
malt, hops, starch, water	malt, houblon, fécule, eau	mout, hop, zetmeel, w
5,50%	5,50%	5,50%
slightly yellowish	légèrement jaunâtre	licht gelig
Pour into a clean, degreased glass, avoiding contact between bottle and foam.	Verser dans un verre propre, dégraissé sans que la bouteille touche l'écume.	Uitschenken in een zu ontvet glas zonder da fles het schuim raakt.
36 - 39 °F	2 - 4 °C	2 - 4 °C
Refreshing thirst-quencher. Smooth Pilsner taste with bitter background.	Désaltérant rafraîchissant. Saveur moelleuse de pils avec un arrière-fond amer.	Verfrissende dorstless Zachte pilssmaak met re achtergrond.
First regional product from the Limburg Kempen (2005).	Premier produit régional des Limburgse Kempen (2005).	Eerste streekproduct v Limburgse Kempen (2

OPS-ALE
OPS-ALE
MET GOUD BEKROOND
BROUWERIJ St. JOZEF
Alc. 5,5%
e 25 cl.
OPS-ALE

Original Cannabier

	top-fermentation re-fermented in the bottle	fermentation haute refermentation en bouteille	hoge gisting hergisting op de fles
	herbal beer	bière aux épices	kruidenbier
	Brouwerij Den Hopperd Westmeerbeek	Brouwerij Den Hopperd Westmeerbeek	Brouwerij Den Hopper Westmeerbeek
	barley malt, yeast, cane sugar, hemp blossom, water. (free of THC)	malt d'orge, levure, sucre de canne, fleurs de chanvre, eau. (sans THC)	gerstemout, gist, rietsu hennepbloesem, water. (THC vrij)
	6,50%	6,50%	6,50%
	–	–	–
	–	–	–
	–	–	–
	–	–	–
	Boutique beer.	Brassée de façon artisanale.	Ambachtelijk gebrouw

Ambachtelijk gebrouwen
original
Cannabier
since 2006
33 cl - 6,5 % vol. alc. - Cat. S

Orval

	top-fermentation re-fermented in the bottle	fermentation haute refermentation en bouteille	hoge gisting hergisting op de fles
	Trappist	trappiste	trappist
	Brasserie d'Orval Villers d'Orval	Brasserie d'Orval Villers d'Orval	Brasserie d'Orval Villers d'Orval
	Barley malt, pale malt, caramel malt, white candy sugar, hops (Hallertau, Styrie), top yeast, Orval yeast (re-fermentation in the barrel), water from the Mathild well.	Malt d'orge, malt pâle, malt caramélisé, sucre candi blanc, houblon (Hallertau, Styrie), levure haute, levure d' Orval (refermentation au réservoir), eau de la source de Mathilde.	Gerstemout, bleekmo ramelmout, witte kan ker, hop (Hallertau, St hoge gist, Orvalgist (n ting op tank), water va Mathildebron.
	6,20%	6,20%	6,20%
	creamy foam head	faux col crémeux	romige schuimkraag
	Pour the sediment separately.	Verser le dépôt séparément.	Het bezinksel afzonde uitschenken.
	54 - 57 °F	12 - 14 °C	12 - 14 °C
	Specific taste of Orval yeast and hoppy aroma.	Saveur spécifique de la levure d'Orval, et d'arôme houblonné.	Specifieke smaak van valgist en hoppig aror
	Store in a dark room at 10 to 15 °C. The label refers to the legend of Orval.	Conserver à l'abri de la lumière à 10 à 15 °C. L'étiquette renvoie à la légende d'Orval.	Donker bewaren bij 1C 15 °C. Het etiket verwijst naa legende van Orval.

TRAPPISTENBIER · TRAPPIST ALE
ORVAL
CONTIENT MALT D'ORGE · BEVAT GERSTEMOUT
orval

Oud Zottegems Bier

	top-fermentation	fermentation haute	hoge gisting
	amber	ambrée	amber
	Brouwerij Strubbe for Brouwerij Crombé Zottegem	Brouwerij Strubbe pour Brouwerij Crombé Zottegem	Brouwerij Strubbe voo Brouwerij Crombé Zottegem
	–	–	–
	6,50%	6,50%	6,50%
	amber	ambrée	amber
	–	–	–
	–	–	–
	Bittersweet beer with taste evolution.	Bière douce-amère avec évolution de la saveur.	Bitterzoet bier met sm evolutie.
	–	–	–

Oud
Zottegems
Bier
Hospitaalstraat 10 B9620 Zottegem - Tel. 09 360 02 40

Zottegems

Oude Geuze Boon

	spontaneous fermentation. Re-fermented in the bottle by the young Lambic which contains fermentable sugars.	fermentation spontanée. Refermentation en bouteille par le lambic jeune contentant des sucres commutables en levure.	spontane gisting. Nagisting op de fles dc jonge lambiek die verg re suikers bevat.
	Gueuze	gueuze	geuze
	Brouwerij Boon Lembeek	Brouwerij Boon Lembeek	Brouwerij Boon Lembeek
	Selected blend of 90% mellow Lambic (at least 18 months), 5% of 3-year old beer full of character, 5% very young Lambic.	Mélange sélectionné de 90% de lambic doux (au moins 18 mois), 5% de bière de caractère de 3 ans, 5% de lambic très jeune.	Geselecteerde mengel van 90% malse lambie (minstens 18 maand), 5% karaktervol bier va jaar, 5% heel jonge lar
%	6,50%	6,50%	6,50%
	–	–	–
	–	–	–
°C	cellar temperature	température de cave	keldertemperatuur
	–	–	–
i	Only champagne bottles are suitable for Gueuze because of the high pressure. If stored under good conditions and at cellar temperature, this beer can keep for more than 20 years.	Seules les bouteilles de champagne résistent à la haute pression de la gueuze. Se conserve plus de 20 ans dans de bonnes conditions et à température de cave.	Enkel champagnefless kunnen weerstaan aar hoge druk van de geu: Kan in goede omstanc heden meer dan 20 ja bewaard worden op ke temperatuur.

2003-2004
BROUWSEIZOEN
OUDE
GEUZE
BOON
MALSE LAMBIEK 100% LAMBIC MOELLEUX

Geuze
Boon

Oude Geuze Cuvée René

	spontaneous fermentation	fermentation spontanée	spontane gisting
	Gueuze Lambic	gueuze lambic	geuze lambiek
	Brouwerij Lindemans Vlezenbeek	Brouwerij Lindemans Vlezenbeek	Brouwerij Lindemans Vlezenbeek
	malt, wheat, hops, water	malt, froment, houblon, eau	mout, tarwe, hop, wat
	5,50%	5,50%	5,50%
	golden blond clear	blond doré claire	goudblond helder
	Pour into a Gueuze or champagne glass.	Verser dans un verre de gueuze ou de champagne.	In een geuze- of champ glas uitschenken.
	41 °F	5 °C	5 °C
	Smoothly sourish. Sparkling, slightly sourish and well-balanced taste with a dry, refreshingly sourish aftertaste.	Moelleux, acidulé. Saveur pétillante, douce, acidulée et équilibrée avec une fin de bouche sèche, fraîche et acidulée.	Zacht zurig. Sprankelende, zachtzu en uitgebalanceerde s met een droge, fris zu afdronk.
	This beer can be kept for many years due to the re-fermentation in the bottle.	Par la refermentation en bouteille, cette bière peut se conserver pendant des années; tout comme le vin, elle subit une évolution de la saveur.	Dit bier is jaren houdb door hergisting op de Het ondergaat een sm evolutie net als wijn.

ALC. 5 % VOL. 750 ML
GRAND CRU
GUEUZE LAMBIC BEER
CUVÉE RENÉ
EST. 1877
BROUWERIJ
LINDEMANS
VLEZENBEEK BELGIUM
MET SMAAK EVOLUTIE - FERMENTATION EN BOUTEILLE
Lindemans

Oude Geuze De Cam

	spontaneous fermentation	fermentation spontanée	spontane gisting
	Gueuze Lambic	gueuze lambic	geuze lambiek
	Geuzestekerij De Oude Cam, Gooik	Geuzestekerij De Oude Cam, Gooik	Geuzestekerij De Oud Gooik
	1, 3 and 5-year old Lambic. Brewed in 4 different breweries. 65% wheat, 35% barley malt, water.	Lambic de 1, 3 et 5 ans d'âge. Brassé en 4 brasseries différentes. 65% froment, 35% malt d'orge, eau.	Lambiek van 1, 3 en 5 oud, gebrouwen in 4 v schillende brouwerije 65% tarwe, 35% gerste water.
	6%	6%	6%
	Golden blond. Sparkling like champagne if served following the rules.	Blond doré. Perlant comme le champagne si versée selon les règles de l'art.	Goudblond. Parelend champagne indien ui schonken volgens de r van de kunst.
	Remove the cork slantwise and do not let the bottle pop. Fill the glasses in one fluent movement. Let the foam overflow and leave the sediment in the bottle or serve it in a shot glass.	Enlever le bouchon en position oblique sans le faire exploser. Remplir les verres en un seul mouvement fluide, laisser la bière déborder et laisser le dépôt dans la bouteille ou le servir dans un petit verre.	Het kurk schuin verw ren en niet laten ploff glazen in 1 vloeiende ging inschenken, het l laten overschuimen e bezinksel in de fles lat of in een borrelglaasje serveren.
	54 - 57 °F	12 - 14 °C	12 - 14 °C
	Velvety soft with a winelike bouquet, sourish.	Velouté avec un bouquet de vin, frais et acidulé.	Fluweelzacht met een achtig boeket, friszur
	Old Gueuze can be kept up to 20 years.	La vieille gueuze peut se conserver 20 ans.	Oude geuze kan tot 2 bewaard worden.

H.O.R.A.L.
HOge Raad
Ambachtelijke Lambikbieren
EXCLUSIEF
OUDE GEUZE
1 fles = 3 jaar werk
DE CAM
Gooik
Belgisch
bier

GEUZE- KRIEK
DE CAM GOOIK

Oude Geuze 3 fonteinen

	spontaneous fermentation spontaneous fermentation in the bottle	fermentation spontanée fermentation spontanée en bouteille	spontane gisting spontane wilde gisting de fles
	Gueuze	gueuze	geuze
	Brouwerij 3 fonteinen Beersel	Brouwerij 3 fonteinen Beersel	Brouwerij 3 fonteinen Beersel
	60% barley malt, 40% wheat, more than one year old hops, water. A blend of 1, 2 and 3-year old Lambic, matured in oak barrels.	60% malt d'orge, 40% froment, houblon suranné, eau. Mélange de lambic de 1, 2 et 3 ans d'âge, mûrit en fûts en bois de chêne.	60% gerstemout, 40% t overjaarse hop, water. Mengeling van 1, 2 en oude lambiek gerijpt o kenhouten vaten.
%	6%	6%	6%
	unfiltered	non filtrée	ongefilterd
	Open the bottle carefully.	Ouvrir la bouteille prudemment.	De fles voorzichtig ope
°C	–	–	–
	–	–	–
i	Can be kept for at least 10 years after the bottling date. Old Gueuze is a protected brand (E.U.). 3 fonteinen is a traditional gueuze blender.	Peut se conserver au moins 10 ans après la date de la mise en bouteille. Vieille Gueuze est une appellation protégée (U.E.). 3 fonteinen est un coupeur artisanal de gueuze.	Kan minstens tot 10 ja na botteldatum worde waard. Oude Geuze is een beschermde benaming (E De 3 fonteinen is een a bachtelijke geuzesteke

OUDE
GEUZE
www.3fonteinen.be

Oude Gueuze Hanssens

	spontaneous fermentation re-fermented in the bottle	fermentation spontanée refermentation en bouteille	spontane gisting hergisting in de fles
	Gueuze	gueuze	geuze
	Hanssens Geuzestekerij Dworp	Hanssens Geuzestekerij Dworp	Hanssens Geuzestekerij Dworp
	Hops, barley malt, wheat, water. A blend of the finest Lambic varieties. 100% matured in oak barrels.	Houblon, malt d'orge, froment, eau. Mélange des lambics les plus fins. Mûri 100% en fûts de chêne.	Hop, gerstemout, tarwe, water. Mengeling van de fijnste lambiek. 100% gerijpt op eiken va
	6%	6%	6%
	–	–	–
	–	–	–
	–	–	–
	–	–	–
	Hanssens boutique Gueuze blender since 1896.	Hanssens Artisanal depuis 1896.	Hanssens Artisanaal sin 1896.

Hanssens Artisanaal
sinds 1896
Oude Gueuze
Mengeling van de fijnste Lambiek,
100% gerijpt op eiken vaten, spontane hergisting in de fles.
Mélange du plus fin Lambiek,
100% mûri en futs de chêne, refermentée en bouteille.
Gebotteld te / Mise en bouteille à Dworp
GUEUZE-KRIEK
HANSSENS
DWORP

Oude Geuze Oud Beersel

	spontaneous fermentation	fermentation spontanée	spontane gisting
	Gueuze Lambic	gueuze lambic	geuze lambiek
	Geuzestekerij Oud Beersel Beersel	Geuzestekerij Oud Beersel Beersel	Geuzestekerij Oud Beer Beersel
	wheat, barley malt, hops, water	froment, malt d'orge, houblon, eau	tarwe, gerstemout, hop water
%	6%	6%	6%
	gold-yellow	jaune doré	goudgeel
	Pour carefully into a degreased, dry glass. Keep the glass tilted and revolve it in your hand to obtain a nice foam head. Leave the yeast sediment in the bottle.	Verser prudemment dans un verre dégraissé et sec. Tenir le verre en oblique et le tourner dans la paume au moment de verser la bière pour obtenir un beau faux col. Laisser le dépôt de levure dans la bouteille.	Voorzichtig uitschenke een ontvet droog glas. glas schuin houden en de handpalm draaien t dens het schenken voor een mooie schuimkraa De gistfond in de fles la
°C	46 - 54 °F	8 - 12 °C	8 - 12 °C
	Rich, refreshing, complex and intriguing. Hoppy flavour with the typical smell of wild yeasts. A taste of pleasant bitterness with a sourish and smooth character.	Riche, frais, complexe et intrigant. Arôme houblonné avec un parfum typique de levures sauvages. Saveur amère agréable avec un caractère acidulé et doux.	Rijk, fris, complex en in gerend. Hoppig aroma met typi geur van wilde gisten. Een smaak van aangen bitterheid met een zuri zacht karakter.
i	Matured in chestnut barrels.	Mûrit en fûts de châtaignier.	Gerijpt op kastanjehou vaten.

OUDE GEUZE VIEILLE
Oud Beersel

Oude Geuze vintage 3 fonteinen

	spontaneous fermentation spontaneous fermentation in the bottle	fermentation spontanée fermentation spontanée sauvage en bouteille	spontane gisting spontane wilde gisting op fles
	Gueuze	gueuze	geuze
	Brouwerij 3 fonteinen Beersel	Brouwerij 3 fonteinen Beersel	Brouwerij 3 fonteinen Beersel
	60% barley malt, 40% wheat, more than one year old hops, water. A blend of 1, 2 and 3-year old Lambic, matured in oak barrels.	60% malt d'orge, 40% froment, houblon suranné, eau. Mélange de lambic de 1, 2 et 3 ans d'âge mûri en fûts en bois de chêne.	60% gerstemout, 40% t overjaarse hop, water. Mengeling van 1, 2 en oude lambiek gerijpt o eikenhouten vaten.
	6%	6%	6%
	unfiltered	non filtrée	ongefilterd
	–	–	–
	–	–	–
	–	–	–
	Can be kept for at least ten years after the bottling date. Old Gueuze is a protected brand (E.U.). De 3 fonteinen is a traditional gueuze blender.	Peut se conserver au moins dix ans après la date de la mise en bouteilles. Vieille Gueuze est une appellation protégée (U.E.). 3 fonteinen est un coupeur artisanal de gueuze.	Kan minstens tot 10 ja na botteldatum worde waard. Oude Geuze is een beschermde benaming (E De 3 fonteinen is een a bachtelijke geuzesteke

brouweri
fontein
OUDE
GEUZE
vintage
www.3fonteinen.be

Oude Kriek Boon

	spontaneous fermentation re-fermented in the bottle	fermentation spontanée refermentation en bouteille	spontane gisting hergisting op de fles
	fruit beer	bière fruitée	fruitbier
	Brouwerij Boon Lembeek	Brouwerij Boon Lembeek	Brouwerij Boon Lembeek
	A blend of young and old Lambic, matured in oak barrels. Real cherries (300 g per litre), bottled with yeast.	Mélange de jeune et vieux lambic mûri en fûts de chêne. De vraies cerises (300 g par litre), mises en bouteilles avec de la levure.	Versnijding van jonge oude lambiek gerijpt eikenhouten vaten. Echte krieken (300 g p liter), gebotteld op gis
%	6,50%	6,50%	6,50%
	red	rouge	rood
	–	–	–
°C	–	–	–
	Refreshing, non-foaming sweet-and-sour cherry taste, pure and unsweetened.	Frais, sans écume. Saveur de cerises aigre-douce, pure et non sucrée.	Fris, niet schuimend. Zuurzoete kriekensma puur en ongezoet.
i	Originally created with Schaarbeek cherries, now mainly with North cherries, and Lambic that is at least 6 months old.	A l'origine fabriquée avec des cerises de Schaerbeek, aujourd'hui surtout avec des cerises du Nord et du lambic d'au minimum 6 mois.	Oorspronkelijk gemaa met Schaarbeekse krie nu vooral met Noordk ken, en lambiek van m mum 6 maanden oud

2004
300g
OUDE
KRIEK
BOON
OUDE LAMBIEK 100% VIEUX LAMBIC

KRIEK
BOON

Oude Kriek Cuvée René

	spontaneous fermentation	fermentation spontanée	spontane gisting
	fruit beer Lambic	bière fruitée lambic	fruitbier lambiek
	Brouwerij Lindemans Vlezenbeek	Brouwerij Lindemans Vlezenbeek	Brouwerij Lindemans Vlezenbeek
	malt, wheat, hops, Belgian cherries, water	malt, froment, houblon, cerises belges, eau	mout, tarwe, hop, Belg krieken, water
	5,50%	5,50%	5,50%
	red clear	rouge claire	rood helder
	Pour into a Gueuze or champagne glass. Open carefully and leave the yeast sediment in the bottle.	Verser dans un verre de gueuze ou de champagne. Ouvrir prudemment et laisser le dépôt de levure dans la bouteille.	In een geuze- of champ glas uitschenken. Voorzichtig openen en gistdepot in de fles late
	41 °F	5 °C	5 °C
	Smoothly sourish. Sparkling, smoothly sourish and well-balanced taste with a fruity cherry touch and a dry, refreshingly sourish aftertaste.	Moelleux, acidulé. Saveur pétillante, douce, acidulée et équilibrée avec une touche fruitée de cerises et une fin de bouche sèche, fraîche et acidulée.	Zacht zurig. Sprankelende, zachtzu en uitgebalanceerde sr met een fruitige toets v krieken en een droge fi zurige afdronk.
	This beer can be kept for many years due to the refermentation in the bottle. Like wine, it experiences a taste evolution.	Cette bière peut se conserver pendant des années par sa refermentation en bouteille; tout comme le vin, elle subit une évolution de la saveur.	Dit bier is jaren houdb door hergisting op de f Het ondergaat een sma evolutie net als wijn.

GRAND CRU
KRIEK
LINDEMANS

Oude Kriek De Cam

	spontaneous fermentation	fermentation spontanée	spontane gisting
	Lambic beer	bière lambic	lambiekbier
	Geuzestekerij De Oude Cam Gooik	Geuzestekerij De Oude Cam Gooik	Geuzestekerij De Oude Gooik
	65% wheat, 35% barley malt, more than one year old hops, min. 35% cherries with pip. No artificial sweetening, juices, other fruits or colouring agents.	65% froment, 35% malt d'orge, houblon suranné, min. 35% de cerises avec noyau. Pas de sucres artificiels, jus, autres fruits ou colorants.	65% tarwe, 35% gersten overjaarse hop, min. 35 krieken met pit. Geen kunstmatige suik sappen, andere vruchte kleurstoffen.
%	6,50%	6,50%	6,50%
	ruby red	rouge rubis	robijnrood
	Remove the cork slantwise and do not let the bottle pop. Fill the glasses in one fluent movement. Let the foam overflow and leave the sediment in the bottle or serve it in a shot glass.	Enlever le bouchon en position oblique sans le faire exploser. Remplir les verres en un seul mouvement fluide, laisser la bière déborder et laisser le dépôt dans la bouteille ou le servir dans un petit verre.	Het kurk schuin verwij ren en niet laten ploffe glazen in 1 vloeiende b ging inschenken, het b laten overschuimen en bezinksel in de fles late of in een borrelglaasje serveren.
°C	50 °F	10 °C	10 °C
	Complex character, vanilla and almond flavour.	Caractère complexe, touches de vanille et d'amande.	Complex karakter, toet van vanille en amande
	–	–	–

H.O.R.A.L.
HOge Raad
Ambachtelijke Lambikbieren
NIET ZOET
exceptioneel
OUDE KRIEK
bevat 100% echte krieken
DE CAM
Gooik

Oude Kriek 3 fonteinen

	spontaneous fermentation spontaneous re-fermentation in the bottle	fermentation spontanée fermentation spontanée en bouteille	spontane gisting spontane hergisting o
	fruit beer	bière fruitée	fruitbier
	Brouwerij 3 fonteinen Beersel	Brouwerij 3 fonteinen Beersel	Brouwerij 3 fonteinen Beersel
	60% barley malt, 40% wheat, more than one year old hops, full cherries (35%), water. A blend of young Lambic and Schaarbeek cherries.	60% malt d'orge, 40% froment, houblon surané, cerises entières (35%), eau. Un assemblage de jeune lambic et de cerises de Schaerbeek.	60% gerstemout, 40% t overjaarse hop, volle k ken (35%), water. Een assemblage van jo lambiek met Schaarbe krieken.
%	5%	5%	5%
	red unfiltered	rouge non filtrée	rood ongefilterd
	Open the bottle carefully.	Ouvrir la bouteille prudemment.	De fles voorzichtig ope
°C	–	–	–
	–	–	–
i	Can be kept for at least ten years after the bottling date. Oude Kriek is a protected brand (E.U.). De 3 fonteinen is a boutique Gueuze blender.	Peut se conserver au moins 10 ans après la date de la mise en bouteilles. Oude Kriek est une appellation protégée (U.E.). 3 fonteinen est un coupeur artisanal de gueuze.	Kan minstens tot 10 ja na botteldatum worde bewaard. Oude Kriek is een besch de benaming (E.G.). De 3 fonteinen is een a bachtelijke geuzesteker

OUDE
KRIEK
www.3fonteinen.be

Oude Kriek Hanssens

	spontaneous fermentation re-fermented in the bottle	fermentation spontanée refermentation en bouteille	spontane gisting hergisting in de fles
	fruit beer	bière fruitée	fruitbier
	Hanssens Geuzestekerij Dworp	Hanssens Geuzestekerij Dworp	Hanssens Geuzesteker[i] Dworp
	Hops, barley malt, wheat, fresh cherries, water. A blend of the finest Lambic varieties, 100% matured in oak barrels.	Houblon, malt d'orge, froment, cerises fraîches, eau. Mélange des lambics les plus fins. Mûri 100% en fûts de chêne.	Hop, gerstemout, tarw[e] verse krieken, water. Mengeling van de fijns[te] lambieksoorten. 100% gerijpt op eiken v[aten]
%	6%	6%	6%
	red	rouge	rood
	–	–	–
	–	–	–
	–	–	–
i	Hanssens boutique Gueuze blender since 1896.	Hanssens Artisanal depuis 1896.	Hanssens Artisanaal si[nds] 1896.

Hanssens Artisanaal
sinds 1896
Oude Kriek
Mengeling van de fijnste Lambiek
100% gerijpt op eiken vaten, spontane hergisting in de fles
Mélange du plus fin Lambiek
100% mûrit en futs de chêne, refermentée en bouteille
Gebotteld te / Mise en bouteille à Dworp

GUEUZE-KRIEK
HANSSENS
DWORP

Oude Kriek Mort Subite

	spontaneous	fermentation spontanée	spontane gisting
	fruit beer	bière fruitée	fruitbier
	Alken Maes corporation Brewsite Mort Subite Kobbegem	Alken Maes corporation Brewsite Mort Subite Kobbegem	Alken Maes Corporati Brewsite Mort Subite Kobbegem
	Authentic blend of old and young Lambic with Belgian Krieks.	Mélange authentique de vieux et de jeune lambic avec des cerises belges.	Authentieke mengeli oude en jonge lambie Belgische krieken.
%	–	–	–
	bright red	rouge vif	helrood
	Empty in a degreased, rinsed and wet bulb jar, avoiding contact between bottle and foam. Let the glass overflow and skimm off. Rince the bottom of the glass, pat it dry and present it with the bottle.	Verser complètement dans un verre ballon dégraissé, rincé et mouillé sans que la bouteille touche l'écume. Laisser déborder et écumer. Rincer le verre, le sécher et le présenter avec la bouteille.	Helemaal uitschenker een ontvet, gespoeld e ballonglas zonder dat fles het schuim raakt. overlopen en afschuin Het glas spoelen, droc pen en samen met de presenteren.
°C	36 - 39 °F	2 - 4 °C	2 - 4 °C
	Refreshing sweet-and-sour with the flavour of fresh cherries.	Frais, aigre-doux avec la saveur de cerises fraîches.	Fris zuurzoet met de s van verse krieken.
i	The name Mort Subite refers to the last throw in the dice game 'mort subite' that was played at the Brussels Café 'La Cour Royale'.	Le nom Mort Subite renvoie au dernier coup dans le jeu de dés 'mort subite' joué dans le café bruxellois 'La Cour Royale'.	De naam Mort Subite ve naar de laatste worp in teerlingspel 'mort subi gespeeld werd in het Br Café 'La Cour Royale'.

ANNO 1686
MORT
SUBITE
LAMBIC
Oude Kriek
A L'ANCIENNE

MORT
SUBITE
LAMBIC

Oude Kriek Oud Beersel

	spontaneous fermentation	fermentation spontanée	spontane gisting
	Gueuze Lambic	gueuze lambic	geuze lambiek
	Geuzestekerij Oud Beersel Beersel	Geuzestekerij Oud Beersel Beersel	Geuzestekerij Oud Bee Beersel
	wheat, barley malt, hops, 400 g cherries/litre, water	froment, malt d'orge, houblon, 400 g de cerises/ litre, eau	tarwe, gerstemout, ho 400 g krieken/liter, wa
%	6,50%	6,50%	6,50%
	deep red	rouge intense	dieprood
	Pour carefully into a de-greased, dry glass. Keep the glass tilted and revolve it in your hand to obtain a nice foam head. Leave the yeast sediment in the bottle.	Verser prudemment dans un verre dégraissé et sec. Tenir le verre en oblique et le tourner dans la paume au moment de verser la bière pour obtenir un beau faux col. Laisser le dépôt de levure dans la bouteille.	Voorzichtig uitschenk een ontvet droog glas. glas schuin houden en de handpalm draaien dens het schenken voc mooie schuimkraag. De gistfond in de fles l
°C	46 - 54 °F	8 - 12 °C	8 - 12 °C
	Rich, fresh, fruity and intriguing. An overwhelming fruitiness of cherry with a touch of almond from the cherry stones.	Riche, frais, fruité et intrigant. Goût fruité éblouissant de cerises avec une touche d'amande du noyau.	Rijk, fris, fruitig en in gerend. Overweldigende fruiti van krieken met amar toets van de pit.
i	–	–	–

OUDE KRIEK VIEILLE
Oud Beersel

Oude Lambiek De Cam

	spontaneous fermentation	fermentation spontanée	spontane gisting
	Lambic	lambic	lambiek
	Geuzestekerij De Oude Cam Gooik	Geuzestekerij De Oude Cam Gooik	Geuzestekerij De Oud Gooik
	5-year old Lambic. 65% wheat, 35% barley malt, more than 1 year old hops, water.	Lambic de 5 ans. 65% froment, 35% malt d'orge, houblon suranné, eau.	Lambiek van 5 jaar ou 65% tarwe, 35% gerste overjaarse hop, water.
%	5%	5%	5%
	straw-yellow, beer without carbon dioxide	jaune paille bière sans acide carbonique	strogeel, plat bier zor koolzuurgas
	First rinse the glass with hot water, then cold, to remove all the detergent. Next, dry it. Leave the bottle for 3 weeks in an upright position and put it in a basket before serving.	Rincer le verre d'abord à l'eau chaude et puis à l'eau froide pour enlever le détergent et sécher. Laisser reposer la bouteille 3 semaines en position verticale. Utiliser un panier verseur pour servir.	Het glas eerst met wa dan met koud water s len om alle detergent te verwijderen en daa afdrogen. De fles 3 we rechtopstaand laten r Voor het schenken in mandje leggen.
°C	43 - 46 °F	6 - 8 °C	6 - 8 °C
	Very smooth with a wine bouquet. Evolution of apple to calvados or sherry. Surprising due to the lack of carbon dioxide.	Velouté avec un bouquet de vin. Saveur de pomme passant au calvados ou au xérès. Surprenant par le manque de gaz carbonique.	Fluweelzacht met een achtig boeket. Evolue van appel naar calvad sherry. Verrassend do gebrek aan koolzuurg
i	Lambic is called the missing link between beer and wine.	Le lambic est souvent appelé 'le missing link' entre la bière et le vin.	Lambiek wordt wel ee missing link tussen b wijn genoemd.

H.O.R.A.L.
HOge Raad
exceptioneel
OUDE LAMBIEK
ons vakmanschap, uw trots
DE CAM
Gooik
OUDE LAMBIC
Belgisch

Palm Dobbel

	top-fermentation	fermentation haute	hoge gisting
	amber Christmas beer	bière de Noël ambrée	amber kerstbier
	Palm Breweries Site Palm Steenhuffel	Palm Breweries Site Palm Steenhuffel	Palm Breweries Site Palm Steenhuffel
	special palm malts, fine aromatic hops, palm yeasts, water	malts Palm spéciaux, houblons aromatiques fins, levures Palm, eau	speciale palmmouten, fijne aromahoppen, pa gisten, water
%	6%	6%	6%
	amber	ambrée	amber
	Serve in a typical Palm snifter with a fine foam head.	Servir dans un verre ballon Palm typique avec un faux col fin.	Serveren in een typisc Palm bolglas met een schuimkraag.
	41 - 50 °F	5 - 10 °C	5 - 10 °C
	Pronounced malty and hoppy character. A stronger version of Palm Spéciale.	Caractère malté et houblonné prononcé. Version plus forte de la Palm Spéciale.	Uitgesproken mout- en karakter. Zwaardere versie van Spéciale.
i	Created in 1947 for the 200th anniversary of Brouwerij Palm.	Créée en 1947 à l'occasion du bicentenaire de la Brasserie Palm.	Gecreëerd in 1947 ter genheid van het 200-j. bestaan van Brouwerij Palm.

PALM
Dobbel
ANNO 1747
PALM
Dobbel
STEENHUFFEL
BELGIUM

Palm Green

	top-fermentation	fermentation haute	hoge gisting
	Spéciale Belge amber	spéciale belge ambrée	speciale belge amber
	Palm Breweries Site Palm Steenhuffel	Palm Breweries Site Palm Steenhuffel	Palm Breweries Site Palm Steenhuffel
	Special palm malts, fine, aromatic hops (among other places from Kent), palm yeasts, water	malts Palm spéciaux, houblons aromatiques fins (e.a. de Kent), levures Palm, eau	speciale palmmouten, ne aromahoppen (o.a. Kent), palmgisten, wat
%	<0,25%	<0,25%	<0,25%
	amber-coloured	couleur ambrée	amberkleurig
	Serve in a typical Palm snifter with a thick foam head. The bottle can be emptied.	Servir dans un verre ballon Palm typique avec un bon faux col. Peut être complètement versée.	Serveren in een typisc Palm bolglas met een schuimkraag. Mag voll uitgeschonken worden
°C	41 °F	5 °C	5 °C
	Smooth like honey.	Doux comme du miel.	Honingzacht.
i	Non-alcoholic version.	Version sans alcool.	Alcoholvrije versie.

PALM
Green
ALCOHOLVRIJ / SANS ALCOOL
ANNO
PALM

Palm Royale

	top-fermentation re-fermented in the bottle	fermentation haute refermentation en bouteille	hoge gisting nagisting op de fles
	amber	ambrée	amber
	Palm Breweries Site Palm Steenhuffel	Palm Breweries Site Palm Steenhuffel	Palm Breweries Site Palm Steenhuffel
	special palm malts, fine, aromatic hops, palm yeasts, water	malts Palm spéciaux, houblons aromatiques fins, levures Palm, eau	speciale palmmouten, fijne aromahoppen, pa gisten, water
%	7,50%	7,50%	7,50%
	copper-blond	blond cuivre	koperblond
	Serve in a typical Palm snifter with a thick foam head.	Servir dans un verre calice Palm typique avec un bon faux col.	Serveren in een typisc Palm kelkglas met een flinke schuimkraag.
°C	41 - 50 °F	5 - 10 °C	5 - 10 °C
	Pronounced fruitiness due to fermentation.	Caractère fruité prononcé dû à la fermentation.	Nadrukkelijke gistings fruitigheid.
i	Created for brewer Alfred Van Roy's 90th birthday. Brewed with Palm yeasts, selected by him.	Créée à l'occasion du quatre-vingt-dixième anniversaire du brasseur Alfred Van Roy et brassée à base de levures Palm sélectionnées par lui-même.	Gecreëerd ter gelegenh van de 90e verjaardag brouwer Alfred Van Rc gebrouwen op basis va zijn zelf geselecteerde gisten.

PALM
Royale
ANNO 1747
PALM
Royale
7,5% vol
BELGIUM
PALM
Royale

Palm Speciale

	top-fermentation	fermentation haute	hoge gisting
	Spéciale Belge amber	spéciale belge ambrée	speciale belge amber
	Palm Breweries Site Palm Steenhuffel	Palm Breweries Site Palm Steenhuffel	Palm Breweries Site Palm Steenhuffel
	special palm malts, fine, aromatic hops (e.g. from Kent), palm yeasts, water	malts Palm spéciaux, houblons aromatiques fins (e.a. de Kent), levures Palm, eau	speciale palmmouten, ne aromahoppen (o.a. Kent), palmgisten, wat
%	5,40%	5,40%	5,40%
	amber-coloured	couleur ambrée	amberkleurig
	Serve in a typical Palm snifter with a thick foam head.	Servir dans un verre ballon Palm typique avec un bon faux col.	Serveren in een typisch Palm bolglas met een schuimkraag.
°C	41 - 50 °F	5 - 10 °C	5 - 10 °C
	Easy to drink and harmonious. Honey-like tenderness (palm mouts) and fruity fermentation aroma (palm yeasts).	Facilement buvable et harmonieux. Caractère doux de miel (malts Palm) et arôme de fermentation fruité (levures Palm).	Laat zich vlot drinken harmonieus. Honingachtige malshe (palmmouten) en fruit gistingsaroma (palmgis
i	–	–	–

PALM
BELGIUM
ANNO
PALM
BELGIUM
PALM

Pannepøt

	top-fermentation re-fermented in the bottle	fermentation haute refermentation en bouteille	hoge gisting met nagisting in de fle
	Belgian strong ale	Belgian strong ale	Belgian strong ale
	at Brouwerij Deca De Struise Brouwers De Panne	chez Brouwerij Deca De Struise Brouwers La Panne	bij Brouwerij Deca De Struise Brouwers De Panne
	Pilsner malt, special B, carafa, cane sugar, yeast, water, hops (Bramling Cross, Hallertauer Mittelfrueh), herbs (cinnamon, sweet orange rind, thyme, coriander, vanilla, massis banda).	Malt de pils, B spécial, carafa, sucre de canne, levure, eau, houblon (Bramling Cross, Hallertauer Mittelfrueh), herbes (cannelle, écorce d'orange, thym, coriandre, vanille, massis banda).	Pilsmout, special B, ca rietsuiker, gist, water, (Bramling Cross, Haller er Mittelfrueh), kruide (kaneel, zoete sinaassc tijm, koriander, vanille massis banda).
	10%	10%	10%
	dark brown (84 EBC) unfiltered creamy foam head	brun foncé (84 EBC) non filtrée faux col crémeux	donkerbruin (84 EBC) ongefilterd romige schuimkraag
	–	–	–
	–	–	–
	Very malty flavour, soft and spicy with accents of dried fruit. Generous taste with touches of caramel, fruits, herbs, liquorice, hops and nutmeg.	Arôme très malté, doucement relevé avec des accents de fruits séchés. Saveur généreuse avec des touches de caramel, fruits, réglisse, houblon, muscade.	Zeer moutig aroma, zac kruidig met accenten va gedroogd fruit. Genereu smaak met toetsen van mel, vruchten, kruiden, hout, hop, muskaatnoot
	Originally created for the International Beer Festival of Copenhague, 2006.	Créée à l'occasion du festival international de la bière à Copenhague en 2006.	Ontwikkeld t.g.v. het In nationaal bierfestival in penhagen in 2006.
	....		

PANNEPØT
AUTHENTIC
DSB
2006
by the Struise Brouwers for Vdaco bvba
DSB
Struisebrouwers.be

Pannepot

	top-fermentation unpasteurised	fermentation haute non pasteurisée	hoge gisting niet gepasteuriseerd
	Belgian strong Ale	Belgian strong ale	Belgian strong ale
	at Brouwerij Deca De Struise Brouwers De Panne	chez Brouwerij Deca De Struise Brouwers La Panne	bij Brouwerij Deca De Struise Brouwers De Panne
	Pilsner malt, caramel malt, carafa, coffee, chocolate, corn flocks, yeast, water, candy sugar, cane sugar, cinnamon, thyme, coriander, sweet orange rind, hops (Bramling Cross, Hallertauer Mittelfrueh).	malt de pils et de caramel, carafa, café, chocolat, flocons de maïs, levure, eau, sucre candi, sucre de canne, cannelle, thym, coriandre, écorce d'orange doux, houblon (Bramling Cross, Hallertau Mittelfrueh).	pilsmout, karamelmou carafa, koffie, chocolad maisvlokken, gist, wate kandijsuiker, rietsuiker neel, tijm, koriander, zo sinaasschil, hop (Braml Cross, Hallertauer Mittelfrueh).
	10%	10%	10%
	almost black (99 EBC) creamy foam head unfiltered	presque noire (99 EBC) faux col crémeux non filtrée	bijna zwart (99 EBC) romige schuimkraag ongefilterd
	–	–	–
	–	–	–
	Flavour of gingerbread, caramel, coffee, liquorice, almond cake. Sweet, complex taste due to the herbs (wood, caramel, coffee, gingerbread) with a fruity, light alcoholic taste near the end.	Arôme de pain de gingembre, caramel, café, réglisse, gâteau d'amande. Goût doux et complexe dû aux herbes (bois, caramel, café, pain d'épice) aboutissant à un goût fruité, alcoolisé.	Aroma van gemberbroo karamel, koffie, zoetho amandelcake. Zoete en plexe smaak door de kr den (hout, karamel, kof peperkoek) die eindigt i een fruitige alcoholsma
	–	–	–

PANNEPOT
2006
DSB
ALE BREWED
WITH SPICES
11.2 FL. OZ. - 10% ALC./VOL
DSB
Struisebrouwers.be

Passion Max

	spontaneous fermentation	fermentation spontanée	spontane gisting
	fruit beer	bière fruitée	fruitbier
	Brouwerij Bockor Bellegem	Brouwerij Bockor Bellegem	Brouwerij Bockor Bellegem
	barley malt, wheat, hops, yeast, fruit juices, nature-identical flavouring, water	malt d'orge, froment, houblon, levure, jus de fruits, arômes naturels, eau	gerstemout, tarwe, hop gist, vruchtensappen, natuuridentische arom water
	3%	3%	3%
	cloudy orange	orange trouble	troebel oranje
	Rinse the glass with cold water, tilt it a little and pour carefully half of the bottle. Next keep the glass upright and pour the rest of the bottle in one single movement.	Rincer le verre à l'eau froide, le tenir légèrement incliné et le remplir prudemment à moitié. Relever le verre et vider la bouteille en un seul mouvement.	Het glas koud spoelen, schuin houden en voor tig half inschenken. Daarna het glas recht houden en de rest in 1 weging inschenken.
	41 - 46 °F	5 - 8 °C	5 - 8 °C
	Refreshingly fruity character. Fruity sweetness with a clearly recognisable citric taste.	Caractère frais et fruité. Fruité et doux avec une saveur reconnaissable d'agrumes.	Frisfruitig karakter. Fruitzoetig met herken citrusvruchtensmaak.
	–	–	–

passion MAX
New Taste
passion
MAX
Jacobins

MAX

Pater Lieven blond

	top-fermentation re-fermented in the bottle	fermentation haute refermentation en bouteille	hoge gisting hergisting op de fles
	abbey beer blond	bière d'abbaye blonde	abdijbier blond
	Brouwerij Van Den Bossche St-Lievens-Esse	Brouwerij Van Den Bossche St-Lievens-Esse	Brouwerij Van Den Boss St-Lievens-Esse
	hops, yeast, fermentable sugar, water, malt varieties (Pilsner, caramel, Pale Ale).	malt, houblon, sucre fermentescible, eau, sortes de malt (pils, caramélisé, pale ale).	hop, gist, vergistbare su water, moutsoorten (pi karamel, pale ale).
%	6,50%	6,50%	6,50%
	Pale yellow. Gentle carbon dioxide sparkling, creating a fine, white foam.	Jaune pâle. Léger pétillement d'acide carbonique créant une écume fine blanche.	Bleekgeel. Rustige kool gaspareling die fijn, wi schuim geeft.
	Pour slowly for a nice foam head with hat. Leave a small amount in the bottle and present it with the glass.	Verser lentement pour obtenir un beau faux col avec chapeau. Laisser un peu de bière dans la bouteille et l'offrir également.	Langzaam inschenken een mooie schuimkraa met -hoed. Een restje i fles laten en de fles me aanbieden.
°C	43 - 46 °F	6 - 8 °C	6 - 8 °C
	Pleasant aroma of malt and flowers with a touch of spicy bitterness. Tastes sweet and bitter at the same time. Dry and bitter aftertaste that reminds of grapefruit.	Parfum agréable de malt et de fleurs avec une touche amère relevée. Saveur à la fois douce et amère. Fin de bouche sèche et amère rappelant la pamplemousse.	Aangename geur van r en bloemen met een v kruidige bitterheid. Sm tegelijk zoet en bitter. en bittere afdronk die pompelmoes doet denk
i	Brewed for the first time in 1957 for the Saint Livinus festivities.	Brassée pour la première fois en 1957 à l'occasion des fêtes de St-Livinus.	Voor de eerste keer geb wen in 1957 ter gelege van de St-Livinusfeeste

Anno 1897
Pater
Lieven
Blond - Blonde
Anno 1897
Pater
Lieven
Blond - Blonde
Belgisch Bier - Bière Belge

Pater
Lieven

Pater Lieven bruin

	top-fermentation re-fermented in the bottle	fermentation haute refermentation en bouteille	hoge gisting hergisting op de fles
	abbey beer brown	bière d'abbaye brune	abdijbier bruin
	Brouwerij Van Den Bossche St-Lievens-Esse	Brouwerij Van Den Bossche St-Lievens-Esse	Brouwerij Van Den Bos St-Lievens-Esse
	hops, yeast, fermentable sugar, water, malt varieties (Pilsner, caramel, roast).	malt, houblon, sucre fermentescible, eau, sortes de malt (pils, caramélisé, grillé).	hop, gist, vergistbare su water, moutsoorten (pi karamel, roost).
%	6,50%	6,50%	6,50%
	dark brown fine, stable, beige foam	brun foncé écume fine, beige, stable	donkerbruin fijn, stabiel beige schui
	Pour slowly for a nice foam head. Leave a small amount in the bottle and present the bottle with the glass.	Verser lentement pour obtenir un beau faux col. Laisser un peu de bière dans la bouteille et l'offrir également.	Langzaam inschenken een mooie schuimkraa Een restje in de fles lat de fles mee aanbieden.
°C	43 - 46 °F	6 - 8 °C	6 - 8 °C
	Smell of black chocolate with nuts, rolled oats, raisins and cacao powder. Intense taste of bitter chocolate and cacao, complemented by liquorice. Aftertaste: cacao.	Parfum de chocolat noir avec noisettes, flocons d'avoine, raisins secs et poudre de cacao. Saveur intense de chocolat amer, de cacao et de réglisse. Fin de bouche avec goût de cacao.	Geur van zwarte choco met nootjes, havermo rozijntjes en cacaopoe Intense smaak van bitt re chocolade en cacao gevuld met drop. Afdr met nasmaak van caca
i	Brewed for the first time in 1957 for the Saint Livinus festivities.	Brassée pour la première fois en 1957 à l'occasion des fêtes de St-Livinus.	Voor de eerste keer gebr wen in 1957 ter gelegen van de St-Livinusfeesten

Anno 1897
Pater
Lieven
Bruin - Brune
Anno 1897
Pater
Lieven
Bruin - Brune

Pater
Lieven

Pater Lieven tripel

	top-fermentation re-fermented in the bottle	fermentation haute refermentation en bouteille	hoge gisting hergisting op de fles
	abbey beer Tripel	bière d'abbaye triple	abdijbier tripel
	Brouwerij Van Den Bossche St-Lievens-Esse	Brouwerij Van Den Bossche St-Lievens-Esse	Brouwerij Van Den Bos St-Lievens-Esse
	hops, yeast, fermentable sugar, water, malt varieties (Pilsner, Pale Ale, caramel, wheat).	malt, houblon, sucre fermentescible, eau, sortes de malt (pils, pale ale, caramel, froment).	hop, gist, vergistbare s water, moutsoorten (p pale ale, karamel, tarv
	8%	8%	8%
	pale amber nice foam head, between white and off-white	ambré pâle beau faux col entre blanc et blanc cassé	bleekamber mooie schuimkraag tu wit en gebroken wit
	Pour slowly for a nice foam head. Leave a small amount in the bottle and present it with the glass.	Verser lentement pour obtenir un beau faux col. Laisser un peu de bière dans la bouteille et l'offrir aussi.	Langzaam inschenken een mooie schuimkra Een restje in de fles la de fles mee aanbieden
	43 - 46 °F	6 - 8 °C	6 - 8 °C
	The aroma is dominated by a spicy bitterness, complemented by floral touches. Slightly sweet malt and alcohol accents. Long-lasting, intensely bitter aftertaste.	Goût et parfum amers et relevés, complétés par des touches fleuries. Accents légèrement doux de malt et d'alcool. Fin de bouche longue, intense et amère.	Kruidige, bittere geur aroma, aangevuld me rale toetsen. Lichtzoe centen van mout en a hol. Lange afdronk me intense bitterheid.
	Brewed for the first time in 1957 for the Saint Livinus festivities.	Brassée pour la première fois en 1957 à l'occasion des fêtes de St-Livinus.	Voor de eerste keer geb wen in 1957 ter gelege van de St-Livinusfeeste
	....		

Anno 1897
Pater Lieven
Tripel-Triple
Anno 1897
Pater Lieven
Tripel - Triple
Belgisch Bier - Bière Belge

Pater Lieven

Pater Lieven witbier

	top-fermentation	fermentation haute	hoge gisting
	Witbier/wheat beer	bière blanche/de froment	witbier/tarwebier
	Brouwerij Van Den Bossche Sint-Lievens-Esse	Brouwerij Van Den Bossche Sint-Lievens-Esse	Brouwerij Van Den Bos Sint-Lievens-Esse
	Pilsner malt, wheat, oat, hops, herbs, yeast, fermentable sugar, water. Aromatised with orange rind and coriander.	Malt de pils, froment, avoine, houblon, herbes, levure, sucré fermentescible, eau. Aromatisé avec écorce d'orange et coriandre.	Pilsmout, tarwe, haver kruiden, gist, vergistba suiker, water. Gearomatiseerd met si schil en koriander.
%	4,50%	4,50%	4,50%
	yellow-white cloudy (wheat and oat) unfiltered	jaune blanc trouble (froment et avoine) non filtrée	geelwit troebel (tarwe en have niet gefilterd
	Pour the beer slowly and avoid sloshing. Shake the bottle to loosen the yeast and pour it along with the beer. Form a nice foam head.	Verser la bière lentement sans la laisser glougLouter. Secouer pour dégager le fond de levure et le verser également. Former un beau faux col.	Het bier langzaam uitschenken zonder het t ten klokken. De gistbo losschudden en mee i het glas gieten. Een m schuimkraag vormen.
°C	37 - 43 °F	3 - 6 °C	3 - 6 °C
	Pleasant fruity taste and thirst-quenching character obtained by the orange and the coriander.	Caractère agréable fruité et désaltérant par l'orange et le coriandre.	Aangenaam fruitig en dorstlessend karakter de sinaas en koriande
i	As the beer is unfiltered, it contains living yeast cells.	Contient des cellules de levure vivantes parce que la bière n'est pas filtrée.	Het bier bevat levende cellen omdat het niet filterd is.
	....		

Anno 1897
Pater
Lieven
Wit - Blanche
Anno 1897
Pater
Lieven
Wit - Blanche
Belgisch Bier - Bière Belge

Pater
Lieven

Paulus

	top-fermentation	fermentation haute	hoge gisting
	old brown	vieille brune	oud bruin
	Brouwerij Leroy Boezinge	Brouwerij Leroy Boezinge	Brouwerij Leroy Boezinge
	malt, sweetener, hops, caramel, water	malt, édulcorant, houblon, caramel, eau	mout, zoetstof, hop, karamel, water
	6%	6%	6%
	dark brown	brun foncé	donkerbruin
	Pour slowly in a single, smooth movement, in a degreased glass. Keep the glass tilted and avoid sloshing. Skim off the foam	Verser lentement en un seul mouvement fluide dans un verre dégraissé tenu en oblique. Ne pas laisser la bière glouglouter. Ecumer le verre.	Traag en in 1 vloeiend weging uitschenken in een vetvrij glas dat wo schuingehouden. Het b niet laten klotsen. Het glas afschuimen.
	41 - 43 °F	5 - 6 °C	5 - 6 °C
	Summery session beer. Sweet-and-sour with a full character.	Bière d'été facilement buvable. Aigre-doux avec un caractère plein.	Zomers doordrinkbier. Zuurzoet met een vol karakter.
	Named after Paul Priem, one of the salesmen of the brewery.	Son nom provient de Paul Priem, un des vendeurs de la brasserie.	Genoemd naar Paul Pr een van de verkopers b brouwerij.

natuurlijk bier van hoge gisting ~ fermentation haute sur lie
Paulus
OUD BRUIN VIEILLE BRUNE
bier gebrouwd naar oude traditie
bière brassée selon vieille tradition
CONT. 25cl. INH.
H.R.V.18804

Pauwel Kwak

	top-fermentation	fermentation haute	hoge gisting
	specialty beer	bière spéciale	speciaalbier
	Brouwerij Bosteels Buggenhout	Brouwerij Bosteels Buggenhout	Brouwerij Bosteels Buggenhout
	barley malts, candy sugar, hops, water	malts d'orge, sucre candi, houblon, eau	gerstemouten, kandijs hop, water
%	8,10%	8,10%	8,10%
	deep, clear amber colour consistent, cream-coloured foam head	couleur ambrée intense faux col cohérant, couleur crème	diepe, heldere amberk consistente, crèmekle schuimkraag
	Slightly tilt the glass and fill it. When the foam head reaches the edge of the glass, there must be 2 cm of foam left in the globe of the glass. After 15 seconds the foam head will have pulled up to approx. 7 cm from the edge.	Tenir le verre légèrement incliné et le remplir. Quand le faux col atteint le bord du verre, il doit rester encore 2 cm d'écume dans le ballon du verre. Après 15 secondes, le faux col se stabilise à ca. 7 cm du bord supérieur du verre kwak.	Het glas licht schuin hc en volschenken. Wanne schuimkraag de rand v glas bereikt, moet er nc cm schuim in de bol va glas zitten. Na 15 secon stabiliseert de schuimk zich op ca. 7 cm van de venkant van het kwakg
°C	41 - 43 °F	5 - 6 °C	5 - 6 °C
	Smooth, fruity initial nougat flavour, light spicy character with a touch of liquorice turning into a warm and bitter aftertaste that reminds of caramelized bananas.	Saveur initiale douce et fruitée de nougat, caractère légèrement relevé avec une touche de réglisse aboutissant à une fin de bouche chaleureuse et amère qui fait penser à des bananes caramélisées.	Zachte, fruitige, noga- ge smaakaanzet, licht dig karakter met zoet toets die overgaat in e warme en bittere afdr die aan gekaramellise banaan doet denken.
i	–	–	–

Anno 1791
Pauwel
Kwak
Pauwel Kwak

Pax Pils

	bottom-fermentation	fermentation basse	lage gisting
	Pilsner	pils	pils
	Brouwerij Sint-Jozef Opitter	Brouwerij Sint-Jozef Opitter	Brouwerij Sint-Jozef Opitter
	malt, hops, starch, water	malt, houblon, fécu-le, eau	mout, hop, zetmeel, w
%	5,10%	5,10%	5,10%
	light-yellowish	légèrement jaunâtre	licht gelig
	Pour into a clean, de-greased glass, avoiding contact between the bot-tle and the foam.	Verser dans un verre pro-pre, dégraissé sans que la bouteille touche l'écume.	Uitschenken in een zu ontvet glas zonder dat fles het schuim raakt.
°C	36 - 39 °F	2 - 4 °C	2 - 4 °C
	Refreshing thirst-quencher. Smooth Pilsner taste.	Désaltérant rafraîchis-sant. Saveur moelleuse de pils.	Verfrissende dorstlesse Zachte pilssmaak.
i	–	–	–

PAX
PILS
PAX
PILS
JOZEF - ITTERPLEIN 19 - B-3960 BREE
PAX
OPITTER

Pecheresse Lindemans

	spontaneous fermentation	fermentation spontanée	spontane gisting
	fruit beer based on Lambic	bière fruitée à base de lambic	fruitbier op basis van lambiek
	Brouwerij Lindemans Vlezenbeek	Brouwerij Lindemans Vlezenbeek	Brouwerij Lindemans Vlezenbeek
	malt, wheat, hops, peach juice (30%), fructose, water	malt, froment, houblon, jus de pêches (30%), fructose, eau	mout, tarwe, hop, perz sap (30%), fructose, wa
	2,50%	2,50%	2,50%
	golden blond slightly hazy	blond doré légèrement voilée	goudblond licht gesluierd
	Pour into a flute-glass.	Verser dans une flûte.	In een fluitglas uitschenken.
	37 - 39 °F	3 - 4 °C	3 - 4 °C
	Fruity character. Lively and strong onset turning into a balance of sweet (fruit) and smooth sour (Lambic).	Caractère fruité. Début vif et corsé passant à un équilibre de douceur (fruits) et d'acidulité légère (lambic).	Fruitig karakter. Levendige en sterke aa die overgaat in een eve wicht van zoet (fruit) e zacht zuur (lambiek).
	Suitable as an aperitif and as a thirst-quencher.	Convient comme apéritif et boisson désaltérante.	Geschikt als aperitief e dorstlesser.

PECHERESSE
Lindemans
GEBROUWEN EN GEBOTTELD DOOR BROUWERIJ
BRASSÉE ET EMBOUTEILLÉE PAR LA BRASSERIE
LINDEMANS B 1602 VLEZENBEEK BELGIUM
PECHERESSE
LINDEMANS

Père Noël

	top-fermentation	fermentation haute	hoge gisting
	Christmas beer amber	bière de Noël ambrée	kerstbier amber
	Brouwerij De Ranke Wevelgem	Brouwerij De Ranke Wevelgem	Brouwerij De Ranke Wevelgem
	3 malts, hop flowers, in- dustrial yeast, liquorice	3 malts, fleurs de houblon, levure de culture, réglisse	3 mouten, hopbloeme cultuurgist, zoethout
%	7%	7%	7%
	amber slightly cloudy	ambrée légèrement trouble	amber licht troebel
	–	–	–
	Moderately cooled.	Rafraîchie modérément.	Medium koel.
	Bittersweet, hoppy and spicy.	Doux-amer, houblonné et relevé.	Bitterzoet, hoppig en dig.
i	–	–	–

PÈRE NOËL
33 cl. e
Speciaal Kerstbrouwsel • Brassin spécial de Noël
Embouteillage 5 ans avant date de
J F M A M J J A S O N D
DE RANKE

Petrus aged pale

	top-fermentation, mixed	fermentation haute mixte	hoge gisting gemengd
	unblended base beer for red-brown	bière de base non coupée pour brune-rouge	onversneden basisbier voor roodbruin
	Brouwerij Bavik Bavikhove	Brouwerij Bavik Bavikhove	Brouwerij Bavik Bavikhove
	barley malt (only pale malt), hops, yeast, pure spring water	malt d'orge (seulement malt pâle), houblon, levure, eau de source pure	gerstemout (enkel bleke mout), hop, gist, zui bronwater
%	7,30%	7,30%	7,30%
	bronze, old yellow	bronze, vieux jaune	brons, oud geel
	Pour into a dry glass avoiding contact between bottle and foam.	Verser dans un verre sec sans que la bouteille touche le faux col.	Uitschenken in een dr glas zonder dat de fles schuim raakt.
°C	46 - 54 °F	8 - 12 °C	8 - 12 °C
	Oak aroma with a touch of sherry and fruit (mainly pears). Classical, slightly sour but complex taste. Low carbon dioxide content.	Arôme de chêne avec une pointe de xéres et de fruits (surtout des poires). Goût classique légèrement acidulé mais complexe. Teneur basse en gaz carbonique.	Eikachtig aroma met e vleugje sherry en fruit (vooral peren). Klassieke lichtzurige m complexe smaak. Laag koolzuurgehalte.
i	An unblended beer that has matured 24 to 30 months in oak barrels. It is bottled straight from the barrel, which is why the brewer describes it as Lambic.	Une bière de base non coupée mûrie pendant 24 à 30 mois en fûts de chêne. Vu qu'elle est mise directement en bouteilles à partir des fûts en bois, le brasseur la décrit comme une bière lambic.	Een onversneden basis dat 24 à 30 maanden g rijpt heeft op eiken va Het wordt rechtstreeks botteld vanuit de hout foeders. Vanuit die cor wordt het door de bro omschreven als 'lambi

PETRUS
PETRUS
AGED PALE
GRAND RESERVE - GRANDE RESERVE

Petrus blond

	top-fermentation	fermentation haute	hoge gisting
	blond	blonde	blond
	Brouwerij Bavik Bavikhove	Brouwerij Bavik Bavikhove	Brouwerij Bavik Bavikhove
	barley malt, hops, yeast, pure spring water	malt d'orge, houblon, levure, eau de source pure	gerstemout, hop, gist, ver bronwater
	6,60%	6,60%	6,60%
	Beautiful bronze colour with a solid foam head. Clear blond.	Jolie couleur de bronze avec un faux col solide. Blond clair.	Mooie bronskleur met vaste schuimkraag. Helder blond.
	Pour into a degreased, rinsed and wet glass, avoiding contact between bottle and foam.	Verser dans un verre dégraissé, rincé et mouillé sans que la bouteille touche le faux col.	Uitschenken in een on gespoeld en nat glas zonder dat de fles het schuim raakt.
	46 - 54 °F	8 - 12 °C	8 - 12 °C
	Smooth, full taste with a light, pleasant bitterness. Hoppy character.	Saveur douce et pleine avec un goût amer léger et agréable. Caractère houblonné.	Zachte volle smaak me lichte, aangename bitterheid. Hoppig karakter.
	–	–	–

PETRUS
PETRUS
PETRUS
BLOND

Petrus dubbel bruin

	top-fermentation	fermentation haute	hoge gisting
	dubbel brown	double brune	dubbel bruin
	Brouwerij Bavik Bavikhove	Brouwerij Bavik Bavikhove	Brouwerij Bavik Bavikhove
	barley malt, hops, yeast, pure spring water	malt d'orge, houblon, levure, eau de source pure	gerstemout, hop, gist, [illegible]ver bronwater
	6,50%	6,50%	6,50%
	dark, mahogany	foncée, couleur acajou	donker, mahoniekleur
	Pour into a degreased, rinsed and wet glass avoiding contact between bottle and foam.	Verser dans un verre dégraissé, rincé et mouillé sans que la bouteille touche le faux col.	Uitschenken in een on[illegible] gespoeld en nat glas zonder dat de fles het schuim raakt.
	46 - 54 °F	8 - 12 °C	8 - 12 °C
	Bittersweet caramel and black chocolate. Full and creamy character.	Caramel amer-sucré et chocolat foncé. Caractère plein et crémeux.	Bitterzoete karamel en [illegible]kere chocolade. Vol en romig karakter.
	–	–	–

PETRUS
PETRUS
DUBBEL BRUIN

Petrus gouden tripel

top-fermentation traditionally re-fermented in the bottle	fermentation haute refermentation tradition-nelle en bouteille	hoge gisting tradionele hergisting i de fles
triple Ale	triple ale	triple ale
Brouwerij Bavik Bavikhove	Brouwerij Bavik Bavikhove	Brouwerij Bavik Bavikhove
barley malt, hops, yeast, pure spring water	malt d'orge, houblon, le-vure, eau de source pure	gerstemout, hop, gist, ver bronwater
7,50%	7,50%	7,50%
pale yellow	jaune pâle	bleekgeel
Pour into a dry glass and leave the sediment in the bottle.	Verser dans un verre sec. Laisser le dépôt de levure dans la bouteille.	Uitschenken in een dro glas. Het bezinksel in de fles
46 - 54 °F	8 - 12 °C	8 - 12 °C
Full, round taste of green apples and ripe pears, with a spicy, fresh and strong aroma.	Saveur pleine et ronde de pommes vertes et de poi-res mûres avec un arôme relevé, frais et corsé.	Volle, ronde smaak va groene appels en rijpe ren met een kruidig, f krachtig aroma.
–	–	–

PETRUS
THE KEY TO HEAVEN
PETRUS
GOUDEN TRIPEL
TRIPLE D'OR · GOLDEN TRIPLE ALE · GOLDENES TRIPEL · TRIPLE DE ORO
PETRUS

Petrus oud bruin

	top-fermentation, mixed	fermentation haute mixte	hoge gisting gemengd
	red old brown	vieille brune-rouge	rood oud bruin
	Brouwerij Bavik Bavikhove	Brouwerij Bavik Bavikhove	Brouwerij Bavik Bavikhove
	barley malt, hops, yeast, pure spring water	malt d'orge, houblon, levure, eau de source pure	gerstemout, hop, gist, z ver bronwater
	5,50%	5,50%	5,50%
	dark, mahogany	foncée, couleur acajou	donker, mahoniekleur
	Pour into a degreased, rinsed and wet glass.	Verser dans un verre dégraissé, rincé et mouillé.	Uitschenken in een on gespoeld en nat glas.
	46 - 54 °F	8 - 12 °C	8 - 12 °C
	Perfect balance between sour and sweet, with chocolate touches and a light, delicate vanilla flavour. Full and rich character with a refreshing sourness.	Equilibre parfait entre acidité et douceur, touches de chocolat et pointe de vanille. Caractère plein et riche avec un goût acidulé frais.	Perfecte balans tussen en zoet, chocoladetoets en een snufje vanille. Vol en rijk karakter me frisse zurigheid.
	The mature, amber-coloured, lactic acidulous base beer is blended with a young beer.	Coupage de la bière de base mûre, lactique et de couleur ambrée avec une bière jeune.	Versnijding van het be gen, amberkleurig, me rig basisbier met een j gebrouwen bier.

PETRUS
THE KEY TO HEAVEN
PETRUS
OUD BRUIN
VIEILLE BRUNE · OLD BROWN · ALT BRAUN · VIEJA OSCURA

Petrus speciale

	top-fermentation	fermentation haute	hoge gisting
	amber	ambrée	amber
	Brouwerij Bavik Bavikhove	Brouwerij Bavik Bavikhove	Brouwerij Bavik Bavikhove
	barley malt, hops (Vienna hop varieties), yeast, pure spring water, coriander	malt d'orge, houblon (variétés de houblon viennois), levure, eau de source pure, coriandre	gerstemout, hop (Weens hopvariëteiten), gist, zu bronwater, koriander
%	5,50%	5,50%	5,50%
	amber-coloured with a solid foam head	couleur ambrée avec un faux col solide	amberkleurig met een v schuimkraag
	Pour into a degreased, rinsed and wet glass, avoiding contact between bottle and foam.	Verser dans un verre dégraissé, rincé et mouillé sans que la bouteille touche le faux col.	Uitschenken in een ontv gespoeld en nat glas zonder dat de fles het schuim raakt.
°C	43 - 50 °F	6 - 10 °C	6 - 10 °C
	Fruity, creamy flavour with a dry, malty background. Spicy with a slightly bitter aftertaste.	Arôme fruité et crémeux avec un arrière-fond sec et malté. Corsé avec une fin de bouche légèrement amère.	Fruitig en romig aroma met een droge moutach achtergrond. Pittig met een licht bitt afdronk.
i	–	–	–

PETRUS
PETRUS
PETRUS
SPECIALE

Petrus winter

	top-fermentation re-fermented in the bottle	fermentation haute refermentation en bouteille	hoge gisting hergisting in de fles
	dark winter beer	bière hivernale foncée	donker winterbier
	Brouwerij Bavik Bavikhove	Brouwerij Bavik Bavikhove	Brouwerij Bavik Bavikhove
	barley malt, hops, yeast, pure spring water	malt d'orge, houblon, levure, eau de source pure	gerstemout, hop, gist ver bronwater
%	6,50%	6,50%	6,50%
	caramel-red	rouge caramel	karamelrood
	Pour into a dry glass avoiding contact between bottle and foam. Leave the sediment in the bottle.	Verser dans un verre sec sans que la bouteille touche l'écume. Laisser le dépôt de levure dans la bouteille.	Uitschenken in een d glas zonder dat de fle schuim raakt. Het bezinksel in de fl laten.
°C	46 - 54 °F	8 - 12 °C	8 - 12 °C
	Smooth, slightly hoppy taste with a touch of roasty malt. Spicy and slightly bitter character.	Saveur douce, légèrement houblonnée avec une touche de malt brûlé. Corsé et de caractère légèrement amer.	Zachte smaak, licht h met een toets van geb de mout. Pittig en licht bitter karakter.
i	Is only brewed at the end of the year, following a very old recipe.	Cette bière n'est brassée qu'à la fin de l'année d'après une recette ancienne.	Wordt enkel op het einde van het jaar ge wen naar een aloud r

PETRUS
THE KEY TO HEAVEN
PETRUS
WINTER

Piet-Agoras

	top-fermentation re-fermented in the bottle	fermentation haute refermentation en bouteille	hoge gisting hergisting op de fles
	specialty beer unpasteurised light amber	bière spéciale non pasteurisée légèrement ambrée	speciaalbier niet gepasteuriseerd licht amber
	at Picobrouwerij Alvinne Het Alternatief Izegem	chez Picobrouwerij Alvinne Het Alternatief Izegem	bij Picobrouwerij Alvi Het Alternatief Izegem
	5 malt varieties, 3 hop varieties, wheat, hops, yeast, granulated sugar, brewing water, no additives	5 sortes de malt, 3 sortes de houblon, froment, houblon, levure, sucre cristallisé, eau de brassage, pas d'additifs	5 soorten mout, 3 ho ten, tarwe, hop, gist, talsuiker, brouwwate additieven
	9%	9%	9%
	dark blond (15 EBC) unfiltered	blond foncé (15 EBC) non filtrée	donkerblond (15 EBC niet gefilterd
	Pour carefully in the Alternatief glass.	Verser prudemment dans le verre Alternatief.	Voorzichtig uitschen het Alternatiefglas.
	46 - 50 °F	8 - 10 °C	8 - 10 °C
	Warming beer with malty and hoppy character. Taste and aroma: spices, pepper, caramel, alcohol.	Bière réchauffante avec un caractère malté et houblonné. Saveur et arômes: herbes, poivre, caramel, alcool.	Verwarmend bier me tig en hoppig karakte Smaak en aroma: kru peper, karamel, alco
	–	–	–

Piet-Agoras
alternatief
Botteldatum: 1 2 3 4 5 6 7 8 9 10 11 12 07 08 09

Pilaarbijter Blond

	top-fermentation re-fermented in the bottle	fermentation haute refermentation en bouteille	hoge gisting nagisting in de fles
	blond	blonde	blond
	Brouwerij Bavik Bavikhove	Brouwerij Bavik Bavikhove	Brouwerij Bavik Bavikhove
	barley malt, hops, yeast, pure spring water	malt d'orge, houblon, levure, eau de source pure	gerstemout, hop, gist, z ver bronwater
	7,50%	7,50%	7,50%
	very light yellow	jaune très clair	zeer licht geel
	Pour into a dry glass avoiding contact between bottle and foam. Leave the sediment in the bottle.	Verser dans un verre sec sans que la bouteille touche le faux col. Laisser le dépôt de levure dans la bouteille.	Uitschenken in een dr glas zonder dat de fles schuim raakt. Het bezinksel in de fles ten.
	46 - 54 °F	8 - 12 °C	8 - 12 °C
	Full, fruity taste with a well-balanced hoppy bitterness. Slightly spicy. Malty, strong and creamy, full character.	Saveur pleine et fruitée avec un goût houblonné équilibré et légèrement relevé. Malté, prononcé et crémeux, plein de caractère.	Volle en fruitige smaak een evenwichtige hopp bitterheid en licht gek Moutig, sterk en romig karakter.
	Brewed under licence of the diocese of Bruges.	Brassée sous licence de l'Evêché de Bruges.	Gebrouwen onder lice van het Bisdom Brugg

pilaarbijter
Bier met een ziel

pilaarbijter

Pilaartbijter Bruin

	top-fermentation re-fermented in the bottle	fermentation haute refermentation en bouteille	hoge gisting hergisting in de fles
	dubbel	double	dubbel
	Brouwerij Bavik Bavikhove	Brouwerij Bavik Bavikhove	Brouwerij Bavik Bavikhove
	barley malt, hops, yeast, pure spring water	malt d'orge, houblon, levure, eau de source pure	gerstemout, hop, gist, z ver bronwater
	6,50%	6,50%	6,50%
	burgundy slightly cloudy	bordeaux légèrement trouble	bordeaux licht troebel
	Pour into a dry glass avoiding contact between bottle and foam.	Verser dans un verre sec sans que la bouteille touche le faux col.	Uitschenken in een dro glas zonder dat de fles schuim raakt.
	46 - 54 °F	8 - 12 °C	8 - 12 °C
	Oak-like, juicy, roasted, Armagnac-like taste. Solid and full.	Goût de chêne savoureux et grillé renvoyant à l'Armagnac. Solide et plein.	Eikachtige, sappige, ge te smaak die doet denk aan Armagnac. Stevig en vol.
	Brewed under licence of the diocese of Bruges.	Brassée sous licence de l'Evêché de Bruges.	Gebrouwen onder licen van het Bisdom Brugge

BRUIN BRUNE
Bier met een ziel
pilaarbijter

Pils Pick-up natuurbier

	bottom-fermentation	fermentation basse	lage gisting
	Pilsner natural beer	pils bière naturelle	pilsbier natuurbier
	Brouwerij Walrave Laarne	Brouwerij Walrave Laarne	Brouwerij Walrave Laarne
	barley malt, yeast, sugar, hops, water	malt d'orge, houblon, sucre, levure, eau	gerstemout, gist, suike[r], hop, water
%	5%	5%	5%
	clear	claire	helder
	Pour carefully into a goblet and leave the yeast sediment in the bottle.	Verser complètement dans un verre dégraissé, rincé et mouillé sans que la bouteille touche l'écume.	Helemaal uitschenken [in] een ontvet, gespoeld, [n…] glas zonder dat de fles [het] schuim raakt.
°C	37 - 41 °F	3 - 5 °C	3 - 5 °C
	Refreshing and thirst-quenching. Aroma of hop and typical taste of unpasteurised beer.	Frais et désaltérant. Arômes de houblon et goût typique de bière non pasteurisée.	Fris en dorstlessend. Aroma van hop en typ[…] smaak van ongepasteu[ri]seerd bier.
i	This beer does not contain any preservatives and is not pasteurised. Therefore, it can only be kept for about four weeks in the refrigerator.	La bière ne contient pas de produits conservateurs et n'est pas pasteurisée; elle se conserve seulement 4 semaines au réfrigérateur.	Het bier bevat geen be[…] middelen en wordt ni[et ge]pasteuriseerd waardo[…] maar een 4-tal weken [h…]baar is op koelkasttem[pe]ratuur.
	....		

BROUWERIJ
BIER
PICK - UP
5%VOL.ALC
WALRAVE
NATUURBIER
PILS

BROUWERIJ
PICK - UP
WALRAVE

Pink Killer

	top-fermentation	fermentation haute	hoge gisting
	fruity Witbier	bière blanche fruitée	fruitig witbier
	Brasserie de Silly Silly	Brasserie de Silly Silly	Brasserie de Silly Silly
	malt, wheat, pink grapefruit juice, flavouring, sugar, yeast, coriander, orange rind, Hallertau hops, water	malt, froment, jus de pamplemousse rose, arômes, sucre, levure, coriandre, écorce d'orange, houblon Hallertau, eau	mout, tarwe, roze-pom moessap, aroma's, suil gist, koriander, sinaas Hallertauhop, water
%	4,70% 11° plato	4,70% 11° plato	4,70% 11° plato
	pink (25 EBC) cloudy	rose (25 EBC) trouble	roze (25 EBC) troebel
	–	–	–
	39 - 45 °F	4 - 7 °C	4 - 7 °C
	Fruity and thirst-quenching, sugared but not excessively sweet. Bitter grapefruit touch.	Fruité et désaltérant, sucré mais pas excessivement doux. Touche amère de pamplemousse.	Fruitig en dorstlessen suikerd maar niet over ven zoet. Bittere toets pompelmoes.
i	–	–	–

Pink Killer
Pink grapefruit
flavoured beer
Pink Killer

Piraat

	top-fermentation re-fermented in the bottle	fermentation haute refermentation en bouteille	hoge gisting hergisting in de fles
	strong blond	blonde forte	sterk blond
	Brouwerij Van Steenberge Ertvelde	Brouwerij Van Steenberge Ertvelde	Brouwerij Van Steenbe Ertvelde
	barley malt, hops, yeast, water	malt d'orge, houblon, levure, eau	gerstemout, hop, gist,
	10,50% - 23° plato	10,50% - 23° plato	10,50% - 23° plato
	light amber	ambré clair	licht amber
	Pour in one fluent movement, leaving 1 cm of yeast sediment in the bottle. The sediment can be poured, making the beer cloudy.	Verser en un seul mouvement fluide et doux et laisser 1 cm de dépôt de levure dans la bouteille. Le depôt de levure peut être versé et rend la bière trouble.	Uitschenken in 1 vloei zachte beweging en 1 gistdepot in de fles lat De gistfond kan worde geschonken en maakt bier troebel.
	50 - 54 °F	10 - 12 °C	10 - 12 °C
	Complex, rich taste. Spicy, light sweetness, richly balanced by a solid hoppy bitterness.	Saveur complexe et riche. Goût relevé, légèrement sucré et richement équilibré par un goût amer houblonné solide.	Complexe en rijke sma Kruidige, lichte zoetig die rijkelijk gebalance wordt met een stevige bitterheid.
	A lively beer with a powerful nutritional value, like the beers the Vikings used to drink whilst sailing. Also has a 9% version. Very much appreciated by American connoisseurs.	Une bière vive avec forte valeur nutritive comme les bières que buvaient les Vikings en mer. Existe aussi dans une version 9%. Cotée très haut par les connaisseurs américains.	Een levendig bier met hoge voedingswaarde de bieren die de Vikin op zee dronken. Besta in een versie van 9%. Superhoog gekwoteer Amerikaanse bierkenr

10,5°
Piraat
Belgisch Bier- Bière Belge
CAT. S

Piraat

Pissenlit

(fermentation)	top-fermentation	fermentation haute	hoge gisting
(type)	Saisons boutique beer	bière de saison artisanale	saison, artisanaal bie
(brewery)	Brasserie Fantôme Soy	Brasserie Fantôme Soy	Brasserie Fantôme Soy
(ingredients)	dandelions, barley malt, hops, yeast, water	pissenlits, malt d'orge, houblon, levure, eau	paardenbloemen, ger stemout, hop, gist, wa
%	8%	8%	8%
(colour)	amber yellow	jaune ambré	ambergeel
(glass)	Serve in a tulip-shaped glass (cfr. Duvel).	Verser dans un verre tulipe (voir Duvel).	Uitschenken in een t (cfr. Duvel).
°C	–	–	–
(taste)	Strong, savoury beer with a pronounced hoppy touch.	Bière forte et pleine de goût avec une touche houblonnée forte.	Sterk en smaakvol bie een sterke hoptoets.
i	Fantôme beers are very hard to find in Belgium. Even the brewer only has a small stock.	Les bières de Fantôme sont difficiles à trouver en Belgique, même le brasseur a peu de stock.	De bieren van Fantôn in België heel moeilij vinden, zelfs de brou heeft weinig op voorr

1PT 9.4 FL.OZ
Bière artisanale
Ssenlit
bière de Saison -
100 % naturelle
fabriquée à Soy - Printemps 2003

Plokkersbier

	top-fermentation	fermentation haute	hoge gisting
	amber	ambrée	amber
	Brouwerij De Bie Loker	Brouwerij De Bie Loker	Brouwerij De Bie Loker
	malt, hops, wheat, candy sugar, yeast, herbs, water	malt, houblon, froment, sucre candi, levure, herbes, eau	mout, hop, tarwe, kar suiker, gist, kruiden,
%	7%	7%	7%
	amber	ambrée	amber
	–	–	–
	43 °F	6 °C	6 °C
	Spicy.	Goût relevé.	Kruidig.
i	Very suitable for cooking. 'Plokker' refers to the Plokkers route in Watou. 'Plokken' means to pluck, a reference to the hop harvesting.	Convient particulièrement pour la cuisine à la bière. 'Plokker' se réfère à la route des Plokkers à Watou. 'Plokken' signifie cueillir et renvoie au houblon.	Heel geschikt voor de keuken. De naam Plo refereert aan de de Pl kersroute in Watou. P ken betekent plukken verwijzing naar de hc

Brouwerij De Bie
B-8958 Loker • Tel. 0475 23 47 95
Plokkersbier
Cat.S.
Gebotteld
Mise en bouteille

Plokkersbier

Podge Belgian Imperial Stou

	top-fermentation	fermentation haute	hoge gisting
	imperial Stout regional beer	imperial stout bière régionale	imperial stout streekbier
	Picobrouwerij Alvinne Ingelmunster	Picobrouwerij Alvinne Ingelmunster	Picobrouwerij Alvinn Ingelmunster
	malt (Pilsner, wheat, amber, chocolate, flavouring, Munich, black), candy sugar, granulated sugar, hops, yeast, water	malt (pils, froment, ambré, chocolat, arômes, Munich, noir), sucre candi, sucre cristallisé, houblon, levure, eau	mout (pils, tarwe, am chocolade, aroma, m black), kandijsuiker, suiker, hop, gist, wate
%	10,50%	10,50%	10,50%
	black	noire	zwart
	Pour into a tulip-shaped glass or goblet. Leave the yeast (approx. 1 cm) at the bottom of the bottle. Pour slowly to obtain a nice foam head.	Verser dans un verre tulipe ou calice. Laisser la levure (environ 1 cm) au fond de la bouteille. Verser lentement de sorte qu'un beau faux col se forme.	Uitschenken in een t of kelkvormig glas. D (ca. 1 cm) op de boden de fles laten. Langzaa schenken zodat er zic mooie schuimkraag v
	46 °F	8 °C	8 °C
	Aroma and flavour of chocolate, coffee and alcohol. Full-bodied and alcoholic character.	Arômes et saveurs de chocolat, café et alcool. Caractère plein et alcoolisé.	Chocolade, koffie en hol in aroma en smaa Volmondig en alcoho karakter.
i	–	–	–

2003
ALVINNE
Picobrouwerij
vzw
INGELMUNSTER
BELGIAN IMPERIAL STOUT
Alc 10,5% vol
Picobrouwerij Alvinne, Oostrozebekestraat 114, 8770

Postel Blond

	top-fermentation re-fermented in the bottle	fermentation haute refermentation en bouteille	hoge gisting hergisting op de fles
	recognised Belgian abbey beer	Bière d'abbaye belge reconnue	Erkend Belgisch abdij blond
	Brouwerij Affligem Opwijk	Brouwerij Affligem Opwijk	Brouwerij Affligem Opwijk
	barley malt, hops, yeast, water	malt d'orge, houblon, levure, eau	gerstemout, hop, gist
%	7%	7%	7%
	golden blond	blond doré	goudblond
	Pour slowly, leaving the yeast in the bottle.	Verser lentement et laisser la levure dans la bouteille.	Langzaam uitschenke en de gist in de fles la
°C	46 - 50 °F	8 - 10 °C	8 - 10 °C
	Hoppy nose, smoothly bitter, balance between malt and hops.	Parfum houblonné, doux-amer, équilibre entre malt et houblon.	Hoppige neus, zacht bitter, evenwicht tuss mout en hop.
i	The abbey of Postel is located on the Belgian-Dutch border.	L'abbaye de Postel est située à la frontière entre la Belgique et les Pays-Bas.	De abdij van Postel lig op de Belgisch-Nederlandse grens.

POSTEL
1140

BLOND
Abdij
bier
BLONDE
bière
d'Abbaye
Abdij
bier
Anno
1140
POSTEL
33 cl ℮
11,6 FL.OZ.

POSTEL
11 40

Postel Dubbel

	top-fermentation re-fermented in the bottle	fermentation haute refermentation en bouteille	hoge gisting hergisting op de fles
	recognised Belgian abbey beer	Bière d'abbaye belge reconnue	Erkend Belgisch abdij[illegible] dubbel
	Brouwerij Affligem Opwijk	Brouwerij Affligem Opwijk	Brouwerij Affligem Opwijk
	barley malt, hops, yeast, water	malt d'orge, houblon, levure, eau	gerstemout, hop, gist,
%	7%	7%	7%
	red-brown	brun rouge	roodbruin
	Slowly pour, leaving the yeast in the bottle.	Verser lentement et laisser la levure dans la bouteille.	Langzaam uitschenke en de gist in de fles la
°C	46 - 50 °F	8 - 10 °C	8 - 10 °C
	Spicy with a sweet touch, smooth mouthfeel with full aftertaste.	Goût relevé avec une touche douce, sensation moelleuse dans la bouche avec une fin de bouche pleine.	Kruidig met een zoete zacht in de mond me volle afdronk.
i	The abbey of Postel is located on the Belgian-Dutch border.	L'abbaye de Postel est située à la frontière entre la Belgique et les Pays-Bas.	De abdij van Postel lig op de Belgisch-Nederlandse grens.

DOBBEL
Abdij
bier
Abdij
bier
Anno
1140
POSTEL
POSTEL

Postel Tripel

	top-fermentation re-fermented in the bottle	fermentation haute refermentation en bouteille	hoge gisting hergisting op de fles
	recognised Belgian abbey beer	bière d'abbaye belge reconnue	Erkend Belgisch abdijb tripel
	Brouwerij Affligem Opwijk	Brouwerij Affligem Opwijk	Brouwerij Affligem Opwijk
	barley malt, hops, yeast, water	malt d'orge, houblon, levure, eau	gerstemout, hop, gist,
	8,50%	8,50%	8,50%
	deep gold	doré intense	diepgoud
	Pour slowly, leaving the yeast in the bottle.	Verser lentement et laisser la levure dans la bouteille.	Langzaam uitschenke en de gist in de fles lat
	46 - 50 °F	8 - 10 °C	8 - 10 °C
	Typical bitterness and full round aftertaste. Spicy character with flavours of malt and spices.	Goût amer typique et fin de bouche ronde pleine. Caractère corsé avec des arômes de malt et d'herbes.	Typische bitterheid en volronde afdronk. Pittig karakter met ar van mout en kruiden.
	The abbey of Postel is located on the Belgian-Dutch border.	L'abbaye de Postel est située à la frontière entre la Belgique et les Pays-Bas.	De abdij van Postel lig op de Belgisch-Nederlandse grens.

POSTEL
1140
TRIPEL
Abdij bier
bière d'Abbaye
Abdij bier
Anno 1140
POSTEL
33 cl
11
40

Potteloereke

	top-fermentation	fermentation haute	hoge gisting
	dark Ale	ale foncée	donkere ale
	De Proefbrouwerij for brouwerij St-Canarus Gottem	De Proefbrouwerij pour brouwerij St-Canarus Gottem	De Proefbrouwerij voor brouwerij St-Cana Gottem
	Pilsner malt, cara and Munich malts, Vlamertinge hops, brown candy sugar, yeast, water	malt de pils, cara et Munich, houblon de Vlamertinge, sucre candi brun, levure, eau	pilsmout, cara en mur mouten, Vlamertingse bruine kandijsuiker, g water
%	8%	8%	8%
	deep brown, clear	brun intense, claire	diepbruin, helder
	Pour carefully into a goblet and leave the yeast sediment in the bottle. The latter can be drunk separately. Pour into a clean, degreased glass, avoiding contact between bottle and foam.	Laisser reposer la bière quelques jours avant la dégustation. Verser prudemment dans un verre calice et laisser le dépôt de levure dans la bouteille. Le dépôt de levure peut être bu séparément.	Het bier voor het degu ren een paar dagen lat rusten. Voorzichtig uitschenk een kelkglas en de gist bodem in de fles laten De gistbodem kan afzo lijk worden uitgedronk
°C	50 - 57 °F	10 - 14 °C	10 - 14 °C
	Intense, heart-warming and pleasantly sweet.	Intense, réchauffant et agréablement doux.	Intens, hartverwarme aangenaam zoet.
i	Brewed by order of the pottery 't Hoveke from Deinze. Therefore, it is served in a specific, handmade stone jug.	Brassée à la demande de la poterie 't Hoveke de Deinze et pour cette raison bue dans un pot en pierre fait à la main.	Gebrouwen op vraag v Pottenbakkerij 't Hove Deinze en daarom ged ken uit een handgedra stenen pot.

POTTELOEREKE
POTTENBAKKERSBIER

Premium Cassis St Louis

	spontaneous fermentation	fermentation spontanée	spontane gisting
	fruit beer with Gueuze Lambic as a base	bière fruitée à base de gueuze lambic	fruitbier op basis van geuze lambiek
	Castle Brewery Van Honsebrouck Ingelmunster	Castle Brewery Van Honsebrouck Ingelmunster	Castle Brewery Van Honsebrouck Ingelmunster
	malt, wheat, sugar, hops, peach juice, flavour, water	malt, froment, sucre, houblon, jus de baies noires, arômes, eau	mout, tarwe, suiker, h zwartebessensap, aron water
	3,20%	3,20%	3,20%
	intense red-blue clear	rouge-bleu intense claire	intens roodblauw helder
	Pour into a newly rinsed glass, keeping it tilted first and in a vertical position at the end.	Verser dans un verre rincé tenu d'abord en oblique et à la fin en position verticale.	Uitschenken in een ve spoeld glas dat eerst sc gehouden wordt en op einde verticaal gehoud wordt.
	41 °F	5 °C	5 °C
	Refreshing. Pronounced blackcurrant.	Rafraîchissant. Cassis prononcé.	Verfrissend. Uitgesproken cassis.
	–	–	–

PREMIUM
CASSIS
St Louis
PREMIUM
CASSIS
St Louis
BIERE BELGE • BELGISCH BIER
- CASSIS - FARO -
PREMIUM
St Louis

Premium Faro St Louis

	spontaneous fermentation	fermentation spontanée	spontane gisting
	Faro	faro	faro
	Castle Brewery Van Honsebrouck Ingelmunster	Castle Brewery Van Honsebrouck Ingelmunster	Castle Brewery Van Honsebrouck Ingelmunster
	malt, wheat, candy sugar, hops, water	malt, froment, sucre candi, houblon, eau	mout, tarwe, kandijsui hop, water
%	3,20%	3,20%	3,20%
	amber clear	ambrée claire	amber helder
	Pour into a newly rinsed glass, keeping it tilted first and in a vertical position at the end.	Verser dans un verre rincé tenu d'abord en oblique et à la fin en position verticale.	Uitschenken in een ver spoeld glas dat eerst sc gehouden wordt en op einde verticaal gehoud wordt.
	41 °F	5 °C	5 °C
	Refreshing. Sweet-and-sour with the taste of candy sugar.	Frais. Aigre-doux avec la saveur de sucre de candi.	Fris. Zuur en zoet met de sn van kandijsuiker.
i	–	–	–

PREMIUM
FARO
St Louis
BIERE BELGE · BELGISCH BIER
- CASSIS - FARO -
PREMIUM

Premium Framboise St Louis

	spontaneous fermentation	fermentation spontanée	spontane gisting
	fruit beer based on Gueuze Lambic	bière fruitée à base de gueuze lambic	fruitbier op basis van geuze lambiek
	Castle Brewery Van Honsebrouck Ingelmunster	Castle Brewery Van Honsebrouck Ingelmunster	Castle Brewery Van Honsebrouck Ingelmunster
	malt, wheat, sugar, hops, raspberry juice, water	malt, froment, sucre, houblon, jus de framboises, eau	mout, tarwe, suiker, hc frambozensap, water
%	2,80%	2,80%	2,80%
	dark red clear	rouge foncé claire	donkerrood helder
	Pour into a newly rinsed glass, keeping it tilted first and in a vertical position at the end.	Verser dans un verre rincé tenu d'abord en oblique et à la fin en position verticale.	Uitschenken in een ver spoeld glas dat eerst sc gehouden wordt en op einde verticaal gehoud wordt.
°C	41 °F	5 °C	5 °C
	Refreshing and fruity. Strong raspberry flavour and aroma with a fruity aftertaste.	Rafraîchissant et fruité. Saveur et arômes de framboises et arrière-bouche fruitée.	Verfrissend en fruitig. Sterke frambozensmaa en -aroma met fruitige nasmaak.
i	–	–	–

PREMIUM
FRAMBOISE
St Louis
BIERE BELGE • BELGISCH BIER
KRIEK
PREMIUM

Premium Kriek St Louis

	spontaneous fermentation	fermentation spontanée	spontane gisting
	fruit beer based on Gueuze Lambic	bière fruitée à base de gueuze lambic	fruitbier op basis van geuze lambiek
	Castle Brewery Van Honsebrouck Ingelmunster	Castle Brewery Van Honsebrouck Ingelmunster	Castle Brewery Van Honsebrouck Ingelmunster
	malt, wheat, sugar, hops, cherries, water	malt, froment, sucre, houblon, cerises, eau	mout, tarwe, suiker, krieken, water
%	3,20%	3,20%	3,20%
	dark red clear	rouge foncé claire	donkerrood helder
	Pour into a newly rinsed glass, keeping it tilted first and in a vertical position at the end.	Verser dans un verre rincé tenu d'abord en oblique et à la fin en position verticale.	Uitschenken in een ‹ spoeld glas dat eerst gehouden wordt en ‹ einde verticaal geho‹ wordt.
°C	41 °F	5 °C	5 °C
	Fresh and very fruity. Sweet-and-sour with a deep cherry taste and strong, refreshing aftertaste.	Frais et fruité. Aigre-doux avec une saveur profonde de cerises et une arrière-bouche très rafraîchissante.	Fris en fruitig. Zuurzoet met diepe kriekensmaak en ste verfrissende nasmaa
i	–	–	–

PREMIUM
KRIEK
St Louis
BIERE BELGE • BELGISCH BIER
PREMIUM
KRIEK
St Louis

P

Premium Pêche St Louis

	spontaneous fermentation	fermentation spontanée	spontane gisting
	fruit beer based on Gueuze Lambic	bière fruitée à base de gueuze lambic	fruitbier op basis van geuze lambiek
	Castle Brewery Van Honsebrouck Ingelmunster	Castle Brewery Van Honsebrouck Ingelmunster	Castle Brewery Van Honsebrouck Ingelmunster
	malt, wheat, sugar, hops, peach juice, water	malt, froment, sucre, houblon, jus de pêches, eau	mout, tarwe, suiker, perzikensap, water
	2,60%	2,60%	2,60%
	amber clear	ambrée claire	amber helder
	Pour into a newly rinsed glass, keeping it tilted first and in a vertical position at the end.	Verser dans un verre rincé tenu d'abord en oblique et à la fin en position verticale.	Uitschenken in een v spoeld glas dat eerst gehouden wordt en c einde verticaal geho wordt.
	41 °F	5 °C	5 °C
	Refreshing and fruity. Full flavour and aroma of peach, with a slightly sourish aftertaste.	Frais et fruité. Saveur et arôme pleins de pêche avec une fin de bouche légèrement acidulée.	Verfrissend en fruiti Volle smaak en arom perzik met lichte zur in de nasmaak.
	–	–	–

PREMIUM
PECHE
St Louis
PREMIUM
PECHE
St Louis
BIERE BELGE • BELGISCH BIER
MBOISE - PÊCHE -
PREMIUM

Prima

	bottom-fermentation	fermentation basse	lage gisting
	table beer Tripel	bière de table triple	tafelbier tripel
	Brouwerij Leroy Boezinge	Brouwerij Leroy Boezinge	Brouwerij Leroy Boezinge
	malt, rice, hops, water	malt, riz, houblon, eau	mout, rijst, hop, water
%	3,25%	3,25%	3,25%
	blond clear	blonde claire	blond helder
	Pour slowly in a single, smooth movement in a degreased glass. Keep the glass tilted and avoid sloshing. Skim off the foam.	Verser lentement en un seul mouvement fluide dans un verre dégraissé tenu en oblique. Ne pas laisser la bière glouglouter. Ecumer le verre.	Traag en in 1 vloeiend beweging uitschenker een vetvrij glas dat wc schuingehouden. Het niet laten klotsen. Het glas afschuimen.
°C	37 °F	3 °C	3 °C
	Distinctive. Malt flavour and slightly bitter aftertaste.	Plein de caractère. Arôme malté et fin de bouche légèrement amère.	Karaktervol. Moutig aroma en lich tere afdronk.
i	–	–	–

SUPER
LIB
BOCK
LIB
PRIMA
LEROY

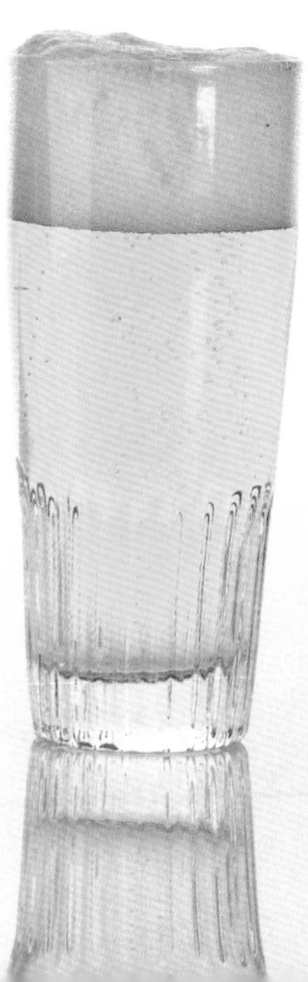

Primus

	bottom-fermentation	fermentation basse	lage gisting
	premium Pilsner	premium pils	premium pils
	Brouwerij Haacht Boortmeerbeek	Brouwerij Haacht Boortmeerbeek	Brouwerij Haacht Boortmeerbeek
	barley malt from Belgium, the Netherlands or France, corn, Belgian and German hop varieties, water from the brewery's well	malt d'orge de la Belgique, des Pays-Bas ou de la France, maïs, sortes de houblon belges et allemandes, eau de propre source	gerstemout uit België, . derland of Frankrijk, m Belgische en Duitse ho soorten, water uit eige bron
%	5,20%	5,20%	5,20%
	clear light blond foam head with fine bubbles	blond clair faux col avec des bulles fines	helder lichtblond schuimkraag met fijne bellen
	Pour carefully into a rinsed, wet Primus glass, avoiding contact between bottle and foam.	Verser prudemment dans un verre Primus rincé et mouillé sans que la bouteille touche l'écume.	Voorzichtig uitschenke een gespoeld, nat Prim glas zonder dat de fles schuim raakt.
°C	37 °F	3 °C	3 °C
	Typical bitterness and hoppy flavour. Taste: sweet and slightly bitter, turning into a dry, thirst-quenching aftertaste.	Goût amer typique et arômes de houblon. Saveur initiale légèrement douce avec un goût amer retenu évoluant vers une fin de bouche sèche, désaltérante.	Typische bitterheid en aroma's. Smaak die licht zoet b met ingetoomde bitter en evolueert naar een ge, dorstlessende afdrc
i	Refers to Jan Primus, Duke of Brabant. Until 1975 the beer was called Super 8.	Réfère à Jan Primus, duc du Brabant. Avant 1975, cette bière était brassée sous le nom de Super 8.	Verwijst naar Jan Prim hertog van Brabant.Vóc 1975 werd dit bier gebr wen onder de naam Su

BREWED AND
BOTTLED IN BELGIUM
BREWED IN BELGIUM
PRIMUS
Premium Pils
HAACHT

BRABANT
PRIMUS
HAACHT

Prinsesken

top-fermentation re-fermented in the bottle	fermentation haute refermentation en bouteille	hoge gisting hergisting op de fles
fruit beer	bière fruitée	fruitbier
Huisbrouwerij Boelens Belsele	Huisbrouwerij Boelens Belsele	Huisbrouwerij Boelens Belsele
–	–	–
5,50%	5,50%	5,50%
strawberry pink clear	rose fraises claire	aardbeiroze helder
Pour carefully so that the yeast sediment stays at the bottom of the bottle.	Verser prudemment pour garder le dépôt de levure au fond de la bouteille.	Voorzichtig uitschenke om het gistbezinksel o bodem te houden.
39 - 43 °F	4 - 6 °C	4 - 6 °C
Light, sour and non-sweet strawberry taste.	Saveur légère, acidulée et non sucrée de fraises.	Licht, zuur, niet zoete beiensmaak.
Season's beer brewed by order of the Melsele Strawberry Committee.	Bière de saison brassée à la demande du comité des fraises de Melsele.	Seizoensbier gebrouwer opdracht van het aardb comité van Melsele.

Prinsesken
Meilses Eïerebezenbier
door Huisbrouwerij Boelens — Belsele 03 772 03 80
Boelens

Prosit

	bottom-fermentation	fermentation basse	lage gisting
	premium Pilsner	pils premium	premium pils
	Brouwerij Bosteels Buggenhout	Brouwerij Bosteels Buggenhout	Brouwerij Bosteels Buggenhout
	barley malt, corn, hops, yeast, water	malt d'orge, maïs, houblon, levure, eau	gerstemout, mais, hop water
%	5,20%	5,20%	5,20%
	blond	blonde	blond
	–	–	–
	cool	frais	fris
	–	–	–
	–	–	–

Prosit
Prosit
Premium Pils
rustig gerijpt · murie lentement
Anno 1791
Prosit

Quintine Ambrée

	top-fermentation re-fermented in the bottle	fermentation haute refermentation en bouteille	hoge gisting nagisting in de fles
	specialty beer	bière spéciale	speciaalbier
	Brasserie des Légendes Brewsite Quintine Ellezelles	Brasserie des Légendes Brewsite Quintine Ellezelles	Brasserie des Légendes Brewsite Quintine Ellezelles
	pale malt, caramel malt, hops, yeast, water	malt pâle, malt caraméli-sé, houblon, levure, eau	bleke mout, karamelm[illegible] hop, gist, water
%	8,50%	8,50%	8,50%
	amber hazy	ambrée voilée	amber gesluierd
	–	–	–
	46 - 54 °F	8 - 12 °C	8 - 12 °C
	Very smooth character. Dry malt and caramel flavour.	Caractère très doux. Arômes de malt sec et de caramel.	Zeer zacht karakter. Droge mout en karamelaroma.
i	–	–	–

La Bière des Collines
QUINTINE
AMBRÉE
Brasserie Ellezelloise
La Bière des Collines
QUINTINE®
AMBRÉE
Brasserie Ellezelloise
Alc. 8,5% vol
e 33 cl
S.P.R.L.
B.V.B.A.
Bière Belge • Belgisch Bier • Belgian Beer • Cerveza Extra
B-7890 ELLEZELLES

Quintine blonde

	top-fermentation; unfiltered, centrifuged or pasteurised; re-fermented in the bottle	fermentation haute; non filtrée, centrifugée ni pasteurisée; refermentation en bouteille	hoge gisting; niet gefilterd, gecentri- geerd of gepasteuriseer hergisting in de fles
	specialty beer	bière spéciale	speciaalbier
	Brasserie des Légendes Brewsite Quintine Ellezelles	Brasserie des Légendes Brewsite Quintine Ellezelles	Brasserie des Légendes Brewsite Quintine Ellezelles
	malt, hops, yeast, water	malt, houblon, levure, eau	mout, hop, gist, water
%	8%	8%	8%
	blond hazy	blonde voilée	blond gesluierd
	–	–	–
°C	46 - 54 °F	8 - 12 °C	8 - 12 °C
	Smooth, robust and hoppy. Earthy, creamy flavour, dry malt and hop-py aftertaste.	Doux et robuste avec un goût de houblon prononcé. Arôme terreux et crémeux, malt sec et arrière-bouche houblonnée.	Zacht en robuust met delijke hop. Gronderig en romig aroma, droge mout en hoppige afdronk.
i	The name refers to the folklore from Ellezelles: Quintine is a witch who was burnt at the stake in 1610.	Le nom renvoie au folkore d'Ellezelles: Quintine est une sorcière qui est morte sur le bûcher en 1610.	De naam verwijst naar de folklore van Ellezel-les: Quintine is een he die in 1610 op de bran pel stierf.

La Bière des Collines
QUINTINE®
BLONDE
Brasserie Ellezelloise
Alc. 8 % vol.
℮ 33 cl
S.P.R.L.
B.V.B.A.
Bière Belge • Belgisch Bier • Belgian Beer • Cerveza Extra

La Bière des Collines

Rédor Pils

	bottom-fermentation unpasteurised	fermentation basse non pasteurisée	lage gisting niet gepasteuriseerd
	Pilsner	pils	pils
	Brasserie Dupont Tourpes-Leuze	Brasserie Dupont Tourpes-Leuze	Brasserie Dupont Tourpes-Leuze
	pure beer, brewed with barley malt	brassée seulement avec du malt d'orge	puur met gerstemout gebrouwen
%	5%	5%	5%
	blond filtered	blonde filtrée	blond gefilterd
	–	–	–
°C	Cooled.	Rafraîchie.	Gekoeld.
	Pleasantly bitter.	Goût amer agréable.	Aangenaam bitter.
i	Can be kept for approximately three months.	Possibilité de conserver pendant 3 mois environ.	Beperkt houdbaar (ci maanden).

DUPONT
Dupont
BRASSERIE DUPONT - TOURPES R.C.I. 39.753
DUPONT

Regal christmas

	top-fermentation re-fermentation in the bottle.	fermentation haute refermentation en bouteille	hoge gisting nagisting in de fles
	specialty beer strong brown	bière spéciale brune forte	speciaalbier sterk bruin
	Brasserie du Bocq Purnode-Yvoir	Brasserie du Bocq Purnode-Yvoir	Brasserie du Bocq Purnode-Yvoir
	barley malt, hop varieties, yeast, herbs, water	malt d'orge, sortes de houblon, levure, herbes, eau	gerstemout, hoppesoo gist, kruiden, water
%	8,10%	8,10%	8,10%
	dark coloured (70 EBC), clear, with fine, generous white foam head	foncé (70 EBC), claire, avec faux col blanc, fin et abondant	donkerkleurig (70 EBC helder, met fijne, overvloedige, witte kr
	Gently pour into a perfectly degreased glass. Leave the yeast sediment (due to natural re-fermenting) in the bottle.	Verser doucement dans un verre parfaitement dégraissé. Laisser le dépôt de levure (refermentation naturelle) dans la bouteille.	Zacht uitschenken in een perfect ontvet gla Het gistbezinksel (nat lijke hergisting) in de laten.
°C	46 - 54 °F	8 - 12 °C	8 - 12 °C
	Rich nose with a touch of coriander and liquorice. Full-bodied, delicious aroma of typical, special malts. Bitterness: 32 EBU.	Bouquet riche avec une touche de coriandre et de réglisse. Franc, arôme exquis de malts spéciaux typiques. Amertume 32 EBU.	Rijke neus met een to van koriander en zoet Volmondig, heerlijk a van typische, speciale ten. Bitterheid 32 EBL
i	Typical New Year's beer, Season's beer.	Bière typique de fin d'année, bière de saison.	Typisch eindejaarsbie seizoensbier.

REGAL
Christmas
REGAL
Christmas

Reinaert blond

	top-fermentation re-fermented in the bottle	fermentation haute refermentation en bouteille	hoge gisting hergisting in de fles
	amber - Belgian Ale	ambrée - Belgian ale	amber - Belgian ale
	De Proefbrouwerij/Andelot Lochristi	De Proefbrouwerij/Andelot Lochristi	De Proefbrouwerij/An Lochristi
	–	–	–
%	7%	7%	7%
	–	–	–
	–	–	–
°C	–	–	–
	–	–	–
i	–	–	–

DRINK MATIG MAAR REGELMATIG
Reinaert
BIER
GEBROUWEN
MET
NATUURLIJKE
PRODUKTEN
BELGISCH BIER · BIERE BELGE
DRINK MATIG MAAR REGELMATIG
Reinaert

Reinaert grand cru

	top-fermentation re-fermented in the bottle	fermentation haute refermentation en bouteille	hoge gisting hergisting in de fles
	Belgian strong Ale	Belgian strong ale	Belgian strong ale
	De Proefbrouwerij/Andelot Lochristi	De Proefbrouwerij/Andelot Lochristi	De Proefbrouwerij/An Lochristi
	full-malt	pur malt	volmout
%	9,50%	9,50%	9,50%
	dark red	rouge foncé	donkerrood
	Serve in a Trappist or tulip-shaped glass.	Verser dans un verre trappiste ou tulipe.	Uitschenken in een tr pist- of tulpglas.
°C	–	–	–
	–	–	–
i	–	–	–

DRINK MATIG MAAR REGELMATIG
Reinaert
DRINK MATIG MAAR REGELMATIG
Reinaert®
Grand Cru
BELGISCH BIER · BIERE BELGE

Reinaert tripel

	top-fermentation re-fermented in the bottle	fermentation haute refermentation en bouteille	hoge gisting hergisting in de fles
	Tripel	triple	tripel
	De Proefbrouwerij/Andelot Lochristi	De Proefbrouwerij/Andelot Lochristi	De Proefbrouwerij/And Lochristi
	full-malt	pur malt	volmout
%	9%	9%	9%
	blond	blonde	blond
	–	–	–
°C	–	–	–
	–	–	–
i	–	–	–

DRINK MATIG MAAR REGELMATIG
Reinaert
Tripel
BELGISCH BIER · BIERE BELGE

DRINK MATIG MAAR REGELMATIG
Reinaert

Revolución Cubana

	bottom-fermentation	fermentation basse	lage gisting
	aromatised specialty beer	bière spéciale aromatisée	gearomatiseerd specia bier
	Brouwerij Timmermans/ Timmermans Itterbeek	Brouwerij Timmermans/ Timmermans Itterbeek	Brouwerij Timmerma Timmermans Itterbeek
	barley malt, corn, sugar, hops, flavouring, water	malt d'orge, maïs, sucre, houblon, arômes, eau	gerstemout, maïs, suik hop, aroma's, water
	5%	5%	5%
	amber-coloured yellow	jaune ambré	amberkleurig geel
	–	–	–
	37 - 43 °F	3 - 6 °C	3 - 6 °C
	Flavour of brown rum. Tingling and exotic taste.	Arôme de rhum brun. Goût pétillant et exotique.	Aroma van bruine run Prikkelende en exotisc smaak.
	–	–	–

CUBANA'59®
REVOLUCIÓN

Revolución Mexicana

	bottom-fermentation	fermentation basse	lage gisting
	aromatised specialty beer	bière spéciale aromatisée	gearomatiseerd speciaa bier
	Brouwerij Timmermans/ Timmermans Itterbeek	Brouwerij Timmermans/ Timmermans Itterbeek	Brouwerij Timmermans Timmermans Itterbeek
	barley malt, corn, sugar, hops, flavouring, water	malt d'orge, maïs, sucre, houblon, arômes, eau	gerstemout, maïs, suike hop, aroma's, water
%	5%	5%	5%
	blond	blonde	blond
	–	–	–
°C	37 - 43 °F	3 - 6 °C	3 - 6 °C
	Tequila and lime in the background. Touch of sugar in the aftertaste.	Arrière-fond de tequila et de citron vert. Touche sucrée dans la fin de bouche.	Tequila en limoen op de achtergrond. Toets van ker in de afdronk.
	–	–	–

REVOLUCIÓN
MEXICANA'10

Ridder

	bottom-fermentation	fermentation basse	lage gisting
	low alcohol content	pauvre en alcool	alcoholarm
	Brouwerij Leroy Boezinge	Brouwerij Leroy Boezinge	Brouwerij Leroy Boezinge
	malt, rice, hops, water	malt, riz, houblon, eau	mout, rijst, hop, water
%	2,25%	2,25%	2,25%
	blond clear	blonde claire	blond helder
	Pour slowly in a single, smooth movement into a degreased glass. Keep the glass tilted and avoid sloshing. Skim off the foam.	Verser lentement et en un seul mouvement fluide dans un verre dégraissé tenu en oblique. Ne pas laisser la bière glouglouter. Ecumer le verre.	Traag en in 1 vloeiend[illegible] beweging uitschenken in een vetvrij glas dat wordt schuingehoude[illegible] Het bier niet laten klot[illegible] Het glas afschuimen.
°C	37 °F	3 °C	3 °C
	Thirst-quencher with low alcohol content. Fresh, aromatic and slightly bitter.	Désaltérant légèrement alcoolisé. Frais, parfumé et légèrement amer.	Licht alcoholische dorstlesser. Fris, geurig en licht bit[illegible]
i	–	–	–

Zeer Fijn Bier
Bière Très Fine
NEVEJAN
Streekbier · Bière Régionale
2,25% vol. alc.
25cl e
NEVEJAN

Riebedebie

	top-fermentation	fermentation haute	hoge gisting
	Tripel	triple	tripel
	Brouwerij De Bie Loker	Brouwerij De Bie Loker	Brouwerij De Bie Loker
	malt, hops, sugar, yeast, herbs, water	malt, houblon, sucre, levure, herbes, eau	mout, hop, suiker, gist, kruiden, water
%	9%	9%	9%
	blond clear	blonde claire	blond helder
	–	–	–
°C	–	–	–
	–	–	–
i	–	–	–

Riebedebie
De Bie

Rodenbach

	mixed fermentation	fermentation mixte	gemengde gisting
	Flemish red-brown	brune-rouge flamande	Vlaams roodbruin
	Palm Breweries Site Rodenbach Roeselare	Palm Breweries Site Rodenbach Roulers	Palm Breweries Site Rodenbach Roeselare
	special malts, fine aromatic hops, mixed yeasts, water. A blend of 3/4 young beer and 1/4 beer that has matured in oak barrels for 24 months.	malts spéciaux, houblons aromatiques fins, levures mélangées, eau. Mélange de 3/4 bière jeune et 1/4 bière mûrie en fûts de chêne pendant 24 mois.	speciale mouten, fijne mahoppen, gemengde ten, water. Blend van jong bier en 1/4 bier d maand gerijpt is op ei
%	5,20%	5,20%	5,20%
	red-brown	brun rouge	roodbruin
	Serve in a tall goblet with stem.	Servir dans un verre calice haut à pied.	Serveren in een hoog glas op voet.
°C	ca. 43 °F	ca. 6 °C	ca. 6 °C
	Very refreshing. Acidity and complex volatile fruitiness of wine (due to the symbiosis of top yeasts and lactic acid flora and to the fermentation on oak).	Très rafraîchissant. Degré d'acidité et goût fruité, complexe et volatile de vin (résultat de la symbiose de levures mixtes et de la flore d'acide lactique d'une part et de la maturation en fûts de chêne d'autre part).	Zeer verfrissend. Zuur graad en complexe, vl ge fruitigheid van wij gevolg van de symbios hoge gisten en melkz flora enerzijds en de r op eik anderzijds).
	Recognised regional product.	Produit régional reconnu.	Erkend streekproduct

RODENBACH
RODENBACH

Rodenbach Grand Cru

	mixed fermentation	fermentation mixte	gemengde gisting
	Flemish red-brown	brune-rouge flamande	Vlaams roodbruin
	Palm Breweries Site Rodenbach Roeselare	Palm Breweries Site Rodenbach Roulers	Palm Breweries Site Rodenbach Roeselare
	special malts, fine, aromatic hops, mixed yeasts, water. Blend of 3/4 young beer and 1/4 beer that has matured in oak barrels for 24 months	malts spéciaux, houblons aromatiques fins, levures mixtes, eau. Mélange de 3/4 bière jeune et 1/4 bière mûrie en fûts de chêne pendant 24 mois.	speciale mouten, fijne mahoppen, gemengde ten, water. Blend van 3/4 jong bier 1/4 bier dat 24 maand rijpt is op eik.
	6%	6%	6%
	red-brown	brun rouge	roodbruin
	Serve in the typical Grand Cru goblet.	Servir dans un verre calice typique 'Grand Cru'.	Serveren in de typische 'Grand Cru' kelk.
°C	ca. 43 °F	ca. 6 °C	ca. 6 °C
	Very refreshing. Acidity and complex volatile fruitiness of wine (due to the symbiosis of top yeasts and lactic acid flora and to the fermentation on oak).	Très rafraîchissant. Degré d'acidité et goût fruité, complexe et volatile de vin (résultat de la symbiose de levures hautes et de la flore d'acide lactique d'une part et de la maturation en fûts de chêne d'autre part).	Zeer verfrissend. Zuurt graad en complexe vlu ge fruitigheid van wijn gevolg van de symbiose hoge gisten en melkzu flora enerzijds en de ri op eik anderzijds).
i	Recognised regional product.	Produit régional reconnu.	Erkend streekproduct.

GRAND CRU
GRAND CRU
RODENBACH
GRAND CRU
RODENBACH

Romy Pils

	bottom-fermentation	fermentation basse	lage gisting
	Pilsner	pils	pilsbier
	Brouwerij Roman Mater	Brouwerij Roman Mater	Brouwerij Roman Mater
	barley malt, hops, corn, yeast, spring water	malt d'orge, houblon, maïs, levure, eau de source	gerstemout, hop, mais bronwater
%	5,10%	5,10%	5,10%
	light yellow clear and shiny	jaune clair claire et brillante	lichtgeel helder en blinkend
	Pour slowly into a degreased, rinsed beer glass.	Verser lentement dans un verre de bière dégraissé et rincé.	Langzaam uitschenken in een ontvet en gespo bierglas.
°C	37 °F	3 °C	3 °C
	Spicy thirst-quencher with a fruity flavour. Pleasant malty onset turning into a bitterish taste.	Désaltérant corsé avec un arôme fruité. Début malté agréable passant à une saveur plutôt amère.	Pittige dorstlesser met fruitig aroma. Aangenaam moutige a zet die overgaat in een terige smaak.
i	Store in a dark, cool room.	Conserver à l'abri de la lumière et de la chaleur.	Donker en koel bewar

Romy
PILS
PREMIUM
LAGER BEER
Romy
PILS
BR. ROMAN - OUDENAARDE
Romy
PILS

Rosé de Gambrinus

	spontaneous fermentation naturally re-fermented in the bottle	fermentation haute refermentation naturelle en bouteille	spontane gisting natuurlijke hergisting de fles
	fruit beer, Lambic	bière fruitée, lambic	fruitbier, lambiek
	Brouwerij Cantillon Brussel	Brouwerij Cantillon Bruxelles	Brouwerij Cantillon Brussel
	barley malt, wheat, more than one year old hops, fresh raspberries	malt d'orge, froment, houblon suranné, framboises fraîches	gerstemout, tarwe, overjaarse hop, verse frambozen
%	5,50%	5,50%	5,50%
	dark pink	rose foncé	donkerroze
	The use of a wine basket is recommended if the bottle was stored horizontally. Place the bottle in an upright position 48 hours before serving. .	Un panier verseur est recommandé si la bouteille a été conservée en position horizontale. Mettre la bouteille 48 heures avant de servir dans une position verticale pour faire descendre le dépôt de levure.	Een schenkmandje is a gewezen wanneer de fl horizontaal bewaard w De fles 48 uur voor het schenken verticaal pla om het bezinksel te decanteren.
°C	cellar temperature (54 - 61 °F)	température de cave (12 - 16 °C)	keldertemperatuur (12 - 16 °C)
	Intensely fruity, sourish flavour and pronounced raspberry aroma.	Goût fruité intense, saveur acidulée et arôme de framboises prononcé.	Intense fruitigheid, zurige smaak en uitge sproken frambozenarc
i	–	–	–

CANTILLON
CANTILLON
Rosé de Gambrinus

Rose des Remparts

	top-fermentation re-fermented in the bottle unpasteurised	fermentation haute refermentation en bouteille non pasteurisée	hoge gisting hergisting in de fles niet gepasteuriseerd
	fruit beer	bière fruitée	fruitbier
	Brasserie La Binchoise Binche	Brasserie La Binchoise Binche	Brasserie La Binchoise Binche
	perfumed with raspberry	parfumé aux framboises	geparfumeerd met fra boos
%	4,50%	4,50%	4,50%
	pink-red	rouge rose	rozerood
	–	–	–
°C	–	–	–
	Smooth, light and re- freshing.	Doux, léger et rafraîchis- sant.	Zacht, licht en verfriss
i	–	–	–

BIÈRE BELGE
rose
DES REMPARTS
LA BINCHOISE
A LA FRAMBOISE
rose
DES REMPARTS
LA BINCHOISE
A LA FRAMBOISE

Saint-Denis

	top-fermentation re-fermented in the bottle	fermentation haute refermentation en bouteille	hoge gisting hergisting op de fles
	Ale	ale	ale
	Brasserie Artisanale Millevertus Toernich	Brasserie Artisanale Millevertus Toernich	Brasserie Artisanale Millevertus Toernich
	different malt, hop and yeast varieties, water	différentes sortes de malt, de houblon et de levures, eau	verschillende mout-, h en gistsoorten, water
%	7,50%	7,50%	7,50%
	orange blond	blond orange	oranjeblond
	–	–	–
	45 or 54 °F	7 ou 12 °C	7 of 12 °C
	Smooth but surprising beer, well-balanced between malty round and hoppy flavours.	Bière douce mais surprenante. Bon équilibre entre les arômes de malt et de houblon.	Zacht maar verrassen Goed evenwicht tusse mout- en hoparoma's
	–	–	–

SAINT DENIS
Brasserie Artisanale
MMMH!!
MILLEVERTUS

Saint-Monon ambrée

	top-fermentation re-fermented in the bottle	fermentation haute refermentation en bouteille	hoge gisting nagisting op de fles
	amber	ambrée	amber
	Brasserie Saint-Monon Ambly-Nassogne	Brasserie Saint-Monon Ambly-Nassogne	Brasserie Saint-Monon Ambly-Nassogne
	special malts, Pilsner malt, hop varieties, sugar, yeast, water	malts spéciaux, malt de pils, sortes de houblon, sucre, levure, eau	speciale mouten, pilsm hopsoorten, suiker, gis water
	6,50%	6,50%	6,50%
	amber clear with a white foam head	ambrée claire avec un faux col blanc	amber helder met witte schui kraag
	Pour slowly, leaving the yeast sediment in the bottle. Whilst pouring, move the bottle away from the glass to obtain a nice foam head.	Verser lentement et laisser le dépôt de levure dans la bouteille. Séparer la bouteille du verre au moment de verser pour obtenir un beau faux col.	Traag uitschenken en gistdepot in de fles lat Tijdens het schenken van het glas verwijder voor een mooie schuimkraag.
	43 - 50 °F	6 - 10 °C	6 - 10 °C
	Bitter and thirst-quenching with an aftertaste of caramelized malt. Hoppy flavour.	Amer et désaltérant avec une arrière-bouche de malt caramélisé. Arôme houblonné.	Bitter en dorstlessend een nasmaak van gekarameliseerde mo Hoparoma.
	–	–	–

la
Saint-Monon
Bière Ambrée
Amber Bier

la
Saint-Monon

S

Saint-Monon au miel

	top-fermentation re-fermented in the bottle	fermentation haute refermentation en bouteille	hoge gisting nagisting op de fles
	Tripel	triple	tripel
	Brasserie Saint-Monon Ambly-Nassogne	Brasserie Saint-Monon Ambly-Nassogne	Brasserie Saint-Monon Ambly-Nassogne
	malt varieties, hop varieties, yeast, local honey, sugar, water	sortes de malt, sortes de houblon, levure, miel de la région, sucre, eau	moutsoorten, hopsoo gist, honing van de st suiker, water
%	8%	8%	8%
	honey-coloured	couleur miel	honingkleur
	Pour slowly, leaving the yeast sediment in the bottle. Keep the bottle upright near the end to obtain a nice foam head.	Verser lentement et laisser le dépôt de levure dans la bouteille. Tenir la bouteille à la fin en position verticale pour obtenir un beau faux col.	Traag uitschenken en gistdepot in de fles lat Op het einde van het s ken de fles rechthoud voor een mooie schui kraag.
°C	43 - 50 °F	6 - 10 °C	6 - 10 °C
	Full and smooth taste, balanced by a fine bitterness. Flavours of yeast, hop and malt.	Saveur pleine et moelleuse équilibrée par un goût amer raffiné. Arômes de levure, de houblon et de malt.	Volle en zachte smaak lanceerd door een fijn terheid. Aroma van gist, hop e mout.
i	–	–	–

La Saint-Monon
au Miel - met Honing
La Saint-Monon

Saint-Monon brune

	top-fermentation re-fermented in the bottle	fermentation haute refermentation en bouteille	hoge gisting nagisting op de fles
	dubbel	double	dubbel
	Brasserie Saint-Monon Ambly-Nassogne	Brasserie Saint-Monon Ambly-Nassogne	Brasserie Saint-Monon Ambly-Nassogne
	Pilsner malt, roasted and caramelised malt, hop varieties, sugar, yeast, herbs, water	malt de pils, malt brûlé et caramélisé, sortes de houblon, sucre, levure, herbes, eau	pilsmout, gebrande en gekaramelliseerde hopsoorten, suiker, gi kruiden, water
%	7,50%	7,50%	7,50%
	dark brown white foam head	brun foncé faux col blanc	donkerbruin witte schuimkraag
	While pouring, keep the glass tilted first and in a vertical position at the end. The yeast sediment can be drunk afterwards.	Au moment de verser, tenir le verre d'abord en oblique et à la fin en position verticale. Le dépôt de levure peut être bu par la suite.	Tijdens het uitschenk het glas eerst schuin houden en tegen het einde recht houden. De gistfond kan achte worden uitgedronken
°C	43 - 50 °F	6 - 10 °C	6 - 10 °C
	Smooth and caramelized taste. Long and well-balanced aftertaste of roasty malt and bitterness.	Saveur moelleuse et caramélisée. Arrière-bouche longue et équilibrée de malt brûlé et de goût amer.	Zachte en gekaramell de smaak. Lange en evenwichtig smaak van gebrande en bitterheid.
	–	–	–

la
Saint-Monon
Bière Brune
Bruin Bier
Belgien speciaal bier • Cervezo espacial Belga
brasserie Saint-Monon • B-6953 Ambly/Nassogne
la
Saint-Monon

Saison 1900

	top-fermentation	fermentation haute	hoge gisting
	Saisons	saison	saison
	Brasserie Lefebvre Quenast	Brasserie Lefebvre Quenast	Brasserie Lefebvre Quenast
	barley malt, candy sugar, hops, yeast, water	malt d'orge, sucre candi, houblon, levure, eau	gerstemout, kandijsui[illegible] hop, gist, water
%	5,20%	5,20%	5,20%
	–	–	–
	Pour into a conic glass, with a thick foam head.	Verser dans un verre conique et prévoir un large faux col.	Uitschenken in een ko[illegible] glas en een ruime sch[illegible] kraag laten.
°C	39 - 43 °F	4 - 6 °C	4 - 6 °C
	–	–	–
i	–	–	–

Saison
1900
BIÈRE BELGE AMBRÉE - BELGIAN AMBER BEER
Saison
1900
un nom!
un renom!

Saison
1900
IMPORTED FROM
BELGIUM

Saison 2000

	top-fermentation re-fermented in the bottle	fermentation haute refermentation en bouteille	hoge gisting nagisting in de fles
	Saisons	saison	saison
	Brasserie des Légendes Brewsite Quintine Ellezelles	Brasserie des Légendes Brewsite Quintine Ellezelles	Brasserie des Légendes Brewsite Quintine Ellezelles
	pale malt, hops, yeast, water	malt pâle, houblon, levure, eau	bleke mout, hop, gist,
%	6,50%	6,50%	6,50%
	bronze	bronze	brons
	–	–	–
°C	41 - 46 °F	5 - 8 °C	5 - 8 °C
	Dry and thirst-quenching. Very fruity with a touch of nuts. Dry and lively aftertaste.	Sec et désaltérant. Très fruité, touche de noix. Fin de bouche sèche et vive.	Droog en dorstlessend Zeer fruitig en toets va noten. Droge en levendige afdronk.
i	–	–	–

La Bière des Collines
SAISON
2000
Brasserie Ellezelloise
La Bière des Collines
SAISON
2000
Brasserie Ellezelloise
Alc.6,5% vol.
e 33 cl
S.P.R.L.
B.V.B.A.
Bière Belge • Belgisch Bier • Belgian Beer • Cerveza Extra
Guinaumont 75 • B-7890 ELLEZELLES • +32 (0)68 54 31 60

La Bière des Collines
SAISON
2000
Brasserie Ellezelloise

Saison biologique Dupont

	top-fermentation re-fermented in the bottle	fermentation haute refermentation en bouteille	hoge gisting nagisting in de fles
	blond	blonde	blond
	Brasserie Dupont Tourpes-Leuze	Brasserie Dupont Tourpes-Leuze	Brasserie Dupont Tourpes-Leuze
	–	–	–
%	5,50%	5,50%	5,50%
	blond	blonde	blond
	–	–	–
°C	cellar temperature (54 °F) or slightly chilled	température de cave (12 °C) ou légèrement rafraîchie	keldertemperatuur (12 of lichtgekoeld
	Thirst-quenching with an exceptional dryness and bitterness. Citric touches (mainly grapefruit).	Désaltérant avec une saveur sèche et amère exceptionnelle. Touches d'agrumes (principalement pamplemousse).	Dorstlessend met uitz derlijke droogheid en bitterheid. Citrustoets (vooral pompelmoes).
i	Beer with label of Biogarantie®. The production is supervised by Ecocert®.	La production est contrôlée par Ecocert®. Avec le label Biogarantie®.	De productie wordt ge troleerd door Ecocert® Met label Biogarantie®

SAISON
DUPONT
Biologique
e25cl
Alc.5,5% Vol.
bière non filtrée
ongefilterd bier

Saison
Dupont

Saison de Mai

	top-fermentation	fermentation haute	hoge gisting
	Saisons boutique beer	saison artisanale	saison artisanaal
	Brasserie Saint-Monon for Arelbières Arlon	Brasserie Saint-Monon pour Arelbières Arlon	Brasserie Saint-Monon voor Arelbières Arlon
	malt varieties, hop varieties, sweet woodruff, herbs, yeast, water	sortes de malt, sortes de houblon, aspérule odorante, herbes, levure, eau	moutsoorten, hopsoor[ten,] lievevrouwbedstro, kruiden, gist, water
%	8,30%	8,30%	8,30%
	amber slightly cloudy	ambrée légèrement trouble	amber licht troebel
	–	–	–
°C	46 °F	8 °C	8 °C
	Bitter, flowery character. Taste of sweet woodruff with a touch of orange. Spring flavours.	Caractère amer, fleuri. Saveur d'aspérule odorante avec une touche d'orange. Arômes printaniers.	Bitter, bloemig karakt[er.] Smaak van lievevrouw[-] bedstro met een toets van sinaasappel. Lentearoma's.
i	–	–	–

SAISON
SAISON
DE MAI
Ambrée à l'aspérule du pays d'Arlon

Saison de Pipaix

	top-fermentation	fermentation haute	hoge gisting
	Saisons	saison	saison
	Brasserie à Vapeur Pipaix	Brasserie à Vapeur Pipaix	Brasserie à Vapeur Pipaix
	–	–	–
	6%	6%	6%
	–	–	–
	–	–	–
	–	–	–
	Dry beer, neutral hops, slightly sour and very spicy (pepper, ginger, smooth orange rind, curaçao).	Bière sèche, houblon neutre, légèrement acidulé et très relevé (poivre, gingembre, écorce d'orange doux, curaçao).	Droog bier, neutrale ho[illegible] lichtzuur en zeer gekru[illegible] (peper, gember, zachte s[illegible] naasschil, curaçao).
	Brewed since the foundation of the brewery in 1785.	Brassée dépuis 1785, au moment où la brasserie a été fondée.	Wordt gebrouwen seder[illegible] 1785 toen de brouwerij werd opgericht.

SAISON DE PIPAIX
MARQUE DÉPOSÉE
BRASSERIE
A VAPEUR
BRASSERIE A VAPEUR
PIPAIX

Saison d'Epeautre

	top-fermentation re-fermented in the bottle	fermentation haute refermentation en bouteille	hoge gisting hergisting in de fles
	specialty beer	bière spéciale	speciaalbier
	Brasserie de Blaugies Blaugies-Dour	Brasserie de Blaugies Blaugies-Dour	Brasserie de Blaugies Blaugies-Dour
	Malt, spelt, hops, yeast, water. Boutique beer without herbs or additives.	Malt, épeautre, houblon, levure, eau. Produit artisanal sans herbes ou additifs.	Mout, spelt, hop, gist, water. Artisanaal produ[illegible] zonder kruiden of additieven.
%	6%	6%	6%
	blond unfiltered	blonde non filtrée	blond niet gefilterd
	–	–	–
°C	43 - 46 °F	6 - 8 °C	6 - 8 °C
	Digestive and refreshing. Fine bitterness and plenty of body, despite the medium alcohol content.	Digestif et rafraîchissant. Saveur amère raffinée et assez de corps malgré la basse teneur en alcool.	Digestief en verfrissend[illegible] Fijne bitterheid en vold[illegible] de body ondanks het m[illegible]delmatige alcoholgeha[illegible]
i	–	–	–

Blaugies
SAISON
D'EPEAUTRE
6 %
BIERE - BIER
e
75 cl
Épeautre et orge du Pays donnent à cette bière artisanale belge, non filtrée, son caractère authentique. Refermentation en bouteille. Servir frais.
La Moneuse
BLAUGIES

Saison d'Erpe-Mere

	top-fermentation re-fermented in the bottle	fermentation haute refermentation en bouteille	hoge gisting nagisting op de fles
	Saisons	saison	saison
	Brouwerij De Glazen Toren Erpe-Mere	Brouwerij De Glazen Toren Erpe-Mere	Brouwerij De Glazen Tc Erpe-Mere
	Pilsner malt, wheat malt, sugar, hops, yeast, water	malt de pils, malt de froment, sucre, houblon, levure, eau	pilsmout, tarwemout, suiker, hop, gist, water
%	6,90%	6,90%	6,90%
	Straw-yellow, slightly hazy, very sparkling. Solid foam head that sticks to the glass.	Jaune paille, légèrement voilé, très pétillant. Faux col solide collant au verre.	Strogeel, licht gesluier sterk parelend. Stevige schuimkraag di aan het glas plakt.
	Pour carefully into a dry, tall glass (e.g. a tulip-shaped glass). Keep the bottle horizontally.	Verser prudemment dans un verre sec, oblong (p. ex. tulipe). Tenir la bouteille en position horizontale.	Voorzichtig uitschenke een droog, langwerpig tulpvormig) glas. De fles horizontaal ho
°C	43 °F	6 °C	6 °C
	Dry and thirst-quenching. Citric, bitter in the nose, dry and bitter in the mouth, long-lasting aftertaste.	Sec et désaltérant. Agrumes, parfum amer, saveur sèche et amère dans la bouche. Fin de bouche longue.	Droog en dorstlessend. Citrusachtig, bitter in de neus, droog en bitte in de mond. Lange afd
i	Specialty from the province of Hainaut.	Spécialité de la province du Hainaut.	Specialiteit van de provincie Henegouwer

KLEINBROUWERIJ
DE GLAZEN TOREN

Saison Dupont

	top-fermentation re-fermented in the bottle	fermentation haute refermentation en bouteille	hoge gisting nagisting in de fles
	Saisons	saison	saison
	Brasserie Dupont Tourpes-Leuze	Brasserie Dupont Tourpes-Leuze	Brasserie Dupont Tourpes-Leuze
	–	–	–
%	6,50%	6,50%	6,50%
	copper blond	blond cuivré	koperblond
	–	–	–
°C	cellar temperature (54 °F) or slightly cooled	température de cave (12 °C) ou légèrement rafraîchie	keldertemperatuur (12 of lichtgekoeld
	Thirst-quencher with dry bitterness and fine hoppy flavour.	Désaltérant avec un goût amer sec et des arômes de houblon raffinés.	Dorstlesser met droge terheid en fijne hoparoma's.
i	This beer was originally brewed in the winter as a thirst-quencher for the seasonal workers at the farm during the summer.	A l'origine brassée en hiver comme désaltérant pour les ouvriers saisonniers à la ferme en été.	Werd oorspronkelijk g brouwen in de winter dorstlesser voor de seizoensarbeiders op de hoeve in de zomer.

Saison
Dupont

Saison Regal

	top-fermentation re-fermented in the bottle	fermentation haute refermentation en bouteille	hoge gisting met hergisting in de fle
	specialty amber beer - saison	bière spéciale ambrée - saison	speciaalbier amber - saison
	Brasserie du Bocq Purnode-Yvoir	Brasserie du Bocq Purnode-Yvoir	Brasserie du Bocq Purnode-Yvoir
	barley malt, wheat starch, hop varieties, yeast, herbs, water	malt d'orge, fécule de fro-ment, sortes de houblon, levure, herbes, eau	gerstemout, tarwezetn hoppesoorten, gist, kruiden, water
%	5,50%	5,50%	5,50%
	amber-coloured and clear (30 EBC) fine, compact foam head	couleur ambrée et claire (30 EBC) faux col fin et épais	amberkleurig en helde (30 EBC) fijne, dichte schuimkra
	Gently pour into a per-fectly degreased glass. Leave the yeast sediment (due to natural re-fer-menting) in the bottle.	Verser doucement dans un verre parfaitement dégraissé. Laisser le dépôt de levure (refermentation naturel-le) dans la bouteille.	Zacht uitschenken in e perfect ontvet glas. Het gistbezinksel (natu lijke hergisting) in de f laten.
°C	41 - 54 °F	5 - 12 °C	5 - 12 °C
	Versatile nose, hoppy base with a fruity touch. Thirst-quenching and light with a clearly bitter taste (30 EBU).	Bouquet varié à base de houblon avec une touche fruitée. Désaltérant et lé-ger avec une saveur amère prononcée (30 EBU).	Veelzijdige neus, hopb met een fruitig tintje. Dorstlessend en licht n een duidelijke bitterhe de smaak (30 EBU).
i	–	–	–

SAISON
REGAL
SAISON
REGAL
Anno 1858

SAISON
REGAL

Saison Silly

	top-fermentation	fermentation haute	hoge gisting
	Saisons	saison	saison
	Brasserie de Silly Silly	Brasserie de Silly Silly	Brasserie de Silly Silly
	aromatic malt, sugar, yeast, Kent and Hallertau hops, water	malt aromatique, sucre, levure, houblon Kent et Hallertau, eau	aromatische mout, suiker, gist, Kent en Hallertauhop, wate
%	5% 11,3° plato	5% 11,3° plato	5% 11,3° plato
	brown (45 EBC)	brune (45 EBC)	bruin (45 EBC)
	–	–	–
°C	39 - 48 °F	4 - 9 °C	4 - 9 °C
	Light, both fruity and slightly sugared, with a fresh aftertaste.	Léger, à la fois fruité et légèrement sucré avec une arrière-bouche fraîche.	Licht, tegelijk fruitig e licht gesuikerd met fri nasmaak.
i	–	–	–

SILLY
SAISON
BRASSERIE DE SILLY BROUWERIJ
SILLY
SAISON

Saison Voisin

	top-fermentation re-fermented in the bottle unfiltered	fermentation haute refermentation en bouteille non filtrée	hoge gisting nagisting in de fles niet gefilterd
	Saisons	saison	saison
	Brasserie des Légendes Brewsite Gouyasse Irchonwelz (Ath)	Brasserie des Légendes Brewsite Gouyasse Irchonwelz (Ath)	Brasserie des Légendes Brewsite Gouyasse Irchonwelz (Ath)
	pale malt, caramel malt, hops, yeast, water	malt pâle, malt caramélisé, houblon, levure, eau	bleekmout, karamelm hop, gist, water
%	5%	5%	5%
	amber	ambrée	amber
	Degrease the glass, rinse with hot water and dry. With yeast sediment: smoothly revolve the bottle before serving the last third. Without yeast sediment: pour carefully and leave the sediment in the bottle.	Dégraisser le verre, bien le rincer à l'eau chaude et sécher. Avec dépôt de levure: tourner le dernier tiers de bière avant de le verser. Sans dépôt de levure: verser prudemment et laisser le fond de levure dans la bouteille.	Het glas ontvetten, goe spoelen met warm wa drogen. Met gistbezink het laatste derde in de walsen voor het uitsch ken. Zonder gistbezink voorzichtig schenken fond in de fles laten.
°C	41 - 46 °F	5 - 8 °C	5 - 8 °C
	Very dry beer with pronounced, long-lasting bitterness. Malt, hop and caramel flavours.	Bière très sèche avec un goût amer durable. Arômes de malt, de houblon et de caramel.	Zeer droog bier met ui sproken bitterheid die blijft hangen. Aroma's mout, hop en karamel
i	Brewed following an original recipe from 1884.	Brassée selon la recette originale de 1884.	Gebrouwen volgens ee gineel recept van 1884

BRASSERIE DES
GÉANTS
Château-Brasserie
Saison
Voisin
Belgisch Bier - Bière Belge - Belgian

Saison
Voisin

Santa Bee

	top-fermentation re-fermented in the bottle	fermentation haute refermentation en bouteille	hoge gisting hergisting op de fles
	dark winter beer	bière hivernale foncée	donker winterbier
	Huisbrouwerij Boelens Belsele	Huisbrouwerij Boelens Belsele	Huisbrouwerij Boelens Belsele
	–	–	–
	8,70%	8,70%	8,70%
	dark clear	foncée claire	donker helder
	Pour carefully so that the yeast sediment stays at the bottom of the bottle.	Verser prudemment pour garder le dépôt de levure au fond de la bouteille.	Voorzichtig uitschenke om het gistbezinksel o bodem te houden.
	45 °F	7 °C	7 °C
	Spicy, caramel malt, winter spices. Deliciously creamy with a rich bouquet.	Goût relevé de malt caramélisé, herbes d'hiver. Délicieusement crémeux avec un bouquet riche.	Kruidig, karamelmout terse specerijen. Heerlijk romig met ee boeket.
	–	–	–

Donker Kerstbier van Brouwerij Boelens
Kerkstraat 7 • B-9111 Belsele
Boelens

Sara blond

	top-fermentation re-fermented in the bottle	fermentation haute refermentation en bouteille	hoge gisting nagisting op de fles
	specialty beer buckwheat beer	bière spéciale bière de sarrasin	speciaalbier boekweitbier
	Brasserie de Silenrieux Silenrieux	Brasserie de Silenrieux Silenrieux	Brasserie de Silenrieux Silenrieux
	barley, buckwheat (25%), hops, herbs, water	orge, sarrasin (25%), houblon, herbes, eau	gerst, boekweit (25%), [illegible] kruiden, water
%	6%	6%	6%
	blond amber cloudy (unfiltered) compact foam head	blond ambré trouble (non filtrée) faux col dense	blond amber troebel (niet gefilterd) dichte schuimkraag
	Softly revolve or shake the bottle before opening to obtain a cloudy beer.	Tourner légèrement ou secouer la bouteille avant de l'ouvrir pour obtenir une bière trouble.	De fles licht draaien o[illegible] schudden voor het op[illegible] om een troebel bier te[illegible] komen.
°C	45 - 50 °F	7 - 10 °C	7 - 10 °C
	Fruity, aromatic thirst-quencher. Full-bodied, slightly hopped, buckwheat taste and slightly bitter.	Désaltérant fruité aromatique. Franc, légèrement houblonné, goût de sarrasin et légèrement amer.	Fruitige, aromatische lesser. Volmondig, licht geh[illegible] boekweitsmaak en lic[illegible] bitter.
i	Organic beer. Buckwheat has a high nutritional value, stimulating digestion and lowering blood pressure.	Bière biologique. Le sarrasin a une valeur nutritive élevée, stimule la digestion et baisse la tension artérielle.	Biologisch bier. Boekweit heeft een h[illegible] voedingswaarde, bevo[illegible] de spijsvertering en w[illegible] bloeddrukverlagend.

SERVIR A 8°
6% alc vol
DE
Sara

Sara bruin

	top-fermentation re-fermented in the bottle	fermentation haute refermentation en bouteille	hoge gisting nagisting op de fles
	specialty beer buckwheat beer	bière spéciale bière de sarrasin	speciaalbier boekweitbier
	Brasserie de Silenrieux Silenrieux	Brasserie de Silenrieux Silenrieux	Brasserie de Silenrieux Silenrieux
	barley, buckwheat, hops, herbs, water	orge, sarrasin, houblon, herbes, eau	gerst, boekweit, hop, kruiden, water
%	6%	6%	6%
	brown cloudy (unfiltered)	brune trouble (non filtrée)	bruin troebel (niet gefilterd)
	Softly revolve or shake the bottle before opening to obtain a cloudy beer.	Tourner légèrement ou secouer la bouteille avant de l'ouvrir pour obtenir une bière trouble.	De fles licht draaien o schudden voor het ope om een troebel bier te bekomen.
°C	45 - 50 °F	7 - 10 °C	7 - 10 °C
	Refreshing. Slight bitter, buckwheat taste.	Rafraîchissant. Légèrement amer, goût de sarrasin.	Verfrissend. Licht bitter, boekweitsmaak.
i	–	–	–

Sara
BRASSERIE
DE
SILENRIEUX
Sara

Sas Export

	bottom-fermentation	fermentation basse	lage gisting
	export	export	export
	Brouwerij Leroy Boezinge	Brouwerij Leroy Boezinge	Brouwerij Leroy Boezinge
	malt, rice, hops, water	malt, riz, houblon, eau	mout, rijst, hop, water
%	5%	5%	5%
	amber	ambrée	amber
	Pour slowly in a single, smooth movement into a degreased glass. Keep the glass tilted and avoid sloshing. Skim off the foam.	Verser lentement en un seul mouvement fluide dans un verre dégraissé tenu en oblique. Ne pas laisser la bière clapoter. Ecumer le verre.	Traag en in 1 vloeiend beweging uitschenken een vetvrij glas dat wo schuingehouden. Het niet laten klotsen. Het glas afschuimen.
°C	37 °F	3 °C	3 °C
	Powerful and refreshing. Malt flavour with a bitter aftertaste.	Corsé et rafraîchissant. Arôme malté avec une fin de bouche amère.	Krachtig en verfrissen Moutig aroma met bit afdronk.
i	–	–	–

SAS
EXPORT

SAS
EXPORT

Sas Pils

	bottom-fermentation	fermentation basse	lage gisting
	Pilsner	pils	pils
	Brouwerij Leroy Boezinge	Brouwerij Leroy Boezinge	Brouwerij Leroy Boezinge
	malt, rice, hops, water	malt, riz, houblon, eau	mout, rijst, hop, water
	5%	5%	5%
	blond clear	blonde claire	blond helder
	Pour slowly in a single, smooth movement into a degreased glass. Keep the glass tilted and avoid sloshing. Skim off the foam.	Verser lentement en un seul mouvement fluide dans un verre dégraissé tenu en oblique. Ne pas laisser la bière clapoter. Ecumer le verre.	Traag en in 1 vloeiend[illegible] beweging uitschenken [illegible] een vetvrij glas dat wo[illegible] schuingehouden. Het [illegible] niet laten klotsen. Het glas afschuimen.
	37 °F	3 °C	3 °C
	Powerful and refreshing. Malty flavour with bitter aftertaste.	Corsé et rafraîchissant. Arôme malté avec une fin de bouche amère.	Krachtig en verfrissen[illegible] Moutig aroma met bit[illegible] afdronk.
	–	–	–

Premium
Pils
BELGIAN PREMIUM LAGER BEER
SAS
Pils
Brouwerij Leroy . B 8904 Boezinge

1720
SAS
Pils

Sasbräu

	bottom-fermentation	fermentation basse	lage gisting
	Dortmunder Pilsner	Pils Dortmunder	Dortmunder pils
	Brouwerij Leroy Boezinge	Brouwerij Leroy Boezinge	Brouwerij Leroy Boezinge
	malt, hops, water	malt, houblon, eau	mout, hop, water
%	6,30%	6,30%	6,30%
	blond clear	blonde claire	blond helder
	Pour slowly in a single, smooth movement into a degreased glass. Keep the glass tilted and avoid sloshing. Skim off the foam.	Verser lentement en un seul mouvement fluide dans un verre dégraissé tenu en oblique. Ne pas laisser la bière clapoter. Ecumer le verre.	Traag en in 1 vloeiend beweging uitschenker een vetvrij glas dat wc schuingehouden. Het niet laten klotsen. Het glas afschuimen.
°C	37 °F	3 °C	3 °C
	Solid and aromatic. Strong malty and hoppy flavour.	Corsé et parfumé. Arôme prononcé de malt et de houblon.	Stevig en geurig. Sterk mout- en hoparc
i	One of the few Dortmunders left in Belgium.	Une des peu Dortmunders subsistant encore en Belgique.	Een van de weinige D munders die nog over ven in België.

1720
Sasbräu
dortmunder type
MALZ LAGER BIER
BR. LEROY B - 8904 BOEZINGE
ALC. 6,3 % VOL.
e 25cl

BLB
Sasbräu
Dortmunder Type

Satan Gold

	top-fermentation, unpasteurised re-fermented in the bottle	fermentation haute non pasteurisée refermentation en bouteille	hoge gisting niet gepasteuriseerd hergisting op de fles
	strong blond	blonde forte	sterk blond
	Brouwerij De Block Peizegem-Merchtem	Brouwerij De Block Peizegem-Merchtem	Brouwerij De Block Peizegem-Merchtem
	wheat, malt, hops, yeast, water	froment, malt, houblon, levure, eau	tarwe, mout, hop, gist water
	8%	8%	8%
	blond clear	blonde claire	blond helder
	cfr chimay	voir chimay	cfr. chimay
	43 - 46 °F	6 - 8 °C	6 - 8 °C
	Fresh and deep, full character. Rich palette of yeast with a considerable fruit and flower touch.	Caractère frais, profond et plein. Palette riche de levure et touche profonde fruitée et fleurie.	Fris en diep, vol karak Rijk palet van gist en d toets van fruit en bloe
	Store the beer upright.	Conserver la bière en position verticale.	Het bier verticaal bew

of Belgium • Prod
• België • Belgio •
satan
GOLD
Brewery DE BLOCK
Alc. 8% vol.
℮ 33 cl.
Bier • Biere • Beer • Cerveza • Birra
satan

Satan red

	top-fermentation unpasteurised re-fermented in the bottle	fermentation haute non pasteurisée refermentation en bouteille	hoge gisting niet gepasteuriseerd hergisting op de fles
	Flemish brown	brune flamande	Vlaams bruin
	Brouwerij De Block Peizegem-Merchtem	Brouwerij De Block Peizegem-Merchtem	Brouwerij De Block Peizegem-Merchtem
	wheat, malt, hops, yeast, water	froment, malt, houblon, levure, eau	tarwe, mout, hop, gis water
	8%	8%	8%
	red, clear	rouge, clair	rood, helder
	cfr. Chimay	voir chimay	cfr. chimay
	43 - 46 °F	6 - 8 °C	6 - 8 °C
	Fresh, deep and full character. Rich palette of yeast with a considerable fruit and flower touch.	Caractère frais, profond et plein. Palette riche de levure et touche profonde fruitée et fleurie.	Fris, diep en vol kara Rijk palet van gist en toets van fruit en blo
	Store the beer upright. This beer is described by the brewer as a strong red beer.	Conserver la bière en position verticale. Le brasseur décrit Satan Red comme une bière rouge forte.	Het bier verticaal bev De brouwer omschrij als zwaar rood bier.

of Belgium •
• België • Belgio •
satan
RED
8% vol
satan

Saxo

	top-fermentation	fermentation haute	hoge gisting
	strong blond	blonde forte	sterk blond
	La Brasserie Caracole Falmignoul	La Brasserie Caracole Falmignoul	La Brasserie Caracole Falmignoul
	Pilsner malt, wheat malt, barley malt, coriander, Saaz hops, yeast, water	malt de pils, malt de froment, malt d'orge, coriandre, houblon Saaz, levure, eau	pilsmout, tarwemout, gerstemout, koriander, Saazhop, gist, water
%	7,50%	7,50%	7,50%
	golden blond	blond doré	goudblond
	–	–	–
°C	cool not chilled	fraîche, mais pas trop froide	fris maar niet te koud
	Light, fruity and vegetable nose with green apple flavours. Flexible and refined, with a strong but delicate bitterness.	Parfum légèrement fruité et végétal avec des arômes de pommes vertes. Souple et raffiné avec une touche amère corsée mais délicate.	Licht fruitige en vegeta neus met aroma's van groene appels. Soepel en geraffineerd met een sterke maar delicate bitterheid.
i	Exists in an organic version.	Existe aussi dans une version bio.	Bestaat ook in een bioversie.

SAXO
Bière • Bier • Beer
Cerveza • Birra doppio malto
BELGIAN BEER
SAXO

Scotch Silly

	top-fermentation	fermentation haute	hoge gisting
	Scottish style	scotch	scotch
	Brasserie de Silly Silly	Brasserie de Silly Silly	Brasserie de Silly Silly
	pale malt, caramelised malt, aromatic malt, sugar, Kent and Hallertau hops, yeast, water	malt pâle, malt caramélisé, malt aromatique, sucre, houblon Kent et Hallertau, levure, eau	bleke mout, gekaramell seerde mout, aromatisc mout, suiker, Kent en Hallertau hop, gist, wat
%	7,80% 17,2° plato	7,80% 17,2° plato	7,80% 17,2° plato
	dark brown (62 EBC)	brun foncé (62 EBC)	donkerbruin (62 EBC)
	Pour carefully in a wide goblet.	Verser tranquillement dans un verre calice large.	Rustig uitschenken in e breed kelkglas.
°C	43 - 48 °F	6 - 9 °C	6 - 9 °C
	Woody aroma with a touch of hazelnut. Bitter and with a fuller taste than the traditional British Scottish style.	Parfum boisé renvoyant à la noisette. Saveur amère et plus pleine que celle de la Scotch anglaise traditionnelle.	Houtachtige geur die refereert aan hazelnoot. Bittere en vollere smaak dan de traditionele Britse scotch.
i	–	–	–

SCOTCH
SILLY
SCOTCH
SILLY
SCOTCH
SILLY

Season Mortal

	top-fermentation re-fermented in the bottle	fermentation haute refermentation en bouteille	hoge gisting hergisting op de fles
	Saisons	saison	saison
	Mortal's Beers Jamagne	Mortal's Beers Jamagne	Mortal's Beers Jamagne
	malt, sugar, hops, fruit, yeast, water	malt, sucre, houblon, fruits, levure, eau	mout, suiker, hop, fruit gist, water
%	7,20%	7,20%	7,20%
	golden yellow	jaune doré	goudgeel
	–	–	–
	39 - 43 °F	4 - 6 °C	4 - 6 °C
	Smooth, fruity with smooth hoppy flavours.	Moelleux, fruité avec arômes houblonnés doux.	Zacht, fruitig met zach hoparoma's.
	–	–	–

WWW.MORTALSBEERS.BE
MORTALS BEERS

Serafijn donker

	top-fermentation re-fermented in the bottle	fermentation haute refermentation en bouteille	hoge gisting met hergisting op de fl
	dubbel	double	dubbel
	Microbrouwerij Achilles Itegem	Microbrouwerij Achilles Itegem	Microbrouwerij Achille Itegem
	coloured malt, aromatic hops, yeast, water	malt coloré, houblon aromatique, levure, eau	kleurmout, aromatisch hop, gist, water
%	8%	8%	8%
	dark brown-purple	brun-violet foncé	donker paarsbruin
	–	–	–
°C	–	–	–
	Spicy with smooth bitterness. Distinctive taste owing to the roasted barley varieties, which give this beer its colour in a natural way.	Relevé avec un goût légèrement amer. Goût plein de caractère par les types d'orge brûlée donnant aussi de façon naturelle à la bière sa couleur.	Kruidig met zachte bit heid. Karaktervolle smaak d de gebrande gerstsoort die ook op natuurlijke ze dit bier kleuren.
i	–	–	–

Serafijn
DONKER
HERGISTING OP FLES • FLASCHENGÄRUNG • BIÈRE DE FERMENTATION HAUTE • REFERMENTATION IN BOTTLE • BIRRA RIFERMENTATA IN BOTTIGLIA

Serafijn gold

	top-fermentation re-fermented in the bottle	fermentation haute refermentation en bouteille	hoge gisting met hergisting op de fl
	blond	blonde	blond
	Microbrouwerij Achilles Itegem	Microbrouwerij Achilles Itegem	Microbrouwerij Achille Itegem
	coloured malt, aromatic hops, yeast, coriander, water	malt coloré, houblon aromatique, levure, coriandre, eau	kleurmout, aromatisc hop, gist, koriander, w
%	7%	7%	7%
	blond beer with a firm foam head	bière blonde avec un beau faux col	blond bier mooie schuimkraag
	–	–	–
°C	–	–	–
	Rich, stimulating taste. Sweetish, spicy flower aroma. Slowly disappearing aftertaste with a slightly bitter touch.	Saveur riche, pétillante. Arômes fleuris sucrés et relevés. Arrière-bouche disparaissant lentement avec une touche légèrement amère.	Rijke, prikkelende sma Zoetig en kruidig bloemenaroma. Langzaam wegvloeien nasmaak met licht bittere toets.
i	–	–	–

Serafijn
GOLD
ERGISTING OP FLES • FLASCHENGARUNG • BIÈRE
DE FERMENTATION HAUTE • REFERMENTATION IN
BOTTLE • BIRRA RIFERMENTATA IN BOTTIGLIA

Serafijn tripel

	top-fermentation re-fermented in the bottle	fermentation haute refermentation en bouteille	hoge gisting met hergisting op de fle
	Tripel	triple	tripel
	Microbrouwerij Achilles Itegem	Microbrouwerij Achilles Itegem	Microbrouwerij Achilles Itegem
	coloured malt, aromatic hops, yeast, water	malt coloré, houblon aromatique, levure, eau	kleurmout, aromatisch hop, gist, water
	8%	8%	8%
	deep golden	doré intense	diepgoud
	–	–	–
	–	–	–
	Flower aroma. Natural bitterness caused by the hops, that presents itself on the sides of the tongue and then smoothly fades away.	Arôme de fleurs. Goût amer naturel par le goût de houblon persistant aux bords de la langue et disparaissant lentement par la suite.	Aroma van bloemen. Natuurlijke bitterheid de hop die licht blijft h gen op de zijkant van d tong en daarna zacht w vloeit.
	–	–	–

Serafijn
TRIPEL
HERGISTING OP FLES • FLASCHENGARUNG • BIERE DE FERMENTATION HAUTE • REFERMENTATION IN BOTTLE • BIRRA RIFERMENTATA IN BOTTIGLIA
Serafijn

Sezoens Blond

	top-fermentation	fermentation haute	hoge gisting
	specialty beer	bière spéciale	speciaalbier
	Brouwerij Martens Bocholt	Brouwerij Martens Bocholt	Brouwerij Martens Bocholt
	malt, hops, water	malt, houblon, eau	mout, hop, water
%	6%	6%	6%
	gold-coloured clear	dorée claire	goudkleurig helder
	cfr. abbey beer	voir bière d'abbaye	cfr. abdijbier
	36 °F	2 °C	2 °C
	Remarkable hoppy character obtained by dry-hopping.	Caractère houblonné remarquable par le dryhopping.	Opmerkelijk hopkarak[t] door dryhopping.
i	–	–	–

BROUWERIJ MARTENS BOCHOLT
SEZOENS
ANNO 1758
BLOND
BROUWERIJ MARTENS BOCHOLT
SEZOENS
ANNO 1758

Sezoens Quattro

	top-fermentation	fermentation haute	hoge gisting
	strong amber	ambrée forte	sterk amber
	Brouwerij Martens Bocholt	Brouwerij Martens Bocholt	Brouwerij Martens Bocholt
	malt, hops, water	malt, houblon, eau	mout, hop, water
%	8%	8%	8%
	dark	foncée	donker
	Cfr. abbey beer	voir bière d'abbaye	cfr. abdijbier
°C	39 °F	4 °C	4 °C
	Coffee-like onset, then pure fruitiness and an intense finale. Well-bound hoppy dryness, not a thirst-quencher.	Goût café au début, puis fruité et pur, fin de bouche intense. Caractère sec, houblonné bien lié. Pas de désaltérant.	Koffie-achtige start, da[illegible] een zuivere fruitigheid en een intense finale. Goed gebonden hoppig droogheid. Geen dorstlesser.
i	–	–	–

BROUWERIJ MARTENS BOCHOLT
SEZOENS
ANNO 1758
QUATTRO
SEZOENS

Silly Pils

bottom-fermentation	fermentation basse	lage gisting
Pilsner	pils	pils
Brasserie de Silly Silly	Brasserie de Silly Silly	Brasserie de Silly Silly
pale malt, yeast, Saaz and Hallertau hops, water	malt pâle, levure, houblon Saaz et Hallertau, eau	bleke mout, gist, Saaz e Hallertauhop, water
5% 11,2° plato	5% 11,2° plato	5% 11,2° plato
7 EBC clear	7 EBC claire	7 EBC helder
–	–	–
37 - 43 °F	3 - 6 °C	3 - 6 °C
Malty thirst-quencher with a hoppy bitter touch.	Désaltérant malté avec une touche amère houblonnée.	Moutige dorstlesser m hoppig bittere toets.
No provision beer.	Pas de bière de conservation.	Geen bewaarbier.

Silly
Pils
Silly
Pils
5% Vol.
250ml
SILLY

Sinpalsken blond

	top-fermentation re-fermented in the bottle	fermentation haute refermentation en bouteille	hoge gisting hergisting op de fles
	regional beer	bière régionale	streekbier
	at Brouwerij Van Steen- berge Brouwerij De Cock Sint-Pauwels	chez Brouwerij Van Steen- berge Brouwerij De Cock Sint-Pauwels	bij Brouwerij Van Stee berge Brouwerij De Cock Sint-Pauwels
	Malt, hops, yeast, water. No preservatives added.	Malt, houblon, levure, eau. Sans conservateurs.	Mout, hop, gist, water Zonder bewaarmiddel
%	8,50%	8,50%	8,50%
	clear golden blond (12 EBC) nice, full foam head	claire blond doré (12 EBC) beau faux col plein	helder goudblond (12 EBC) mooie, volle schuimk
	–	–	–
°C	46 °F	8 °C	8 °C
	Soft beer with a typical hoppy flavour, fairly full-bodied.	Bière moelleuse avec un arôme houblonné typique et un caractère légèrement franc.	Zacht biertje met een pisch hoparoma en ee beetje volmondigheid
i	–	–	–

Sinpalsken
DE COCK
1996
Sinpalsken
Blond
Hergist in de fles

Sinpalsken donker

	top-fermentation re-fermented in the bottle	fermentation haute refermentation en bouteille	hoge gisting hergisting op de fles
	regional beer	bière régionale	streekbier
	at Brouwerij Van Steen- berge Brouwerij De Cock Sint-Pauwels	chez Brouwerij Van Steen- berge Brouwerij De Cock Sint-Pauwels	bij Brouwerij Van Steen- berge Brouwerij De Cock Sint-Pauwels
	Malt, hops, yeast, roasted malt, water. No preservatives added.	Malt, houblon, levure, malt grillé, eau. Sans conservateurs.	Mout, hop, gist, geroo[illegible] mout, water. Zonder bewaarmiddel
%	8,50%	8,50%	8,50%
	clear red-brown nice, full foam head	claire brun rouge beau faux col plein	helder roodbruin mooie, volle schuimk[illegible]
	–	–	–
	46 °F	8 °C	8 °C
	Slightly roasted taste with a touch of sweetness and a light bitterness in the aftertaste.	Légèrement brûlé avec une touche sucrée et une fin de bouche légèrement amère.	Lichtgebrand met een vleugje zoetigheid en lichte bitterheid in de smaak.
i	–	–	–

Sinpalsken
DE COCK
1996
Sinpalsken
Donker
Hergist in de fles

Sint Canarus Tripel

	top-fermentation re-fermented in the bottle	fermentation haute refermentation en bouteille	hoge gisting nagisting op de fles
	Tripel	triple	tripel
	De Proefbrouwerij for Sint Canarus Gottem	De Proefbrouwerij pour Sint Canarus Gottem	De Proefbrouwerij voor Sint Canarus Gottem
	Pilsner malt, special malts, Vlamertinge hops, yeast, water	malt de pils, malts spéciaux, houblon de Vlamertinge, levure, eau	pilsmout, speciale mo Vlamertingse hop, gist water
	7,50%	7,50%	7,50%
	golden blond, clear	blond doré, claire	goudblond, helder
	Pour carefully into a goblet and leave the yeast sediment in the bottle. The latter can be drunk separately. Let the beer rest for a few days before tasting.	Laisser reposer la bière quelques jours avant la dégustation. Verser prudemment dans un verre calice et laisser le dépôt de levure dans la bouteille. Le dépôt de levure peut être bu séparément.	Het bier voor het degu ren een paar dagen la rusten. Voorzichtig ui schenken in een kelkg en de gistbodem in de laten. De gistbodem k afzonderlijk worden u dronken.
	46 - 54 °F	8 - 12 °C	8 - 12 °C
	Triple session beer. Well-balanced, smoothly bitter, fruity.	Triple facilement buvable. Equilibré, moelleux, amer, fruité.	Doordrinktripel. Evenwichtig, zacht bi fruitig.
	'Canarus' is dog Latin for 'canard', which means drunk in the local dialect.	En latin de cuisine, 'Canarus' veut dire 'canard', ce qui signifie 'ivre' dans le dialecte local.	'Canarus' is potjeslati voor canard, wat in he kale dialect 'dronken' tekent.

SINT CANARUS
SINT CANARUS
TRIPEL
SINT CANARUS

Sint Gummarus Dubbel

	top-fermentation re-fermented in the bottle	fermentation haute refermentation en bouteille	hoge gisting nagisting op de fles
	specialty beer	bière spéciale	speciaalbier
	Brouwerij Sint-Jozef Opitter	Brouwerij Sint-Jozef Opitter	Brouwerij Sint-Jozef Opitter
	malt, hops, sugar, herbs, water	malt, houblon, sucre, herbes, eau	mout, hop, suiker, kruiden, water
%	7%	7%	7%
	dark	foncée	donker
	Pour into a clean, degreased glass, avoiding contact between bottle and foam.	Verser dans un verre propre, dégraissé sans que la bouteille touche l'écume.	Uitschenken in een zu ontvet glas zonder dat fles het schuim raakt.
°C	36 - 39 °F	2 - 4 °C	2 - 4 °C
	Full and spicy flavour with a strong aftertaste.	Saveur pleine et corsée avec une fin de bouche forte.	Volle en pittige smaak sterke afdronk.
i	–	–	–

SINT
GUMMARUS
Dubbel
SINT
GUMMARUS
HERGIST
OP DE FLES

Sint Gummarus Tripel

	top-fermentation re-fermented in the bottle	fermentation haute refermentation en bouteille	hoge gisting nagisting op de fles
	strong blond	blonde forte	zwaar blond
	Brouwerij Sint-Jozef Opitter	Brouwerij Sint-Jozef Opitter	Brouwerij Sint-Jozef Opitter
	malt, hops, sugar, herbs, water	malt, houblon, sucre, herbes, eau	mout, hop, suiker, kruiden, water
	8%	8%	8%
	yellowish and shiny	jaunâtre et brillante	gelig en blinkend
	Pour carefully into a goblet, avoiding contact between bottle and foam.	Verser dans un verre propre, dégraissé sans que la bouteille touche l'écume.	Uitschenken in een zu ontvet glas zonder da fles het schuim raakt.
°C	36 - 39 °F	2 - 4 °C	2 - 4 °C
	Full-bodied and spicy flavour with strong aftertaste.	Saveur franche et corsée avec une fin de bouche forte.	Volle en pittige smaak sterke afdronk.
	–	–	–

SINT
GUMMARUS
SINT
GUMMARUS

Slaapmutske blond

	top-fermentation re-fermented in the bottle	fermentation haute refermentation en bouteille	hoge gisting hergisting op de fles
	regional beer, blond	bière régionale blonde	streekbier blond
	De Proefbrouwerij for Slaapmutske, Melle	De Proefbrouwerij pour Slaapmutske, Melle	De Proefbrouwerij voo Slaapmutske, Melle
	Pilsner malt, wheat malt, aromatic hop varieties, yeast, water	malt de pils, malt de froment, sortes de houblon aromatiques, levure, eau	pilsmout, tarwemout, matische hopsoorten, water
%	6,40%	6,40%	6,40%
	blond with possibly a light cloudiness when served very cold	blonde, aspect légèrement trouble est possible si la bière est très froide	blond, lichte koudetro heid is mogelijk
	Pour into a dry glass in a single, fluent movement, and avoid sloshing. Leave 2 cm in the bottle and serve it alongside the glass of beer. The yeast sediment can be added to the beer afterwards.	Verser en un seul mouvement fluide dans un verre sec sans que la bière clapote. Laisser 2 cm de bière dans la bouteille et la servir avec le verre rempli. Le dépôt de levure dans la bouteille peut être ajouté selon le goût.	In 1 vlotte beweging uit schenken in een droog zonder dat het bier klok 2 cm in de fles laten en men met het ingeschon glas serveren. Het gistre in de fles kan desgewen teraf worden bijgeschor
°C	43 °F	6 °C	6 °C
	Refreshing and thirst-quenching smooth bitter character beer. 35 EBU. Smooth, mild full-malt flavour with fine aromatic, slightly citric hoppy touch.	Bière de caractère rafraîchissante et légèrement amère. 35 EBU. Saveur maltée moelleuse avec des arômes de houblon aromatiques et une touche légère d'agrumes.	Verfrissend en dorstle zachtbitter karakterbi 35 EBU. Zachte en ma volmoutsmaak met fij matisch, licht citrusa hoparoma.
i	–	–	–

BIERE BELGE - BELGISCH BIER
BLOND
SLAAPMUTSKE
6,4 Vol%

SLAAPMUTSKE

Slaapmutske bruin

	top-fermentation re-fermented in the bottle	fermentation haute refermentation en bouteille	hoge gisting hergisting op de fles
	regional beer, dubbel	bière régionale double	streekbier dubbel
	De Proefbrouwerij for Slaapmutske, Melle	De Proefbrouwerij pour Slaapmutske, Melle	De Proefbrouwerij voc Slaapmutske, Melle
	different kinds of coloured malts, Pilsner malt, hops, coriander, yeast, water	différentes sortes de malt coloré, malt de pils, houblon, coriandre, levure, eau	verschillende soorten mouten, pilsmout, ho koriander, gist, water
	6%	6%	6%
	red-brown clear and slightly sparkling; compact, solid and creamy foam head	brun rouge, clair et legèrement perlant; faux col dense, solide et crémeux	roodbruin, helder en licht parele compacte, stevige en romige schuimkra
	Pour into a dry glass in a single, fluent movement, and avoid sloshing. Leave 2 cm in the bottle and serve it along with the glass of beer.	Verser en un seul mouvement fluide dans un verre sec sans que la bière clapote. Laisser 2 cm de bière dans la bouteille et la servir avec le verre rempli.	In 1 vlotte beweging u schenken in een droo zonder dat het bier kl 2 cm in de fles laten e samen met het ingesc ken glas serveren.
	48 °F	9 °C	9 °C
	Spicy and full-bodied character beer. 30 EBU. Full-bodied, slighty sweetish with a spicy aftertaste (colour malt and coriander touch).	Bière de caractère relevée et franche avec une amertume de 30 EBU. Franc, légèrement doux avec une fin de bouche corsée et relevée (malts colorés et touche de coriandre).	Kruidig en volmondig rakterbier met een bit heid van 30 EBU. Volmondig, licht zoeti een pittige, kruidige afdronk (kleurmouter en koriandertoets).
	–	–	

BIERE BELGE - BELGISCH BIER - BELGIAN BEER
BRUIN
SLAAPMUTSKE
6,0 Vol%

SLAAPMUTSKE

Slaapmutske tripel

	top-fermentation re-fermented in the bottle	fermentation haute refermentation en bouteille	hoge gisting hergisting op de fles
	regional beer tripel	bière régionale triple	streekbier tripel
	De Proefbrouwerij for Slaapmutske, Melle	De Proefbrouwerij pour Slaapmutske, Melle	De Proefbrouwerij voor Slaapmutske, Melle
	Pilsner malt, coloured malt, two strong aromatic hop varieties, yeast, water	malt de pils, malt coloré, 2 sortes de houblon très aromatiques, levure, eau	pilsmout, kleurmout, 2 sterk aromatische hops ten, gist, water
%	8,10%	8,10%	8,10%
	golden blond clear	blond doré claire	goudblond helder
	Pour into a dry glass in a single, fluent movement and avoid sloshing. Leave 2 cm in the bottle and serve it along with the glass of beer.	Verser en un seul mouvement fluide dans un verre sec sans que la bière clapote. Laisser 2 cm de bière dans la bouteille et la servir avec le verre rempli.	In 1 vlotte beweging ui schenken in een droog zonder dat het bier klo 2 cm in de fles laten en samen met het ingesch ken glas serveren.
	46 °F	8 °C	8 °C
	Fresh hoppy aroma and a spicy, bitter taste. Malty aftertaste with evolution toward a pleasantly bitter mouthfeel.	Arôme houblonné frais et saveur corsée, amère. Fin de bouche maltée aboutissant à une sensation amère agréable dans la bouche.	Fris hoparoma en een p ge, bittere smaak. Mou afdronk die uitvloeit in aangenaam bitter mon gevoel.
i	Triple Nightcap is the brand name for the American market.	Sur le marché américain cette bière se vend sous le nom de Triple Nightcap.	Op de Amerikaanse ma wordt dit bier verkocht onder de naam Triple Nightcap.

BIERE BELGE - BELGISCH BIER - BELGIAN BEER
TRIPEL
SLAAPMUTSKE
8,1 Vol%
SLAAPMUTSKE

Slag Pils

	bottom-fermentation unpasteurised	fermentation basse non pasteurisée	lage gisting ongepasteuriseerd
	Pilsner	pils	pils
	Brouwerij Slaghmuylder Ninove	Brouwerij Slaghmuylder Ninove	Brouwerij Slaghmuylde Ninove
	barley malt, yeast, water, hop varieties (Belgian Hallertau, Czech Styrie). The main fermentation starts at 8 °C: powder yeast and yeast flakes merge and evolve during the 2 month lagering.	malt d'orge, levure, eau, sortes de houblon (Hallertau belge, Styrie tchèque). La fermentation principale commence à 8 °C: la levure en poudre et en flocons s'unissent et évoluent pendant la conservation, qui prend plus de 2 mois.	gerstemout, gist, water, hopsoorten (Belgische H lertau, Tsjechische Styr De hoofdgisting start bi 8 °C: stofgist en vlokgist komen samen en evolu tijdens de lagering die r dan 2 maanden duurt.
%	5%	5%	5%
	Blond. Slightly saturated. Also available unfiltered.	Blonde. Légèrement saturée. Egalement disponible dans une version non filtrée.	Blond. Licht gesatureerd. Ook ongefilterd verkrijg baar.
	Pour in one fluent, smooth movement.	Verser en un seul mouvement fluide et doux.	Uitschenken in 1 vloeie zachte beweging.
°C	43 - 50 °F	6 - 10 °C	6 - 10 °C
	Smooth, bitter pils with a unique taste when unfiltered.	Pils moelleuse, amère qui a une saveur unique si elle est non filtrée.	Zachte, bittere pils die gefilterd een unieke sm heeft.
i	Perfect as an aperitif: the typical bitterness sharpens the appetite.	Idéal comme apéritif: le goût amer stimule la sensation de faim.	Ideaal als aperitief : de sche bitterheid scherpt hongergevoel aan.

25 cl ℮
Alc. 5% Vol.
Sedert
1860
“SLAG”
LAGER BIER
n.v. Brouwerij Slaghmuylder - B-9400 Ninove
LOT
à consommer de préférence avant fin:
ten minste houdbaar tot einde:
B C D J F M A M J J A S O N D 07 08 09

BIEREN SLAG
SEDERT
1860
NINOVE

Slaghmuylder's Kerstbier

	bottom-fermentation unpasteurised	fermentation basse non pasteurisée	lage gisting ongepasteuriseerd
	luxury/premium Pilsner Christmas beer	pils de luxe/premium bière de Noël	luxe/premium pils kerstbier
	Brouwerij Slaghmuylder Ninove	Brouwerij Slaghmuylder Ninove	Brouwerij Slaghmuyld Ninove
	barley malt, yeast, water hop varieties (Belgian Hallertau, Czech Styrie). Heavy brewing technique, with extra local hops.	malt d'orge, levure, eau, sortes de houblon (Hallertau belge, Styrie tchèque). Brassage fort, extra houblonné avec du houblon de la propre région.	gerstemout, gist, water, hopsoorten (Belgische Hallertau, Tsjechische Styr Zwaar gebrouwen en extra gehopt met ho uit eigen streek.
%	5,20%	5,20%	5,20%
	Blond with a stable foam head. Crystal-clear with gentle bubbles. Also available in an unfiltered version.	Blonde avec faux col stable. Claire comme du cristal et perlant tranquillement. Egalement disponible dans une version non filtrée.	Blond met stabiele schuimkraag. Kristalhe en rustig parelend. Ook ongefilterd verkrijgbaa
	Pour in one single, smooth movement.	Verser en un seul mouvement fluide et doux.	Uitschenken in 1 vloeie zachte beweging.
°C	43 - 50 °F	6 - 10 °C	6 - 10 °C
	Hop aroma in the bitter aftertaste.	Arômes houblonnés dans la fin de bouche amère.	Aroma's van hop in de bittere afdronk.
i	Recognised regional product. An exceptional product: blond low-fermenting Christmas beer.	Reconnu comme produit régional. Produit exceptionnel: bière blonde de Noël à fermentation basse.	Erkend als streekprodu Een uitzonderlijk prod blond van lage gisting a kerstbier.

SLAGHMUYLDER NV
Belgium
witkap.be
Slaghmuylder's
Kerstbier
Christmas
5,2% vol.

Slaghmuylder's Paasbier

	bottom-fermentation	fermentation basse	lage gisting
	premium Pilsner	pils de luxe/premium	luxe/premium pilsner
	Brouwerij Slaghmuylder Ninove	Brouwerij Slaghmuylder Ninove	Brouwerij Slaghmuylde Ninove
	barley malt, yeast, water, hop varieties (Belgian Hallertau, Czech Styrie). Heavy brewing technique with extra local hops. Main fermentation and lagering take 3 months.	malt d'orge, levure, eau, sortes de houblon (Hallertau belge, Styrie tchèque). Brassage fort, extra houblonné avec du houblon de la propre région. La conservation et la fermentation principale durent 3 mois.	gerstemout, gist, water hopsoorten (Belgische lertau, Tsjechische Sty Zwaar gebrouwen en e gehopt met hop uit eig streek. 3 maanden lagering en hoofdgisti
%	5,20%	5,20%	5,20%
	blond with a stable foam head. Crystal-clear with fine bubbles. Also available in an unfiltered version.	Blonde avec un faux col stable. Claire comme du cristal et légèrement perlant. Egalement disponible dans une version non filtrée.	Blond met stabiele sch kraag. Kristalhelder en parelend. Ook ongefilt verkrijgbaar.
	Pour in 1 fluent, smooth movement.	Verser en un seul mouvement fluide et doux.	Uitschenken in 1 vloei zachte beweging.
	43 - 50 °F	6 - 10 °C	6 - 10 °C
	Hoppy luxury Pilsner. Hop aroma in the bitter aftertaste.	Pils de luxe houblonnée. Arômes de houblon dans la fin de bouche amère.	Hoppige luxepils. Aroma's van hop in de bittere afdronk.
i	–	–	–

SLAGHMUYLDER'S
Paasbier
5,2% vol.

Sloeber

	top-fermentation re-fermented in the bottle	fermentation haute refermentation en bouteille	hoge gisting nagisting op de fles
	strong blond	blonde forte	sterk blond
	Brouwerij Roman Mater	Brouwerij Roman Mater	Brouwerij Roman Mater
	barley malt, hops, sugars, yeast, spring water	malt d'orge, houblon, sucres, levure, eau de source	gerstemout, hop, suike gist, bronwater
%	7,50%	7,50%	7,50%
	blond	blonde	blond
	Pour carefully in a single, smooth movement, avoiding contact between bottle and foam. Leave the yeast sediment in the bottle.	Verser prudemment en un seul mouvement fluide sans que la bouteille touche le faux col. Laisser le dépôt de levure dans la bouteille.	Voorzichtig uitschenk in 1 vlotte beweging z der dat de fles de schu kraag raakt. De gistfond in de fles l
°C	43 °F	6 °C	6 °C
	Sipping beer with a spicy, full-bodied taste and a powerful alcoholic aftertaste.	Bière de dégustation avec une saveur corsée, franche et une fin de bouche corsée, alcoolisée.	Degustatiebier met ee tige, volmondige smaa een krachtige alcoholi afdronk.
i	Store in a dark, cool room.	Conserver à l'abri de la lumière et de la chaleur.	Donker en koel bewar

Sloeber
Sloeber

't Smisje BBBourgondiër

	top-fermentation re-fermented in the bottle	fermentation haute refermentation en bouteille	hoge gisting hergisting op de fles
	barley wine	vin d'orge	gerstewijn
	Brouwerij De Regenboog Brugge	Brouwerij De Regenboog Bruges	Brouwerij De Regenboc Brugge
	5 malt varieties, Hallertau and Challenger hops, dark candy sugar, valerian, lemon balm, yeast, water	5 sortes de malt, houblon Hallertau et Challenger, sucre candi foncé, valériane, citronnelle, levure, eau	5 moutsoorten, Hallert en Challenger hop, dor kandijsuiker, valeriaan citroenmelisse, gist, w
	12%	12%	12%
	dark, unfiltered	foncée, non filtrée	donker, niet gefilterd
	–	–	–
	50 °F	10 °C	10 °C
	Very malty and complex aroma, obtained by the herbs. Spicy, hoppy and caramel-like taste.	Arôme très malté et complexe dû aux herbes. Saveur relevée, houblonnée et caramélisée.	Zeer moutig en compl aroma door de kruide Kruidige, hoppige en k melachtige smaak.
	Boutique beer. The name BBBourgondiër refers to the B's in the name of the website www.babblebelt.com	Bière artisanale. Le nom BBBourgondiër renvoie aux 3 B du site web www.babblebelt.com.	Artisanaal bier. De naa BBBourgondiër verwijs naar de letters B van d website www.babblebe com.

't Smisje
B
B
Bourgondier
'T SMISJE

't Smisje blond

	top-fermentation re-fermented in the bottle	fermentation haute refermentation en bouteille	hoge gisting hergisting op de fles
	blond	blonde	blond
	Brouwerij De Regenboog Brugge	Brouwerij De Regenboog Bruges	Brouwerij De Regenboc Brugge
	Pilsner/barley malt, Challenger hops, candy sugar, lime blossoms, yeast, water	malt de pils/d'orge, houblon Challenger, sucre candi, fleurs de tilleul, levure, eau	pils-/gerstemout, Chall ger hop, kandijsuiker, l bloesems, gist, water
%	6%	6%	6%
	blond unfiltered	blonde non filtrée	blond niet gefilterd
	–	–	–
°C	50 °F	10 °C	10 °C
	Hop-bitter with a long-lasting, bitter aftertaste.	Amer-houblonné avec une longue fin de bouche amère.	Hopbitter met een lan bittere afdronk.
i	Boutique beer that can be kept up to three years after bottling date. The label was designed by the American comic artist Bill Coleman.	Bière artisanale qui se conserve jusqu'à 3 ans après la date de la mise en bouteilles. L'étiquette est conçue par le cartooniste américain Bill Coleman.	Artisanaal bier, 3 jaar l baar na botteldatum. Het etiket is ontworpe door de Amerikaanse s tekenaar Bill Coleman.

't Smisje Blond
Gebrouwen door
De Regenboog
Brugge 050-37.38.33
Smisje@pandora.be
33 cl℮ Cat S 6% vol
5425004552013
'T SMISJE

't Smisje Catherine The great imperial stout

	top-fermentation re-fermented in the bottle	fermentation haute refermentation en bouteille	hoge gisting hergisting op de fles
	American Imperial Stout	Imperial Stout américain	Amerikaanse Imperial stout
	Brouwerij De Regenboog Brugge	Brouwerij De Regenboog Bruges	Brouwerij De Regenboo Brugge
	7 malt varieties, 4 hop varieties, brewer's yeast, oat, water	7 sortes de malt, 4 variétés de houblon, levure de bière, avoine, eau	7 moutsoorten, 4 hops ten, biergist, haver, wa
%	10%	10%	10%
	almost black unfiltered	presque noire non filtrée	bijna zwart niet gefilterd
	–	–	–
°C	43 - 50 °F	6 - 10 °C	6 - 10 °C
	Complex aroma and taste. Full-bodied with a long-lasting, bitter aftertaste.	Arômes et goûts complexes. Franc avec une longue fin de bouche amère.	Complexe aroma's en smaak. Volmondig met ge en bittere afdronk.
i	Boutique beer that can be kept up to 5 years after bottling date. The label, designed by the American comic artist Bill Coleman, is a parody of the Russian tsarina Catherine the Great.	Bière artisanale qui se conserve jusqu'à 5 ans après la date de la mise en bouteilles. L'étiquette est conçue par le cartooniste américain Bill Coleman et est une parodie sur la tsarine russe Cathérine La Grande.	Artisanaal bier, 5 jaar baar na botteldatum. Het etiket is ontworpe door de Amerikaanse s tekenaar Bill Coleman een parodie op de Russ tsarina Katarina de Gr

't Smisje Catherine
The Great Imperial Stout
De Regenboog
Brugge Belgium
33 cl e Cat S 10% vol
5425004 259998
'T SMISJE

’t Smisje dubbel

	top-fermentation re-fermented in the bottle	fermentation haute refermentation en bouteille	hoge gisting hergisting op de fles
	dubbel	double	dubbel
	Brouwerij De Regenboog Brugge	Brouwerij De Regenboog Bruges	Brouwerij De Regenbo Brugge
	3 malt varieties (Pilsner, cara, roasted), Hallertau hops, fresh dates, candy, honey, yeast, water	3 sortes de malt (pils, cara, grillé), houblon Hallertau, dattes fraîches, sucre candi, miel, levure, eau	3 moutsoorten (pils-, ca geroosterde), Hallertau verse dadels, kandij, hc gist, water
	9%	9%	9%
	copper-coloured, dark amber, unfiltered	cuivre, ambré foncé, non filtrée	koperkleurig, donker amber, niet gefilterd
	–	–	–
	50 °F	10 °C	10 °C
	Fruity taste with a touch of figs. Full-bodied. Bitter aftertaste.	Saveur fruitée avec une touche de figues. Plein. Fin de bouche amère.	Fruitige smaak met to van vijgen. Volmondig Bittere afdronk.
	Boutique beer that can be kept up to five years after bottling date. The label was designed by the American comic artist Bill Coleman.	Bière artisanale qui se conserve jusqu’à 5 ans après la date de la mise en bouteilles. L’étiquette est conçue par le cartooniste américain Bill Coleman.	Artisanaal bier, 5 jaar baar na botteldatum. Het etiket is ontworpe door de Amerikaanse s tekenaar Bill Coleman

't Smisje Dubbel
33 cl ℮ Cat S 9% vol
5 425004 253019
'T SMISJE

't Smisje Fiori

	top-fermentation re-fermented in the bottle	fermentation haute refermentation en bouteille	hoge gisting hergisting op de fles
	amber specialty beer	bière spéciale ambrée	speciaalbier amber
	Brouwerij De Regenboog Brugge	Brouwerij De Regenboog Bruges	Brouwerij De Regenbo Brugge
	2 malt varieties (Pilsner and cara), 2 hop varieties (Hallertau and Challenger), candy sugar, one flower variety, brewer's yeast, water	2 sortes de malt (pils et cara), 2 variétés de houblon (Hallertau et Challenger), sucre candi, 1 variété de fleurs, levure de bière, eau	2 moutsoorten (pils e ra), 2 hopsoorten (Hal en Challenger), kandijsuiker, 1 bloem soort, biergist, water
	7%	7%	7%
	amber, unfiltered	ambrée, non filtrée	amber, niet gefilterd
	–	–	–
°C	43 - 50 °F	6 - 10 °C	6 - 10 °C
	Fruity with a very spicy touch.	Saveur fruitée avec une touche très relevée.	Fruitig met zeer kruid ge toets.
	Boutique beer that can be kept up to two years after the bottling date. The label was designed by the American comic artist Bill Coleman. This beer was made upon the request of an Italian client. 'Fiori' means 'flowers' in Italian.	Bière artisanale qui se conserve jusqu'à 2 ans après la date de la mise en bouteilles. L'étiquette est conçue par le cartooniste américain Bill Coleman. Cette bière a été créée à la demande d'un client italien. 'Fiori' est le mot italien pour 'fleurs'.	Artisanaal bier, 2 jaar baar na botteldatum. Het etiket is ontworpe door de Amerikaanse tekenaar Bill Colema Dit bier werd gemaak verzoek van een Italia klant: 'Fiori' is de Ital vertaling van 'bloeme

't Smisje Fiori
Gebrouwen door, brassée par, brewed by
De Regenboog
Brugge Belgium
33 cl ℮ Cat S 7% vol
5 425004 552013
'T Smisje

't Smisje Halloween

	top-fermentation re-fermented in the bottle	fermentation haute refermentation en bouteille	hoge gisting hergisting op de fles
	strong blond pumpkin/Halloween beer	blonde forte citrouille/bière d'Halloween	sterk blond pompoen/halloweenb
	Brouwerij De Regenboog Brugge	Brouwerij De Regenboog Bruges	Brouwerij De Regenb Brugge
	Pilsner malt, Hallertau hops, candy sugar, pumpkin (pulp and rind), pumpkin seeds, brewer's yeast, water	malt de pils, houblon Hallertau, sucre candi, citrouille (chair et peau), graines de citrouille, levure de bière, eau	pilsmout, Hallertau h kandijsuiker, pompoe (vruchtvlees en schil), poenpitten, biergist,
%	10,50%	10,50%	10,50%
	blond, unfiltered	blonde, non filtrée	blond, niet gefilterd
	–	–	–
	50 °F	10 °C	10 °C
	Fruity and spicy with a light pumpkin aroma. Full-bodied, sweetish (pumpkin) with a very full-bodied aftertaste.	Saveur fruitée et relevée avec un parfum de citrouille léger. Franc, doux (citrouille) avec une fin de bouche très franche.	Fruitig en kruidig me lichte neus van pomp Volmondig, zoetig (pc poen) met een heel vc dige afdronk.
i	Boutique beer that can be kept up to five years after the bottling date. The label was designed by the American comic artist Bill Coleman. Halloween beer is especially popular in the USA.	Se conserve jusqu'à 5 ans après la date de la mise en bouteilles. L'étiquette est conçue par le cartooniste américain Bill Coleman. La bière Halloween est surtout populaire aux Etats-Unis.	Artisanaal bier, 5 jaar baar na botteldatum. etiket is ontworpen d Amerikaanse striptek Bill Coleman. Hallowe bier is vooral populai Verenigde Staten.

't Smisje Halloween
ALC. VOL 10,5 %
33 cl e
Blond bier van hoge gisting; drinktemp 10° C
bier met smaakevolutie.
gebrouwen door
de Regenboog - Brugge
smisje@pandora.be
ingrediënten:
mout, hop, kandij, pompoen en pompoenpitten, biergist en water
2010 2011 2012 2013 2014 2015 2016
'T SMISJE

't Smisje Honing

	top-fermentation re-fermented in the bottle	fermentation haute refermentation en bouteille	hoge gisting hergisting op de fles
	amber honey beer	bière de miel ambrée	honingbier, amber
	Brouwerij De Regenboog Brugge	Brouwerij De Regenboog Bruges	Brouwerij De Regenbo Brugge
	3 malt varieties (Pilsner, Munich, cara), Hallertau hops, a lot of honey, brewer's yeast, water	3 sortes de malt (pils, Munich, cara), houblon Hallertau, beaucoup de miel, levure de bière, eau	3 moutsoorten (pils, m nich, cara), Hallertau veel honing, biergist,
%	6%	6%	6%
	amber-coloured unfiltered	ambrée non filtrée	amberkleurig niet gefilterd
	–	–	–
	50 °F	10 °C	10 °C
	Sweet-and-sour aroma of flowers and honey. Smoothly bitter taste with vanilla touches. Soft aftertaste.	Arôme aigre-doux de fleurs et de miel. Goût: légèrement amer avec des touches de vanille. Fin de bouche douce.	Zoetzurig aroma van men en honing. Smaak: zachtbitter m toetsen van vanille. Zachte afdronk.
	The very first beer of the Regenboog brewery (1995) and the result of the brewer's hobbies in that time: brewer and bee-keeper. Boutique beer.	La toute première bière de la brasserie Regenboog (1995) et le résultat des passe-temps favoris du brasseur à l'époque: apiculteur et brasseur. Brassage artisanal.	Het allereerste bier va brouwerij De Regenbc (1995) en de combinat van de toenmalige ho van de brouwer: imke brouwer. Artisanaal gebrouwen

't Smisje Honing
Gebrouwen door
33 cl ℮ Cat S 6% vol
5 425004 251015
'T Smisje

't Smisje Kerst

	top-fermentation re-fermented in the bottle	fermentation haute refermentation en bouteille	hoge gisting hergisting op de fles
	dark Christmas beer	bière de Noël foncée	kerstbier donker
	Brouwerij De Regenboog Brugge	Brouwerij De Regenboog Bruges	Brouwerij De Regenbo Brugge
	4 malt varieties (crystal, cara, Pilsner, wheat), Hallertau and Challenger hops, candy, two sorts of herbs, yeast, water	4 sortes de malt (cristal, cara, pils, froment), houblon Hallertau et Challenger, sucre candi, 2 sortes d'herbes, levure, eau	4 moutsoorten (kristal ra, pils, tarwe), Hallert Challenger hop, kandi 2 soorten kruiden, gis water
%	10%	10%	10%
	dark unfiltered	foncée non filtrée	donker niet gefilterd
	–	–	–
°C	50 °F	10 °C	10 °C
	Fruity, malty and sweet aroma. Taste: caramel, sweet, spicy with a very long-lasting, bitter aftertaste. Full-bodied beer.	Arôme fruité, houblonné et doux. Goût: caramel, doux, herbes avec une fin de bouche très longue, amère. Bière franche.	Fruitig, moutig en zoe aroma. Smaak: karamel, zoet, dig met zeer lange, bi afdronk. Volmondig bier.
i	Boutique beer that can be kept up to 5 years after the bottling date. The label was designed by the American comic artist Bill Coleman.	Bière artisanale qui se conserve jusqu'à 5 ans après la date de la mise en bouteilles. L'étiquette est conçue par le cartooniste Américain Bill Coleman.	Artisanaal bier, 5 jaar baar na botteldatum. Het etiket is ontworpe door de Amerikaanse tekenaar Bill Coleman

't Smisje Kerst
33 cl e Cat S 11% vol
5 425004 259598
'T SMISJE

't Smisje Sleedoorn

	top-fermentation re-fermented in the bottle	fermentation haute refermentation en bouteille	hoge gisting hergisting op de fles
	specialty beer fruit beer	bière spéciale fruitée	speciaalbier fruitbier
	Brouwerij De Regenboog Brugge	Brouwerij De Regenboog Bruges	Brouwerij De Regenbo Brugge
	Barley malt, Hallertau hops, brewer's yeast, water. Maturation on blackthorn during 2 months. Before bottling, candy sugar is added for re-fermentation.	Malt d'orge, houblon Hallertau, levure de bière, eau. Maturation de 2 mois avec des baies de prunellier. Au moment de la mise en bouteilles, du sucre est ajouté pour la refermentation.	Gerstemout, Hallerta biergist, water. 2 maa gerijpt op sleedoorn. dijsuiker voor de herg wordt toegevoegd bij botteling.
	6%	6%	6%
	Pink. Evolution from cloudy to crystal-clear. Unfiltered.	Rose. Evolue de trouble à claire comme du cristal. Non filtrée.	Roze. Evolueert van t naar kristalhelder. Niet gefilterd.
	–	–	–
	43 - 50 °F	6 - 10 °C	6 - 10 °C
	Fruity and slightly sourish due to the blackthorn berries. May have a woody, dry taste.	Fruité et légèrement acidulé par les baies de prunellier. Peut avoir un goût boisé, sec.	Fruitig en zachtzurig de sleedoornbessen. K een houtachtige, drog smaak hebben.
	Boutique beer, to be kept up to 3 years after the bottling date. The label was designed by the American comic artist Bill Coleman.	Bière artisanale, se conserve 3 ans après la date de la mise en bouteilles. L'étiquette est conçue par le cartooniste américain Bill Coleman.	Artisanaal bier, 3 jaar baar na botteldatum. Het etiket is ontworp door de Amerikaanse tekenaar Bill Colema

't Smisje
Sleedoorn
Gebrouwen door,
brassée par, brewed by
De Regenboog
33 cl e
Cat S 6% vol
5425004259097
'T Smisje

't Smisje tripel

	top-fermentation re-fermented in the bottle	fermentation haute refermentation en bouteille	hoge gisting hergisting op de fles
	Tripel blond	triple blonde	tripel blond
	Brouwerij De Regenboog Brugge	Brouwerij De Regenboog Bruges	Brouwerij De Regenbo Brugge
	Pilsner malt, white candy sugar, Hallertau hops, brewer's yeast, water	malt de pils, sucre candi blanc, houblon Hallertau, levure de bière, eau	pilsmout, witte kandij ker, Hallertau hop, bie gist, water
%	9%	9%	9%
	blond unfiltered	blonde non filtrée	blond niet gefilterd
	–	–	–
	43 - 50 °F	6 - 10 °C	6 - 10 °C
	Fruity and a little hoppy.	Fruité et un peu houblonné.	Fruitig en zacht hoppi
i	Boutique beer that can be kept up to 5 years after the bottling date. The label was designed by the American comic artist Bill Coleman.	Bière artisanale qui se conserve jusqu'à 5 ans après la date de la mise en bouteilles. L'étiquette est conçue par le cartooniste américain Bill Coleman.	Artisanaal bier, 5 jaar baar na botteldatum. Het etiket is ontworpe door de Amerikaanse tekenaar Bill Coleman

't Smisje Tripel
Gebrouwen door,
brassée par, brewed by
De Regenboog
Astridlaan 134 - Brugge Belgium
33 cl e Cat S 9% vol
5425004254016
'T SMISJE

Special 6 Block

	top-fermentation re-fermented in the bottle	fermentation haute refermentation en bouteille	hoge gisting met hergisting op de
	amber / brown-red blended beer	ambrée / bière de coupage brune-rouge	amber / bruinrood versnijbier
	Brouwerij De Block Peizegem-Merchtem	Brouwerij De Block Peizegem-Merchtem	Brouwerij De Block Peizegem-Merchtem
	wheat, malt, hops, yeast, water	froment, malt, houblon, levure, eau	tarwe, mout, hop, gist water
	6%	6%	6%
	red, clear	rouge, claire	rood, helder
	Cfr. Chimay: in a goblet with a stem.	Voir chimay, dans un ver- re calice à pied.	Zoals chimay, in een glas met voet.
	43 - 46 °F	6 - 8 °C	6 - 8 °C
	Fruity and fresh. Full aroma, with pome- granate flavour.	Fruité et frais. Plein d'arômes, goût de grenade.	Fruitig en fris. Vol aroma, smaak van naatappel.
	Store the beer in an up- right position. According to the brewer, it is an Old Flemish red beer, blend- ed with young beer. Beer connoisseurs however, claim that it has recent- ly been reintroduced and would better belong in the 'amber' category.	Conserver la bière en po- sition verticale. Selon le brasseur, Special 6 est une vieille bière rouge flaman- de coupée avec une biè- re jeune. Des amateurs de bière réagissent en disant qu'elle vient d'être relan- cée sur le marché et qu'elle appartient mieux à la caté- gorie des bières ambrées.	Het bier verticaal bew Volgens de brouwer is een Oud Vlaams rood versneden met jong bi Vanuit kringen van bi naten komt de reactie het bier recent opnieu op de markt gebracht beter past in de catego 'amber'.

DE FIJNSTE MOUTEN DER WERELD WORDEN VOOR HET BROUWEN VAN DIT SPECIAAL BIER GEBRUIKT
SPECIAL-BLOCK
6
BROUWERIJ DE BLOCK
BVBA
DE BLOCK-PEISEGEM
e33cl.
Alc. 6% vol
BIERE BELGE - BELGIAN ALE - BIRRA SPECIALE
SPECIAL-BLOCK
6

Special De Ryck

	top-fermentation re-fermented in the bottle	fermentation haute refermentation en bouteille	hoge gisting nagisting op de fles
	Ale - amber beer	ale - bière ambrée	ale - amberbier
	Brouwerij De Ryck Herzele	Brouwerij De Ryck Herzele	Brouwerij De Ryck Herzele
	malt, hops, yeast, sucrose, water	malt, houblon, levure, sucrose, eau	mout, hop, gist, sucros water
%	5,50%	5,50%	5,50%
	light amber slightly hazy	ambré clair légèrement voilée	licht amber licht gesluierd
	Rinse the glass with cold water, take it by the handle and tilt it slightly. Pour slowly in a single movement, avoiding contact between bottle and glass or foam. Leave the 1 cm yeast sediment in the bottle or pour it.	Rincer le verre à l'eau froide et le tenir légèrement en oblique par l'anse. Verser la bière lentement et en un seul mouvement sans que la bouteille touche le verre ou l'écume. Laisser un dépôt de levure de 1 cm dans la bouteille ou la vider.	Het glas koud spoelen, bij het oor vastnemen en licht schuin houder Het bier traag en in 1 beweging inschenker zonder dat de fles het g of schuim raakt. Het gistdepot van 1 cm de fles laten of uitsche
°C	39 - 43 °F	4 - 6 °C	4 - 6 °C
	Rich, fresh and slightly alcoholic character. Fruity, hoppy aroma. A typical combination of a malty, full-bodied flavour and a smoothly bitter aftertaste.	Caractère riche, frais et légèrement alcoolisé. Arôme houblonné fruité. Combinaison typique d'un goût houblonné franc et d'une fin de bouche légèrement amère.	Rijk, fris en licht alcoh lisch karakter. Fruithoppig aroma. Typische combinatie v moutige volmondighe zachtbittere afdronk.
i	The draught version of this beer is clear (filtered).	La bière au fût est claire (filtrée).	Van het vat is het bier der (gefilterd).

«special»
DE RYCK
«special»
DE RYCK

"SPECIAL"
DE RYCK
DA'S NOG ECHT BIER!

Special Roman

	top-fermentation	fermentation haute	hoge gisting
	Flemish brown Oudenaards	brune flamande d'Audenarde	Vlaams bruin Oudenaards
	Brouwerij Roman Mater	Brouwerij Roman Mater	Brouwerij Roman Mater
	barley malt, corn, hops, candy sugar, yeast, spring water	malt d'orge, maïs, houblon, sucre candi, levure, eau de source	gerstemout, mais, hop, dijsuiker, gist, bronwat
%	5,50%	5,50%	5,50%
	red-brown clear	brun rouge claire	roodbruin helder
	Slowly pour into a degreased, rinsed beer glass, making a nice foam head.	Verser lentement dans un verre de bière dégraissé et rincé et former un beau faux col.	Langzaam uitschenken een ontvet en gespoeld glas en een mooie schu kraag vormen.
°C	46 °F	8 °C	8 °C
	Sipping beer with a full-bodied, bittersweet taste. Smoothly aromatic, slightly frivolous and yet very spicy.	Bière de dégustation avec un goût franc, doux-amer. Doucement aromatique, un peu frivole et quand même très corsé.	Degustatiebier met een volmondige, zoetbitter smaak. Zacht aromatisch, iets vool en toch zeer pittig
i	Store in a dark, cool room.	Conserver à l'abri de la lumière et de la chaleur.	Donker en koel beware

Special
Roman
anno
R
1545
Special
Roman

Special
Roman

Special spelt Leireken

	top-fermentation	fermentation haute	hoge gisting
	spelt beer	bière d'épeautre	speltbier
	Brouwerij Silenrieux for Guldenboot Opwijk	Brouwerij Silenrieux pour Guldenboot Opwijk	Brouwerij Silenrieux voor Guldenboot Opwijk
	organic barley malt, organic spelt, organic sucrose, hops, yeast, water	malt d'orge bio, épeautre bio, sucrose bio, houblon, levure, eau	biogerstemout, biospelt biosucrose, hop, gist, w
%	5,40%	5,40%	5,40%
	5 EBC cloudy	5 EBC trouble	5 EBC troebel
	Keep the glass tilted (45°) whilst pouring.	Tenir le verre incliné (45 °) au moment de verser.	Het glas schuin houden (45 °) bij het inschenke
°C	37 °F	3 °C	3 °C
	Fresh thirst-quencher, hoppy.	Désaltérant frais, houblonné.	Frisse dorstlesser, hopp
i	–	–	–

SPECIAL SPELT
Leireken
2008
0,10 €

Speciale 1900

	top-fermentation	fermentation haute	hoge gisting
	Spéciale Belge amber	spéciale belge ambrée	spéciale belge amber
	Brouwerij Haacht Boortmeerbeek	Brouwerij Haacht Boortmeerbeek	Brouwerij Haacht Boortmeerbeek
	barley malt, wheat malt, corn, sugar, hops, herbs, water	malt d'orge, malt de froment, maïs, sucre, houblon, herbes, eau	gerstemout, tarwemo mais, suiker, hop, kru water
	5%	5%	5%
	amber to copper-coloured	ambrée à couleur cuivre	amber tot koperkleur
	Pour carefully into a rinsed, wet Speciale glass, avoiding contact between bottle and foam.	Verser prudemment dans un verre Speciale rincé et mouillé sans que la bouteille touche l'écume.	Voorzichtig uitschenk een gespoeld, nat Spec glas zonder dat de fles schuim raakt.
	37 °F	3 °C	3 °C
	Typical Belgian Speciale with a spicy touch, a pronounced hoppy bitterness and a fairly dry aftertaste.	Spéciale belge typique avec une touche relevée, une amertume houblonnée prononcée et une fin de bouche plutôt sèche.	Typische spéciale belg een kruidige toets, een gesproken hopbitterhe een eerder droge afdrc
	–	–	–

Speciale
1900
Speciale
1900
Speciale
1900

Spéciale Noël

	top-fermentation re-fermented in the bottle	fermentation haute refermentation en bouteille	hoge gisting hergisting in de fles
	winter beer	bière hivernale	winterbier
	Brasserie La Binchoise Binche	Brasserie La Binchoise Binche	Brasserie La Binchoise Binche
	–	–	–
	9%	9%	9%
	amber clear	ambrée brillante	amber helder
	–	–	–
	Chilled.	Très frais.	Zeer fris.
	Very aromatic with a complex taste and fine bitterness. Sipping beer, suitable as an aperitif.	Très aromatique avec un goût complexe et une amertume fine. Bière de dégustation qui se boit également comme apéritif.	Zeer aromatisch met complexe smaak en fijne bitterheid. Degustatiebier dat ook als aperitief geschikt is.
	–	–	–

LA BINCHOISE
SINCE 1987
LA BINCHOISE
BIÈRE BELGE
REFERMENTÉE EN BOUTEILLE
ARTISANALE
9% vol. alc.

Speciale Op-ale

	top-fermentation	fermentation haute	hoge gisting
	amber	ambrée	amber
	Brouwerij Affligem Opwijk	Brouwerij Affligem Opwijk	Brouwerij Affligem Opwijk
	barley malt, yeast, water	malt d'orge, levure, eau	gerstemout, gist, water
%	5%	5%	5%
	copper colour fine foam head	couleur cuivre faux col fin	koperkleur fijne schuimkraag
	–	–	–
	45 °F	7 °C	7 °C
	Spicy, hoppy and slightly fruity with a dry aftertaste.	Corsé, houblonné et légèrement fruité avec une fin de bouche sèche.	Pittig, hoppig en licht fruitig met droge afdronk.
	Produced for the local market.	Destinée au marché local.	Bestemd voor de lokale markt.

BIER · BIERE
BIRRA
SPECIALE
OP-ALE
1832
Speciale
Op-Ale

Spelziale

	top-fermentation	fermentation haute	hoge gisting
	Ale	ale	ale
	Brasserie Artisanale Millevertus Toernich	Brasserie Artisanale Millevertus Toernich	Brasserie Artisanale Millevertus Toernich
	different malt, hop and yeast varieties, water	différentes sortes de malt, de houblon et de levure, eau	verschillende mout-, h[illegible] en gistsoorten, water
	4,50%	4,50%	4,50%
	blond	blonde	blond
	–	–	–
	39 °F	4 °C	4 °C
	Light but round spelt beer with austere bitterness and hop flavours.	Bière d'épeautre légère mais ronde avec une amertume sobre et des arômes houblonnés.	Licht maar rond spelt[illegible] met sobere bitterheid [illegible] hoparoma's.
	–	–	–

Brasserie Artisanale
MMMH!!
MILLEVERTUS

St. Arnoldus Tripel

	top-fermentation	fermentation haute	hoge gisting
	Tripel	triple	tripel
	Brouwerij Liefmans Oudenaarde/Dentergem	Brouwerij Liefmans Audenarde/Dentergem	Brouwerij Liefmans Oudenaarde/Denterge
	barley malt, sugar, corn, hops, yeast, water	malt d'orge, sucre, maïs, houblon, levure, eau	gerstemout, suiker, ma hop, gist, water
%	7,50%	7,50%	7,50%
	golden yellow clear	jaune doré claire	goudgeel helder
	–	–	–
°C	46 - 50 °F	8 - 10 °C	8 - 10 °C
	Malty character. Slightly nut-like with a dry aftertaste.	Caractère malté. Touches légères de noix et fin de bouche ronde, sèche.	Moutig karakter. Licht nootachtig met a ronde droge afdronk.
i	In Belgium the beer is sold under the name of Flanders Abbey, because the name of Sint-Arnoldus is already patented by another brewery.	En Belgique, cette bière est vendue sous le nom de Flanders Abbey, parce que le nom Sint-Arnoldus est déjà breveté par une autre brasserie.	In België wordt het bie kocht onder het etiket ders Abbey omdat de n Sint-Arnoldus gepaten is door een andere bro werij.

St. Arnoldus
TRIPLE
TRIPLE

St Benoit Blonde

	top-fermentation re-fermented in the bottle	fermentation haute refermentation en bouteille	hoge gisting met hergisting in de fle
	blond abbey beer	bière d'abbaye blonde	abdijbier blond
	Brasserie du Bocq Purnode-Yvoir	Brasserie du Bocq Purnode-Yvoir	Brasserie du Bocq Purnode-Yvoir
	barley malt, hop varieties, yeast, herbs, water	malt d'orge, sortes de houblon, levure, herbes, eau	gerstemout, hoppesoor gist, kruiden, water
%	6,30%	6,30%	6,30%
	Nice straw-yellow colour (10,5 EBC) with a fine, white foam head.	jolie couleur jaune paille (10,5 EBC) avec un faux col fin blanc	mooie strogele kleur (10,5 EBC) met fijne witte kraag
	Gently pour into a perfectly degreased glass. Leave the yeast sediment (due to natural refermenting) in the bottle.	Verser doucement dans un verre parfaitement dégraissé. Laisser le dépôt de levure (refermentation naturelle) dans la bouteille.	Zacht uitschenken in e perfect ontvet glas. Het gistbezinksel (natu lijke hergisting) in de f laten.
°C	41 - 54 °F	5 - 12 °C	5 - 12 °C
	Fruity flavour with a light hoppy aroma. Smooth, pleasant and fine beer, slightly bitter (22 EBU).	Arôme fruité avec un parfum légèrement houblonné. Bière douce, agréable et fine avec une légère amertume (22 EBU).	Fruitig aroma met een te hopgeur. Zacht bier, aangenaam fijn met een lichte bitt heid (22 EBU).
i	–	–	–

Bière d'Abbaye • Abdijbier
St Benoît
Blonde • Blond
Une tradition de brasseurs depuis 1858
Een brouwerstraditie sinds 1858

Bière d'Abbaye • Abdijbier
St Benoît

St Benoît Brune

	top-fermentation re-fermented in the bottle	fermentation haute refermentation en bouteille	hoge gisting hergisting in de fles
	dark abbey beer	bière d'abbaye foncée	abdijbier donker
	Brasserie du Bocq Purnode-Yvoir	Brasserie du Bocq Purnode-Yvoir	Brasserie du Bocq Purnode-Yvoir
	barley malt, wheat starch, hop varieties, yeast, herbs, water	malt d'orge, fécule de froment, sortes de houblon, levure, herbes, eau	gerstemout, tarwezet hoppesoorten, gist, kruiden, water
%	6,30%	6,30%	6,30%
	dark brown (70 EBC) clear fine, nice, solid foam head	brune foncée (70 EBC) claire faux col fin, joli, solide	donkerbruin (70 EBC) helder fijne, mooie, vaste kra
	Gently pour into a perfectly degreased glass. Leave the yeast sediment (due to natural re-fermenting) in the bottle.	Verser doucement dans un verre parfaitement dégraissé. Laisser le dépôt de levure (refermentation naturelle) dans la bouteille.	Zacht uitschenken in perfect ontvet glas. Het gistbezinksel (nat lijke hergisting) in de laten.
°C	46 - 54 °F	8 - 12 °C	8 - 12 °C
	Pleasant flavour of dark malt. Slightly fruity. Bitterness: 28 EBU.	Arôme agréable de malt foncé. Amertume 28 EBU. Légèrement fruité.	Aangenaam aroma va kere mout. Licht fruit Bitterheid 28 EBU.
i	–	–	–

Bière d'Abbaye • Abdijbier
St Benoît
BRUNE • BRUIN
Bière d'Abbaye • Abdijbier
St Benoît

St. Bernardus Abt 12

	top-fermentation re-fermented in the bottle	fermentation haute refermentation en bouteille	hoge gisting hergisting op de fles
	Belgian abbey beer	bière d'abbaye belge	Belgisch abdijbier
	Brouwerij St-Bernardus Watou	Brouwerij St-Bernardus Watou	Brouwerij St-Bernardus Watou
	Malt varieties, hops, sugar, yeast and 'historical' water (rain water fallen in Jeanne d'Arc's time, pumped in Watou)	sortes de malt, houblon, sucre, levure et eau 'historique' (pompée à Watou et provenant de la pluie de l'époque de Jeanne d'Arc)	moutsoorten, hop, suik[illegible] gist en 'historisch' wat[illegible] (opgepompt in Watou [illegible] komstig van de regenv[illegible] de tijd van Jeanne d'Ar[illegible]
%	10,50%	10,50%	10,50%
	dark ivory, unfiltered	ivoire foncé, non filtrée	donker ivoor, ongefilte[illegible]
	Pour into a glass, rinsed with cold water. Leave the glass upright and pour the beer carefully in a single, fluent movement. The yeast sediment can be left in the bottle and drunk separately.	Verser la bière prudemment et en un seul mouvement dans un verre rincé à l'eau froide et tenu en position verticale. Laisser le dépôt de levure (peut être bu séparément) dans la bouteille.	Het bier voorzichting i[illegible] 1 vloeiende beweging [illegible] schenken in een met k[illegible] water gespoeld glas da[illegible] rechtop staat. Het gist[illegible] (kan apart worden ged[illegible] ken) in de fles laten.
°C	43 - 50 °F	6 - 10 °C	6 - 10 °C
	Fruity aroma and smooth full-bodied taste.	Arôme fruité et goût doux et franc.	Fruitig aroma en zach[illegible] mondige smaak.
i	The name of the brewery refers to the shelter, erected in Watou in the 1900s, by the abbey community of Catsberg who had been elbowed out of France.	Le nom de la brasserie renvoie au refuge établi à Watou au début du 20ième siècle par la communauté abbatiale de Catsberg refoulée de France.	De naam van de brouwe[illegible] verwijst naar de refuge [illegible] gin 20e eeuw in Watou [illegible] opgericht door de abdij[illegible] meenschap van Catsber[illegible] in Frankrijk werd verdr[illegible]

St. Bernardus
Abt 12
Abdijbier
St. Bernardus
Abt 12
St. Bernardus

St. Bernardus Christmas Ale

	top-fermentation re-fermented in the bottle	fermentation haute refermentation en bouteille	hoge gisting hergisting op de fles
	dark Christmas beer	bière de Noël foncée	donker kerstbier
	Brouwerij St-Bernardus Watou	Brouwerij St-Bernardus Watou	Brouwerij St-Bernardu Watou
	malt varieties, hops, sugar, yeast and historical' water (rain water fallen in Jeanne d'Arc's time, pumped in Watou)	sortes de malt, houblon, sucre, levure et eau 'historique' (pompée à Watou et provenant de la pluie de l'époque de Jeanne d'Arc)	moutsoorten, hop, su gist en 'historisch' wa (opgepompt in Watou komstig van de regen de tijd van Jeanne d'A
	10%	10%	10%
	deep brown	brun foncé	diepbruin
	Empty in a glass rinsed with cold water. Leave the glass upright and pour the beer carefully in one single movement. Leave the yeast sediment in the bottle or serve it separately.	Verser la bière prudemment et en un seul mouvement dans un verre rincé à l'eau froide et tenu verticalement. Laisser le dépôt de levure (peut être bu séparément) dans la bouteille.	Het bier voorzichting 1 vloeiende beweging schenken in een met water gespoeld glas d rechtop staat. Het gis (kan apart worden ge ken) in de fles laten.
	43 - 50 °F	6 - 10 °C	6 - 10 °C
	Malty, fruity, full taste, with an aftertaste that is more sweet than bitter.	Houblonné-fruité, saveur pleine, fin de bouche plutôt douce qu'amère.	Moutfruitig, volle sm eerder zoete dan bitte dronk.
	The name of the brewery refers to the shelter, erected in Watou in the 1900s, by the abbey community of Catsberg.	Le nom de la brasserie renvoie au refuge établi à Watou au début du 20ième siècle par la communauté abbatiale de Catsberg.	De naam van de brouw verwijst naar de refuge gin 20e eeuw in Watou opgericht door de abdij meenschap van Catsbe

Christmas Ale
St. Bernardus
Christmas Ale
BELGIAN
St. Bernardus

St. Bernardus Pater 6

	top-fermentation re-fermented in the bottle	fermentation haute refermentation en bouteille	hoge gisting hergisting op de fles
	Belgian abbey beer	bière d'abbaye belge	Belgisch abdijbier
	Brouwerij St-Bernardus Watou	Brouwerij St-Bernardus Watou	Brouwerij St-Bernardu Watou
	malt varieties, hops, sugar, yeast and 'historical' water (rain fallen in Jeanne d'Arc's time, pumped in Watou)	sortes de malt, houblon, sucre, levure et eau 'historique' (pompée à Watou, provenant de la pluie de l'époque de Jeanne d'Arc)	moutsoorten, hop, sui gist en 'historisch' wa (opgepompt in Watou komstig van de regen de tijd van Jeanne d'A
%	6,70%	6,70%	6,70%
	chestnut	marron	kastanjekleur
	Pour into a glass, rinsed with cold water. Leave the glass upright and pour the beer carefully in a single, fluent movement. The yeast sediment can be left in the bottle or drunk separately.	Verser la bière prudemment et en un seul mouvement dans un verre rincé à l'eau froide et tenu en position verticale. Laisser le dépôt de levure (peut être bu séparément) dans la bouteille.	Het bier voorzichting 1 vloeiende beweging schenken in een met water gespoeld glas d rechtop staat. Het gist (kan apart worden ge ken) in de fles laten.
°C	43 - 50 °F	6 - 10 °C	6 - 10 °C
	Full taste.	Goût plein.	Volle smaak.
i	The name of the brewery refers to the shelter, erected in Watou in the 1900s, by the abbey community of Catsberg who had been elbowed out of France.	Le nom de la brasserie renvoie au refuge établi à Watou au début du 20ième siècle par la communauté abbatiale de Catsberg refoulée de France.	De naam van de brouw verwijst naar de refuge gin 20e eeuw in Watou opgericht door de abdij meenschap van Catsbe in Frankrijk werd verdr

St. Bernardus
Pater 6

Abdijbier
St. Bernardus

Pater 6

St. Bernardus Prior 8

	top-fermentation re-fermented in the bottle	fermentation haute refermentation en bouteille	hoge gisting hergisting op de fles
	Belgian abbey beer	bière d'abbaye belge	Belgisch abdijbier
	Brouwerij St-Bernardus Watou	Brouwerij St-Bernardus Watou	Brouwerij St-Bernardus Watou
	malt varieties, hops, sugar, yeast and 'historical' water (rain water fallen in Jeanne d'Arc's time, pumped in Watou)	sortes de malt, houblon, sucre, levure et eau 'historique' (pompée à Watou, provenant de la pluie de l'époque de Jeanne d'Arc)	moutsoorten, hop, sui gist en 'historisch' wat (opgepompt in Watou komstig van de regenv de tijd van Jeanne d'Ar
%	8%	8%	8%
	ruby purple,unfiltered, nice round foam head	violet rubis, non filtrée, joli faux col rond	robijnpaars, ongefilter mooie ronde schuimk
	Pour into a glass, rinsed with cold water. Leave the glass upright and pour the beer carefully. The yeast sediment can be drunk separately.	Verser la bière prudemment dans un verre rincé à l'eau froide et tenu en position verticale. Le dépôt de levure peut être bu séparément.	Het bier voorzichtig u schenken in een met k water gespoeld glas da rechtop staat. Het gist pot kan apart worden dronken.
°C	43 - 50 °F	6 - 10 °C	6 - 10 °C
	Malty, fruity, full taste and bittersweet aftertaste.	Goût de houblon fruité, plein et fin de bouche douce-amère.	Moutfruitige, volle sm en zoetbittere nasmaa
i	The name of the brewery refers to the shelter, erected in Watou in the 1900s, by the abbey community of Catsberg who had been elbowed out of France.	Le nom de la brasserie renvoie au refuge établi à Watou au début du 20ième siècle par la communauté abbatiale de Catsberg refoulée de France.	De naam van de brouwe verwijst naar de refuge gin 20e eeuw in Watou opgericht door de abdij meenschap van Catsber in Frankrijk werd verdr
	....		

St. Bernardus
Prior 8
Abdijbier
St. Bernardus
Prior 8
WATOU
St. Bernardus

St. Bernardus tripel

	top-fermentation re-fermented in the bottle	fermentation haute refermentation en bouteille	hoge gisting hergisting op de fles
	Belgian abbey beer	bière d'abbaye belge	Belgisch abdijbier
	Brouwerij St-Bernardus Watou	Brouwerij St-Bernardus Watou	Brouwerij St-Bernardu Watou
	malt varieties, hops, sugar, yeast and 'historical' water (rain water fallen in Jeanne d'Arc's time, pumped in Watou)	sortes de malt, houblon, sucre, levure et eau 'historique' (pompée à Watou, provenant de la pluie de l'époque de Jeanne d'Arc)	moutsoorten, hop, sui gist en 'historisch' wat (opgepompt in Watou komstig van de regenv de tijd van Jeanne d'Ar
%	8%	8%	8%
	amber/blonde, unfiltered thick, smooth foam head	ambrée/blonde, non filtrée faux col crémeux	amber/blond, ongefilt smeuïge schuimkraag
	Leave the glass upright and pour the beer carefully in a single movement. The sediment can be left in the bottle or drunk separately	Laisser le verre en position verticale et verser la bière prudemment. Laisser le dépôt (peut être bu séparément) dans la bouteille .	Het glas rechtop laten en het bier in voorzich uitschenken. Het gistd (kan apart worden uit dronken) in de fles lat
°C	39 - 46 °F	4 - 8 °C	4 - 8 °C
	flowery, fruity aroma, bittersweet balance, well-balanced aftertaste	Arôme fleuri et fruité, équilibre doux-amer, fin de bouche équilibrée.	Bloemig, fruitig arom zoetbitter evenwicht, balanceerde nasmaak.
i	The name of the brewery refers to the shelter, erected in Watou in the 1900s, by the abbey community of Catsberg.	Le nom de la brasserie renvoie au refuge établi à Watou au début du 20ième siècle par la communauté abbatiale de Catsberg.	De naam van de brouv rij verwijst naar de ref die begin 20e eeuw in tou werd opgericht do de abdijgemeenschap Catsberg.

St. Bernardus
Tripel
Abdijbier
St. Bernardus
Tripel

St. Bernardus witbier

top-fermentation re-fermented in the bottle	fermentation haute refermentation en bouteille	hoge gisting hergisting op de fles
Witbier	bière blanche	witbier
Brouwerij St-Bernardus Watou	Brouwerij St-Bernardus Watou	Brouwerij St-Bernardu Watou
malt, wheat, hops, yeast, water	malt, froment, houblon, levure, eau	mout, tarwe, hop, gist, water
5,50%	5,50%	5,50%
Clear yellow and slightly cloudy, produced by the wheat. Off-white foam head.	Couleur jaune clair, quelque peu trouble due au froment. Le faux col est blanc cassé.	Heldergele, ietwat tro kleur door de tarwe. De schuimkraag is geb ken wit.
Pour into a tall glass, rinsed with cold water. Leave the glass upright and pour the beer carefully in a single, fluent movement.	Verser dans un verre haut rincé à l'eau froide. Laisser le verre en position verticale et verser la bière prudemment en un seul mouvement fluide.	Uitschenken in een m koud water gespoeld h glas. Het glas rechtop l staan en het bier in 1 v ende beweging voorzic uitschenken.
36 - 43 °F	2 - 6 °C	2 - 6 °C
Light and refreshing.	Légère et rafraîchissante.	Licht en verfrissend.
Developed in collaboration with Pierre Celis, the father of the Hoegaarden Witbier and Celis White.	Développée en collaboration avec Pierre Celis, le 'père' de la bière blanche Hoegaarden et Celis White.	Ontwikkeld in samenv king met Pierre Celis, 'vader' van Hoegaarde witbier en Celis White

St. Bernardus
BIERE BLANCHE
WITBIER

St. Bernardus
WATOU

S

St Feuillien Blonde

	top-fermentation re-fermented in the bottle	fermentation haute refermentation en bouteille	hoge gisting hergisting in de fles
	recognised Belgian abbey beer	Bière d'abbaye belge reconnue	Erkend Belgisch abdijbi
	Brasserie Saint-Feuillien Le Roeulx	Brasserie Saint-Feuillien Le Roeulx	Brasserie Saint-Feuillier Le Roeulx
	barley malt, sugar, hops, yeast, vitamin C, brewing water	malt d'orge, sucre, houblon, levure, vitamine C, eau de brassage	gerstemout, suiker, hop gist, vitamine C, brouw water
	7,50%	7,50%	7,50%
	deep golden colour	doré intense	diepe goudkleur
	Dry goblet.	Verre ballon sec.	Droog ballonglas.
	43 °F or 54 °F	6 °C ou 12 °C	6 °C of 12 °C
	Digestive with a very perfumed aroma. Intense, distinctive bitterness and prominent malt flavour with a full mouthfeel. Dry and hoppy aftertaste.	Digestif, avec un arôme très parfumé. Amertume intense, très caractéristique et pleine. Le goût malté dominant laisse une impression pleine dans la bouche. Arrière-bouche sèche et houblonnée.	Digestief met zeer gepa meerd aroma. Intense, karakteristieke volle bi heid. De dominante mc smaak laat een volle in na in de mond. Droge en hoppige afdrc
	–	–	–

St Feuillien
anno 1125
BLONDE
BLOND
BIÈRE D'ABBAYE - ABDIJBIER
Bière
d'abbaye
St Feuillien
Abdijbier

St Feuillien Brune

	top-fermentation re-fermented in the bottle	fermentation haute refermentation en bouteille	hoge gisting hergisting in de fles
	recognised Belgian abbey beer	Bière d'abbaye belge reconnue	Erkend Belgisch abdijbi
	Brasserie Saint-Feuillien Le Roeulx	Brasserie Saint-Feuillien Le Roeulx	Brasserie Saint-Feuillier Le Roeulx
	barley malt, sugar, hops, yeast, vitamin C, brewing water	malt d'orge, sucre, houblon, levure, vitamine C, eau de brassage	gerstemout, suiker, hop gist, vitamine C, brouwwater
%	7,50%	7,50%	7,50%
	ruby-brown	brun rubis	robijnbruin
	Dry goblet.	Verre ballon sec.	Droog ballonglas.
°C	43 °F or 54 °F	6 °C ou 12 °C	6 °C of 12 °C
	Exceptional sensual palette with a hoppy taste and powerful flavour. Touches of fruit in harmony with the prominent liquorice and caramel.	Palette exceptionnellement sensorielle avec une saveur houblonnée et un arôme fort. Touches fruitées en harmonie avec la dominance de réglisse et de caramel.	Uitzonderlijk zintuiglij let met een hoppige sm en een krachtig aroma. Toetsen van fruit in ha nie met de dominantie zoethout en karamel.
i	–	–	–

StFeuillien
anno 1125
BRUNE
BRUIN
BIERE D'ABBAYE - ABDIJBIER
Bière d'abbaye
StFeuillien
Abdijbier

St Feuillien Cuvée de Noël

	top-fermentation re-fermented in the bottle	fermentation haute refermentation en bouteille	hoge gisting hergisting in de fles
	recognised Belgian abbey beer	Bière d'abbaye belge reconnue	Erkend Belgisch abdijbi
	Brasserie Saint-Feuillien Le Roeulx	Brasserie Saint-Feuillien Le Roeulx	Brasserie Saint-Feuillier Le Roeulx
	barley malt, sugar, hops, yeast, vitamin C, brewing water, roasted and caramelised malt	malt d'orge, sucre, houblon, levure, vitamine C, eau de brassage, malt brûlé et caramélisé	gerstemout, suiker, hop gist, vitamine C, brouw- water, gebrande en gekaramelliseerde mou
	9%	9%	9%
	Deep ruby-brown colour, brownish due to the roasted malt.	Couleur rubis profonde, brunâtre de malt brûlé.	Diep robijnrode, bruinachtige kleur van gebrande mout.
	Dry goblet.	Verre ballon sec.	Droog ballonglas.
	46 - 54 °F	8 - 12 °C	8 - 12 °C
	Round and smooth. Intense, perfumed aroma. Harmonious taste, with some bitterness in the background.	Rond et moelleux. Arôme intensément parfumé. Saveur harmonieuse avec une amertume à l'arrière-plan.	Rond en zacht. Intens geparfumeerd ar ma. Harmonieuze smaa waar de bitterheid op d achtergrond blijft.
	–	–	–

Cuvée de Noël
St Feuillien
Bière d'abbaye
Abdijbier
St Feuillien
Abdijbier

St Feuillien Triple

	top-fermentation re-fermented in the bottle	fermentation haute refermentation en bouteille	hoge gisting hergisting in de fles
	recognised Belgian abbey beer	Bière d'abbaye belge reconnue	Erkend Belgisch abdijb
	Brasserie Saint-Feuillien Le Roeulx	Brasserie Saint-Feuillien Le Roeulx	Brasserie Saint-Feuillie Le Roeulx
	barley malt, sugar, hops, yeast, vitamin C, brewing water	malt d'orge, sucre, houblon, levure, vitamine C, eau de brassage	gerstemout, suiker, hop gist, vitamine C, brouwwater
%	8,50%	8,50%	8,50%
	light amber	ambré clair	licht amber
	Dry goblet.	Ballon sec.	Droog ballonglas.
°C	43 °F or 54 °F	6 °C ou 12 °C	6 °C of 12 °C
	Sipping beer with a very perfumed and fruity aroma of hop, spices and yeast. Powerful taste, exceptional mouthfeel.	Bière de dégustation avec des arômes très parfumés et fruités de houblon, herbes et levure. Saveur forte et fin de bouche exceptionnelle.	Degustatiebier met zee geparfumeerd en fruit aroma van hop, kruide gist. Krachtige smaak e uitzonderlijke afdronk
i	–	–	–

St Feuillien
anno 1125
TRIPLE
TRIPEL
BIERE D'ABBAYE - ABDIJBIER
Bière d'abbaye
St Feuillien
Abdijbier

St-Idesbald Réserve Ten Duinen blond

	top-fermentation re-fermented in the bottle	fermentation haute refermentation en bou-teille	hoge gisting hergisting in de fles
	Belgian abbey beer blond	bière d'abbaye belge blonde	Belgisch abdijbier blond
	Brouwerij Huyghe Melle	Brouwerij Huyghe Melle	Brouwerij Huyghe Melle
	malt, hops, yeast, water	malt, houblon, levure, eau	mout, hop, gist, water
%	6,50%	6,50%	6,50%
	blond clear	blonde claire	blond helder
	Serve in a goblet.	Verser dans un verre calice.	Uitschenken in een ke glas.
°C	–	–	–
	Fairly light, malty and bitter. A thirst-quencher.	Assez léger, malté et amer. Désaltérant.	Tamelijk licht, moutig bitter. Dorstlessend.
i	Brewed following an ancient tradition based on a recipe of Saint Idesbald, the third abbot of the Duinen Abbey (ca. 1130).	Brassée selon une tradition séculaire d'après une recette de St-Idesbald, 3ième abbé de l'Abbaye des Dunes (vers 1130).	Gebrouwen volgens eeuwenoude traditie r een recept van St-Idesb 3e abt van de Duinena (ca 1130).

St Idesbald
BLOND
ABBATIA DE DUNIS
KOKSIJDE ANNO 1138
St-IDESBALD

St-Idesbald Réserve Ten Duinen dubbel

	top-fermentation re-fermented in the bottle	fermentation haute refermentation en bouteille	hoge gisting hergisting in de fles
	Belgian abbey beer dubbel	bière d'abbaye belge double	Belgisch abdijbier dubbel
	Brouwerij Huyghe Melle	Brouwerij Huyghe Melle	Brouwerij Huyghe Melle
	malt, hops, yeast, water	malt, houblon, levure, eau	mout, hop, gist, water
%	8%	8%	8%
	brown	brune	bruin
	Serve in a goblet.	Verser dans un verre calice.	Uitschenken in een ke[illegible] glas.
°C	–	–	–
	Character and taste are similar to Flemish oudbruin with a discrete, pleasant sourness. Bitter caramel and fine bitterness.	Caractère et goût semblables aux vieilles brunes flamandes, avec une acidulité discrète et agréable. Caramel amer et amertume fine.	Neigt qua karakter en smaak naar Vlaams ou[illegible] bruin met discrete aa[illegible] name zurigheid. Bittere karamel en fijn[illegible] terheid.
i	Brewed following an ancient tradition based on a recipe of Saint Idesbald, the third abbot of the Duinen Abbey (ca. 1130).	Brassée selon une tradition séculaire d'après une recette de St-Idesbald, 3ième abbé de l'Abbaye des Dunes (vers 1130).	Gebrouwen volgens eeuwenoude traditie n[illegible] een recept van St-Ides[illegible] 3e abt van de Duinen[illegible] (ca 1130).

DUBBEL
ABBATIA DE DUNIS
KOKSIJDE ANNO
St-IDESBALD
Abdijbier
Bière d'abbaye

St Idesbald
Abdij
Abbaye

St-Idesbald Réserve Ten Duinen tripel

	top-fermentation re-fermented in the bottle	fermentation haute refermentation en bouteille	hoge gisting hergisting in de fles
	Belgian abbey beer Tripel	bière d'abbaye belge triple	Belgisch abdijbier tripel
	Brouwerij Huyghe Melle	Brouwerij Huyghe Melle	Brouwerij Huyghe Melle
	malt, hops, yeast, water	malt, houblon, levure, eau	mout, hop, gist, water
	9%	9%	9%
	blond cloudy	blonde trouble	blond troebel
	Serve in a goblet.	Verser dans un verre calice.	Uitschenken in een kelkglas.
	–	–	–
	Velvety soft with a light bitterness.	Velouté avec une amertume légère.	Fluweelzacht met lich bitterheid.
	Brewed following an ancient tradition based on a recipe of Saint Idesbald, the third abbot of the Duinen Abbey (ca. 1130).	Brassée selon une tradition séculaire d'après une recette de St-Idesbald, 3ième abbé de l'Abbaye des Dunes (vers 1130).	Gebrouwen volgens eeuwenoude traditie n een recept van St-Idesb 3e abt van de Duinena (ca 1130).

TRIPLE
ABBATIA DE DUNIS
KOKSIJDE ANNO 1138
St-IDESBALD
Réserve TEN DUINEN
Belgisch Abdijbier
Bière d'abbaye belg
St Idesbald
Abdij
Abbaye

St. Paul blond

	top-fermentation re-fermented in the bottle	fermentation haute refermentation en bouteille	hoge gisting hergisting in de fles
	blond abbey beer	bière d'abbaye blonde	blond abdijbier
	Collega-brouwers for Brouwerij Sterkens Meer	Collega-brouwers pour Brouwerij Sterkens Meer	Collega-brouwers voor Brouwerij Sterker Meer
	malt, hops, yeast, water	malt, houblon, levure, eau	mout, hop, gist, water
	5,30%	5,30%	5,30%
	light blond unfiltered, cloudy	blond clair non filtrée, trouble	lichtblond ongefilterd, troebel
	Pour carefully with a generous foam head.	Verser prudemment avec un faux col large.	Voorzichtig uitschenk met ruime schuimkra
	43 - 50 °F	6 - 10 °C	6 - 10 °C
	Fairly high saturation. Mild and soft. Flavours of coriander, lime and green apple. Refreshing taste with a dry aftertaste.	Saturation assez haute, moelleuse et douce. Arômes de coriandre, de citron vert et de pomme verte. Saveur rafraîchissante avec une fin de bouche sèche.	Vrij hoog gesatureerd, en zacht. Aroma's van riander, limoen en gro appel. Verfrissende sm met droge afdronk.
	More than 90 % is destined for export. Since 4 years, production and bottling have been done done (temporarily) at Du Bocq and elsewhere.	Plus de 90% est destiné à l'exportation. La production et la mise en bouteilles sont réalisées (provisoirement) depuis 4 ans chez Du Bocq et d'autres brasseries.	Meer dan 90% is beste voor export. Productie bottelen gebeurt sinds viertal jaar (voorlopig) Du Bocq en andere bro werijen.

St. Paul
St. Paul
BLOND
Abbey Ale • Abdijbier • Klosterbier
Bière Spéciale • Cerveza Especial
e33cl.
PRODUCT OF BELGIUM

St. Paul

St. Paul double

	top-fermentation re-fermented in the bottle	fermentation haute refermentation en bouteille	hoge gisting hergisting in de fles
	dubbel abbey beer	bière d'abbaye double	dubbel abdijbier
	Collega-brouwers for Brouwerij Sterkens Meer	Collega-brouwers pour Brouwerij Sterkens Meer	Collega-brouwers voor Brouwerij Sterker Meer
	malt, hops, yeast, water	malt, houblon, levure, eau	mout, hop, gist, water
%	6,90%	6,90%	6,90%
	brown, filtered	brune, filtrée	bruin, gefilterd
	Pour carefully with a generous foam head.	Verser prudemment avec un faux col large.	Voorzichtig uitschenk met ruime schuimkra
°C	43 - 50 °F	6 - 10 °C	6 - 10 °C
	Sweet and bitter. Caramel malt perfume with light fruit aromas. Hops and herbs touches. Full malt taste. Touches of chocolate, nuts, fruit and wood.	Doux et amer. Parfum de malt caramélisé avec des arômes fruités légers. Touches de houblon et d'herbes. Goût malté plein, touches de chocolat, de noix, de fruits et de bois.	Zoet en bitter. Parfum karamelmout met lich fruitaroma's. Toetsen hop en kruiden. Volle smaak, toetsen van ch de, noten, fruit en ho
i	More than 90 % is destined for export. Since 4 years, production and bottling have been done (temporarily) at Du Bocq and elsewhere.	Plus de 90% est destiné à l'exportation. La production et la mise en bouteilles sont réalisées (provisoirement) depuis 4 ans chez Du Bocq et d'autres brasseries.	Meer dan 90% is beste voor export. Productie bottelen gebeurt sinds viertal jaar (voorlopig) Du Bocq en andere.

St. Paul
St. Paul
DOUBLE
Abbey Ale • Abdijbier • Klosterbier
Bière Spéciale • Cerveza Especial
e33cl.
PRODUCT OF BELGIUM

St. Paul

St. Paul speciale

	top-fermentation re-fermented in the bottle	fermentation haute refermentation en bouteille	hoge gisting hergisting in de fles
	amber abbey beer	bière d'abbaye ambrée	amber abdijbier
	Collega-brouwers for Brouwerij Sterkens Meer	Collega-brouwers pour Brouwerij Sterkens Meer	Collega-brouwers voor Brouwerij Sterke Meer
	malt, hops, yeast, water	malt, houblon, levure, eau	mout, hop, gist, water
%	5,50%	5,50%	5,50%
	amber-coloured, filtered	couleur ambrée, filtrée	amberkleurig, gefilter
	Pour carefully with a generous foam head.	Verser prudemment avec un faux col large.	Voorzichtig uitschenk met ruime schuimkra
°C	43 - 50 °F	6 - 10 °C	6 - 10 °C
	–	–	–
i	More than 90 % is destined for export. Since 4 years, production and bottling have been done (temporarily) at Du Bocq and elsewhere.	Plus de 90% est destiné à l'exportation. La production et la mise en bouteilles sont réalisées (provisoirement) depuis 4 ans chez Du Bocq et d'autres brasseries.	Meer dan 90% is beste voor export. Productie en bottelen beurt sinds een vierta (voorlopig) bij Du Boc andere brouwerijen.

St. Paul
St. Paul
SPECIALE
Abbey Ale • Abdijbier • Klosterbier
Bière Spéciale • Cerveza Especial
e33cl.
PRODUCT OF BELGIUM
St. Paul

St. Paul tripel

	top-fermentation re-fermented in the bottle	fermentation haute refermentation en bouteille	hoge gisting hergisting in de fles
	Tripel abbey beer	bière d'abbaye triple	tripel abdijbier
	Collega-brouwers for Brouwerij Sterkens Meer	Collega-brouwers pour Brouwerij Sterkens Meer	Collega-brouwers voor Brouwerij Sterker Meer
	malt, hops, yeast, water	malt, houblon, levure, eau	mout, hop, gist, water
%	7,60%	7,60%	7,60%
	light blonde, filtered	blond clair, filtrée	lichtblond, gefilterd
	Pour carefully with a generous foam head.	Verser prudemment avec faux col large.	Voorzichtig uitschenke een ruime schuimkraa
°C	43 - 50 °F	6 - 10 °C	6 - 10 °C
	Refreshing, very drinkable Tripel. Aroma of flowers, malt, herbs and citrus. Full malty, creamy taste.	Triple rafraîchissante qui se boit facilement. Arômes de fleurs, de malt, d'herbes et d'agrumes. Goût houblonné plein, crémeux.	Verfrissende tripel die gemakkelijk laat drink Aroma's van bloemen, mout, kruiden en citr Volmoutige, romige sr
i	More than 90 % is destined for export. Since 4 years, production and bottling have been done (temporarily) at Du Bocq and elsewhere.	Plus de 90% est destiné à l'exportation. La production et la mise en bouteilles sont réalisées (provisoirement) depuis 4 ans chez Du Bocq et d'autres brasseries.	Meer dan 90% is beste voor export. Productie bottelen gebeurt sinds viertal jaar (voorlopig) Du Bocq en andere bro werijen.

St. Paul
St. Paul
TRIPLE
Abbey Ale • Abdijbier • Klosterbier
Bière Spéciale • Cerveza Especial
e33cl.
PRODUCT OF BELGIUM

St. Paul

St. Sebastiaan dark

	top-fermentation re-fermented in the bottle	fermentation haute refermentation en bouteille	hoge gisting hergisting in de fles
	dubbel abbey beer	bière d'abbaye double	dubbel abdijbier
	Collega-brouwers for Brouwerij Sterkens Meer	Collega-brouwers pour Brouwerij Sterkens Meer	Collega-brouwers voor Brouwerij Sterken Meer
	malt, hops, yeast, water	malt, houblon, levure, eau	mout, hop, gist, water
%	6,90%	6,90%	6,90%
	dark brown, filtered	brun foncé, filtrée	donkerbruin, gefilterd
	Pour carefully with a generous foam head.	Verser prudemment avec un faux col large.	Voorzichtig uitschenke met ruime schuimkraa
°C	43 - 50 °F	6 - 10 °C	6 - 10 °C
	Well-balanced and very drinkable. Aroma of caramel and nuts. Light bitter nose. Taste of caramel, chocolate and dark malt.	Bien équilibré, se boit facilement. Arômes de caramel et de noix, parfum légèrement amer. Goût de caramel, chocolat et malt foncé.	Goed gebalanceerd, laa zich makkelijk drinker Aroma van karamel en noten, lichtbittere neu Smaak van karamel, cl lade en donkere mout.
i	More than 90 % is destined for export. Since 4 years, production and bottling have been done (temporarily) at Du Bocq and elsewhere.	Plus de 90% est destiné à l'exportation. La production et la mise en bouteilles sont réalisées (provisoirement) depuis 4 ans chez Du Bocq et d'autres brasseries.	Meer dan 90% is bestem voor export. Productie bottelen gebeurt sinds viertal jaar (voorlopig) Du Bocq en andere bro werijen.

ST. SEBASTIAAN
ST. SEBASTIAAN
DARK

St. Sebastiaan Grand Cru

	top-fermentation re-fermented in the bottle	fermentation haute refermentation en bouteille	hoge gisting hergisting in de fles
	strong blond, abbey beer	blonde forte, bière d'abbaye	sterk blond, abdijbier
	Collega-brouwers for Brouwerij Sterkens Meer	Collega-brouwers pour Brouwerij Sterkens Meer	Collega-brouwers voor Brouwerij Sterken Meer
	malt, hops, yeast, water	malt, houblon, levu- re, eau	mout, hop, gist, water
%	7,60%	7,60%	7,60%
	golden blond, filtered	blond doré, filtrée	goudblond, gefilterd
	Pour carefully with a generous foam head.	Verser prudemment avec un faux col large.	Voorzichtig uitschenke met ruime schuimkraa
°C	43 - 50 °F	6 - 10 °C	6 - 10 °C
	Heavy sipping beer. Sweet flavour with apricot and grapefruit touches. Softly malty but full-bodied with a touch of honey and sweet fruit.	Bière de dégustation forte. Arôme doux avec des touches d'abricot et de pamplemousse. Légèrement houblonné mais franc avec une touche de miel et de fruits doux.	Zwaar degustatiebier. Z aroma met toetsen van abrikoos en pompelmo Zachtmoutig maar toch mondig met een vleug ning en zoet fruit.
i	More than 90 % is destined for export. Since 4 years, production and bottling have been done (temporarily) at Du Bocq and elsewhere.	Plus de 90% est destiné à l'exportation. La production et la mise en bouteilles sont réalisées (provisoirement) depuis 4 ans chez Du Bocq et d'autres brasseries.	Meer dan 90% is bestem voor export. Productie e bottelen gebeurt sinds e viertal jaar (voorlopig) b Bocq en andere brouwe

ST. SEBASTIAAN
GRAND CRU
BR. STERKENS MEER - PRODUCT OF BELGIUM

ST. SEBASTIAAN

Steenbrugge Dubbel bruin

	top-fermentation re-fermented in the bottle	fermentation haute refermentation en bouteille	hoge gisting hergisting op de fles
	Dubbel abbey beer	bière d'abbaye double	dubbel abdijbier
	Palm Breweries Steenhuffel	Palm Breweries Steenhuffel	Palm Breweries Steenhuffel
	–	–	–
%	6,5 %	6,5%	6,5 %
	ruby	rubis	robijnkleur
	Leave 1 cm of yeast sediment in the bottle.	Laisser 1 cm de dépôt de levure dans la bouteille.	1 cm gistdepot in de fl laten.
°C	46 - 54 °F	8 - 12 °C	8 - 12 °C
	Frank, full taste. Malty.	Saveur franche, pleine. Malté.	Rondborstige, volle sm Moutig.
i	The founder of the abbey of Steenbrugge, Saint Arnoldus, is the patron saint of the brewers.	Le fondateur de l'abbaye de Steenbrugge, le Saint Arnould, est le patron des brasseurs.	De stichter van de abd van Steenbrugge, de h Arnoldus, is de patroo lige van de brouwers.

Steenbrugge
dubbel
bruin

Steenbrugge

Steenbrugge Tripel blond

	top-fermentation re-fermented in the bottle	fermentation haute refermentation en bouteille	hoge gisting hergisting op de fles
	blond abbey beer	bière d'abbaye blonde	blond abdijbier
	Palm Breweries Steenhuffel	Palm Breweries Steenhuffel	Palm Breweries Steenhuffel
	–	–	–
	8,5 %	8,5%	8,5 %
	golden blond	blond doré	goudblond
	Leave 1 cm of yeast sediment in the bottle.	Laisser 1 cm de dépôt de levure dans la bouteille.	1 cm gistdepot in de fl[illegible] laten.
	–	–	–
	Spicy flavour with a noble aftertaste.	Arôme relevé et fin de bouche noble.	Kruidig aroma en nob[illegible] afdronk.
	–	–	–

tripel
blond
Steenbrugge
tripel
blond
Steenbrugge

Steendonk Brabants Witbier

	top-fermentation	fermentation haute	hoge gisting
	Witbier	bière blanche	witbier
	Duvel Moortgat Corp. Puurs	Duvel Moortgat Corp. Puurs	Duvel Moortgat Corp. Puurs
	malted barley, unmalted wheat, coriander, curaçao, water	orge maltée, froment non malté, coriandre, curaçao, eau	gemoute gerst, ongemoute tarwe, koriander, curaçao, wa
%	4,50%	4,50%	4,50%
	cloudy	trouble	troebel
	Pour in a single movement into a cool glass, previously rinsed with pure, cold water. Let the foam run over the rim of the glass and skim off the excess foam and big bubbles with a spatula or knife (big carbon dioxide bubbles cause the foam head to disappear more quickly).	Verser d'un seul trait dans un verre rafraîchi rincé à l'avance à l'eau froide propre. Laisser déborder et enlever l'écume redondante ainsi que les grosses bulles avec une spatule ou un couteau (de grandes bulles de dioxyde de carbone font disparaître l'écume).	In 1 keer uitschenken een koel glas dat voora gespoeld is met koud, zuiver water. Laten overschuimen e het overtollige schuin en grove bellen met e spatel of mes van de r van het glas afhalen (grote koolzuurbellen het schuim verdwijne
°C	37 - 39 °F	3 - 4 °C	3 - 4 °C
	Flavour and aroma refined by the double fermentation process. Slightly hopped thirst-quencher.	La saveur et les arômes sont raffinés par la double fermentation. Désaltérant légèrement houblonné.	Smaak en aroma zijn fijnd door het procéde dubbele gisting. Licht gehopte dorstle
i	–	–	–

Steendonk
Brabants Witbier
Steendonk
Bière Blanche du Brabant
N.V. BROUWERIJ S.A. BRASSERIE STEENDONK
Steendonk

Stella Artois

	bottom-fermentation	fermentation basse	lage gisting
	Pilsner	pils	pilsbier
	Inbev Belgium Brewsite Stella Artois	Inbev Belgium Brewsite Stella Artois	Inbev Belgium Brewsite Stella Artois
	pale malt, corn, hops, yeast, water	malt pâle, maïs, houblon, levure, eau	bleekmout, maïs, hop, water
%	5,20%	5,20%	5,20%
	blond	blonde	blond
	Rinse the glass in cold water, tilt it and smoothly pour the beer. Skim off if desired.	Rincer le verre à l'eau froide, le tenir incliné et verser la bière doucement. Ecumer selon le goût.	Het glas onder koud w spoelen, schuin houde het bier zacht uitscher Desgewenst afschuime
	37 °F	3 °C	3 °C
	The character of Czech hop and a vague impression of recently mowed hay. Fresh, full taste with a fine bitterness.	Caractère de houblon tchèque et vague impression de foin coupé. Goût frais, plein avec une amertume fine.	Karakter van Tsjechisc hop en vage impressie pas gemaaid hooi. Frisse, volle smaak met fijne bitterheid.
i	–	–	–

STELLA
ARTOIS
PREMIUM LAGER BEER
ANNO 1366
STELLA
ARTOIS
LEUVEN
BELGIUM'S ORIGINAL BEER

ANNO 1366
STELLA
ARTOIS

Stille Nacht

	top-fermentation re-fermented in the bottle unfiltered or centrifuged	fermentation haute refermentation en bouteille non filtrée, ni centrifugée	hoge gisting nagisting op de fles, niet gefilterd of gecentr fugeerd
	specialty beer winter beer	bière spéciale bière hivernale	speciaalbier winterbier
	De Dolle Brouwers Diksmuide	De Dolle Brouwers Dixmude	De Dolle Brouwers Diksmuide
	pale malt, white candy sugar, Golding hops	malt pâle, sucre candi blanc, houblon Golding	bleke mout, witte kandi suiker, Golding hop
%	12%	12%	12%
	amber	ambrée	amber
	Serve in an Oerbeer glass or wine glass.	Servir dans un verre oer-bier ou un verre de vin.	Serveren in een oerbier of wijnglas.
°C	50 - 54 °F	10 - 12 °C	10 - 12 °C
	Flavour of alcohol, malt and hops. Smooth and strong.	Arôme d'alcool, de malt et de houblon. Doux et fort.	Aroma van alcohol, mo en hop. Zacht en straf.
i	Can be kept for 20 years or longer.	Se conserve jusqu'à 20 ans et plus.	Houdbaar tot 20 jaar en meer.

BREWED &
ANNO 1980
oerbier
NAT EN
HOGE GISTING MET NAGISTING IN DE FLES
MET WATER, MOUT, KANDIJ, HOP EN GIST.
NON PASTEURIZED - WITH TASTE EVOLUTION
NON PASTEURISEE - AU GOUT EVOLUTIF

Stout Leroy

	bottom-fermentation	fermentation basse	lage gisting
	sweet Stout	stout douce	zoete stout
	Brouwerij Leroy Boezinge	Brouwerij Leroy Boezinge	Brouwerij Leroy Boezinge
	malt, rice, hops, caramel, water	malt, riz, houblon, caramel, eau	mout, rijst, hop, karame water
%	5%	5%	5%
	dark brown	brun foncé	donkerbruin
	Pour slowly in a single, smooth movement, into a degreased glass. Keep the glass tilted to avoid sloshing. Skim off the foam.	Verser lentement en un seul mouvement fluide dans un verre dégraissé tenu en oblique. Ne pas laisser la bière clapoter. Ecumer le verre.	Traag en in 1 vloeiende beweging uitschenken i een vetvrij glas dat word schuingehouden. Het bi niet laten klotsen. Het glas afschuimen.
°C	41 - 43 °F	5 - 6 °C	5 - 6 °C
	Sweet session beer. Sweet toffee taste with a hint of liquorice.	Bière douce facilement buvable. Goût de caramel doux avec une touche de réglisse.	Zoet doordrinkbier. Zoete toffeesmaak met hint van zoethout.
i	During storage, the beer goes through an evolution similar to wine, developing a nut-like flavour.	Pendant la conservation, la bière 'vinifie' et développe un goût de noix.	Tijdens het bewaren 've wijnt' het bier en ontwi kelt het een notensmaa

stout
LIB
stout
LEROY

Stout
Leroy

Stoute Bie

top-fermentation	fermentation haute	hoge gisting
sweet Stout	stout douce	zoete stout
Brouwerij De Bie Loker	Brouwerij De Bie Loker	Brouwerij De Bie Loker
–	–	–
5,50%	5,50%	5,50%
–	–	–
–	–	–
–	–	–
–	–	–
–	–	–

Stoute Bie
Brouwerij De Bie
B-8958 Loker
Tel.: 0475 23 47 95
www.brijdebie.be
D.B

Stouterik
The Brussels stout

	top-fermentation re-fermented in the bottle	fermentation haute refermentation en bouteille	hoge gisting hergisting op de fles
	Stout	stout	stout
	at De Ranke Brasserie de la Senne Brussel	chez De Ranke Brasserie de la Senne Bruxelles	bij De Ranke Brasserie de la Senne Brussel
	malt, barley, hops, yeast, water	malt, orge, houblon, levure, eau	mout, gerst, hop, gist, w ter
	4,50%	4,50%	4,50%
	dark black unfiltered	noire non filtrée	donker zwart ongefilterd
	Serve in the corresponding glass.	Verser dans le verre approprié.	Uitschenken in het bij sende glas.
	41 °F	5 °C	5 °C
	Bitter, strong beer with a touch of coffee.	Une bière forte, amère avec une touche de café.	Een bitter, sterk bier m een vleugje koffie.
	–	–	–

STOUTERIK
THE BRUSSELS STOUT
BRASSERIE DE LA SENNE

Strubbe pils

	bottom-fermentation	fermentation basse	lage gisting
	Pilsner	pils	pilsbier
	Brouwerij Strubbe Ichtegem	Brouwerij Strubbe Ichtegem	Brouwerij Strubbe Ichtegem
	Pilsner malt, corn, sugar, hops, water	malt de pils, maïs, sucre, houblon, eau	pilsmout, mais, suiker, water
%	5,20%	5,20%	5,20%
	blond clear (filtered)	blonde claire (filtrée)	blond helder (gefilterd)
	–	–	–
	39 °F	4 °C	4 °C
	Malty, pure, slightly bitter, thirst-quenching.	Malté, pur, légèrement amer, désaltérant.	Moutig, zuiver, lichtbit dorstlessend.
	–	–	–

STRUBBE
5 VOL. %
BROUWERIJ STRUBBE
8480 ICHTEGEM
BELGIUMS FINEST PILS BEER
Best before: see cap
Ingr.: water, malt, sugars, hops and yeast
STRUBBE
Ichtegem

Struise Rosse

	top-fermentation unpasteurised	fermentation haute non pasteurisée	hoge gisting niet gepasteuriseerd
	Belgian Pale Ale	Belgian Pale Ale	Belgian pale ale
	at Brouwerij Deca De Struise Brouwers De Panne	chez Brouwerij Deca De Struise Brouwers La Panne	bij Brouwerij Deca De Struise Brouwers De Panne
	Pilsner malt, Vienna malt, Munich malt, cara Munich, corn flocks, yeast, water. Hops: Brewers gold, Challenger. Herbs: sweet orange rind, coriander, cloves.	malt de pils, malt vienna, malt Munich, cara Munich, flocons de maïs, levure, eau. Houblon: Brewers gold, Challenger. Herbes: écorce d'orange doux, coriandre, girofle.	Pilsmout, viennamout, nichmout, caramunich, maisvlokken, gist, water Hop: Brewers gold, Chal ger. Kruiden: zoete sinaasschil, koriander, kruidnagel.
	5%	5%	5%
	amber (29 EBC) cloudy (unfiltered)	ambrée (29 EBC) trouble (non filtrée)	amber (29 EBC) troebel (ongefilterd)
	–	–	–
	–	–	–
	Pronounced nose of roasted nuts with a fine touch of brewer's yeast. Refreshing taste with a dry character, forest aroma. 20 IBU. The aftertaste is elegant and very well-balanced.	Parfum prononcé de noix grillées avec une touche légère de levure de bière. Saveur rafraîchissante avec un caractère sec, boisé. 20 IBU. La fin de bouche est élégante et très équilibrée.	Uitgesproken neus van roosterde noten met ee ne toets van biergist. Ve frissende smaak met ee droog, bosgeurig karakt 20 IBU. De afdronk is el gant en zeer gebalancee
	De Rosse is the result of a mistake made by the brewer... with positive consequences.	La Rosse est le résultat d'une erreur du brasseur; la suite a été une réussite.	De Rosse is het gevolg v een brouwersfoutje, gel kig met goede afloop.

AUTHENTIC
STRUISE
ROSSE
2007
by De Struise Brouwers for Vdaco bvba
DSB
Struisebrouwers.be

Struise Witte

	top-fermentation wild yeasts unpasteurised	fermentation haute levures sauvages non pasteurisée	hoge gisting wilde gisten niet gepasteuriseerd
	wheat beer	bière de froment	tarwebier
	at Brouwerij Deca De Struise Brouwers, De Panne	chez Brouwerij Deca De Struise Brouwers La Panne	bij Brouwerij Deca De Struise Brouwers, De Panne
	Pilsner malt, wheat malt, corn flocks, yeast, water. Hops: Bramling Cross, Hallertauer Mittelfrueh. Herbs: bitter orange rind, coriander.	Malt de pils et de froment, flocons de maïs, levure, eau. Houblon: Bramling Cross, Hallertauer Mittelfrueh. Herbes: écorce d'orange amer, coriandre.	Pilsmout, tarwemout, vlokken, gist, water. H Bramling Cross, Halle Mittelfrueh. Kruiden: bittere sinaa koriander.
%	5%	5%	5%
	yellow-gold (6EBC) unfiltered creamy foam head	jaune doré (6 EBC) non filtrée faux col crémeux	geelgoud (6 EBC) ongefilterd romige schuimkraag
	–	–	–
°C	–	–	–
	Nose: complex with flavours of fine malt, lemon rind, yeast and exotic herbs. Refreshing thirst-quencher. 15 IBU.	Parfum: complexe avec des arômes nobles de malt fin, écorce de citron, levure et herbes exotiques. Désaltérant rafraîchissant. 15 IBU.	Neus: complex met nc aroma's van fijne mou troenschil, gist en exo kruiden. Verfrissende lesser. 15 IBU.
i	–	–	–

AUTHENTIC
STRUISE
WITTE
WITBIER
VAN
ALTER
Vleteren by De Struise Brouwers for Vdaco bvba
DSB
Struisebrouwers.be

Sun Mortal

	top-fermentation re-fermented in the bottle	fermentation haute refermentation en bouteille	hoge gisting hergisting op de fles
	blond	blonde	blond
	Mortal's Beers Jamagne	Mortal's Beers Jamagne	Mortal's Beers Jamagne
	malt, sugar, hops, fruit, yeast, water	malt, sucre, houblon, fruits, levure, eau	mout, suiker, hop, frui[illegible] gist, water
%	5,60%	5,60%	5,60%
	golden yellow	jaune doré	goudgeel
	–	–	–
°C	39 - 43 °F	4 - 6 °C	4 - 6 °C
	Smooth, fruity with smooth hop flavours.	Moelleux, fruité avec des arômes de houblon doux.	Zacht, fruitig met zach[illegible] hoparoma's.
i	–	–	–

WWW.MORTALSBEERS.BE
Alc. 5,6 % vol.
WWW.MORTALSBEERS.BE
MORTALS BEERS

Super 64

	top-fermentation	fermentation haute	hoge gisting
	amber	ambrée	amber
	Brasserie de Silly Silly	Brasserie de Silly Silly	Brasserie de Silly Silly
	aromatic malt, sugar, yeast, Kent and Hallertau hops, water	malt aromatique, sucre, levure, houblon Kent et Hallertau, eau	aromatische mout, su gist, Kent en Hallerta water
%	5% 11,3° plato	5% 11,3° plato	5% 11,3° plato
	amber (8 EBC)	ambré (8 EBC)	amber (8 EBC)
	–	–	–
	39 - 48 °F	4 - 9 °C	4 - 9 °C
	Subtle malt and hop flavour and aroma, slightly bitter with grain and caramel touches.	Saveur et arômes subtiles de malt et de houblon, légèrement amers avec des touches de blé et de caramel.	Subtiele smaak en ar van mout en hop, lic ter met toetsen van g en karamel.
i	Provision beer.	Bière de conservation.	Bewaarbier.

Silly
ARTISANAL
BELGIAN
BEER
Brasserie de Silly Brouwerij
Super
64
25 cl. 250 ml
Alc.5,2vol.%

br.SILLY
Super
64

Super des fagnes blonde

	top-fermentation re-fermented in the bottle unpasteurised	fermentation haute refermentation en bouteille non pasteurisée	hoge gisting hergisting op de fles ongepasteuriseerd
	regional blond beer	bière régionale blonde	streekbier blond
	Brasserie des fagnes Mariembourg	Brasserie des fagnes Mariembourg	Brasserie des fagnes Mariembourg
	roasted malt, barley malt, yeast, hops (Germany), water	malt brûlé, malt d'orge, levure, houblon (Allemagne), eau	gebrande mout, gerstemout, gist, hop (Duitsland), water
%	7,50%	7,50%	7,50%
	Blond, gold-coloured.	blonde, dorée	blond, goudkleurig
	–	–	–
°C	43 - 50 °F	6 - 10 °C	6 - 10 °C
	Lively beer with a smooth and fruity taste. Fine coriander and liquorice flavour.	Bière vivante avec une saveur moelleuse et fruitée. Arômes fins de coriandre et de réglisse.	Levend bier met zacht fruitige smaak. Fijne aroma's van kor en zoethout.
i	Boutique beer.	Brassée de façon artisanale.	Ambachtelijk gebrou

Super des Fagnes
Super des Fagnes
Super des Fagnes

Super des fagnes brune

	top-fermentation re-fermented in the bottle unpasteurised	fermentation haute refermentation en bouteille non pasteurisée	hoge gisting hergisting op de fles ongepasteuriseerd
	regional beer	bière régionale	streekbier
	Brasserie des fagnes Mariembourg	Brasserie des fagnes Mariembourg	Brasserie des fagnes Mariembourg
	roasted malt, barley malt, yeast, hops (Germany), water	malt brûlé, malt d'orge, levure, houblon (Allemagne), eau	gebrande mout, gerstemout, gist, hop (Duitsland), water
%	7,50%	7,50%	7,50%
	brown, ruby red	brune, rouge rubis	bruin, robijnrood
	–	–	–
°C	43 - 50 °F	6 - 10 °C	6 - 10 °C
	–	–	–
i	Boutique beer.	Brassée de façon artisanale.	Ambachtelijk gebrouw

Super des Fagnes
Brune · Bruin
Super
des Fagnes

Super des fagnes Griottes

	top-fermentation	fermentation haute	hoge gisting
	fruit beer	bière fruitée	fruitbier
	Brasserie des fagnes Mariembourg	Brasserie des fagnes Mariembourg	Brasserie des fagnes Mariembourg
	roasted malt, barley malt, yeast, hops (Germany), aromatised with real cherries (7%), water.	malt brûlé, malt d'orge, levure, houblon (Allemagne), aromatisé avec de vraies cerises (7%), eau	gebrande mout, gerstemout, gist, hop (Duitsland), gearomatiseerd met ec krieken (7%), water
%	4,80%	4,80%	4,80%
	red	rouge	rood
	–	–	–
°C	39 - 46 °F	4 - 8 °C	4 - 8 °C
	Lively beer with taste evolution and cherry flavour.	Bière vivante et évolutive avec saveur de cerises.	Levendig en evolueren bier met kersensmaak.
i	Boutique beer.	Brassée de façon artisanale.	Ambachtelijk gebrouw

Super des Fagnes
Super des Fagnes
Griottes
Super des Fagnes

Taras Boulba extra hoppy ale

	top-fermentation	fermentation haute	hoge gisting
	Belgian Pale Ale - bitter Ale	Pale Ale belge - bitter ale	Belgische pale ale - bitter ale
	at De Ranke Brasserie de la Senne Brussel	chez De Ranke Brasserie de la Senne Bruxelles	bij De Ranke Brasserie de la Senne Brussel
	malt, hops, yeast, water	malt, houblon, levure, eau	mout, hop, gist, water
	4,25%	4,25%	4,25%
	clear blond	blond clair	helder blond
	Serve in the corresponding glass.	Verser dans le verre approprié.	Uitschenken in het bij[illegible] sende glas.
	41 °F	5 °C	5 °C
	Bitter and refreshing.	Amer et rafraîchissant.	Bitter en verfrissend.
	–	–	–

BRASSERIE DE LA SENNE – DE ZENNE BROUWERIJ
TARAS BOULBA
EXTRA HOPPY ALE
Smeirlap !

BRASSERIE DE LA SENNE

Ten Duinen - Réserve St Idesbald rousse

	top-fermentation re-fermented in the bottle	fermentation haute refermentation en bouteille	hoge gisting hergisting in de fles
	Belgian abbey beer rousse	bière d'abbaye belge rousse	Belgisch abdijbier rousse
	Brouwerij Huyghe Melle	Brouwerij Huyghe Melle	Brouwerij Huyghe Melle
	malt, hops, yeast, water	malt, houblon, levure, eau	mout, hop, gist, water
	7%	7%	7%
	red-brown	brun rouge	roodbruin
	Serve in a goblet.	Verser dans un verre calice.	Uitschenken in een ke glas.
	–	–	–
	–	–	–
	Brewed following an ancient tradition based on a recipe of Saint Idesbald, the third abbot of the Duinen Abbey (around 1130).	Brassée selon une tradition séculaire d'après une recette de St-Idesbald, 3ième abbé de l'Abbaye des Dunes (vers 1130).	Gebrouwen volgens eeuwenoude traditie n een recept van St-Idesb 3e abt van de Duinena (ca 1130).

ROUSSE
ABBATIA DE DUNIS
KOKSIJDE ANNO 1138
Ten DUINEN
Réserve St-Idesbald
Belgisch Abdijbier Bière d'abbaye belge

ABBATIA DE DUNIS
Ten DUINEN

Ter Dolen blond

	top-fermentation	fermentation haute	hoge gisting
	abbey beer blond	bière d'abbaye blonde	abdijbier blond
	Kasteelbrouwerij De Dool Houthalen-Helchteren	Kasteelbrouwerij De Dool Houthalen-Helchteren	Kasteelbrouwerij De Dc Houthalen-Helchteren
	2 malt varieties, 2 noble hop varieties, water	2 sortes de malt, 2 variétés précieuses de houblon, eau	2 moutsoorten, 2 edele soorten, water
%	6,10%	6,10%	6,10%
	clear blond	blond clair	helder blond
	Lift the bottle and pour in a single, smooth movement to obtain a nice foam head.	Verser de haut et en un seul mouvement fluide de façon à obtenir un beau faux col.	Hoog en vloeiend uitsc ken om een mooie sch kraag te bekomen.
°C	39 - 41 °F	4 - 5 °C	4 - 5 °C
	Velvety smooth with a full taste, suitable as a thirst-quencher. Refreshing with neutral taste and bittersweet touch.	Velouté avec une saveur pleine, également désaltérant. Rafraîchissant avec une saveur neutre et une touche douce-amère.	Fluweelzacht met volle smaak, ook gesch als dorstlesser. Verfrissend met neutra smaak en zoetbittere t
i	–	–	–

Ter Dolen
ABDIJBIER
www.terdolen.be
KASTEEL
BROUWERIJ
Ter Dolen
BLOND
Ter Dolen

Ter Dolen donker

	top-fermentation re-fermented in the bottle	fermentation haute refermentation en bouteille	hoge gisting nagisting op de fles
	abbey beer dark	bière d'abbaye foncée	abdijbier donker
	Kasteelbrouwerij De Dool Houthalen-Helchteren	Kasteelbrouwerij De Dool Houthalen-Helchteren	Kasteelbrouwerij De Do Houthalen-Helchteren
	3 malt varieties, 2 hop varieties, light and dark candy sugar, water	3 sortes de malt, 2 sortes de houblon, sucre candi clair et foncé, eau	3 moutsoorten, 2 hopsc ten, lichte en donkere k dijsuiker, water
%	7,10%	7,10%	7,10%
	clear dark	foncé clair	helder donker
	Lift the bottle and pour in a single, smooth movement to obtain a nice foam head.	Verser de haut et en un seul mouvement fluide de façon à obtenir un beau faux col.	Hoog en vloeiend uitsc ken om een mooie schu kraag te bekomen.
	41 - 50 °F	5 - 10 °C	5 - 10 °C
	Full and smooth taste, neutral fruity beer. Rich, powerful and well-balanced flavour.	Saveur pleine et douce, bière neutre fruitée. Arôme riche, corsé et équilibré.	Vol en zacht van smaak neutraal fruitig bier. Rijk, krachtig en evenw tig aroma.
i	–	–	–

Ter Dolen
ABDIJBIER
KASTEEL
BROUWERIJ
CASTLE BREWERY
CHATEAU BRASSERIE
Ter Dolen
DONKER
Hergist op fles

Ter Dolen

Ter Dolen kriek

	top-fermentation	fermentation haute	hoge gisting
	abbey beer Kriek	bière d'abbaye kriek	abdijbier kriek
	Kasteelbrouwerij De Dool Houthalen-Helchteren	Kasteelbrouwerij De Dool Houthalen-Helchteren	Kasteelbrouwerij De Dc Houthalen-Helchteren
	1 malt variety, wheat, 2 hop varieties, coriander, orange rind, fresh cherry juice, water	1 sorte de malt, froment, 2 sortes de houblon, coriandre, écorce d'orange, jus de cerises frais, eau	1 moutsoort, tarwe, 2 h soorten, koriander, sina appelschil, vers krieken sap, water
%	4,50%	4,50%	4,50%
	unfiltered red	rouge non filtrée	ongefilterd rood
	Lift the bottle and pour in a single, smooth movement to obtain a nice foam head.	Verser de haut et en un seul mouvement fluide de façon à obtenir un beau faux col.	Hoog en vloeiend uitsc ken om een mooie schu kraag te vormen.
°C	39 - 41 °F	4 - 5 °C	4 - 5 °C
	Sweet and deliciously refreshing. Fruit beer with citric acid touch that does not overpower the beer taste.	Doux et agréablement rafraîchissant. Bière fruitée avec une touche acidulée de citron ne reniant pas la saveur de bière.	Zoet en lekker verfrisse Fruitbier met citroenzu toets die de biersmaak verloochent.
i	The only kriek abbey beer in the world.	La seule bière d'abbaye kriek au monde.	Het enige kriek-abdijbi ter wereld.

Ter Dolen
ABDIJBIER
www.terdolen.be
KASTEEL
BROUWERIJ
CASTLE-BREWERY
CHATEAU-BRASSERIE
Ter Dolen
KRIEK

Ter Dolen

Ter Dolen tripel

	top-fermentation re-fermented in the bottle	fermentation haute refermentation en bouteille	hoge gisting nagisting op de fles
	abbey beer Tripel	bière d'abbaye triple	abdijbier tripel
	Kasteelbrouwerij De Dool Houthalen-Helchteren	Kasteelbrouwerij De Dool Houthalen-Helchteren	Kasteelbrouwerij De Do Houthalen-Helchteren
	2 malt varieties, 3 hop varieties, coriander, curaçao, grains of paradise, water	2 sortes de malt, 3 variétés de houblon, coriandre, curaçao, graines de paradis, eau	2 moutsoorten, 3 hopso ten, koriander, curaçao, paradijszaad, water
%	8,10%	8,10%	8,10%
	clear copper-blond	blond cuivre clair	helder koperblond
	Lift the bottle and pour in a single, smooth movement to obtain a nice foam head.	Verser de haut et en un seul mouvement fluide de façon à obtenir un beau faux col.	Hoog en vloeiend uitsch ken om een mooie schu kraag te bekomen.
	41 °F	5 °C	5 °C
	Lively character. Young, fruity flavour with a smooth aftertaste.	Caractère corsé. Saveur jeune, fruitée avec une fin de bouche douce.	Pittig karakter. Jonge, fruitige smaak m zachte afdronk.
i	–	–	–

ABDIJBIER
www.terdolen.be
KASTEEL
BROUWERIJ
Ter Dolen
TRIPEL
Hergist op fles
Ter Dolen

Terracotta

	top-fermentation re-fermented in the bottle unpasteurised	fermentation haute refermentation en bouteille non pasteurisée	hoge gisting hergisting op de fles niet gepasteuriseerd
	specialty beer blond	bière spéciale blonde	speciaalbier blond
	Brouwerij De Regenboog Brugge	Brouwerij De Regenboog Bruges	Brouwerij De Regenboc Brugge
	Pilsner/barley malt, Hallertau hops, candy sugar, elderberry blossom, yeast, water	malt de pils et d'orge, houblon Hallertau, sucre candi, fleurs de sureau, levure, eau	pils-/gerstemout, Hallei hop, kandijsuiker, vliei sem, gist, water
%	7%	7%	7%
	blond unfiltered	blonde non filtrée	blond niet gefilterd
	–	–	–
	41 °F	5 °C	5 °C
	Very fruity, cider-like, refreshing summer beer with slightly sour touches.	Très fruité, caractère de cidre, bière d'été rafraîchissante avec des touches légèrement acidulées.	Zeer fruitig, ciderachti verfrissend zomerbier lichtzurige toetsen.
i	Boutique beer that can be kept up to two years after bottling date. The label was designed by the American comic artist Bill Coleman.	Bière artisanale qui se conserve jusqu'à 2 ans après la date de la mise en bouteilles. L'étiquette est conçue par le cartooniste américain Bill Coleman.	Artisanaal bier, 2 jaar baar na botteldatum. Het etiket is ontworpe door de Amerikaanse s tekenaar Bill Coleman.
	....		

Terracotta
nieuw recept!
Gebrouwen door
33 cl e Cat.S 7% vol 5425004259011
'T SMISJE

Timmermans Framboise Lambic

	spontaneous fermentation	fermentation spontanée	spontane gisting
	fruit beer	bière fruitée	fruitbier
	Brouwerij Timmermans/ Timmermans Itterbeek	Brouwerij Timmermans/ Timmermans Itterbeek	Brouwerij Timmermar Site Timmermans Itterbeek
	barley malt, sugar, wheat, hops, fruit juices, water	malt d'orge, sucre, froment, houblon, jus de fruits, eau	gerstemout, suiker, tar hop, fruitsappen, wate
%	4%	4%	4%
	raspberry colour	couleur framboise	frambozenkleur
	–	–	–
	37 - 43 °F	3 - 6 °C	3 - 6 °C
	Very ripe raspberries hiding the sourness of the Lambic.	Framboises très mûres qui cachent le goût acidulé du lambic.	Zeer rijpe frambozen c zuurheid van de lamb verbergen.
i	–	–	–

TIMMERMANS
TRADITION
Framboise
LAMBIC
TIMMERMANS

Timmermans Kriek

	spontaneous fermentation	fermentation spontanée	spontane gisting
	fruit beer	bière fruitée	fruitbier
	Brouwerij Timmermans/ Timmermans Itterbeek	Brouwerij Timmermans/ Timmermans Itterbeek	Brouwerij Timmerman Timmermans Itterbeek
	barley malt, sugar, wheat, hops, fruit juices, water	malt d'orge, sucre, froment, houblon, jus de fruits, eau	gerstemout, suiker, tar hop, fruitsappen, wate
	4%	4%	4%
	red	rouge	rood
	–	–	–
	37 - 43 °F	3 - 6 °C	3 - 6 °C
	Sweet and velvety.	Doux et velouté.	Zoet en fluwelig.
	–	–	–

TIMMERMANS
ANNO 1781
LAMBIC
KRIEK
TIMMERMANS
ANNO 1781

Timmermans Krieklight

	spontaneous fermentation	fermentation spontanée	spontane gisting
	fruit beer	bière fruitée	fruitbier
	Brouwerij Timmermans/ Timmermans Itterbeek	Brouwerij Timmermans/ Timmermans Itterbeek	Brouwerij Timmerman Timmermans Itterbeek
	barley malt, sugar, wheat, hops, fruit juices, water	malt d'orge, sucre, froment, houblon, jus de fruits, eau	gerstemout, suiker, tar hop, fruitsappen, wate
	2,50%	2,50%	2,50%
	red	rouge	rood
	–	–	–
	37 - 43 °F	3 - 6 °C	3 - 6 °C
	Fruity aroma and low calories content. Taste of cherries and sugar.	Arôme fruité, pauvre en calories. Saveur de cerises et de sucre.	Fruitig aroma en laag c riegehalte. Smaak van kersen en s ker.
	–	–	–

TIMMERMANS
beer by TIMMERMANS
25 CL

Timmermans Pêche

	spontaneous fermentation	fermentation spontanée	spontane gisting
	fruit beer	bière fruitée	fruitbier
	Brouwerij Timmermans/ Timmermans Itterbeek	Brouwerij Timmermans/ Timmermans Itterbeek	Brouwerij Timmerman Timmermans Itterbeek
	barley malt, sugar, wheat, hops, fruit juices, water	malt d'orge, sucre, froment, houblon, jus de fruits, eau	gerstemout, suiker, tar hop, fruitsappen, wate
	4%	4%	4%
	blond	blonde	blond
	–	–	–
	37 - 43 °F	3 - 6 °C	3 - 6 °C
	Very fruity aroma. Taste of fruit and sugar with a touch of bitterness owing to peach skin and stone.	Arôme très fruité. Saveur de fruits et de sucre avec une pointe d'amertume de l'écorce et du noyau de la pêche.	Zeer fruitig aroma. Smaak van fruit en sui met een vleugje bitter van de schil en pit van perzik.
	–	–	–

TIMMERMANS
ITTERBEEK – BELGIUM
ANNO
1781
LAMBIC
PECHE
TIMMERMANS
ANNO
1781

Timmermans Tradition Blanche Lambicus

	spontaneous fermentation	fermentation spontanée	spontane gisting
	Lambic Witbier	lambic bière blanche	lambiek witbier
	Brouwerij Timmermans/ Timmermans Itterbeek	Brouwerij Timmermans/ Timmermans Itterbeek	Brouwerij Timmerman Timmermans Itterbeek
	barley malt, sugar, wheat, hops, flavouring, water	malt d'orge, sucre, froment, houblon, arômes, eau	gerstemout, suiker, tar hop, aroma's, water
%	4,40%	4,40%	4,40%
	white cloudy	blanche trouble	wit troebel
	–	–	–
	37 - 43 °F	3 - 6 °C	3 - 6 °C
	Slightly sour but round taste. Sugary touch. A thirst-quencher.	Saveur légèrement acidulée mais arrondie. Touche sucrée. Désaltérant.	Lichtzure maar ronde smaak. Toets van suike Dorstlesser.
i	–	–	–

TIMMERMANS
TRADITION
Lambicus
BLANCHE

TIMMERMANS
ANNO
1781

Timmermans Tradition Faro

	spontaneous fermentation	fermentation spontanée	spontane gisting
	Faro Lambic	faro lambic	faro lambiek
	Brouwerij Timmermans/ Timmermans Itterbeek	Brouwerij Timmermans/ Timmermans Itterbeek	Brouwerij Timmermar Timmermans Itterbeek
	barley malt, sugar, wheat, hops, fruit juice, water	malt d'orge, sucre, froment, houblon, jus de fruits, eau	gerstemout, suiker, ta hop, fruitsap, water
%	4%	4%	4%
	amber	ambrée	amber
	–	–	–
°C	37 - 43 °F	3 - 6 °C	3 - 6 °C
	Smooth beer, perfect thirst-quencher.	Bière moelleuse, désaltérant idéal.	Zacht bier, perfecte dc lesser.
i	–	–	–

TIMMERMANS
ANNO
1781
TRADITION
Faro
LAMBIC

TIMMERMANS
ANNO
1781

Timmermans Tradition Gueuze Lambic

	spontaneous fermentation	fermentation spontanée	spontane gisting
	Gueuze	gueuze	geuze
	Brouwerij Timmermans/ Timmermans Itterbeek	Brouwerij Timmermans/ Timmermans Itterbeek	Brouwerij Timmerma Timmermans Itterbeek
	barley malt, wheat, hop extract, water	malt d'orge, froment, extraits de houblon, eau	gerstemout, tarwe, hopextract, water
	5,50%	5,50%	5,50%
	amber	ambrée	amber
	–	–	–
	37 - 43 °F	3 - 6 °C	3 - 6 °C
	Pronounced sourness without being sharp. Discrete touch of bitterness and full mouthfeel.	Goût acidulé prononcé sans être trop aigu. Touche amère discrète en pleine bouche.	Uitgesproken zuurhei der te scherp te zijn. Discrete toets van bitt heid in volle mond.
	–	–	–

TIMMERMANS

TRADITION
Gueuze
LAMBIC

TIMMERMANS

Timmermans Tradition Kriek Nouveau Lambic

	spontaneous fermentation	fermentation spontanée	spontane gisting
	fruit beer Lambic	bière fruitée lambic	fruitbier lambiek
	Brouwerij Timmermans/ Timmermans Itterbeek	Brouwerij Timmermans/ Timmermans Itterbeek	Brouwerij Timmerma Timmermans Itterbeek
	barley malt, sugar, wheat, hops, fruit juice, water	malt d'orge, sucre, froment, houblon, jus de fruits, eau	gerstemout, suiker, ta hop, fruitsap, water
%	5%	5%	5%
	red	rouge	rood
	–	–	–
	37 - 43 °F	3 - 6 °C	3 - 6 °C
	Wonderful symbiosis of old Lambic on the palate. The Sint-Truiden cherries caress the tongue.	Symbiose splendide du vieux lambic se faisant sentir au palais et de cerises de Saint-Trond caressant la langue.	Prachtige symbiose va de lambiek die zich la voelen op het geheme kersen van Sint-Truid de tong strelen.
i	–	–	–

TIMMERMANS
TRADITION
Kriek Nouveau
LAMBIC

TIMMERMANS

Timmermans Tradition Pêche Lambic

	spontaneous fermentation	fermentation spontanée	spontane gisting
	fruit beer	bière fruitée	fruitbier
	Brouwerij Timmermans/ Timmermans Itterbeek	Brouwerij Timmermans/ Timmermans Itterbeek	Brouwerij Timmerman Timmermans Itterbeek
	barley malt, sugar, wheat, hops, fruit juice, water	malt d'orge, sucre, froment, houblon, jus de fruits, eau	gerstemout, suiker, tar hop, fruitsap, water
%	5%	5%	5%
	Peach colour.	Couleur de pêche.	Perzikkleur.
	–	–	–
°C	37 - 43 °F	3 - 6 °C	3 - 6 °C
	–	–	–
i	–	–	–

TIMMERMANS
TRADITION
Pêche
LAMBIC

TIMMERMANS

T

Titje

	top-fermentation	fermentation haute	hoge gisting
	Witbier	bière blanche	witbier
	Brasserie de Silly Silly	Brasserie de Silly Silly	Brasserie de Silly Silly
	malt, wheat, sugar, yeast, coriander, dried orange rind, Hallertau hops, water	malt, froment, sucre, levure, coriandre, écorce d'orange séché, houblon Hallertau, eau	mout, tarwe, suiker, g koriander, gedroogde naasschil, Hallertauhc water
	4,70% 11° plato	4,70% 11° plato	4,70% 11° plato
	white (14 EBC) cloudy	blanche (14 EBC) trouble	wit (14 EBC) troebel
	–	–	–
	39 - 45 °F	4 - 7 °C	4 - 7 °C
	Refreshening thirst-quencher with coriander effect. The orange rind gives a long-lasting, stimulating flavour.	Saveur extrêmement rafraîchissante. Le coriandre désaltère, l'écorce d'orange séché caresse la langue.	Uiterst verfrissende sm De koriander fungeert dorstlesser, de gedroog sinaasappelschil streelt de tong.
	–	–	–

BIERE BELGE
SUR LIE
BIERE BLANCHE • WIT BIER
OP GIST
250 ml
TITJE
Brasserie de Silly SA, Rue Ville Basse 2,
BIERE BLANCHE • WIT BIER
TITJE
BR. DE SILLY

Tjeeses

top-fermentation unpasteurised	fermentation haute non pasteurisée	hoge gisting niet gepasteuriseerd
blond Christmas beer	bière de Noël blonde	blond kerstbier
at Brouwerij Deca De Struise Brouwers De Panne	chez Brouwerij Deca De Struise Brouwers La Panne	bij Brouwerij Deca De Struise Brouwers De Panne
Pilsner, cara Munich, and wheat malt, cane sugar, yeast, water. Hops: Brewers Gold, Marynka, Bramling Cross. Sweet orange rind, massis banda, mint.	malt de pils et de froment, cara Munich, sucre de canne, levure, eau, houblon (Brewers Gold, Marynka, Bramling Cross), herbes (écorce d'orange doux, massis banda, menthe).	pilsmout, caramunich, wemout, rietsuiker, gis water, hop (Brewers Go Marynka, Bramling Cr kruiden (zoete sinaass massis banda, munt).
10%	10%	10%
golden blond (14 EBU) unfiltered	blond doré (14 EBC) non filtrée	goudblond (14 EBC) ongefilterd
–	–	–
–	–	–
Elegant aroma with touches of fruit, herbs, noble hop. 32 IBU (soft bitter). Strong, pronounced and complex taste. Pleasant, long-lasting aftertaste.	Arôme élégant avec touches de fruits, d'herbes et de houblon précieux. 32 EBU. Saveur forte, prononcée et goût très complexe. Fin de bouche avec chaleur subsistante.	Elegant aroma met toe van fruit, kruiden, edele hop. 32 IBU. Ster uitgesproken en zeer c plexe smaak. Aangena nagloeiende afdronk.
When the brewer tasted the beer, he exclaimed: 'Tsjeeses wat een lekker biertje!' (Gee, what a nice little beer!').	En dégustant la bière de Noël le maître de brassage s'est écrié 'Tsjeeses quelle bière agréable!'.	Bij het proeven van he kerstbier riep de brouv 'Tsjeeses wat een lekke biertje!'.

Tsjeeses
DSB
Struisebrouwers.be

Toernichoise fumée

	top-fermentation re-fermented in the bottle	fermentation haute refermentation en bouteille	hoge gisting hergisting op de fles
	Ale Rauch beer	ale bière Rauch	ale Rauchbier
	Brasserie Artisanale Millevertus Toernich	Brasserie Artisanale Millevertus Toernich	Brasserie Artisanale Millevertus Toernich
	peaty malt and other malt varieties, different hop and yeast varieties, water	malt tourbeux et d'autres sortes de malt, différentes sortes de houblon et de levures, eau	turfachtige mout en a moutsoorten, verschil hop- en gistsoorten, w
	6,50%	6,50%	6,50%
	dark amber	ambré foncé	donker amber
	Pour at cellar temperature.	Verser à température de cave.	Uitschenken op kelder peratuur.
	54 °F	12 °C	12 °C
	Very complex owing to the use of 8 malt types and 3 hop species. Smoky aroma.	Très complexe par l'utilisation de 8 sortes de malt et de 3 sortes de houblon. Goût fumée.	Zeer complex door het bruik van 8 moutsoort 3 hopsoorten. Rooksm
	The only smoke beer in Belgium, analogous to the German Rauchbier (Bamberg region).	Unique bière 'fumeur' en Belgique par analogie avec la Rauchbier de la région de Bamberg (Allemagne).	Enige rookbier in Belgi naar analogie met Rau bier uit de streek van B berg (Duitsland).

TOERNICHOISE
Brasserie Artisanale
MMMH!!
MILLEVERTUS

Tongerlo blond

top-fermentation re-fermented in the bottle	fermentation haute refermentation en bouteille	hoge gisting hergisting op de fles
recognised Belgian blond abbey beer	Bière d'abbaye belge reconnue, double blonde	Erkend Belgisch abdijbi blond dubbel
Brouwerij Haacht Boortmeerbeek	Brouwerij Haacht Boortmeerbeek	Brouwerij Haacht Boortmeerbeek
barley malt, sugar, hops, herbs, water	malt d'orge, sucre, houblon, herbes, eau	gerstemout, suiker, hop kruiden, water
6%	6%	6%
amber	ambrée	amber
Pour carefully and tilt the glass. With yeast sediment: smoothly revolve the bottle before serving the last third. Without yeast sediment: pour carefully and leave the sediment in the bottle.	Verser prudemment en tenant le verre incliné. Avec dépôt de levure: tourner le dernier tiers de bière avant de le verser. Sans dépôt de levure: verser prudemment et laisser le fond dans la bouteille.	Voorzichtig inschenker het glas schuin houden Met gistbezinkel: laatst derde in de fles walsen het uitschenken. Zonder gistbezinksel: v zichtig schenken en de fond in de fles laten.
48 °F	9 °C	9 °C
Honey aroma and a full-bodied taste with a smooth aftertaste. Pronounced taste and aroma obtained by weeks of re-fermentation and fermentation in the bottle.	Arôme de miel et saveur franche. Saveur et arôme prononcés par la refermentation et le mûrissement de plusieurs semaines en bouteille.	Aroma van honing en e volmondige smaak die zacht uitvloeit. Uitgesproken smaak en ma door wekenlange h ting en rijping op de fl
–	–	–

....

DE NORBERTIJNEN VAN · LES PRÉMONTRÉS DE
Tongerlo

Tongerlo

Tongerlo bruin

	top-fermentation re-fermented in the bottle	fermentation haute refermentation en bouteille	hoge gisting hergisting op de fles
	recognised Belgian dark abbey beer	Bière d'abbaye belge reconnue, double foncée	Erkend Belgisch abdijbi dubbel donker
	Brouwerij Haacht Boortmeerbeek	Brouwerij Haacht Boortmeerbeek	Brouwerij Haacht Boortmeerbeek
	barley malt, sugar, corn, water	malt d'orge, sucre, maïs, eau	gerstemout, suiker, mai water
%	6%	6%	6%
	red-brown	brun rouge	roodbruin
	Pour carefully and tilt the glass. With yeast sediment: smoothly revolve the bottle before serving the last third. Without yeast sediment: pour carefully and leave the sediment in the bottle.	Verser prudemment en tenant le verre incliné. Avec dépôt de levure: tourner le dernier tiers de bière avant de le verser. Sans dépôt de levure: verser prudemment et laisser le fond dans la bouteille.	Voorzichtig inschenken het glas schuin houden Met gistbezinkel: laatste derde in de fles wals voor het uitschenken. Z der gistbezinksel: voorz tig schenken en fond in fles laten.
°C	52 °F	11 °C	11 °C
	Sweetish aroma, full taste, slightly roasty aftertaste. Pronounced taste and aroma obtained by weeks of re-fermentation and fermentation in the bottle.	Arôme doux, saveur pleine, fin de bouche légèrement grillée. Saveur et arôme prononcés par la refermentation et le mûrissement de plusieurs semaines en bouteille.	Zoetig aroma, volle sma licht geroosterde afdror Uitgesproken smaak en ma door wekenlange he ting en rijping op de fle
i	–	–	–

6°
ABBAYE · ABDIJBIER
DE NORBERTIJNEN VAN · LES PRÉMONTRÉS DE
Tongerlo
ANNO 1133
BRUIN – BRUNE
DOPPIO MALTO BRUNA

Tongerlo

Tongerlo Christmas

	top-fermentation re-fermented in the bottle	fermentation haute refermentation en bouteille	hoge gisting hergisting op de fles
	recognised Belgian dark dubbel abbey beer	Bière d'abbaye belge reconnue, double foncée	Erkend Belgisch abdijbi dubbel donker
	Brouwerij Haacht Boortmeerbeek	Brouwerij Haacht Boortmeerbeek	Brouwerij Haacht Boortmeerbeek
	barley malt, sugar, hops, herbs, water	malt d'orge, sucre, houblon, herbes, eau	gerstemout, suiker, ho kruiden, water
	6,50%	6,50%	6,50%
	amber-coloured	ambrée	amberkleurig
	Pour carefully and tilt the glass. With yeast sediment: smoothly revolve the bottle before serving the last third. Without yeast sediment: pour carefully and leave the sediment in the bottle.	Verser prudemment en tenant le verre incliné. Avec dépôt de levure: tourner le dernier tiers de bière avant de le verser. Sans dépôt de levure: verser prudemment et laisser le fond dans la bouteille.	Voorzichtig inschenke en het glas schuin hou Met gistbezinkel: laatst derde in de fles walsen het uitschenken. Zond gistbezinksel: voorzich schenken en de fond in fles laten.
	48 °F	9 °C	9 °C
	Pure summer barley, aroma with vanilla touch, fruity and complex taste, smooth aftertaste. Pronounced taste and aroma obtained by weeks of re-fermentation and fermentation in the bottle.	Orge d'été pure, arôme avec touche de vanille, saveur fruitée et complexe. Fin de bouche douce. Saveur et arôme prononcés par la refermentation et le mûrissement de plusieurs semaines en bouteille.	Zuivere zomergerst, ar met vanilletoets, fruiti complexe smaak. Zachte afdronk. Uitgesproken smaak en ma door wekenlange h ting en rijping op de fle
	–	–	–

6,5°
HERGIST IN DE FLES
BIERE D'ABBAYE · ABDIJBIER
DE NORBERTIJNEN VAN · LES PRÉMONTRÉS DE
Tongerlo
Christmas
BLOND – BLONDE
DOPPIO MALTO BIONDA

Tongerlo

Tongerlo tripel

	top-fermentation re-fermented in the bottle	fermentation haute refermentation en bouteille	hoge gisting hergisting op de fles
	recognised Belgian abbey beer, Tripel	Bière d'abbaye belge reconnue, triple	Erkend Belgisch abdijbi tripel
	Brouwerij Haacht Boortmeerbeek	Brouwerij Haacht Boortmeerbeek	Brouwerij Haacht Boortmeerbeek
	barley malt, sugar, corn, water	malt d'orge, sucre, maïs, eau	gerstemout, suiker, ma water
%	8%	8%	8%
	blond	blonde	blond
	Pour carefully and tilt the glass. With yeast sediment: smoothly revolve the bottle in circles before serving the last third. Without yeast sediment: pour carefully and leave the sediment in the bottle.	Verser prudemment en tenant le verre incliné. Avec dépôt de levure: tourner le dernier tiers de bière avant de le verser. Sans dépôt de levure: verser prudemment et laisser le fond dans la bouteille.	Voorzichtig inschenken het glas schuin houder Met gistbezinkel: laatst derde in de fles walsen het uitschenken. Zonder gistbezinksel: voorzichtig schenken en de fond in de fles la
°C	45 °F	7 °C	7 °C
	Fruity, hoppy aroma and a round, well-balanced taste. Slightly bitter aftertaste. Pronounced taste and aroma obtained by weeks of re-fermentation and fermentation in the bottle.	Arôme houblonné, fruité et saveur ronde, équilibrée. Fin de bouche légèrement amère. Saveur et arôme prononcés par la refermentation et le mûrissement de plusieurs semaines en bouteille.	Fruitig, hoppig aroma e een ronde, evenwichtig smaak. Licht bittere afdronk. Uitgesproken smaak e ma door wekenlange h ting en rijping op de fl
i	–	–	–

8
DE NORBERTIJNEN VAN · LES PRÉMONTRÉS DE
Tongerlo
Tongerlo

Tonneke

	top-fermentation	fermentation haute	hoge gisting
	typical Belgian Ale	belgian ale typique	typical belgian ale
	Brouwerij Contreras Gavere	Brouwerij Contreras Gavere	Brouwerij Contreras Gavere
	barley malt, hop (Hallertau, Styrian, Brewers gold) top-fermenting yeast, water	malt d'orge, houblon (Hallertau, Styrian, Brewers gold), levure de fermentation haute, eau	gerstemout, hop (Halle Styrian, Brewers gold), hogegistingsgist, wate
%	5%	5%	5%
	orange-amber clear	orange-ambrée claire	oranje-amber helder
	Empty in a degreased, rinsed and dry glass. Tilt the glass about 45° and pour the beer, avoiding contact between the bottle and the foam. Provide a foam head of approx. 5 cm.	Verser complètement dans un verre dégraissé, rincé et sec. Tenir le verre incliné à 45° et verser la bière sans que la bouteille touche l'écume. Prévoir un faux col de 5 cm environ.	Helemaal uitschenken i ontvet, gespoeld en dro glas. Het glas 45° schui houden, het bier uitsch ken zonder dat de fles h schuim raakt. Een schu kraag van ca. 5 cm voor
°C	39 - 43 °F	4 - 6 °C	4 - 6 °C
	Malty, sweet, fruity.	Malté, doux, fruité.	Moutig, zoet, fruitig.
i	Available in 30 litre oak barrels.	Egalement disponible en fûts de chêne de 30 litres.	Ook verkrijgbaar op ei houten vaatjes van 30

TONNEKE
TONNEKE
CONTRERAS
NATUURBIER

Toria

	top-fermentation re-fermented in the bottle	fermentation haute refermentation en bouteille	hoge gisting hergisting op de fles
	specialty beer	bière spéciale	speciaalbier
	at De Graal De Hoevebrouwers Zottegem	chez De Graal De Hoevebrouwers Zottegem	bij De Graal De Hoevebrouwers Zottegem
	malt (Pilsner, wheat), hops (EK Goldings, Hallertau), yeast (T58), water	malt (pils, froment), houblon (EK Goldings, Hallertau), levure (T58), eau	mout (pils, tarwe), hop Goldings, Hallertau), g (T58), water
%	6,50%	6,50%	6,50%
	blond clear	blonde claire	blond helder
	Pour into a degreased goblet in a single movement, avoiding contact between bottle and foam. Leave approx. 1 cm of beer in the bottle.	Verser en un seul mouvement dans un verre calice dégraissé sans toucher le verre et l'écume. Laisser environ 1 cm de bière dans la bouteille.	In 1 beweging in een ve kelkglas gieten zonder glas en het schuim te r Ongeveer 1 cm bier in fles laten.
°C	43 - 50 °F	6 - 10 °C	6 - 10 °C
	Light and refreshing. Dry with a bitter aftertaste.	Léger et rafraîchissant. Sec avec une fin de bouche amère.	Licht en verfrissend. D met een bittere afdron
i	Toria was a popular character from Zottegem, who forecasted the weather.	Toria était une figure populaire et un monsieur météo de Zottegem.	Toria was een Zottegen volksfiguur en weervo speller.

6,5 % vol.alc.
Toria
Info@dehoevebrouwers.be

Totentrekker

	mixed fermentation re-fermentation in the bottle (top fermentation, wild yeasts)	fermentation mixte refermentation en bouteille (fermentation haute et levures sauvages)	gemengde gisting hergisting in de fles (hoge gisting en wilde g
	old brown Kriek	bière kriek vieille brune	oud bruin kriekbier
	Proefbrouwerij in Lochristi for Buitenlust Zulte	Proefbrouwerij à Lochristi pour Buitenlust Zulte	Proefbrouwerij in Loch voor Buitenlust Zulte
	malt (Munchner, cara, Pilsner), Poperinge hops, water, yeasts, sour concentrated cherry juice, saccharin, naturally fermented lactic acid (0,5%)	malt (Munchner, cara, pils), houblon de Poperinge, eau, levures, jus de cerises concentré, saccharine et acide lactique fermenté de façon naturelle (0,5%)	mout (munchner, cara pils), Poperingse hop, w gisten, zuur kriekensap geconcentreerde vorm charine en natuurlijk v gist melkzuur (0,5%)
%	5,00%	5,00%	5%
	light to dark-red	rouge clair à foncé	licht- tot donkerrood
	Smoothly pour in a single movement. The sediment can be served separately.	Verser doucement en un seul mouvement. Le dépôt de levure peut être servi séparément.	Zacht uitschenken in 1 weging. Het gistdepot afzonderlijk geserveerd worden.
°C	43 - 50 °F or 39 °F	6 - 10 °C ou 4 °C	6 - 10 °C of 4 °C
	Beer with taste evolution. Slightly hoppy. 15 EBU. Sweet-and-sour, the sour fruit slightly stronger than the malt sugar.	Bière avec saveur évolutive. Légèrement houblonné. 15 EBU. Aigre-doux où l'acide (fruits) dépasse légèrement la douceur (sucre de malt).	Bier met smaakevoluti Lichte hopsmaak. 15 EB Zuurzoet waarbij het z (fruit) net boven het zo (moutsuiker) uitkomt.
i	Store in a dark place, with constant temperature and vibration-free.	Conserver à l'abri de la lumière et des tremblements à une température constante.	Donker en trillingsvrij bewaren op een consta temperatuur.

TOTENTREKKER

Tournay

	top-fermentation re-fermented in the bottle	fermentation haute refermentation en bouteille	hoge gisting hergisting op de fles
	regional beer	bière régionale	streekbier
	Brasserie de Cazeau Templeuve	Brasserie de Cazeau Templeuve	Brasserie de Cazeau Templeuve
	malt: blond and caramel 4 hop varieties	malt: blond et caramélisé 4 sortes de houblon	mout: blond en karam 4 hopsoorten
%	7,20%	7,20%	7,20%
	gold-coloured slightly cloudy at the bottom of the bottle	doré légèrement trouble au fond de la bouteille	goudkleurig licht troebel onderaan de fles
	Keep the glass upright and pour the beer. Hold the glass tilted at the end.	Tenir le verre d'abord en position verticale, verser la bière et incliner le verre à la fin.	Het glas eerst verticaa den, het bier uitschen en het glas schuin hou op het einde.
°C	46 - 50 °F	8 - 10 °C	8 - 10 °C
	Well-balanced. Fruity nose, well-balanced aromas, hoppy and fairly dry aftertaste.	Equilibré. Parfum fruité, arômes de goût équilibrés, fin de bouche houblonnée et assez sèche.	Evenwichtig. Fruitige neus, evenwic smaakaroma's, hoppig vrij droge afdronk.
i	–	–	–

TOURNAY
TOURNAY
Blonde - Blond

Tournay de Noël

	top-fermentation re-fermented in the bottle	fermentation haute refermentation en bouteille	hoge gisting hergisting op de fles
	Stout	stout	stout
	Brasserie de Cazeau Templeuve	Brasserie de Cazeau Templeuve	Brasserie de Cazeau Templeuve
	malt varieties: blond, light caramel, strong caramel, roasted 2 hop varieties	sortes de malt: blond, caramélisé clair, caramélisé prononcé, brûlé 2 sortes de houblon	moutsoorten: blond, l karamel, uitgesproken mel, gebrand 2 hopsoorten
%	8,20%	8,20%	8,20%
	black	noire	zwart
	Keep the glass upright and pour the beer. Hold it tilted at the end.	Tenir le verre d'abord en position verticale, verser la bière et incliner le verre à la fin.	Het glas eerst verticaa den, het bier uitschen en het glas schuin ho op het einde.
	50 - 54 °F	10 - 12 °C	10 - 12 °C
	Powerful character. Pronounced bitterness (hop and roasty malt) with chocolate and malt perfumes in the mouth. Very clear roasty aftertaste.	Caractère corsé. Goût amer prononcé (houblon et malt brûlé) avec parfums de chocolat et de houblon dans la bouche. Arrière-bouche brûlée très prononcée.	Krachtig karakter. Uitgesproken bitterhe (hop en gebrande mo met parfums van chocolade en hop in de mond. Zeer duideli gebrande nasmaak.
i		–	–

TOURNAY

Tourtel Blond

	bottom-fermentation	fermentation basse	lage gisting
	non-alcoholic Pilsner	pils sans alcool	alcoholvrije pils
	Alken Maes corporation Alken	Alken Maes corporation Alken	Alken Maes corporatic Alken
	brewed with 100% pure malt	brassée 100% pur malt	100% puur malt gebro
%	0,30%	0,30%	0,30%
	gold-yellow	jaune doré	goudgeel
	Empty in a degreased, rinsed and wet glass. Let overflow and skim off the foam.	Verser complètement dans un verre dégraissé, rincé et mouillé. Laisser déborder et écumer.	Helemaal uitschenker een ontvet, gespoeld e nat glas. Laten overlopen en afs men.
	36 - 39 °F	2 - 4 °C	2 - 4 °C
	Fresh malty flavour with a touch of bitterness.	Saveur fraîche, maltée, légèrement amère.	Frisse, moutige smaak lichte bitterheid.
	Non-alcoholic beer.	Bière sans alcool.	Alcoholvrij bier.

TOURTEL
1839
PREMIUM BLOND BIER
TOURTEL
MALT
BIÈRE BLONDE PREMIUM
TOURTEL
MALT

Trappist Westmalle dubbel

	top-fermentation re-fermented in the bottle	fermentation haute refermentation en bouteille	hoge gisting nagisting op de fles
	Trappist dubbel	trappiste double	trappist dubbel
	Brouwerij der Trappisten van Westmalle Westmalle	Brouwerij der Trappisten van Westmalle Westmalle	Brouwerij der Trappis van Westmalle Westmalle
	barley malt, yeast, sugar, hops, water	malt d'orge, houblon, sucre, levure, eau	gerstemout, gist, suik hop, water
%	7%	7%	7%
	dark red amber	ambré rouge foncé	donkerrode amberkle
	Let the beer rest for a few days before tasting. Pour carefully into a goblet and leave the yeast sediment in the bottle. The latter can be drunk separately.	Laisser reposer la bière avant la dégustation. Verser prudemment dans un verre calice et laisser le dépôt de levure dans la bouteille. Ce dépôt peut être bu séparément.	Het bier voor het degu ren laten rusten. Voor tig uitschenken in eer glas en de gistbodem fles laten. De gistbode kan afzonderlijk word uitgedronken.
°C	46 - 54 °F	8 - 12 °C	8 - 12 °C
	Not too sweet. A well fermented beer with a refined, matching hop taste. Harmoniously bitter to slightly sweet with a caramel touch.	Saveur pas trop douce. Bière bien fermentée avec un goût houblonné nuancé, approprié. Harmonieusement amer à légèrement doux avec touche de caramel.	Niet te zoete smaak. E goed uitvergist bier m een genuanceerde, pa de hopsmaak. Harmonieus bitter to zoet met karameltoet
i	The taste evolution of the 75 cl bottle is different due to the synthetic cork and a narrow neck.	L'évolution de la saveur de la bouteille 75 cl varie par l'emploi du bouchon synthétique et la colonne d'air plus petite.	De smaakevolutie van cl-fles verschilt door h bruik van kunststofkı de kleinere luchthals.

Westmalle
TRAPPIST
Dubbel
33 CL
Westmalle
trappist

Trappist Westmalle tripel

	top-fermentation re-fermented in the bottle	fermentation haute refermentation en bouteille	hoge gisting nagisting op de fles
	Trappist tripel	trappiste triple	trappist tripel
	Brouwerij der Trappisten van Westmalle Westmalle	Brouwerij der Trappisten van Westmalle Westmalle	Brouwerij der Trappis van Westmalle Westmalle
	barley malt, yeast, sugar, hops, water	malt d'orge, sucre, levure, houblon, eau	gerstemout, gist, suik hop, water
	9,50%	9,50%	9,50%
	gold-yellow with solid foam head, clear	jaune doré avec un faux col solide, clair	goudgeel met vaste sc kraag, helder
	Let the beer rest before tasting. Pour carefully into a goblet and leave the yeast sediment in the bottle. The latter can be drunk separately.	Laisser reposer la bière avant la dégustation. Verser prudemment et laisser le dépôt de levure dans la bouteille (peut être bu séparément).	Het bier een paar dage ten rusten. Voorzichtig schenken en de gistboc de fles laten (kan afzor lijk worden uitgedronk
	46 - 54 °F	8 - 12 °C	8 - 12 °C
	Very refined hop nose and strong bitterness, supported by the fruit aroma. The taste is fruity and strongly-hopped. Long-lasting aftertaste.	Parfum houblonné très nuancé et goût amer corsé soutenu par l'arôme fruité. Saveur fruitée et franche, fortement houblonnée avec une arrière-bouche longue.	Zeer genuanceerde hc en sterke bitterheid ge gen door het fruitaror smaak is fruitig en vo dig, sterk gehopt met lange afdronk.
	The taste evolution of the 75 cl bottle is different due to the synthetic cork and the narrow neck.	L'évolution de la saveur de la bouteille 75 cl varie par l'emploi du bouchon synthétique et la colonne d'air plus petite.	De smaakevolutie van cl-fles verschilt door h bruik van kunststofku de kleinere luchthals

Westmalle
TRAPPIST
Tripel
ALC. 9,5%
33 CL

Westmalle
trappist

Trappist Westvleteren 8

	top-fermentation re-fermented in the bottle	fermentation haute refermentation en bouteille	hoge gisting nagisting op de fles
	dark Trappist	trappiste foncée	trappist donker
	Abdij Sint-Sixtus Westvleteren	Abdij Sint-Sixtus Westvleteren	Abdij Sint-Sixtus Westvleteren
	malt, hops, sugar, yeast, water	malt, houblon, sucre, levure, eau	mout, hop, suiker, gist water
%	8%	8%	8%
	red-brown clear	brun rouge claire	roodbruin helder
	Pour carefully into a goblet.	Verser prudemment dans un verre calice.	Voorzichtig uitschenk een kelkglas.
°C	54 - 61 °F	12 - 16 °C	12 - 16 °C
	Sweetish, fruity aroma with a melon accent.	Arôme sucré, fruité avec accent de melon.	Zoetig, fruitig aroma een meloenaccent.
i	Store the bottles upright in a dark room between 12 and 18 °C.	Conserver les bouteilles en position verticale à l'abri de la lumière entre 12 et 18 °C.	De flessen verticaal op donkere plaats beware sen 12 en 18 °C.

Westvleteren

Trappist Westvleteren 12

	top-fermentation re-fermented in the bottle	fermentation haute refermentation en bouteille	hoge gisting nagisting op de fles
	dark Trappist	trappiste foncée	trappist donker
	Abdij Sint-Sixtus Westvleteren	Abdij Sint-Sixtus Westvleteren	Abdij Sint-Sixtus Westvleteren
	malt, hops, sugar, yeast, water	malt, houblon, sucre, levure, eau	mout, hop, suiker, gis water
	10%	10%	10%
	red-brown clear	brun rouge claire	roodbruin helder
	Pour carefully into a goblet.	Verser prudemment dans un verre calice.	Voorzichtig uitschenk een kelkglas.
	54 - 61 °F	12 - 16 °C	12 - 16 °C
	Full, creamy aroma. Rich, caramel-like and malt flavour palette.	Arôme plein et crémeux. Palette de saveurs riche, caramélisée et maltée.	Vol, romig aroma. Rijk, karamelachtig e moutig smaakpalet.
	Store the bottles upright in a dark room between 12 and 18 °C.	Conserver les bouteilles en position verticale à l'abri de la lumière entre 12 et 18 °C.	De flessen verticaal op donkere plaats beware sen 12 en 18 °C.

Trappist
Westvleteren

Trappist Westvleteren blond

	top-fermentation re-fermented in the bottle	fermentation haute refermentation en bouteille	hoge gisting nagisting op de fles
	blond Trappist	trappiste blonde	trappist blond
	Abdij Sint-Sixtus Westvleteren	Abdij Sint-Sixtus Westvleteren	Abdij Sint-Sixtus Westvleteren
	malt, hops, sugar, yeast, water	malt, houblon, sucre, levure, eau	mout, hop, suiker, gist, water
%	5,80%	5,80%	5,80%
	blond clear	blonde claire	blond helder
	Pour carefully into a goblet.	Verser prudemment dans un verre calice.	Voorzichtig uitschenke een kelkglas.
°C	54 - 61 °F	12 - 16 °C	12 - 16 °C
	Hoppy, spicy aroma. Slightly smooth taste with pronounced bitter aftertaste.	Arôme houblonné, relevé. Saveur légèrement moelleuse avec une fin de bouche amère prononcée.	Hoppig, kruidig aroma Lichtzacht van smaak geaccentueerde bittere dronk.
i	Store the bottles upright in a dark room between 12 and 18 °C.	Conserver les bouteilles en position verticale à l'abri de la lumière entre 12 et 18 °C.	De flessen verticaal op donkere plaats beware sen 12 en 18 °C.

Trappist

Trappistes Rochefort 6

	top-fermentation	fermentation haute	hoge gisting
	dark Trappist	trappiste foncée	trappist donker
	Abbaye Notre-Dame de Saint-Remy, Rochefort	Abbaye Notre-Dame de Saint-Remy, Rochefort	Abbaye Notre-Dame de Saint-Remy, Rochefc
	barley malt, grain starch, sugar, yeast, hops, spring water	malt d'orge, fécule de blé, sucre, levure, houblon, eau de source	gerstemout, zetmeel va graan, suiker, gist, hop bronwater
	7,50%	7,50%	7,50%
	red-brown	brun rouge	roodbruin
	Pour slowly into a slightly tilted glass at eye level. Move the bottle away from the glass to obtain a nice foam head. Pour the last part (1/10th), which contains the yeast, separately.	Verser lentement dans un verre tenu légèrement incliné à hauteur d'yeux. Séparer la bouteille du verre pour obtenir un beau faux col. Verser séparément la dernière portion riche en vitamines (1/10e) qui contient la levure.	Traag uitschenken in e licht schuingehouden op ooghoogte. De fles v het glas verwijderen vo een mooie schuimkraa Het laatste, vitamineri deel (1/10e) met gist afzonderlijk uitschenk
	54 - 57 °F	12 - 14 °C	12 - 14 °C
	Smooth, full-bodied taste, evolving against the palate. Fruity touch.	Goût doux, plein dans la bouche évoluant au palais. Touche fruitée.	Zachte, volmondige sm die evolueert tegen het hemelte. Fruitige toets
i	The figure 6 does not indicate the alcohol content but is the value of the malt density before the fermentation process.	Le chiffre 6 n'indique pas la teneur en alcool, mais correspond à la valeur indiquant la densité des malts avant la fermentation.	Het cijfer 6 verwijst nie naar het alcoholpercen ge maar stemt overeen de waarde die de dicht van de mouten aandui vòòr het gistingsproces

ABBAYE ST-REMY B-5580 ROCHEFORT
Trappistes
Rochefort
L 25 10 11
14:08
6
BIERE
BIER
33 cl
ALC. 7,5% VOL.

Trappistes Rochefort 8

	top-fermentation	fermentation haute	hoge gisting
	dark Trappist	trappiste foncée	trappist donker
	Abbaye Notre-Dame de Saint-Remy, Rochefort	Abbaye Notre-Dame de Saint-Remy, Rochefort	Abbaye Notre-Dame de Saint-Remy, Rochefc
	barley malt, grain starch, sugar, yeast, hops, spring water	malt d'orge, fécule de blé, sucre, levure, houblon, eau de source	gerstemout, zetmeel va graan, suiker, gist, hop bronwater
%	9,20%	9,20%	9,20%
	brown, tawny	brune, fauve	bruin, fauve
	Slowly pour into a slightly tilted glass at eye level. Move the bottle away from the glass to obtain a nice foam head. Pour the last part (1/10th), which contains the yeast, separately.	Verser lentement dans un verre tenu légèrement incliné à hauteur d'yeux. Séparer la bouteille du verre pour obtenir un beau faux col. Verser séparément la dernière portion riche en vitamines (1/10e) qui contient la levure.	Traag uitschenken in e licht schuingehouden op ooghoogte. De fles v het glas verwijderen vc een mooie schuimkraa Het laatste, vitamineri deel (1/10e) met gist afzonderlijk uitschenk
°C	54 - 57 °F	12 - 14 °C	12 - 14 °C
	Pronounced taste, richer fruitiness, a touch of fig, strong aftertaste.	Saveur plus prononcée, fruitée avec une touche de figue. Bonne fin de bouche.	Meer uitgesproken sm fruitiger, een vleugje v Goede afdronk.
i	The figure 8 does not indicate the alcohol content but is the value of the malt density before the fermentation process.	Le chiffre 8 n'indique pas la teneur en alcool, mais correspond à la valeur indiquant la densité des malts avant la fermentation.	Het cijfer 8 verwijst ni naar het alcoholvolum maar stemt overeen m de waarde die de dich van de mouten aandu vòòr het gistingsproce

ABBAYE ST-REMY B-5580 ROCHEFORT
Trappistes
Rochefort
L18 10 11
11:16
8
BIERE
BIER
33 cl
ALC. 9,2% VOL.

Trappistes Rochefort 10

	top-fermentation	fermentation haute	hoge gisting
	dark Trappist	trappiste foncée	trappist donker
	Abbaye Notre-Dame de Saint-Remy, Rochefort	Abbaye Notre-Dame de Saint-Remy, Rochefort	Abbaye Notre-Dame de Saint-Remy, Rochefo
	barley malt, grain starch, sugar, yeast, hops, well water	malt d'orge, fécule de blé, sucre, levure, houblon, eau de source	gerstemout, zetmeel va graan, suiker, gist, hop, bronwater
%	10,30%	10,30%	10,30%
	deep red-brown	brun rouge intense	diep roodbruin
	Slowly pour into a slightly tilted glass at eye level. Move the bottle away from the glass to obtain a nice foam head. Pour the last part (1/10th) which contains the yeast, separately.	Verser lentement dans un verre tenu légèrement incliné à hauteur d'yeux. Séparer la bouteille du verre pour obtenir un beau faux col. Verser séparément la dernière portion (1/10e) qui contient la levure.	Traag uitschenken in ee licht schuingehouden g op ooghoogte. De fles va het glas verwijderen vo een mooie schuimkraag Het laatste deel (1/10de) met gist afzonderlijk uitschenken.
°C	54 - 57 °F	12 - 14 °C	12 - 14 °C
	Honey evolving to very fruity (pears, bananas, raisins) with touches of fondant chocolate. Long-lasting aftertaste.	Saveur de miel évoluant à très fruitée (poire, bananes, raisins secs) et une touche de chocolat noir. Fin de bouche longue.	Honingsmaak evoluere naar heel fruitig (peer, b naan, rozijn) en een toe van zwarte chocolade. L ge afdronk.
i	The figure 10 does not indicate the alcohol content but is the value of the malt density before the fermentation process.	Le chiffre 10 n'indique pas la teneur en alcool, mais correspond à la densité des malts avant la fermentation.	Het cijfer 10 verwijst ni naar het alcoholvolume maar stemt overeen me dichtheid van de mout vòòr het gistingsproces

ABBAYE ST-REMY B-5580 ROCHEFORT
Trappistes Rochefort
10
BIERE
BIER
33cl
ALC. 11,3% VOL.

Trappistes Rochefort

Tripel Abdijbier Dendermon

	top-fermentation re-fermented in the bottle	fermentation haute refermentation en bouteille	hoge gisting hergisting op de fles
	recognised Belgian abbey beer, Tripel	Bière d'abbaye belge reconnue, triple	Erkend Belgisch Abdijb tripel
	Brouwerij De Block Peizegem-Merchtem	Brouwerij De Block Peizegem-Merchtem	Brouwerij De Block Peizegem-Merchtem
	wheat, malt, hops, yeast, water	froment, malt, houblon, levure, eau	tarwe, mout, hop, gist, water
%	8%	8%	8%
	copper, amber full, creamy foam head	cuivre, ambrée faux col plein, crémeux	koper, amber volle, romige schuimk
	cfr chimay	voir chimay	cfr. chimay
	43 - 46 °F	6 - 8 °C	6 - 8 °C
	Full-bodied and fruity. Rich with a slightly caramelized taste.	Franc et fruité. Goût riche, légèrement caramélisé.	Volmondig en fruitig. Rijke, licht gekaramell de smaak.
i	–	–	–

Abdij-Abbaye
Dendermonde
benedictijnen

Abdij
Abbaye
Dendermonde

Tripel Karmeliet

	top-fermentation re-fermented in the bottle	fermentation haute refermentation en bouteille	hoge gisting hergisting op de fles
	Tripel 3-grains	triple 3-grains	tripel 3-granen
	Brouwerij Bosteels Buggenhout	Brouwerij Bosteels Buggenhout	Brouwerij Bosteels Buggenhout
	wheat, haver, barley, hops, water	froment, avoine, orge, houblon, eau	tarwe, haver, gerst, hop water
	8,10%	8,10%	8,10%
	complex gold- to bronze- coloured nice, creamy foam head	couleur bronze-dorée complexe beau faux col crémeux	complex goud- tot bron kleurig mooie, romige kraag
	Slightly tilt the glass and fill carefully. Leave a yeast sediment of approx. 1/2 cm at the bottom of the bottle. The yeast sediment can be drunk separately.	Tenir le verre légèrement incliné et le remplir prudemment. Laisser dans la bouteille un fond de levure de 1/2 cm environ. Ce dépôt peut être bu.	Het glas licht schuinho den en voorzichtig volschenken. 1/2 cm gistb dem in de fles laten. He gistdepot mag uitgedr ken worden.
	41 - 43 °F	5 - 6 °C	5 - 6 °C
	Light freshness of wheat, creamy oat, citric dryness. Complex, refined flavour (grains and yeast, hops). Touches of vanilla mixed with citric flavours.	Goût légèrement frais de froment, crémeux d'avoine et sec de citron. Arôme raffiné et complexe (grains et levure, houblon). Touches de vanille et de citron.	Lichte frisheid van tar romigheid van haver, citroenachtige droogh Verfijnd en complex ar (granen en huisgist, ho Toetsen van vanille en citrusachtige arom
	Historical 3-grain beer brewed following a Carmelite recipe from 1679.	Bière 3-grains historique brassée selon une recette des Carmélites de 1679.	Historisch 3-granenbie brouwen volgens een K lietenrecept uit 1679.

1679
Karmeliet
Authentiek 3 granenbier, nog steeds gebrouwen volgens een 17e eeuws Dendermonds Karmelietenrecept
Tripel
Gerst
Haver
3 Granen
Orge
Froment
3 Grains
Karmeliet®
Bière "3 grains", toujours brassée selon une recette du 17e siècle de l'ancien cloître de Carmes de Termonde
Tripel
16
79
Karmeliet

Triple moine

	top-fermentation re-fermented in the bottle	fermentation haute refermentation en bouteille	hoge gisting met hergisting in de fl
	specialty beer Tripel	bière spéciale triple	speciaalbier tripel
	Brasserie du Bocq Purnode-Yvoir	Brasserie du Bocq Purnode-Yvoir	Brasserie du Bocq Purnode-Yvoir
	barley malt, wheat starch, hop varieties, yeast, herbs, water	malt d'orge, fécule de froment, sortes de houblon, levure, herbes, eau	gerstemout, tarwezetm hoppesoorten, gist, kruiden, water
%	7,30%	7,30%	7,30%
	blond, lively beer (9EBC) fine, full foam head	blonde (9 EBC), vivante, brillante, mousse fine et généreuse	blond, levendig bier (9 fijne, volle kraag
	Gently pour into a perfectly degreased glass. Leave the yeast sediment (natural re-fermenting) in the bottle	Verser doucement dans un verre parfaitement dégraissé. Laisser le dépôt de levure (refermentation naturelle) dans la bouteille.	Zacht uitschenken in e perfect ontvet glas. Het gistbezinksel (nat lijke hergisting) in de laten.
°C	41 - 54 °F	5 - 12 °C	5 - 12 °C
	Well-balanced mixture of green apple and fine hops. Smooth character beer, low bitterness (25 EBU).	Mélange équilibré de pommes vertes et de houblon fin. Bière pleine de caractère avec une saveur peu amère (25 EBU).	Evenwichtige mengeli van groene appel en fi hop. Zacht bier vol ka ter met weinig bitterh (25 EBU).
i	–	–	–

Triple
Moine
Une tradition de brasseurs depuis 1858
Een brouwerstraditie sinds 1858

Triple Moine

Triverius

	top-fermentation re-fermented in the bottle	fermentation haute refermentation en bouteille	hoge of bovengisting nagisting op de fles
	specialty beer wheat double white	bière spéciale froment double white	speciaalbier tarwe double white
	Brouwerij De Graal Brakel	Brouwerij De Graal Brakel	Brouwerij De Graal Brakel
	malt, wheat, hops, coriander, orange, powerful yeast. 40% more malt and wheat than common Witbier.	malt, froment, houblon, coriandre, orange, levure forte. 40% plus de malt et de froment que dans la bière blanche ordinaire.	mout, tarwe, hop, kori der, sinaas, krachtige g 40% meer mout en tar dan gewoon witbier.
%	6,80%	6,80%	6,80%
	blond, clear	blonde, claire	blond, helder
	Pour carefully in a single, smooth movement and leave the yeast sediment in the bottle.	Verser prudemment en un seul mouvement fluide et laisser le dépôt de levure dans la bouteille.	In 1 vloeiende bewegir voorzichtig uitschenke en het gistdepot in de laten.
°C	46 - 50 °F	8 - 10 °C	8 - 10 °C
	Refreshing, smooth and slightly bitter wheat beer. Non-sweet, dry flavours of special yeast and wheat with coriander. Spicy lime and a dry, citrus-like aftertaste.	Bière de froment rafraîchissante, douce légèrement amère. Goût non sucré, sec, arômes de levure spéciale et froment au coriandre. Citron vert relevé, fin de bouche sèche avec goût d'agrumes.	Verfrissend, zacht en l bitter tarwebier. Niet zoet, droog, arom van speciale gist en ta met koriander. Kruidige limoen en ee ge, citrusachtige afdro
i	Store the bottle upright in a dark, cool room.	Conserver la bouteille verticalement, à l'abri de la lumière et de la chaleur.	De Fles verticaal bewar een donkere, koele pla

TARWEBIER
BIERE BLANCHE
500
TRIVERIUS
Alc 6,8% Vol
de graal

Troubadour blond

	top-fermentation re-fermented in the bottle	fermentation haute refermentation en bouteille	hoge gisting hergisting op de fles
	Belgian specialty beer	bière spéciale belge	Belgisch speciaalbier
	De Proefbrouwerij, Lochristi for The Musketeers, Ursel	De Proefbrouwerij, Lochristi pour The Musketeers, Ursel	De Proefbrouwerij, Lochristi voor The Musketeers Ursel
	–	–	–
%	6,50%	6,50%	6,50%
	blond	blonde	blond
	–	–	–
°C	41 - 46 °F	5 - 8 °C	5 - 8 °C
	–	–	–
	–	–	–

SPECIAALBIER • BELG AN SPECIALTY
Troubadour
BLOND
Alc. 6.5% by Vol.
BELGE SPECIALE • CERVEZA BELGA

Troubadour obscura

	top-fermentation re-fermented in the bottle	fermentation haute refermentation en bouteille	hoge gisting hergisting op de fles
	Belgian specialty beer	bière spéciale belge	Belgisch speciaalbier
	De Proefbrouwerij, Lochristi for The Musketeers, Ursel	De Proefbrouwerij, Lochristi pour The Musketeers, Ursel	De Proefbrouwerij, Lochristi voor The Musketeers, Ursel
	–	–	–
%	8,20%	8,20%	8,20%
	dark brown	brun foncé	donkerbruin
	–	–	–
°C	43 - 50 °F	6 - 10 °C	6 - 10 °C
	–	–	–
i	–	–	–

SPECIAALBIER • BELGIAN
Troubadour
OBSCURA
Alc. 8.2% by Vol.
BELGE SPECIALE • CERVEZA BELGA

Troublette

	top-fermentation	fermentation haute	hoge gisting
	Witbier	bière blanche	witbier
	La Brasserie Caracole Falmignoul	La Brasserie Caracole Falmignoul	La Brasserie Caracole Falmignoul
	barley malt, wheat, Pilsner malt, aromatic hops, lemon rind, yeast, water	malt d'orge, froment, malt de pils, houblon aromatique, écorce de citron, levure, eau	gerstemout, tarwe, pil mout, aromatische ho citroenschil, gist, wate
%	5,50%	5,50%	5,50%
	light blond	blond clair	lichtblond
	–	–	–
°C	refrigerated	température de réfrigérateur	frigotemperatuur
	Light and refreshing with a lemon touch. A real thirst-quencher.	Léger et rafraîchissant avec une touche de citron, désaltérant.	Licht en verfrissend m citroentoets, dorstless
i	Also has an organic version.	Existe également dans une version bio.	Bestaat ook in een bioversie.

Troublette
Alc. 5,5% vol.
Bière • Bier • Beer
Cerveza • Birra doppio malto
BELGIAN BEER

Troublette

Uitzet 1730

	top-fermentation re-fermented in the bottle	fermentation haute refermentation en bouteille	hoge gisting met nagisting in de fle
	Tripel	triple	tripel
	Brouwerij Van Steenberge for Microbrouwerij Paeleman, Wetteren	Brouwerij Van Steenberge pour Microbrouwerij Paeleman, Wetteren	Brouwerij Van Steenbe voor Microbrouwerij Paeleman, Wetteren
	malt, oat, hops, yeast, herbs, water	malt, avoine, houblon, levure, herbes, eau	mout, haver, hop, gist, den, water
%	6,80%	6,80%	6,80%
	unfiltered, generous fine foam head	non filtrée, faux col fin abondant	ongefilterd, overvloedi fijne schuimkraag
	–	–	–
°C	–	–	–
	Boutique beer, bitter with a fruity flavour and a touch of coriander.	Bière artisanale amère avec un arôme fruité et une pointe de coriandre.	Ambachtelijk bitter bi met een fruitig aroma een vleugje koriander.
i	Sipping beer with taste evolution. Store in a cool, dark room.	Bière de dégustation avec évolution de saveur. Conserver à l'abri de la chaleur et de la lumière.	Degustatiebier met sm evolutie. Bewaren op e koele donkere plaats.

1730
Uitzet
een levende Wetterse tripel
1730
Uitzet
een levend bier

Ulricher

	bottom-fermentation	fermentation basse	lage gisting
	Lager / Pilsner	lager/pils	lager/pils
	Brouwerij Girardin Sint-Ulriks-Kapelle	Brouwerij Girardin Sint-Ulriks-Kapelle	Brouwerij Girardin Sint-Ulriks-Kapelle
	barley malt, rice, hops, water	malt d'orge, riz, houblon, eau	gerstemout, rijst, hop, water
%	5%	5%	5%
	gold-yellow, darker than common Pilsner (slightly roasted, direct flame under the beerkettle). Clear.	jaune doré, plus foncé que la pils traditionnelle (légèrement brûlée, flamme directement sous la marmite). Claire.	goudgeel, donkerder d gewone pils (licht gebr directe vlam onder de ketel). Helder.
	cfr Pilsner	voir pils	cfr. Pils
	Cool.	Frais.	Fris.
	Refreshing. Dry, malty, slightly bitter and roasty.	Rafraîchissant. Sec, malté, légèrement amer et légèrement brûlé.	Verfrissend. Droog, moutig, licht b Licht gebrand.
i	–	–	–

BIÈRE
BELGE
Ulricher
EXTRA

Ultra ambrée

	top-fermentation re-fermented in the bottle	fermentation haute refermentation en bouteille	hoge gisting hergisting in de fles
	amber - Ale	ambrée - ale	amber - ale
	Brasserie d'Ecaussinnes Ecaussinnes d'Enghien	Brasserie d'Ecaussinnes Ecaussinnes d'Enghien	Brasserie d'Ecaussinne Ecaussinnes d'Enghie
	malts, hops, candy sugar, yeast, spring water	malts, houblon, sucre candi, levure, eau de source	mouten, hop, kandijsu gist, bronwater
%	7%	7%	7%
	yellow-copper unfiltered	cuivre jaune non filtrée	geelkoper niet gefilterd
	–	–	–
°C	37 °F	3 °C	3 °C
	Pronounced malt and rind aroma. Taste: initially malty, turning into dry bitterness. No long-lasting aftertaste.	Arôme malté prononcé sur fond d'écorce. Introduction principalement maltée, rejointe en milieu de bouche par un amer sec, sans prolongation excessive.	Geprononceerd mouta schil op de achtergron De smaak begint mou en vloeit over in een d bitterheid. Geen te lar afdronk.
i	–	–	–

Ultra
ambrée
d'Ecaussinnes
Brasserie d'Ecaussinnes
7190 Ecaussinnes -BELGIUM
Ultra
des
Ecaussinnes

Ultrablonde

	top-fermentation re-fermented in the bottle	fermentation haute refermentation en bouteille	hoge gisting hergisting in de fles
	strong blond	blonde forte	sterk blond
	Brasserie d'Ecaussinnes Ecaussinnes d'Enghien	Brasserie d'Ecaussinnes Ecaussinnes d'Enghien	Brasserie d'Ecaussinne Ecaussinnes d'Enghie
	selected pale malt varieties, hops, candy sugar, yeast, well water	sortes sélectionnées de malt pâle, houblon, sucre candi, levure, eau de source	geselecteerde bleke m soorten, hop, kandijsu gist, bronwater
%	8%	8%	8%
	gold-coloured	dorée	goudkleurig
	–	–	–
	37 °F	3 °C	3 °C
	Subtle, fruity character. Pronounced malty character combined with a fine bitterness.	Caractère fruité subtile. Caractère malté prononcé combiné avec un goût amer raffiné.	Subtiel fruitig karakte Geprononceerd mout ter gekoppeld aan een bitterheid.
i	–	–	–

Ultrablonde
33cl
Brasserie d'Ecaussinnes
7190 Ecaussinnes -BELGIUM
Restaumont 118
+32(0)67/34 22 77

Ultra
des
Ecaussinnes

Ultrabrune

	top-fermentation re-fermented in the bottle	fermentation haute refermentation en bouteille	hoge gisting hergisting in de fles
	Scottish style - strong brown	scotch - brune forte	scotch - sterk bruin
	Brasserie d'Ecaussinnes Ecaussinnes d'Enghien	Brasserie d'Ecaussinnes Ecaussinnes d'Enghien	Brasserie d'Ecaussinne Ecaussinnes d'Enghier
	Malts, hops, candy sugar, yeast, spring water. Based on hop varieties from Poperinge. Triple fermentation.	Malts, houblon, sucre candi, levure, eau de source. A base de sortes de houblon de Poperinge. Triple fermentation.	Mouten, hop, kandijsu gist, bronwater. Op basis van hopsoort Poperinge. Drievoudige fermenta
%	10%	10%	10%
	brown, almost black filtered	brune, presque noire filtrée	bruin, bijna zwart gefilterd
	–	–	–
	50 - 54 °F	10 - 12 °C	10 - 12 °C
	Strong perfume of liquorice and alcohol. Taste of roasty malt varieties, coffee with liquorice and bitter orange rind.	Parfum fort de réglisse et d'alcool. Goût de sortes de malt brûlé, café avec réglisse et écorce d'orange amer.	Sterk parfum van zoet en alcohol. Smaak van gebrande r soorten, koffie met zo hout en bittere sinaas
	–	–	–

PRODUCT OF BELGIUM
Ultrabrune
d Ecaussinnes
Brasserie d Ecaussinnes
Restaumont 118
7190 Ecaussinnes -BELGIUM
Ultra
des
Ecaussinnes

Ultradélice

	top-fermentation re-fermented in the bottle	fermentation haute refermentation en bouteille	hoge gisting hergisting in de fles
	regional beer brown	bière citadine ou régionale, brune	stads- of streekbier bruin
	Brasserie d'Ecaussinnes Ecaussinnes d'Enghien	Brasserie d'Ecaussinnes Ecaussinnes d'Enghien	Brasserie d'Ecaussinne Ecaussinnes d'Enghier
	malts, hops, candy sugar, yeast, spring water	malts, houblon, sucre candi, levure, eau de source	mouten, hop, kandijsu gist, bronwater
%	8%	8%	8%
	dark brown	brun foncé	donkerbruin
	–	–	–
	46 °F	8 °C	8 °C
	Slightly sugared flavour. Light touch of sugar with special spices.	Arôme légèrement sucré. Touche légèrement sucrée avec un goût relevé spécial.	Licht gesuikerd aroma Lichte suikertoets met ciale kruidensmaak.
	This beer won 'Le coq de cristal 2003' for being the best brown beer.	La bière a gagné 'Le coq de cristal 2003' comme meilleure bière brune.	Dit bier won 'Le coq de tal 2003' als beste brui bier.
	....		

PRODUCT OF BELGIUM
Ultradélice
d'Ecaussinnes
Brasserie d'Ecaussinnes
7190 Ecaussinnes -BELGIUM
Restaumont 118
33CL

Ultra
des
Ecaussinnes

Ultra Fraîche

	top-fermentation re-fermented in the bottle	fermentation haute refermentation en bouteille	hoge gisting hergisting in de fles
	blond	blonde	blond
	Brasserie d'Ecaussinnes Ecaussinnes d'Enghien	Brasserie d'Ecaussinnes Ecaussinnes d'Enghien	Brasserie d'Ecaussinnes Ecaussinnes d'Enghien
	malts, hops, candy sugar, yeast, spring water	malts, houblon, sucre candi, levure, eau de source	mouten, hop, kandijsu gist, bronwater
%	3,50%	3,50%	3,50%
	blond	blonde	blond
	–	–	–
	36 - 37 °F	2 - 3 °C	2 - 3 °C
	Pronounced taste despite the very low alcohol content.	Saveur prononcée malgré la faible teneur en alcool.	Uitgesproken smaak o danks het minieme alc volume.
i	–	–	–

PRODUCT OF BELGIUM
Ultra Fraîche
d'Ecaussinnes
33CL
Brasserie d'Ecaussinnes
7190 Ecaussinnes -BELGIUM
Restaumont 118
+32(0)67/34 22 77

Ultra
des
Ecaussinnes

Ultramour

	top-fermentation	fermentation haute	hoge gisting
	blond fruit beer	blonde bière fruitée	blond fruitbier
	Brasserie d'Ecaussinnes Ecaussinnes d'Enghien	Brasserie d'Ecaussinnes Ecaussinnes d'Enghien	Brasserie d'Ecaussinnes Ecaussinnes d'Enghien
	malts, hops, candy sugar, 3 kinds of red fruits, lemon juice, yeast, spring water	malts, houblon, sucre candi, 3 sortes de fruits rouges, jus de citron, levure, eau de source	mouten, hop, kandijsui 3 soorten rode vruchte troensap, gist, bronwat
%	5%	5%	5%
	hazy reddish unfiltered	rougeâtre, voilée non filtrée	gesluierd roodachtig niet gefilterd
	–	–	–
	37 °F	3 °C	3 °C
	Very perfumed aroma. Light touch of white candy sugar, long-lasting fruit taste, not bitter at all.	Arôme très parfumé. Touche légère de sucre candi blanc, goût fruité qui reste longtemps dans la bouche, pas du tout amer.	Zeer geparfumeerd aro Lichte toets van witte kandijsuiker, fruitsma die lang in de mond bl niets bitter.
	–	–	–

Ultramour
BELGIAN FRUIT BEER
Ultramour

Ultra Soif

	top-fermentation re-fermented in the bottle	fermentation haute refermentation en bouteille	hoge gisting hergisting in de fles
	blond	blonde	blond
	Brasserie d'Ecaussinnes Ecaussinnes d'Enghien	Brasserie d'Ecaussinnes Ecaussinnes d'Enghien	Brasserie d'Ecaussinnes Ecaussinnes d'Enghien
	malts, hops, candy sugar, yeast, spring water	malts, houblon, sucre candi, levure, eau de source	mouten, hop, kandijsui gist, bronwater
	5%	5%	5%
	blond	blonde	blond
	–	–	–
	37 °F	3 °C	3 °C
	A young beer with a pronounced taste that reminds of Witbier. Refreshing with a malty taste and a touch of hop.	Bière jeune avec une saveur prononcée renvoyant à la bière blanche. Rafraîchissant avec un goût malté et une pointe de houblon.	Jong bier met uitgespro ken smaak die refereer witbier. Verfrissend met moutig smaak en een tikje hop
	Boutique beer.	Bière artisanale.	Artisanaal bier.

Ultra Soif
Ultra
des
Ecaussinnes

Urchon

	top-fermentation re-fermented in the bottle	fermentation haute refermentation en bouteille	hoge gisting nagisting in de fles
	specialty beer	bière spéciale	speciaalbier
	Brasserie des Légendes Brewsite Gouyasse Irchonwelz (Ath)	Brasserie des Légendes Brewsite Gouyasse Irchonwelz (Ath)	Brasserie des Légendes Brewsite Gouyasse Irchonwelz (Ath)
	pale malt, caramel malt, roasted malt, hops, yeast, water	malt pâle, malt caramélisé, malt brûlé, houblon, levure, eau	bleekmout, karamelm gebrande mout, hop, g water
	7,50%	7,50%	7,50%
	brown	brune	bruin
	Degrease the glass with some detergent, rinse thoroughly with hot water and dry. With yeast sediment: smoothly revolve the bottle before serving. Without yeast sediment: pour carefully, leaving the sediment in the bottle.	Dégraisser les verres avec un peu de détergent, bien les rincer à l'eau chaude et sécher. Avec dépôt de levure: tourner le dernier tiers de bière avant de le verser. Sans dépôt: verser prudemment et laisser la levure dans la bouteille.	Het glas ontvetten (bee je detergent), goed spo met warm water en dr Met gistbezinkel: het l derde in de fles walsen het uitschenken. Zonder gistbezinksel: voorzichtig schenken en de fond in de fles la
	45 - 50 °F	7 - 10 °C	7 - 10 °C
	Dry character: coffee and caramel. Aroma of roasty malt and pronounced bitterness.	Caractère sec: café et caramel. Arôme de malt brûlé et goût amer prononcé.	Droog karakter: koffie karamel. Aroma van gebrande n en duidelijke bitterhei
	–	–	–

BRASSERIE DES GÉANTS
Château-Brasserie
URCHON
Bière Belge
URCHON

Urthel donker parlus magnificum

	top-fermentation re-fermented in the bottle	fermentation haute refermentation en bouteille	hoge gisting nagisting op de fles
	dubbel	double	dubbel
	at Brouwerij De Konings-hoeven (NL) Brouwerij De Leyerth Ruiselede	chez Brouwerij De Konings-hoeven (NL) Brouwerij De Leyerth Ruiselede	bij Brouwerij De Konin hoeven (NL) Brouwerij De Leyerth Ruiselede
	malt, yeast, hops, water	malt, levure, houblon, eau	mout, gist, hop, water
%	7,50%	7,50%	7,50%
	dark brown clear	brun foncé claire	donkerbruin helder
	Slowly pour into a tilted Urthel glass and preferably leave the yeast sediment in the bottle. The rich foam head can take more or less half of the glass.	Verser lentement dans un verre Urthel tenu en oblique et laisser de préférence le fond de levure dans la bouteille. Le riche faux col peut prendre environ la moitié du verre.	Langzaam uitschenker een schuingehouden U thelglas en de gistfond voorkeur in de fles late De rijkelijke schuimkr mag ongeveer de helft het glas innemen.
°C	43 - 46 °F	6 - 8 °C	6 - 8 °C
	Roasty malt, warm after-taste and fondant chocolate impressions.	Malt brûlé, fin de bouche chaleureuse et impressions de chocolat fondant.	Gebrande mout, warm dronk en impressies va fondantchocolade.
i	Parlus magnificum is the Erthels' forefather (see remark to Urthel triple).	Parlus magnificum est l'ancêtre des Erthels (voir remarque Urthel triple).	Parlus magnificum is stamvader van de Erth (zie opmerking bij Urt tripel).

7,5
DONKER-DARK
SPRAKELIJK DONKER
DARK ALE WITH A BITE
7,5
Urthel
Parlus Magnificum

Urthel hop-it

	top-fermentation re-fermented in the bottle	fermentation haute refermentation en bouteille	hoge gisting nagisting op de fles
	strong blond	blonde forte	sterk blond
	at Brouwerij De Konings-hoeven (NL) Brouwerij De Leyerth Ruiselede	chez Brouwerij De Konings-hoeven (NL) Brouwerij De Leyerth Ruiselede	bij Brouwerij De Konin hoeven (NL) Brouwerij De Leyerth Ruiselede
	malt, yeast, European hops, water	malt, levure, houblon européen, eau	mout, gist, Europese h water
	9,50%	9,50%	9,50%
	pale blond clear	blond pâle claire	bleekblond helder
	Slowly pour into a tilted Urthel glass and preferably leave the yeast sediment in the bottle. The rich foam head can take more or less half of the glass.	Verser lentement dans un verre Urthel tenu en oblique et laisser de préférence le fond de levure dans la bouteille. Le riche faux col peut prendre environ la moitié du verre.	Langzaam uitschenker een schuingehouden U thelglas en de gistfond voorkeur in de fles late De rijkelijke schuimkr mag ongeveer de helft het glas innemen.
°C	43 - 46 °F	6 - 8 °C	6 - 8 °C
	Very hoppy and bitter.	Très houblonné et amer.	Zeer hoppig en bitter.
i	A fairly recent beer, created in 1995 for the American market, but now also sold in Belgium.	Une bière plutôt récente développée en 1995 pour le marché américain mais actuellement également distribuée en Belgique.	Een vrij recent bier da 1995 werd ontwikkeld de Amerikaanse mark maar nu ook in België wordt verdeeld.

SUPERIEUR HOPPIG BLOND
BREWERS EXCELLENT SELECTION OF HOPS
Urthel
HOP-IT

Urthel Samaranth

	top-fermentation re-fermented in the bottle	fermentation haute refermentation en bouteille	hoge gisting nagisting op de fles
	barley wine	vin d'orge	gerstewijn
	at Brouwerij De Konings-hoeven (NL) Brouwerij De Leyerth Ruiselede	chez Brouwerij De Konings-hoeven (NL) Brouwerij De Leyerth Ruiselede	bij Brouwerij De Konin hoeven (NL) Brouwerij De Leyerth Ruiselede
	malts (pale, cara and chocolate), yeast, hops, water	malts (pâle, cara et chocolat), levure, houblon, eau	mout (bleek, cara en c lade), gist, hop, water
	11,50%	11,50%	11,50%
	deep amber, clear	ambré intense, claire	diep amberkleurig, he
	Slowly pour into a tilted Urthel glass and preferably leave the yeast sediment in the bottle. The rich foam head can take more or less half of the glass.	Verser lentement dans un verre Urthel tenu en oblique et laisser de préférence le fond de levure dans la bouteille. Le riche faux col peut prendre environ la moitié du verre.	Langzaam uitschenke een schuingehouden U thelglas en de gistfond voorkeur in de fles late De rijkelijke schuimkr mag ongeveer de helft het glas innemen.
	46 - 50 °F	8 - 10 °C	8 - 10 °C
	Aroma of malt chocolate and ripe summer fruits. Exceptionally round and full taste with a light sweet liqueur-like aftertaste.	Arôme de chocolat malté et de fruits mûrs d'été. La saveur est particulièrement ronde et pleine, avec une fin de bouche légèrement douce de liqueur.	Aroma van moutige c lade en rijpe zomervru ten. De smaak is bijzo rond en vol, met een l zoete likeurachtige afdronk.
	Samaranth is the language Erthels speak (see remark to Urthel Tripel).	Samaranth est la langue des Erthels (voir remarque Urthel tripel).	Samaranth is de taal v Erthels (zie opmerkin Urthel tripel).

12
QUADRIUM
12
QUADRIUM
Urthel
Samaranth

Urthel

Urthel tripel hibernus quentum

	top-fermentation re-fermented in the bottle	fermentation haute refermentation en bouteille	hoge gisting nagisting op de fles
	Tripel	triple	tripel
	at Brouwerij De Konings-hoeven (NL) Brouwerij De Leyerth Ruiselede	chez Brouwerij De Konings-hoeven (NL) Brouwerij De Leyerth Ruiselede	bij Brouwerij De Konin[illegible] hoeven (NL) Brouwerij De Leyerth Ruiselede
	malt, yeast, hops, water	malt, levure, houblon, eau	mout, gist, hop, water
%	9%	9%	9%
	blond, clear	blonde, claire	blond, helder
	Pour slowly into a tilted Urthel glass and preferably leave the yeast sediment in the bottle. The rich foam head can take more or less half of the glass.	Verser lentement dans un verre Urthel tenu en oblique et laisser de préférence le fond de levure dans la bouteille. Le riche faux col peut prendre environ la moitié du verre.	Langzaam uitschenken [illegible] een schuingehouden U[illegible] helglas en de gistfond [illegible] voorkeur in de fles late[illegible] De rijkelijke schuimkr[illegible] mag ongeveer de helft [illegible] het glas innemen.
°C	43 - 46 °F	6 - 8 °C	6 - 8 °C
	Full-bodied and fruity.	Franc et fruité.	Volmondig en fruitig.
i	Brewed by one of the few women-brewers, Hildegard van Ostaden. Urthel is the drink of the Erthels: tiny little men from a story, created and drawn by the brewer's husband.	Brassée par une des peu de brasseurs féminins, Hildegard van Ostaden. Urthel est la boisson des Erthels: les petits personnages du récit créé et dessiné par l'époux du brasseur.	Gebrouwen door een v[illegible] weinige vrouwelijke br[illegible] wers, Hildegard van Os[illegible] den. Urthel is de dran[illegible] de Erthels: kleine man[illegible] tjes in een verhaal gec[illegible] eerd en getekend door [illegible] echtgenoot van de bro[illegible]
	....		

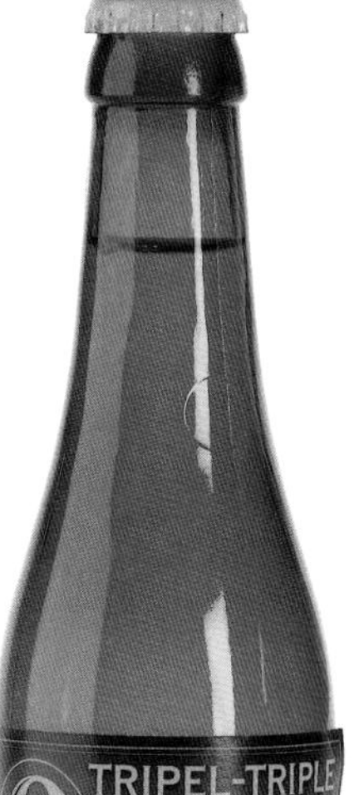
9
TRIPEL-TRIPLE
Urthel
Hibernus Quentum

BREWERIES
Urthel

Val-Dieu blonde

	top-fermentation re-fermented in the bottle	fermentation haute refermentation en bouteille	hoge gisting hergisting op de fles
	recognised Belgian abbey beer, blond	Bière d'abbaye belge reconnue, blonde	Erkend Belgisch abdijb blond
	Brasserie Abbaye du Val-Dieu, Aubel	Brasserie Abbaye du Val-Dieu, Aubel	Brasserie Abbaye du Val-Dieu, Aubel
	malt, two traditional hop varieties, yeast, water	malt, 2 sortes traditionnelles de houblon, levure, eau	mout, 2 traditionele h soorten, gist, water
%	6%	6%	6%
	light yellow slightly hazy	jaune clair légèrement voilée	lichtgeel licht gesluierd
	Whilst pouring, first keep the glass slightly tilted, then slowly straighten it to obtain a white, smooth-edged foam head.	Tenir le verre d'abord légèrement en oblique et le redresser doucement par la suite pour obtenir un faux col blanc pas trop large.	Tijdens het uitschenke glas eerst licht schuin den en zacht recht bre voor een witte maar ni hoge schuimkraag.
°C	43 - 50 °F	6 - 10 °C	6 - 10 °C
	Very refreshing digestive. Initial sugar taste which evolves into light bitterness and ends in a short, slightly bitter aftertaste. Perfumed and slightly stimulating aroma.	Très rafraîchissant et disgestif. Goût initial sucré évoluant à un goût légèrement amer et une arrière-bouche courte, légèrement amère. Arôme parfumé et légèrement stimulant.	Zeer verfrissend en dis tief. Aanzet van suiker evolueert naar lichte b heid en een korte, lich tere nasmaak. Geparfumeerd en lich kelend aroma.
i	A traditional recipe dating back from 1216, when the abbey was founded.	Une recette traditionnelle datant de 1216, quand l'abbaye a été fondée.	Een traditioneel recep dateert van 1216 toen dij gesticht werd.

Abbaye - Abdij
du
Val-Dieu
Anno 1216
Bier gebrouwen
in de Abdij
33 cl
Blonde
Bière brassée
à l'Abbaye
Abbaye du
Val-Dieu

V Val-Dieu brune

	top-fermentation re-fermented in the bottle	fermentation haute refermentation en bouteille	hoge gisting hergisting op de fles
	recognised Belgian abbey beer, brown	Bière d'abbaye belge reconnue, brune	Erkend Belgisch abdij bruin
	Brasserie Abbaye du Val-Dieu, Aubel	Brasserie Abbaye du Val-Dieu, Aubel	Brasserie Abbaye du Val-Dieu, Aubel
	malt, hops, yeast, water	malt, houblon, levure, eau	mout, hop, gist, water
%	8%	8%	8%
	deep ruby, despite its name	rubis foncé malgré son nom	donker robijn ondank naam
	Whilst pouring, first keep the glass slightly tilted, then slowly straighten it to obtain a brownish foam head.	D'abord tenir le verre légèrement en oblique et le redresser doucement par la suite pour obtenir un faux col brunâtre.	Tijdens het uitschenk glas eerst licht schuin den en zacht recht bre voor een bruinachtige schuimkraag.
°C	50 - 54 °F	10 - 12 °C	10 - 12 °C
	Rich and energetic. Slightly stimulating coffee flavour that seeps away without a trace of bitterness.	Riche et énergique. Arôme légèrement stimulant de café absorbé dans le goût sans laisser de goût amer.	Rijk en energiek. Licht prikkelend arom van koffie dat wegebt de smaak en geen bitt heid laat.
i	A traditional recipe dating back from 1216, when the abbey was founded.	Une recette traditionnelle datant de 1216, quand l'abbaye a été fondée.	Een traditioneel recep dateert van 1216 toen dij gesticht werd.

Abbaye Abdij
du
Val-Dieu
Anno 1216
Bier gebrouwen
in de Abdij
Bière brassée
à l'Abbaye
Brune
33 cl

Abbaye du
Val-Dieu

Val-Dieu Noël

	top-fermentation re-fermented in the bottle	fermentation haute refermentation en bouteille	hoge gisting hergisting op de fles
	recognised Belgian abbey beer	Bière d'abbaye belge reconnue	Erkend Belgisch abdij
	Brasserie Abbaye du Val-Dieu, Aubel	Brasserie Abbaye du Val-Dieu, Aubel	Brasserie Abbaye du Val-Dieu, Aubel
	malt, hops, yeast, water	malt, houblon, levure, eau	mout, hop, gist, water
	7%	7%	7%
	warm amber-yellow gentle bubbles	jaune ambré chaud perle tranquillement	warm ambergeel rustige pareling
	Whilst pouring, first keep the glass slightly tilted, then slowly straighten it to obtain a nice, white foam head.	D'abord tenir le verre légèrement en oblique et le redresser doucement par la suite pour obtenir un faux col blanc.	Tijdens het uitschenk glas eerst licht schuin den en zacht recht br voor een witte schuim kraag.
	46 - 54 °F	8 - 12 °C	8 - 12 °C
	Easily digestible. Captivatingly smooth with fine, well-balanced flavours. A pronounced aroma of yeast and malt varieties.	Facilement digestible. Douceur envoûtante comprenant de fines saveurs nuancées. Arôme prononcé de levure et de sortes de malt.	Licht verteerbaar. Onweerstaanbaar zac met een genuanceerd smaak. Uitgesproken aroma gist en moutsoorten.
	–	–	–

Abbaye du
Val-Dieu
Bière de Noël
33 cl
Abbaye du
Val-Dieu

Val-Dieu Triple

	top-fermentation re-fermented in the bottle	fermentation haute refermentation en bouteille	hoge gisting hergisting op de fles
	recognised Belgian abbey beer	Bière d'abbaye belge reconnue	Erkend Belgisch abdijt
	Brasserie Abbaye du Val-Dieu, Aubel	Brasserie Abbaye du Val-Dieu, Aubel	Brasserie Abbaye du Val-Dieu, Aubel
	malt, hops, yeast, water	malt, houblon, levure, eau	mout, hop, gist, water
%	9%	9%	9%
	warm yellow slightly hazy	jaune chaud légèrement voilée	warmgeel licht gesluierd
	Whilst pouring, first keep the glass slightly tilted, then slowly straighten it to obtain a nice, white but not too creamy foam head.	D'abord tenir le verre légèrement en oblique et le redresser doucement par la suite pour obtenir un faux col blanc mais pas trop onctueux.	Tijdens het uitschenk glas eerst licht schuin den en zacht recht bre voor een mooie witte niet te smeuïge schui kraag.
°C	52 - 55 °F	11 - 13 °C	11 - 13 °C
	Easily digestible. Agreeably spicy. Light touch of sugar in the middle, sometimes with alcohol, bitter and soft.	Facilement digestible. Agréablement corsé. Légère touche sucrée au centre, parfois avec de l'alcool, goût amer et moelleux.	Licht verteerbaar. Aan naam kruidig. Lichte toets van suike het midden soms met hol, bitter en zacht.
i	A traditional recipe dating back from 1216, when the abbey was founded. Winner of the 2005 Superior Taste Award.	Une recette traditionnelle datant de 1216, quand l'abbaye a été fondée. A gagné le 'Superior Taste Award' en 2005.	Een traditioneel recep dat dateert van 1216 t de abdij gesticht werd Won de 'Superior Tast Award' in 2005.

Abbaye Abdij
du
Val-Dieu
Anno 1216
Bier gebrouwen
in de Abdij
Bière brassée
à l'Abbaye
Triple
33 cl
Abbaye du
Val-Dieu

Valeir blond

	top-fermentation re-fermented in the bottle (and the barrel)	fermentation haute refermentation en bouteille (et au fût)	hoge gisting hergisting op de fles (e het vat)
	blond specialty beer	bière spéciale blonde	blond speciaalbier
	Brouwerij Contreras Gavere	Brouwerij Contreras Gavere	Brouwerij Contreras Gavere
	Barley malt, hops (Saaz), sugar (for re-fermentation), top-fermenting yeast, water. Dry-hopped.	malt d'orge, houblon (Saaz), sucre (pour refermentation), levure de fermentation haute, eau. Dry-hopped.	Gerstemout, hop (Saaz suiker (voor hergisting hogegistingsgist, wate Ge-dry-hopped.
%	6,50%	6,50%	6,50%
	orange-blond, clear	blond orange, claire	oranjeblond, helder
	Pour into a degreased, rinsed and dry glass. Tilt the glass about 45° and gently pour the beer, avoiding contact between bottle and foam. Provide a foam head of about 2.5 cm and leave 1 cm of beer in the bottle. Present the bottle along with the glass.	Verser dans un verre dégraissé, rincé et sec. Tenir le verre incliné à 45° et verser la bière doucement sans que la bouteille touche l'écume. Prévoir un faux col de 2,5 cm et laisser 1 cm de bière dans la bouteille. Servir la bouteille avec le verre rempli.	Schenken in ontvet, ge en droog glas. Het glas schuin houden en het zacht inschenken zond de fles het schuim raak schuimkraag van ca. 2, voorzien en 1 cm bier fles laten. De fles samen het glas serveren.
°C	43 °F	6 °C	6 °C
	Spicy and hoppy. Pleasantly refreshing.	Relevé et houblonné. Agréablement rafraîchissant.	Kruidig en hoppig. Aangenaam verfrisser
i	Store upright to ensure that the yeast congeals at the bottom of the bottle.	Conserver en position verticale pour tenir la levure au fond.	Verticaal bewaren om gist op de bodem te h den.

VALEIR
BLOND

VALEIR
1453

Valeir divers

	top-fermentation re-fermented in the bottle (and the barrel)	fermentation haute refermentation en bouteille (et au fût)	hoge gisting hergisting op de fles (e het vat)
	Tripel	triple	tripel
	Brouwerij Contreras Gavere	Brouwerij Contreras Gavere	Brouwerij Contreras Gavere
	barley malt, hops (Saaz), sugar (for re-fermentation), top-fermenting yeast, water	malt d'orge, houblon (Saaz), sucre (pour refermentation), levure de fermentation haute, eau	gerstemout, hop (Saaz) suiker (voor hergisting hogegistingsgist, wate
	8,50%	8,50%	8,50%
	light blond	blond clair	lichtblond
	Pour into a degreased, rinsed and dry glass. Tilt the glass about 45° and gently pour the beer, avoiding contact between bottle and foam. Provide a foam head of about 2.5 cm and leave 1 cm of beer in the bottle. Present the bottle along with the glass.	Verser dans un verre dégraissé, rincé et sec. Tenir le verre incliné à 45° et verser la bière doucement sans que la bouteille touche l'écume. Prévoir un faux col de 2,5 cm et laisser 1 cm de bière dans la bouteille. Servir la bouteille avec le verre rempli.	Schenken in ontvet, ges en droog glas. Het glas schuin houden en het zacht inschenken zond de fles het schuim raak schuimkraag van ca. 2, voorzien en 1 cm bier i fles laten. De fles samen het glas serveren.
	43 °F	6 °C	6 °C
	Silky smooth. Dry and hoppy.	Soyeux. Sec et houblonné.	Zijdezacht. Droog en hoppig.
	Store upright to ensure that the yeast settles on the bottom of the bottle.	Conserver en position verticale pour tenir la levure au fond.	Verticaal bewaren om gist op de bodem te h den.

VALEIR
DIVERS
1453
VALEIR
1453

Valeir donker

	top-fermentation re-fermented in the bottle	fermentation haute refermentation en bouteille	hoge gisting hergisting op de fles
	dark specialty beer	bière spéciale foncée	donker speciaalbier
	Brouwerij Contreras Gavere	Brouwerij Contreras Gavere	Brouwerij Contreras Gavere
	barley malt, hops (Hallertau, Styrian, Brewers gold), sugar, top-fermenting yeast, water	malt d'orge, houblon (Hallertau, Styrian, Brewers gold), sucre, levure de fermentation haute, eau	gerstemout, hop (Halle Styrian, Brewers gold), suiker, hogegistingsgis water
%	6,50%	6,50%	6,50%
	chestnut	brun marron	kastanjebruin
	Pour into a degreased, rinsed and dry glass. Tilt the glass about 45° and gently pour the beer, avoiding contact between bottle and foam. Provide a foam head of about 2.5 cm and leave 1 cm of beer in the bottle. Present the bottle along with the glass.	Verser dans un verre dégraissé, rincé et sec. Tenir le verre incliné à 45° et verser la bière doucement sans que la bouteille touche l'écume. Prévoir un faux col de 2,5 cm et laisser 1 cm de bière dans la bouteille. Servir la bouteille avec le verre rempli.	Schenken in een ontvet gespoeld en droog glas. Het glas 45° schuin ho en het bier zacht insch ken zonder dat de fles l schuim raakt. Een schu kraag van ca. 2,5 cm vo zien en 1 cm bier in de laten. De fles samen me het glas serveren.
°C	45 °F	7 °C	7 °C
	Caramel malt. Smooth and bitter.	Caramel malté. Moelleux et amer.	Karamelmoutig. Zacht en bitter.
i	Store upright to ensure that the yeast settles on the bottom of the bottle.	Conserver en position verticale pour tenir la levure au fond.	Verticaal bewaren om gist op de bodem te ho den.

VALEIR
1453
VALEIR
DONKER
1453

Vapeur en folie

	top-fermentation re-fermented in the bottle unpasteurised	fermentation haute refermentation en bouteille non pasteurisée	hoge gisting hergisting op de fles niet gepasteuriseerd
	strong blond	blonde forte	sterk blond
	Brasserie à Vapeur Pipaix	Brasserie à Vapeur Pipaix	Brasserie à Vapeur Pipaix
	barley malt, hops, yeast, herbs, water	malt d'orge, houblon, levure, herbes, eau	gerstemout, hop, gist, [illegible]den, water
%	8%	8%	8%
	blond unfiltered	blonde non filtrée	blond niet gefilterd
	–	–	–
°C	55 - 64 °F	13 - 18 °C	13 - 18 °C
	Strong and round with a moderate flavour of hops and spices (cummin, smooth orange rind).	Corsé et rond avec une portion modérée de houblon et d'herbes (cumin, écorce d'orange doux).	Sterk en rond met matige hop en kruiden (komijn, zachte sinaas-pelschil).
i	Natural boutique beer that can be stored for a long time.	Bière naturelle brassée de façon traditionnelle qui se conserve longtemps.	Op traditionele wijze gebrouwen natuurbier dat lang houdbaar is.

(11,2 Fl.OZ.)
8% alc./vol.
Vapeur en FOLiE
BRASSERIE A VAPEUR
PIPAIX

Vapeur Légère

	top-fermentation re-fermented in the bottle unpasteurised	fermentation haute refermentation en bouteille non pasteurisée	hoge gisting hergisting op de fles niet gepasteuriseerd
	light blond	blonde légère	lichtblond
	Brasserie à Vapeur Pipaix	Brasserie à Vapeur Pipaix	Brasserie à Vapeur Pipaix
	barley malt, hops, yeast, herbs, water	malt d'orge, houblon, levure, herbes, eau	gerstemout, hop, gist, k[illegible]den, water
%	5%	5%	5%
	blond unfiltered	blonde non filtrée	blond niet gefilterd
	–	–	–
°C	55 - 64 °F	13 - 18 °C	13 - 18 °C
	Light and dry with fine hops and subtle cinnamon and vanilla touches. Beer with taste evolution.	Léger et sec avec houblon fin et une touche subtile de cannelle et de vanille. Bière avec évolution de la saveur.	Licht en droog met fijn[illegible] hop en subtiele toets v[illegible] kaneel en vanille. Bier met smaakevoluti[illegible]
i	Natural boutique beer that can be kept for a long time. The original brand name was 'Watt 5'.	Bière naturelle brassée de façon traditionnelle qui se conserve longtemps. Son nom originel était Watt 5.	Op traditionele wijze g[illegible] brouwen natuurbier d[illegible] lang houdbaar is. Vroeger werd dit bier g[illegible] commercialiseerd ond[illegible] naam Watt 5.

Vapeur
Légère
11.2 Fl.oz.
BRASSERIE A VAPEUR
PIPAIX

Vedett

	bottom-fermentation	fermentation basse	lage gisting
	premium Pilsner	premium pils	premium pils
	Duvel Moortgat Corp. Puurs	Duvel Moortgat Corp. Puurs	Duvel Moortgat Corp. Puurs
	barley malt, rice grits, hops (Saaz), lager yeast, water	malt d'orge, semoule de riz, houblon (Saaz), levure de basse fermentation, eau	gerstemout, griesmeel rijst, hop (Saaz), lagergi water
	5,20%	5,20%	5,20%
	blond	blond	blond
	Pour in a single movement in a cool glass, previously rinsed with pure, cold water. Let the foam run over the rim of the glass and skim off the excess foam and big bubbles with a spatula or knife (big carbon dioxide bubbles cause the foam head to disappear more quickly).	Verser d'un seul trait dans un verre refroidi rincé à l'avance à l'eau froide propre. Laisser déborder et enlever l'écume redondante ainsi que les grosses bulles avec une spatule ou un couteau (de grandes bulles de dioxyde de carbone font disparaître l'écume).	In 1 keer uitschenken i een koel glas dat voora spoeld is met koud, zui ver water. Laten overschuimen en het overtollige schuim grove bellen met een s tel of mes van de rand van het glas afhalen (g te koolzuurbellen doen schuim verdwijnen).
	32 - 41 °F	0 - 5 °C	0 - 5 °C
	Sweet, fruity and hoppy background. Typical taste of Saaz hop and lager yeast.	Touche douce, fruitée et houblonnée sur le fond. Saveur typique de houblon Saaz et de levure de basse fermentation.	Zoete, fruitige en hopp achtergrondtoets. Typische smaak van Saazhop en lagergist.
	–	–	–

EXTRA BLOND
VEDETT
WWW.VEDETT.COM
GEWAARBORGD ZONDER SCHEIKUNDIGE PRODUCTEN
GARANTIE SANS ADDITIFS NUISIBLES
ALC.5.2% VOL
33cl

Verhaeghe Pils

	bottom-fermentation	fermentation basse	lage gisting
	Pilsner	pils	pilsbier
	Brouwerij Verhaeghe Vichte	Brouwerij Verhaeghe Vichte	Brouwerij Verhaeghe Vichte
	malt, hops, yeast, corn, water	malt, houblon, levure, maïs, eau	mout, hop, gist, maïs, w
%	5,10%	5,10%	5,10%
	golden yellow filtered	jaune doré filtrée	goudgeel gefilterd
	Pour carefully into a degreased, rinsed, wet glass.	Verser prudemment en un seul mouvement dans un verre dégraissé et mouillé.	Voorzichtig uitschenke 1 beweging in een nat, vet glas.
	37 °F	3 °C	3 °C
	Bitter and malty.	Amer et houblonné.	Bitter en moutig.
i	–	–	–

VERHAEGHE
Pils
VERHAEGHE
Pils

BROUWERIJ - BRASSERIE
VERHAEGHE

Vicardin

	top-fermentation re-fermented in the bottle	fermentation haute refermentation en bouteille	hoge gisting hergisting op de fles
	Tripel Gueuze	gueuze triple	tripel-geuze
	De Proefbrouwerij for Brouwerij Dilewyns Grembergen	De Proefbrouwerij pour Brouwerij Dilewyns Grembergen	De Proefbrouwerij voor Brouwerij Dilewyns Grembergen
	Malt, barley, hops, yeast, sugar, Gueuze from Girardin brewery, water. No herbs or syrups added.	Malt, orge, houblon, levure, sucre, gueuze de la brasserie Girardin, eau. Sans adjonction d'herbes, ni de sirops.	Mout, gerst, hop, gist, s ker, geuze van brouwer Girardin, water. Er worden geen kruide siropen toegevoegd.
	7%	7%	7%
	orange-yellow clear	jaune orange claire	oranjegeel helder
	Keep the glass tilted and pour the beer slowly, with or without yeast sediment.	Tenir le verre en oblique et verser la bière lentement, avec ou sans dépôt de levure.	Het glas schuinhouden het bier langzaam insc ken, met of zonder gist-depot.
	43 - 48 °F	6 - 9 °C	6 - 9 °C
	Summer beer with added Gueuze. Fruity and refreshing with a smooth aftertaste.	Bière d'été avec une petite extra par l'adjonction de gueuze. Fruité, frais avec une fin de bouche moelleuse.	Zomerbier met een extraatje door de toegevo de geuze. Fruitig, fris met zachte dronk.
	–	–	–

VICARDIN
TRIPEL - GUEUZE
VICARDIN
TRIPEL - GUEUZE

Vicaris generaal

	top-fermentation re-fermented in the bottle	fermentation haute refermentation en bouteille	hoge gisting hergisting op de fles
	dark specialty beer	bière spéciale foncée	speciaalbier donker
	De Proefbrouwerij for Brouwerij Dilewyns Grembergen	De Proefbrouwerij pour Brouwerij Dilewyns Grembergen	De Proefbrouwerij voor Brouwerij Dilewyns Grembergen
	Barley, malt, hops, sugar, water. No herbs or syrups added.	orge, malt, houblon, sucre, eau. Sans adjonction d'herbes, ni de sirops.	Gerst, mout, hop, suike water. Er worden geen kruide siropen toegevoegd.
%	8,80%	8,80%	8,80%
	red-brown clear	brun rouge claire	roodbruin helder
	Keep the glass tilted and pour the beer slowly, with or without yeast sediment.	Tenir le verre en oblique et verser la bière lentement, avec ou sans dépôt de levure.	Het glas schuinhouden het bier langzaam insc ken, met of zonder gis depot.
°C	43 - 48 °F	6 - 9 °C	6 - 9 °C
	Roasty malt flavour, suggesting a Christmas beer.	Arôme de malt brûlé, ce qui fait penser à une bière de Noël.	Aroma van gebrande n wat doet denken aan e kerstbier.
i	–	–	–

VICARIS
GENERAAL

Vicaris tripel

	top-fermentation re-fermented in the bottle	fermentation haute refermentation en bouteille	hoge gisting hergisting op de fles
	Tripel	triple	tripel
	De Proefbrouwerij for Brouwerij Dilewyns Grembergen	De Proefbrouwerij pour Brouwerij Dilewyns Grembergen	De Proefbrouwerij voor Brouwerij Dilewyns Grembergen
	Barley, malt, hops, sugar, water. No herbs or syrups added.	Orge, malt, houblon, su- cre, eau . Sans adjonction d'herbes ou de sirops.	Gerst, mout, hop, suike water. Er worden geen kruide siropen toegevoegd.
%	8,50%	8,50%	8,50%
	golden yellow clear	jaune doré claire	goudgeel helder
	Keep the glass tilted and pour the beer slowly, with or without yeast sediment.	Tenir le verre en oblique et verser la bière lente- ment, avec ou sans dépôt de levure.	Het glas schuinhouden het bier langzaam insc ken, met of zonder gist depot.
°C	43 - 48 °F	6 - 9 °C	6 - 9 °C
	A perfectly well-balanced beer with a fruity fla- vour, not too bitter or too sweet.	Bière parfaitement équili- brée avec un arôme frui- té pas trop amer, ni trop doux.	Perfect uitgebalanceer bier met een fruitig ar dat niet te bitter en ni zoet is.
i	–	–	–

VICARIS
VICARIS
TRIPEL

Vichtenaar

	mixed fermentation	fermentation mixte	gemengde gisting
	West-Flanders red-brown – Flemish ale	brune-rouge de la Flandre-Occidentale – Flemish ale	Westvlaams roodbruin Flemish ale
	Brouwerij Verhaeghe Vichte	Brouwerij Verhaeghe Vichte	Brouwerij Verhaeghe Vichte
	Malt, hops, wheat, water. Matured in oak barrels for an average of eight months.	Malt, houblon, froment, eau. Mûrit en moyenne 8 mois en fûts de chêne.	Mout, hop, tarwe, wate Gemiddeld 8 maanden rijpt op eikenhouten va
%	5,10%	5,10%	5,10%
	red-brown filtered	brun rouge filtrée	roodbruin gefilterd
	Pour carefully in a cold, rinsed glass.	Verser prudemment dans un verre refroidi et rincé.	Voorzichtig uitschenke een koud, gespoeld gla
°C	39 °F or 46 - 54 °F	4 °C ou 8 - 12 °C	4 °C of 8 - 12 °C
	Thirst-quencher. Refreshing taste with a slightly sweet and fruity aftertaste.	Désaltérant. Saveur fraîche avec une fin de bouche légèrement douce et fruitée.	Dorstlesser. Frisse smaak met een zoete en fruitige afdro
i	–	–	–

Vichtenaar

Vichtenaar

Villers tripel

	top-fermentation re-fermented in the bottle	fermentation haute refermentation en bouteille	hoge gisting hergisting in de fles
	regional beer Tripel abbey beer	bière régionale bière d'abbaye triple	streekbier abdijbier tripel
	Brouwerij Huyghe Melle	Brouwerij Huyghe Melle	Brouwerij Huyghe Melle
	barley malt, hops, yeast, re-fermentation sugar, water, coriander and orange rind	malt d'orge, houblon, levure, sucre de refermentation, eau, coriandre et écorce d'orange	gerstemout, hop, gist, h gistingssuiker, water, koriander en sinaassch
	8%	8%	8 %
	blond slightly cloudy with fine bubbly foam	blonde légèrement trouble avec faux col légèrement perlant	blond lichttroebel met fijn pa schuim
	–	–	–
	–	–	–
	Taste of hops, coriander and orange rind. Aftertaste: controlled bitterness, pleasant freshness, alcohol.	Goût de houblon, coriandre et écorce d'orange. Fin de bouche: goût amer contrôlé, fraîcheur agréable, alcool.	Smaak van hop, korian en sinaasschil. Afdronk: gecontroleer bitterheid, aangename heid, alcohol.
	Also available in a brown version 'Vieille Villers'.	Egalement disponible dans une version brune 'Vieille Villers'.	Bestaat ook in een bru versie 'Vieille Villers'.

Abdij-
Bier
Bière de
l'Abbaye
Anno 1727
VILLERS
TRIPPEL
TRIPLE

Vlaamsche Leeuw

	top-fermentation re-fermented in the bottle	fermentation haute refermentation en bouteille	hoge gisting hergisting op de fles
	Tripel	triple	tripel
	Brouwerij Van Steenberghe for De Brouwerij van Vlaanderen, Schilde	Brouwerij Van Steenberghe pour De Brouwerij van Vlaanderen, Schilde	Brouwerij Van Steenbe voor De Brouwerij van Vlaanderen, Schild
	barley malt, Saaz hops, sugar, aromatic hops, water	malt d'orge, houblon Saaz, sucre, houblons aromatiques, eau	gerstemout, Saaz hop, ker, aromahoppen, wa
%	8,50%	8,50%	8,50%
	blond slightly cloudy	blonde légèrement trouble	blond lichttroebel
	Empty the bottle carefully.	Verser complètement et prudemment.	Voorzichtig helemaal schenken.
	43 °F	6 °C	6 °C
	Stimulating beer with full taste and fruity aftertaste.	Bière corsée avec un goût plein et une fin de bouche fruitée.	Pittig bier met volle sn en fruitige afdronk.
i	Vlaamsche Leeuw also offers a blond and a brown beer.	Vlaamsche Leeuw a aussi une blonde et une bière foncée.	Vlaamsche Leeuw heef een blond en een bruir

Vlaamsche
Leeuw
Vlaamsche
Leeuw
Natuurlijk en ambachtelijk gebrouwen blond bier

Vlaskop gerstebier

top-fermentation re-fermented in the bottle	fermentation haute refermentation en bouteille	hoge gisting nagisting op de fles
Witbier	bière blanche	witbier
Brouwerij Strubbe Ichtegem	Brouwerij Strubbe Ichtegem	Brouwerij Strubbe Ichtegem
40% unmalted barley, wheat, oat, rye, herbs, hops, yeast, water	40 % orge non maltée, froment, avoine, orge, herbes, houblon, levure, eau	40 % ongemoute gerst, tarwe, haver, rogge, kr den, hop, gist, water
5,50%	5,50%	5,50%
blond cloudy (unfiltered)	blonde trouble (non filtrée)	blond troebel (ongefilterd)
–	–	–
43 °F	6 °C	6 °C
Fruity. Refreshing, thirst-quenching session beer.	Fruité. Bière facilement buvable fraîche et désaltérante.	Fruitig. Fris en dorstlessend doordrinkbier.
Unlike most Witbier brands, this one is based on unmalted barley instead of wheat.	Contrairement à la plupart des bières blanches, cette bière est produite à base d'orge non maltée au lieu de froment.	In tegenstelling tot de meeste witbieren is Vl kop gemaakt op basis ongemoute gerst in pl van tarwe.

VLAS
KOP
GERSTEBIER
VLAS
KOP
GERSTEBIER

Vleteren alt

	top-fermentation re-fermented in the bottle	fermentation haute refermentation en bouteille	hoge gisting hergisting op de fles
	dark Ale	ale foncée	ale donker
	Brouwerij Deca Woesten-Vleteren	Brouwerij Deca Woesten-Vleteren	Brouwerij Deca Woesten-Vleteren
	barley malt, hops, candy sugar, yeast, water	malt d'orge, houblon, sucre candi , levure, eau	gerstemout, hop, kand ker, gist, water
%	8%	8%	8%
	dark brown	brun foncé	donkerbruin
	Bottle can be emptied.	Peut être versée complètement.	Mag helemaal uitgescl ken worden.
°C	43 - 50 °F	6 - 10 °C	6 - 10 °C
	–	–	–
i	–	–	–

Vleteren
Alt

Vondel

	top-fermentation re-fermented in the bottle	fermentation haute refermentation en bouteille	hoge gisting nagisting in de fles
	strong dark brown Ale	ale brune forte, foncée	sterke donkere bruine ale
	Brouwerij Liefmans Oudenaarde/Dentergem	Brouwerij Liefmans Audenarde/Dentergem	Brouwerij Liefmans Oudenaarde/Denterge
	Barley malt, dark caramel malts, corn, sugar, hops, yeast, herbs, water. Fermentation lasts 1.5 months.	Malt d'orge, malts caramélisés foncés, maïs, sucre, houblon, levure, herbes, eau. La fermentation dure 1,5 mois.	Gerstemout, donkere k melmouten, mais, suil hop, gist, kruiden, wat De gisting duurt 1,5 m
	8,50% high density	8,50% haute densité	8,50% hoge densiteit
	dark brown slightly cloudy	brun foncé légèrement trouble	donkerbruin licht troebel
	Leave the yeast in the bottle.	Laisser la levure dans la bouteille.	De gist in het flesje lat
	46 - 50 °F	8 - 10 °C	8 - 10 °C
	Soft taste with a touch of liquorice and toffee. Spicy, caramel-like aroma.	Saveur moelleuse avec une touche de réglisse et de caramel. Arôme caramélisé, relevé.	Zachte smaak met toe drop en toffee. Kruidig, karamelachti aroma.
	Can be kept for years if stored horizontally at cellar temperature. Winner of the World Beer Cup 2004 Gold Award.	Se conserve pendant des années en position horizontale à température de cave. World Beer Cup 2004 Gold Award.	Horizontaal op kelder peratuur gedurende ja houdbaar. World Beer Cup 2004 (Award.

BRUIN BIER
SCURA BELGA
BIÈRE BRUNE FORTE
BELGIAN STRONG
Vondel
Brassée et embouteillée par / Brewed and bottled by
Liefmans Breweries, B-8720 Dentergem
8,5% ALC
Vondel

Vuuve

	top-fermentation re-fermented in the bottle	fermentation haute refermentation en bouteille	hoge gisting hergisting op de fles
	Witbier with herbs	bière blanche aux épices	witbier met kruiden
	Brouwerij De Regenboog Brugge	Brouwerij De Regenboog Bruges	Brouwerij De Regenbo Brugge
	60% barley malt, 40% wheat, Hallertau hops, coriander, fresh orange rind, brewer's yeast, water	60 % malt d'orge, 40 % de froment, houblon Hallertau, coriandre, zeste d'orange frais, levure de bière, eau	60 % gerstemout, 40 % we, Hallertau hop, kor der, verse sinaasschil, gist, water
%	5%	5%	5%
	blond, unfiltered non-cloudy Witbier	blonde, non filtrée bière blanche non trouble	blond, niet gefilterd niet troebel witbier
	–	–	–
°C	refrigerated	température de réfrigérateur	frigofris
	Fruity nose, dominated by citrus, coriander and wheat. Typical Witbier taste with citric and orange touches.	Parfum fruité dominé par des agrumes, du coriandre et du froment. Goût typique de bière blanche avec des touches d'agrumes et d'orange.	Fruitige neus met voo trus, koriander en tar Typische witbiersmaal met toetsen van citrus sinaas.
i	Boutique beer, brewed for the brewery's fifth anniversary in 2005. 'Vuuve' means 'five' in the Bruges' dialect. Very successful in the USA but hard to find in Belgium.	Bière artisanale brassée à l'occasion du 5ième anniversaire de la brasserie en 2005. 'Vuuve' veut dire 'cinq' en dialecte brugeois. Cette bière a beaucoup de succès aux Etats-Unis mais est difficile à trouver en Belgique.	Artisanaal bier, gebrou n.a.v. het 5-jarig bestaa van de brouwerij in 20 'Vuuve' is het Brugse lect voor 'vijf'. Erg suc vol in de Verenigde St maar moeilijk verkrijg in België.

CA REDEMPTION VALUE:
5% Alc./Vol.
ALE BREWED WITH SPICES
vuuve
BREWED & BOTTLED BY
DE REGENBOOG, BRUGGE, BELGIUM
IMPORTED BY B. UNITED INT. INC.
REDDING CT 06896
11.2 FL.OZ PRODUCT OF BELGIUM
vuuve

Waaslander

	top-fermentation re-fermented in the bottle	fermentation haute refermentation en bouteille	hoge gisting hergisting op de fles
	Witbier	bière blanche	witbier
	Huisbrouwerij Boelens Belsele	Huisbrouwerij Boelens Belsele	Huisbrouwerij Boelen Belsele
	barley malt, wheat malt, citric herbs, hops, brewer's yeast, water	malt d'orge, malt de froment, herbes de citron, houblon, levure de bière, eau	gerstemout, tarwemo citruskruiden, hop, biergist, water
%	6,50%	6,50%	6,50%
	blond slightly cloudy	blonde légèrement trouble	blond licht troebel
	Pour carefully, so the yeast sediment remains at the bottom of the bottle.	Verser prudemment pour tenir le dépôt de levure au fond de la bouteille.	Voorzichtig uitschenk om het gistbezinksel bodem te houden.
°C	45 °F	7 °C	7 °C
	Very spicy summer beer, smooth and light, with a complex taste due to the use of citrus, coriander and curaçao. Typical wheat aftertaste.	Bière d'été très relevée, douce et légère, goût complexe par l'utilisation d'agrumes, de coriandre et de curaçao. Arrière-bouche typique de froment.	Zeer kruidig zomerbi zacht en licht, comple smaak door het gebru van citrus, koriander en curaçao. Typische tarweafdron
i	–	–	–

Boelens
Waaslander

Wase wolf

	top-fermentation re-fermented in the bottle	fermentation haute refermentation en bouteille	hoge gisting hergisting op de fles
	Witbier amber	bière blanche ambrée	witbier amber
	Huisbrouwerij Boelens Belsele	Huisbrouwerij Boelens Belsele	Huisbrouwerij Boelens Belsele
	wheat, caramel malt, coriander, yeast, water	froment, malt de caramel, coriandre, levure, eau	tarwe, karamelmout, k ander, gist, water
	6,50%	6,50%	6,50%
	amber clear	ambrée claire	amber helder
	Pour carefully, so the yeast sediment remains at the bottom of the bottle.	Verser prudemment pour tenir le dépôt de levure au fond de la bouteille.	Voorzichtig uitschenk om het gistbezinksel c bodem te houden.
	41 - 45 °F	5 - 7 °C	5 - 7 °C
	Very spicy amber beer with a touch of coriander. The added caramel is noticeable in the taste.	Bière ambrée très relevée avec une touche de coriandre. L'adjonction de caramel se traduit dans la saveur.	Sterk gekruid amberbi met een toets van kori der. De toevoeging van karamel vertaalt zich i de smaak.
	Refers to the legend of 'The Wolf of the Waasland' anno 2000.	Renvoie à la légende du 'Loup du Waasland' anno 2000.	Verwijst naar de legen van 'De Wolf van het W land' anno 2000.

BIER UIT HET WAASLAND
WAASE WOLF
Gebrouwen door • Brassée par • Brewed by
Brouwerij Boelens
Kerkstraat 7 • B-9111 Belsele

Watou Tripel

	top-fermentation re-fermented in the bottle	fermentation haute refermentation en bouteille	hoge gisting hergisting op de fles
	Tripel Belgian abbey beer	bière d'abbaye belge triple	Belgisch abdijbier trip
	Brouwerij St-Bernardus Watou	Brouwerij St-Bernardus Watou	Brouwerij St-Bernardu Watou
	malt varieties, hops, sugar, yeast and 'historical' water (rain water fallen in Jeanne d'Arc's time, pumped in Watou)	sortes de malt, houblon, sucre, levure et eau 'historique' (pompée à Watou et provenant de l'époque de Jeanne d'Arc)	moutsoorten, hop, sui gist en 'historisch' wat (opgepompt in Watou komstig uit de tijd dat ne d'Arc leefde)
	7,50%	7,50%	7,50%
	amber/blond unfiltered	ambrée/blonde non filtrée	amber/blond ongefilterd
	Pour into a glass, rinsed with cold water. Keep the glass upright and pour the beer carefully in a single movement. The yeast sediment can be left in the bottle or drunk separately.	Verser dans un verre rincé à l'eau froide. Laisser le verre en position verticale et verser la bière prudemment en un seul mouvement. Laisser le dépôt de levure dans la bouteille ou le boire séparément.	Uitschenken in een me water gespoeld glas. He rechtop laten staan en bier in 1 vloeiende bew voorzichtig uitschenke gistdepot (kan desgewe apart worden uitgedro in de fles laten.
	39 - 46 °F	4 - 8 °C	4 - 8 °C
	Agreeably smooth flavour, slightly bitter and well-balanced, with a fruity orange touch and fresh aftertaste.	Arôme doux agréable, légèrement amer et équilibré avec une touche fruitée d'orange et une fin de bouche fraîche.	Aangenaam zacht aro licht bitter en evenwic met fruitige sinaastoe frisse afdronk.
	–	–	–
	....		

Watou
Tripel
Watou
Tripel
St. Bernardus

Watou's Wit Bier

	top-fermentation	fermentation haute	hoge gisting
	Witbier	bière blanche	witbier
	Brouwerij Van Eecke Watou	Brouwerij Van Eecke Watou	Brouwerij Van Eecke Watou
	malt, wheat, spices, yeast, water	malt, froment, condiments, levure, eau	mout, tarwe, specerij gist, water
%	5%	5%	5%
	light yellow, cloudy	jaune clair, trouble	lichtgeel, troebel
	Pour slowly in a single, smooth movement in a degreased glass. Keep the glass tilted to avoid sloshing. Leave the last 4 cm in the bottle. Next, revolve the bottle to loosen the yeast sediment. Empty the bottle and skim off the foam.	Verser lentement et en un seul mouvement fluide dans un verre dégraissé tenu en oblique. Ne pas laisser la bière clapoter. Laisser les derniers 4 cm de bière dans la bouteille et secouer pour dégager le dépôt de levure. Vider la bouteille et écumer le verre.	Traag en in 1 vloeien weging uitschenken i een vetvrij glas dat w schuingehouden. Het niet laten klotsen. De ste 4 cm in de fles lat en rondwalsen om de sluier los te maken. D leegschenken en het schuimen.
°C	37 °F	3 °C	3 °C
	Refreshing thirst-quencher. Sourish taste with fruity coriander.	Désaltérant frais. Saveur légèrement acidulée avec une touche de coriandre fruitée.	Frisse dorstlesser. Lichtzure smaak met ge koriander.
i	–	–	–

Wit
Bier
5 412896 000111
Watou's
Wit Bier
Bière Blanche
25 CL. e

Watou's
Wit
Bière Blanche

Winter Koninck

	top-fermentation	fermentation haute	hoge gisting
	winter beer	bière hivernale	winterbier
	Brouwerij De Koninck Antwerpen	Brouwerij De Koninck Anvers	Brouwerij De Koninck Antwerpen
	malt, hops, yeast, organic cane sugar, water	malt, houblon, levure, sucre de canne biologique, eau	mout, hop, gist, biologi rietsuiker, water
	6,50%	6,50%	6,50%
	dark red clear creamy foam head	rouge foncé claire faux col couleur crème	donkerrood helder crème-achtige schuimk
	Lift the bottle high when pouring starts, then lower it slowly, until a nice foam head is formed.	Tenir la bouteille haut au début et la baisser lentement jusqu'à la formation d'un beau faux col.	De fles hoog houden bi start, en langzaam late zakken tot er een mooi schuimkraag is gevorm
	43 - 50 °F	6 - 10 °C	6 - 10 °C
	Perfect balance between sweet, bitter and roasty. Soft, warm start. Full-bodied with touches of roasted malt. Bitter aftertaste because of the Saaz hops.	Equilibre parfait entre doux, amer et brûlé. Goût initial doux, chaleureux. Franc avec des touches de malt brûlé. Fin de bouche amère par le houblon Saaz.	Perfecte balans tussen bitter en gebrand. Zach te, warme start. Volmo met toetsen van gebrar mout. Afdronk bitter d de Saaz hop.
	–	–	–

DE KONINCK
1833
DE KONINCK
1833
Winter
Koninck
DE KONINCK
1833

Winterkoninkske

	top-fermentation re-fermented in the bottle unpasteurised	fermentation haute refermentation en bouteillee non pasteurisée	hoge gisting nagisting op de fles niet gepasteuriseerd
	specialty beer winter beer	bière spéciale bière hivernale	speciaalbier winterbier
	Brouwerij Kerkom Sint-Truiden	Brouwerij Kerkom Sint-Trond	Brouwerij Kerkom Sint-Truiden
	7 malt varieties, includ- ing oat malt, 2 Belgian hop varieties, including Saaz	7 sortes de malt dont malt d'avoine, 2 sortes de houblon belge dont Saaz.	7 moutsoorten waaron havermout, 2 Belgische hopsoorten waaronder Saaz.
%	8,30%	8,30%	8,30%
	dark unfiltered	foncée non filtrée	donker ongefilterd
	–	–	–
°C	–	–	–
	Deep and full-bodied with a refreshing taste, ob- tained by the oats. Pleasant and smooth bit- terness due to the differ- ent hop varieties. Full, pure, slightly sweetish taste and long, smoothly bitter aftertaste.	Saveur franche profon- de et rafraîchissante par les flocons d'avoine. Goût amer agréable et moel- leux par les sortes de hou- blon utilisées. Saveur plei- ne, pure et légèrement douce, fin de bouche lon- gue et légèrement amère.	Diepe volmondigheid e verfrissende smaak doo havermout. Aangename en zachte b terheid door de hopsoo Volle, zuivere, lichtzoet smaak en lange zachtbi re afdronk.
i	–	–	–

gebrouwen streekbier van hoge gisting
Nagisting in de fles. Met
brouwwater, mout, havermout, gist,
: 0495/38.12.14 Sint-Truiden

Brouwerij

Witbier Haacht

	top-fermentation	fermentation haute	hoge gisting
	Witbier	bière blanche	witbier
	Brouwerij Haacht Boortmeerbeek	Brouwerij Haacht Boortmeerbeek	Brouwerij Haacht Boortmeerbeek
	barley malt, wheat malt, unmalted wheat, sugar, hops, herbs (coriander), orange rind, yeast, water	malt d'orge et de froment, froment non malté, sucre, houblon, herbes (coriandre), écorce d'orange, levure, eau	gerstemout, tarwemou gemoute tarwe, suiker, kruiden (koriander), gis sinaasappelschil, water
%	5,10%	5,10%	5,10%
	slightly cloudy (unfiltered)	légèrement trouble (non filtrée)	licht troebel (ongefilter
	Pour carefully into a rinsed, wet glass, avoiding contact between bottle and foam.	Verser prudemment dans un verre rincé et mouillé sans que la bouteille touche l'écume.	Voorzichtig uitschenke in een gespoeld, nat gla zonder dat de fles het schuim raakt.
	37 °F	3 °C	3 °C
	Volatile, fruity components due to the top-fermenting process. The mouthfeel is fuller than the density suggests, owing to the proteins and yeast cells.	Composantes volatiles et fruitées par la fermentation haute. La sensation dans la bouche est plus pleine que ce que la densité laisse présumer vu la présence des protéines et des cellules de fermentation.	Vluchtige, fruitige com nenten door het hogegi tingsproces. Het mondgevoel is volle dan de densiteit laat ve moeden door de aanwe eiwitten en gistcellen.
i	The sower's emblem has existed ever since Brouwerij Haacht was founded in 1898.	L'emblème du semeur trouve son origine dans la Brasserie Haacht en 1898.	Het embleem van de za er vindt zijn oorsprong het ontstaan van Brouw Haacht in 1898.

Bière de
froment
avec levure
HAACHT
25cl.e
alc.5,1%vol
1898
HAACHT
WITBIER · BLANCHE
1898
HAACHT
WITBIER · BLANCHE

Witkap - Dubbele Pater

	top-fermentation naturally re-fermented in the bottle	fermentation haute avec refermentation naturelle en bouteille	hoge gisting met natuu ke hergisting op de fles
	dark abbey beer	bière d'abbaye foncée	abdijbier donker
	Brouwerij Slaghmuylder Ninove	Brouwerij Slaghmuylder Ninove	Brouwerij Slaghmuylde Ninove
	Barley malt, yeast, water hop varieties (Belgian Hallertau, Czech Styrie).	Malt d'orge, levure, eau, sortes de houblon (Hallertau belge, Styrie tchèque).	Gerstemout, gist, wate hopsoorten (Belgische lertau, Tsjechische Sty
%	7%	7%	7%
	dark brown with cream-coloured foam head	brun foncé avec un faux col couleur crème	donkerbruin met crèm kleurige schuimkraag
	Pour carefully in a single, fluent and smooth movement. Leave the yeast sediment in the bottle.	Verser prudemment en un seul mouvement fluide et doux. Laisser le dépôt de levure dans la bouteille.	Voorzichtig uitschenke in 1 vloeiende, zachte beweging. Het gistdepc in de fles laten.
°C	46 - 54 °F	8 - 12 °C	8 - 12 °C
	Lively beer with taste evolution, that matches bitter chocolate. Full-bodied with touches of caramel and fine bitter aftertaste.	Bière vivante avec évolution de la saveur qui se marie parfaitement avec le chocolat amer. Franc avec des touches caramélisées et une fin de bouche amère, raffinée.	Levend bier met smaak evolutie dat past bij bi chocolade. Volmondig toetsen van karamel er ne bittere afdronk.
i	–	–	–

WITKAP · PATER
WITKAP · PATER
DUBBELE PATER
LEVEND BIER
BIERE VIVANTE

Witkap - Pater Stimulo

	top-fermentation naturally re-fermented in the bottle	fermentation haute avec refermentation naturelle en bouteille	hoge gisting met natuu ke hergisting op de fles
	blond abbey beer	bière d'abbaye, blonde	abdijbier, blond
	Brouwerij Slaghmuylder Ninove	Brouwerij Slaghmuylder Ninove	Brouwerij Slaghmuylde Ninove
	barley malt, yeast, water hop varieties (Belgian Hallertau, Czech Styrie).	malt d'orge, levure, eau sortes de houblon (Hallertau belge, Styrie tchèque).	gerstemout, gist, water hopsoorten (Belgische H lertau, Tsjechische Styr
%	6%	6%	6%
	Gold-coloured with a creamy foam head. Clear bubbles when served gently. Possibly cloudy when cold (due to the proteins).	Dorée avec un faux col crémeux. Clairement perlant si on verse doucement. Possiblement trouble si la bière est froide (par les protéines).	Goudkleurig met romig schuimkraag. Helder pa relend indien zacht uit schonken. Koudetroebe mogelijk (eiwitten).
	Pour carefully in a single, fluent and smooth movement. Leave the yeast sediment in the bottle.	Verser prudemment en un seul mouvement fluide et doux. Laisser le dépôt de levure dans la bouteille.	Voorzichtig uitschenke in 1 vloeiende, zachte beweging. Het gistdepo in de fles laten.
°C	46 - 54 °F	8 - 12 °C	8 - 12 °C
	Lively beer with taste evolution, a unique thirst-quencher. Velvety smooth mouthfeel and pleasant hoppy bitter aftertaste.	Bière vivante avec évolution de la saveur, désaltérant unique. Sensation de bouche veloutée et fin de bouche houblonnée, amère.	Levend bier met smaak evolutie, unieke dorstle Fluweelzacht mondgev en aangename hopbitt afdronk.
i	One of the few abbey beers that are not pasteurised and re-fermented in the barrel.	Une des rares bières d'abbaye non pasteurisées et sans refermentation au fût.	Een van de weinige abd bieren dat niet gepaste seerd is en hergist is op

WITKAP · PATER
STIMULO
LEVEND BIER
BIERE VIVANTE
Alc. 6% vol.
Bevat gerstemout - Contient du malt d'orge
LOT
WITKAP · PATER

Witkap - Pater Tripel

	top-fermentation naturally re-fermented in the bottle	fermentation haute avec refermentation naturelle en bouteille	hoge gisting met natu ke hergisting op de fle
	Tripel blond	triple blonde	tripel blond
	Brouwerij Slaghmuylder Ninove	Brouwerij Slaghmuylder Ninove	Brouwerij Slaghmuylc Ninove
	barley malt, yeast, water hop varieties (Belgian Hallertau, Czech Styrie).	malt d'orge, levure, eau, sortes de houblon (Hallertau belge, Styrie tchèque).	gerstemout, gist, wate hopsoorten (Belgische lertau, Tsjechische Sty
%	7,50%	7,50%	7,50 %
	gold-yellow with fine, white foam, clear and gentle CO_2 bubbles	jaune doré avec écume fine blanche, bulles CO_2 claires et tranquilles	goudgeel met fijn wit schuim, heldere en ru CO_2 parels
	Pour carefully in one fluent movement. Leave the yeast sediment in the bottle.	Verser prudemment en un seul mouvement fluide. Laisser le dépôt de levure dans la bouteille.	Voorzichtig uitschenk 1 vloeiende, zachte be ging. Het gistdepot in fles laten.
°C	46 - 54 °F	8 - 12 °C	8 - 12 °C
	Lively beer with a fruity nose, a wide range of flowery and spicy aromas and a complex taste, due to the fermentation. Long, dry, bitter aftertaste due to the hops from Aalst.	Bière vivante avec un parfum fruité, une multitude d'arômes (fleuris et relevés) et une saveur complexe par la fermentation. Arrière-bouche longue, sèche et amère par les houblons d'Alost.	Levend bier met fruiti neus, een veelheid aa ma's (bloemig en krui en een complexe sma door de gisting. Lange ge, bittere afdronk do Aalsterse hop.
i	Classified by the New York Times as the nr. 8 of the 'best Tripels in the world'.	Classée par le New York Times à la 8ième place parmi les 'Meilleures Triples du Monde'.	Door New York Times nummer 8 gerangschi de 'Beste Tripels ter w

WITKAP·PATER
TRIPEL
LEVEND BIER
BIERE VIVANTE
7,5% vol.
LOT
Bevat gerstemout - Contient du malt d'orge
www.witkap.
WITKAP · PATER

Wittekerke Rosé

	top-fermentation	fermentation haute	hoge gisting
	Witbier with fruit	bière blanche fruitée	witbier met fruit
	Brouwerij Bavik Bavikhove	Brouwerij Bavik Bavikhove	Brouwerij Bavik Bavikhove
	malt, hops, wheat, fructose, flavouring, raspberry juice, aspartame, water	malt, houblon, froment, fructose, arômes, jus de framboises, aspartame, eau	mout, hop, tarwe, fruc aroma's, frambozensap partaam, water
	4,30%	4,30%	4,30%
	Pink with a nice, solid, white to light pink foam head.	Rose avec un beau faux col solide, blanche à rose clair.	Roze met een mooi ste witte tot lichtroze schu kraag.
	Empty in a degreased, rinsed and wet glass, avoiding contact between bottle and foam.	Verser complètement dans un verre dégraissé, rincé et mouillé sans que la bouteille touche le faux col.	Helemaal uitschenken een ontvet, gespoeld er glas zonder dat de fles schuim raakt.
	39 - 43 °F	4 - 6 °C	4 - 6 °C
	Sweet-and-sour with a clearly recognisable raspberry taste. Naturally refreshing, with a smooth and full-bodied character.	Aigre-doux avec une saveur de framboises parfaitement reconnaissable. Naturellement rafraîchissant, moelleux et caractère plein dans la bouche.	Zoetzuur met duidelijk kenbare frambozensm Natuurlijk verfrissend, zacht en mondvullend rakter.
	The first fruit beer based on Witbeer.	La première bière fruitée à base de bière blanche.	Het eerste fruitbier op van witbier.

Wittekerke
Rosé
•THE FRUITY PINK BEER•
Wittekerke

Wittekerke Speciale

	top-fermentation	fermentation haute	hoge gisting
	Witbier amber	bière blanche ambrée	witbier amber
	Brouwerij Bavik Bavikhove	Brouwerij Bavik Bavikhove	Brouwerij Bavik Bavikhove
	barley malt, hops, yeast, wheat, pure spring water	malt d'orge, houblon, levure, eau de source pure	gerstemout, hop, gist, we, zuiver bronwater
%	5,80%	5,80%	5,80%
	golden blond Witbier	bière blanche blond doré	goudblond witbier
	Pour into a degreased, rinsed and wet glass, avoiding contact between bottle and foam.	Verser dans un verre dégraissé, rincé et mouillé sans que la bouteille touche le faux col.	Uitschenken in een on gespoeld en nat glas zc der dat de fles het schu raakt.
°C	39 - 43 °F	4 - 6 °C	4 - 6 °C
	Smooth and fruity with a touch of pears and cream. Dry, creamy, powerful character.	Doux et fruité avec une touche de poires et de crème. Caractère sec, crémeux et corsé.	Zacht en fruitig met ee snufje peren en room. Droog, romig, krachtig rakter.
i	–	–	–

De Vurige Witte
La Blanche Ardente
Wittekerke
Speciale
Wittekerke

Wittekerke Wit Bier

	top-fermentation	fermentation haute	hoge gisting
	Witbier - Wheat Ale	bière blanche	witbier
	Brouwerij Bavik Bavikhove	Brouwerij Bavik Bavikhove	Brouwerij Bavik Bavikhove
	barley malt, hops, wheat, fructose, flavouring, pure spring water	malt d'orge, houblon, froment, fructose, arômes, eau de source pure	gerstemout, hop, tarw fructose, aroma's, zuiv bronwater
	5%	5%	5%
	attractive, opalescent light golden green colour	couleur attractive opaline, vert doré clair	aantrekkelijke, opaala ge, licht groengouden
	Pour into a degreased, rinsed and wet glass, avoiding contact between bottle and foam.	Verser dans un verre dégraissé, rincé et mouillé sans que la bouteille touche le faux col.	Uitschenken in een on gespoeld en nat glas z der dat de fles het sch raakt.
	39 - 43 °F	4 - 6 °C	4 - 6 °C
	Very aromatic with a fragrant fruitiness, slightly spicy, with an underlying sweetness and a touch of citrus. Round and complex character.	Très aromatisé: arôme fruité, légèrement épicé avec une douceur sous-jacente, touche d'agrumes. Caractère complexe et rond.	Zeer aromatisch met g ge fruitigheid, lichtjes dig met onderliggend zoetigheid, toets van c Rond en complex kara
	Named after a successful TV soap.	Nommé après un feuilleton télévisé à succès.	Genoemd naar een suc volle TV soap.

Wit Bier - Bière Blanche
Wittekerke
Wheat Ale
Wittekerke

Wittoen

	top-fermentation re-fermented in the bottle	fermentation haute refermentation en bouteille	hoge gisting nagisting op de fles
	Tripel amber	triple ambrée	tripel amber
	Brouwerij Strubbe Ichtegem	Brouwerij Strubbe Ichtegem	Brouwerij Strubbe Ichtegem
	Pilsner malt, caramel malt, candy sugar, hops, gruut (mainly gale and rosemary) yeast, water. Gruut is a mixture of herbs, the predecessor of the hops.	malt de pils, malt caramélisé, sucre candi, houblon, gruyt (surtout myrte bâtard et romarin), levure, eau. Gruyt est un mélange d'herbes et est le précurseur du houblon.	pilsmout, karamelmo[illegible] kandijsuiker, hop, gru[illegible] (vooral gagel en rozem[illegible] rijn), gist, water. Gruu[illegible] een kruidenmengsel, [illegible] voorloper van de hop.
	8,20%	8,20%	8,20%
	amber	ambrée	amber
	Pour into a glass suitable for abbey beers or into a Wittoen-glass.	Verser dans un verre pour bières d'abbaye ou un verre Wittoen.	Uitschenken in een gl[illegible] voor abdijbieren of Wi[illegible] toenglas.
	46 °F	8 °C	8 °C
	Spicy, full, bittersweet.	Relevé, plein, doux-amer.	Kruidig, vol, zoetbitte[illegible]
	Aromatised with herbs in the same way as the local beers of the Middle Ages. The name refers to the Oostkamp knight Jan Wittoen (or Jan Winteyn) who lived in the 15th century.	Aromatisé aux herbes comme les bières locales du Moyen-Age. Le nom renvoie au chevalier d'Oostkamp Jan Wittoen (ou Jan Winteyn) qui a vécu au 15ième siècle.	Gearomatiseerd met k[illegible] den zoals de lokale bi[illegible] uit de Middeleeuwen. De naam verwijst naa[illegible] Oostkampse ridder Ja[illegible] toen (of Jan Winteyn) leefde in de 15e eeuw.

Wittoen
Wittoen
Oostkamp

Wostyntje Torhouts Mostaard Bier

	top-fermentation re-fermented in the bottle	fermentation haute refermentation en bouteille	hoge gisting hergisting op de fles
	light Tripel	triple légère	lichte tripel
	Brouwerij De Regenboog Brugge	Brouwerij De Regenboog Bruges	Brouwerij De Regenbo Brugge
	barley/Pilsner malt, Munich malt, Hallertau and Challenger hops, dark candy, musterd seed, yeast, water	malt d'orge/de pils, malt Munich, houblon Hallertau et Challenger, sucre candi foncé, graine de moutarde, levure, eau	gerste-/pilsmout, munichmout, Hallertau e Challenger hop, donke kandij, mosterdzaad, g water
%	7%	7%	7%
	dark blond unfiltered	blond foncé non filtrée	donkerblond niet gefilterd
	–	–	–
°C	50 °F	10 °C	10 °C
	Soft Tripel with a very spicy touch of musterd seed.	Triple moelleuse avec une touche très relevée de graines de moutarde.	Zachte tripel met een kruidige toets van mo zaadjes.
i	Boutique beer that can be kept up to three years after the bottling date. The label was designed by the American comic artist Bill Coleman. Initially brewed for the 130th anniversary of the mustard factory Wostyn in Torhout (1999).	Bière artisanale qui se conserve jusqu'à 3 ans après la date de la mise en bouteilles. L'étiquette est conçue par le cartooniste américain Bill Coleman. A l'origine brassée à l'occasion du 130ième anniversaire de la fabrique de moutarde Wostyn à Torhout (1999).	Artisanaal bier, 3 jaar baar na botteldatum. Het etiket is ontworpe door de Amerikaanse tekenaar Bill Coleman Initieel gebrouwen n.a 130e verjaardag van m terdfabriek Wostyn in hout (1999).

Mostyntje
Torhouts Mostaard Bier
33 cl
7% vol
Torhouts Mostaard Bier

XX Bitter

	top-fermentation	fermentation haute	hoge gisting
	bitter blond	blonde amère	bitter blond
	Brouwerij De Ranke Wevelgem	Brouwerij De Ranke Wevelgem	Brouwerij De Ranke Wevelgem
	pale malt, hop flowers, industrial yeast	malt pâle, fleurs de houblon, levure de culture	bleekmout, hopbloem cultuurgist
%	6,20%	6,20%	6,20%
	blond slightly cloudy	blonde légèrement trouble	blond licht troebel
	–	–	–
	Moderately cooled.	Rafraîchie modérément.	Medium koel.
	Hoppy and extra bitter.	Houblonné et extra amer.	Hoppig en extra bitter
i	–	–	–

BROUWERIJ - BRASSERIE
DE RANKE
33 cl
XX
Bitter
Brouwerij De Ranke

Yellow Mortal

	top-fermentation re-fermented in the bottle	fermentation haute refermentation en bouteille	hoge gisting hergisting op de fles
	fruit beer	bière fruitée	fruitbier
	Mortal's Beers Jamagne	Mortal's Beers Jamagne	Mortal's Beers Jamagne
	malt, sugar, hops, fruit, yeast, water	malt, sucre, houblon, fruits, levure, eau	mout, suiker, hop, frui[t], gist, water
%	7,20%	7,20%	7,20%
	golden yellow	jaune doré	goudgeel
	–	–	–
°C	39 - 43 °F	4 - 6 °C	4 - 6 °C
	Smooth and fruity, with soft hop flavours.	Moelleux, fruité avec des arômes houblonnés doux.	Zacht, fruitig met zach[te] hoparoma's.
i	–	–	–

WWW.MORTALSBEERS.BE
Yellow Mortal
Alc. 7,2 % vol.
33 cl
WWW.MORTALSBEERS.BE
MORTALS BEERS

Yperman

	bottom-fermentation	fermentation basse	lage gisting
	Ale	ale	ale
	Brouwerij Leroy Boezinge	Brouwerij Leroy Boezinge	Brouwerij Leroy Boezinge
	malt, spices, sweetener, hops, water	malt, condiments, édulcorant, houblon, eau	mout, specerijen, zoet hop, water
%	5,50%	5,50%	5,50%
	brown	brune	bruin
	Pour slowly in a single, smooth movement, into a degreased glass. Keep the glass tilted to avoid sloshing. Skim off the foam.	Verser lentement en un seul mouvement fluide dans un verre dégraissé tenu en oblique. Ne pas laisser la bière clapoter. Ecumer le verre.	Traag en in 1 vloeiend weging uitschenken in een vetvrij glas dat wo schuingehouden. Het niet laten klotsen. Het glas afschuimen.
°C	41 - 43 °F	5 - 6 °C	5 - 6 °C
	Full-bodied. Light roasty cereal taste.	Franc. Saveur de céréales légèrement fumée.	Volmondig. Licht gerookte graans
i	Named after the medieval surgeon Jan Yperman from Ypres.	Porte le nom du chirurgien médiéval d'Ypres Jan Yperman.	Genoemd naar de mid eeuwse Ieperse chirur Jan Yperman.

5 412896 001996
YPERMAN
YPERMAN

Zatte Bie

top-fermentation	fermentation haute	hoge gisting
dark	brune	donker
Brouwerij De Bie Loker	Brouwerij De Bie Loker	Brouwerij De Bie Loker
malt, hops, candy sugar, yeast, herbs, water	malt, houblon, sucre candi, levure, herbes, eau	mout, hop, kandijsuik gist, kruiden, water
9%	9%	9%
brown	brune	bruin
–	–	–
43 °F	6 °C	6 °C
Spicy.	Epicé.	Kruidig.
–	–	–

Zatte Bie
Brouwerij De Bie
B-8958 Loker
Tel 0475 23 47 95
Gebotteld
Mise en bouteille
Zatte Bie

't Zelfde - La méme chose - The same again

	top-fermentation re-fermented in the bottle	fermentation haute refermentation en bouteille	hoge gisting hergisting op de fles
	regional beer	bière régionale	streekbier
	Brouwerij Bosteels Buggenhout	Brouwerij Bosteels Buggenhout	Brouwerij Bosteels Buggenhout
	barley malts (mainly light-coloured malts combined with two dark malts), hops, water and a limited quantity of wheat	malts d'orge (principalement clairs en combinaison avec 2 malts foncés), houblon, eau et une quantité limitée de froment	gerstemouten (overwe licht gekleurde in com tie met 2 donkere), ho ter en een beperkte ho heid tarwe
%	6,10%	6,10%	6,10%
	amber blond	blond ambré	blond amber
	Pour carefully, with or without the yeast sediment.	Verser prudemment et ajouter le fond de levure selon le goût.	Voorzichtig uitschenk de gistbodem naar keu dan niet toevoegen.
°C	41 - 43 °F	5 - 6 °C	5 - 6 °C
	Fresh, flowery malt aroma. Citric, hoppy taste.	Arôme malté frais et fleuri. Touches houblonnées, d'agrumes.	Fris en fleurig moutar Citrusachtige, hoppige smaaktoetsen.
i	–	–	–

BIER
BIERE
'T ZELFDE
LA
MEME CHOSE
THE
SAME AGAIN

BIER
BIERE
'T ZELFDE
LA
MEME CHOSE
THE
SAME AGAIN

Zinnebir

	top-fermentation re-fermented in the bottle	fermentation haute refermentation en bouteille	hoge gisting hergisting op de fles
	blond - Belgian Ale	blonde - Belgian ale	blond - belgian ale
	at De Ranke Brasserie de la Senne Brussel	chez De Ranke Brasserie de la Senne Bruxelles	bij De Ranke Brasserie de la Senne Brussel
	malt, hops, yeast, water	malt, houblon, levure, eau	mout, hop, gist, water
	6%	6%	6%
	golden blond, unfiltered	blond doré, non filtrée	goudblond, ongefilter
	Serve in the correspond-ing glass.	Verser dans le verre ap-proprié.	Uitschenken in het bij sende glas.
	41 °F	5 °C	5 °C
	Character beer with taste evolution. Round and hoppy. Malty and full at the start, pleasantly bit-ter, long-lasting aftertaste.	Bière de caractère avec évolu-tion de saveur. Rond et hou-blonné. Goût initial franc malté, goût amer agréable, arrière-bouche longue.	Karakterbier met sma evolutie. Rond en hop Aanzet van moutige v heid, aangename bitte heid, lange afdronk.
	Boutique beer. The old micro-brewery Sint Pieters in Sint-Pieters-Leeuw was getting too small. Whilst a new brewery is being built in Brussels (opening in 2008) the beer is produced by brouwerij De Ranke.	Brassée de façon tradi-tionnelle. L'ancienne micro-brasserie Sint-Pieters à Sint-Pieters-Leeuw devenait trop petite; en attendant l'ouverture d'une nouvelle brasserie à Bruxelles (2008) la produc-tion se fait chez De Ranke.	Ambachtelijk gebrouw De oude microbrouwe Sint-Pieters-Leeuw wer klein; in afwachting v de opening van een ni brouwerij in Brussel (2 is de productie naar b werij De Ranke verhui

ZINNE BIR
BRASSERIE DE LA SENNE - DE ZENNE BROUWERIJ

From the brewers' jargon

(Source: Basic Beer Course of the Belgische Brouwers – Brasseurs Belges)

Raw materials

Brewing water – water, one of the main materials in the brewing p ess, can be corrected to guarantee a constant quality and composition. bacteriological purity and the chemical composition of the water ar crucial importance when brewing beer. Some beer types require a spe 'kind' of water. The English Pale Ale, for example, is known for its high r eral content, while the water used for Czech Pilsner contains a very mineral percentage.

Barley – not all varieties are suitable for beer production. Only the row summer barley and the six-row winter barley qualify for malting. gian brewers mainly use imported barley. To produce one litre of 5 % alc. beer (e.g. Pilsner) approximately 250 grams of barley are needed.

Malt/malting – barley grains germinate with water, warmth and After the grain is moistened, it begins to germinate. The germs prod enzymes that convert the starch in the grain into sugars during the b ing process. As soon as the enzymes appear, the germinating process sl down. At this moment the malter stops the germinating process by kiln (or drying) the grain. The higher the kilning temperature, the darker malt: **light-coloured** malt dries at 85 °C, **caramel malt** at 105 °C and **bl** **roasted** malt at approximately 130 °C.

Wheat – after barley the most commonly used grain species. wheat is added to the **mash**. It gives Witbier and Gueuze their typi fresh-sour flavour.

Corn – is used to give specialty beers a fuller-bodied taste. The cor added to germination first because the germ contains a fat that alters

: and the foaming of the beer. Corn and rice are added to the **mash** to 'antee a constant flavour and stability. They increase the starch content ie mash without increasing the protein level. Proteins are important for growth of the yeast and the foaming of the beer.

Rice – broken rice is used to give blond Lager beers a drier, lighter feel ie mouth.

Spelt – a grain species, mainly used as cattle feed and also sporadically ie beer brewing process.

Hops – this 'green gold' is used very sparingly (100 to 300 grams per olitre of beer). It gives the beer its typical fine bitter taste and aroma. s are also meant to keep the beer better for a longer time. Hops (natural ried in pellets) are added during the boil of the **wort**. Only female hop s are used. They contain lupulone, a yellow, very strong bitter compo- t. Hop varieties can be divided into two classes: **bittering hops**, of which a small quantity is needed, and **aroma hops**, which are less bitter and ain a high level of aromatic, volatile oils. The aromatic Hallertau from ria was introduced in Belgium by the priest of Affligem in 1907. The bit- ess of the beer is expressed in EBUs.

EBU – abbreviation of European Bitter Unit. This is a measurement to express the bitterness of the beer. One EBU is equivalent to 1 mg iso- a acids per litre of beer. However, the overall bitterness of the beer is only determined by the hops but also by tanning substances in malt or r grains and the presence or absence of herbs. Beers with a mild bitter- have an EBU value that ranges from 5 to 15. Very bitter beers have an value of 40 or more. A Pilsner with a bitterness of 25 EBUs is already idered bitter.

Hop pellets – grains of ground hops.

Ageing hops – hop cones that are two to three years old and that therefore less bitter. They are mainly used for the production of lambic

Yeasting – the yeast culture or pure culture of every brewery determ the characteristics of the beer or beer style. Every style has its own, spe yeast. E.g. *Saccharomyces Carlsbergensis* is the most suitable yeast for lagers, *Sa romyces Cerevisiae* is used for ales. The yeast converts the sugars in the **wort** alcohol and carbon dioxide. Proteins are important for the growth of the y

Lager yeasts – are pitched to the hopped wort by the brewer. They o ate best at low temperatures (ranging from 6 to 12 °C) and settle to the tom at the end of the fermentation process. They are often referred t bottom-fermenting yeasts. As the chance that wild yeast strains develo rather small, lagers have a stable flavour.

Ale yeasts – are pitched to the hopped wort by the brewer. They ope best at high temperatures (ranging from 15 to 25 °C) and rise to the sur at the end of the fermentation process. Therefore they are often called fermenting yeasts. As there is a higher chance that wild yeast strains d op, there are more differences in taste.

Spontaneous or wild yeasts – are not pitched to the wort by brewer. The **wort** is impregnated with wild yeasts, such as *Brettan ces Bruxellensis* and *Brettanomyces Lambicus*, when in touch with cool These yeasts are only found in certain regions, more precisely ir gions where Lambics are made: the Zenne valley and southwestern bant (Payottenland).

Mixed yeasts – the basis of beers of mixed origin is usually a top-ferm ing beer. After the main fermentation, part of the brew is pumped into barrels called 'foeders' for eighteen months or more. During fermentati lactic acid yeast is produced, while the microorganisms and tannins in l also act on the beer, forming fruity esters. Then, the beer is filtered and ded with young beer. Examples are the Flemish red-brown beers.

e brewing process

lashing – the first step in the brewing process, where the milled malt, d with brewing water, is heated. This way the enzymes in the malt con- the starch in the malt grains into fermentable sugars and the proteins roken down. The tannins in the barley have an influence on the colour flavour of the beer. It is possible to add raw grains to the mash, so the er can increase the quantity of starch without increasing the protein ent. This is favourable to the beer's stability.

Vort – a sugary liquid, ready for fermentation, obtained by the infu- or decoction of farinaceous materials (malt, wheat or other raw grains), wing the brewing procedure and by adding hop during the boil. The **ity** and the colour of the beer are now determined. The colour is ex- ed in **EBC** colour units, the density in degrees Plato.

BC Colour scale – colour scale to determine the colour of beer or wort, ablished by the European Brewery Convention. 1 EBC corresponds to 1 dine per 100 ml of water. In practice the colour of the beer is compared set of tubes that all represent a different colour gradation. The darker eer, the higher the EBC colour value.

ensity – the percentage of sucrose by the weight of the wort. It is ex- ed in degrees **Plato** or **Balling** (percentage of sucrose per 100 grams of rmented wort at a temperature of 20 °C). Density is also referred to as fic gravity or weight of extract.

Vhirlpooling – a centrifugal mechanism separates components of dif- t density from each other. This way the trub (the hops and insoluble components or yeast rests) can be separated from the liquid wort. The m anism can be compared to that of a juice extractor.

Primary fermentation – after the wort has been whirlpooled or filt it is chilled (the temperature depends on the yeast used) and passed thr yeast cells in the fermentation tanks. The yeast converts the sugars int cohol and carbon dioxide. The higher the sugar content, the higher the hol content and the more carbon dioxide. At the end of fermentation s 20 % of unfermentable residual sugars is left. The alcohol stays in the sl ly alcoholised liquid. This is the first time in the brewing process tha product can be called **'beer'**. The carbon dioxide escapes and is collect be added again afterwards, at the moment of bottling.

Lagering or secondary fermentation – after primary fermenta the beer is racked to big lager tanks for further maturation. Here it lowed to sit for up to several months. Some breweries regularly tap yeast, that little by little settles on the bottom of the tank. During stage of the process the flavour, bouquet and character of the beer a fined. The remaining sugars are converted into alcohol and carbon ide to a previously determined percentage that varies for each beer, the beer is saturated.

Alcohol by volume percentage – the number of centilitres of alc per 1 litre of beer.

Filtering – before the beer is bottled or kegged, the protein flocks a moved by filtering, although some breweries offer unfiltered beer.

Pasteurising – filtered beers are usually pasteurised to prevent th velopment of bacteria or possible re-fermentation. Although this has a tain impact on the taste, it makes the taste more constant and is nece for a long storage life, especially where export beer is concerned.

e-fermentation in the bottle – this is the third fermentation, after pri- and secondary fermentation during lagering. Right before bottling or ing some sugar and a minimal quantity of yeast are added in order for eer to continue fermenting while it is stocked in warm storage rooms 22 °C). The taste of a beer that has been re-fermented in the bottle con- ly evolves. After a year it may be totally different from the taste after the month. By re-fermentation an additional quantity of carbon dioxide is ed, producing extra pressure in the bottle and a nice, full foam head.

ry hopping – dry hopping means that hops are added after boiling the Often hop extracts or oil are used, but also dried aroma hops. They are lly added between primary and secondary fermentation to enhance the roma in the beer.

ottling – the bottles or kegs must be filled carefully so as not to lose arbon dioxide. Therefore, the bottles or kegs are first pressurized before are filled with beer. Contact between the beer and air should be avoid- much as possible so that the air in the bottle does not cause the beer idize. Right before bottling it is possible to add certain components to ase the foam head (e.g. carbon dioxide), adjust the colour (e.g. caramel) prove the taste (e.g. saccharin).

Aperçu du jargon des brasseurs

(Source : Cours élémentaire bière des 'Belgische Brouwers – Brasseurs Belges')

Les matières premières

Eau de brassage – l'eau, l'une des plus importantes matières prem dans le brassage, peut être améliorée afin de garantir une qualité et une position constantes. La pureté bactériologique et la composition chimiq l'eau sont primordiales pour le brassage d'une bière. Pour certains types de une eau spécifique est exigée. Ainsi, la Pale Ale anglaise est connue pou haut taux en sel tandis que l'eau de la pils tchèque n'en contient que très

Orge – Toutes les variétés ne conviennent pas pour la productio bière. Seul l'orge d'été à deux rangs et l'orge d'hiver à six rangs entre considération pour être maltés. Les brasseurs belges utilisent surto l'orge provenant de l'étranger. Pour brasser 1 litre de bière à 5 % vol. d'a (telle la Pils), environ 250 grammes d'orge sont nécessaires.

Malt/malts – c'est sous l'influence de l'eau, de la chaleur et de l'ai les grains d'orge germent. Après humidification des grains, ils comme à germer. Au cours du processus de brassage, ces germes produisent de zymes qui transforment l'amidon des grains en sucres. Dès que ces enz sont présents, le processus de germination ralentit. Le malt arrêtera de mer grâce au touraillage du grain (ou séchage). Plus haute est la tempér de séchage, plus sombre est le malt : le **malt clair** est séché en l'occurre 85 °C, le **malt caramel** à 105 °C et le **malt noir brûlé** à environ 130 °C.

Froment – après l'orge, c'est la céréale la plus utilisée. Ajouté à la pa apporte le goût frais caractéristique des bières blanches et de la gueuze

Maïs – on l'utilise pour donner aux bières spéciales un goût plus loppant. Le maïs est dégermé car le germe contient de la graisse qui a le goût et la formation de mousse. Du maïs et du riz sont ajoutés à la

ntissant ainsi la stabilité des bières et un goût constant. Ils veillent à aug-
.ter la teneur en amidon du brassin sans pour autant augmenter la quan-
de protéines. Les protéines jouent un rôle important dans l'activation de
vure et la formation de la mousse.

Riz – le riz brisé est utilisé pour donner aux bières blondes à fermenta-
basse une saveur plus sèche et légère.

:peautre – cette variété de froment est avant tout destinée au fourrage
; elle est occasionnellement utilisée pour le brassage.

Ioublon – appelé 'l'or vert', il est utilisé avec parcimonie (100 à 300
ımes par hectolitre de bière). C'est lui qui donne à la bière son goût
r typique et son arôme raffiné. Grâce au houblon, on peut également
ıx conserver la bière et plus longtemps. Le houblon (naturel, séché ou
ellets) est ajouté pendant l'ébullition du **moût**. Seules les cônes du hou-
femelles sont utilisés. Ils contiennent de la lupuline, une substance
e très corsée et amère. Deux grandes variétés sont utilisées : le **houblon
r** dont seule une petite quantité est nécessaire et les **variétés aromati-**
qui, elles, sont moins amères et contiennent un grand taux d'huiles
ıtielles. Le Hallertau aromatique de Beieren a été introduit pour la pre-
e fois en Belgique en 1907 par le pasteur d'Affligem. L'amertume de la
: est exprimée en EBU.

:BU – abréviation de 'European Bitter Unit'. Elle sert d'indication de
ıre pour l'amertume de la bière. Une unité de mesure est égale à 1 mg
de iso-alpha par litre de bière. Le houblon à lui seul ne détermine pas
: l'amertume de la bière. Les tannins du malt et d'autres grains ainsi que
ıt d'épices jouent également un rôle important à cet égard. Une bière
ement amère a une valeur EBU de 5 à 15, une bière très amère une va-
EBU de 40 ou plus. Une pils avec une amertume de 25 EBU est déjà per-
:omme amère.

Pellets de houblon – grains de houblon moulu.

Houblon suranné – des cônes de houblon âgés de deux à trois ans, qui une amertune réduite. Il est surtout utilisé dans la production de lambic.

Levures – la culture de levure et ses bouillons propres à chaque bra rie donnent à chaque type de bière sa particularité. Chaque type de b a en effet sa levure spécifique : la *Saccharomyces Carlsbergensis* est la mi adaptée aux bières à basse fermentation, la *Saccharomyces Cerevisiaeaux* bières à haute fermentation. La levure transforme les sucres du **moû** alcool et gaz carbonique. Les protéines, quant à elles, sont importa pour l'activation de la levure.

Fermentation basse – les levures sont placées par le brasseur le moût houblonné. Elles sont actives à basse température (6-12 °(descendent au fond à la fin de la fermentation. Les bières à fermenta basse ont un goût très stable car le risque que se développent des lev sauvages est faible.

Fermentation haute – les levures sont placées par le brasseur s moût houblonné. Elles sont actives à des températures plus hautes (15-2 et flottent à la surface en fin de fermentation. C'est pourquoi on les ap souvent bières 'fermentées en haut'. Dans les bières à fermentation ha les différences de goût sont plus marquées car il y a davantage de risque des levures sauvages se développent.

Fermentation spontanée – les levures ne sont pas placées pa brasseur sur le moût. Les levures sauvages comme *Brettanomyces Brux sis* et *Brettanomyces Lambicus* ensemencent le moût au contact de l'air f Ces levures ne sont présentes que dans certaines régions, notamn là où le lambic est fabriqué : la vallée de la Senne et le Brabant du Ouest (Pajottenland).

ermentation mixte – une bière à fermentation haute sert souvent de aux bières à fermentation mixte. Après la fermentation principale, une ie du brassin est transvasée pour dix-huit mois ou plus dans des fûts de e. Durant cette maturation naît une fermentation lactique. Les micro-or-smes et tannins présents dans le bois vont influer sur la bière et former sters fruités. Ensuite, après avoir été filtrée, la bière est coupée avec une jeune. Citons pour exemple les bières rouges-brunes flamandes.

processus de brassage

âte ou saccharification – c'est la première étape du brassage. Le malt é est mélangé avec de l'eau de brassage puis chauffé. Les enzymes trans-ent l'amidon des grains de malt en sucres fermentescibles. Les protéi-ont brisées. Les tannins de l'orge influencent la couleur et le goût de la . Des grains crus pourront être ensuite ajoutés à la pâte. Le brasseur ainsi augmenter la quantité d'amidon sans pour autant augmenter la tité de protéines. Ceci détermine la stabilité d'une bière.

loût – un liquide sucré (la pâte chauffée) servant à la fermentation. Il btenu par infusion ou décoction de matières premières contenant de idon (malt, blé ou autres grains bruts) suite au procédé de brassage et à it de houblon lors de l'ébullition. Il détermine la **densité** et la couleur bière. La couleur est traduite en **EBC**, la densité en degrés Plato.

chelle de couleurs EBC – l'échelle de la couleur de la bière/du moût minée par la Convention Européenne de Brasserie (European Brewery ention). 1 EBC correspond à 1 ml d'iode par 100 ml d'eau. En pratique, on pare la couleur de la bière en la posant à côté de tubes ayant chacun une ation différente. Plus une bière est foncée, plus la valeur EBC est élevée.

ensité primitive – correspond à la proportion de sucre dans le moût. ensité est exprimée en degrés **Plato** ou **balling** (quantité de sucre par

100 grammes de moût non fermenté à une température ambiante de 2(Notons d'autres qualificatifs de la densité : masse volumique, poids, te en extrait.

Centrifugation – en utilisant des forces centrifuges, les substa de densités différentes sont séparées les unes des autres. Ainsi, la dr (le houblon et les composants non dissous) est séparée du moût liquide. fonctionnement est analogue à celui d'une centrifugeuse à jus.

Fermentation principale – il faut d'abord que le moût soit refroi une température dépendant du type de fermentation) et centrifugé o tré. Puis, il est transféré dans des cuves à fermentation où il est ense cé par des souches très pures de levure. Celle ci transforme les sucre moût en alcool et gaz carbonique. Plus la teneur en sucre est élevée, la teneur en alcool sera élevée et davantage de gaz carbonique sera fo A la fin de la fermentation, il reste environ 20 % de sucres résiduels i mentescibles. L'alcool, par contre, reste dans le liquide à présent légèren alcoolisé : l'on peut maintenant parler pour la première fois de 'bière'. L carbonique qui s'échappe est récupéré pour être rajouté ensuite lors mise en bouteille.

Conditionnement ou fermentation secondaire – après la ferm tion principale, la bière entre en maturation pendant quelques mois de grandes cuves de garde. Certaines brasseries enlèvent régulièreme levure amassée au fond de la cuve. Durant cette maturation, le goû bouquet et le caractère mûrissent et s'affinent. Les sucres résiduels sont t formés en alcool et en gaz carbonique, et ce jusqu'à un taux préétabli et q bière soit saturée.

Pourcentage en volume/teneur en alcool – le rapport du nomb centilitres d'alcool par litre de bière.

iltrage – les protéines coagulées (flocon) sont éliminées par filtrage .t que la bière ne soit mise en bouteille ou en fût. Certaines brasseries osent des bières non filtrées.

asteurisation – les bières filtrées sont la plupart du temps pasteurisées d'éviter le développement de bactéries et une nouvelle fermentation. se fait aux dépens du goût (qui reste néanmoins constant) mais est spensable pour une conservation longue en cas d'exportation.

Nouvelle fermentation en bouteille – cette troisième fermentation fait suite ermentation principale et à la fermentation secondaire lors du conditionne- t. Peu avant la mise en bouteille/le remplissage sont ajoutés un peu de sucre e infime quantité de levure. La bière continue ainsi à mûrir lors du stockage hambres chaudes (20 à 22 °C). Une bière qui a subi une nouvelle fermentation outeille verra son goût évoluer avec le temps. Après un an, son goût sera par- otalement différent qu'après un mois. Avec cette fermentation, une quanti- pplémentaire de dioxyde de carbone est formée. Cela génère une pression lémentaire dans la bouteille et garantit un beau faux col plein.

Dry hopping – ou houblonnage à sec. On ajoute du houblon après l'ébul- n du moût. Cela se fait souvent avec des extraits de houblon ou d'huile oublon. De l'arôme de houblon séché est parfois aussi utilisé. Ceci se fait us souvent après la fermentation principale et avant la fermentation se- laire afin d'augmenter l'arôme du houblon de la bière.

Mise en bouteille – le remplissage des bouteilles/fûts doit se faire avec d soin pour ne pas perdre le gaz carbonique. C'est pourquoi les bou- es/fûts sont d'abord mis sous pression avant d'être remplis de bière. La e est mise le moins possible en contact avec l'air pour éviter l'oxydation bière. Juste avant la mise en bouteille, certaines substances sont ajoutées améliorer le faux col (p. ex. du gaz carbonique), pour modifier la couleur x. du caramel), ou pour adapter le goût (p. ex. de la saccharine).

Uit het brouwersjargon

(Bron: Basiscursus Bier van 'Belgische Brouwers – Brasseurs Belges')

De grondstoffen

Brouwwater – water, een van de belangrijkste grondstoffen bij het b wen, kan gecorrigeerd worden om een constante kwaliteit en samenstel te garanderen. De bacteriologische zuiverheid en de scheikundige sa stelling van het water zijn van primordiaal belang voor het brouwen bier. Voor bepaalde biertypen zijn er specifieke 'soorten' water vereis staat bv. de Engelse pale ale bekend om zijn hoog zoutgehalte, terwij water van Tsjechische pils heel weinig zout bevat.

Gerst – niet alle variëteiten zijn geschikt voor de bierproductie, enk tweerijige zomergerst en de zesrijige wintergerst komen in aanmerkin gemout te worden. Belgische brouwers gebruiken vooral gerst uit het tenland. Om 1 liter bier van 5 % vol. alc. (vb. Pils) te brouwen is er circa gram gerst nodig.

Mout/mouten – gerstkorrels kiemen onder invloed van water, warm lucht. Na bevochtiging van het graan begint het te kiemen. De kiemen pr ceren enzymen die het zetmeel uit de korrel tijdens het brouwproces o ten in suikers. Zodra de enzymen aanwezig zijn, vertraagt het kiemingspr Dan stopt de mouter het kiemen door het graan te eesten (of te drogen). hoger de droogtemperatuur, hoe donkerder het mout: **bleke mout** droo 85 °C, **karamelmout** op 105 °C, **zwartgebrande mout** op ongeveer 130 °C

Tarwe – na gerst de meest gebruikte graansoort. Tarwe wordt toegev aan het **beslag**. Het geeft de typische friszurige smaak aan witbier en ge

Maïs – wordt gebruikt om speciaalbieren een vollere smaak te geve maïs wordt ontkiemd omdat de kiem vet bevat die de smaak en schuin ming van het bier verstoort.

: en rijst worden toegevoegd aan het **beslag** waardoor een constante ak en stabiliteit van de bieren kan worden gewaarborgd. Ze zorgen er- dat het zetmeelgehalte van het brouwsel verhoogt zonder de hoeveel- eiwitten erin te vergroten. Eiwitten zijn van belang voor de voeding van ist en de schuimvorming van het bier.

Rijst – breukrijst wordt gebruikt om blonde bieren van lage gisting een er en lichter mondgevoel te geven.

Spelt – een tarwesoort die hoofdzakelijk bestemd is als veevoer en spo- sch ook bij het brouwen gebruikt wordt.

Hop – dit 'groene goud' wordt zeer spaarzaam aangewend (100 tot 300 n per hectoliter bier). Het geeft de typische, fijnbittere smaak en aroma het bier. Dankzij de hop kan men bier ook langer en beter bewaren. De (natuurlijk, gedroogd of in pellets) wordt toegevoegd tijdens het koken het **wort**. Enkel vrouwelijke hopbellen worden gebruikt. Ze bevatten lu- ne, een gele zeer pittig-bittere stof.
jn twee rassen: **bitterhop** waarvan slechts een kleine hoeveelheid nodig . **aromatische variëteiten** die minder bitter zijn en een hoog gehalte aan natische vluchtige oliën bevatten. De aromatische Hallertau uit Beieren l in 1907 voor het eerst in België geïntroduceerd door de pastoor van gem. De bitterheid van het bier wordt uitgegedrukt in EBU.

EBU – afkorting van 'European Bitter Unit'. Het is een maataandui- ; voor de bitterheid van bier. Eén maateenheid is gelijk aan 1 mg alfazuur per liter bier. Maar niet alleen de hop bepaalt de totale bit- eid van het bier. Ook looistoffen uit de mout of andere granen en ventuele toevoeging van kruiden spelen hierbij een rol. Een bier dat k bitter is, heeft een EBU-waarde van 5 tot 15. Een erg bitter bier heeft EBU-waarde van 40 of meer. Een pils met een bitterheid van 25 EBU dt al als bitter ervaren.

Hoppellets – korrels van gemalen hop

Overjaarse hop – hopbellen die twee tot drie jaar oud zijn waardoo bitterheid afgenomen is. Wordt vooral gebruikt bij de productie van laml

Gisting – De gistcultuur van elke brouwerij, de reincultuur, is ve woordelijk voor de eigenheid van de bieren en het biertype. Elk bie heeft zijn specifieke gist: *Saccharomyces Carlsbergensis* is het meest ges voor lage-gistingsbieren, *Saccharomyces Cerevisiae* voor hoge-gistingsbi De gist zet de suikers in het **wort** om tot alcohol en koolzuurgas. Eiw zijn van belang voor de voeding van de gist.

Lage gisten – worden door de brouwer op het gehopte wort geplaat zijn actief bij lage temperaturen (6-12 °C) en zakken op het einde van d ting naar de bodem. Bij lage-gistingsbieren is de smaak van het bier st omdat de kans klein is dat er zich wilde gisten ontwikkelen.

Hoge gisten – worden door de brouwer op het gehopte wort gepl Ze zijn actief bij hogere temperaturen (15-25 °C) en drijven op het eind het gistingsproces aan de oppervlakte. Daarom worden deze bieren ook bovengegiste bieren genoemd. Bij hoge-gistingsbieren komen meer sn verschillen voor omdat de kans groter is dat er zich wilde gisten ontwikk

Spontane of wilde gisten – worden niet door de brouwer op het ge te wort geplaatst. De wildgisten zoals de *Brettanomyces Bruxellensis* en *Bre myces Lambicus* enten zich op het **wort** door contact met de koele lucht. gisten komen enkel in bepaalde regio's voor, namelijk in de regio's waar biek wordt gemaakt: de Zennevallei en Zuidwest-Brabant (Pajottenland)

Gemengde gisten – de basis van gemengde-gistingsbieren is meesta van hoge gisting; een gedeelte van het brouwsel wordt na de hoofdgisting gepompt en gaat voor achttien maanden of langer in eiken vaten en foe ns dit rijpingsproces ontstaat een melkzure gisting, terwijl de micro-ısismen en tannines die in het hout zitten eveneens op het bier gaan ːken en fruitige esters vormen. Daarna wordt het bier gefilterd en versne-net jong bier. Voorbeelden hiervan zijn de Vlaamse roodbruine bieren.

t brouwproces

eslag of versuikering – de eerste stap in het brouwproces waarbij het ge- mout, vermengd met brouwwater, wordt opgewarmd. De enzymen zetten ɜtmeel in de moutkorrels om in vergistbare suikers en de eiwitten worden roken. De looistoffen van de gerst beïnvloeden de kleur en de smaak van ier. Aan het beslag kunnen nog ruwe granen worden toegevoegd, waardoor ɔuwer de hoeveelheid zetmeel kan vergroten zonder dat de hoeveelheid ei-n toeneemt. De stabiliteit van een bier wordt hierdoor gunstig beïnvloed.

/ort – een suikerhoudende vloeistof (het opgewarmde beslag) klaar voor ting. Het wordt verkregen door infusie of decoctie van zetmeelhoudende ɫstoffen (mout, tarwe of andere ruwe granen) volgens het brouwprocédé en toevoeging van hop bij het koken. De **densiteit** en de kleur van het bier zijn paald. De kleur wordt uitgedrukt in **EBC**, de densiteit in graden plato.

3C-kleurenschaal – de schaal voor de bepaling van de kleur van bier/ vastgesteld door de Europese Brouwerij Conventie (European Brewery ention). 1 EBC komt overeen met 1 ml jodium per 100 ml water. In de ijk vergelijkt men de kleur door het bier naast buisjes te leggen die elk ɜrschillende kleurgradatie weergeven. Naarmate een bier donkerder is, het een hogere EBC-waarde.

ensiteit – de verhouding suiker tot het wort. De densiteit wordt uit-ıkt in graden **plato** of **balling** (hoeveelheid suikers per 100 gram onge-/ort bij een temperatuur van 20 °C).
niemen voor densiteit: dichtheid, zwaarte, extractgehalte.

Centrifugeren – door gebruik te maken van ronddraaiende krac
worden stoffen van verschillende dichtheid van elkaar gescheiden. Zo
draf (de hop en onopgeloste bestanddelen) gescheiden van het vloe
wort. De werking kan worden vergeleken met die van een sapcentrifu

Hoofdgisting – het afgekoelde (de temperatuur is afhankelijk v
soort gisting) en gecentrifugeerde of gefilterde wort wordt in de gist
met gistcellen bezaaid. De gist zet de suikers om in alcohol en kool
gas. Hoe hoger het suikergehalte, hoe hoger het alcoholgehalte en hoe
koolzuurgas er wordt gevormd. Bij het einde van de gisting blijft er
veer 20 % onvergistbare restsuiker over. De alcohol blijft in de vloeist
nu licht gealcoholiseerd is en voor het eerst wordt er in het brouwproce
'bier' gesproken . Het koolzuurgas ontsnapt en wordt opgevangen om
te worden toegevoegd bij het bottelen.

Lagering of nagisting – na de hoofdgisting ondergaat het bier ee
pingsproces in grote lagertanks waarin het enkele maanden kan verbl
Sommige brouwerijen tappen de gist, die zich langzamerhand op de bo
van de tank verzamelt, geregeld af.
Tijdens deze rijping verfijnen de smaak, het boeket en het karakter en
den de nog resterende suikers omgezet in alcohol en koolzuurgas, tot o
vooraf per bier vastgesteld percentage, tot het bier verzadigd is.

Volumeprocent/alcoholgehalte – de verhouding van het aantal ce
ters alcohol op 1 liter bier.

Filteren – voor het bier gebotteld of op vat wordt afgevuld, word
eiwitverbindingen (vlokken) verwijderd door filtering. Enkele brouwe
bieden ongefilterd bier aan.

Pasteuriseren – gefilterde bieren worden meestal gepasteuriseer
de ontwikkeling van bacteriën en eventuele hergisting tegen te gaa

ten koste van de smaak (die hiermee wel constant blijft) maar is nood-
.ijk voor een lange houdbaarheid met het oog op de export.

Iergisting op de fles – dit is de derde gisting na de hoofdgisting en de ;ting tijdens het lageren. Vlak voor de botteling/afvulling wordt nog uiker en een minuscule hoeveelheid gist toegevoegd waardoor het bier :r rijpt bij stockage in warme kamers (20 à 22 °C). De smaak van een net hergisting op de fles ontwikkelt zich verder met de tijd. Na een jaar .kt het soms totaal anders dan na een maand. Door de hergisting wordt :en extra hoeveelheid koolzuur gevormd. Die brengt extra druk in het en zorgt voor een mooie, volle schuimkraag.

ry hopping – drooghoppen is het toevoegen van hop na het koken ıet wort. Vaak gebeurt dit met hopextracten of hopolie, maar naar ver- wordt ook wel gedroogde aromahop gebruikt. De hop wordt meestal : hoofdgisting en voor de nagisting toegevoegd om het hoparoma van ier te verhogen.

ottelen – het vullen van de flessen/vaten moet zorgvuldig gebeuren om ınwezige koolzuurgas niet te verliezen. Daarom worden de flessen/vaten onder druk gebracht voor zij met bier worden gevuld. Het bier wordt zo .g mogelijk met lucht in contact gebracht om te vermijden dat de lucht in esje het bier zou laten oxideren. Vlak voor het bottelen worden soms pro- n toegevoegd om de schuimkraag te verbeteren (bv. koolzuurgas), om de bij te sturen (bv. karamel), of om de smaak aan te passen (bv. sacharine).

Definitions & Beer styles

Definitions

Beer – the drink obtained after alcoholic fermentation of a wort, posed mainly of farinaceous and sugary materials, of which at least barley or wheat malt, hop (whether or not processed) and brewing *(Definition according to the Belgian Royal Decree of 1993)*

Gueuze and Lambic (or a combination) – the name can only be for sour beers obtained by spontaneous fermentation. The names **Gueuze** and **Old Lambic** are protected by European regulations and for the authentic, traditional specialty beers that are obtained by taneous fermentation only and that have matured for a long time i wood barrels.

Organic beer – beer that is exclusively made from certified or materials, processed without any chemical additives. The norms are lished in an EEC regulation of 1991 *(Council regulation No 2092/91/EEC June 1991 on organic production of agricultural products and indications ref thereto on agricultural products and foodstuffs, amended by regulation 1991/2 21 December 2006).*

gian beer styles

ent opinions exist about beer styles, their names, definitions and clas-ions. The classification of the 'Belgian Brewers' divides beer styles ac-ıg to yeasting method.

om-fermenting (lagers)

lsner or lager beer – pioneered in the Czech town of Pilsen in 1842. r is brewed with soft water and a light coloured malt (pale malt). It is hopped and has a solid, relatively long-lasting head. The original bit-te has evolved to a refined, hop bitter flavour. The alcohol level ranges 4.5 to 5.2% alc. vol.

ble beer – beer with an extract content between 1 and 4° Plato and ohol level ranging from 0.8 to 2.5% alc. vol. They contain mainly lex sugars. They exist in neutral to bitter versions, in blond and trip-weet table beers usually receive the additional title of brown, faro, or bock.

w-alcohol and non-alcoholic beer – these beers are brewed with a density and less yeast cells are added during fermentation. **Low-alco-**lcohol content between 0.5 and 1.2% alc. vol. **Non-alcoholic**: alcohol nt of maximum 0.5% alc. vol.

ck – especially popular in Germany and originally brewed during the hs that it is not too hot (autumn, winter and spring) because it was ılt to conserve this beer in summer without cooling techniques. Less d than pilsner but with a higher alcohol content: 6.4 to 7.6 alc. vol.

ortmunder or export – beer style from the region of Dortmund. Light-oured, milder and less bitter than Pilsner. The density and the alcohol nt (5.5 to 6 alc. vol.) are higher than in pilsner beers. It is brewed with that is rich in sulphate and minerals.

Rauchbier – typical low-fermenting beer from the German reg Nürnberg-Bamberg. The barley malt is dried above a beech wood fire, the beer its typical burned, smoked or roasted taste. Usually slightly and amber-coloured to very dark. Not common in Belgium

Top-fermenting (ales)

Amber or Speciale Belge – launched after World War I as the lish-style beer of victory'. The specific amber colour is produced by t of colour or cara(mel) malts. The density and alcohol content can be pared to those of Pilsner, although a number of degustation beers higher alcohol content (from 6 to 12% alc. vol.) have been develope the past few years.

Witbier or White beer – Hoegaarden – and especially Pierre Celis started to brew this typical wheat beer again in 1966 – played a pio role in the revival of White beers. The mash contains unmalted wheat sometimes blended with oat. During the boil, coriander and orange (curaçao) may be added to the wort, resulting in the typical, refreshi vour. White beers are usually not filtered and slightly turbid. The a content is, just like in Pilsner, 4.5 to 5% alc. vol.

Trappist ale – beer brewed in abbeys following the traditions Trappist-Cistercian monks (hence the authenticity logo). Exists in thr sions: blond, double/dark or trippel. Worldwide there are only six Tr abbeys left where beer is brewed, all of them in Belgium: Chimay, Orv chefort, Westmalle, Westvleteren and Achel (on the Dutch border).

Abbey beer – collective name used for beers where the brand re an existing or no longer existing abbey. Like trappist beer, abbey beer in three versions, but blond and trippel are slightly more represent order to carry the label of 'Certified Belgian Abbey Beer', beer comm ised after 12 August 1999 must comply with the following conditions:

r the beer is brewed at an existing non-Trappist abbey (or an existing y that commercialises a beer brewed under its responsibility and in li- e in a lay brewery);
e beer is brewed by a lay brewery that has a contractual, legal relation- with an existing abbey to use the abbey's name. Commercialisation is by the lay brewery;
he abbey or order concerned is paid royalties to support charity projects;
it should be based on a historical background (the abbey must have ed beer in the past);
the abbey has the right to monitor the publicity.

lond – light blond to gold-coloured top-fermenting beer with a lightly y, sweet aroma and a fairly neutral, slightly sweet taste. The aftertaste is r bitter. Alcohol content ranges from 2.5 to 7 % alc. vol.

ubbel (double) or dark – originally a beer produced with a double tity of malt, but now evolved toward a light or dark brown beer with et taste and a bitter aftertaste. Aroma of raisins, liquorice and candy a roasted touch. Alcohol content approximately 6 % alc. vol.

ripel (also Trippel) – originally a beer produced with more than twice ormal quantity of malt. Now it stands for a gold-coloured beer with lty, alcoholic and sometimes slightly sweet taste. The alcohol content es between 7 and 9 % alc. vol. The primary fermentation is followed by ondary fermentation at 8 to 10 °C lasting a fortnight. After that the is filtered and bottled, being re-fermented in the bottle at 21 °C for weeks.

trong blond – collective name referring to so-called virtuoso beers excel in their clarity, voluminous head and high alcohol content (7 to and more). They distinguish themselves by the use of aromatic malt , ester-like yeasts and high fermentation and maturation temperatures.

After a cold maturation in lager tanks, the beer is filtered and bottled additional dextrose and some yeast. The result is re-fermentation in the tle during storage in a warm room. After this third fermentation it is st in a cold room for several months allowing it to stabilise.
Strong double also exists.

Saisons – orange-yellow to bronze-coloured summer beer, typically the regions of Hainaut and Walloon-Brabant. It contains a high level o mentable sugars and is submitted to warm maturation with dry hop The raw hop character is compensated by the unfermented sugars tha form the basis of a possible re-fermentation in the bottle, which contri to the sparkling, fruity character of this typical summer beer.

Oud Bruin or Flanders brown – this beer style, originating from th gion of Oudenaarde-Zottegem, is a slightly sweet-sour beer with a su nut-like character. It is created by a blend of old and young beer, matur lager tanks. In this sense, it is also a mixed fermenting beer. This blend antees a constant flavour and re-fermentation is possible. The alcohol tent ranges from 4 to 8.5% alc. vol.

City or regional beer, Barley Wine and specialty beer – beer with ative touch given by the brewer, featuring special herbs, honey, choc different raw or malted wheat types and unique yeasts. These beers u ly have a fairly high alcohol content. They are deeply rooted in the d ent regions and hard to classify because they are unique and unequ Some beers are inspired by champagne, lagered in marl caves or mat following the champagne production method. The 'Brut'-beers or 'c pagne beers', in which the yeast is eliminated from the bottle by 'rem et dégorgement à la méthode originale' are a fine example of that.

Ale – originally an English/Scottish top-fermenting beer style tha be divided into two main varieties: Pale Ale and Mild Ale. Pale Ale is strongly hopped. Mild Ale is a little darker and less hopped. Their alco- :ontent ranges from 4 to 6% alc. vol. Belgium brews its own Ale beers, they have a totally different character than the English ales: they have ;her density and carbon dioxide content because Belgians prefer a nice ı head, rather than the 'plain' English beers. British beers are either ›rted to Belgium in containers and bottled there, or brewed in Bel- ı under licence with an alcohol content and flavour, adapted to the ian market.

Scotch (ale) – hard to find in its country of origin, it has become a spe- y of Walloon-Brabant and Hainaut. Scotch ale is a heavy, strong and . beer, very malty, with a slightly burned character and a sweet taste, ob- ed by the addition of candy sugar.

Stout – originally an Irish beer. Dark, creamy, sweet-bitter with a strong ıed or roasted aroma.

Fruit beers – top-fermentation beers with added fruit, fruit juice or flavor. Some have been sweetened artificially, others ared brewed ac- ing to traditional methods or organically.

Winter or Christmas beer – beers that are especially brewed for the end ar celebrations, with herbs added (honey, cinnamon, cloves and/or liq- :e). Most of these beers are malty.

›ntaneous fermenting

Lambic – one of the oldest beers (early middle ages) with ageing hops. o-organisms that are present in the air between November and March the spontaneous fermentation of the wort. The beer matures for ths or years in oak wood barrels where the secondary fermentation . the *Brettanomyces Lambicus* and *Bruxellensis* begins, giving the Lambic its sour character. Foamless beer.

Gueuze – a blend of old, not completely fermented out Lambic young Lambic that undergoes an additional fermentation in the bott champagne bottle that resists the increased carbon dioxide pressure). S so 'Definitions' p. 1536.

Fruit beer – during the lagering fruits (usually cherries) are added t lambic. As a result the fructose ferments and a fruity, non-sweet taste is c ed. Varieties with raspberry, peach, etc. are normally made with fruit ju

Faro – sour Lambic with added candy sugar, syrup or caramel. S times also a blend of sweetened lambic and top-fermenting beer.

Mixed fermenting

Red-brown ale – beer from southwestern Flanders, based on red barley malts, spicy and less bitter hop varieties and a fresh, slightly yeast with lactic acid bacteria. It has a complex taste and is a blend of yo beer and filtered beer* that has matured in oak wood barrels for 18 mo or more. The tannin and micro-organisms in the barrels act upon the creating fruity esters.

Doctored beer – mix of spontaneous, top- and bottom-fermentation b

* According to this definition, Flanders brown can also be considered as a mixed ferm tion beer. The Belgian Beer Board puts Flanders brown and red-brown in one categor lactid acid beers, as top-fermentation beers.

Beer Judge Certification Program (BJCP Styles) (Belgian) beer style defini- is chiefly focused on the technical aspects of production, but takes also in- :count flavour, colour, look and feel (see: www.bjcp.org). Belgian beers are led into two groups of Ales, each of which contain several subcategories. number of brewers mention these categories, we include them below:

3elgian & French Ale – (Witbier, Belgian Pale Ale, Saison, Bière de le, Belgian Specialty Ale)

3elgian Strong Ale – (Belgian Blond Ale, Belgian Dubbel, Belgian Tripel, ian Golden Strong Ale, Belgian Dark Strong Ale).

Other categories of BJCP Styles that are also applicable to Belgian beers Lager Bock, Ale or Lager Fruit Beer, Lager Pilsner, Ale Stout and Sour To the latter belong Flanders Red Ale, Flanders Brown Ale/Oud Bruin, ght Lambic, Gueuze and Fruit Lambic.

n this classification, Trappist ale and Abbey beer are not regarded as er style or category. Rather, they are considered an 'appellation con- e': an authenticity label.

Définitions & styles de bières belg

Quelques définitions

Bière – boisson obtenue après fermentation alcoolique d'un moût pr rée essentiellement à partir de matières premières amylacées et sucrées au moins 60 % de malt d'orge ou de froment, ainsi qu'à partir de houb éventuellement sous une forme transformée, et d'eau de brassage. *(défin d'après un arrêté royal de 1993)*

Gueuze et lambic (ou mélange) – la dénomination ne peut être sée que pour des bières acides dont la fermentation spontanée interv les dans le processus de fabrication. Les appellations **vieille gueuze** et **v lambic** sont protégées à un niveau européen et désignent les spécia traditionnelles authentiques qui ont à 100 % fermenté spontanémen mûri longtemps en fût de chêne.

Bière biologique – bière pour laquelle on utilise exclusivement de grédients certifiés biologiques sans ajout chimique. Les directives son prises dans une réglementation des EEG de 1991. *(Arrêté nr. 2092/91/EE Conseil du 24 juin 1991 concernant les méthodes de production biologiques et tives relatives aux produits agricoles et produits alimentaires, modifié depuis pa rêté 1991/2006 du 21 décembre 2006)*

ʼles de bières belges

iste une diversité de points de vue au sujet des styles de bières, de leur ›mination, leur définition et répartition en catégories. Le classement de ›sseurs Belges' répartit les bières en catégories en fonction de leur type ›rmentation :

mentation basse

ʼils ou bière blonde – créée en 1842 dans la ville tchèque Pilsen. Les pils brassées avec de l'eau douce et un pâle (malt pils). Cette bière est riche-t houblonnée et a un faux col solide et relativement constant. Son goût r à l'origine a évolué vers une saveur amère et raffinée de houblon. La te-: en alcool varie entre 4,5 et 5,2 % vol.

ʼière de table – bières avec une teneur en extraits située entre 1° et 4° › et une teneur en alcool entre 0,8 et 2,5 % vol qui contiennent surtout ›ucres complexes. Ces bières blondes ou triples varient d'un goût neutre goût plus amer. Les versions sucrées s'accompagnent quant à elles des ›minations complémentaires de bière brune, faro, stout ou bock.

ʼière pauvre en alcool et sans alcool – cette bière est brassée à une den-plus basse et lors de la fermentation, une quantité réduite de levure est tée. **Pauvre en alcool / faiblement alcoolisée** : teneur en alcool entre 0,5 2 % vol. **Sans alcool** : teneur en alcool de maximum 0,5 % vol.

ʼock – populaire surtout en Allemagne, elle était initialement brassée ehors des mois d'été. La raison était que cette bière pouvait difficilement ›nserver en été sans une technique de réfrigération. Moins houblonnée la pils, mais sa teneur en alcool est plus élevée : de 6,4 à 7,6 % vol.

ʼortmunder ou export – style de bière originaire de la région de mund. Plus pâle, plus douce et moins amère que la pils. Sa densité et neur en alcool (5,5 à 6 % vol) sont plus élevées que celles les pils. Elles sont brassées avec une eau riche en sulfate qui contient une quan importante de sels.

Rauchbier – bière typique à fermentation basse provenant d région de Nürnberg-Bamberg en Allemagne. Le malt d'orge est s au-dessus d'un feu de bois d'hêtre. La bière obtient un goût partic de brûlé, de fumé voire de grillé. En général, elle est un peu plus su et de couleur ambrée à très foncée. Cette style de bière est peu cou en Belgique.

Fermentation haute

Ambrée ou Spéciale Belge – bière de style anglais, lancée après la mière Guerre mondiale en tant que 'bière de la victoire'. Sa couleur am spécifique s'obtient par l'utilisation d'un malt coloré ou cara(mélisé). La sité et la teneur en alcool sont comparables à celle des pils, et ce malgré ces dernières années, plusieurs bières de dégustation aient été fabriq avec un taux d'alcool plus élevé (entre 6 et 12 % vol).

Bière blanche – Hoegaarden – et surtout Pierre Celis qui a recomm en 1966 à brasser cette bière de froment typique – a joué un rôle pion dans la renaissance des bières blanches. La pâte est composée à 30 % de ment non malté auquel est parfois mélangé de l'avoine. Lors de l'ébulli on ajoute de la coriandre et des écorces d'oranges (curaçao), ce qui don la bière son goût typique et rafraîchissant. Les bières blanches ne sont g ralement pas filtrées et légèrement troubles. La teneur en alcool e même que celle des pils : de 4,5 à 5 % vol.

Bière trappiste – bière brassée au sein de l'abbaye selon les tradition trappistes cisterciens (logo d'authenticité). Existe en version blonde, dou foncée ou triple. Il n'existe à travers le monde plus que six abbayes trapp qui produisent de la bière et toutes se situent en Belgique : Chimay, Orval chefort, Westmalle, Westvleteren et Achel (à la frontière avec les Pays-Bas

Bière d'abbaye – dénomination commune pour les bières dont la marque ›sée se réfère à une abbaye existante ou disparue. Dans ces bières d'ab-, on retrouve les mêmes types de bières que chez les trappistes mais l'ac- a été davantage porté sur la bière blonde et la triple. Pour qu'une bière : sur le marché après le 12 août 1999 puisse avoir le label de licence 'Bière ›baye belge reconnue', elle doit satisfaire aux conditions suivantes :

la bière est brassée dans une abbaye non trappiste existante (ou une ab- : fait brasser la bière sous sa responsabilité et licence dans une brasserie ue tout en commercialisant elle-même la bière),
la bière est brassée par une brasserie laïque qui est juridiquement liée un contrat avec une abbaye existante pour l'utilisation du nom. La com- cialisation se fait par la brasserie laïque,
es royalties doivent être payées à l'abbaye concernée/à l'ordre qui sou- t avec ces sommes des projets caritatifs,
oit reposer sur des antécédents historiques (l'abbaye en question doit r également brassé de la bière dans le passé),
y a un droit de contrôle de l'abbaye sur la publicité.

Blonde – bière blonde pâle à dorée à fermentation haute. Son arôme x est légèrement malté et son goût neutre ou légèrement sucré. L'arriè- oût est plutôt amer. Sa teneur en alcool se situe entre 5,5 et 7 % vol.

Double ou foncée – à l'origine, on utilisait pour cette bière une double ntité de malt. Elle a évolué vers une bière de couleur brun clair ou foncée : un goût sucré et un arrière-goût amer. Arôme de raisin sec, de réglisse et de li avec une touche de brûlé. Sa teneur en alcool se situe autour de 6 % vol.

Triple – à l'origine, on utilisait pour cette bière une double quantité de t. Aujourd'hui, c'est une bière dorée avec un goût malté, alcoolisé et par- légèrement sucré. Sa teneur en alcool se situe entre 7 à 9 % vol. Après la fer- ›tation principale, commence la seconde fermentation de cinq semaines à une température entre 8 et 10 °C. La bière est ensuite filtrée et mise en teille avec une troisième fermentation pendant trois semaines (à 21 °C).

Blonde forte – une dénomination commune pour les bières 'virtuoses excellent de par leur limpidité, leur faux col volumineux et leur haute te en alcool (7 à 11 % vol et plus). Elles se distinguent par l'utilisation de malts matiques, de levure estérifiée et de températures de fermentation et de ma tion plus élevées. Après une maturation froide dans les cuves de garde, la b est filtrée puis mise en bouteille avec du dextrose et un peu de levure. Ainsi troisième fermentation s'effectue dans la bouteille lors du stockage en ch bre chaude. Elle est entreposée ensuite pendant quelques mois dans un enc froid afin qu'elle se stabilise. Il existe également des bières fortes doubles.

Bière de saison – bière d'été jaune orangée à bronze typique du Hai et du Brabant Wallon. Elle est brassée avec une haute teneur en sucres ferr tescibles et subit une maturation chaude avec houblonnage à cru. Le carac rugueux du houblon est compensé par les sucres non fermentescibles. Ces niers peuvent permettre une nouvelle fermentation en bouteilles. Cette sième fermentation apporte un caractère pétillant et fruité à cette bière d

Bière brune flamande ou vieille brune – ce style de bière est origi re de la région d'Audenarde-Zottegem. Cette bière est légèrement su voire lactique et a un goût subtil de noix. Elle provient d'un mélang vieilles et jeunes bières qui arrivent ensemble à maturation dans les c de garde, et est dès lors le produit d'une fermentation mixte. Ce coupag rantit un goût constant et peut donner lieu à une fermentation second La teneur en alcool se situe entre 4 et 8,5 % vol.

Bières citadines ou régionales, vins d'orge et spécialités – bières por la touche créative du brasseur : ajout d'épices spéciales, miel, chocolat, sieurs grains crus ou moulus, de levures uniques. Elles ont souvent une te en alcool relativement élevée. Ce sont souvent des bières typiquement régi t difficiles à cataloguer puisqu'elles sont tellement uniques et inégalées. ieurs bières sont fabriquées suivant le même procédé que le champagne : litionnées en grotte de marne ou portées à maturation selon la méthode npenoise. Les bières brutes, également appelées bières de champagne, en un parfait exemple. Les levures de ces bières sont enlevées de la bouteille ide de la méthode originale du remuage et du dégorgement.

Ale – à l'origine un type de bière anglaise/écossaise à fermentation haute. Il xiste deux variétés principales : Pale Ale et Mild Ale. Pale Ale est de couleur e et fortement houblonnée ; Mild Ale a une couleur légèrement plus foncée t moins houblonnée. La teneur en alcool des Ales se situe entre 4 et 6 % vol. elgique, diverses variétés de Ale sont également brassées. Elles possèdent efois un caractère totalement différent que les variétés anglaises (densité et ur en gaz carbonique plus élevées vu que nous préférons les bières avec un faux col aux bières anglaises 'plate'). Les bières britanniques sont soit transées en containers et mises en bouteilles en Belgique, soit brassées en Belgisous licence avec un taux d'alcool et un goût adaptés au marché belge.

Scotch (ales) – sont devenues une spécialité du Brabant Wallon et du naut (alors qu'on ne les retrouve presque plus dans leur pays d'origine). bières lourdes, fortes et foncées. Elles sont très maltées et possèdent un r goût de brûlé. Leur saveur est sucrée grâce à l'ajout de sucre candi.

Stout – bière originale irlandaise. Foncée, crémeuse, sucrée et amère. un goût corsé de brûlé ou grillé.

Bières fruitées – bières de fermentation haute auxquelles sont ajoutés fruits, des jus ou des arômes de fruits. Certaines de ces bières sont sus artificiellement, d'autres sont artisanales ou biologiques à 100 %.

Bières hivernales ou de Noël – des bières qui sont brassées pour l'hiver ou les fêtes de fin d'année et qui contiennent des herbes (miel, cannelle, girofle et/ou réglisse). La plupart de ces bières sont des bières de dégustation maltée couleur ambrée ou foncée et ont un pourcentage d'alcool relativement élev

Fermentation spontanée

Lambic – une des plus vieilles bières (du début du Moyen-Âge) avec l'a de houblon suranné. Des micro-organismes dans l'air ambiant (entre no bre et mars) déclenchent la fermentation spontanée du moût. La bière rit des mois ou des années dans des fûts en chêne. C'est là que commen fermentation secondaire avec *Brettanomyces Lambicus* et *Bruxellensis*. Elle ne au lambic son caractère sec et acide. Bière sans mousse.

Gueuze – un mélange de vieux lambic, non complètement ferm avec du jeune lambic qui subit une nouvelle fermentation en bouteille (bouteille de champagne qui résiste à la pression carbonique plus éle Voir également 'Définitions'.

Bière fruitée – des variétés de fruits (souvent des cerises) sont ajou au lambic lors du conditionnement. Leurs sucres vont entièrement fern ter et donner un goût fruité et non sucré. Pour les variétés aux frambo pêches, etc. l'on utilise le plus souvent des jus de fruits.

Faro – lambic pur auquel on a ajouté du sucre candi, du sirop ou cara Parfois aussi, l'on coupe le lambic sucré avec une bière à fermentation ha

Fermentation mixte

Bière brune-rouge – bière du Sud-Ouest des Flandres. A base de m d'orge rougeâtre, de variétés de houblon relevées et moins amères et d vure rafraîchissante et acidulée avec des bactéries lactiques. Elle a un g complexe et résulte du coupage d'une bière jeune avec une bière filtrée*

* Selon cette même définition, les bières brunes flamandes peuvent elles aussi être consid comme étant des bières mixtes. Belgian Beerd Board place les bières flamandes brunes et nes-rouges dans la catégories des bières lactiques en tant que bières à fermentation hau

qui a mûri en fûts de chêne (pendant 18 mois ou plus). Les tannins et mi-
organismes présents dans le bois vont influer et former des esters fruités.

Bière de coupage – coupage/mélange de bières à fermentation sponta-
fermentation haute et fermentation basse.

proche du Beer Judge Certification Program (BJCP Styles) dans la catégo-
ion des styles de bières (belges) est avant tout technique et liée au pro-
, mais tient également compte de l'arôme, de la couleur, de l'aspect exté-
r et de la sensation dans la bouche (voir www.bjcp.org). Les bières belges
réparties en 2 catégories de bières ale qui contiennent à leur tour quel-
sous-catégories. Comme certains brasseurs y reféfèrent, nous en don-
s un bref inventaire :

Belgian & French Ale (bière blanche, Belgian Pale Ale, Saison, Bière de
de, Belgian Specialty Ale),

Belgian Strong Ale (Belgian Blond Ale, Belgian Dubbel, Belgian Tripel,
ian Golden Strong Ale, Belgian Dark Strong Ale).

D'autres catégories BJCP qui s'appliquent aux bières belges sont : Lager
, Ale ou Lager Fruit Beer, Lager Pilsner, Ale Stout et Sour Ale. Dans cet-
rnière catégorie figurent les Flanders Red Ale, Flanders Brown Ale/Oud
n, Straight Lambic, Gueuze et Fruit Lambic.

Dans ce classement, les bières trappistes et les bières d'abbaye ne font pas
tion de style de bière, ni de catégorie. Elles sont plutôt considérées com-
étant une espèce d'"appellation contrôlée', une étiquette d'authenticité.

Definities & Belgische bierstijlen

Enkele definities

Bier – "de drank verkregen na alcoholische gisting van een wort ho
zakelijk bereid uit zetmeel- en suikerhoudende grondstoffen, waarvan
minste 60 % gerst- of tarwemout, alsmede hop, eventueel in verwerkte v
en brouwwater." *(definitie volgens een Koninklijk Besluit van 1993)*

Geuze en lambiek (of combinatie) – de naam mag alleen worden
bruikt voor zure bieren waarin spontane gisting deel uitmaakt van het
ductieproces. De benamingen **'oude geuze'** en **'oude lambiek'** zijn Euro
beschermd en staan voor de echte, traditionele specialiteiten die 100 % s
taan zijn gegist en langdurig gerijpt zijn op eikenhouten vaten.

Biologisch bier – bier waarbij exclusief gebruik wordt gemaakt
grondstoffen met biologisch certificaat die verwerkt worden zonder ch
sche toevoeging. De richtlijnen zijn vervat in een reglementering van de
van 1991. *(Verordening nr. 2092/91/EEG van de Raad van 24 juni 1991 inzake de
logische productiemethode en aanduidingen dienaangaande op landbouwproducte
levensmiddelen, laatst gewijzigd door verordening 1991/2006 van 21 december 200*

r bierstijlen, hun benaming, definiëring en indeling bestaan verschillen-isies. 'Belgische Brouwers' hanteert een indeling waarbij de bierstijlen ens gistingswijze worden onderverdeeld:

ge gisting

Pils- of lagerbier – ontstaan in 1842 in de Tsjechische stad Pilsen. Pils dt gebrouwen met zacht water en een bleke mout (pilsmout). Het is rijk opt en het heeft een stevige en relatief lang blijvende schuimkraag. De inele bittere smaak is geëvolueerd naar een verfijnde hopbittere smaak. alcoholgehalte schommelt tussen de 4,5 en 5,2 vol%.

Tafelbier – bieren met een extractgehalte tussen 1 en 4° Plato en een holgehalte tussen 0,8 en 2,5 vol% die vooral complexe suikers bevatten. estaan in neutrale tot bittere versies, in blond en tripel; zoete tafelbie-krijgen meestal de ondertitel bruin, faro, stout of bock mee.

Alcoholarm en alcoholvrij – dit bier wordt gebrouwen met een lage-ensiteit en er worden minder gistcellen toegevoegd tijdens de gisting. **holarm/laag alcoholisch**: alcoholgehalte tussen 0,5 en 1,2 volumeprocent. **holvrij**: alcoholgehalte van maximum 0,5 volumeprocent.

Bock – vooral populair in Duitsland en aanvankelijk gebrouwen buiten omermaanden omdat het bier zonder koeltechniek moeilijk kon wor-bewaard in de zomer. Minder gehopt dan pils maar wel hoger qua alco-ehalte: 6,4 à 7,6 vol%.

Dortmunder of export – bierstijl afkomstig uit de regio Dortmund. Ble-zachter en minder bitter dan pils. De densiteit en het alcoholgehalte à 6 vol%) zijn hoger dan bij de pilsbieren. Ze worden gebrouwen met sul-rijk water dat veel zouten bevat.

Rauchbier – typisch lage-gistingsbier uit de regio Nürnberg-Bam in Duitsland. Het gerstemout wordt gedroogd boven een beukenhout waardoor het een typische verbrande en gerookte of geroosterde smaak kr Meestal iets zoetig en amberkleurig tot zeer donker. Niet courant in Belgi

Hoge gisting

Amber of Speciale Belge – gelanceerd na de Ie Wereldoorlog als 'over ningsbier in Engelse stijl'. De specifieke amberkleur ontstaat door het geb van kleur- of kara(mel)mouten. De dichtheid en het alcoholgehalte zijn gelijkbaar met die van pils hoewel de laatste jaren een aantal degustatiebi zijn ontwikkeld die hogere alcoholgehaltes hebben (tussen 6 en 12 vol. %).

Witbier – Hoegaarden – en vooral Pierre Celis die in 1966 het typi tarwebier opnieuw is gaan brouwen – heeft een pioniersrol gespeeld b heropleving van de witbieren. Het beslag bestaat voor 30 % uit ongem tarwe waarbij soms haver wordt gemengd. Aan het wort worden tijdens koken koriander en sinaasschillen (curaçao) toegevoegd, wat resulteert i typische, verfrissende smaak. De witbieren worden doorgaans niet gefil en zijn licht troebel. Het alcoholgehalte is zoals bij pils, 4,5 à 5 vol %.

Trappistenbier – bier gebrouwen binnen de abdijmuren volgen tradities van de trappisten-cisterciënzers (authenticiteitslogo). Bestaa blond, dubbel/donker of tripelversie. Wereldwijd zijn er nog zes brouwe trappistenabdijen, alle in België: Chimay, Orval, Rochefort, Westmalle, V vleteren en Achel (op de grens met Nederland).

Abdijbier – verzamelnaam van bieren waarvan de merknaam ver naar een bestaande of verdwenen abdij. Abdijbier heeft dezelfde biert als de trappistbieren, hoewel de klemtoon iets meer op blond en tripel Om het licentielabel 'Erkend Belgisch Abdijbier' te dragen moet het dat na 12 augustus 1999 op de markt werd gebracht, voldoen aan vol de voorwaarden:

el wordt het bier gebrouwen in een bestaande niet-trappistenabdij (ofwel bestaande abdij die onder haar verantwoordelijkheid en in licentie het bier brouwen in een lekenbrouwerij en het bier zelf mee commercialiseert),
el een bier dat gebrouwen wordt door een lekenbrouwerij die een juridi- band heeft via contract met een bestaande abdij voor het gebruik van aam. De commercialisatie gebeurt door de lekenbrouwerij,
r dienen royalties aan de betrokken abdij/orde betaald te worden waar- de orde caritatieve doeleinden ondersteunt,
et bier moet gebaseerd zijn op historische achtergronden (de abdij in stie moet in het verleden ook bier gebrouwen hebben)
r is een controlerecht van de abdij op de publiciteit.

Blond – lichtblond tot goudkleurig bier van hoge gisting met een licht- tig en zoetig aroma en een vrij neutrale, lichtzoetige smaak. De na- ak is eerder bitter. Alcoholpercentage tussen 5,5 en 7 vol%.

Dubbel of donker – oorspronkelijk een bier waarbij een dubbele hoeveel- mout werd gebruikt, maar het is geëvolueerd naar een licht- of donker- n bier met zoetige smaak en bittere nasmaak. Aroma van rozijn, zoet- : en kandij met een gebrande toets. Alcoholpercentage rond de 6 vol%.

Tripel – oorspronkelijk een bier waarbij meer dan een dubbele hoe- heid mout werd gebruikt; nu staat het voor een goudkleurig bier met moutige, alcoholische en soms lichtzoete smaak. Alcoholpercentage 7 à 9 vol %. Na de hoofdgisting volgt een tweede gisting van 5 weken bij 0 °C. Daarna wordt het bier gefilterd en gebotteld met een hergisting op es van 3 weken (bij 21 °C).

Sterk blond – een verzamelnaam van zogenaamde virtuoze bieren die uit- ken door hun grote helderheid, hun volumineuze schuimkraag en hun ho- alcoholgehalte (7 à 11 vol% en meer). Ze onderscheiden zich door het ge- k van aromatische moutsoorten, esterachtige gisten, en hogere gistings- en rijpingstemperaturen. Na een koude rijping in lagertanks wordt het bie filterd en gebotteld met toevoeging van dextrose en een beetje gist. Daar ondergaat het een hergisting op de fles bij stockage in een warme kame deze derde gisting wordt het nog een aantal maanden opgeslagen in een k ruimte om het te laten stabiliseren. Zoals sterk blond is er ook sterk dubb

Saisons – oranjegeel tot bronskleurig zomerbier dat typisch is voo negouwen en Waals-Brabant. Het wordt gebrouwen met een hoog geh aan vergistbare suikers en ondergaat een warme rijping met dry hopp Het ruwe hopkarakter wordt gecompenseerd door de onvergiste sui die de basis kunnen vormen voor een mogelijke hergisting op de fles ze hergisting draagt bij tot het sprankelende en fruitige karakter va typische zomerbier.

Vlaamse bruine bieren of oud bruin – deze bierstijl is afkomstig de regio Oudenaarde-Zottegem en staat voor licht zoetig-(melk)zurig met een subtiel nootachtig karakter. Het ontstaat door een vermen van oud en jong bier gerijpt in lagertanks en is op die manier ook een s 'gemengde gisting'. Deze versnijding garandeert een constante smaak en leiden tot een hergisting. Het alcoholgehalte ligt tussen de 4 en 8,5 vol %

Stads-of streekbier, gerstewijnen en speciaalbier – bieren met creatieve toets van de brouwer: toevoeging van aparte kruiden, hon chocolade, verscheidene graansoorten in ruwe en gemoute vorm, un gisten. Zij hebben meestal een vrij hoog alcoholgehalte. Vaak zijn ze s regionaal verankerd en moeilijk catalogeerbaar omdat zij zo uniek en geëvenaard zijn.
Een aantal bieren zijn geïnspireerd op champagne: gelagerd in me grotten of gerijpt volgens de champagnemethode. De Brutbieren, champagnebieren genoemd, waarbij de gist met 'remuage et dégo ment à la méthode originale' uit de fles wordt verwijderd, zijn hie een uitstekend voorbeeld

\le – van oorsprong een Engelse/Schotse biersoort van hoge gisting zich onderscheidt in twee hoofdsoorten: Pale Ale en Mild Ale. Pale Ale ht van kleur en sterk gehopt; Mild Ale is iets donkerder van kleur en der gehopt. Het alcoholgehalte van Ales ligt tussen de 4 en 6 vol%. in België worden diverse alesoorten gebrouwen maar die hebben een il ander karakter dan de Engelse soorten (hogere dichtheid en hoger zuurgehalte omdat wij nu eenmaal houden van bieren met een mooie imkraag in plaats van de 'platte' Engelse bieren). De Britse bieren len ofwel in containers aangevoerd en daarna in België gebotteld, of- onder licentie in België gebrouwen met een alcoholgehalte en smaak angepast zijn aan de Belgische markt.

Scotch (ales) – uitgegroeid tot een specialiteit uit Waals-Brabant en He- uwen (in hun vaderland zijn ze nog nauwelijks te vinden). Zware, ster- 1 donkere bieren die zeer moutig zijn, een licht gebrand karakter heb- en zoet smaken door de toevoeging van kandijsuiker.

Stout – origineel Iers bier. Donker, romig, zoetbitter met een sterk ge- d of geroosterd aroma.

'ruitbieren – bieren van hoge gisting waaraan fruit, fruitsappen en/of aroma's worden toegevoegd. Sommige zijn artificieel aangezoet, ande- in 100% puur natuurlijk, artisanaal of biologisch.

Vinter- of Kerstbier – bieren gemaakt voor de eindejaarsfeesten en de win- net toevoeging van kruiden (honing, kaneel, kruidnagel, en/of zoethout). neeste zijn moutige degustatiebieren, amber of donker gekleurd, met een ief hoog alcoholgehalte. Er zijn ook winterbieren van lage gisting.

ntane gisting

ambiek – een van de oudste bieren (vroege middeleeuwen) met toevoe- van overjaarse hop. Micro-organismen uit de buitenlucht (tussen november en maart) starten de spontane gisting van het wort. Het bier maanden of jaren in eikenhouten tonnen waar de nagisting met de *Bret myces Lambicus* en *Bruxellensis* begint, waardoor de lambiek zijn droog-z karakter krijgt. Schuimloos bier.

Geuze – een mengeling van oude, nog niet volledig uitgegiste biek met jonge lambiek die een bijkomende gisting krijgt op de fles champagnefles die bestand is tegen verhoogde koolzuurdruk). Zie 'Definities'op p. 1552.

Fruitbier – fruitsoorten (meestal krieken) worden aan de lambiek to voegd tijdens de lagering, waardoor de vruchtensuikers vergisten en e fruitige, niet-zoete smaak ontstaat. Voor variëteiten met framboos, p ken, enz. worden meestal vruchtensappen gebruikt.

Faro – zure lambiek met toevoeging van kandijsuiker, stroop of mel. Soms ook versnijding van gezoete lambiek met hoge-gistingsbier.

Gemengde gisting

Roodbruin bier – bier uit Zuid-West-Vlaanderen, op basis van rood tige gerstemouten, kruidige en minder bittere hopvariëteiten en frisse zure gist met melkzuurbacteriën. Het heeft een complexe smaak en is versnijding van jong bier met gefilterd bier* dat op eikenhouten vaten rijpt (18 maanden of langer). De tannine en micro-organismen in de v gaan inwerken op het bier waardoor fruitige esters ontstaan.

Versnijbier – versnijding/mengeling van bieren van spontane, hog lage gisting.

* Volgens deze definiëring kan ook Vlaams bruin als gemengd bier beschouwd word Belgian Beer Board worden Vlaams bruin en roodbruin in één categorie, de melkzuri ren, als hogegistingsbieren ondergebracht.

ıvalshoek van The Beer Judge Certification Program (BJCP Styles) bij de ıiëring van de (Belgische) bierstijlen is vooral product-technisch maar lt ook rekening met het aroma, de kleur, het uitzicht en het mondgevoel vww.bjcp.org). De Belgische bieren worden hier ingedeeld in twee catego- ı Ale-bieren die elk een aantal subcategorieën bevatten. Omdat een aantal wers eraan refereert, volgt hieronder een summiere opsomming:

Belgian & French Ale – (met witbier, Belgian Pale Ale, Saison, Bière de le, Belgian Specialty Ale),

Belgian Strong Ale – (met Belgian Blond Ale, Belgian Dubbel, Belgian el, Belgian Golden Strong Ale, Belgian Dark Strong Ale).

Andere categorieën bij BJCP styles die ook van toepassing zijn voor Bel- ıe biersoorten zijn Lager Bock, Ale of Lager Fruit Beer, Lager Pilsner, Ale t, en Sour Ale. Bij deze laatste groep horen de Flanders Red Ale, Flanders vn Ale/Oud Bruin, Straight Lambic, Gueuze en Fruit Lambic.

Trappist en abdijbier zijn bij deze indeling niet aan de orde als bierstijl ıtegorie. Ze worden veeleer beschouwd als een soort 'appellation con- ·e' een authenticiteitslabel.

DECA
Brouwerij Deca Services
Elverdingestraat 4
8640 Woesten-vleteren

DE DOCHTER VAN DE KORENAAR
Pastoor de Katerstraat 24
2387 Baarle-Hertog
www.dedochtervandeko-renaar.be

DE DOLLE BROUWERS
Brouwerij De Dolle Brouwers
Roeselarestraat 12b
8600 Esen-Diksmuide
www.dedollebrouwers.be

DE DOOL
Brouwerij De Dool
Eikendreef 21
3530 Houthalen - Helchteren
www.terdolen.be

DE GLAZEN TOREN
Brouwerij De Glazen Toren
Glazen Torenweg 11
9420 Erpe-Mere
www.glazentoren.be

DE GRAAL
Brouwerij De Graal
Warande 15
9660 Brakel
www.degraal.be

DE HALVE MAAN
Brouwerij De Halve Maan
Walplein 26
8000 Brugge
www.halvemaan.be

DE KONINCK
Brouwerij De Koninck
Mechelsesteenweg 291
2018 Antwerpen
www.dekoninck.be

DE RANKE
Brouwerij De Ranke
Brugstraat 43
8560 Wevelgem
www.deranke.be

DE RYCK
Brouwerij De Ryck
Kerkstraat 24
9550 Herzele
www.brouwerijderyck.be

DE TROCH
Brouwerij De Troch
Langestraat 20
1741 Wambeek-Ternat
www.detroch.be

DRIE FONTEINEN
Brouwerij Drie Fonteinen
Hoogstraat 2a
1650 Beersel
www.3fonteinen.be

DU BOCQ
Brasserie Du Bocq
4, Rue de la Brasserie
5530 Purnode-Yvoir
www.bocq.be

DUBUISSON CORPORATION
Brewsite Brasserie Dubuisson
28, Chaussée de Mons
7904 Pipaix-Leuze
www.br-dubuisson.com

DUPONT
Brasserie Dupont
5, Rue Basse
7904 Tourpes-Leuze
www.brasserie-dupont.

DUVEL MOORTGAT CORPORATION
Brewsite Brouwerij Duve Moortgat
Breendonkdorp 58
2870 Breendonk-Puurs
www.duvel.be
Brewsite Brasserie d'Ach
32, Rue du Village
6666 Achouffe-Wibrin
www.achouffe.be

e

ECAUSSINNES
Brasserie d'Ecaussinnes
18, Rue de Restaumont
7190 Ecaussinnes d'Eng
www.brasserieecaussinn

f

FAGNES
Brasserie des Fagnes
26, Route de Nismes
5660 Mariembourg-Co
www.brasseriedesfagne

FANTÔME
Brasserie Fantôme
8, Rue Préal
6997 Soy
www.fantome.be

FERME AU CHÊNE
Brasserie La Ferme Au C
36, Rue Comte d'Ursel
6940 Durbuy

rie Artisanale du Flo
e du Château
lehen-Hannut

NOISE
rie Artisanale
snoise
Basse
rasnes-lez-Buissenal
orasseriefrasnoise.be

RHOPKE
erij 't Gaverhopke
rugstraat 187
tasegem-Harelbeke
gaverhopke.be

rie Gigi
and'Rue
Gérouville

RDIN
erij Girardin
iberg 10
int-Ulriks-Kapelle

N D'ORGE
rie Grain d'Orge
16
Iombourg-Plombières
rasserie-graindorge.be

HT
erij Haacht
ciesteenweg 28
oortmeerbeek
primus.be

HOFBROUWERIJKE
't Hofbrouwerijke
Hoogstraat 149
2580 Beerzel
www.thofbrouwerijke.be

HOPPERD
Brouwerij Den Hopperd
Netestraat 67
2235 Hulshout

HUYGHE
Brouwerij Huyghe
Brusselsesteenweg 282
9090 Melle
www.delirium.be

i

IMPRIMERIE
Brasserie l'Imprimerie
666, Chaussée de St.-Job
1180 Brussel (Ukkel)
www.limprimerie.be

INBEV (BREW COMPANY) CORPORATION
SA Inbev Belgium NV
Vaartkom 31
3000 Leuven
www.stellaartois.be
www.inbev.com
Brewsite Artois
Vaartstraat 94
3000 Leuven
Brewsite S.A. Belle-Vue N.V.
Bergensesteenweg 144
1600 St-Pieters-Leeuw
Brewsite Brouwerij van Hoegaarden
Stoopkensstraat 24
3320 Hoegaarden

Brewsite Brasserie Jupiler
2, Rue des Anciennes Houblonnières
4020 Jupille-sur-Meuse

k

KERKOM
Brouwerij Kerkom
Naamsesteenweg 469
3800 Kerkom-Sint-Truiden
www.brouwerijkerkom.be

l

LEFEBVRE
Brasserie Lefebvre
54, Rue de Croly
1430 Quenast
www.brasserielefebvre.be

LÉGENDES (Brasserie Des) CORPORATION
Brewsite Brasserie des Géants
19, Rue du Castel
7801 Irchonwelz (Ath)
www.brasseriedeslegendes.be
www.brasseriedesgeants.com
Brewsite Brasserie Ellezelloise
75, Guinaumont
7890 Ellezelles
www.brasserie-ellezelloise.be

LEROY
Brouwerij Leroy
Diksmuidesesteenweg 406
8904 Boezinge

LIEFMANS BREWERIES CORP.
Aalststraat 200
9700 Oudenaarde
Wontergemstraat 42
8720 Dentergem
www.liefmans.be

o

ORVAL

Brasserie de l'Abbaye N.D. d'Orval
Orval 2
6823 Villers-devant-Orval
www.orval.be

OXYMORE

Brasserie Oxymore
Rue Verte 1
6670 Limerlé (Gouvy)
www.peripleenlademeure.be

p

PALM BREWERIES CORP.

Brewsite Brewery Palm
Steenhuffeldorp 3
1840 Steenhuffel
www.palm.be

Brewsite Brouwerij Rodenbach
Spanjestraat 133-141
8800 Roeselare
www.rodenbach.be

PROEFBROUWERIJ

De Proefbrouwerij / Andelot
Doornzelestraat 20
9080 Lochristi
www.proefbrouwerij.com

r

REGENBOOG

Brouwerij De Regenboog
Astridlaan 134
8310 Assebroek-brugge

ROCHEFORT

Brasserie de l'Abbaye N.D. de Saint-Rémy
8, Rue de l'Abbaye
5580 Rochefort
www.trappistes-rochefort.com

ROMAN

Brouwerij Roman
Hauwaert 105
9700 Oudenaarde-Mat
www.roman.be

RULLES

Brasserie Artisanale de
36, Rue Maurice Grévis
6724 Rulles (Habay)
www.larulles.be

s

SAINT-FEUILLIEN

Brasserie Saint-Feuillie
20, Rue d'Houdeng
7070 Le Roeulx
www.st-feuillien.com

SAINTE-HÉLÈNE

Brasserie Sainte-Hélène
21, Rue de la Colline
6760 Ethe (Virton)
www.sainte-helene.be

SAINT-MONON

Brasserie Saint-Monon
45, Rue Principale
6953 Ambly-Nassogne

SILENRIEUX

Brasserie de Silenrieux
Rue Noupré 1
5630 Silenrieux

SILLY

Brasserie de Silly
2, Rue Ville Basse
7830 Silly
www.silly-beer.com

LINDEMANS

Brouwerij Lindemans
Lenniksebaan 1479
1602 Vlezenbeek
www.lindemans.be

LOTERBOL

Brouwerij Loterbol
Michel Theysstraat 58a
3290 Diest
www.loterbol.be

m

MALHEUR

Brouwerij Malheur
Mandekensstraat 179
9255 Buggenhout
www.malheur.be

MARTENS

Brouwerij Martens
Reppelerweg 1
3950 Bocholt
www.martens.be

MILLEVERTUS

Brasserie Artisanale Millevertus
8, Ruelle de la Fiels
6700 Toernich-Arlon
www.millevertus.be

MORTAL'S BEERS

Brasserie Mortal's Beers
47a, Belle Ruelle
5600 Jamagne (Philippeville)
www.mortalsbeers.be

BERNARDUS
erij Sint-Bernardus
stenweg 23
Vatou
sintbernardus.be

CANARUS
rouwerij Sint-Canarus
weg 2
Gottem
sintcanarus.be

JOZEF
erij Sint-Jozef
ein 19
Opitter
brouwerijsintjozef.be

HMUYLDER
erij Slaghmuylder
rhoutembaan 2
Ninove
witkap.be

BBE
erij Strubbe
1
chtegem
brouwerij-strubbe.be

ERMANS
MARTIN)
NGSHOEVEN
erij Timmermans
raat 11
tterbeek
anthonymartin.be

V

VAL DE SAMBRE
Brasserie Val de Sambre
273, Rue Emile Vandervelde
6534 Gozée
www.valdesambre.be

VAL-DIEU
Brasserie de l'Abbaye du Val-Dieu
225, Val-Dieu
4880 Aubel
www.val-dieu.com

VAN DEN BOSSCHE
Brouwerij Van den Bossche
Sint-Lievensplein 16
9550 Sint-Lievens-Esse
www.brouwerijvandenbossche.be

VAN EECKE
Brouwerij Van Eecke
Douvieweg 2
8978 Watou
www.brouwerijvaneecke.tk

VAN HONSEBROUCK
Brouwerij Van Honsebrouck
Oostrozebekestraat 43
8770 Ingelmunster
www.kasteelbier.be
www.vanhonsebrouck.be

VAN STEENBERGE
Brouwerij Van Steenberge/Bios
Lindenlaan 25
9940 Ertvelde
www.vansteenberge.com

VAPEUR
Brasserie à Vapeur
1, Rue du Maréchal
7904 Pipaix-Leuze
www.vapeur.com

VERHAEGHE
Brouwerij Verhaeghe
Beukenhofstraat 96
8570 Vichte
www.brouwerijverhaeghe.be

VISSENAKEN
Brouwerij Vissenaken
Metselstraat 74
3300 Vissenaken-Tienen
www.brouwerijvissenaken.net

W

WALRAVE
Brouwerij Walrave
Lepelstraat 36
9270 Laarne

WESTMALLE
Brouwerij van de Abdij der Trappisten
Antwerpsesteenweg 496
2390 Westmalle
www.trappistwestmalle.be

WESTVLETEREN
Brouwerij der Sint-Sixtusabdij
Donkerstraat 12
8640 Westvleteren
www.sintsixtus.be

Contract brewers list (beerfirms)
Liste des sociétés brassicoles | Lijst van de bierfirma's

b

BEER, BED & BREAKFAST JESSENHOFKE
Jessenhofstraat 8
3511 Kuringen-Hasselt
www.jessenhofke.be

BIEREN PIRLOT
Moerstraat 22
2242 Pulderbos

BROUWERIJ CLARYSSE
Krekelput 18
9700 Oudenaarde

BROUWERIJ CORSENDONK NV
Slachthuisstraat 27
2300 Turnhout
www.corsendonk.com

BROUWERIJ CROMBÉ
Hospitaalstraat 10
9620 Zottegem

BROUWERIJ PAELEMAN
Boekakker 1
9230 Wetteren

BROUWERIJ SLAAPMUTSKE
Oefenpleinstraat 15
9090 Melle
www.slaapmutske.be

BROUWERIJ STERKENS
Meerdorp 20
2321 Meer
www.sterkensbrew.be

BROUWERIJ SUBLIM
(bvba Artwi)
Regastraat 44
3000 Leuven
www.brouwerijsublim.com

BROUWERIJ THE MUSKETEERS
Tramstraat 8
9910 Ursel
www.brouwerijdemusketiers.com
www.troubadour.com.be

BUITENLUST BIER VO
Holleweg 111
2950 Kapellen
www.buitenlustbier.be

d

DE BROUWERIJ VAN VLAANDEREN BVBA
Elzendreef 19
2970 Schilde
www.debrouwerijvanvl
deren.be

g

GULDENBOOT NV
Marktstraat 59 bus 5
1745 Opwijk
www.leirekenbier.be

v

VICARIS EVBA
Vijfbunderstraat 31
9200 Grembergen (Der
monde)
www.vicaris.be

Gueuze blenders list | Liste des coupeurs de gueuze
Lijst van de gueuzestekerijen

g

GEUZESTEKERIJ DE CAM
Dorpsstraat 67A
1755 Gooik

GEUZESTEKERIJ HANSSENS
Vroenenbosstraat 15
1653 DWORP

o

OUD BEERSEL BVBA
Laarheidestraat 230
1650 Beersel
www.oudbeersel.com

·wery renters list | Liste des locataires de brasserie
t van de brouwerijhuurders

SPRL
ocus 64c
!aillot
orestinne.be.tf

WERIJ DRUÏDE VOF
straat 37
)eerlijk
lruide.be

WERIJ DE LEYERTH
ıekeerstraat 21
.uiselede
ırthel.com

WERIJ HET
:NATIEF EVBA
esteenweg 65
zegem
·ouwerijhetalternatief.be

d

DE CAM
Dorpsstraat 67a
1755 Gooik
www.decam.be

DE COCK
MEESTERBROUWERS
Potterstraat 10
9170 Sint-Pauwels
www.brouwerijdecock.com

DE HOEVEBROUWERS EVBA
Gentse Steenweg 217
9620 Zottegem
www.dehoevebrouwers.be

o

OUD BEERSEL BVBA
Laarheidestraat 230
1650 Beersel
www.oudbeersel.com

v

VDACO BVBA
DE STRUISE BROUWERS
Landbouwersstraat 18
8660 De Panne
www.struisebrouwers.be

z

ZENNEBROUWERIJ
De Zennebrouwerij
Victor Nonnemansstraat 40a
1600 Sint-Pieters-Leeuw
www.zinnebir.be

resting websites | Des sites internet intéressantes
ele interessante websites

·elgianbeerboard.be
eerparadise.be
ythos.be
jcp.org
atebeer.com

Thanks to
Lambert De Wijngaert, Belgian Brewers
Patrick Beth, Hainaut Développement (Agence de Développement de l'Economie et de l'Environn
de la Province de Hainaut),
Claude Vandereycken, S.P.I.+ (Agence de développement pour la province de Liège),
Yves Vandenbussche, Drankencentrale Waregem,
And in particular to
Filip Geerts, www.belgianbeerboard.be and **Casimir Elsen**, Zythos
for their interesting tips

Concept
Jaak Van Damme

Photography
Group Van Damme bvba, Oostkamp (B)

Text & Compilation
Hilde Deweer

English and French translations
TAAL-AD-VISIE, Brugge

Final editing English
Karolien van Cauwelaert

Final editing French
Eva Joos

Layout and Printing
Group Van Damme bvba, Oostkamp (B)

Published by
Stichting Kunstboek
Legeweg 165
B-8020 Oostkamp
T. +32 (0) 50 46 19 10
F. +32 (0) 50 46 19 18
info@stichtingkunstboek.com
www.stichtingkunstboek.com

Printed on My Sol matt 90 gsm, distributed by Map Belux

ISBN 978-90-5856-242-5
NUR: 448
D/2007/6407/23

BELLEVAUX
BAVIK
TOURTEL
1839
Saint-Monon
BRASSERIE
Abbaye du Val-Dieu
Brune
satan
10
ORVAL
CHIMAY
Trappist
25cl